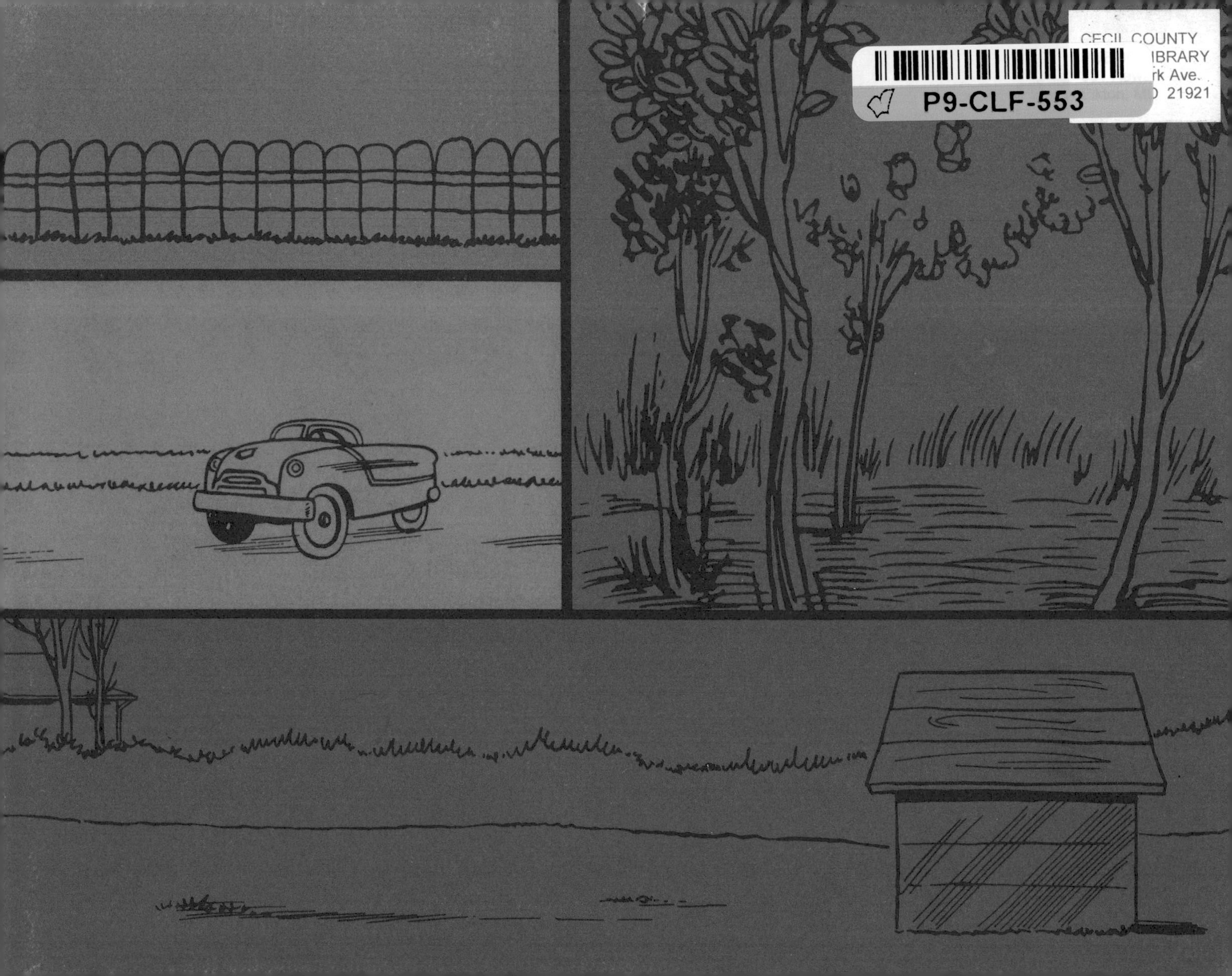

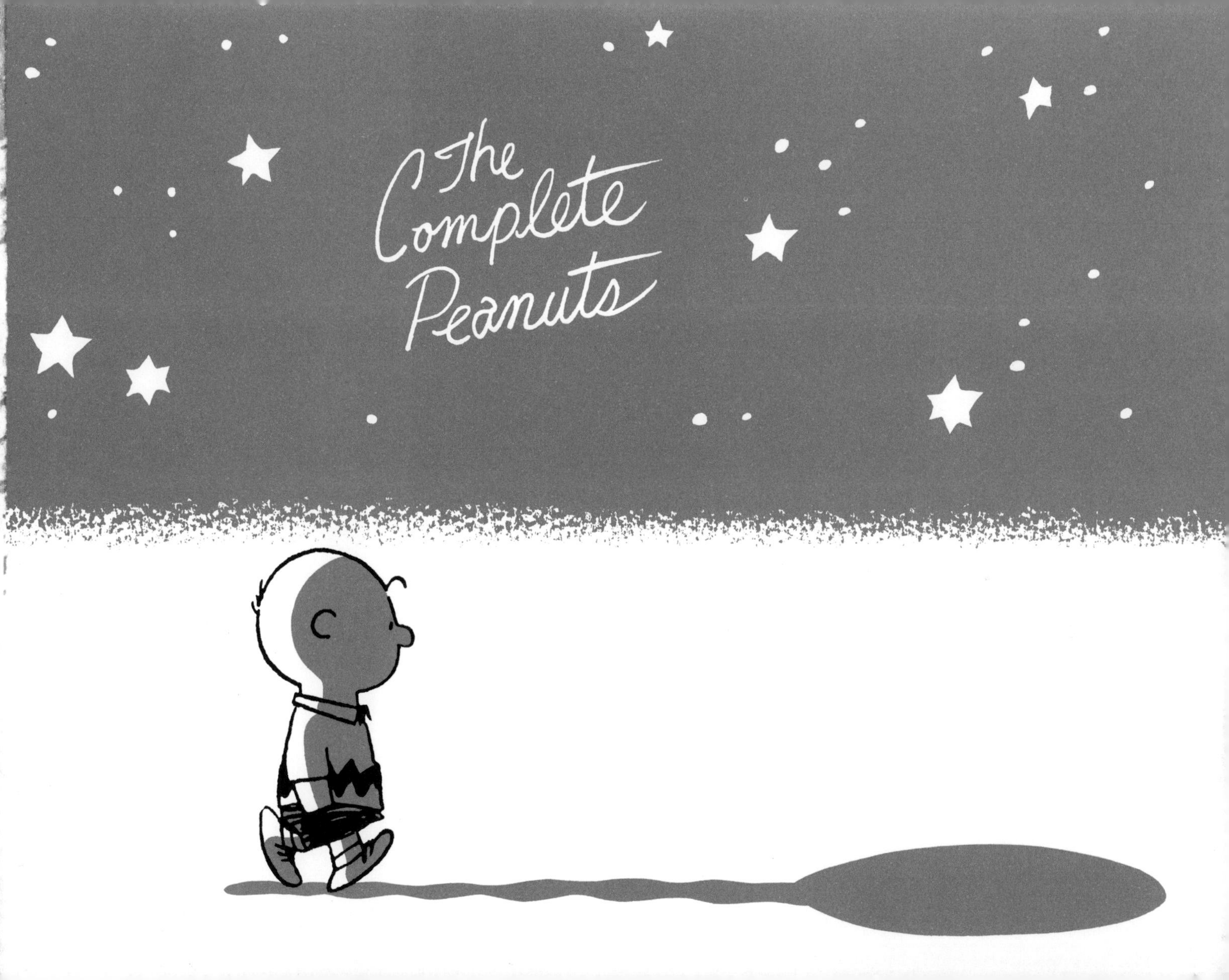
The Complete Peanuts

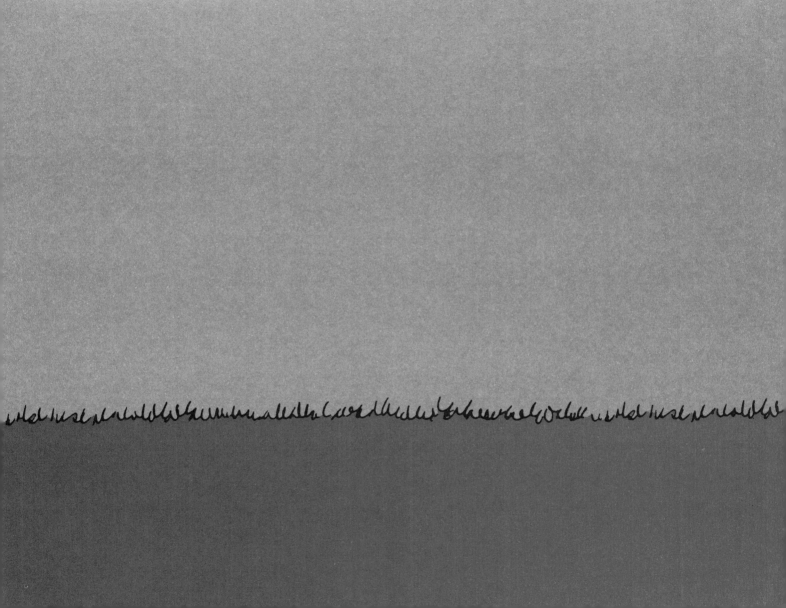

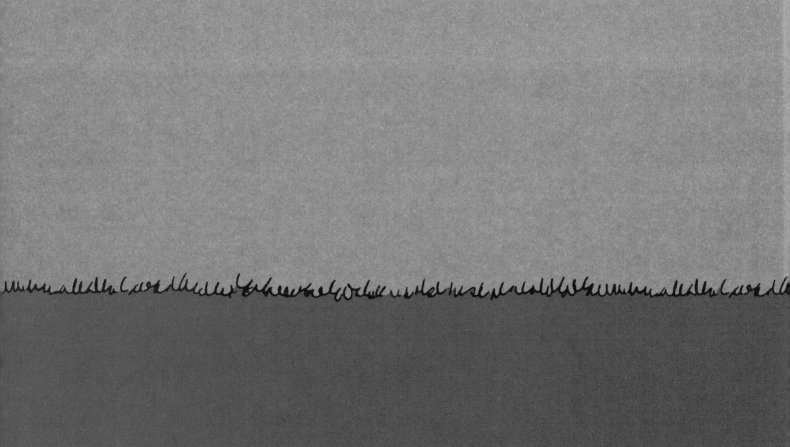

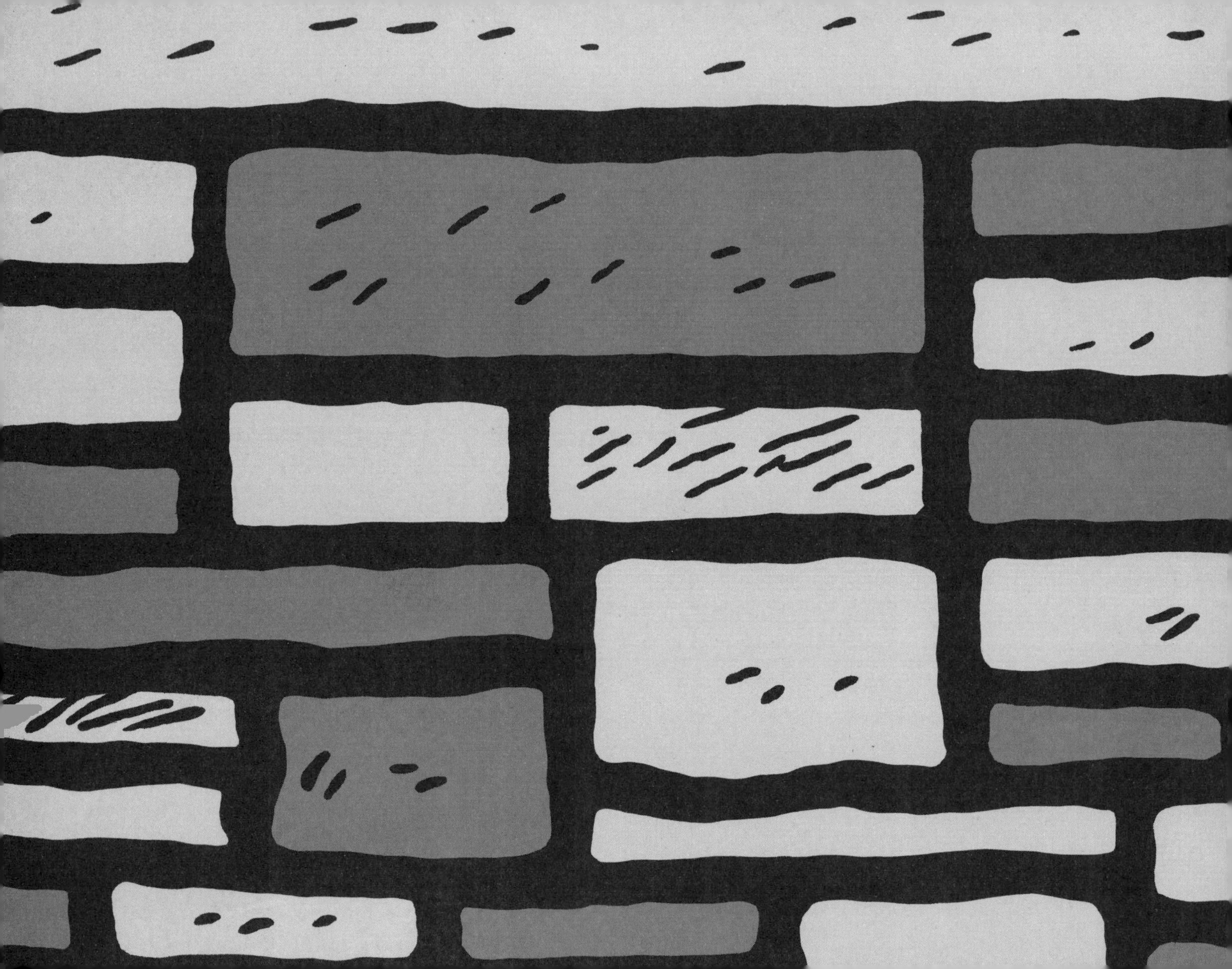

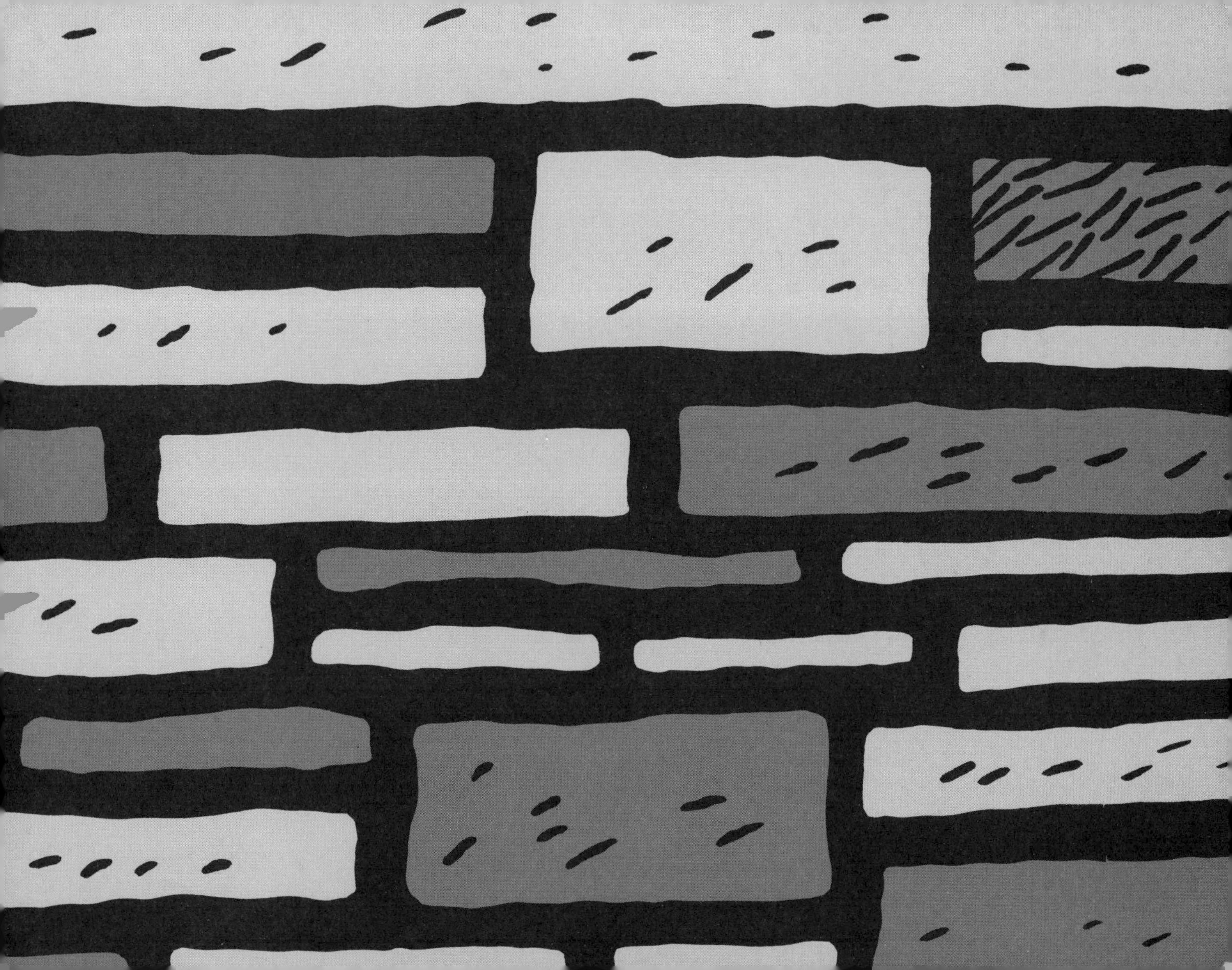

THE COMPLETE PEANUTS
by Charles M. Schulz
published by
Fantagraphics Books

Editor: Gary Groth
Designer: Seth
Production Manager: Kim Thompson
Production, assembly, and restoration: Paul Baresh & Adam Grano
Archival and production assistance: Nat Gertler & Marcie Lee
Index compiled by Houria Kerdioui
Promotion: Eric Reynolds
Publishers: Gary Groth & Kim Thompson

Special thanks to Jeannie Schulz, without whom
this project would not have come to fruition.
Thanks to Timothy Chow, and to
Charles M. Schulz Creative Associates,
especially Paige Braddock and Kim Towner.
Thanks for special support from United Media.

Fantagraphics Books, 7563 Lake City Way, Seattle, WA 98115, USA. For a free full-color catalogue of comics,
call 1-800-657-1100. Our books may be viewed on our website at www.fantagraphics.com.

Distributed to the book trade by:

USA: W.W. Norton and Company, Inc.
500 Fifth Avenue, New York, NY 10010
212-354-5500
Order Department: 800-233-4830

CANADA: Raincoast Books
9050 Shaugnessy Street, Vancouver, British Columbia V6P 6E5
Customer Service: 800-663-5714

ISBN-13: 978-1-56097-671-4   ISBN-10: 1-56097-671-3
First printing: March 2006   Printed in China

CHARLES M. SCHULZ

THE COMPLETE PEANUTS

1959 TO 1960

"WE'RE AFRAID OF
THE FUTURE!"

FANTAGRAPHICS BOOKS

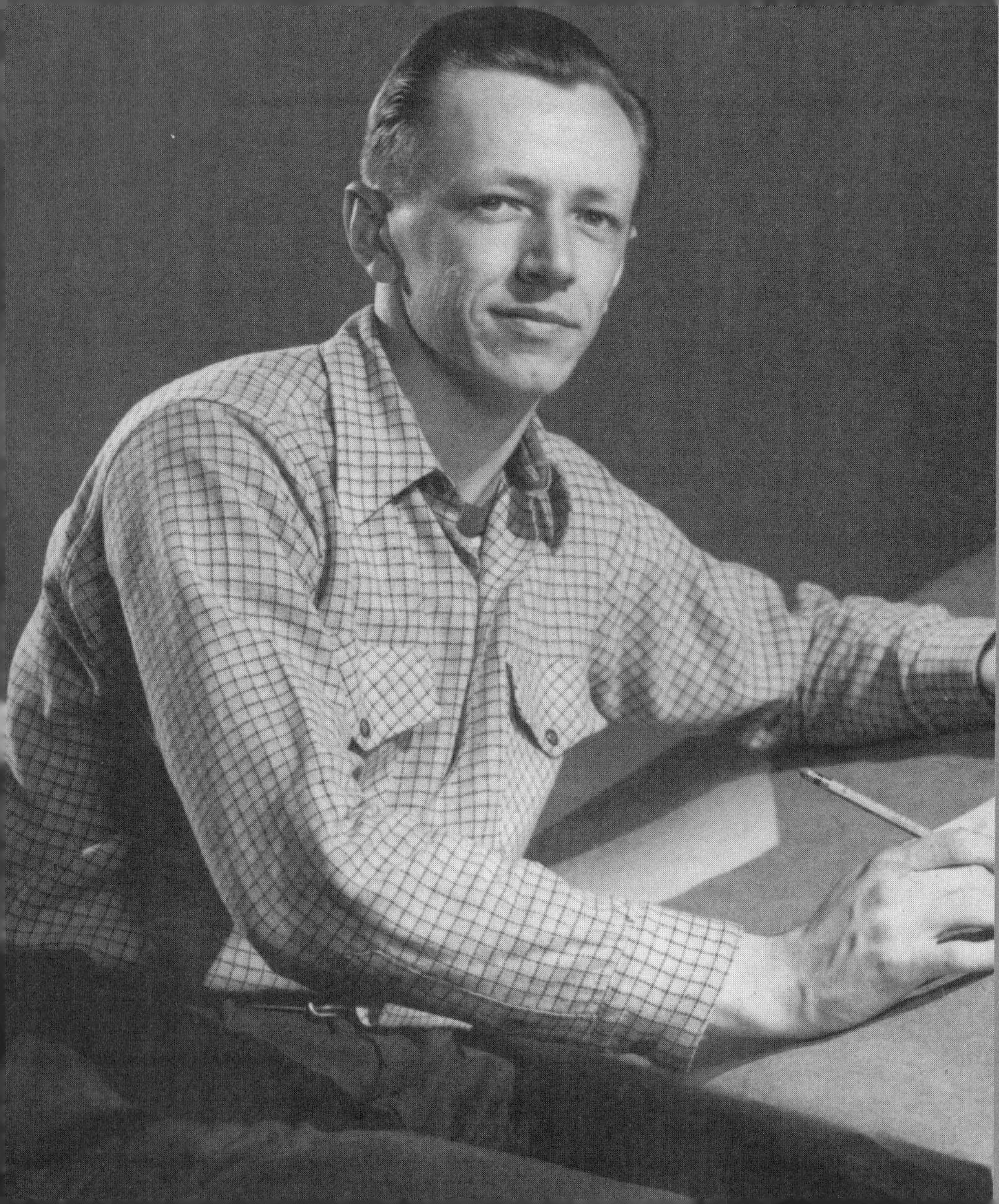

Charles Schulz
circa 1950.

FOREWORD by WHOOPI GOLDBERG

Complete Peanuts editor Gary Groth chatted with Whoopi Goldberg about *Peanuts* in July 2005. Following is an edited transcript of their conversation.

Did you read Peanuts *as a girl?*

    I've always read *everything* as a girl. I had to, because I was never a guy! But yes, all of my life. My mom introduced me to *Peanuts* — it's one of those wonderful things we shared. And of course the television specials started when I was a kid, bringing *Peanuts* to bigger and better life. That's why to this day I can do the Snoopy dance from "A Charlie Brown Christmas."

    I used to have a talk show, and on that talk show I had the joy and privilege of interviewing Charles Schulz. And I bared my breast to Charles Schulz, because I have a tattoo of Woodstock, which I got 28 years ago. He asked

me if I wanted him to color it in. You know, if Charlie Schulz says, *Do you want me to color your tattoo in?* you say, *Sure.*

And did he?

    I'm never gonna tell!

Why Woodstock?

    Because there was something really wonderful about this bird who would just hang out, who wasn't concerned about a lot of stuff. He had a good friend in Snoopy. I thought it would be wonderful to carry that chirp with me, that series of lines. I didn't get the lines put on, but when I see the tattoo I think of him just talking to me, as he would to Snoopy. It's kind of dopey, but I love it.

    Anyway, I thought the guy was somebody I wanted

to meet. I mean, that was the big reason for doing the talk show, so that I could meet the people that I admired. I admired the strip, and he was such a complex gentleman…

Where do you think Charles Schulz's complexity lay?

The fact that Charlie Brown was such an innovative character led me to believe that there was something going on with this gentleman. We'd had Mary Worth, and we'd had Al Capp with Li'l Abner, but no comic strip before *Peanuts* ever felt like it was talking to me. I always felt like I knew Charlie Brown and the other characters, and I understood them in the way that I never did with any other strip. Having grown up with the strip, and having heard periodically that he was a guy who had suffered from depression, I thought, *I gotta meet this guy.* Because I want to know how you work out those things that are in you. So to be able to have the opportunity to sit and talk to Charles Schulz both on and off camera was an extraordinary experience.

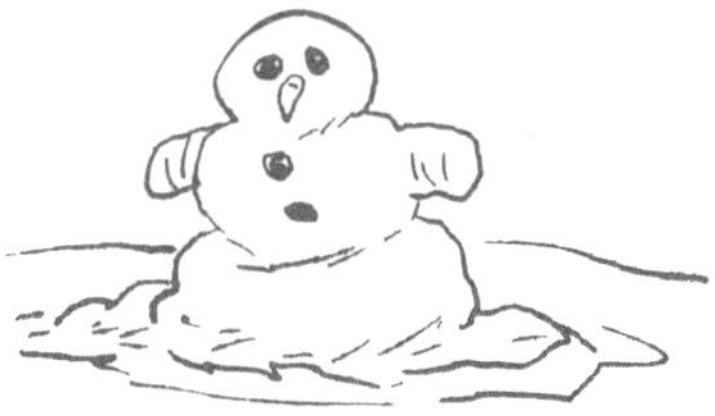

Can you give me your impressions of him and your recollection of what you spoke about?

I won't tell you what we spoke about, but I will tell you that I wish that he had had more time on the earth, because I'd have liked to have spent a lot more time with him, just talking to him.

He was to me just a really, really great man who had no idea why he was great. And it bothered him. The accolades he got he felt weren't his, for some reason. He didn't feel they were…deserved. And I think he didn't feel particularly connected to the world. He was appreciative and very, very loving about all of the good things that came his way but I think he was always mildly surprised.

Was he what you expected?

He was much better drawn, and much richer. But he was also a pretty angry guy. And I gotta love that. I gotta love that because it's something that makes him a great artist. I think he had a lot of rage, and he worked it out the way he worked it out. Very, very smart. Very, very shy. Funny, but not in a "ba-ha-ha" way, but just wit. If he was talking about something he didn't like, you chuckled, but you went, *Oww! I'm glad I'm not on the receiving end of that!*

I would say that he sublimated his anger into the strip, whereas your anger is more front and center.

Well, that's what I know from the theater. When you're on a stage, when you have a physical audience, you sort of have to… Remember, this was in '83. So performance art, the kind of stuff that I was doing, permitted that. I don't know if you could get away with it as richly as I did then. I do it differently now: It's more gentle. You get older, you start to say, *I gotta do this a little bit differently, because I'm tired.* I would love to be able to draw and paint, because there are so many things that you can say and do that are reflective of who you are that don't require you to speak. My medium requires me to physically speak to you. How can I get you to listen? Sometimes I can be in the mode of a really rough and tough kind of character. Sometimes I can be in the mode of a six-year-old who really just wants to be on the "Love Boat." It depends on who I think can deliver the information I want you to have, in a good way.

I loved the *Peanuts* stage play, too. I thought one day I'd get to play Snoopy. But I never got around to doing it.

I was looking at convergences and divergences in your careers. One interesting convergence, I thought, was that you both had a difficult time in school. Sparky suffered a lot in high school. He disliked being considered "sissified" as he called it. I understand that you dropped out of high school within two weeks, and that you were diagnosed with dyslexia, which might have been the cause of some of your turmoil in high school.

I went to high school for about a week, but it was too confining for my mind, because I knew all of the things that I did know, and there weren't really ways to connect these things to the stuff that was on paper, within this very rigid system, in a tangible way. If you weren't within the confines of that system, life was tough. And I'm sure anybody who was an artist at his age, as a kid — you know, being an artist is not football. That's what's so great about the football and the flying of the kite in the strip: There are just some things you can't do! And no matter what you do, no matter how you try, no matter how you bend yourself to the will of others, it's just not going to happen. And that's really the central metaphor of *Peanuts* for me. At some point you just have to say, *You know what? This is what I can do. I can be friends with Peppermint Patty. I can have the greatest dog in the world. I can ponder the moon and the stars and ask the big questions. But I can't fly a kite. Or kick a football.*

So did you identify with his take on failure, which I take to be that you fail but you pick yourself right up and try again?

Well, failure is only somebody else's idea of what you're doing. It wouldn't be failure to us if someone didn't tell us it was failure. The natural state is that if you don't do it the first time the right way, it doesn't work! Then you try it again and you try it again and you try it again until you get it. Then you move on. But once you have all of these folks telling you it's a failure, you're a failure, you're a failure — it's a lot of weight. All you're trying to do is move on.

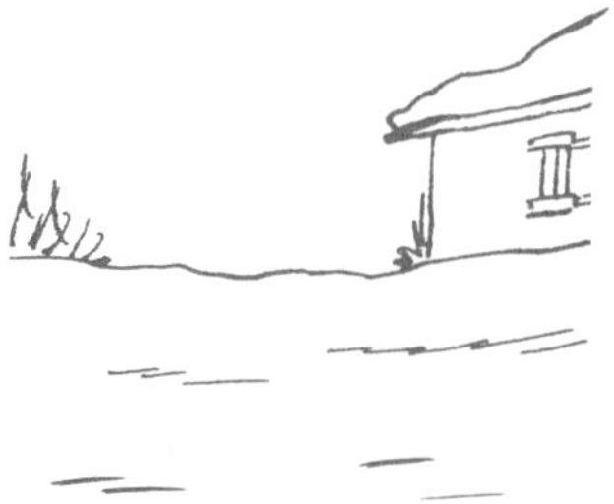

You mentioned Li'l Abner *and* Mary Worth*; did you read comic strips in general when you were a kid?*

Well, that was part of life on a Sunday. You got the Sunday comics. I liked comic books because the pictures and the colors were great. Harvey Comics, where you had Hot Stuff and Baby Huey and Little Dot. Yaw! Boy, I haven't seen a Dot comic in a thousand years.

At what point did you perceive Peanuts *as being a different kind of strip? You said it spoke to you, and at what point did you perceive that it had that existential dimension that the other strips didn't have?*

I think once I became an adult, because it became a different kind of consciousness from the paper to the television. There weren't that many animated features at that time. There'd be Claymation features in the holidays... but in the Peanuts specials you'd have Schroeder and you'd have Snoopy, everybody was together. And you know the song, *Christmas time is here,* then you'd hear *da, da, da, da, da, da, da da...* To this second I can tell you what scene it is if I hear the music. It's in my system. It's part of my absolute consciousness. And of course, in the '60s, when Charlie Brown really sort of got hip and was saying things and you thought, *Well, that would mean this if he was saying it as an adult.* And where Snoopy's up there with the Red Baron and the way he's changed, and Woodstock's introduction. And then seeing the black character get introduced. I mean, it was something. It was just different.

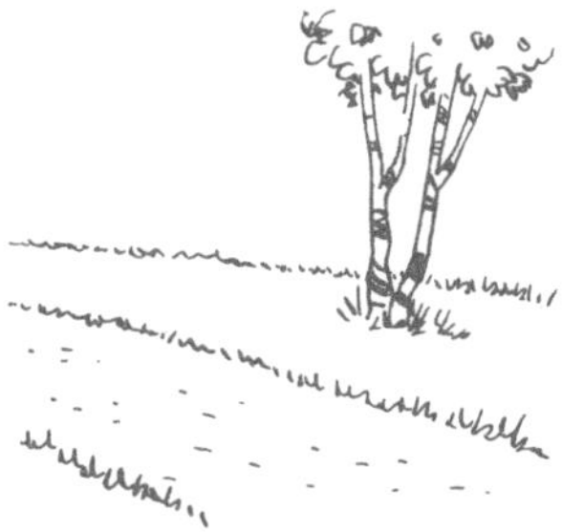

I was going to ask you if the introduction of Franklin in the late '60s was significant for you.

Well, it was just cool to see. I don't remember it feeling odd at all, because Franklin was very hip! Franklin was very hip, as was Peppermint Patty (who I think is gay).

Sparky actually had to fight for the inclusion of Franklin, because some Southern papers threatened to drop the strip. His syndicate wanted him to take Franklin out, and he absolutely refused.

Well, why would he? The world that Charlie Brown inhabits has dogs who think, little children who are virtuosos on the piano, and a black kid. Why wouldn't it? A dog who understands birds. A very dramatic little sister, very much Tallulah Bankhead — you know, Sally.

I think you're both, in your art, trying to tell the truth or find some kernel of truth in your lives.

Find it somewhere, and say it out loud, so it's not this thing which is in the dark and frightening. Just say, *O.K. Here's the world. Here's the good stuff, here's the bad stuff.* It's our world, through the eyes of children. "The psychiatrist is in."

Your modes of expression are almost polar opposites. You're much more of an advocate. You're much louder, in your face. The humor in Peanuts *is gentler, whereas yours is much harsher.*

Well, I think it has to do with the times, really. I wonder what Schulz would have been like had the time period allowed. I don't think he would ever have been as out there as I was, but I do think he might have said things a little differently. But maybe not! Because he needed to say what he needed to say the way he said it, through the kids.

There's no right or wrong of it. I have my characters who speak for me — Fontaine and the handicapped lady and the Jamaican lady and the little girl with the long, luxurious blonde hair. And he had Schroeder and Sally and Charlie Brown and Woodstock and Snoopy and

Snoopy's brother. And we're both speaking to people in two different ways, in many respects, often trying to say the same thing. I think that's why we appreciated each other.

When you say that you were both trying to say the same thing, how would you characterize what you were trying to say?

Well, listen, the world is what it is and here's how we all fit in it. There's nothing wrong with that. There's nothing wrong with being a dog who talks to birds, or being a junkie who travels 6000 miles to get an education about the fact that we're all of one race, and that is the human race. So it's a conversation that occurs all the time in many different ways. And we, as different as our approaches were, really want the best for the world.

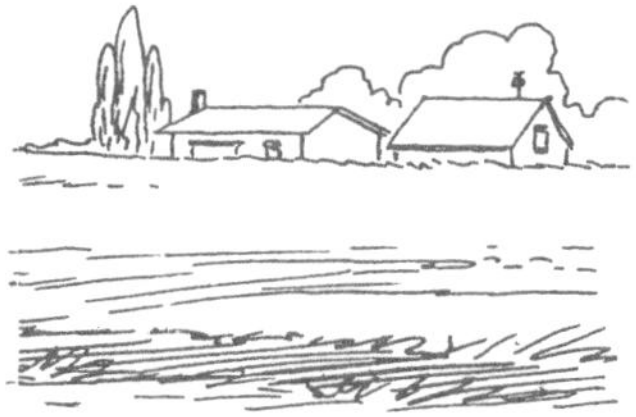

Do you see any direct affinity between your mode of humor and Schulz's?

At its base core, yeah, I think so. Because he also was very smart in the way that he pointed out the stupidity of things. In many ways I wish that we could have seen what he would have made of this president.

It's funny, because Sparky was somewhat conservative.

It never felt that way. It always felt like he wanted after-school programs for kids. You know what I mean? He didn't have to say it.

He probably just preferred that they be privately financed.

Well, in a perfect world, that's the way it should have been. In a perfect world, private financing is what should take care of a lot of stuff. But it isn't a perfect world. Interestingly, you never get the impression from the gang of Peanuts that they're well-to-do or not well-to-do.

I always got the impression that his humanity trumped his politics.

Absolutely.

Did you identify with the aspect of the strip that dealt with alienation?

In hindsight, yes.

Were you that kind of a kid?

No, I was, in a funny way, very oblivious to the fact that I was probably not living up to — not my parents' expectations, but the expectations of other people. It's only in hindsight that I realize the cruelty of adults to children.

Let me ask you a little about the characters in Peanuts. *Do you have any particular favorites? How about Lucy?*

I like Lucy, because as an adult I look at Lucy and I say, *Oh, she's got issues.* She's trying to resolve her own issues and the only way she can protect herself is by being her. And Charlie Brown doesn't have a problem with her being her, he has a problem with him being him. That's the thing about Charlie Brown. He's okay with everybody as they are. They're all freaked out about him. Except for Snoopy. He gets it.

Linus? Gotta love Linus. Who doesn't want something to hold onto?

Did Schroeder's vast talent appeal to you?

Yes, but he's very broody. So you knew he wasn't going to be a whole lot of fun, unless you talked about Beethoven or Schubert. His attitude towards the mundane is very interesting: When he goes to play "Chopsticks" his face changes. It's like, *This is not interesting because it doesn't have any depth to it.* But he doesn't have any problem going to the jazz riff. Whenever I think of him being an adult, I always see him as a '50s beatnik. With the little thing on his chin.

I really like Peppermint Patty. I think she knew that she was going to be different from everybody else. And she was. She looked different and sounded different.

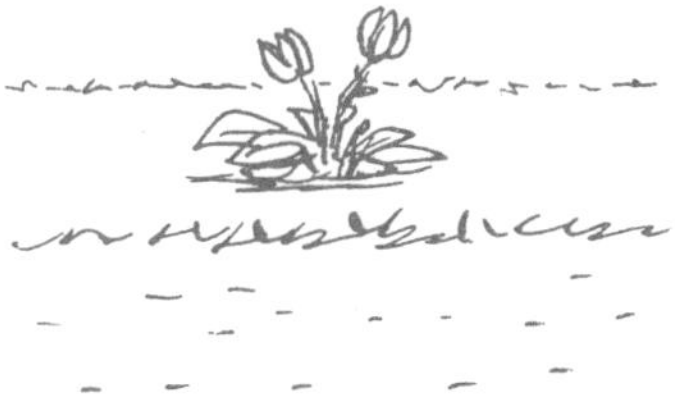

Of course Snoopy gave the strip its fantasy element. Did that appeal to you?

You know, it was only fantasy when you realized his brother was him. I don't think Spike is a separate person. I think Spike is actually his alter-ego. Snoopy is… the internal mind of most artists.

Because he's always in his own imagination?

Yeah. And yet he's contemplating everything. He sees everything, and tries to process it.

Pig-Pen. That's my other guy. We didn't talk about him. Pig-Pen. Is he just a dust cloud? Where did he come from? Where does he live? Is his house a pigpen? Who can say?

Do you have any feelings about how the strip changed or evolved over the years?

I love the visual difference between the early *Peanuts* and the later *Peanuts*. I just feel like it's our world and it's never irrelevant. I guess that's the extraordinary thing: It's for the ages. Like Jules Feiffer.

To what do you attribute your love of the cartooning form? You mentioned Feiffer without any prompting.

I love illustrators. I guess there's something fantastic to me about people like Maxfield Parrish, the illustrators who had magic at their fingers. And so you gotta love it when you see Feiffer's "A Dance to Spring," or two people having an intellectual conversation and one just going, "You're full of it!" and walking away. Or a doghouse with a dog on top who is contemplating life. There's something spectacular about it.

It's the same with Chuck Jones and the Friz Freleng cartoons of the Warner Brothers years and looking at what they were doing, whether it was the "What's Opera, Doc?" or "Coal Black and de Sebben Dwarfs." I love Tex Avery, too.

There are always these incredible voices, and you don't know why you hear them, but you do. The guys that did this kind of work, I hear them. In my own wilderness, I always hear them.

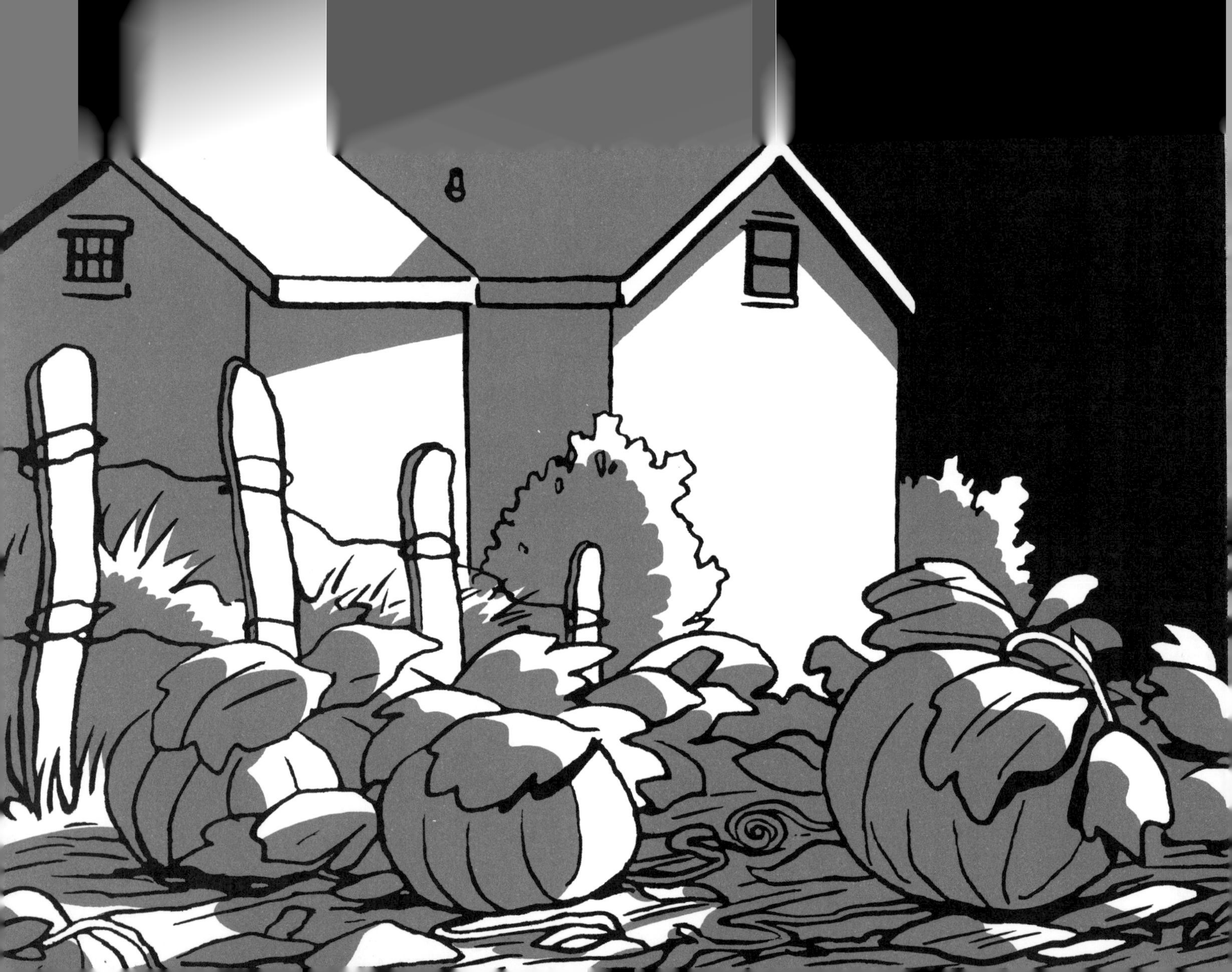

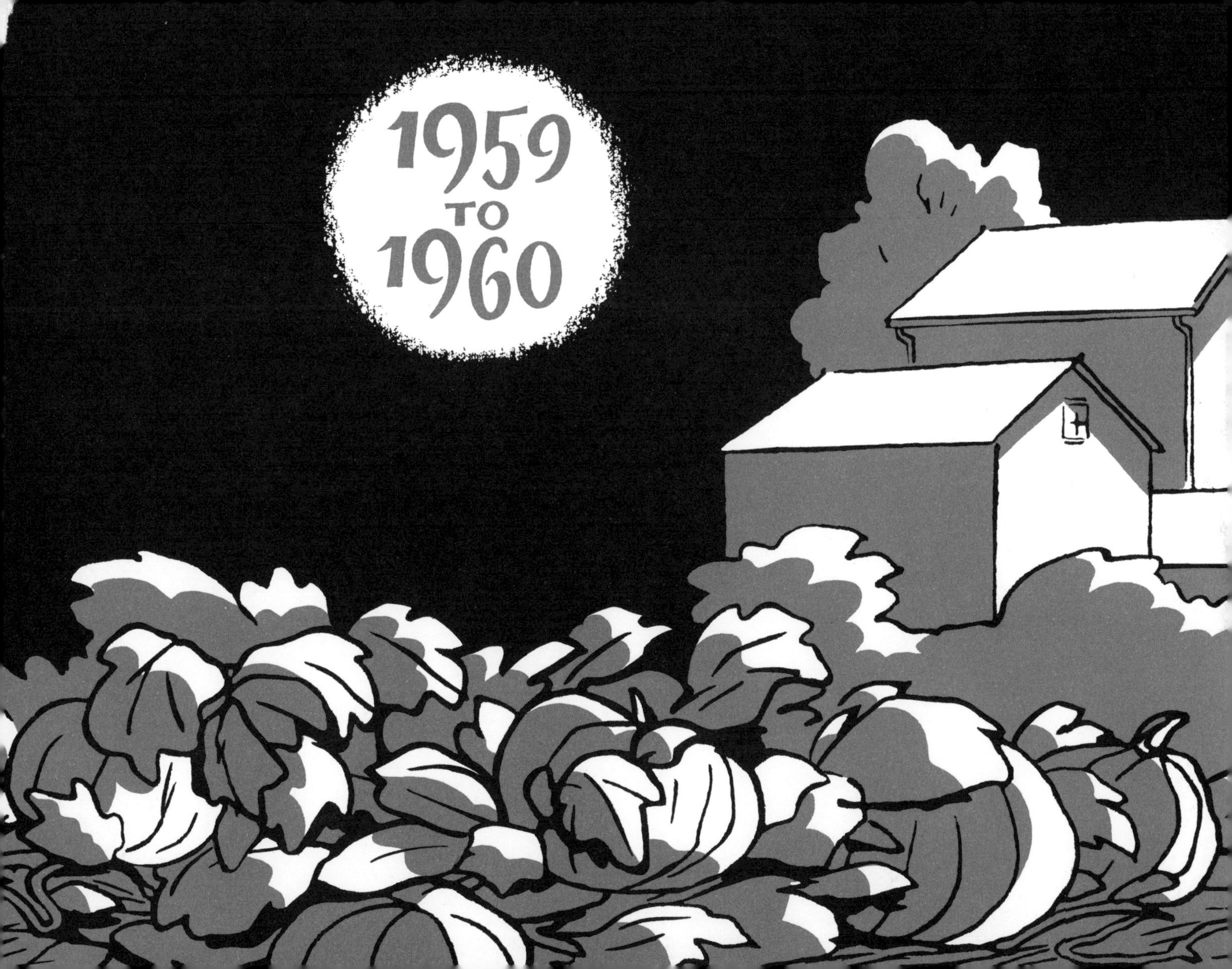
1959
TO
1960

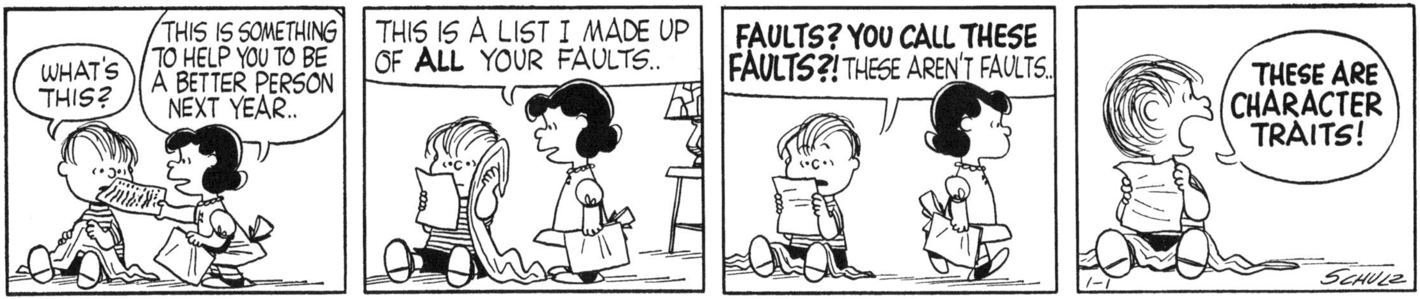
WHAT'S THIS?
THIS IS SOMETHING TO HELP YOU TO BE A BETTER PERSON NEXT YEAR..
THIS IS A LIST I MADE UP OF ALL YOUR FAULTS..
FAULTS? YOU CALL THESE FAULTS?! THESE AREN'T FAULTS..
THESE ARE CHARACTER TRAITS!
1-1
SCHULZ

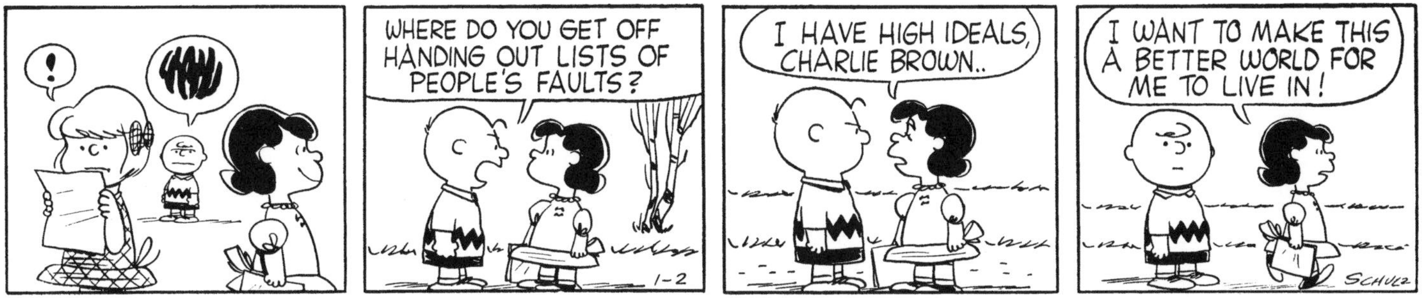
!
WHERE DO YOU GET OFF HANDING OUT LISTS OF PEOPLE'S FAULTS?
1-2
I HAVE HIGH IDEALS, CHARLIE BROWN..
I WANT TO MAKE THIS A BETTER WORLD FOR ME TO LIVE IN!
SCHULZ

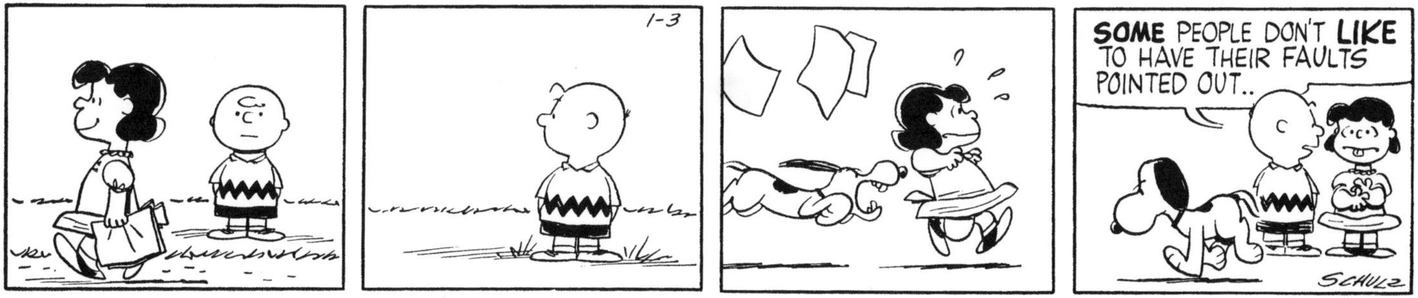
1-3
SOME PEOPLE DON'T LIKE TO HAVE THEIR FAULTS POINTED OUT..
SCHULZ

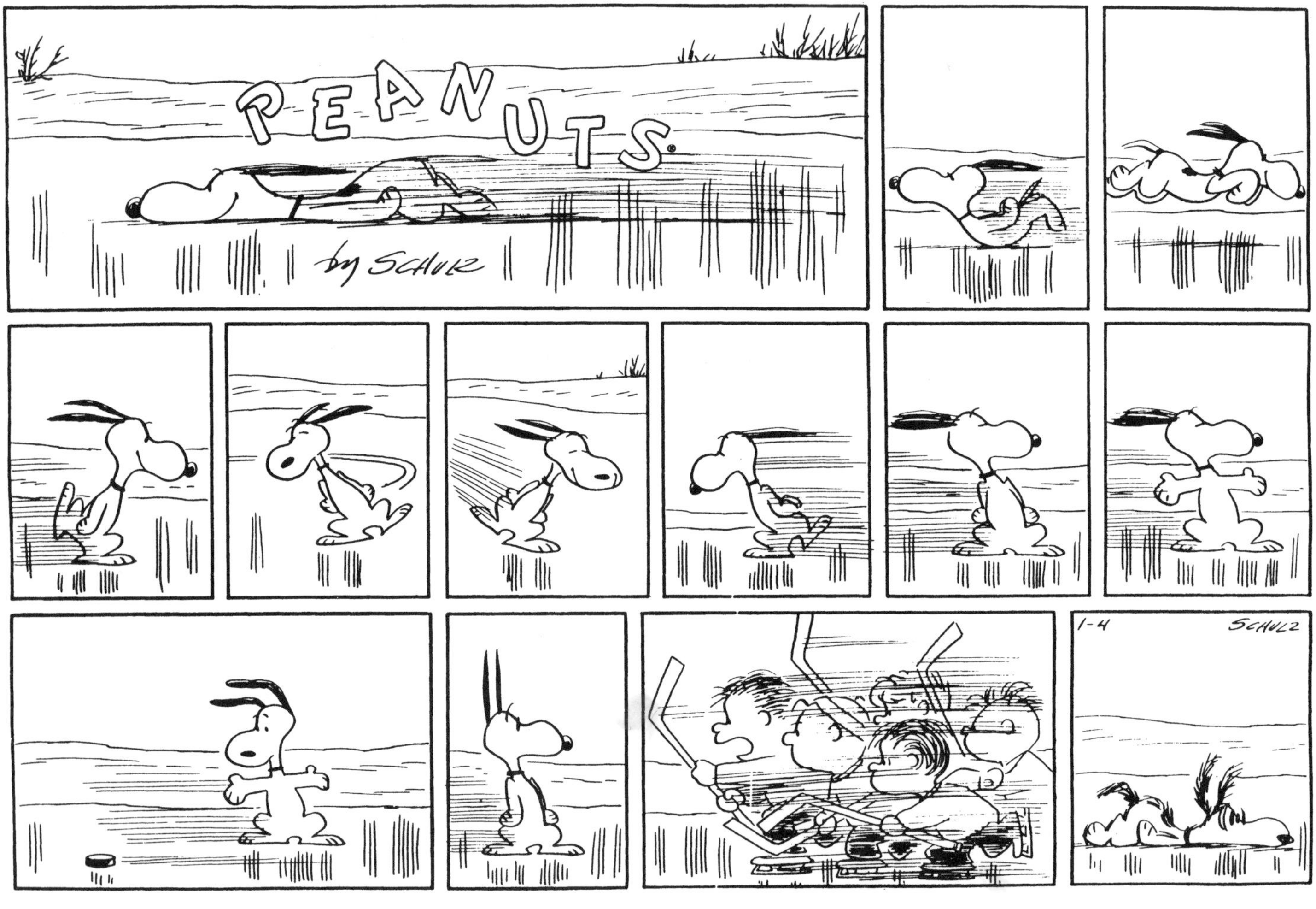
PEANUTS
by SCHULZ
1-4
SCHULZ

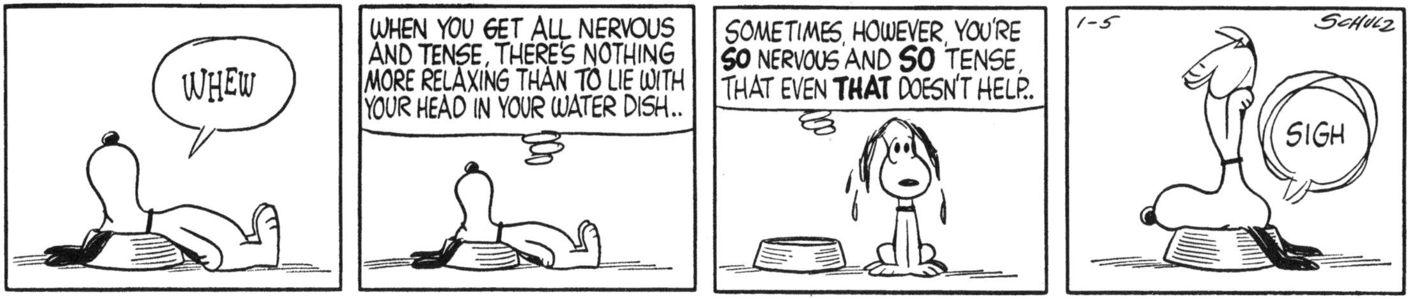
WHEW
WHEN YOU GET ALL NERVOUS AND TENSE, THERE'S NOTHING MORE RELAXING THAN TO LIE WITH YOUR HEAD IN YOUR WATER DISH..
SOMETIMES, HOWEVER, YOU'RE **SO** NERVOUS AND **SO** TENSE, THAT EVEN **THAT** DOESN'T HELP..
1-5
SCHULZ
SIGH

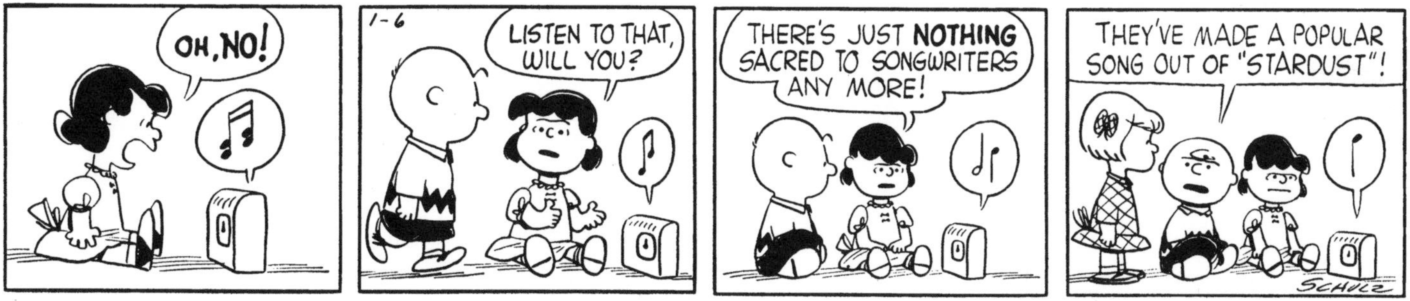
OH, NO!
1-6
LISTEN TO THAT, WILL YOU?
THERE'S JUST **NOTHING** SACRED TO SONGWRITERS ANY MORE!
THEY'VE MADE A POPULAR SONG OUT OF "STARDUST"!
SCHULZ

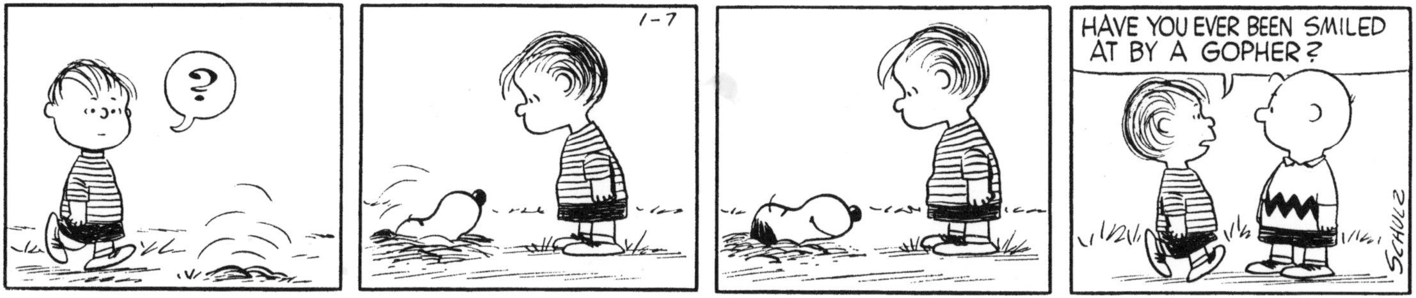
?
1-7
HAVE YOU EVER BEEN SMILED AT BY A GOPHER?
SCHULZ

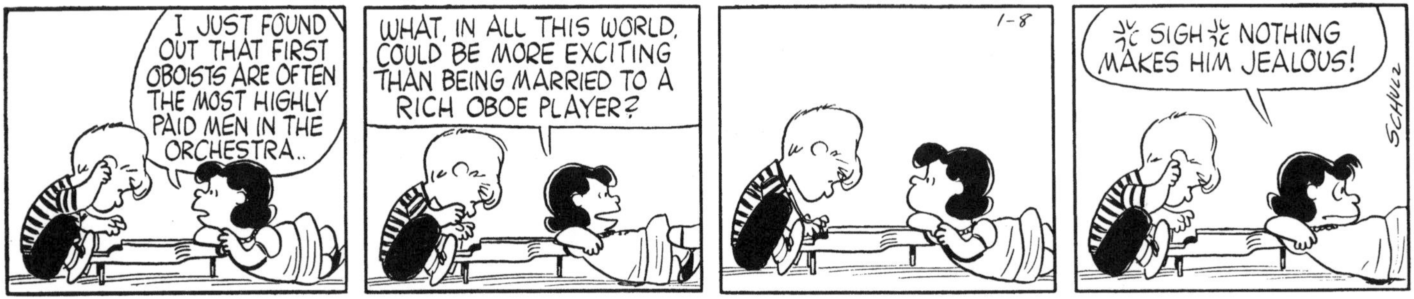
I JUST FOUND OUT THAT FIRST OBOISTS ARE OFTEN THE MOST HIGHLY PAID MEN IN THE ORCHESTRA..
WHAT, IN ALL THIS WORLD, COULD BE MORE EXCITING THAN BEING MARRIED TO A RICH OBOE PLAYER?
1-8
SIGH NOTHING MAKES HIM JEALOUS!
SCHULZ

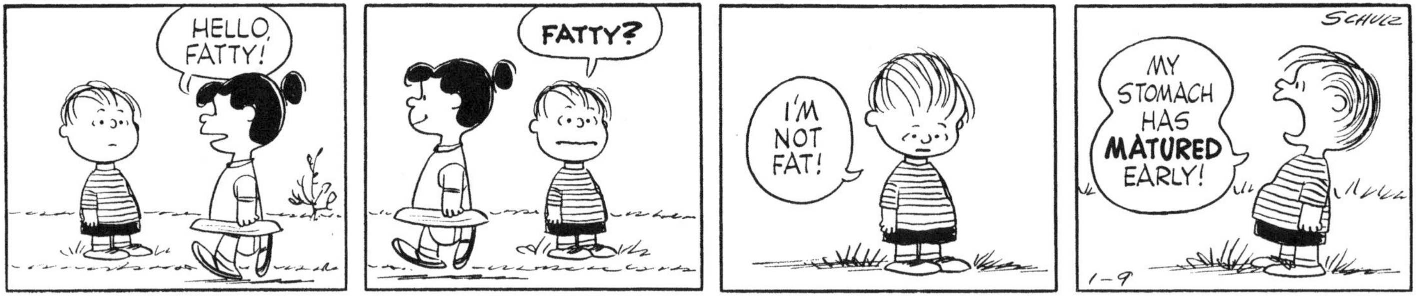
HELLO, FATTY!
FATTY?
I'M NOT FAT!
SCHULZ
MY STOMACH HAS **MATURED** EARLY!
1-9

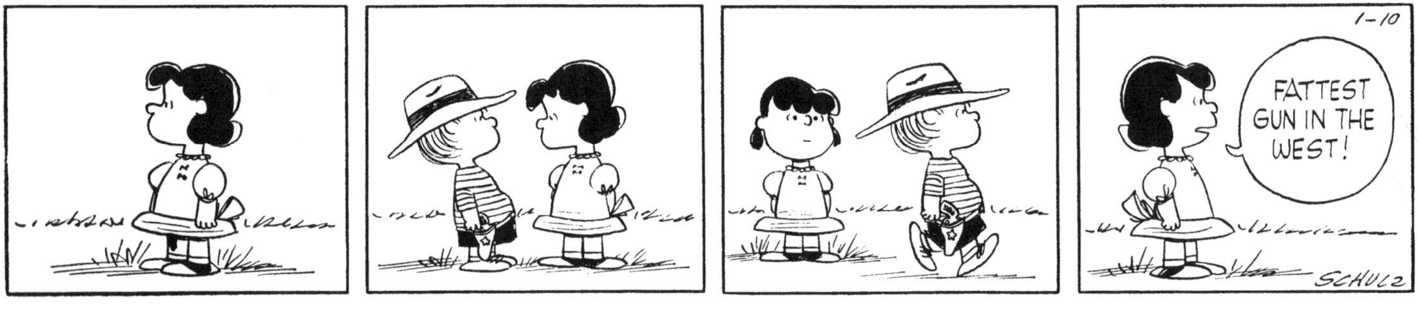
1-10
FATTEST GUN IN THE WEST!
SCHULZ

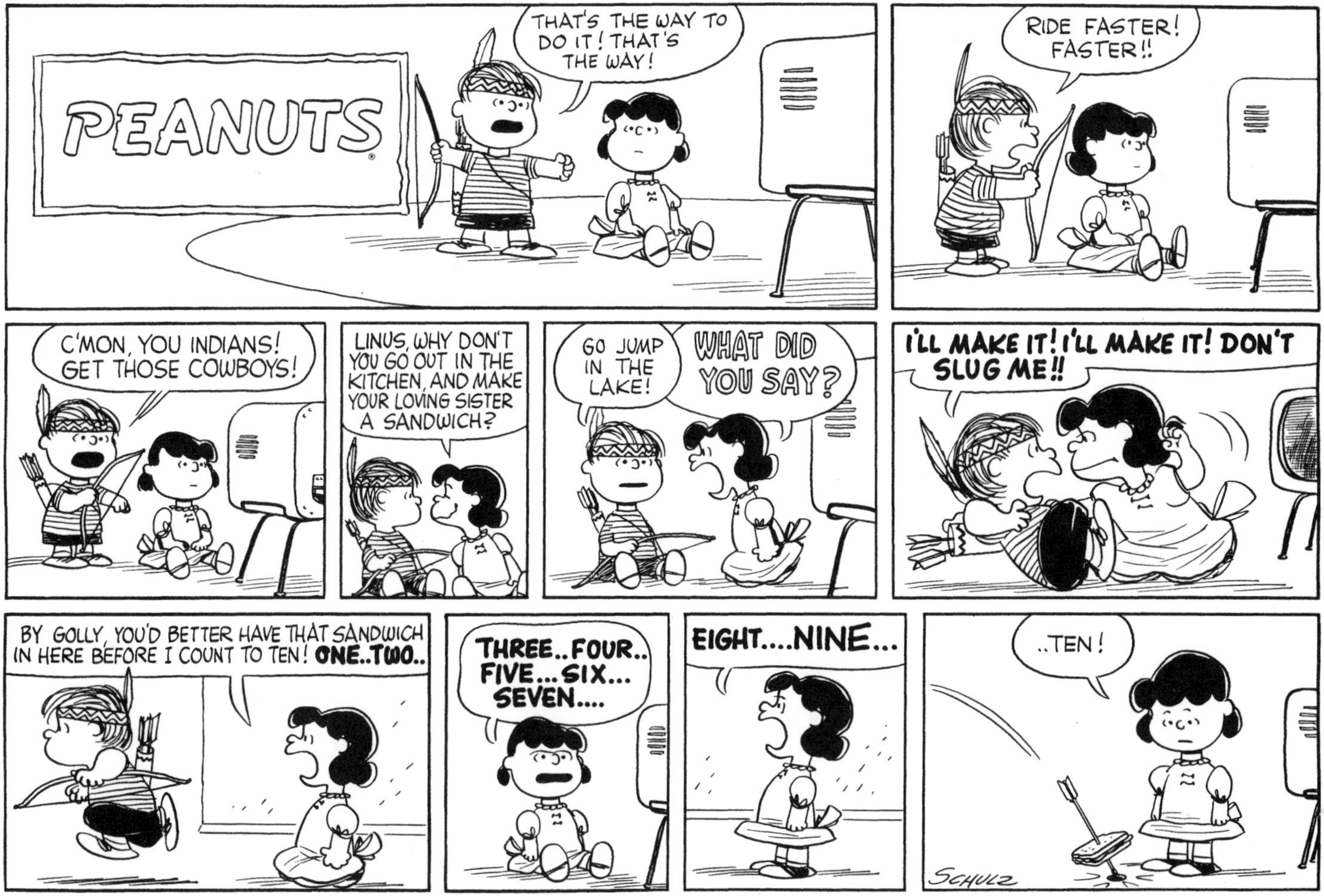
PEANUTS
THAT'S THE WAY TO DO IT! THAT'S THE WAY!
RIDE FASTER! FASTER!!
C'MON, YOU INDIANS! GET THOSE COWBOYS!
LINUS, WHY DON'T YOU GO OUT IN THE KITCHEN, AND MAKE YOUR LOVING SISTER A SANDWICH?
GO JUMP IN THE LAKE!
WHAT DID YOU SAY?
I'LL MAKE IT! I'LL MAKE IT! DON'T SLUG ME!!
BY GOLLY, YOU'D BETTER HAVE THAT SANDWICH IN HERE BEFORE I COUNT TO TEN! ONE..TWO..
THREE..FOUR.. FIVE...SIX... SEVEN....
EIGHT....NINE...
..TEN!
SCHULZ

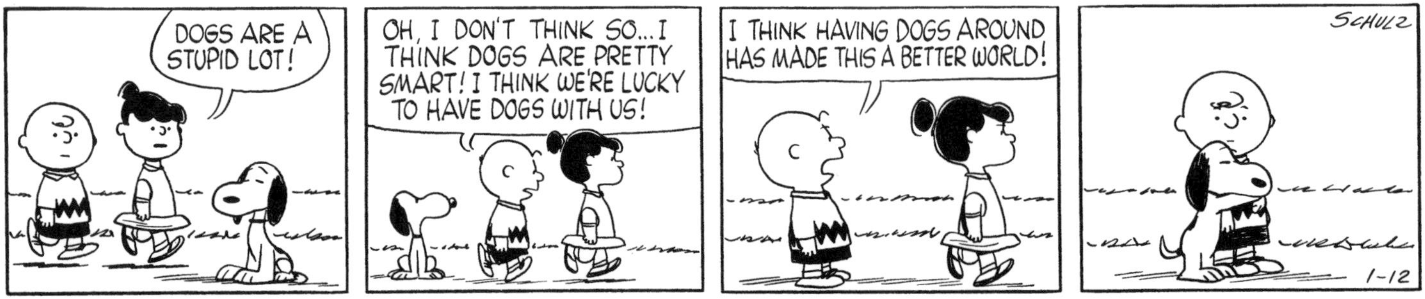
SCHULZ
DOGS ARE A STUPID LOT!
OH, I DON'T THINK SO... I THINK DOGS ARE PRETTY SMART! I THINK WE'RE LUCKY TO HAVE DOGS WITH US!
I THINK HAVING DOGS AROUND HAS MADE THIS A BETTER WORLD!
1-12

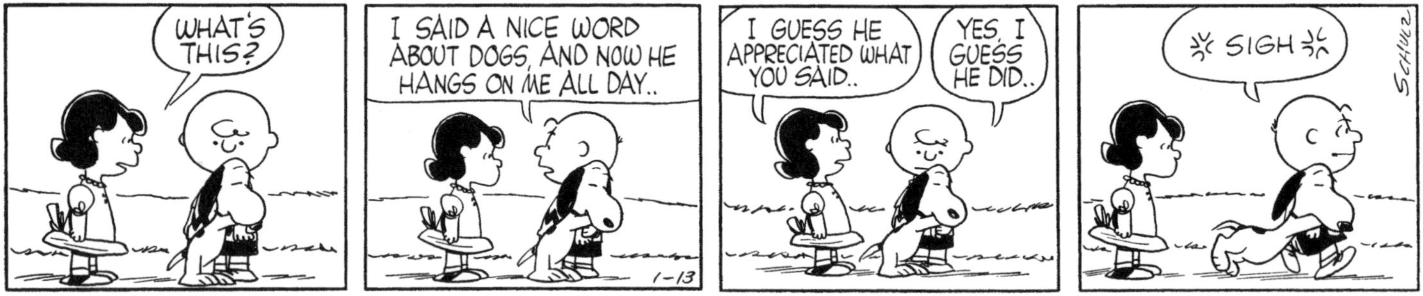
WHAT'S THIS?
I SAID A NICE WORD ABOUT DOGS, AND NOW HE HANGS ON ME ALL DAY..
1-13
I GUESS HE APPRECIATED WHAT YOU SAID..
YES, I GUESS HE DID..
SIGH
SCHULZ

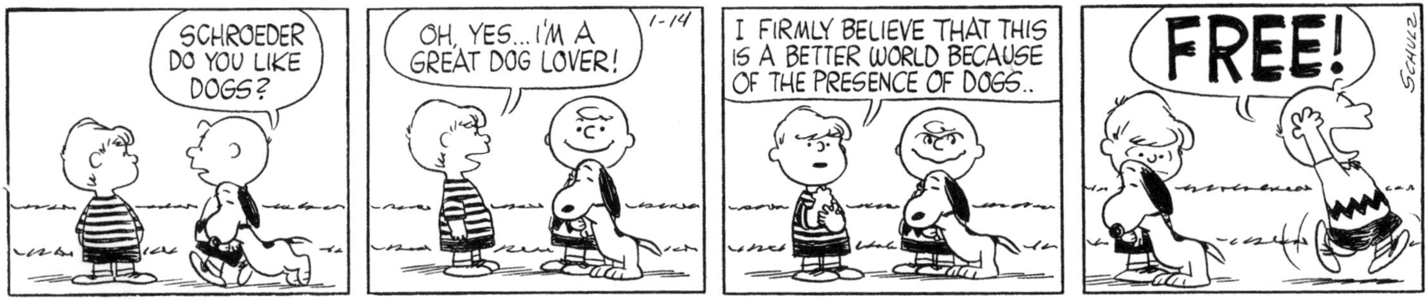
SCHROEDER DO YOU LIKE DOGS?
1-14
OH, YES... I'M A GREAT DOG LOVER!
I FIRMLY BELIEVE THAT THIS IS A BETTER WORLD BECAUSE OF THE PRESENCE OF DOGS..
FREE!
SCHULZ

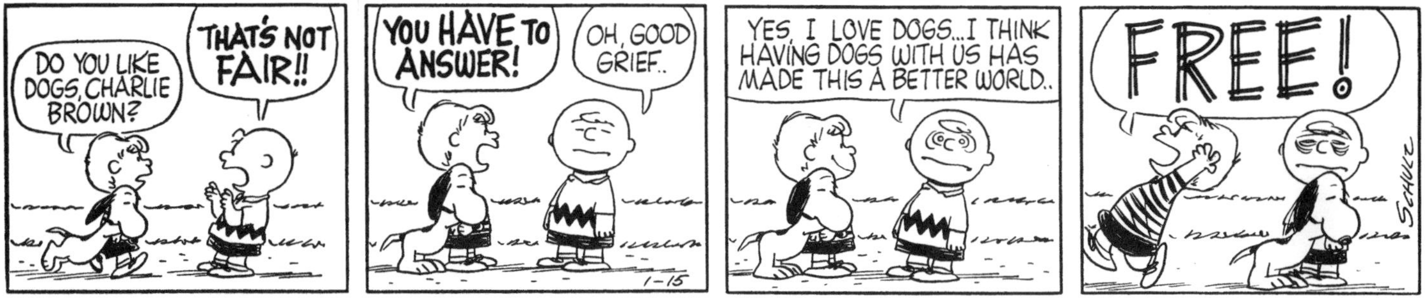
DO YOU LIKE DOGS, CHARLIE BROWN?
THAT'S NOT FAIR!!
YOU HAVE TO ANSWER!
OH, GOOD GRIEF..
1-15
YES, I LOVE DOGS...I THINK HAVING DOGS WITH US HAS MADE THIS A BETTER WORLD..
FREE!
SCHULZ

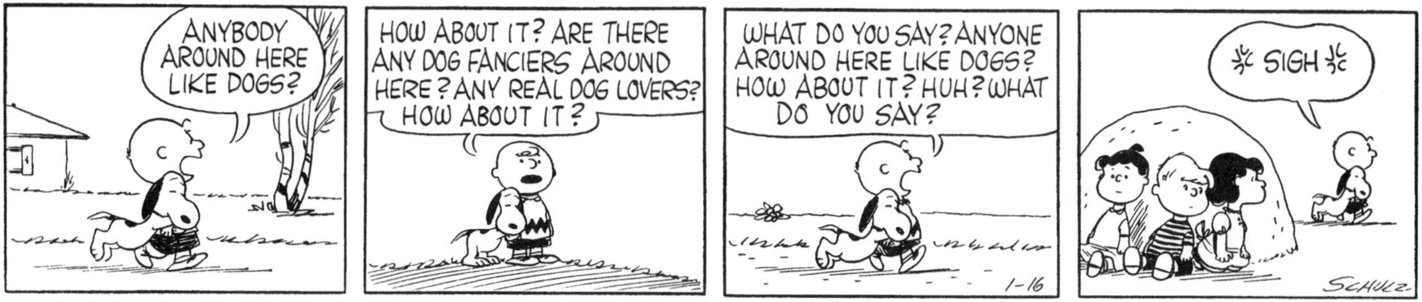
ANYBODY AROUND HERE LIKE DOGS?
HOW ABOUT IT? ARE THERE ANY DOG FANCIERS AROUND HERE? ANY REAL DOG LOVERS? HOW ABOUT IT?
WHAT DO YOU SAY? ANYONE AROUND HERE LIKE DOGS? HOW ABOUT IT? HUH? WHAT DO YOU SAY?
1-16
SIGH
SCHULZ

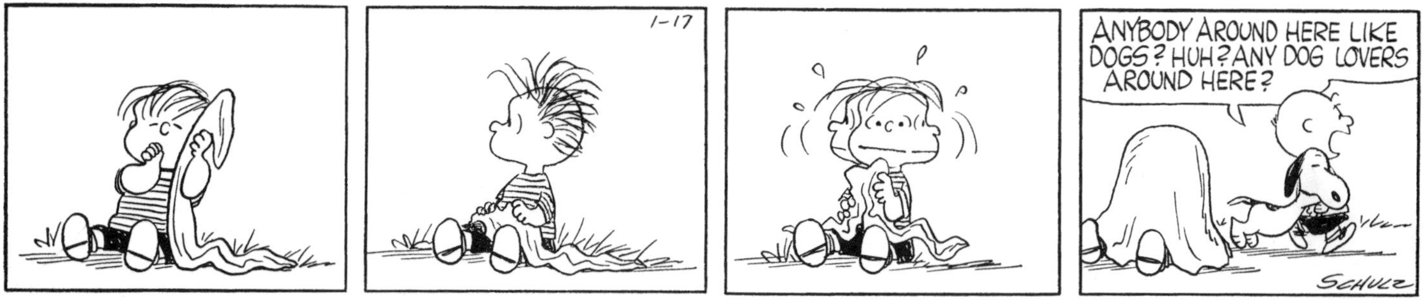
1-17
ANYBODY AROUND HERE LIKE DOGS? HUH? ANY DOG LOVERS AROUND HERE?
SCHULZ

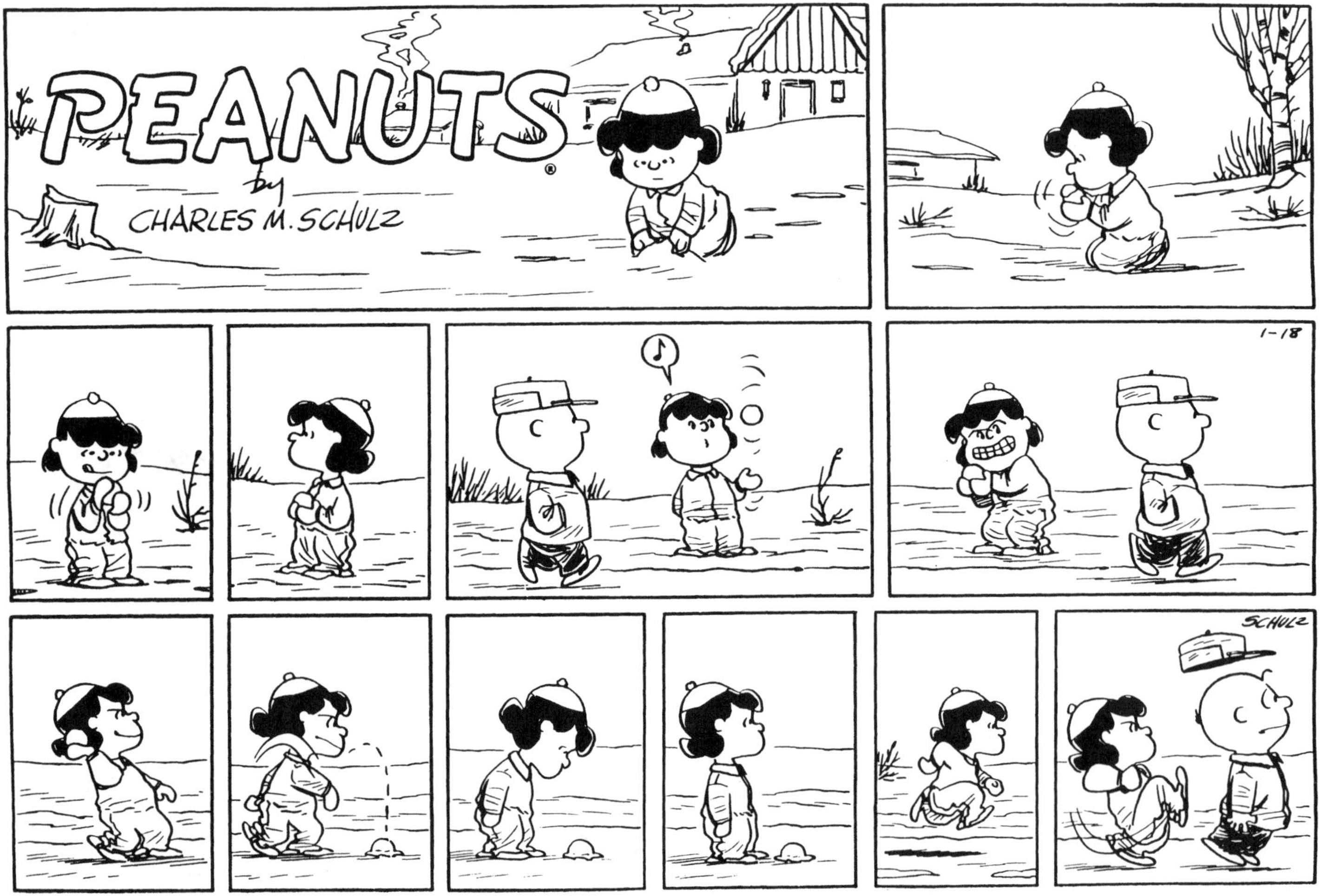
PEANUTS
by
CHARLES M. SCHULZ
1-18
SCHULZ

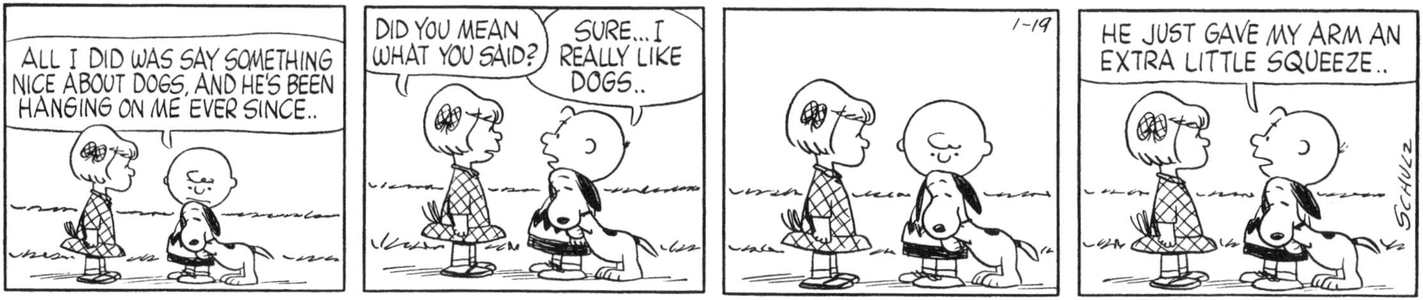
ALL I DID WAS SAY SOMETHING NICE ABOUT DOGS, AND HE'S BEEN HANGING ON ME EVER SINCE..
DID YOU MEAN WHAT YOU SAID?
SURE... I REALLY LIKE DOGS..
1-19
HE JUST GAVE MY ARM AN EXTRA LITTLE SQUEEZE..
SCHULZ

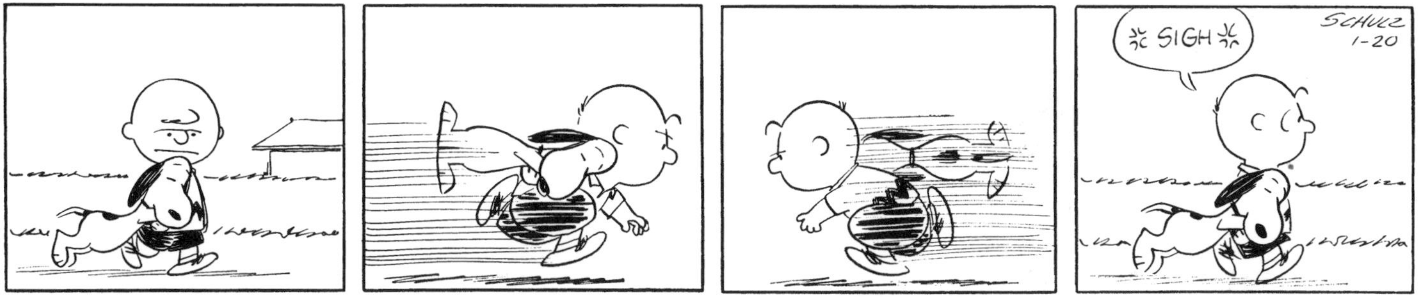
SCHULZ
1-20
SIGH

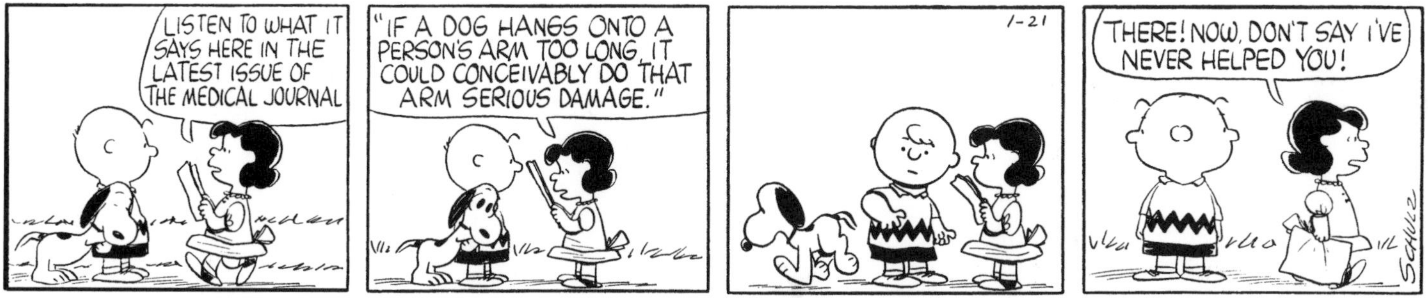
LISTEN TO WHAT IT SAYS HERE IN THE LATEST ISSUE OF THE MEDICAL JOURNAL
"IF A DOG HANGS ONTO A PERSON'S ARM TOO LONG, IT COULD CONCEIVABLY DO THAT ARM SERIOUS DAMAGE."
1-21
THERE! NOW, DON'T SAY I'VE NEVER HELPED YOU!
SCHULZ

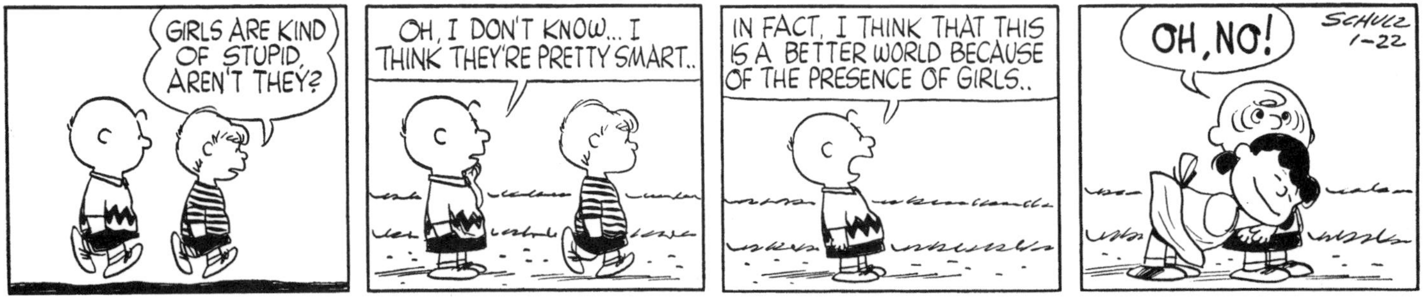
GIRLS ARE KIND OF STUPID, AREN'T THEY?
OH, I DON'T KNOW... I THINK THEY'RE PRETTY SMART..
IN FACT, I THINK THAT THIS IS A BETTER WORLD BECAUSE OF THE PRESENCE OF GIRLS..
OH, NO!
SCHULZ 1-22

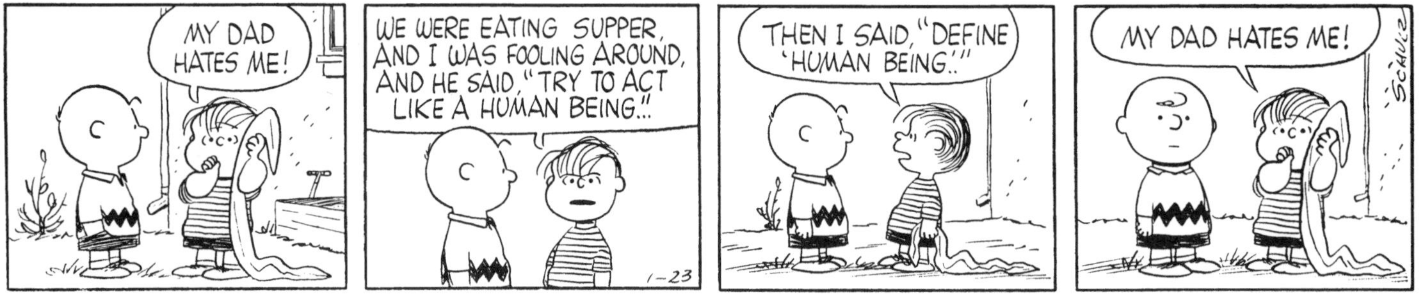
MY DAD HATES ME!
WE WERE EATING SUPPER, AND I WAS FOOLING AROUND, AND HE SAID, "TRY TO ACT LIKE A HUMAN BEING."
1-23
THEN I SAID, "DEFINE 'HUMAN BEING.'"
MY DAD HATES ME!
SCHULZ

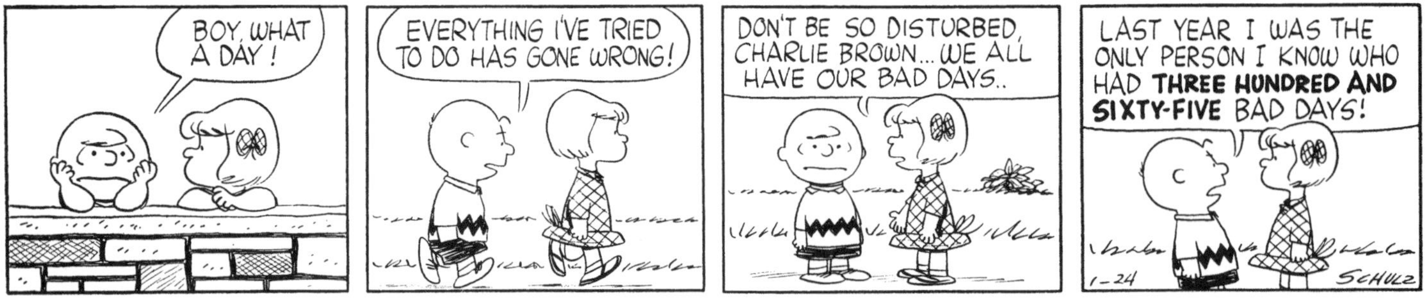
BOY, WHAT A DAY!
EVERYTHING I'VE TRIED TO DO HAS GONE WRONG!
DON'T BE SO DISTURBED, CHARLIE BROWN... WE ALL HAVE OUR BAD DAYS..
LAST YEAR I WAS THE ONLY PERSON I KNOW WHO HAD THREE HUNDRED AND SIXTY-FIVE BAD DAYS!
1-24
SCHULZ

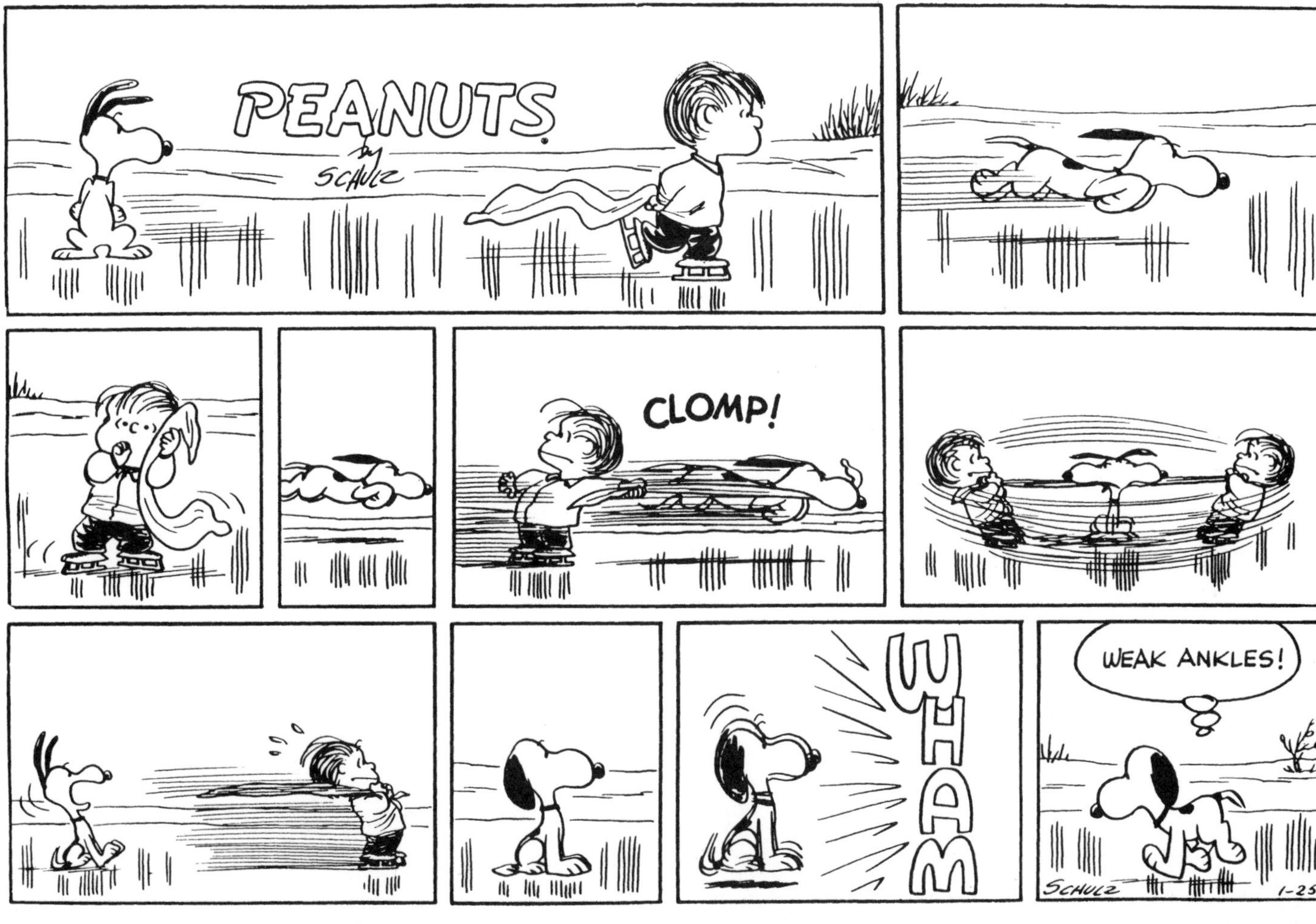
PEANUTS
by SCHULZ
CLOMP!
WHAM
WEAK ANKLES!
SCHULZ
1-25

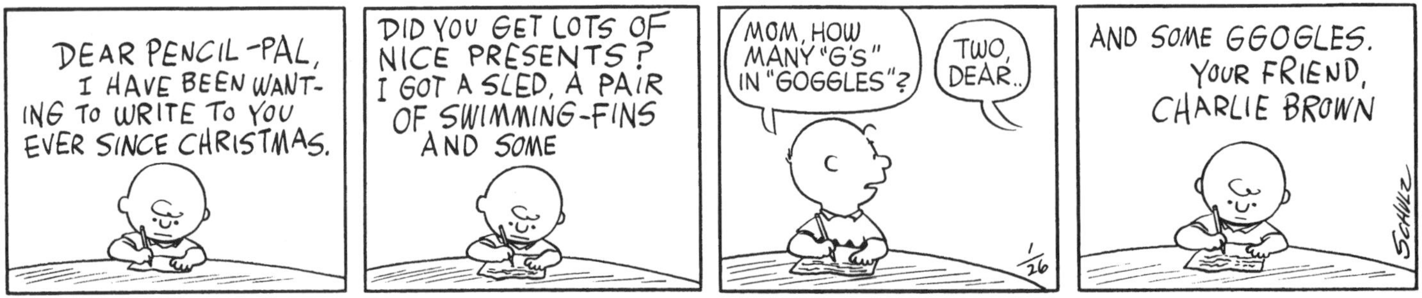
DEAR PENCIL-PAL, I HAVE BEEN WANT-ING TO WRITE TO YOU EVER SINCE CHRISTMAS.
DID YOU GET LOTS OF NICE PRESENTS? I GOT A SLED, A PAIR OF SWIMMING-FINS AND SOME
MOM, HOW MANY "G'S" IN "GOGGLES"?
TWO, DEAR..
AND SOME GGOGLES. YOUR FRIEND, CHARLIE BROWN
SCHULZ
1/26

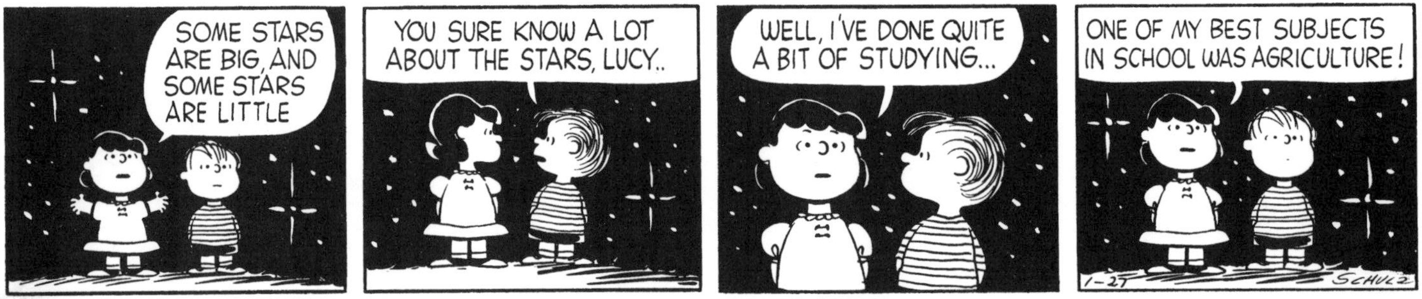
SOME STARS ARE BIG, AND SOME STARS ARE LITTLE
YOU SURE KNOW A LOT ABOUT THE STARS, LUCY..
WELL, I'VE DONE QUITE A BIT OF STUDYING...
ONE OF MY BEST SUBJECTS IN SCHOOL WAS AGRICULTURE!
1-27
SCHULZ

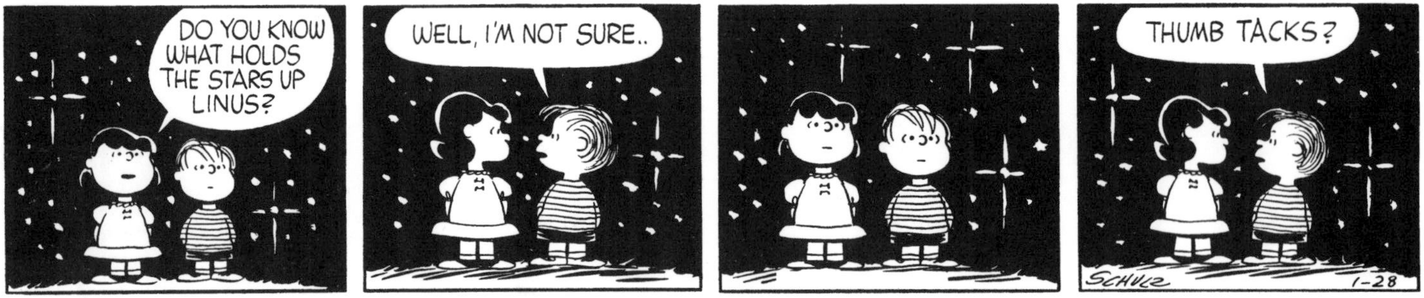
DO YOU KNOW WHAT HOLDS THE STARS UP LINUS?
WELL, I'M NOT SURE..
THUMB TACKS?
SCHULZ
1-28

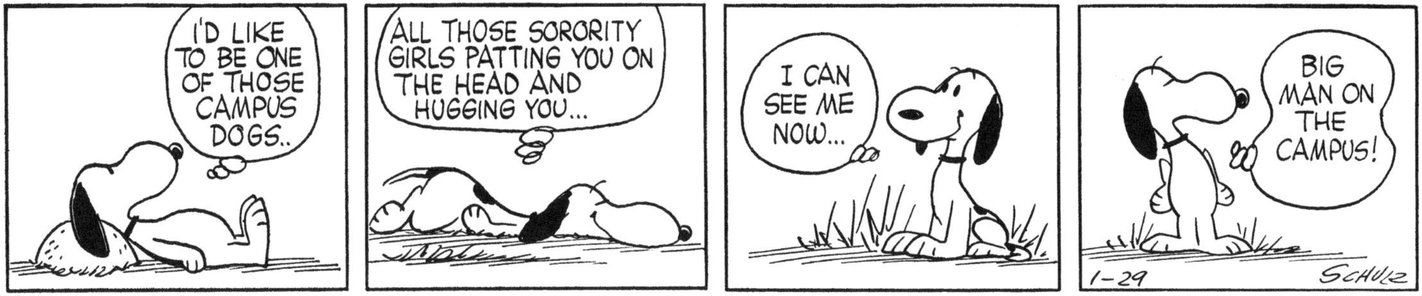
I'D LIKE TO BE ONE OF THOSE CAMPUS DOGS..
ALL THOSE SORORITY GIRLS PATTING YOU ON THE HEAD AND HUGGING YOU...
I CAN SEE ME NOW...
BIG MAN ON THE CAMPUS!
1-29
SCHULZ

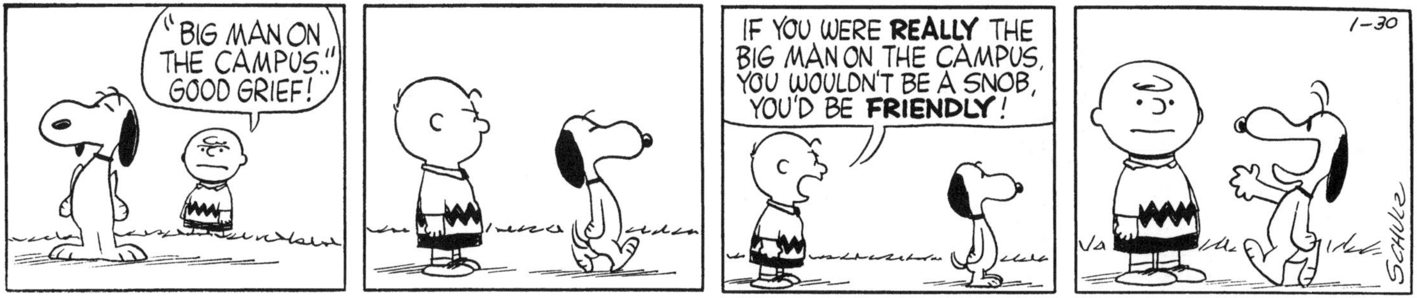
"BIG MAN ON THE CAMPUS.." GOOD GRIEF!
IF YOU WERE **REALLY** THE BIG MAN ON THE CAMPUS, YOU WOULDN'T BE A SNOB, YOU'D BE **FRIENDLY**!
1-30
SCHULZ

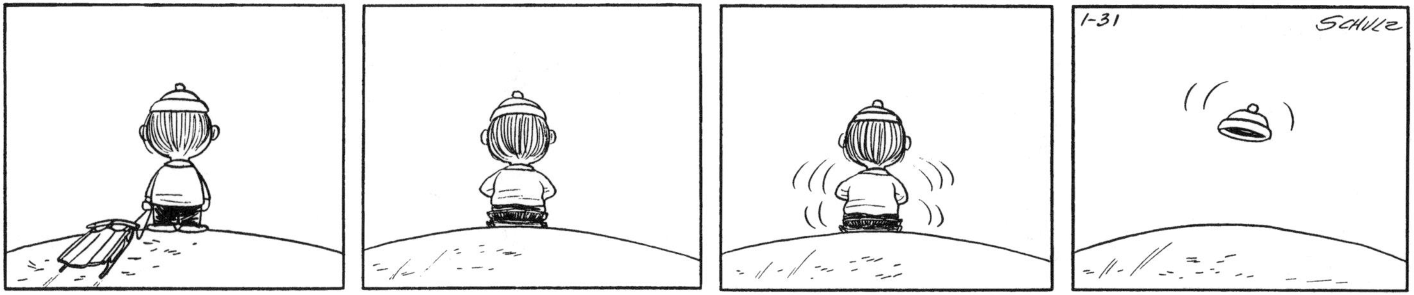
1-31
SCHULZ

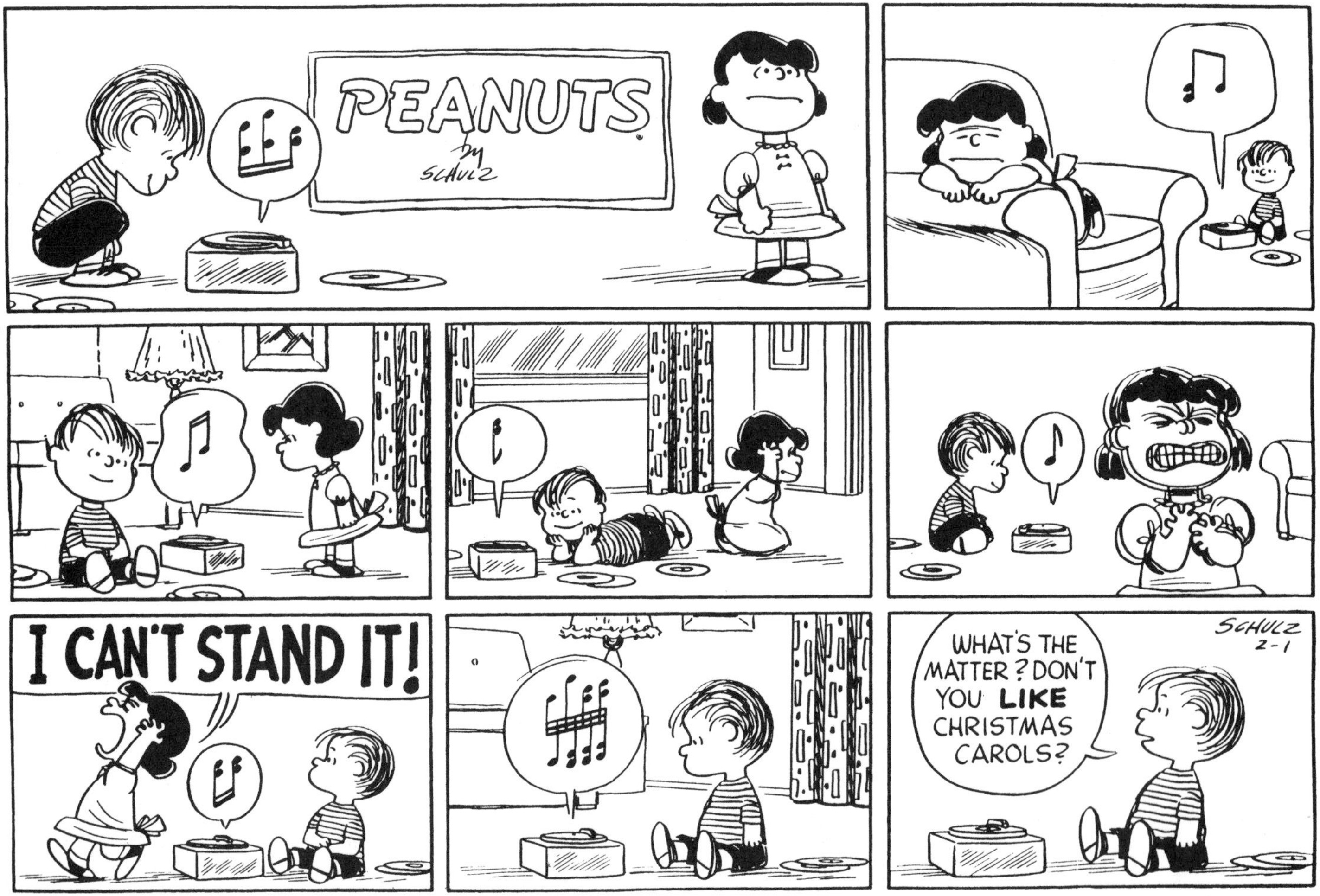
PEANUTS
by SCHULZ
I CAN'T STAND IT!
SCHULZ 2-1
WHAT'S THE MATTER? DON'T YOU LIKE CHRISTMAS CAROLS?

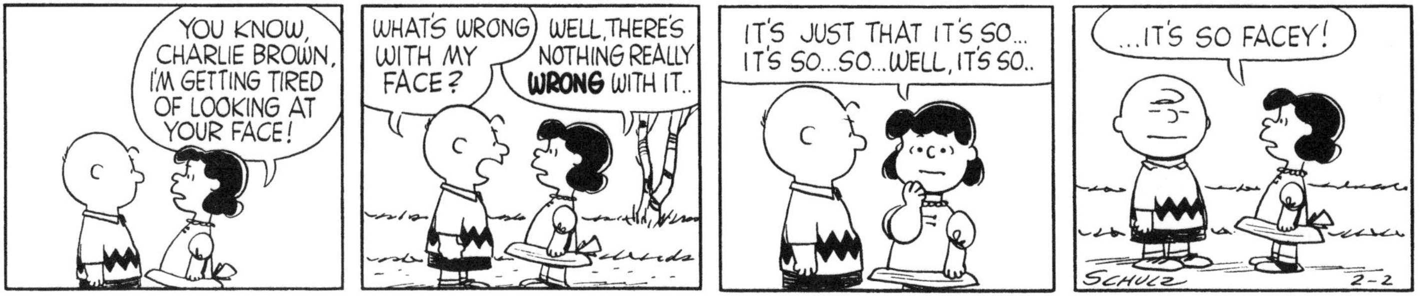
YOU KNOW, CHARLIE BROWN, I'M GETTING TIRED OF LOOKING AT YOUR FACE!
WHAT'S WRONG WITH MY FACE?
WELL, THERE'S NOTHING REALLY **WRONG** WITH IT..
IT'S JUST THAT IT'S SO... IT'S SO...SO...WELL, IT'S SO..
...IT'S SO FACEY!
SCHULZ
2-2

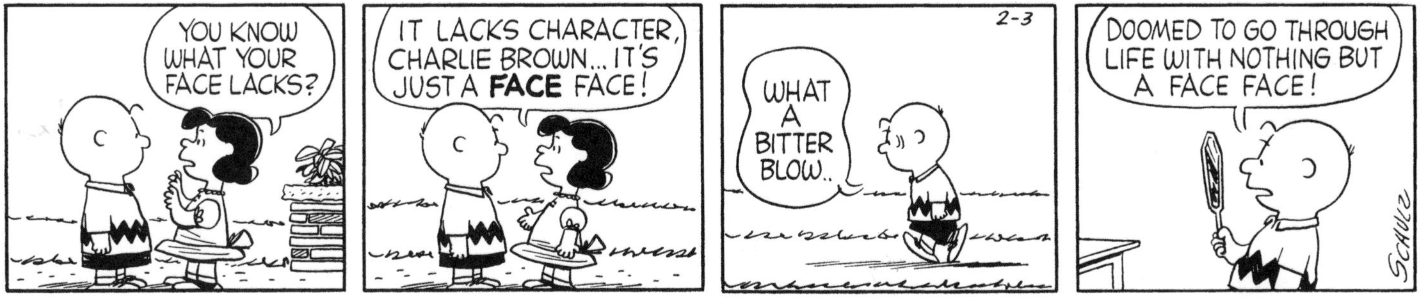
YOU KNOW WHAT YOUR FACE LACKS?
IT LACKS CHARACTER, CHARLIE BROWN... IT'S JUST A **FACE** FACE!
2-3
WHAT A BITTER BLOW..
DOOMED TO GO THROUGH LIFE WITH NOTHING BUT A FACE FACE!
SCHULZ

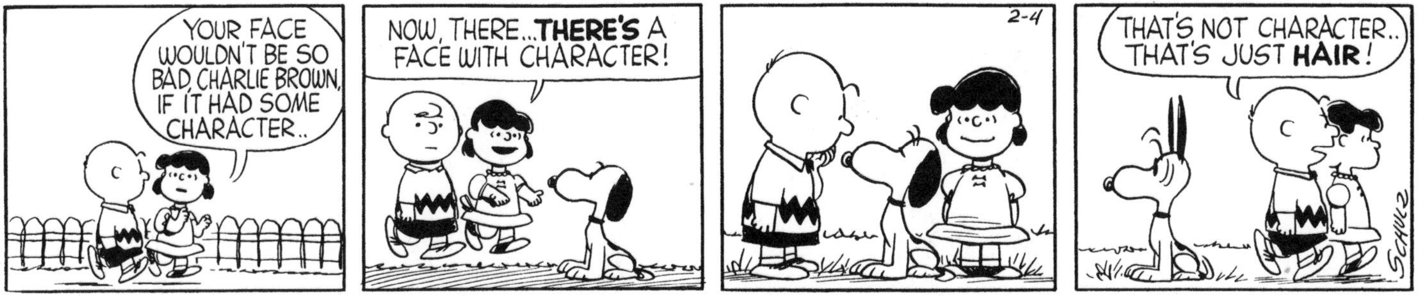
YOUR FACE WOULDN'T BE SO BAD, CHARLIE BROWN, IF IT HAD SOME CHARACTER..
NOW, THERE...**THERE'S** A FACE WITH CHARACTER!
2-4
THAT'S NOT CHARACTER.. THAT'S JUST **HAIR**!
SCHULZ

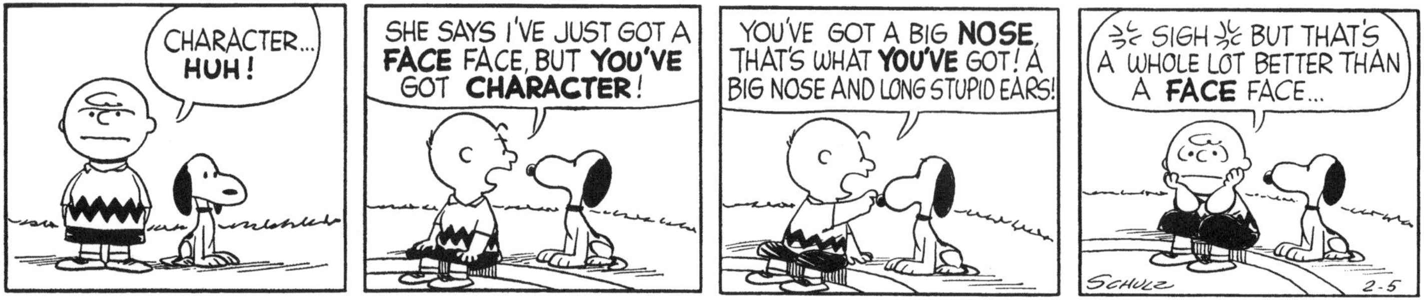
CHARACTER... HUH!
SHE SAYS I'VE JUST GOT A FACE FACE, BUT YOU'VE GOT CHARACTER!
YOU'VE GOT A BIG NOSE, THAT'S WHAT YOU'VE GOT! A BIG NOSE AND LONG STUPID EARS!
SIGH BUT THAT'S A WHOLE LOT BETTER THAN A FACE FACE...
SCHULZ
2-5

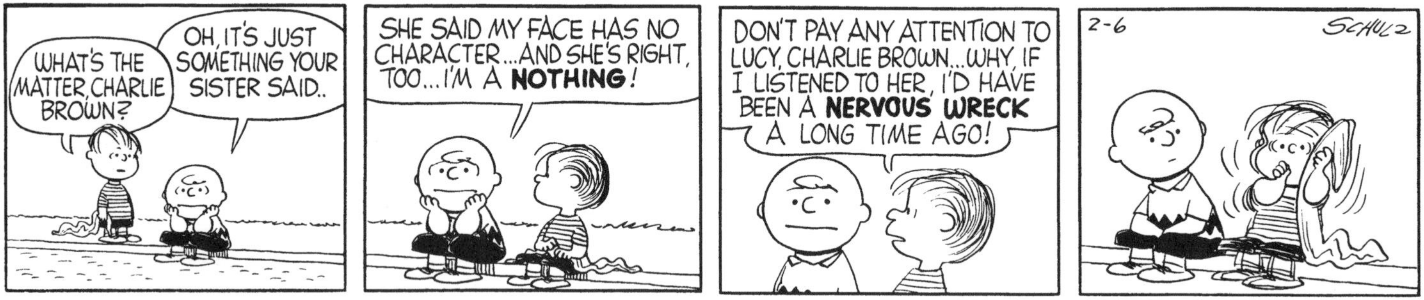
WHAT'S THE MATTER, CHARLIE BROWN?
OH, IT'S JUST SOMETHING YOUR SISTER SAID..
SHE SAID MY FACE HAS NO CHARACTER...AND SHE'S RIGHT, TOO...I'M A NOTHING!
DON'T PAY ANY ATTENTION TO LUCY, CHARLIE BROWN...WHY, IF I LISTENED TO HER, I'D HAVE BEEN A NERVOUS WRECK A LONG TIME AGO!
2-6
SCHULZ

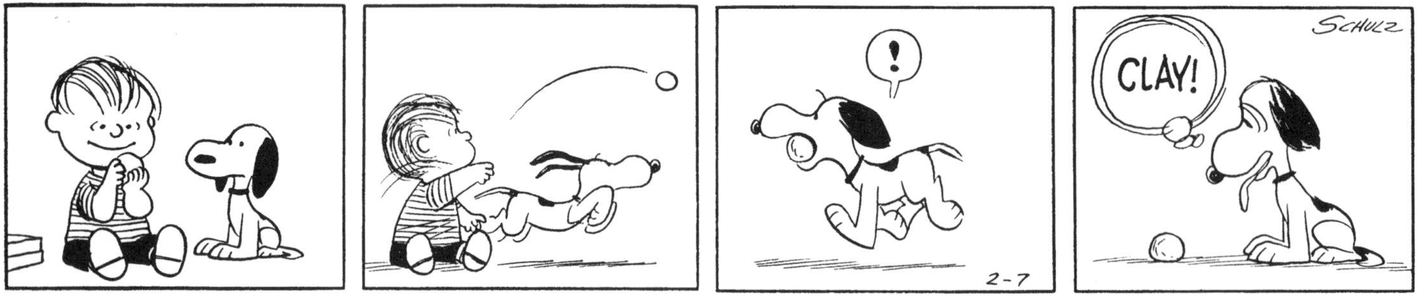
!
2-7
SCHULZ
CLAY!

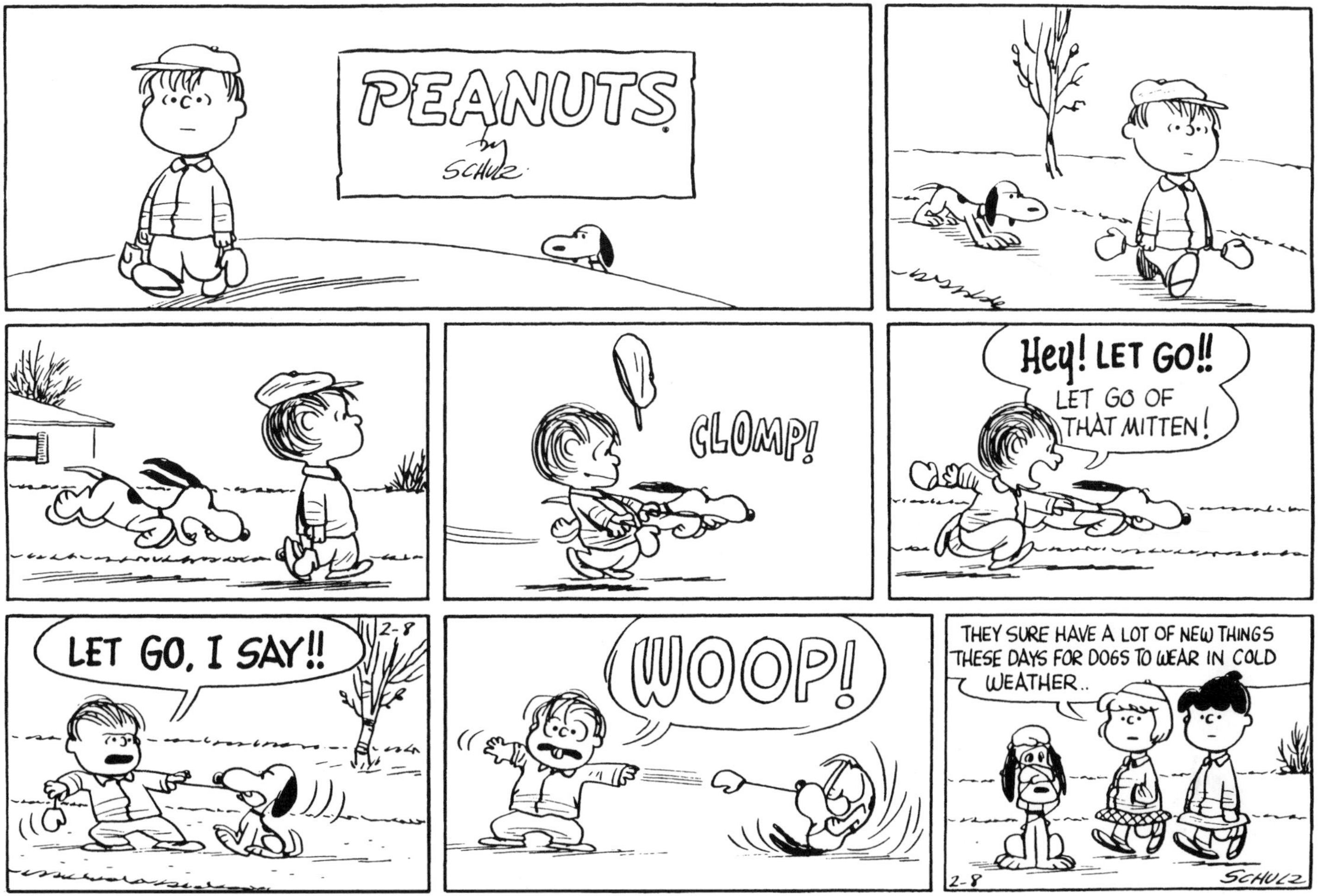
PEANUTS
by SCHULZ
CLOMP!
Hey! LET GO!!
LET GO OF THAT MITTEN!
LET GO, I SAY!!
2-8
WOOP!
THEY SURE HAVE A LOT OF NEW THINGS THESE DAYS FOR DOGS TO WEAR IN COLD WEATHER..
2-8
SCHULZ

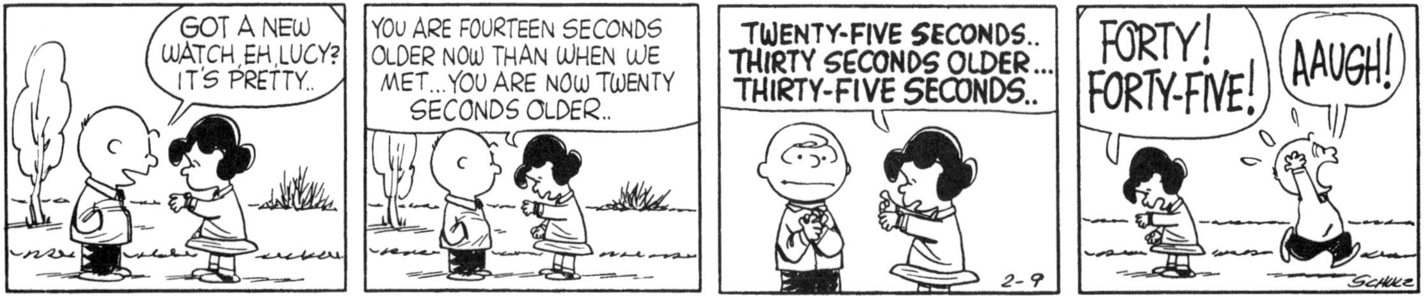
GOT A NEW WATCH, EH, LUCY? IT'S PRETTY..
YOU ARE FOURTEEN SECONDS OLDER NOW THAN WHEN WE MET...YOU ARE NOW TWENTY SECONDS OLDER..
TWENTY-FIVE SECONDS.. THIRTY SECONDS OLDER... THIRTY-FIVE SECONDS..
2-9
FORTY! FORTY-FIVE!
AAUGH!
SCHULZ

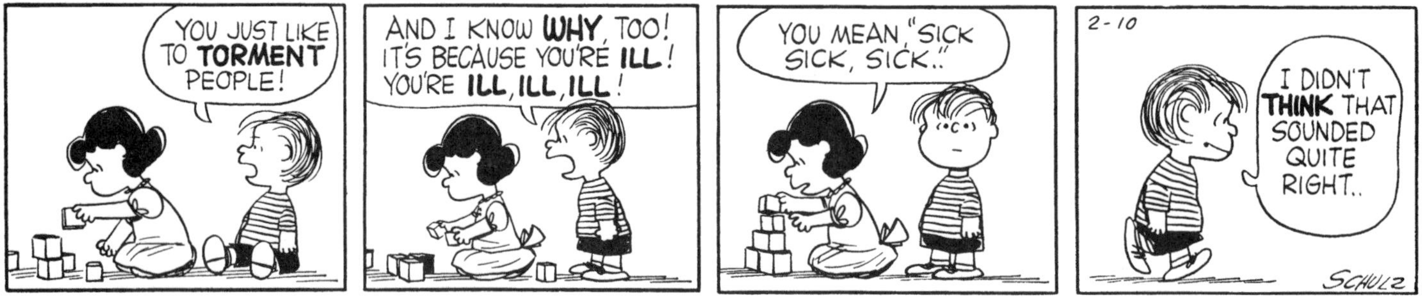
YOU JUST LIKE TO **TORMENT** PEOPLE!
AND I KNOW **WHY**, TOO! IT'S BECAUSE YOU'RE **ILL**! YOU'RE **ILL, ILL, ILL**!
YOU MEAN "SICK SICK, SICK.."
2-10
I DIDN'T **THINK** THAT SOUNDED QUITE RIGHT..
SCHULZ

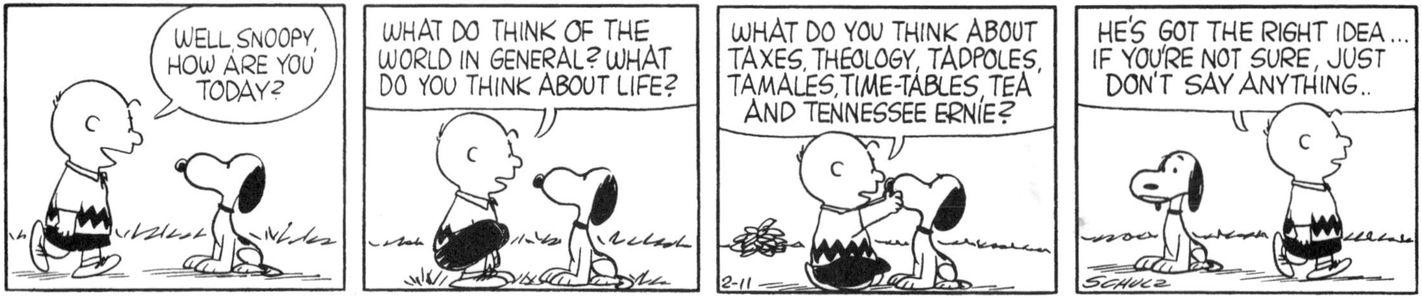
WELL, SNOOPY, HOW ARE YOU TODAY?
WHAT DO THINK OF THE WORLD IN GENERAL? WHAT DO YOU THINK ABOUT LIFE?
WHAT DO YOU THINK ABOUT TAXES, THEOLOGY, TADPOLES, TAMALES, TIME-TABLES, TEA AND TENNESSEE ERNIE?
2-11
HE'S GOT THE RIGHT IDEA... IF YOU'RE NOT SURE, JUST DON'T SAY ANYTHING..
SCHULZ

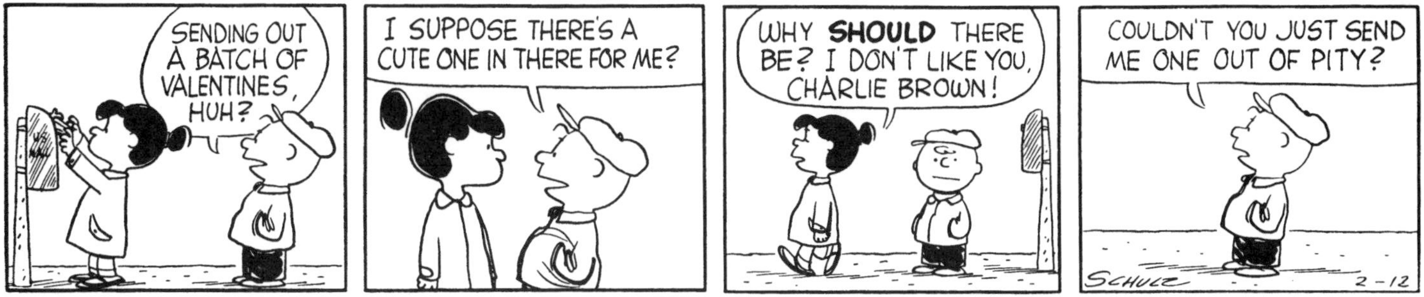
SENDING OUT A BATCH OF VALENTINES, HUH?
I SUPPOSE THERE'S A CUTE ONE IN THERE FOR ME?
WHY **SHOULD** THERE BE? I DON'T LIKE YOU, CHARLIE BROWN!
COULDN'T YOU JUST SEND ME ONE OUT OF PITY?
SCHULZ
2-12

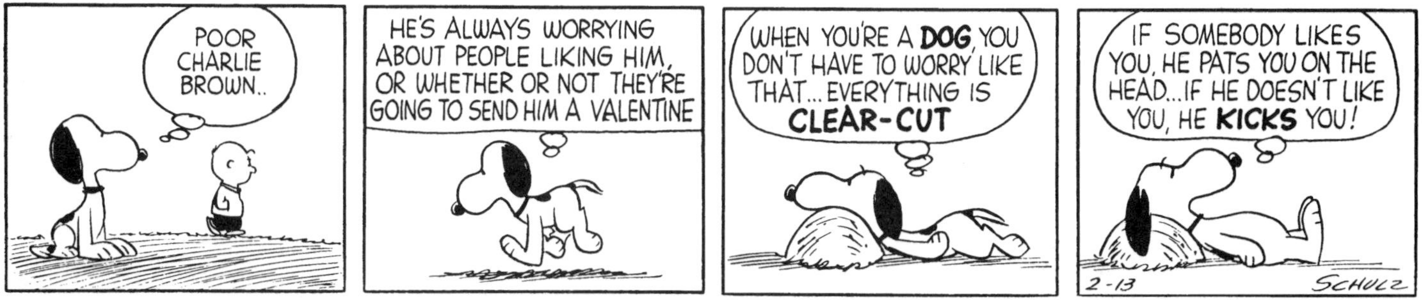
POOR CHARLIE BROWN..
HE'S ALWAYS WORRYING ABOUT PEOPLE LIKING HIM, OR WHETHER OR NOT THEY'RE GOING TO SEND HIM A VALENTINE
WHEN YOU'RE A **DOG**, YOU DON'T HAVE TO WORRY LIKE THAT... EVERYTHING IS **CLEAR-CUT**
IF SOMEBODY LIKES YOU, HE PATS YOU ON THE HEAD...IF HE DOESN'T LIKE YOU, HE **KICKS** YOU!
2-13
SCHULZ

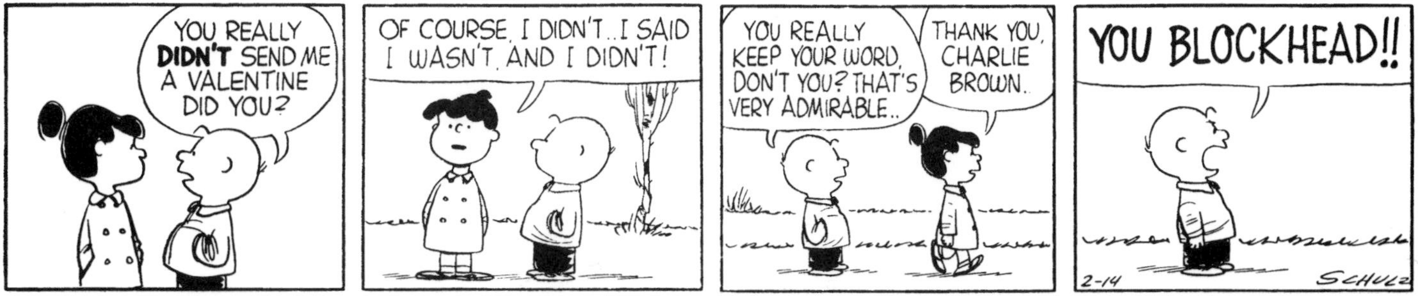
YOU REALLY **DIDN'T** SEND ME A VALENTINE DID YOU?
OF COURSE I DIDN'T..I SAID I WASN'T, AND I DIDN'T!
YOU REALLY KEEP YOUR WORD, DON'T YOU? THAT'S VERY ADMIRABLE..
THANK YOU, CHARLIE BROWN..
YOU BLOCKHEAD!!
2-14
SCHULZ

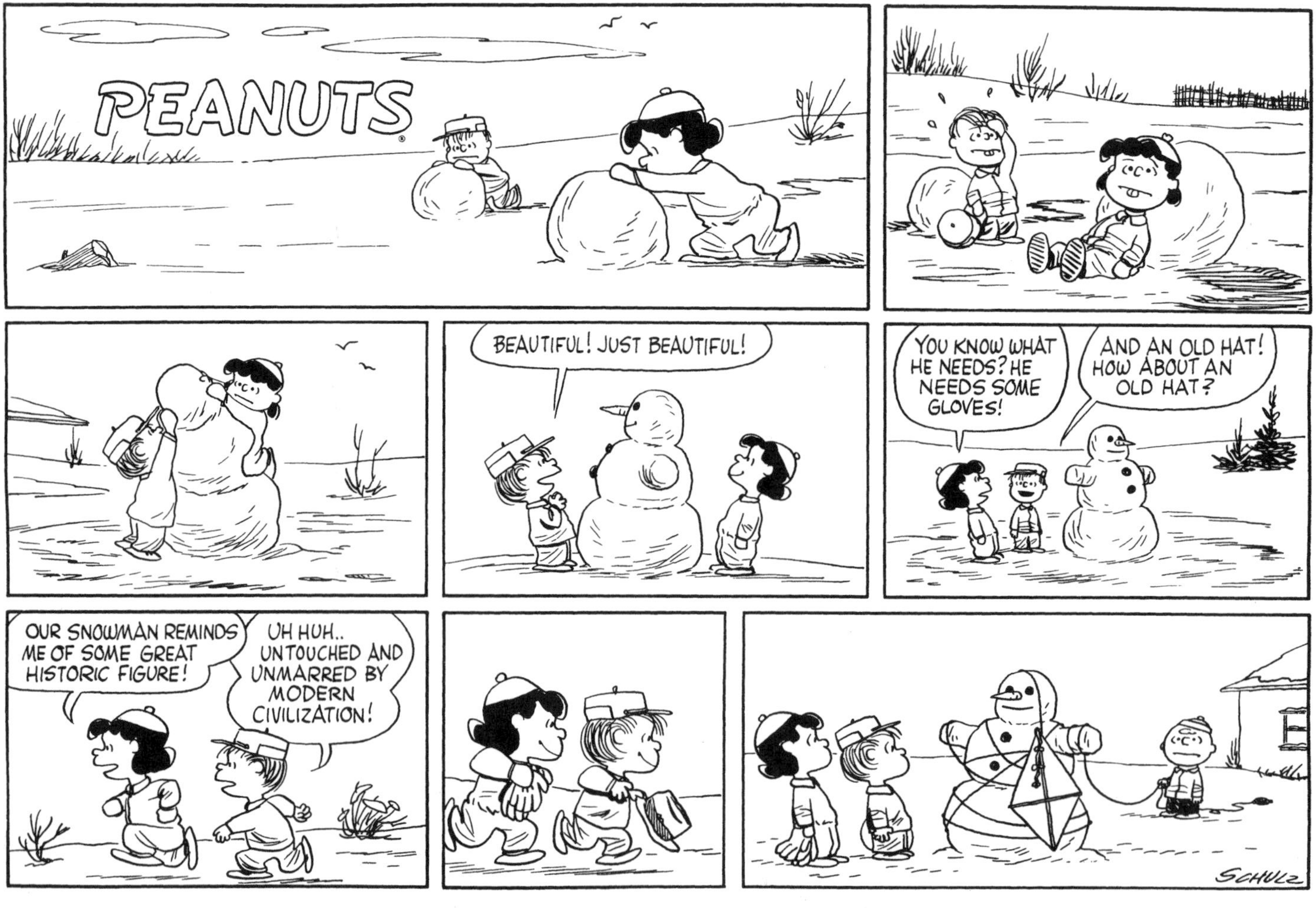
PEANUTS
BEAUTIFUL! JUST BEAUTIFUL!
YOU KNOW WHAT HE NEEDS? HE NEEDS SOME GLOVES!
AND AN OLD HAT! HOW ABOUT AN OLD HAT?
OUR SNOWMAN REMINDS ME OF SOME GREAT HISTORIC FIGURE!
UH HUH.. UNTOUCHED AND UNMARRED BY MODERN CIVILIZATION!
SCHULZ

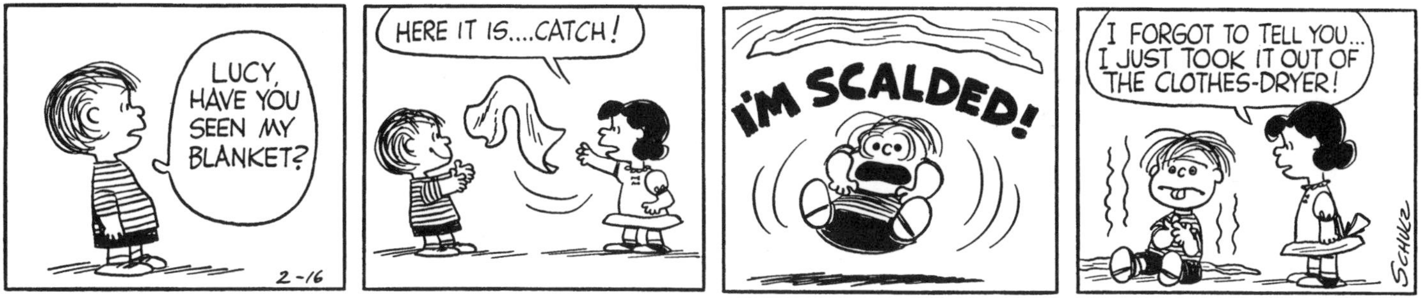
LUCY, HAVE YOU SEEN MY BLANKET?
2-16
HERE IT IS....CATCH!
I'M SCALDED!
I FORGOT TO TELL YOU... I JUST TOOK IT OUT OF THE CLOTHES-DRYER!
SCHULZ

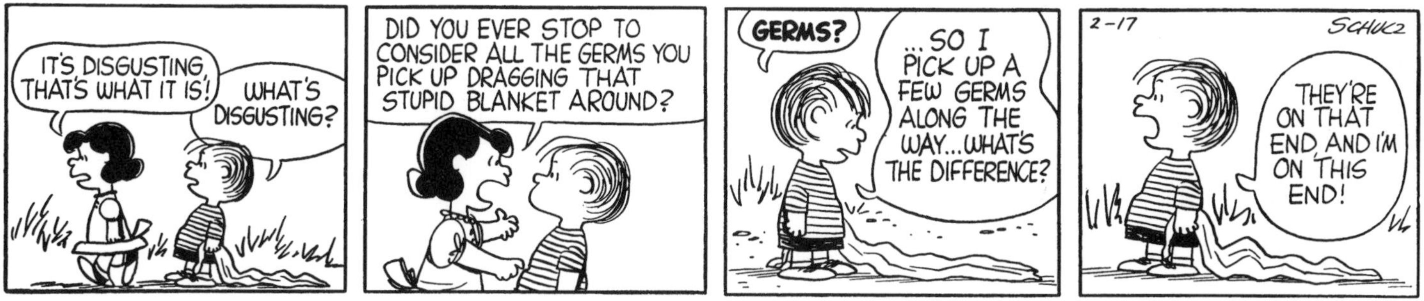
IT'S DISGUSTING, THAT'S WHAT IT IS!
WHAT'S DISGUSTING?
DID YOU EVER STOP TO CONSIDER ALL THE GERMS YOU PICK UP DRAGGING THAT STUPID BLANKET AROUND?
GERMS?
...SO I PICK UP A FEW GERMS ALONG THE WAY...WHAT'S THE DIFFERENCE?
2-17
SCHULZ
THEY'RE ON THAT END, AND I'M ON THIS END!

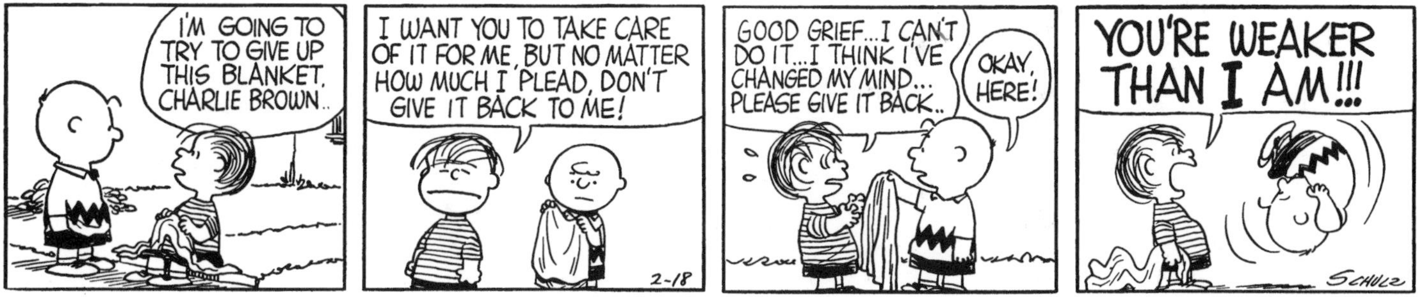
I'M GOING TO TRY TO GIVE UP THIS BLANKET, CHARLIE BROWN..
I WANT YOU TO TAKE CARE OF IT FOR ME, BUT NO MATTER HOW MUCH I PLEAD, DON'T GIVE IT BACK TO ME!
2-18
GOOD GRIEF...I CAN'T DO IT...I THINK I'VE CHANGED MY MIND... PLEASE GIVE IT BACK..
OKAY, HERE!
YOU'RE WEAKER THAN I AM!!!
SCHULZ

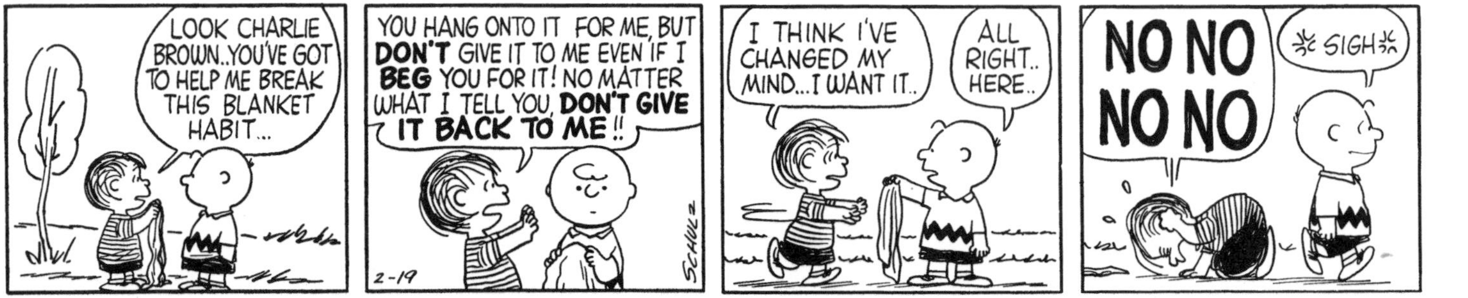
LOOK CHARLIE BROWN..YOU'VE GOT TO HELP ME BREAK THIS BLANKET HABIT...
YOU HANG ONTO IT FOR ME, BUT **DON'T** GIVE IT TO ME EVEN IF I **BEG** YOU FOR IT! NO MATTER WHAT I TELL YOU, **DON'T GIVE IT BACK TO ME**!!
2-19
SCHULZ
I THINK I'VE CHANGED MY MIND...I WANT IT..
ALL RIGHT.. HERE..
NO NO NO NO
SIGH

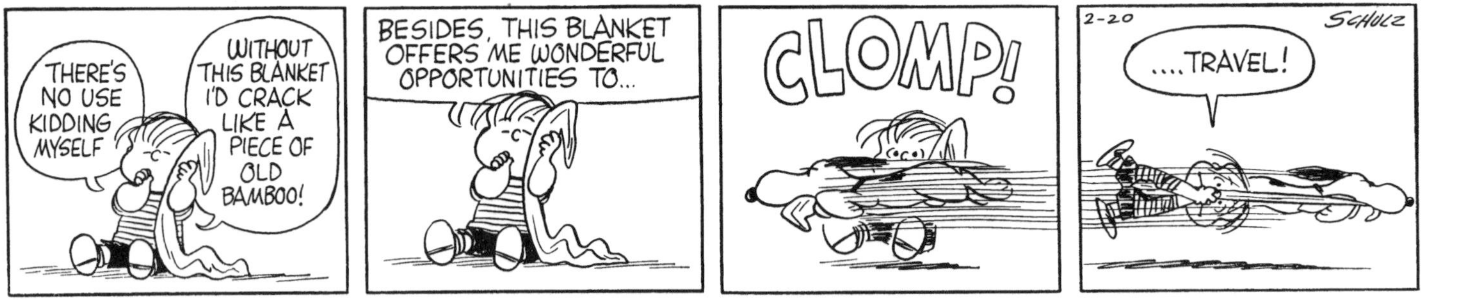
THERE'S NO USE KIDDING MYSELF
WITHOUT THIS BLANKET I'D CRACK LIKE A PIECE OF OLD BAMBOO!
BESIDES, THIS BLANKET OFFERS ME WONDERFUL OPPORTUNITIES TO...
CLOMP!
2-20
SCHULZ
....TRAVEL!

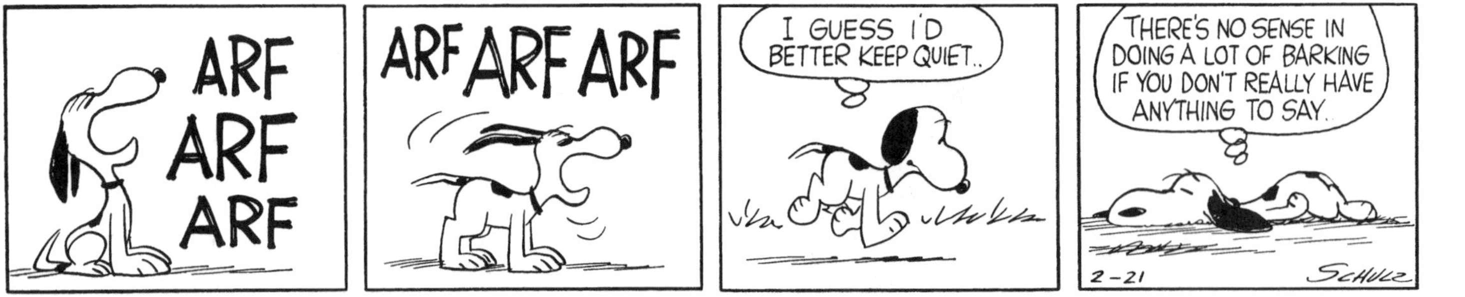
ARF ARF ARF
ARF ARF ARF
I GUESS I'D BETTER KEEP QUIET..
THERE'S NO SENSE IN DOING A LOT OF BARKING IF YOU DON'T REALLY HAVE ANYTHING TO SAY..
2-21
SCHULZ

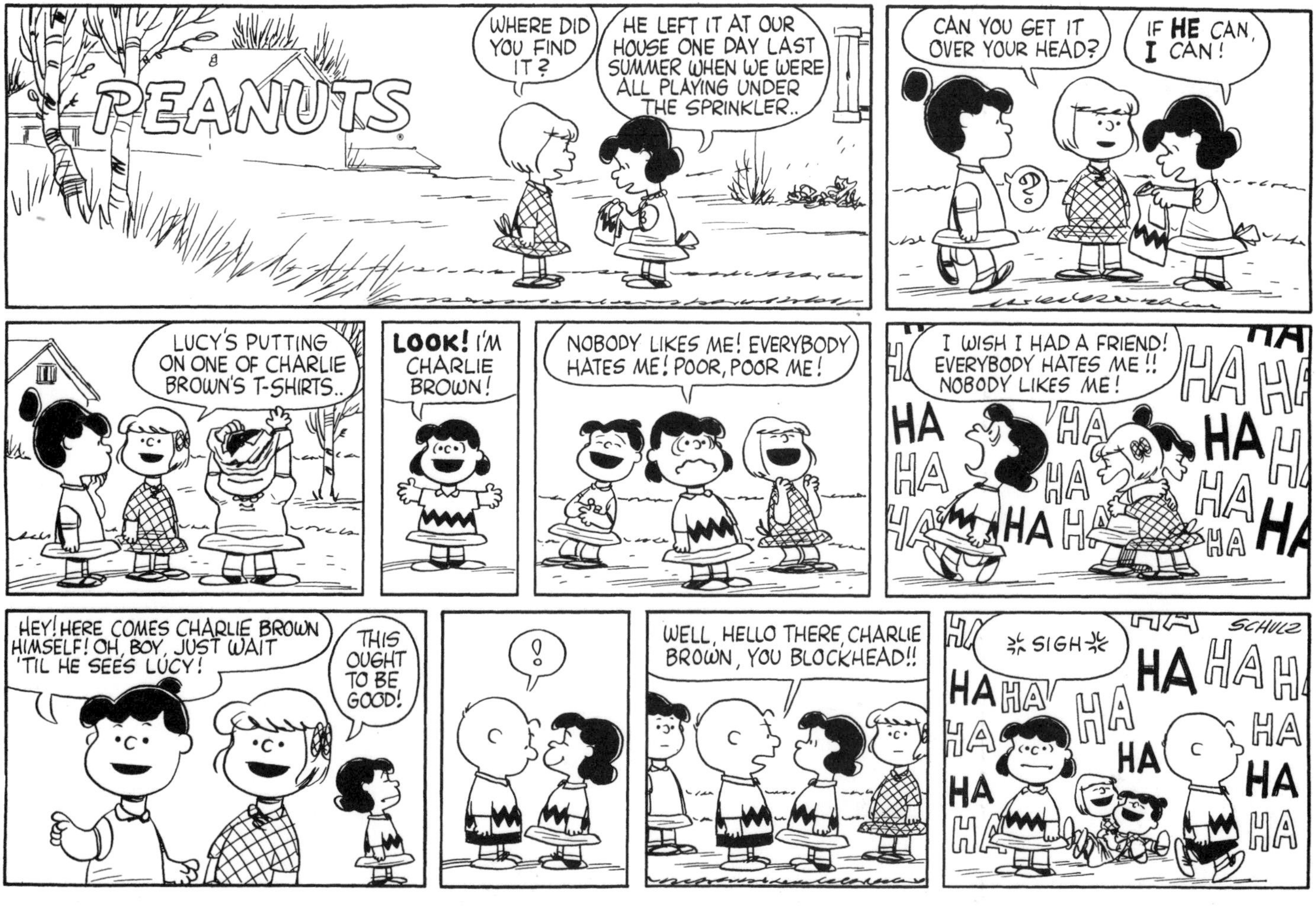
PEANUTS
WHERE DID YOU FIND IT?
HE LEFT IT AT OUR HOUSE ONE DAY LAST SUMMER WHEN WE WERE ALL PLAYING UNDER THE SPRINKLER..
CAN YOU GET IT OVER YOUR HEAD?
IF HE CAN, I CAN!
?
LUCY'S PUTTING ON ONE OF CHARLIE BROWN'S T-SHIRTS..
LOOK! I'M CHARLIE BROWN!
NOBODY LIKES ME! EVERYBODY HATES ME! POOR, POOR ME!
I WISH I HAD A FRIEND! EVERYBODY HATES ME!! NOBODY LIKES ME!
HA HA HA HA HA HA HA HA HA HA HA HA HA HA HA HA HA
HEY! HERE COMES CHARLIE BROWN HIMSELF! OH, BOY, JUST WAIT 'TIL HE SEES LUCY!
THIS OUGHT TO BE GOOD!
!
WELL, HELLO THERE, CHARLIE BROWN, YOU BLOCKHEAD!!
SCHULZ
SIGH
HA HA HA HA HA HA HA HA HA HA HA HA HA HA

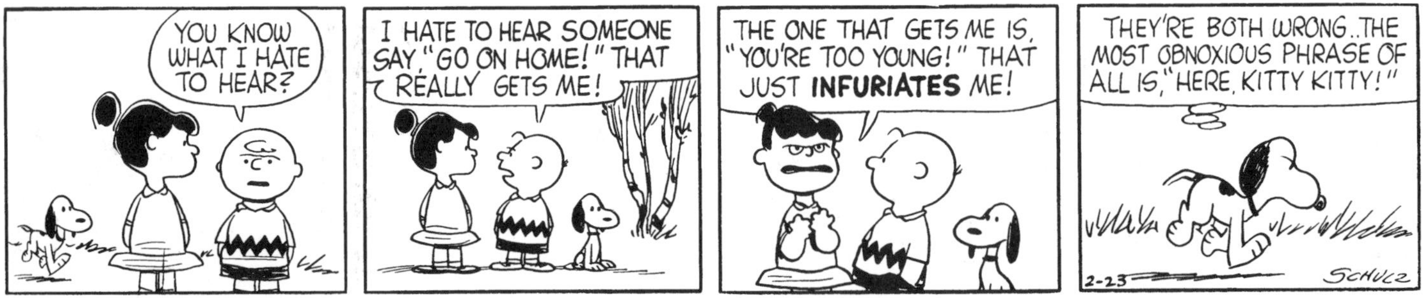
YOU KNOW WHAT I HATE TO HEAR?
I HATE TO HEAR SOMEONE SAY, "GO ON HOME!" THAT REALLY GETS ME!
THE ONE THAT GETS ME IS, "YOU'RE TOO YOUNG!" THAT JUST **INFURIATES** ME!
THEY'RE BOTH WRONG..THE MOST OBNOXIOUS PHRASE OF ALL IS, "HERE, KITTY KITTY!"
2-23
SCHULZ

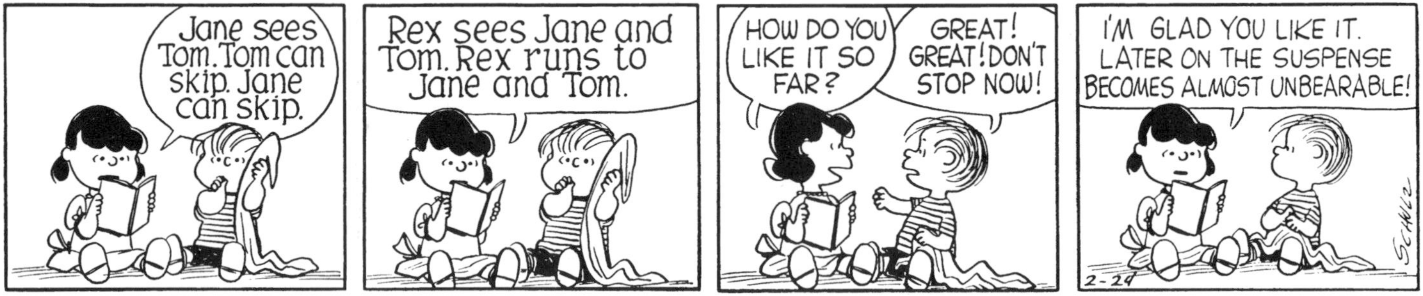
Jane sees Tom. Tom can skip. Jane can skip.
Rex sees Jane and Tom. Rex runs to Jane and Tom.
HOW DO YOU LIKE IT SO FAR?
GREAT! GREAT! DON'T STOP NOW!
I'M GLAD YOU LIKE IT. LATER ON THE SUSPENSE BECOMES ALMOST UNBEARABLE!
2-24
SCHULZ

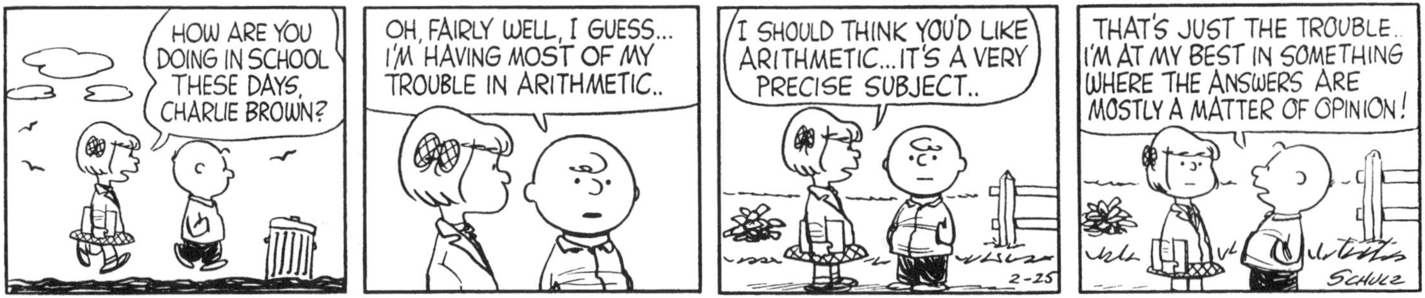
HOW ARE YOU DOING IN SCHOOL THESE DAYS, CHARLIE BROWN?
OH, FAIRLY WELL, I GUESS... I'M HAVING MOST OF MY TROUBLE IN ARITHMETIC..
I SHOULD THINK YOU'D LIKE ARITHMETIC...IT'S A VERY PRECISE SUBJECT..
2-25
THAT'S JUST THE TROUBLE.. I'M AT MY BEST IN SOMETHING WHERE THE ANSWERS ARE MOSTLY A MATTER OF OPINION!
SCHULZ

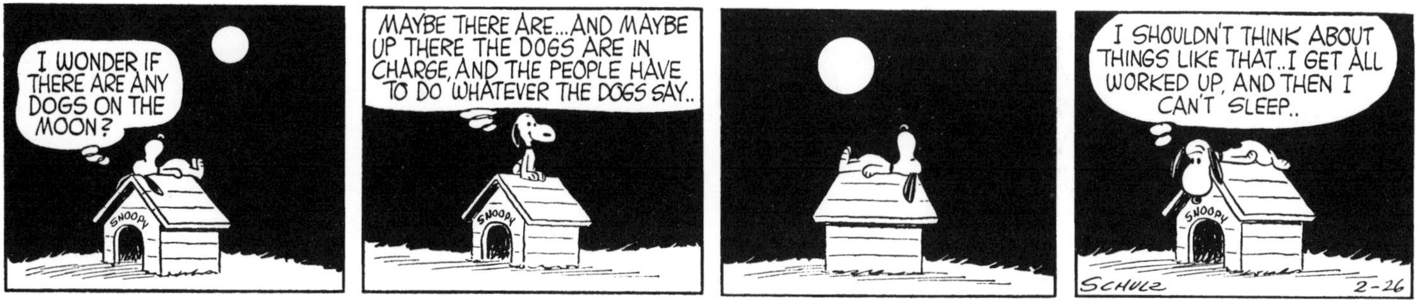
I WONDER IF THERE ARE ANY DOGS ON THE MOON?
SNOOPY
MAYBE THERE ARE...AND MAYBE UP THERE THE DOGS ARE IN CHARGE, AND THE PEOPLE HAVE TO DO WHATEVER THE DOGS SAY..
SNOOPY
I SHOULDN'T THINK ABOUT THINGS LIKE THAT..I GET ALL WORKED UP, AND THEN I CAN'T SLEEP..
SNOOPY
SCHULZ
2-26

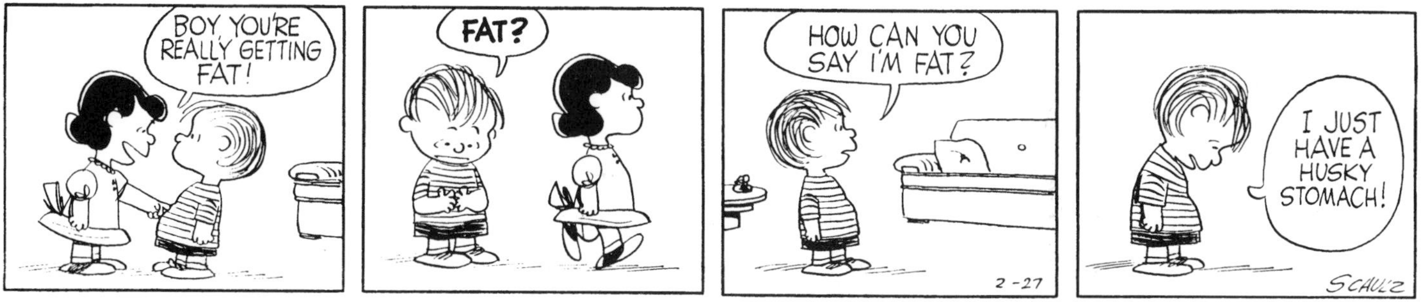
BOY YOU'RE REALLY GETTING FAT!
FAT?
HOW CAN YOU SAY I'M FAT?
2-27
I JUST HAVE A HUSKY STOMACH!
SCHULZ

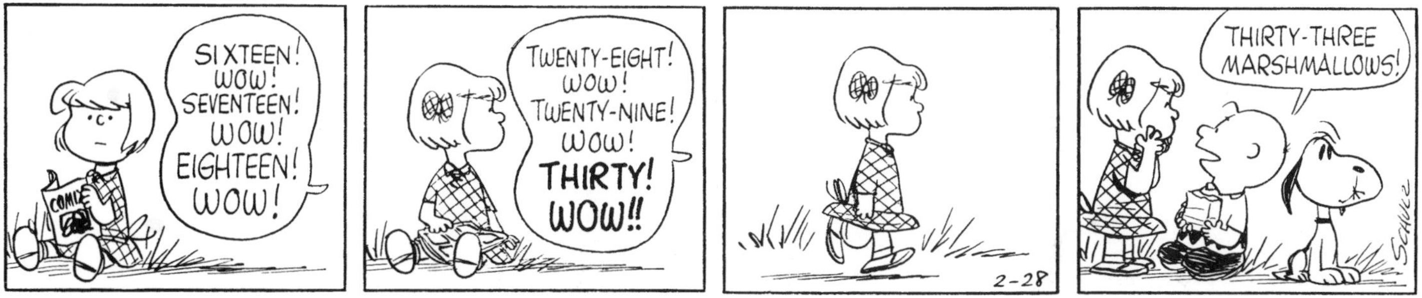
SIXTEEN! WOW! SEVENTEEN! WOW! EIGHTEEN! WOW!
COMIX
TWENTY-EIGHT! WOW! TWENTY-NINE! WOW! THIRTY! WOW!!
2-28
THIRTY-THREE MARSHMALLOWS!
SCHULZ

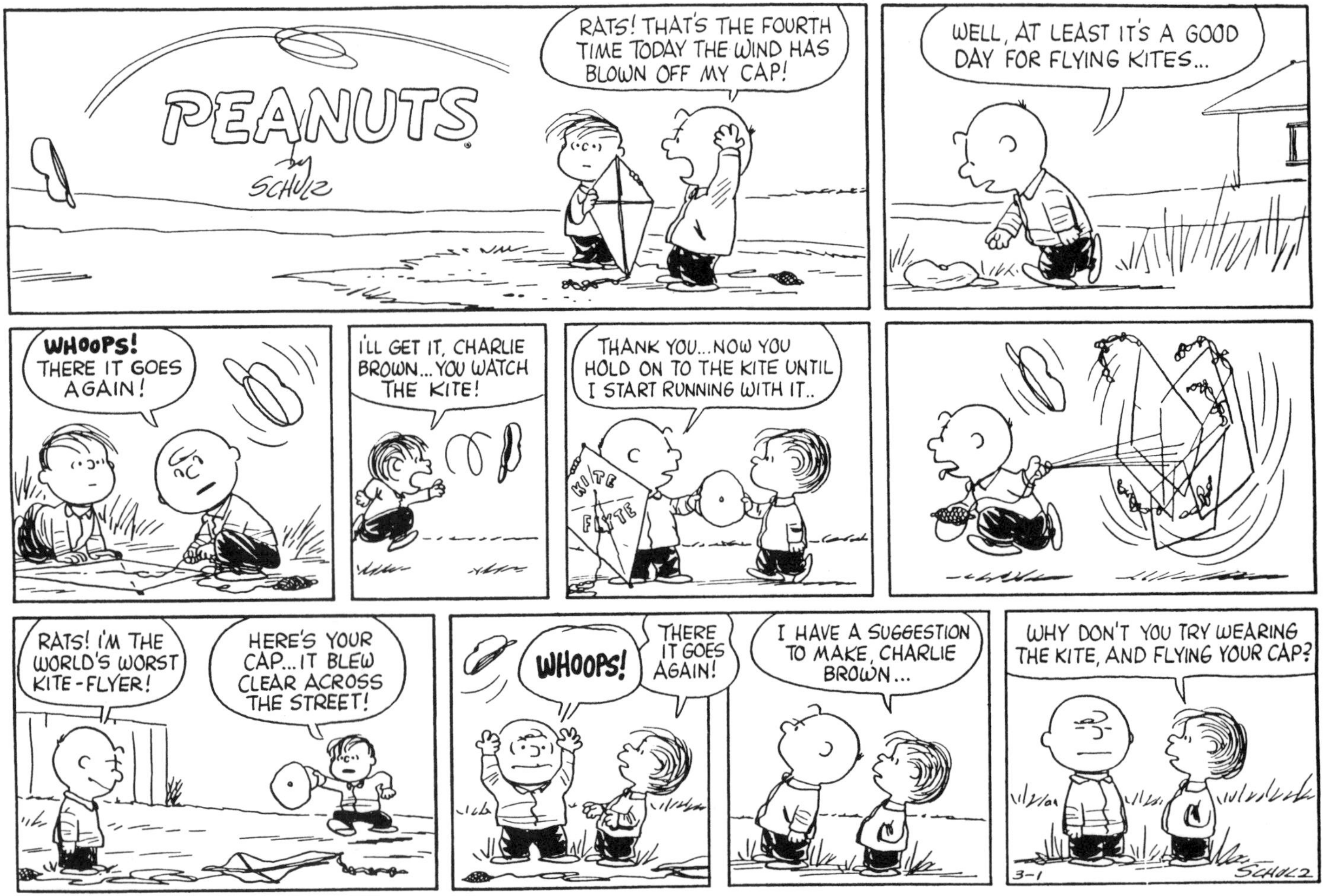
PEANUTS
by SCHULZ
RATS! THAT'S THE FOURTH TIME TODAY THE WIND HAS BLOWN OFF MY CAP!
WELL, AT LEAST IT'S A GOOD DAY FOR FLYING KITES...
WHOOPS! THERE IT GOES AGAIN!
I'LL GET IT, CHARLIE BROWN... YOU WATCH THE KITE!
THANK YOU... NOW YOU HOLD ON TO THE KITE UNTIL I START RUNNING WITH IT..
KITE FLYTE
RATS! I'M THE WORLD'S WORST KITE-FLYER!
HERE'S YOUR CAP... IT BLEW CLEAR ACROSS THE STREET!
WHOOPS!
THERE IT GOES AGAIN!
I HAVE A SUGGESTION TO MAKE, CHARLIE BROWN...
WHY DON'T YOU TRY WEARING THE KITE, AND FLYING YOUR CAP?
3-1
SCHULZ

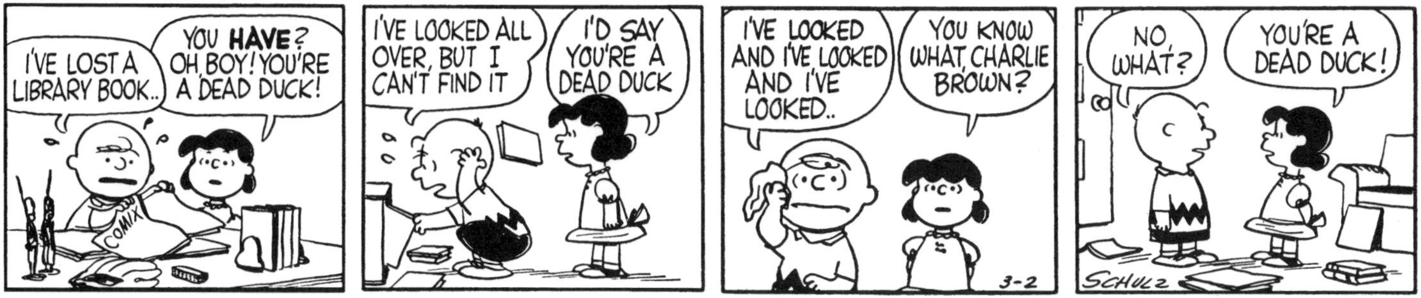
I'VE LOST A LIBRARY BOOK..
YOU **HAVE**? OH, BOY! YOU'RE A DEAD DUCK!
COMIX
I'VE LOOKED ALL OVER, BUT I CAN'T FIND IT
I'D SAY YOU'RE A DEAD DUCK
I'VE LOOKED AND I'VE LOOKED AND I'VE LOOKED..
YOU KNOW WHAT, CHARLIE BROWN?
3-2
NO, WHAT?
YOU'RE A DEAD DUCK!
SCHULZ

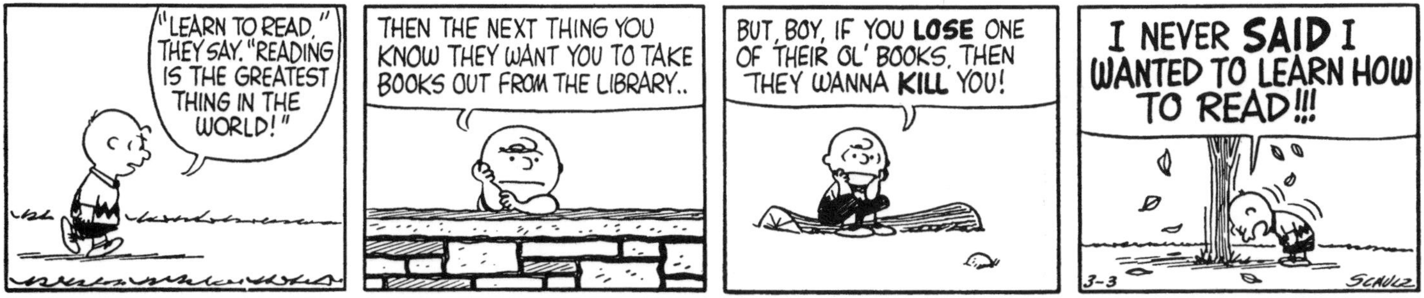
"LEARN TO READ," THEY SAY. "READING IS THE GREATEST THING IN THE WORLD!"
THEN THE NEXT THING YOU KNOW THEY WANT YOU TO TAKE BOOKS OUT FROM THE LIBRARY..
BUT, BOY, IF YOU **LOSE** ONE OF THEIR OL' BOOKS, THEN THEY WANNA **KILL** YOU!
I NEVER **SAID** I WANTED TO LEARN HOW TO READ!!!
3-3
SCHULZ

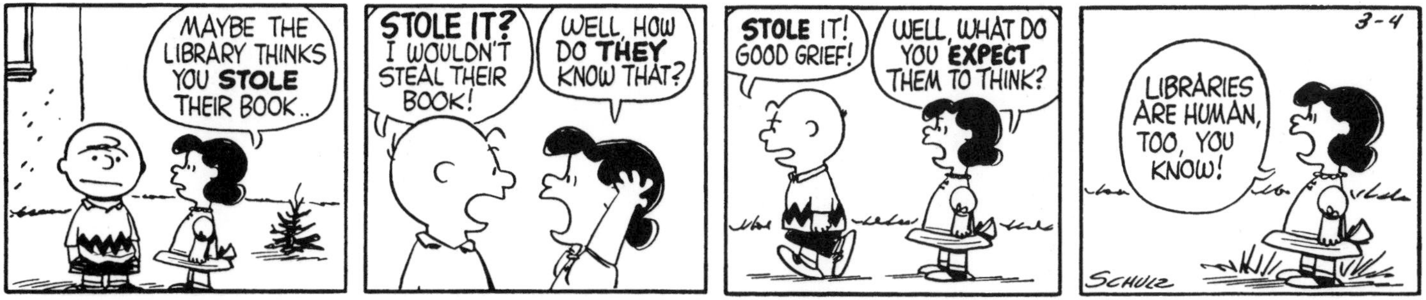
MAYBE THE LIBRARY THINKS YOU **STOLE** THEIR BOOK..
STOLE IT? I WOULDN'T STEAL THEIR BOOK!
WELL, HOW DO **THEY** KNOW THAT?
STOLE IT! GOOD GRIEF!
WELL, WHAT DO YOU **EXPECT** THEM TO THINK?
3-4
LIBRARIES ARE HUMAN, TOO, YOU KNOW!
SCHULZ

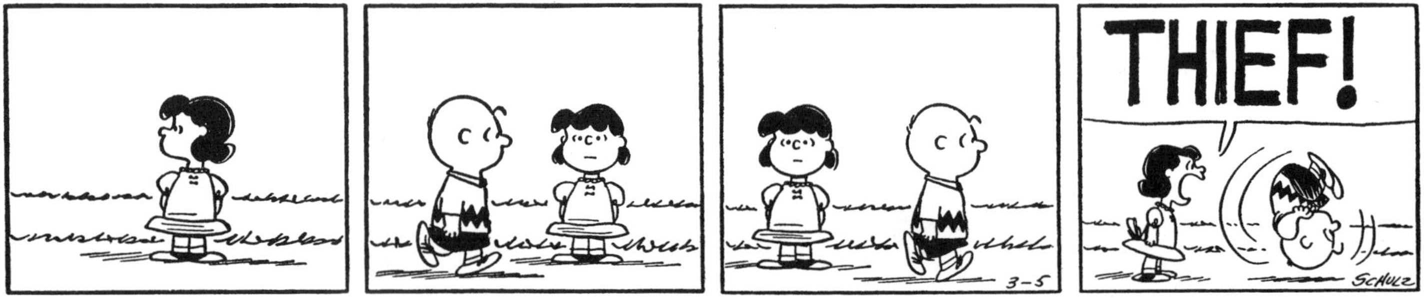
THIEF!

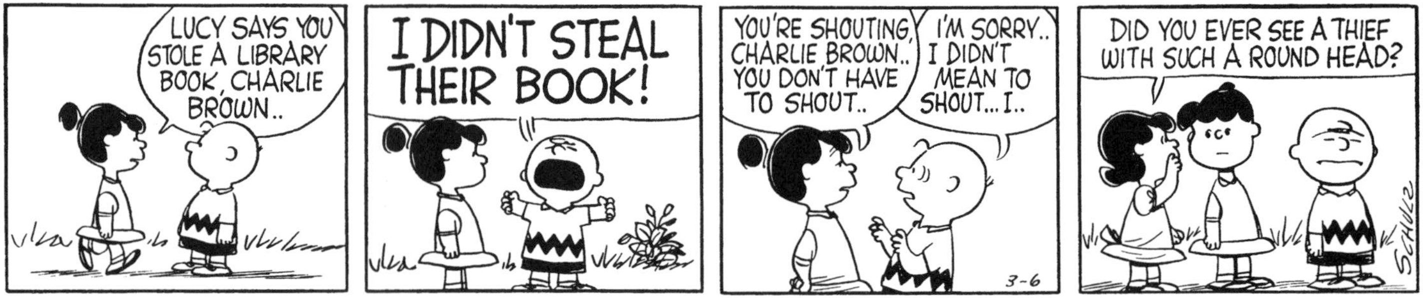
LUCY SAYS YOU STOLE A LIBRARY BOOK, CHARLIE BROWN..
I DIDN'T STEAL THEIR BOOK!
YOU'RE SHOUTING, CHARLIE BROWN.. YOU DON'T HAVE TO SHOUT..
I'M SORRY.. I DIDN'T MEAN TO SHOUT... I..
DID YOU EVER SEE A THIEF WITH SUCH A ROUND HEAD?

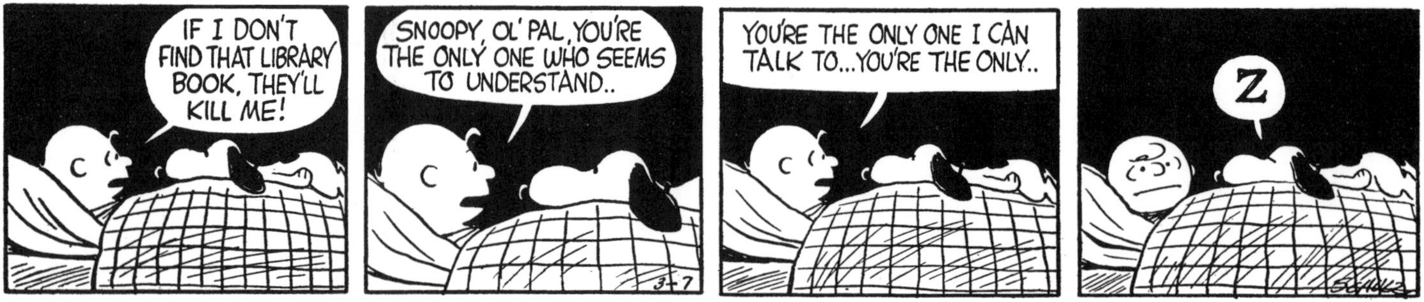
IF I DON'T FIND THAT LIBRARY BOOK, THEY'LL KILL ME!
SNOOPY, OL' PAL, YOU'RE THE ONLY ONE WHO SEEMS TO UNDERSTAND..
YOU'RE THE ONLY ONE I CAN TALK TO... YOU'RE THE ONLY..
Z

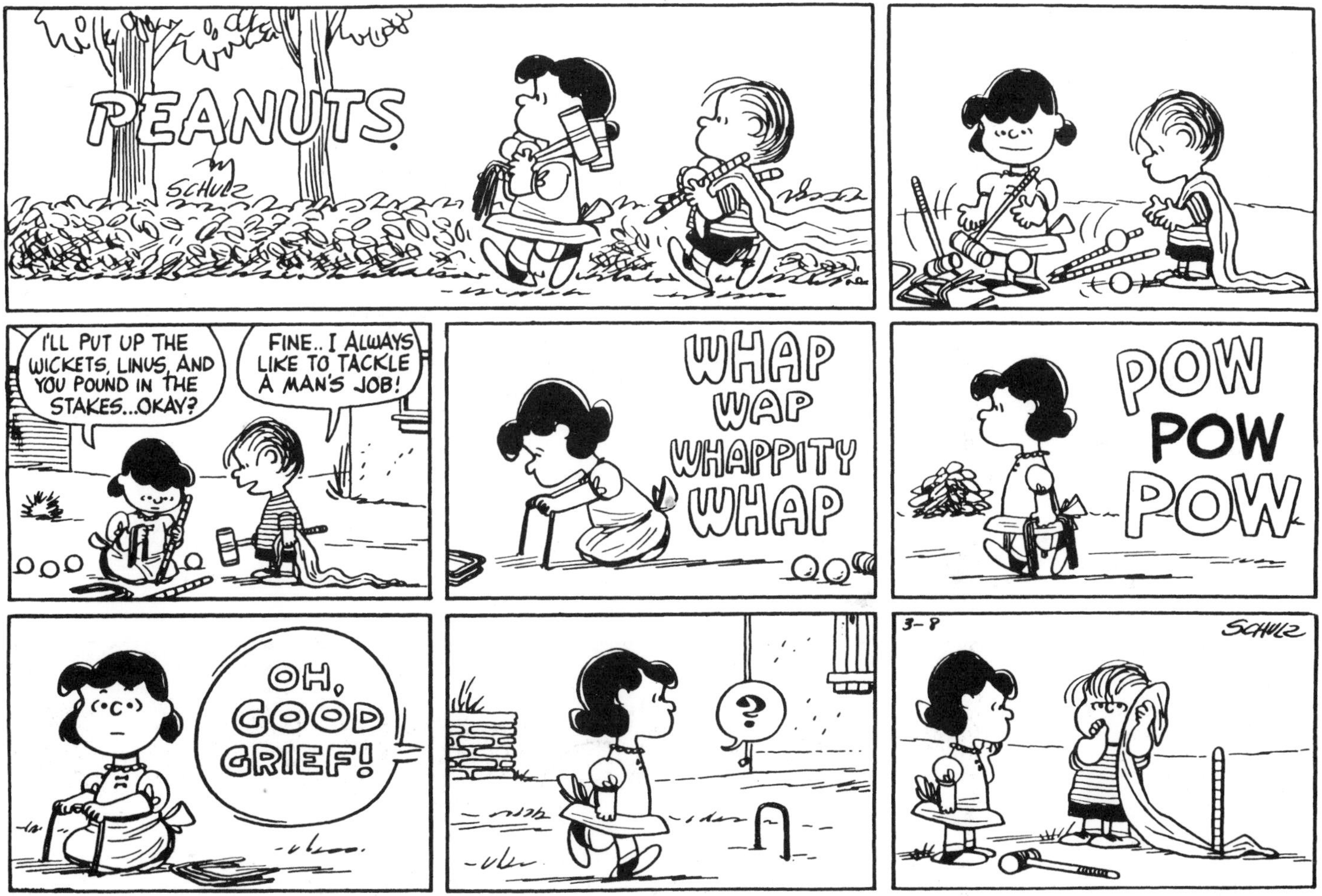
PEANUTS
by SCHULZ
I'LL PUT UP THE WICKETS, LINUS, AND YOU POUND IN THE STAKES...OKAY?
FINE.. I ALWAYS LIKE TO TACKLE A MAN'S JOB!
WHAP WAP WHAPPITY WHAP
POW POW POW
OH, GOOD GRIEF!
?
3-8
SCHULZ

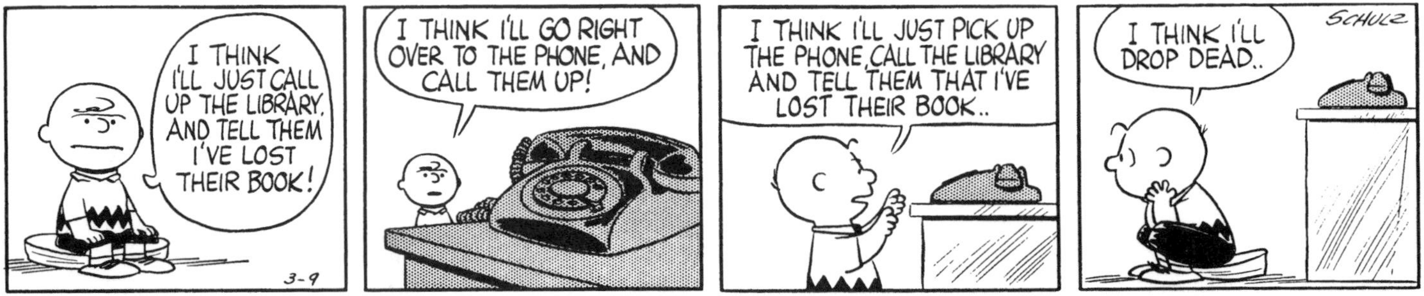
I THINK I'LL JUST CALL UP THE LIBRARY, AND TELL THEM I'VE LOST THEIR BOOK!
3-9
I THINK I'LL GO RIGHT OVER TO THE PHONE, AND CALL THEM UP!
I THINK I'LL JUST PICK UP THE PHONE, CALL THE LIBRARY AND TELL THEM THAT I'VE LOST THEIR BOOK..
I THINK I'LL DROP DEAD..
SCHULZ

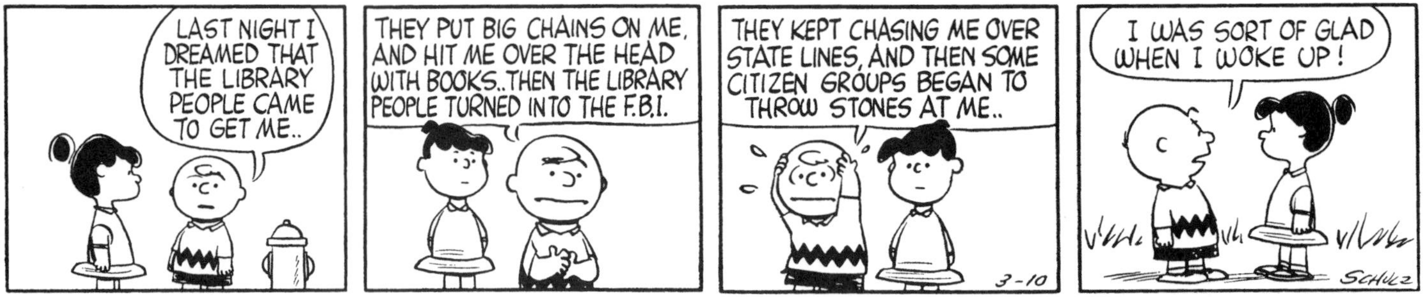
LAST NIGHT I DREAMED THAT THE LIBRARY PEOPLE CAME TO GET ME..
THEY PUT BIG CHAINS ON ME, AND HIT ME OVER THE HEAD WITH BOOKS..THEN THE LIBRARY PEOPLE TURNED INTO THE F.B.I.
THEY KEPT CHASING ME OVER STATE LINES, AND THEN SOME CITIZEN GROUPS BEGAN TO THROW STONES AT ME..
3-10
I WAS SORT OF GLAD WHEN I WOKE UP!
SCHULZ

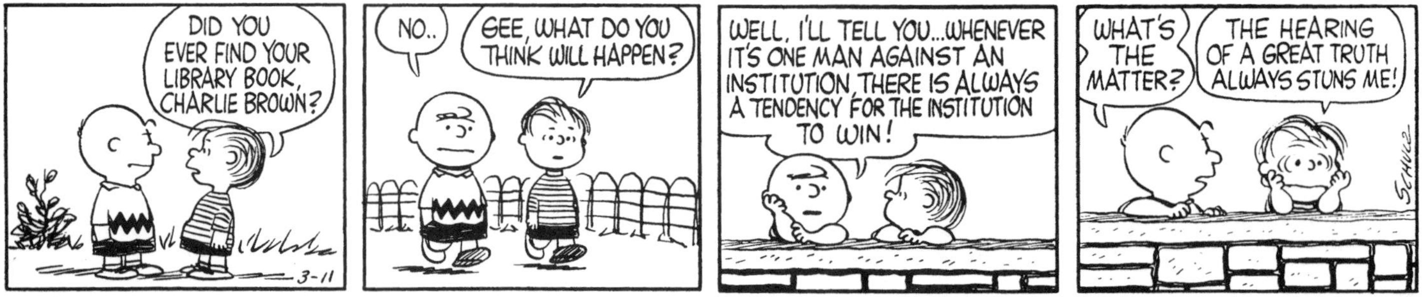
DID YOU EVER FIND YOUR LIBRARY BOOK, CHARLIE BROWN?
3-11
NO..
GEE, WHAT DO YOU THINK WILL HAPPEN?
WELL, I'LL TELL YOU...WHENEVER IT'S ONE MAN AGAINST AN INSTITUTION, THERE IS ALWAYS A TENDENCY FOR THE INSTITUTION TO WIN!
WHAT'S THE MATTER?
THE HEARING OF A GREAT TRUTH ALWAYS STUNS ME!
SCHULZ

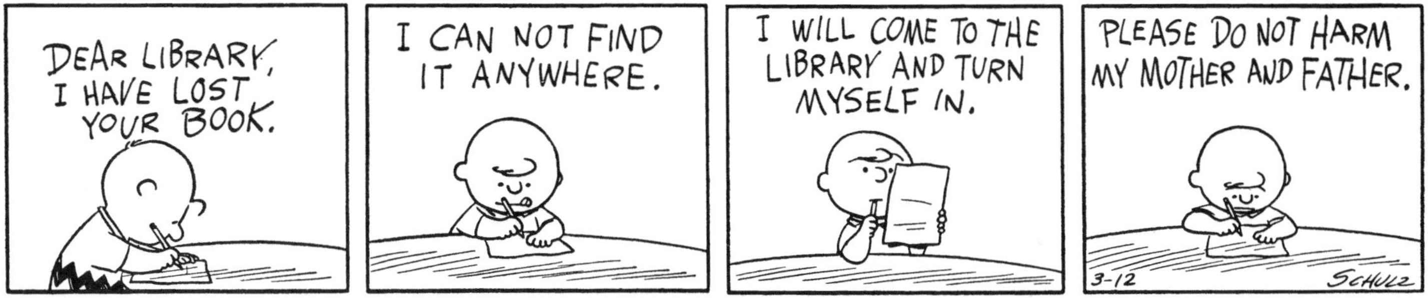
DEAR LIBRARY, I HAVE LOST YOUR BOOK.
I CAN NOT FIND IT ANYWHERE.
I WILL COME TO THE LIBRARY AND TURN MYSELF IN.
PLEASE DO NOT HARM MY MOTHER AND FATHER.
3-12
SCHULZ

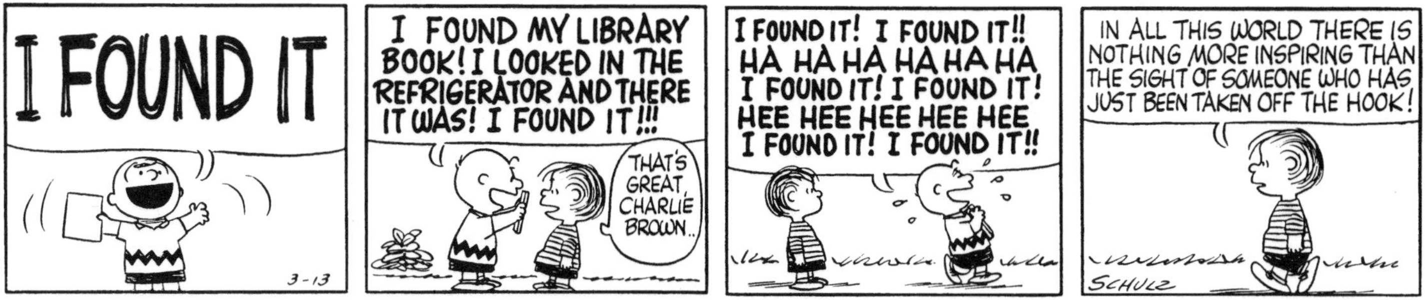
I FOUND IT
3-13
I FOUND MY LIBRARY BOOK! I LOOKED IN THE REFRIGERATOR AND THERE IT WAS! I FOUND IT!!!
THAT'S GREAT, CHARLIE BROWN..
I FOUND IT! I FOUND IT!! HA HA HA HA HA HA I FOUND IT! I FOUND IT! HEE HEE HEE HEE HEE I FOUND IT! I FOUND IT!!
IN ALL THIS WORLD THERE IS NOTHING MORE INSPIRING THAN THE SIGHT OF SOMEONE WHO HAS JUST BEEN TAKEN OFF THE HOOK!
SCHULZ

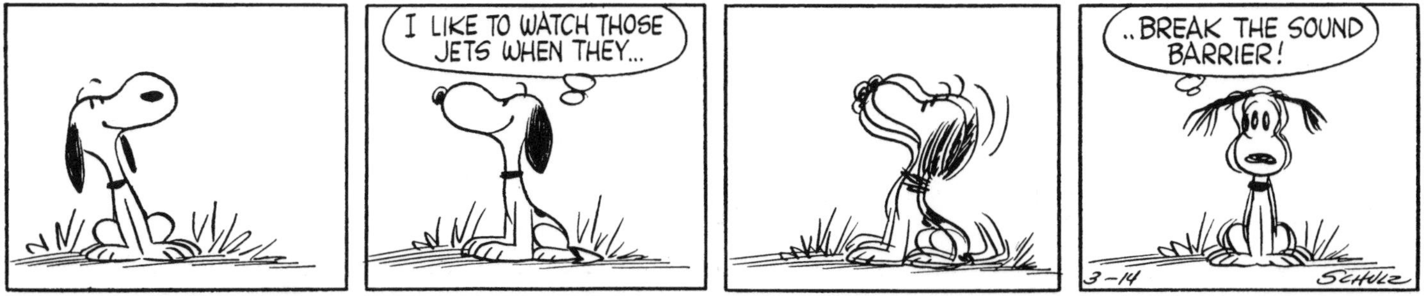
I LIKE TO WATCH THOSE JETS WHEN THEY...
..BREAK THE SOUND BARRIER!
3-14
SCHULZ

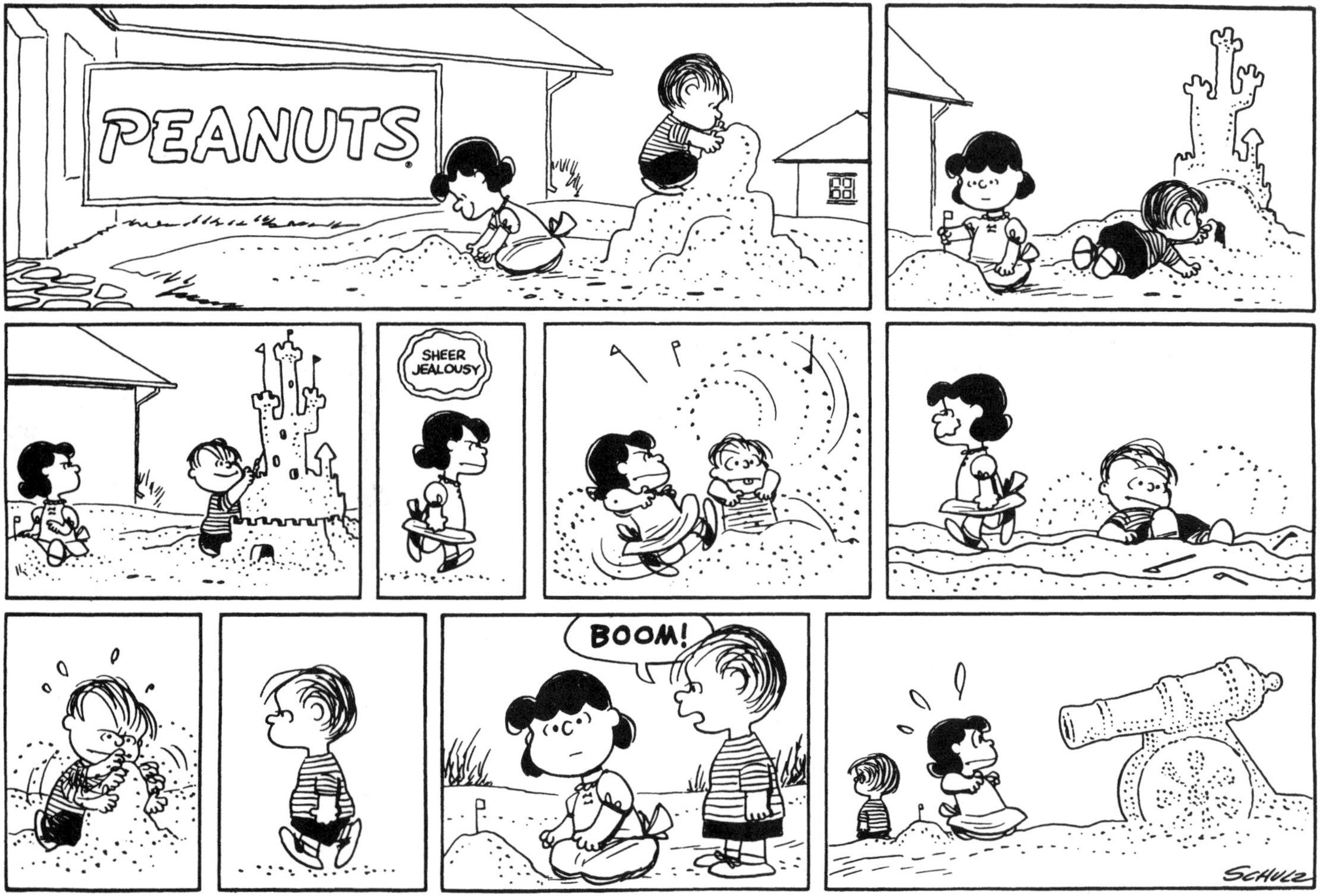
PEANUTS
SHEER JEALOUSY
BOOM!
SCHULZ

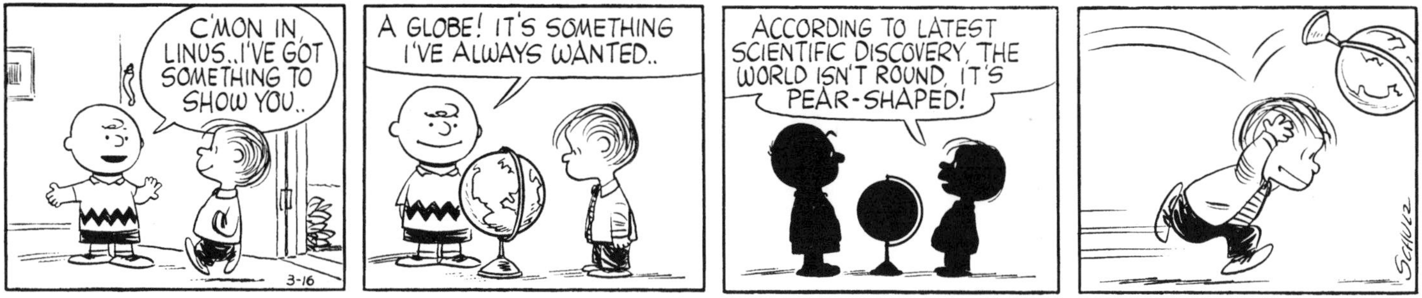
C'MON IN, LINUS..I'VE GOT SOMETHING TO SHOW YOU..
3-16
A GLOBE! IT'S SOMETHING I'VE ALWAYS WANTED..
ACCORDING TO LATEST SCIENTIFIC DISCOVERY, THE WORLD ISN'T ROUND, IT'S PEAR-SHAPED!
SCHULZ

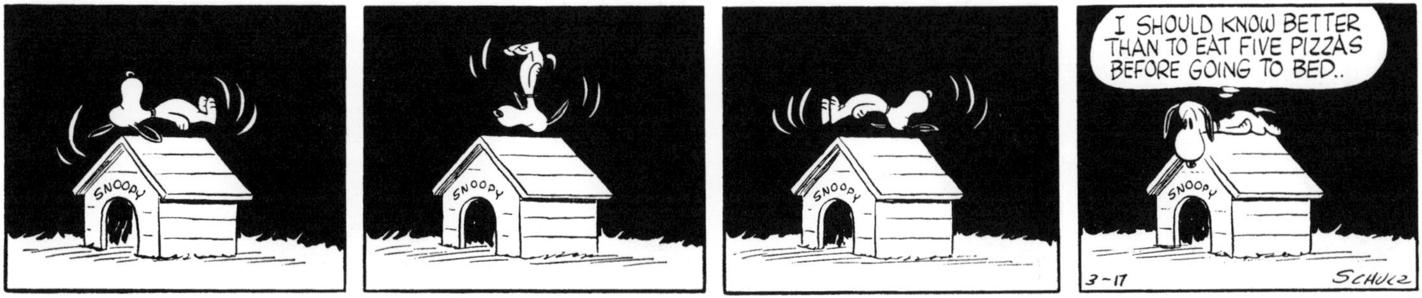
SNOOPY
SNOOPY
SNOOPY
I SHOULD KNOW BETTER THAN TO EAT FIVE PIZZAS BEFORE GOING TO BED..
SNOOPY
3-17
SCHULZ

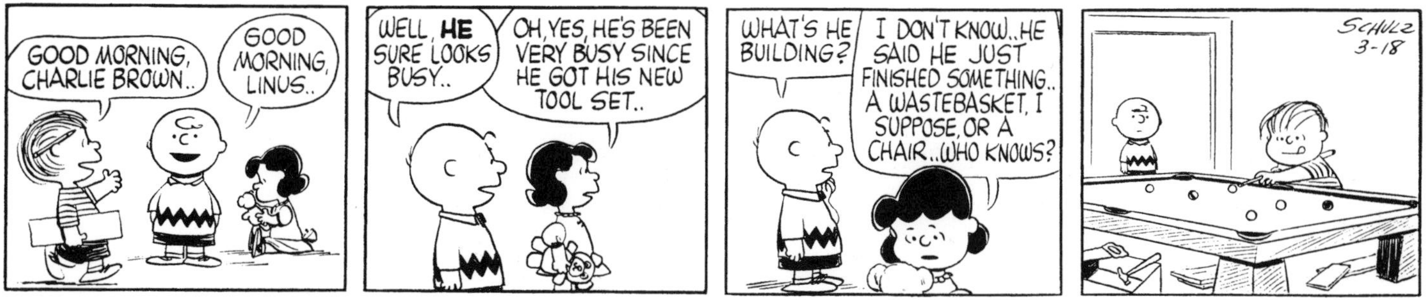
GOOD MORNING, CHARLIE BROWN..
GOOD MORNING, LINUS..
WELL, **HE** SURE LOOKS BUSY..
OH, YES, HE'S BEEN VERY BUSY SINCE HE GOT HIS NEW TOOL SET..
WHAT'S HE BUILDING?
I DON'T KNOW..HE SAID HE JUST FINISHED SOMETHING.. A WASTEBASKET, I SUPPOSE, OR A CHAIR..WHO KNOWS?
SCHULZ 3-18

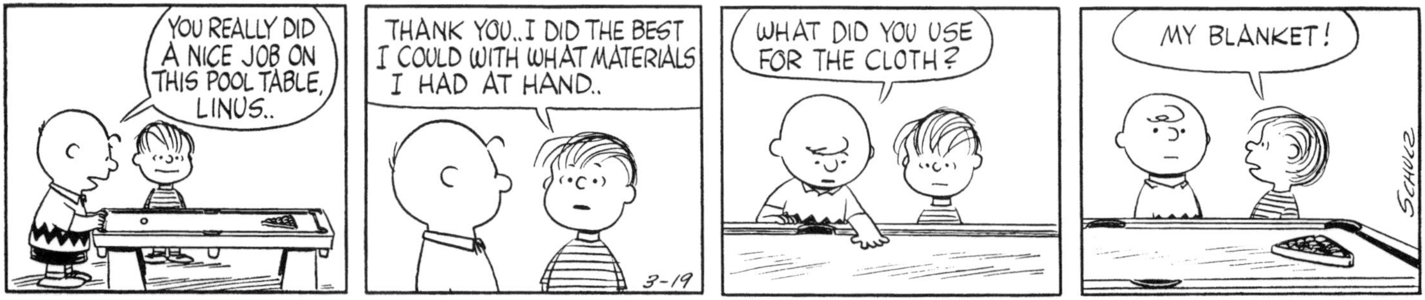
YOU REALLY DID A NICE JOB ON THIS POOL TABLE, LINUS..
THANK YOU..I DID THE BEST I COULD WITH WHAT MATERIALS I HAD AT HAND..
WHAT DID YOU USE FOR THE CLOTH?
MY BLANKET!

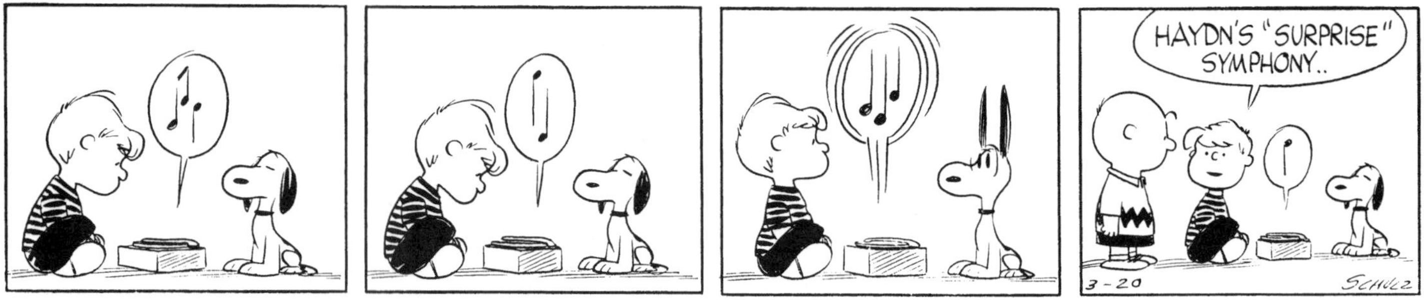
HAYDN'S "SURPRISE" SYMPHONY..

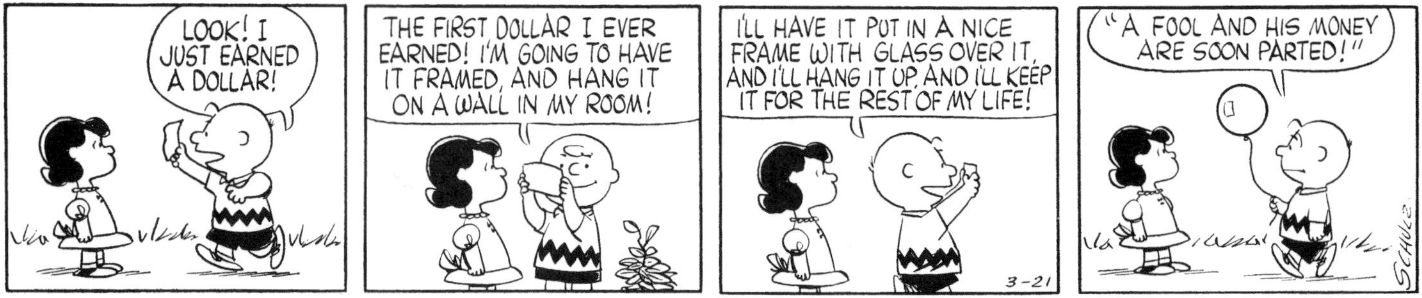
LOOK! I JUST EARNED A DOLLAR!
THE FIRST DOLLAR I EVER EARNED! I'M GOING TO HAVE IT FRAMED, AND HANG IT ON A WALL IN MY ROOM!
I'LL HAVE IT PUT IN A NICE FRAME WITH GLASS OVER IT, AND I'LL HANG IT UP, AND I'LL KEEP IT FOR THE REST OF MY LIFE!
"A FOOL AND HIS MONEY ARE SOON PARTED!"

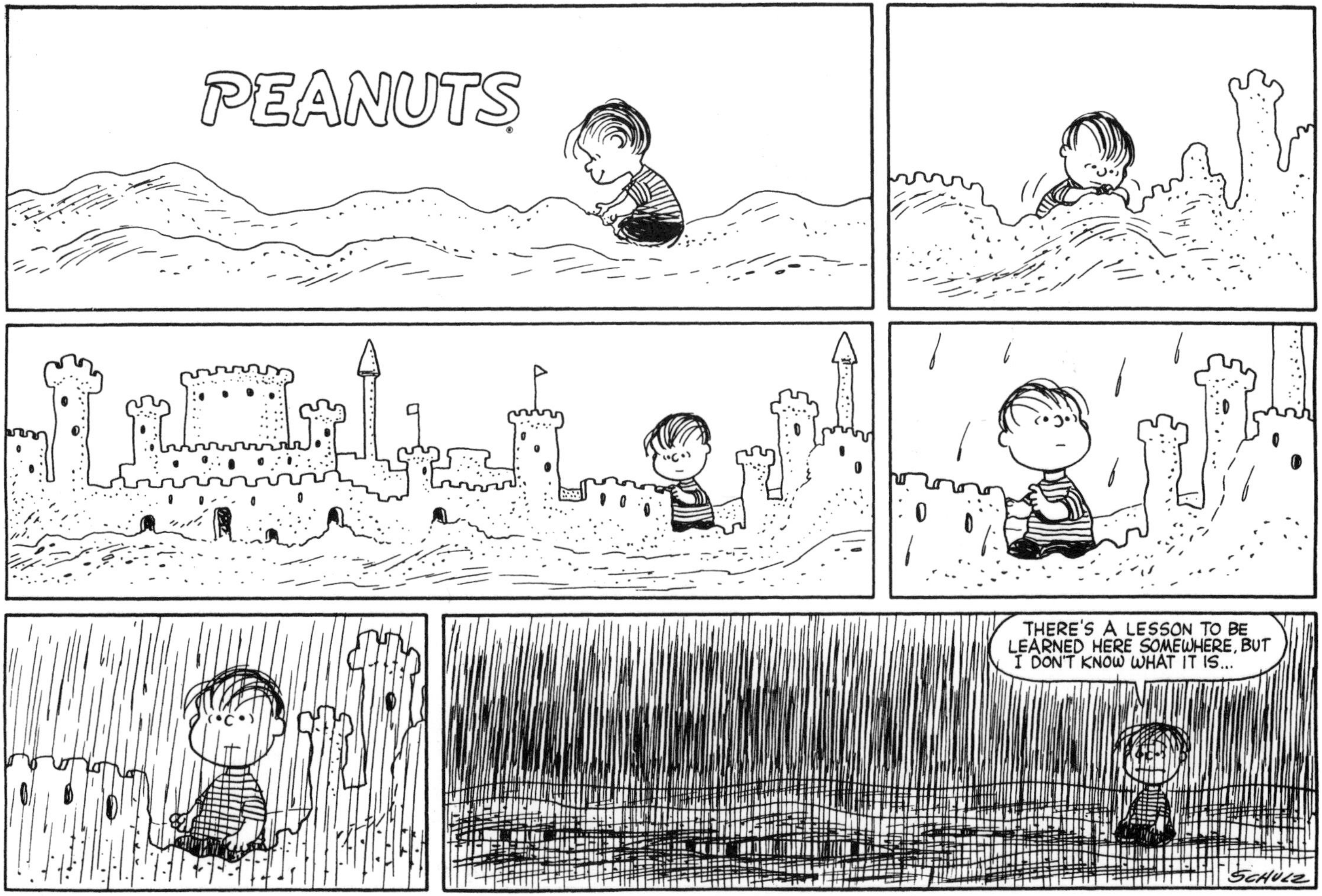
PEANUTS
THERE'S A LESSON TO BE LEARNED HERE SOMEWHERE, BUT I DON'T KNOW WHAT IT IS...
SCHULZ

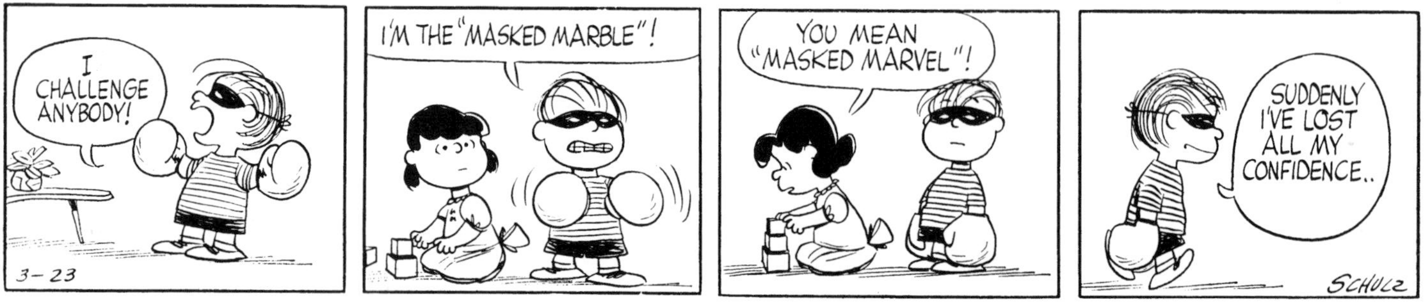
I CHALLENGE ANYBODY!
3-23
I'M THE "MASKED MARBLE"!
YOU MEAN "MASKED MARVEL"!
SUDDENLY I'VE LOST ALL MY CONFIDENCE..
SCHULZ

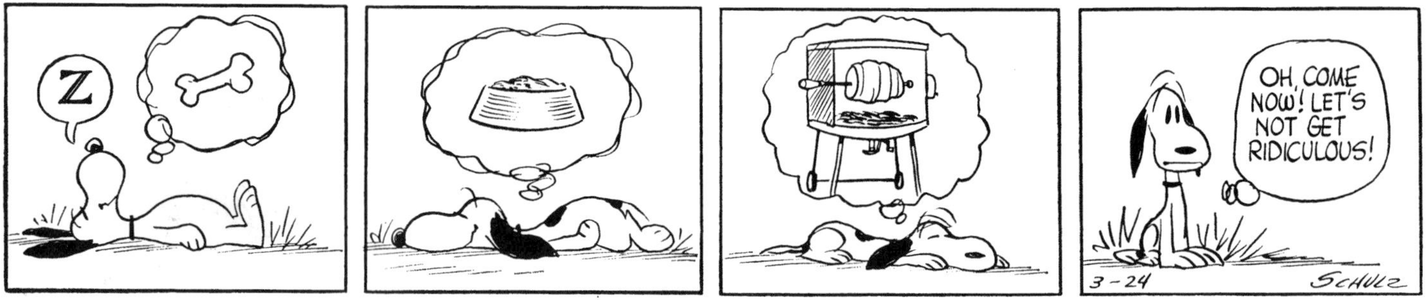
Z
OH, COME NOW! LET'S NOT GET RIDICULOUS!
3-24
SCHULZ

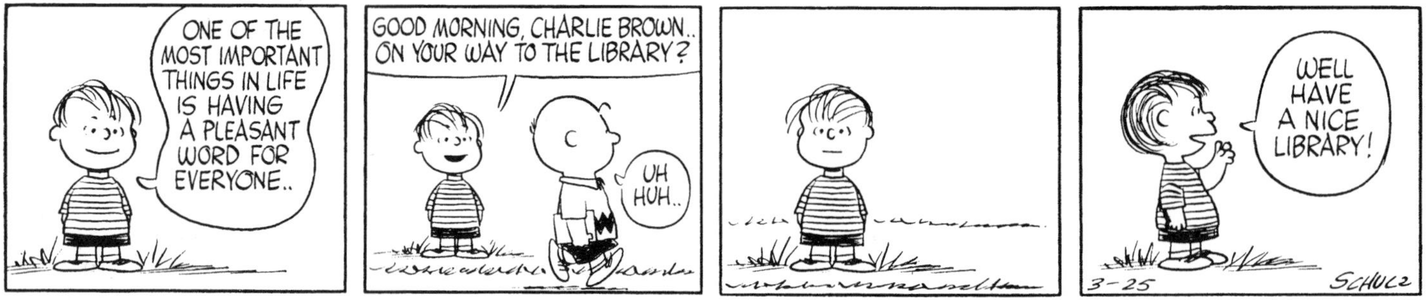
ONE OF THE MOST IMPORTANT THINGS IN LIFE IS HAVING A PLEASANT WORD FOR EVERYONE..
GOOD MORNING, CHARLIE BROWN.. ON YOUR WAY TO THE LIBRARY?
UH HUH..
WELL HAVE A NICE LIBRARY!
3-25
SCHULZ

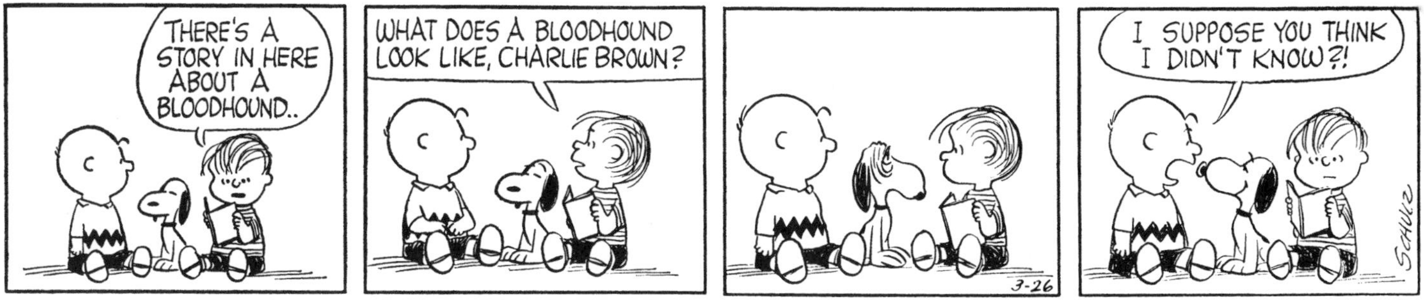
THERE'S A STORY IN HERE ABOUT A BLOODHOUND..
WHAT DOES A BLOODHOUND LOOK LIKE, CHARLIE BROWN?
I SUPPOSE YOU THINK I DIDN'T KNOW?!
3-26
SCHULZ

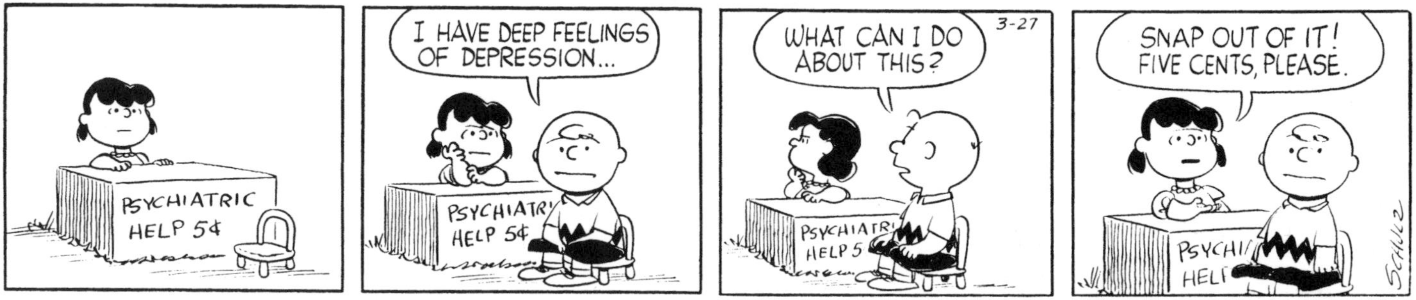
PSYCHIATRIC HELP 5¢
I HAVE DEEP FEELINGS OF DEPRESSION...
WHAT CAN I DO ABOUT THIS?
3-27
SNAP OUT OF IT! FIVE CENTS, PLEASE.
SCHULZ

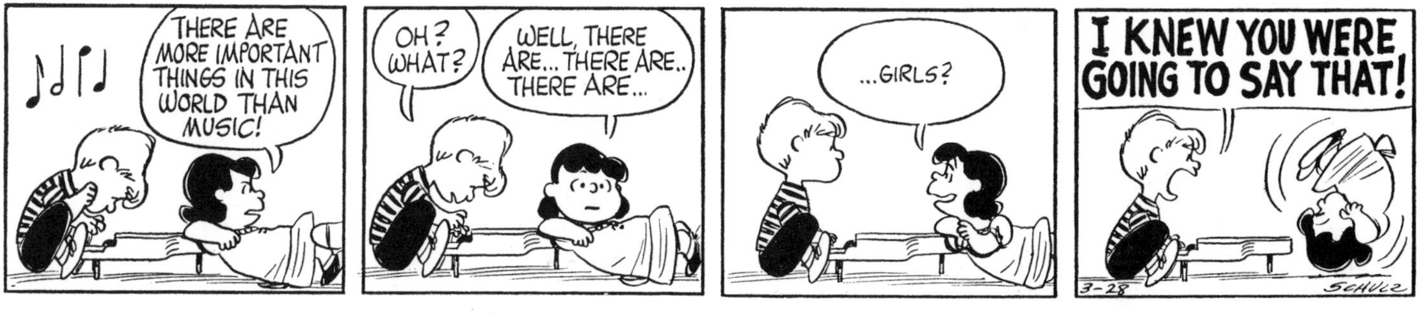
THERE ARE MORE IMPORTANT THINGS IN THIS WORLD THAN MUSIC!
OH? WHAT?
WELL, THERE ARE... THERE ARE.. THERE ARE...
...GIRLS?
I KNEW YOU WERE GOING TO SAY THAT!
3-28
SCHULZ

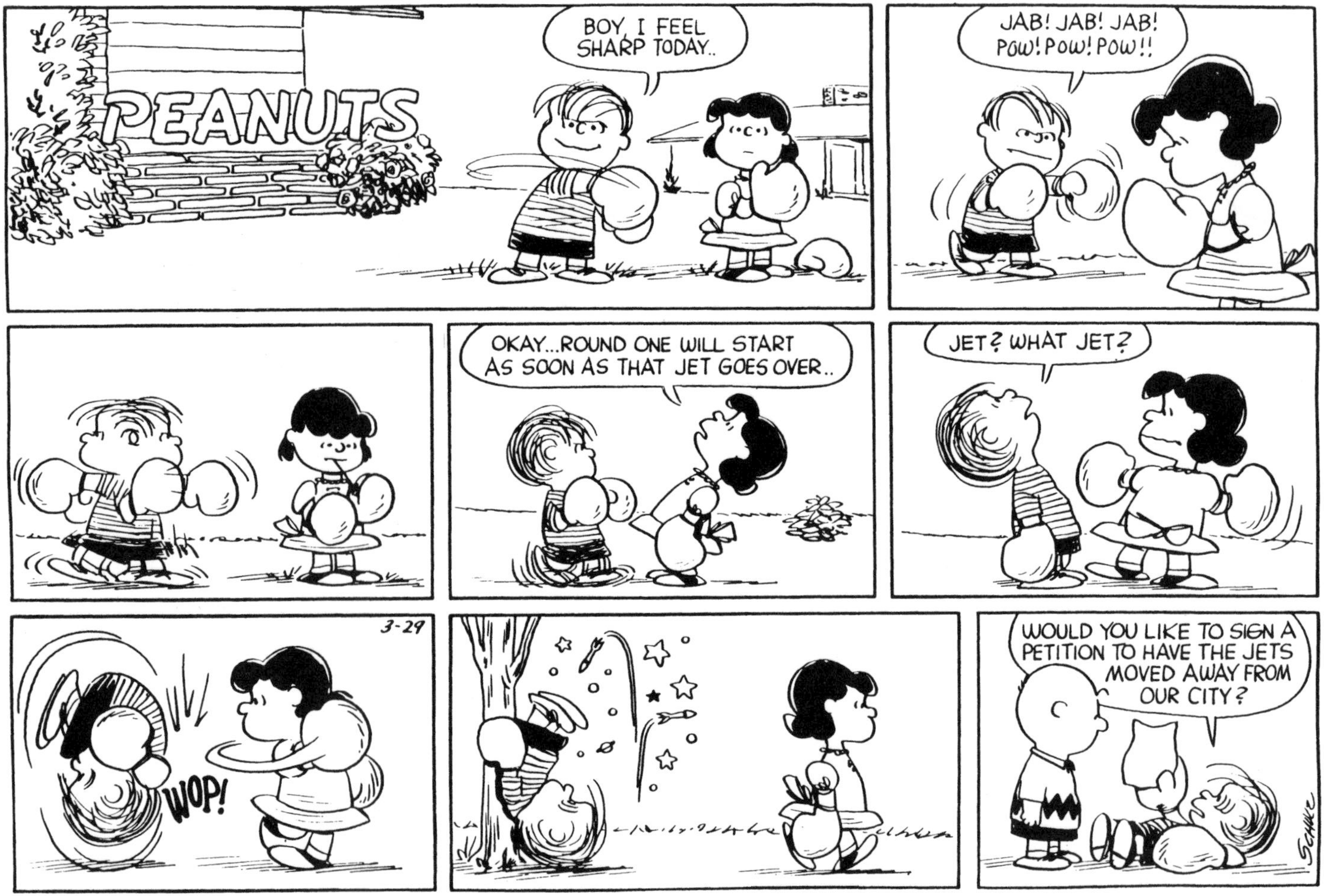
PEANUTS
BOY, I FEEL SHARP TODAY..
JAB! JAB! JAB! POW! POW! POW!!
OKAY...ROUND ONE WILL START AS SOON AS THAT JET GOES OVER..
JET? WHAT JET?
3-29
WOP!
WOULD YOU LIKE TO SIGN A PETITION TO HAVE THE JETS MOVED AWAY FROM OUR CITY?
SCHULZ

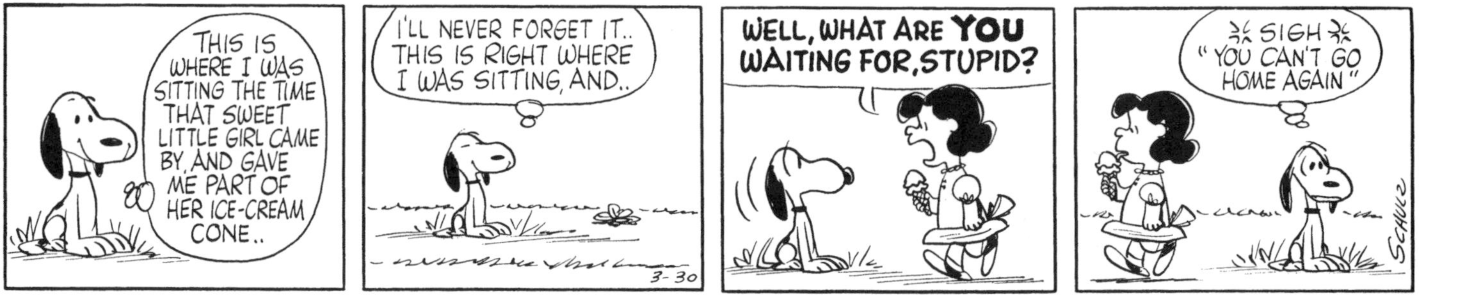
THIS IS WHERE I WAS SITTING THE TIME THAT SWEET LITTLE GIRL CAME BY, AND GAVE ME PART OF HER ICE-CREAM CONE..
I'LL NEVER FORGET IT.. THIS IS RIGHT WHERE I WAS SITTING, AND..
3-30
WELL, WHAT ARE YOU WAITING FOR, STUPID?
SIGH
"YOU CAN'T GO HOME AGAIN"
SCHULZ

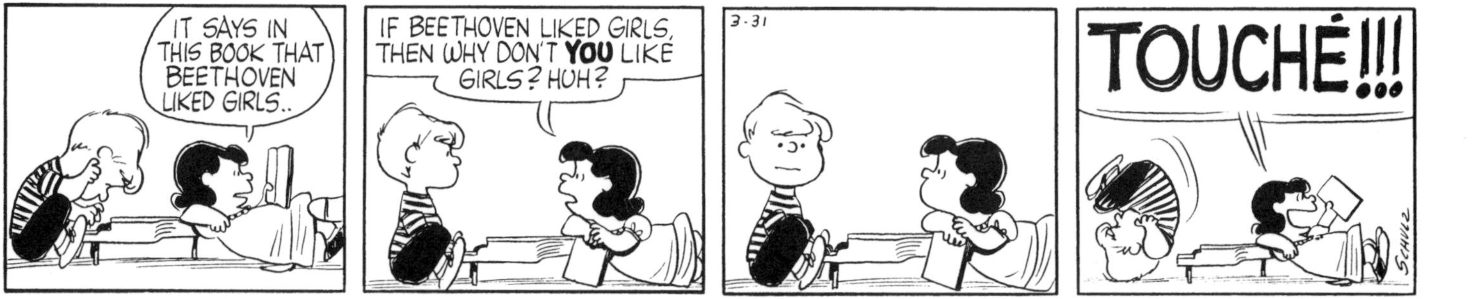
IT SAYS IN THIS BOOK THAT BEETHOVEN LIKED GIRLS..
IF BEETHOVEN LIKED GIRLS, THEN WHY DON'T YOU LIKE GIRLS? HUH?
3-31
TOUCHÉ!!!
SCHULZ

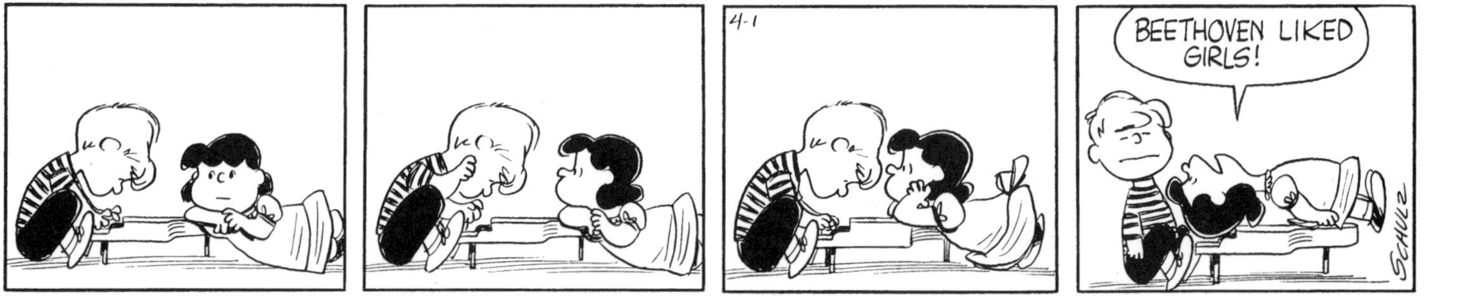
4-1
BEETHOVEN LIKED GIRLS!
SCHULZ

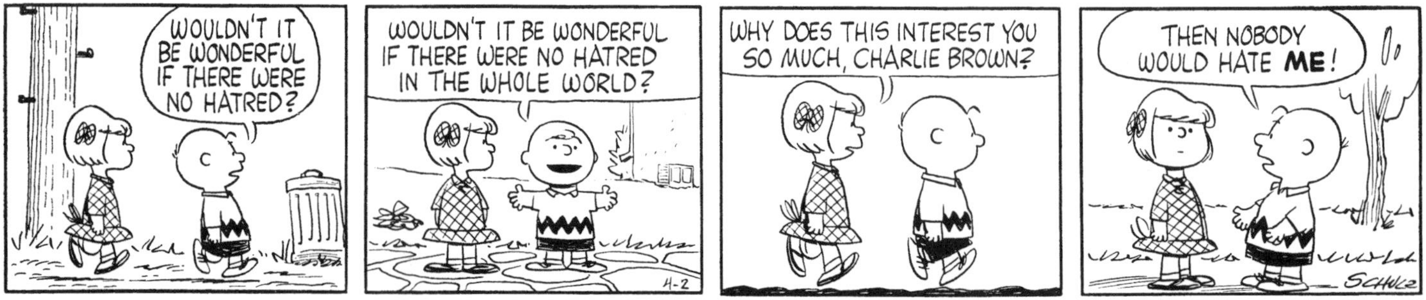
WOULDN'T IT BE WONDERFUL IF THERE WERE NO HATRED?
WOULDN'T IT BE WONDERFUL IF THERE WERE NO HATRED IN THE WHOLE WORLD?
4-2
WHY DOES THIS INTEREST YOU SO MUCH, CHARLIE BROWN?
THEN NOBODY WOULD HATE **ME**!
SCHULZ

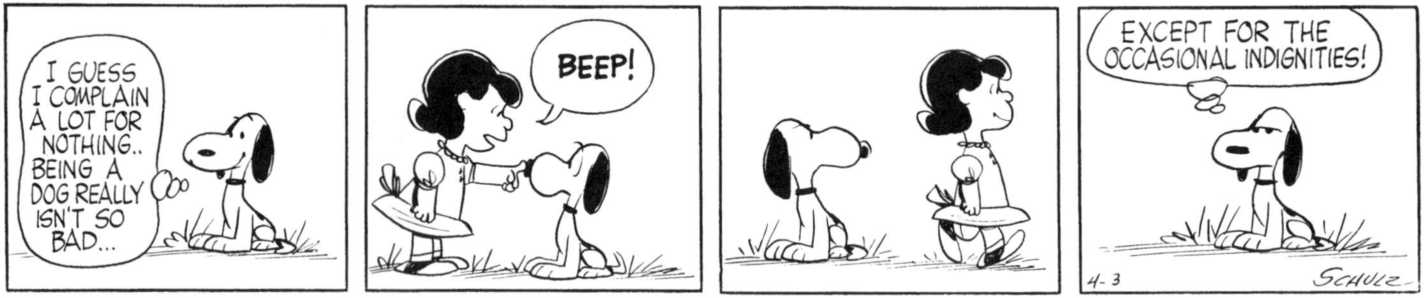
I GUESS I COMPLAIN A LOT FOR NOTHING.. BEING A DOG REALLY ISN'T SO BAD...
BEEP!
EXCEPT FOR THE OCCASIONAL INDIGNITIES!
4-3
SCHULZ

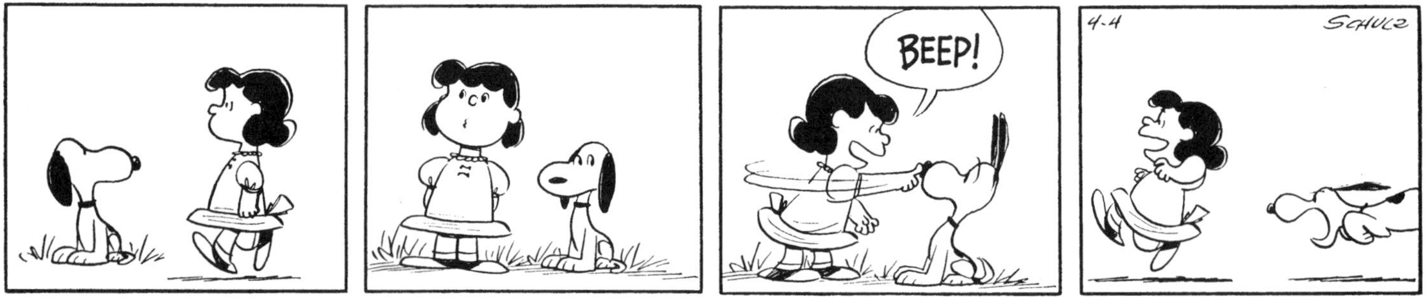
BEEP!
4-4
SCHULZ

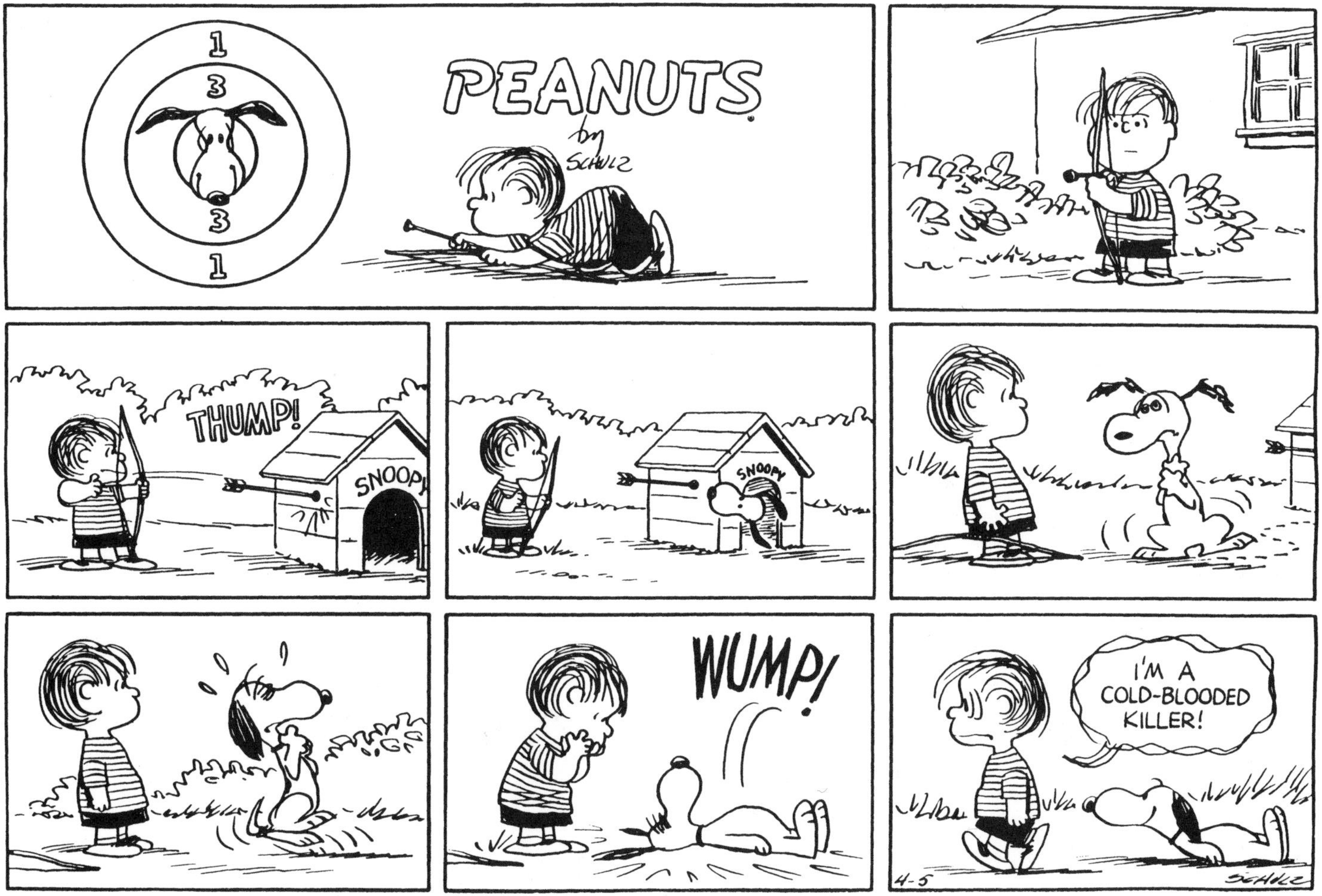
1
3
3
1
PEANUTS
by SCHULZ
THUMP!
SNOOPY
SNOOPY
WUMP!
I'M A COLD-BLOODED KILLER!
4-5
SCHULZ

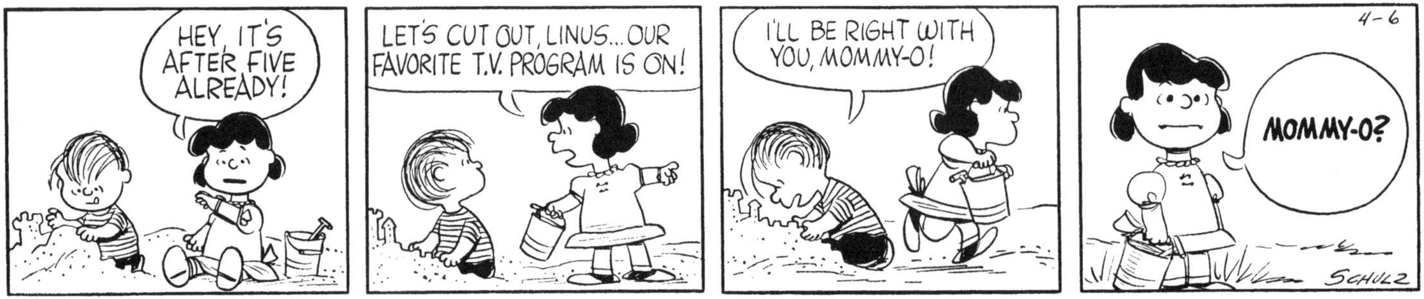
HEY, IT'S AFTER FIVE ALREADY!
LET'S CUT OUT, LINUS...OUR FAVORITE T.V. PROGRAM IS ON!
I'LL BE RIGHT WITH YOU, MOMMY-O!
4-6
MOMMY-O?
SCHULZ

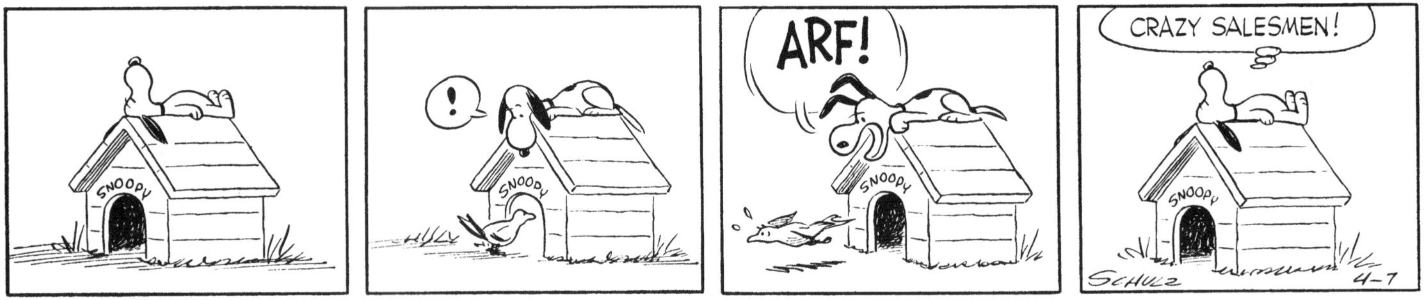
SNOOPY
!
ARF!
CRAZY SALESMEN!
SCHULZ
4-7

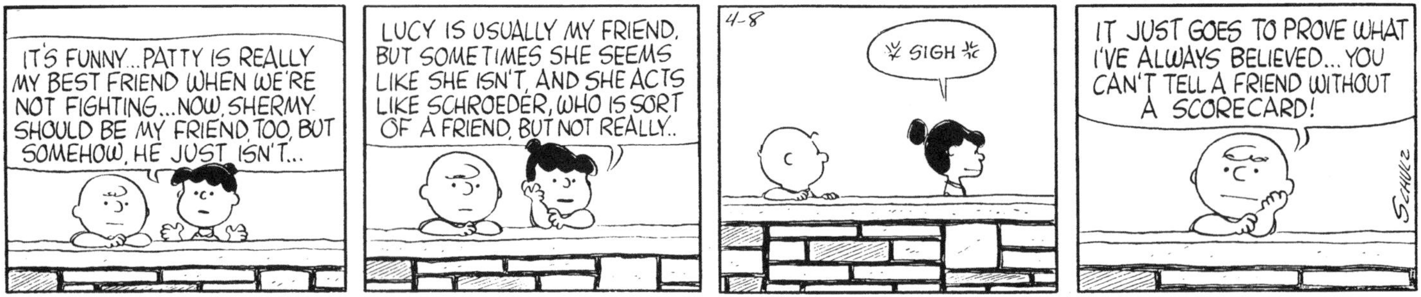
IT'S FUNNY...PATTY IS REALLY MY BEST FRIEND WHEN WE'RE NOT FIGHTING...NOW, SHERMY SHOULD BE MY FRIEND, TOO, BUT SOMEHOW, HE JUST ISN'T...
LUCY IS USUALLY MY FRIEND, BUT SOMETIMES SHE SEEMS LIKE SHE ISN'T, AND SHE ACTS LIKE SCHROEDER, WHO IS SORT OF A FRIEND, BUT NOT REALLY..
4-8
SIGH
IT JUST GOES TO PROVE WHAT I'VE ALWAYS BELIEVED...YOU CAN'T TELL A FRIEND WITHOUT A SCORECARD!
SCHULZ

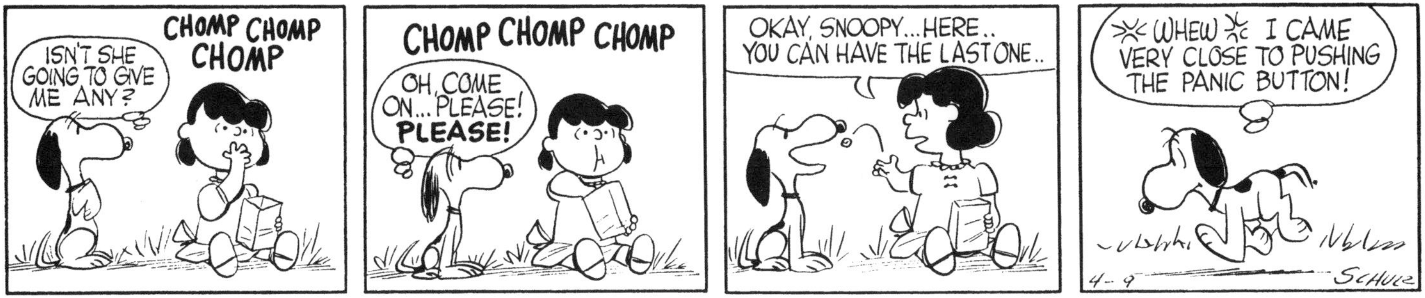
ISN'T SHE GOING TO GIVE ME ANY?
CHOMP CHOMP CHOMP
CHOMP CHOMP CHOMP
OH, COME ON... PLEASE! PLEASE!
OKAY, SNOOPY... HERE.. YOU CAN HAVE THE LAST ONE..
WHEW I CAME VERY CLOSE TO PUSHING THE PANIC BUTTON!
4-9
SCHULZ

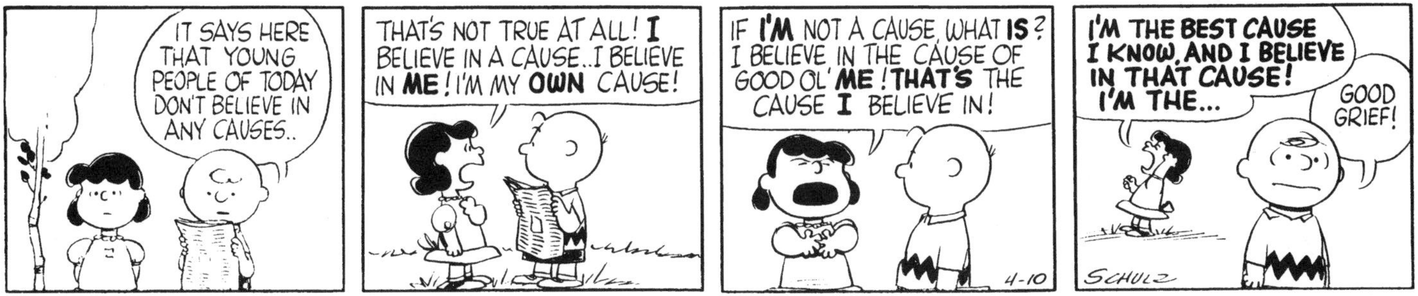
IT SAYS HERE THAT YOUNG PEOPLE OF TODAY DON'T BELIEVE IN ANY CAUSES..
THAT'S NOT TRUE AT ALL! I BELIEVE IN A CAUSE..I BELIEVE IN ME! I'M MY OWN CAUSE!
IF I'M NOT A CAUSE, WHAT IS? I BELIEVE IN THE CAUSE OF GOOD OL' ME! THAT'S THE CAUSE I BELIEVE IN!
4-10
I'M THE BEST CAUSE I KNOW, AND I BELIEVE IN THAT CAUSE! I'M THE...
GOOD GRIEF!
SCHULZ

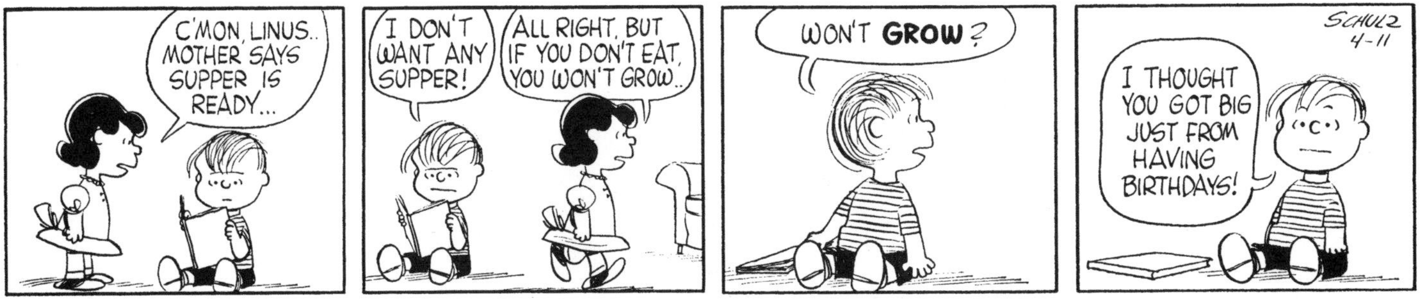
C'MON, LINUS.. MOTHER SAYS SUPPER IS READY...
I DON'T WANT ANY SUPPER!
ALL RIGHT, BUT IF YOU DON'T EAT, YOU WON'T GROW..
WON'T GROW?
SCHULZ 4-11
I THOUGHT YOU GOT BIG JUST FROM HAVING BIRTHDAYS!

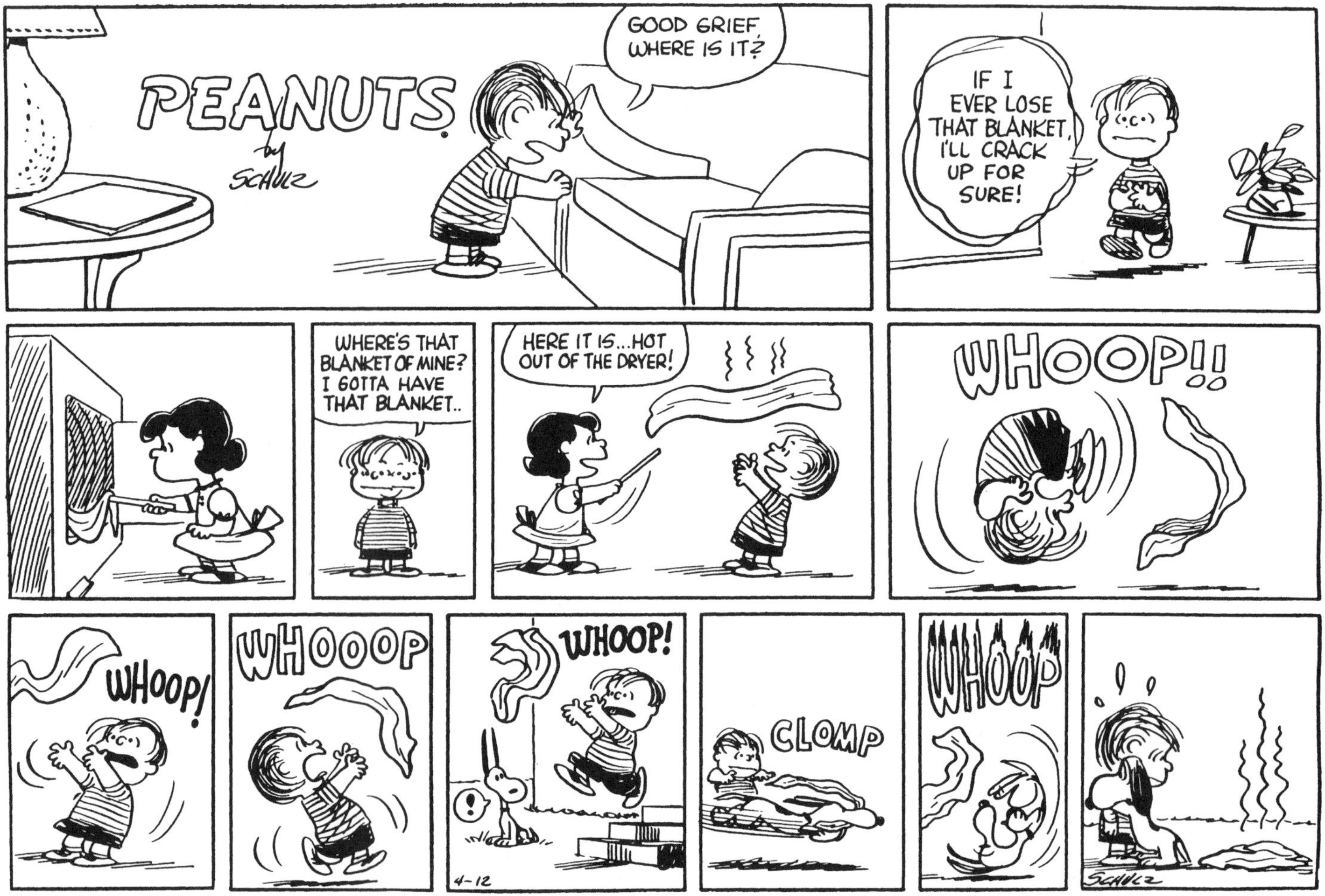
PEANUTS
by SCHULZ
GOOD GRIEF WHERE IS IT?
IF I EVER LOSE THAT BLANKET, I'LL CRACK UP FOR SURE!
WHERE'S THAT BLANKET OF MINE? I GOTTA HAVE THAT BLANKET..
HERE IT IS...HOT OUT OF THE DRYER!
WHOOP!!
WHOOP!
WHOOOP
WHOOP!
4-12
CLOMP
WHOOP
SCHULZ

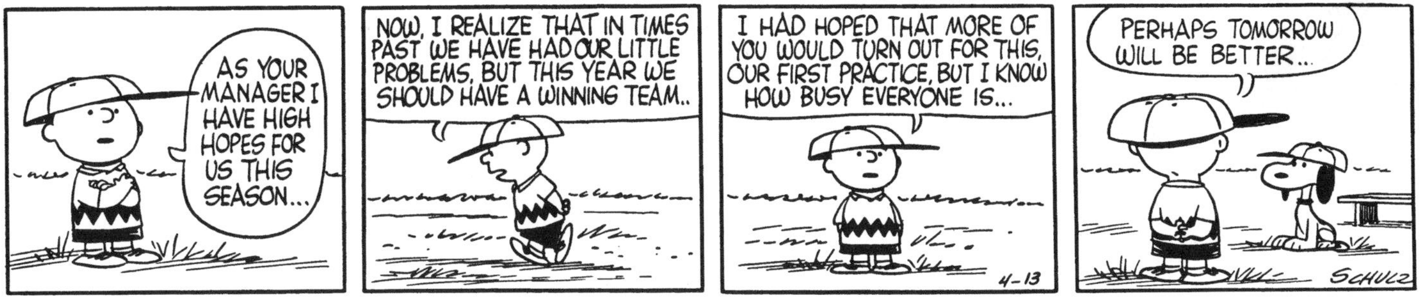
AS YOUR MANAGER I HAVE HIGH HOPES FOR US THIS SEASON...
NOW, I REALIZE THAT IN TIMES PAST WE HAVE HAD OUR LITTLE PROBLEMS, BUT THIS YEAR WE SHOULD HAVE A WINNING TEAM..
I HAD HOPED THAT MORE OF YOU WOULD TURN OUT FOR THIS, OUR FIRST PRACTICE, BUT I KNOW HOW BUSY EVERYONE IS...
4-13
PERHAPS TOMORROW WILL BE BETTER...
SCHULZ

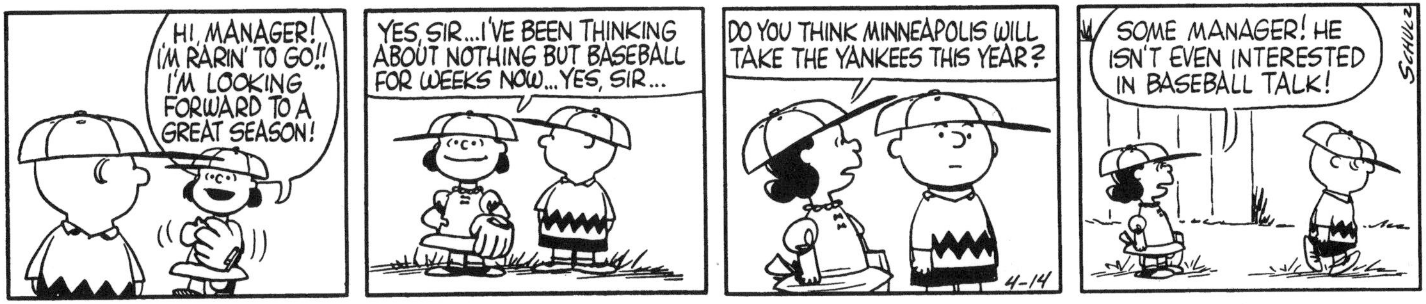
HI, MANAGER! I'M RARIN' TO GO!! I'M LOOKING FORWARD TO A GREAT SEASON!
YES, SIR...I'VE BEEN THINKING ABOUT NOTHING BUT BASEBALL FOR WEEKS NOW...YES, SIR...
DO YOU THINK MINNEAPOLIS WILL TAKE THE YANKEES THIS YEAR?
4-14
SOME MANAGER! HE ISN'T EVEN INTERESTED IN BASEBALL TALK!
SCHULZ

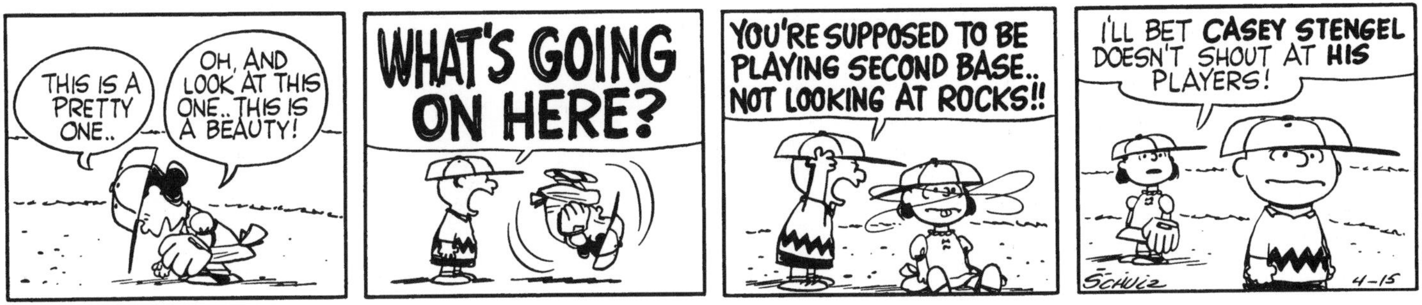
THIS IS A PRETTY ONE..
OH, AND LOOK AT THIS ONE.. THIS IS A BEAUTY!
WHAT'S GOING ON HERE?
YOU'RE SUPPOSED TO BE PLAYING SECOND BASE.. NOT LOOKING AT ROCKS!!
I'LL BET CASEY STENGEL DOESN'T SHOUT AT HIS PLAYERS!
SCHULZ
4-15

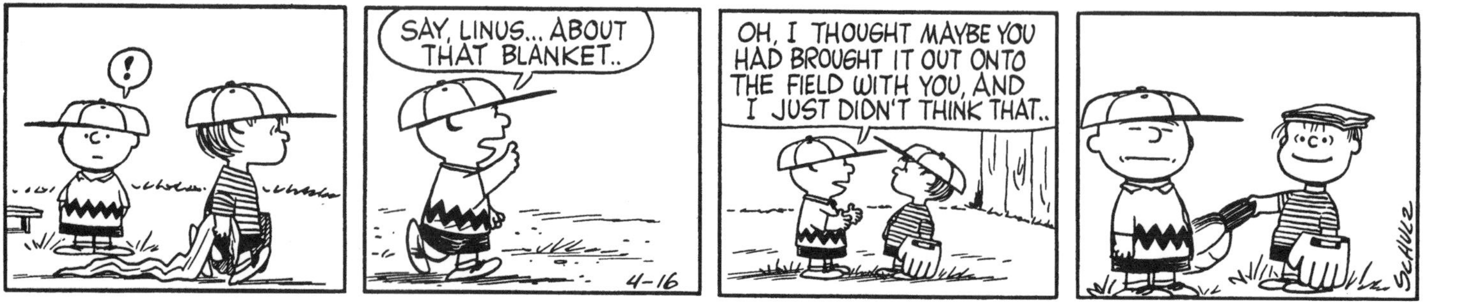
!
SAY, LINUS... ABOUT THAT BLANKET..
4-16
OH, I THOUGHT MAYBE YOU HAD BROUGHT IT OUT ONTO THE FIELD WITH YOU, AND I JUST DIDN'T THINK THAT..
SCHULZ

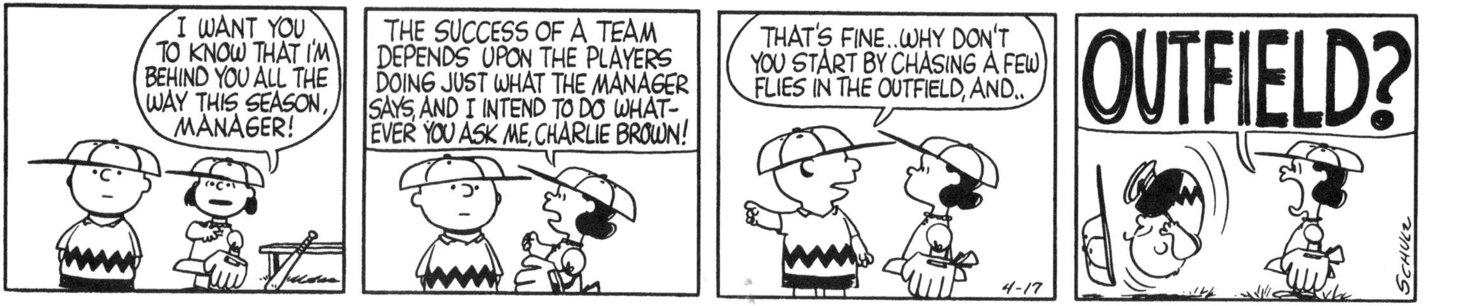
I WANT YOU TO KNOW THAT I'M BEHIND YOU ALL THE WAY THIS SEASON, MANAGER!
THE SUCCESS OF A TEAM DEPENDS UPON THE PLAYERS DOING JUST WHAT THE MANAGER SAYS, AND I INTEND TO DO WHATEVER YOU ASK ME, CHARLIE BROWN!
THAT'S FINE..WHY DON'T YOU START BY CHASING A FEW FLIES IN THE OUTFIELD, AND..
4-17
OUTFIELD?
SCHULZ

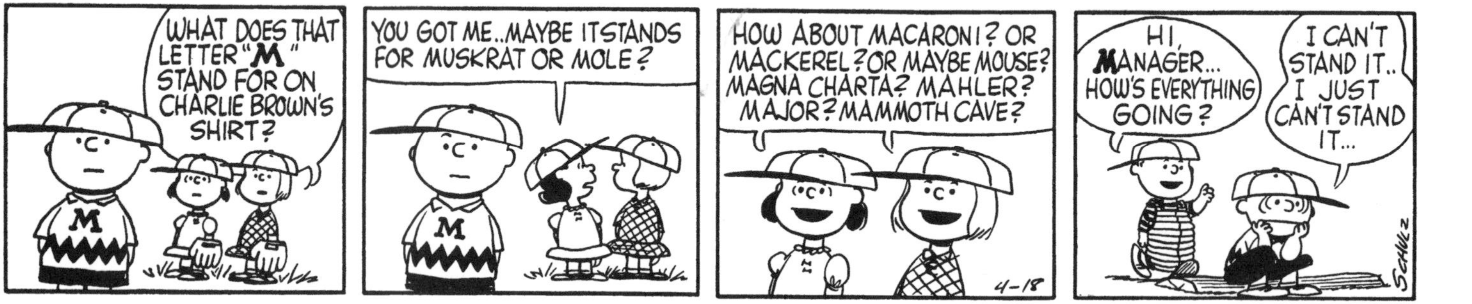
WHAT DOES THAT LETTER "M" STAND FOR ON CHARLIE BROWN'S SHIRT?
YOU GOT ME..MAYBE IT STANDS FOR MUSKRAT OR MOLE?
HOW ABOUT MACARONI? OR MACKEREL? OR MAYBE MOUSE? MAGNA CHARTA? MAHLER? MAJOR? MAMMOTH CAVE?
4-18
HI, MANAGER... HOW'S EVERYTHING GOING?
I CAN'T STAND IT.. I JUST CAN'T STAND IT...
SCHULZ

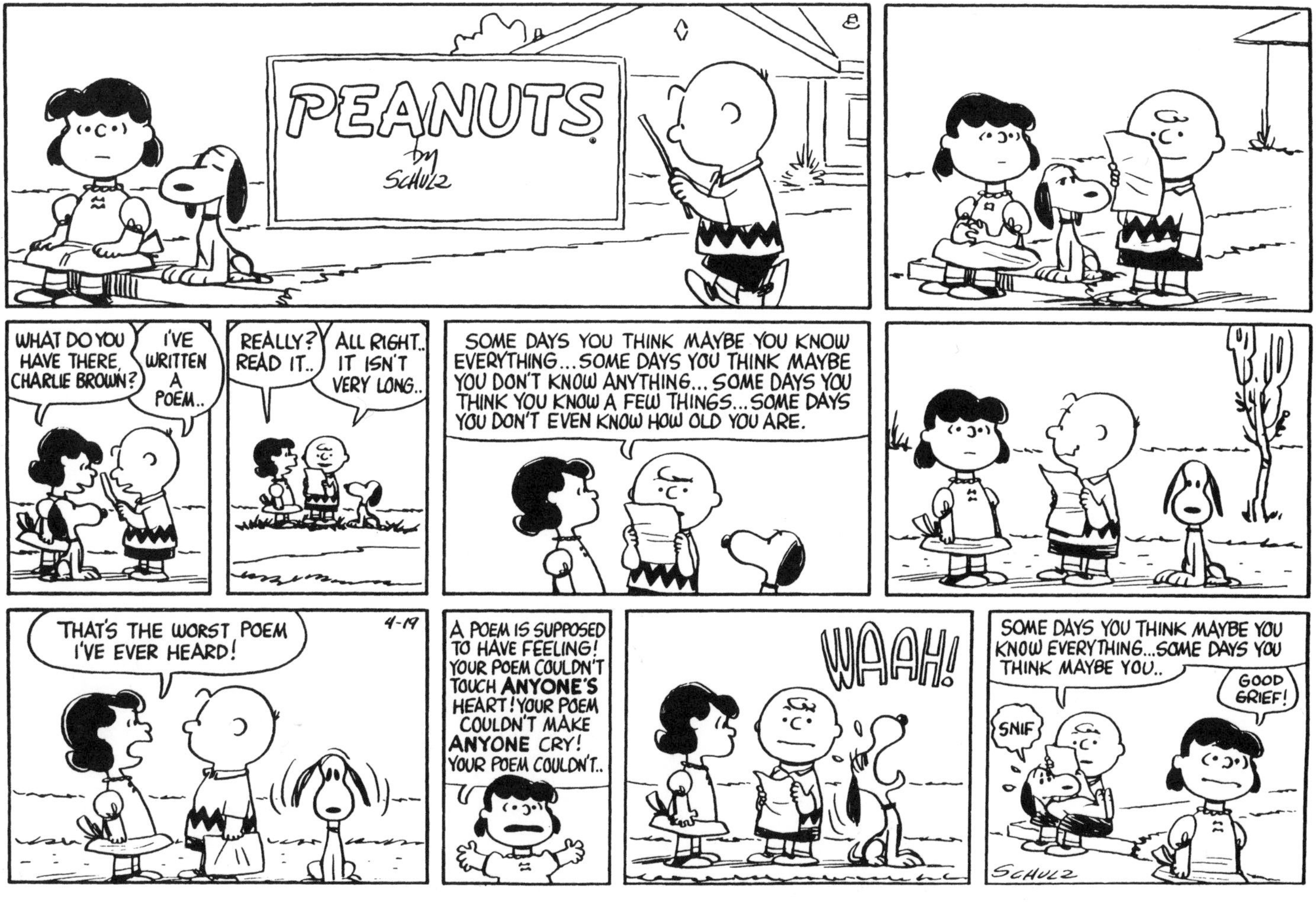
PEANUTS
by SCHULZ
WHAT DO YOU HAVE THERE, CHARLIE BROWN?
I'VE WRITTEN A POEM..
REALLY? READ IT..
ALL RIGHT.. IT ISN'T VERY LONG..
SOME DAYS YOU THINK MAYBE YOU KNOW EVERYTHING... SOME DAYS YOU THINK MAYBE YOU DON'T KNOW ANYTHING... SOME DAYS YOU THINK YOU KNOW A FEW THINGS... SOME DAYS YOU DON'T EVEN KNOW HOW OLD YOU ARE.
THAT'S THE WORST POEM I'VE EVER HEARD!
4-19
A POEM IS SUPPOSED TO HAVE FEELING! YOUR POEM COULDN'T TOUCH ANYONE'S HEART! YOUR POEM COULDN'T MAKE ANYONE CRY! YOUR POEM COULDN'T..
WAAH!
SOME DAYS YOU THINK MAYBE YOU KNOW EVERYTHING...SOME DAYS YOU THINK MAYBE YOU..
SNIF
GOOD GRIEF!
SCHULZ

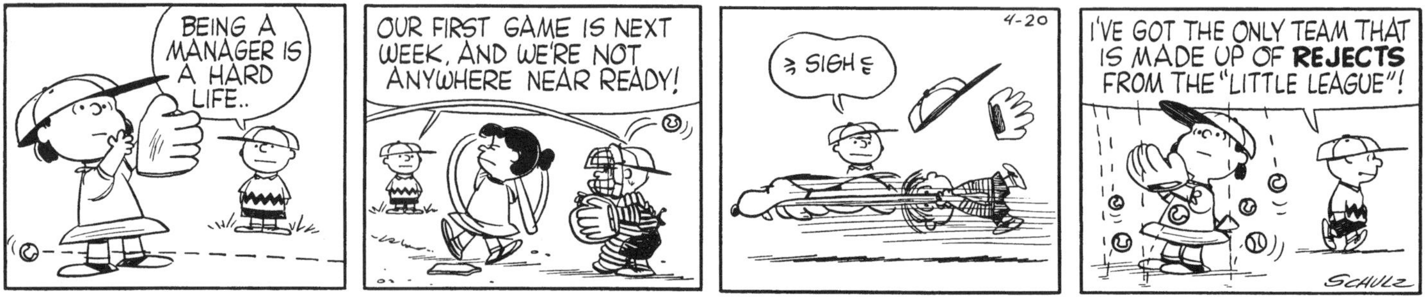
BEING A MANAGER IS A HARD LIFE..
OUR FIRST GAME IS NEXT WEEK, AND WE'RE NOT ANYWHERE NEAR READY!
4-20
SIGH
I'VE GOT THE ONLY TEAM THAT IS MADE UP OF **REJECTS** FROM THE "LITTLE LEAGUE"!
SCHULZ

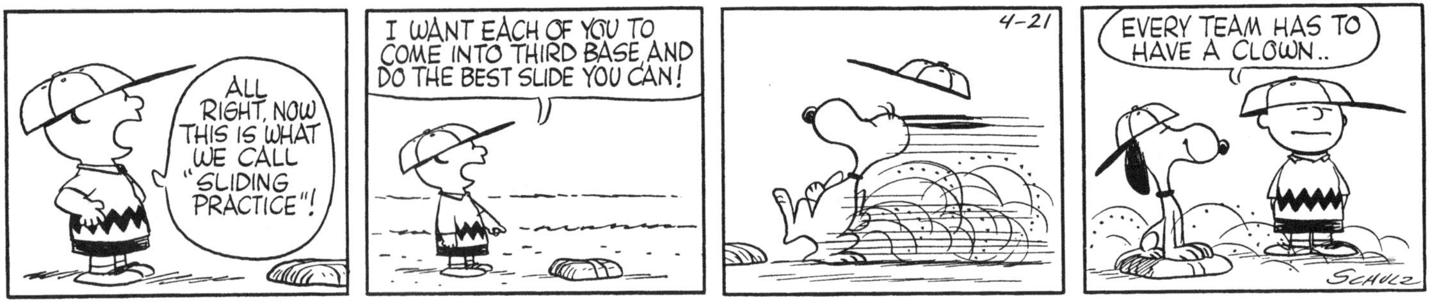
ALL RIGHT, NOW THIS IS WHAT WE CALL "SLIDING PRACTICE"!
I WANT EACH OF YOU TO COME INTO THIRD BASE AND DO THE BEST SLIDE YOU CAN!
4-21
EVERY TEAM HAS TO HAVE A CLOWN..
SCHULZ

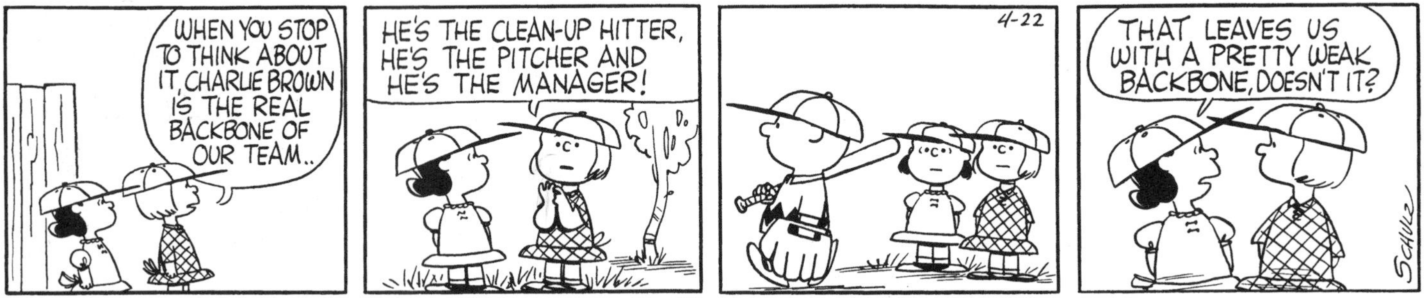
WHEN YOU STOP TO THINK ABOUT IT, CHARLIE BROWN IS THE REAL BACKBONE OF OUR TEAM..
HE'S THE CLEAN-UP HITTER, HE'S THE PITCHER AND HE'S THE MANAGER!
4-22
THAT LEAVES US WITH A PRETTY WEAK BACKBONE, DOESN'T IT?
SCHULZ

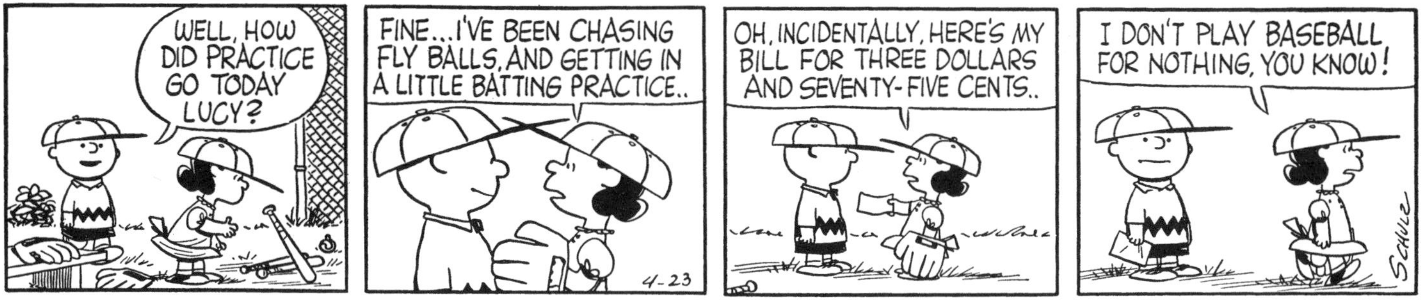
WELL, HOW DID PRACTICE GO TODAY LUCY?
FINE...I'VE BEEN CHASING FLY BALLS, AND GETTING IN A LITTLE BATTING PRACTICE..
OH, INCIDENTALLY, HERE'S MY BILL FOR THREE DOLLARS AND SEVENTY-FIVE CENTS..
I DON'T PLAY BASEBALL FOR NOTHING, YOU KNOW!

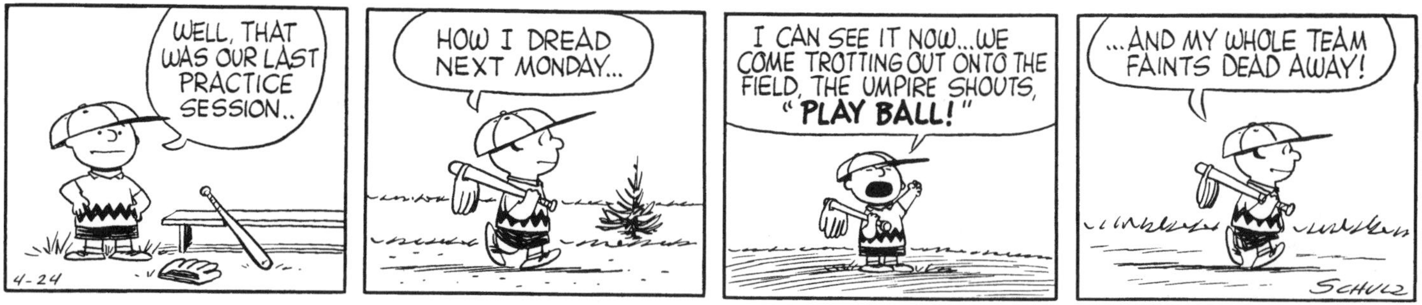
WELL, THAT WAS OUR LAST PRACTICE SESSION..
HOW I DREAD NEXT MONDAY...
I CAN SEE IT NOW...WE COME TROTTING OUT ONTO THE FIELD, THE UMPIRE SHOUTS, "PLAY BALL!"
...AND MY WHOLE TEAM FAINTS DEAD AWAY!

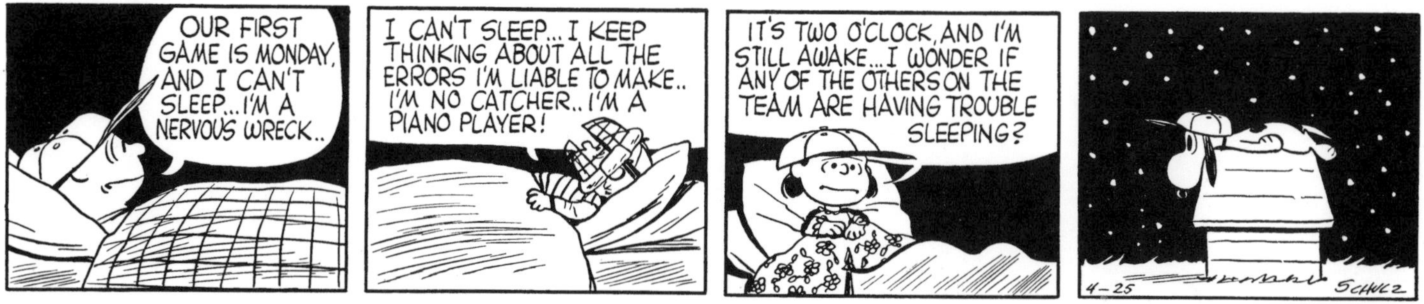
OUR FIRST GAME IS MONDAY, AND I CAN'T SLEEP...I'M A NERVOUS WRECK..
I CAN'T SLEEP... I KEEP THINKING ABOUT ALL THE ERRORS I'M LIABLE TO MAKE.. I'M NO CATCHER.. I'M A PIANO PLAYER!
IT'S TWO O'CLOCK, AND I'M STILL AWAKE...I WONDER IF ANY OF THE OTHERS ON THE TEAM ARE HAVING TROUBLE SLEEPING?

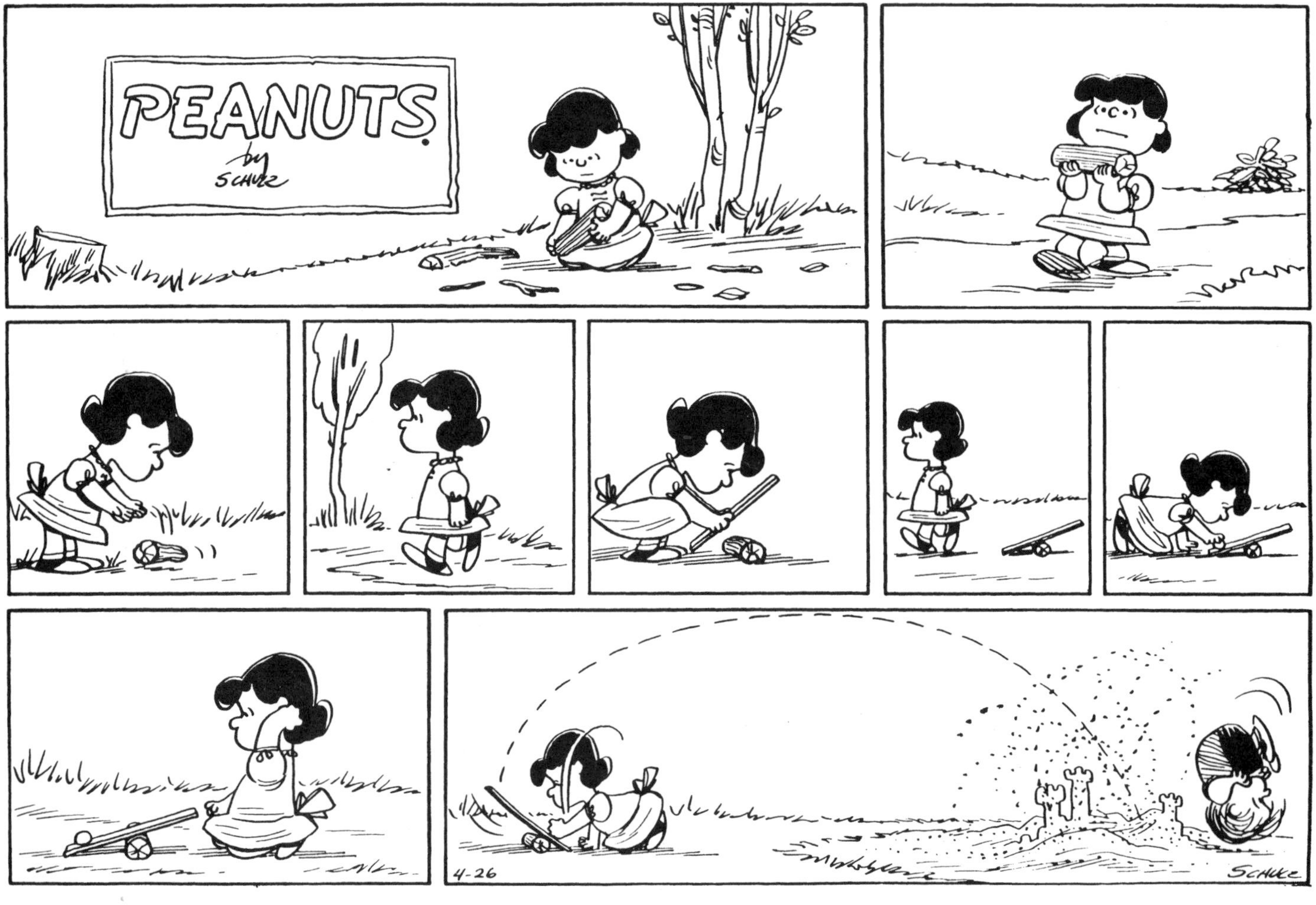
PEANUTS
by
SCHULZ
4-26
SCHULZ

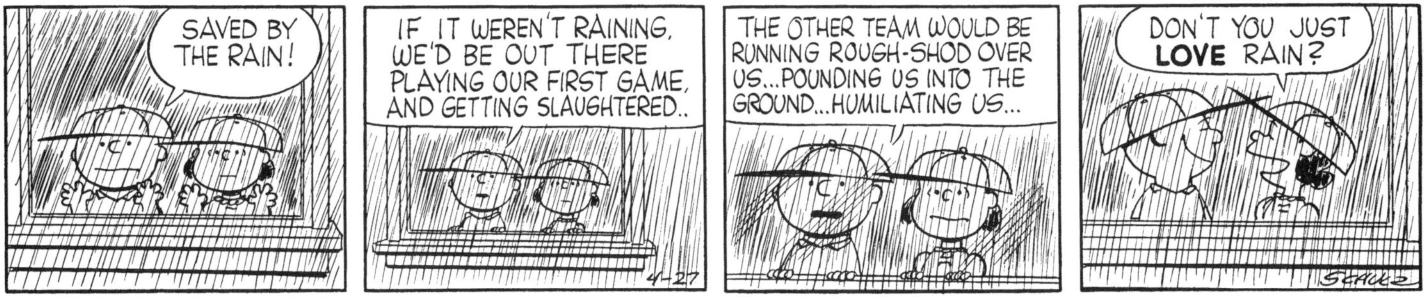
SAVED BY THE RAIN!
IF IT WEREN'T RAINING, WE'D BE OUT THERE PLAYING OUR FIRST GAME, AND GETTING SLAUGHTERED..
4-27
THE OTHER TEAM WOULD BE RUNNING ROUGH-SHOD OVER US...POUNDING US INTO THE GROUND...HUMILIATING US...
DON'T YOU JUST **LOVE** RAIN?
SCHULZ

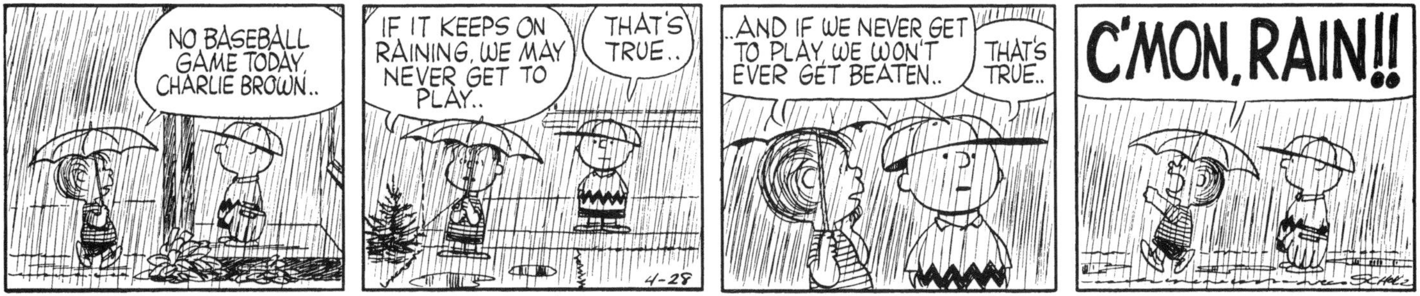
NO BASEBALL GAME TODAY, CHARLIE BROWN..
IF IT KEEPS ON RAINING, WE MAY NEVER GET TO PLAY..
THAT'S TRUE..
4-28
..AND IF WE NEVER GET TO PLAY, WE WON'T EVER GET BEATEN..
THAT'S TRUE..
C'MON, RAIN!!
SCHULZ

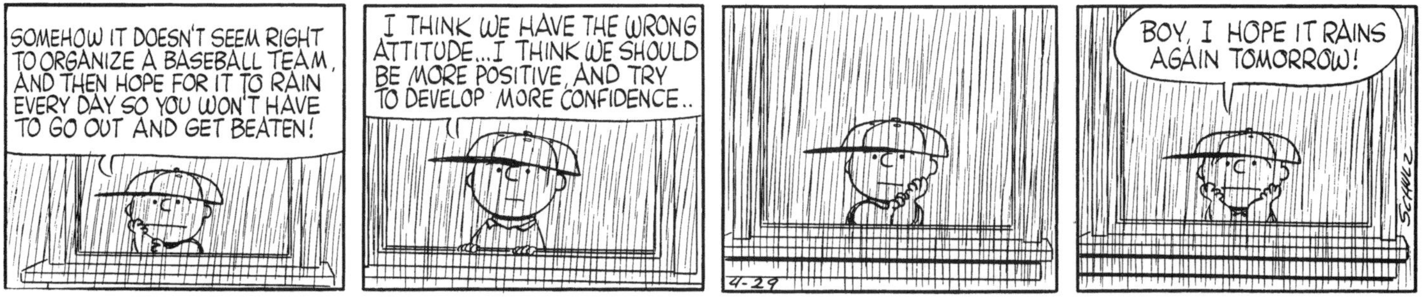
SOMEHOW IT DOESN'T SEEM RIGHT TO ORGANIZE A BASEBALL TEAM, AND THEN HOPE FOR IT TO RAIN EVERY DAY SO YOU WON'T HAVE TO GO OUT AND GET BEATEN!
I THINK WE HAVE THE WRONG ATTITUDE...I THINK WE SHOULD BE MORE POSITIVE, AND TRY TO DEVELOP MORE CONFIDENCE..
4-29
BOY, I HOPE IT RAINS AGAIN TOMORROW!
SCHULZ

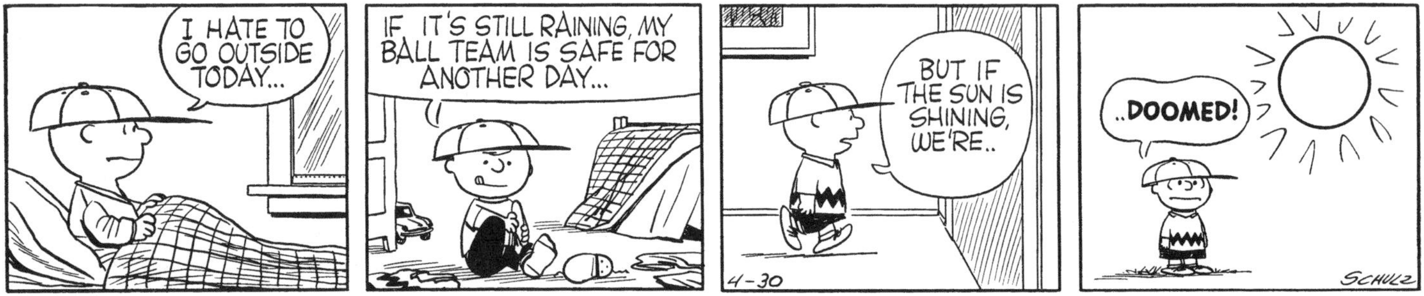
I HATE TO GO OUTSIDE TODAY...
IF IT'S STILL RAINING, MY BALL TEAM IS SAFE FOR ANOTHER DAY...
BUT IF THE SUN IS SHINING, WE'RE..
4-30
..DOOMED!
SCHULZ

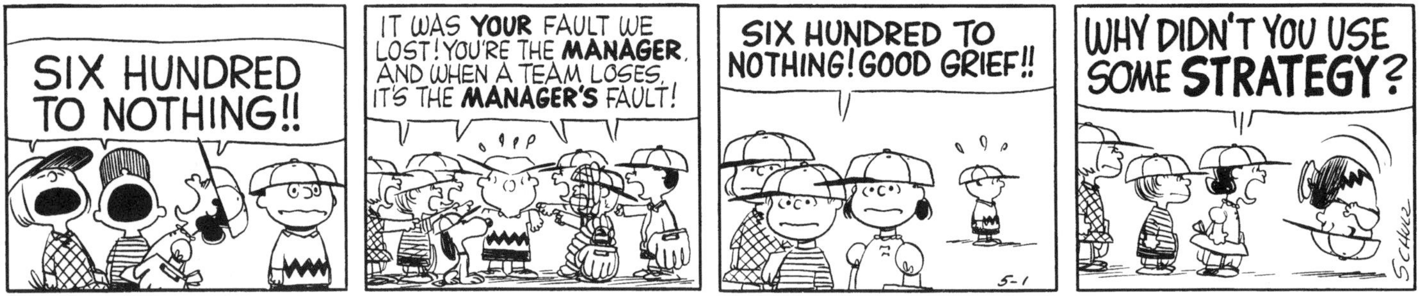
SIX HUNDRED TO NOTHING!!
IT WAS YOUR FAULT WE LOST! YOU'RE THE MANAGER, AND WHEN A TEAM LOSES, IT'S THE MANAGER'S FAULT!
SIX HUNDRED TO NOTHING! GOOD GRIEF!!
5-1
WHY DIDN'T YOU USE SOME STRATEGY?
SCHULZ

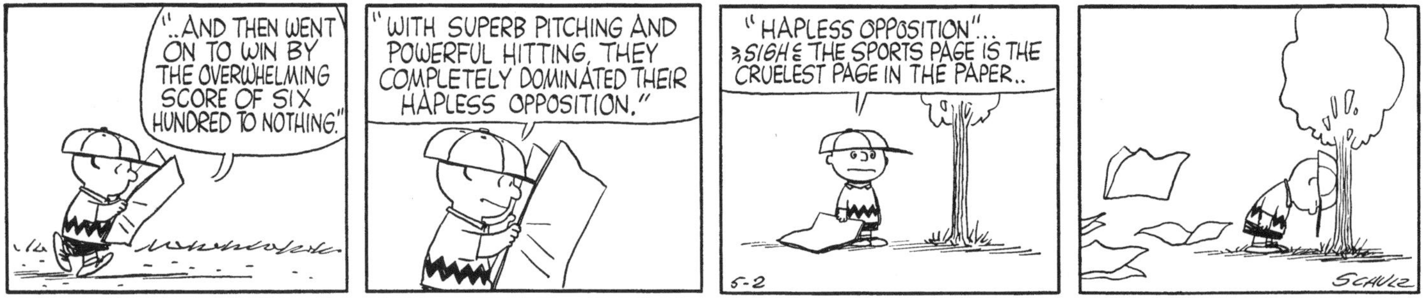
"..AND THEN WENT ON TO WIN BY THE OVERWHELMING SCORE OF SIX HUNDRED TO NOTHING."
"WITH SUPERB PITCHING AND POWERFUL HITTING, THEY COMPLETELY DOMINATED THEIR HAPLESS OPPOSITION."
"HAPLESS OPPOSITION"... SIGH THE SPORTS PAGE IS THE CRUELEST PAGE IN THE PAPER..
5-2
SCHULZ

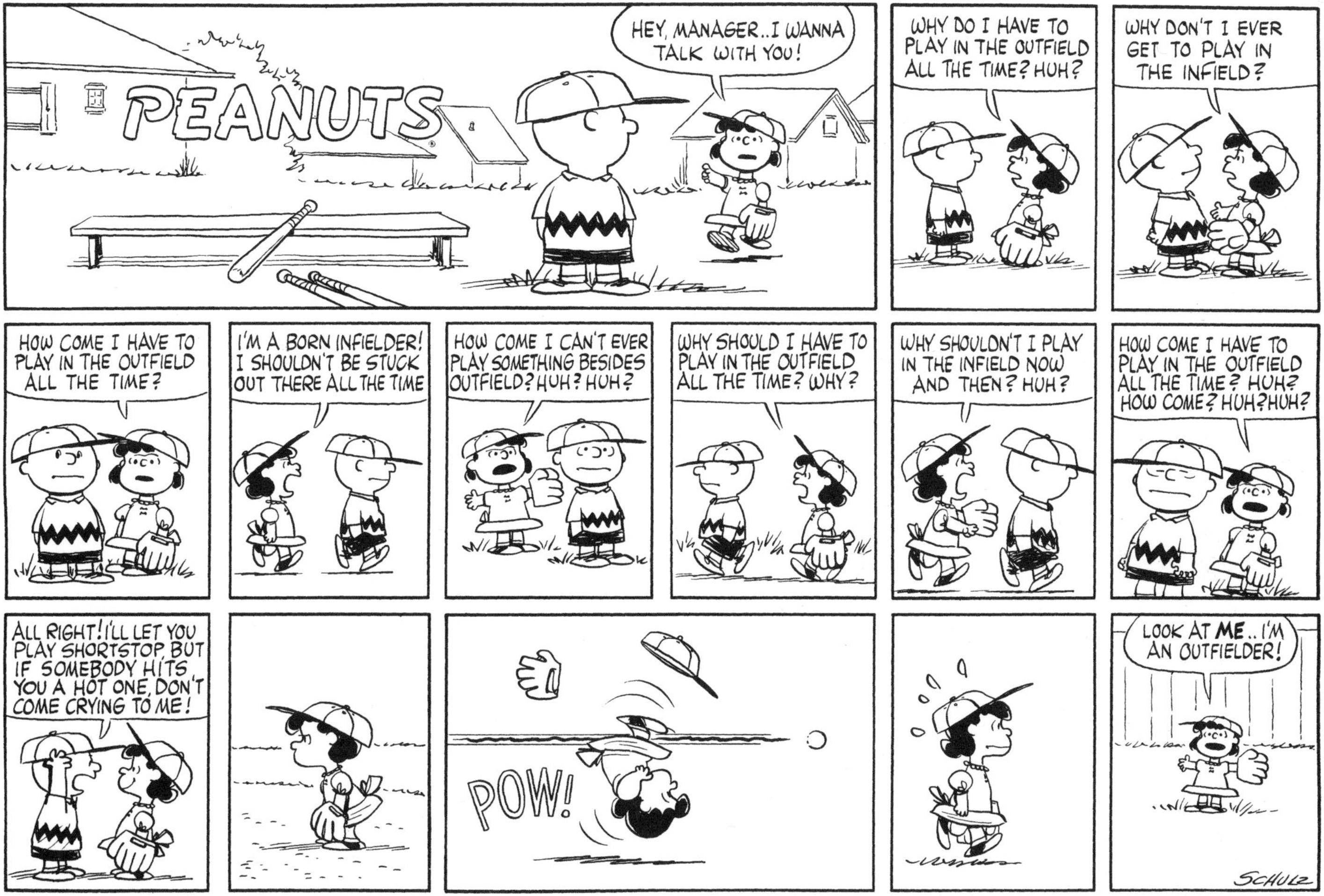
PEANUTS
HEY, MANAGER..I WANNA TALK WITH YOU!
WHY DO I HAVE TO PLAY IN THE OUTFIELD ALL THE TIME? HUH?
WHY DON'T I EVER GET TO PLAY IN THE INFIELD?
HOW COME I HAVE TO PLAY IN THE OUTFIELD ALL THE TIME?
I'M A BORN INFIELDER! I SHOULDN'T BE STUCK OUT THERE ALL THE TIME
HOW COME I CAN'T EVER PLAY SOMETHING BESIDES OUTFIELD? HUH? HUH?
WHY SHOULD I HAVE TO PLAY IN THE OUTFIELD ALL THE TIME? WHY?
WHY SHOULDN'T I PLAY IN THE INFIELD NOW AND THEN? HUH?
HOW COME I HAVE TO PLAY IN THE OUTFIELD ALL THE TIME? HUH? HOW COME? HUH? HUH?
ALL RIGHT! I'LL LET YOU PLAY SHORTSTOP, BUT IF SOMEBODY HITS YOU A HOT ONE, DON'T COME CRYING TO ME!
POW!
LOOK AT **ME**.. I'M AN OUTFIELDER!
SCHULZ

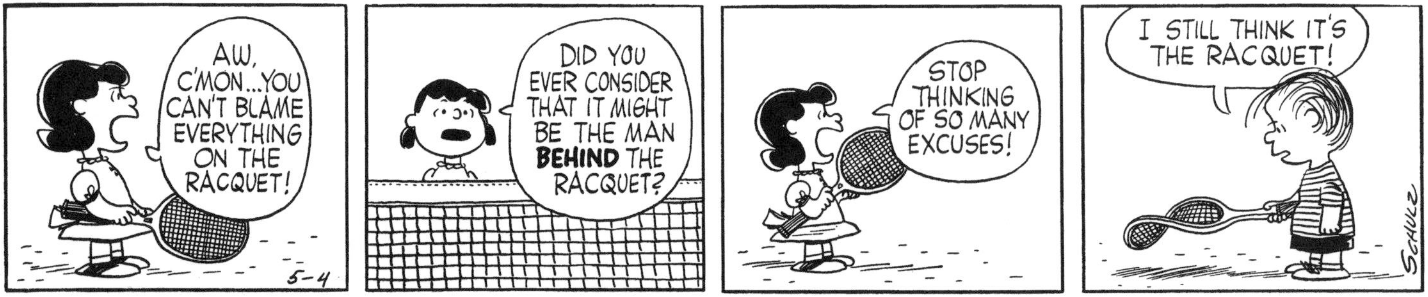
AW, C'MON...YOU CAN'T BLAME EVERYTHING ON THE RACQUET!
5-4
DID YOU EVER CONSIDER THAT IT MIGHT BE THE MAN **BEHIND** THE RACQUET?
STOP THINKING OF SO MANY EXCUSES!
I STILL THINK IT'S THE RACQUET!
SCHULZ

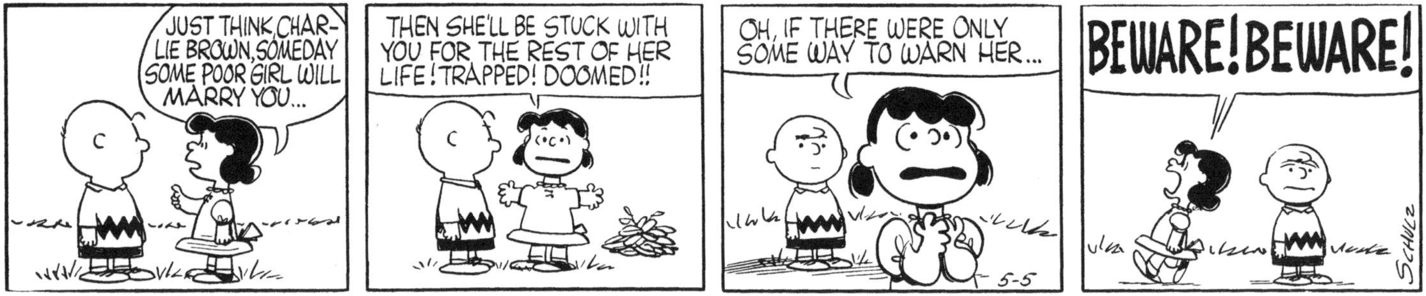
JUST THINK, CHARLIE BROWN, SOMEDAY SOME POOR GIRL WILL MARRY YOU...
THEN SHE'LL BE STUCK WITH YOU FOR THE REST OF HER LIFE! TRAPPED! DOOMED!!
OH, IF THERE WERE ONLY SOME WAY TO WARN HER...
5-5
BEWARE! BEWARE!
SCHULZ

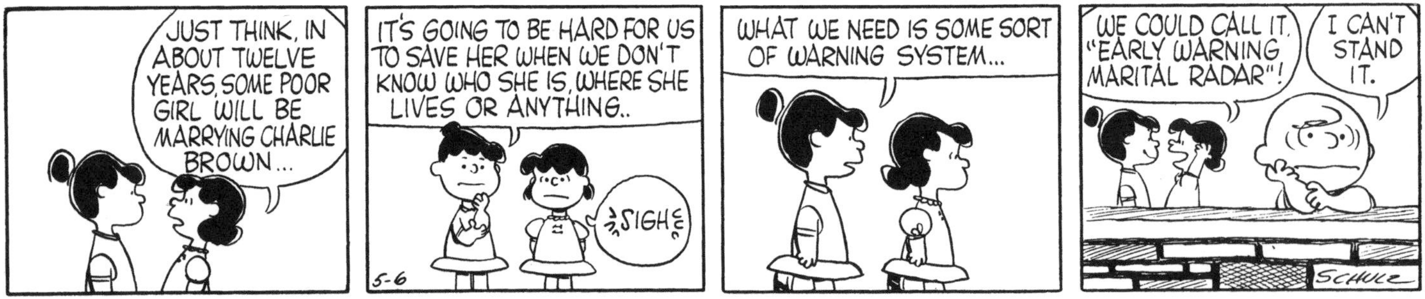
JUST THINK, IN ABOUT TWELVE YEARS, SOME POOR GIRL WILL BE MARRYING CHARLIE BROWN...
IT'S GOING TO BE HARD FOR US TO SAVE HER WHEN WE DON'T KNOW WHO SHE IS, WHERE SHE LIVES OR ANYTHING..
SIGH
5-6
WHAT WE NEED IS SOME SORT OF WARNING SYSTEM...
WE COULD CALL IT "EARLY WARNING MARITAL RADAR"!
I CAN'T STAND IT.
SCHULZ

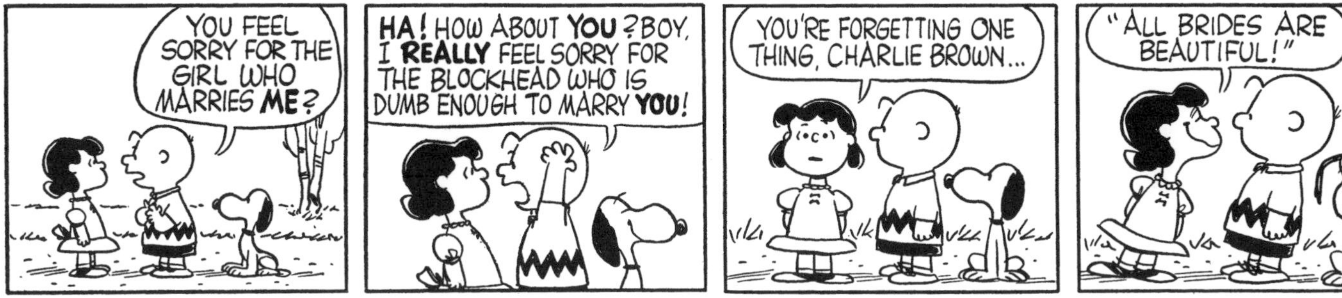
YOU FEEL SORRY FOR THE GIRL WHO MARRIES ME?
HA! HOW ABOUT YOU? BOY, I REALLY FEEL SORRY FOR THE BLOCKHEAD WHO IS DUMB ENOUGH TO MARRY YOU!
YOU'RE FORGETTING ONE THING, CHARLIE BROWN...
"ALL BRIDES ARE BEAUTIFUL!"
5-7
SCHULZ

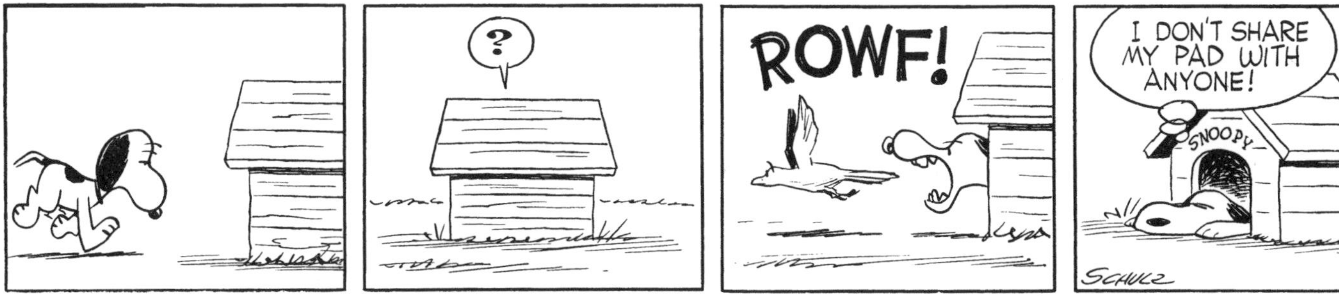
?
ROWF!
I DON'T SHARE MY PAD WITH ANYONE!
SNOOPY
SCHULZ
5-8

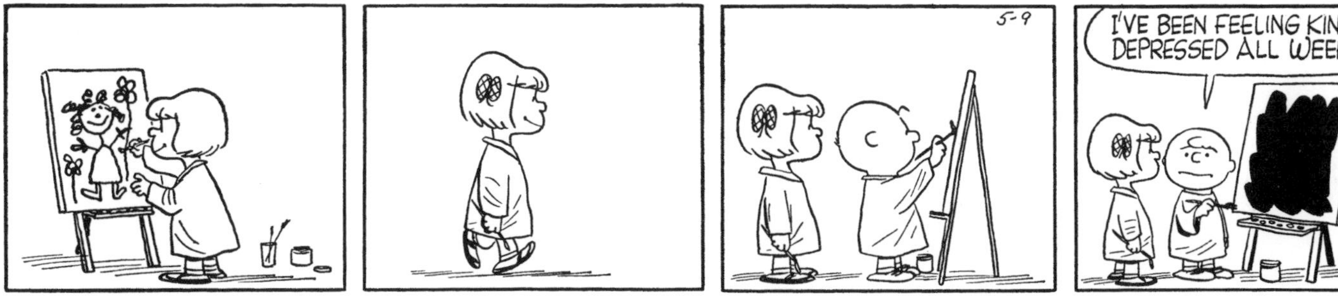
5-9
I'VE BEEN FEELING KIND OF DEPRESSED ALL WEEK..
SCHULZ

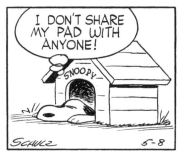

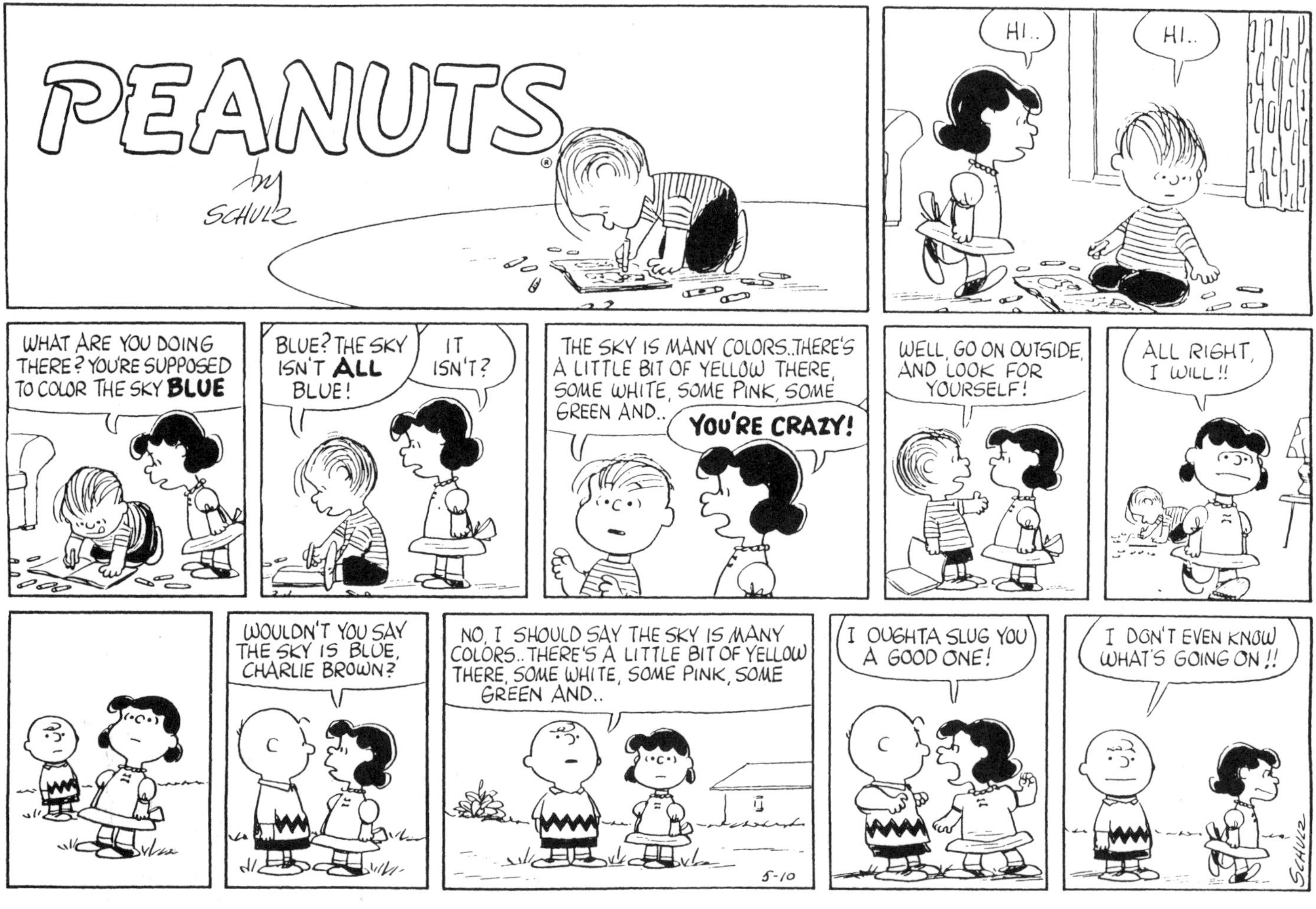

PEANUTS
by SCHULZ
HI..
HI..
WHAT ARE YOU DOING THERE? YOU'RE SUPPOSED TO COLOR THE SKY BLUE
BLUE? THE SKY ISN'T ALL BLUE!
IT ISN'T?
THE SKY IS MANY COLORS..THERE'S A LITTLE BIT OF YELLOW THERE, SOME WHITE, SOME PINK, SOME GREEN AND..
YOU'RE CRAZY!
WELL, GO ON OUTSIDE, AND LOOK FOR YOURSELF!
ALL RIGHT, I WILL!!
WOULDN'T YOU SAY THE SKY IS BLUE, CHARLIE BROWN?
NO, I SHOULD SAY THE SKY IS MANY COLORS..THERE'S A LITTLE BIT OF YELLOW THERE, SOME WHITE, SOME PINK, SOME GREEN AND..
5-10
I OUGHTA SLUG YOU A GOOD ONE!
I DON'T EVEN KNOW WHAT'S GOING ON!!
SCHULZ

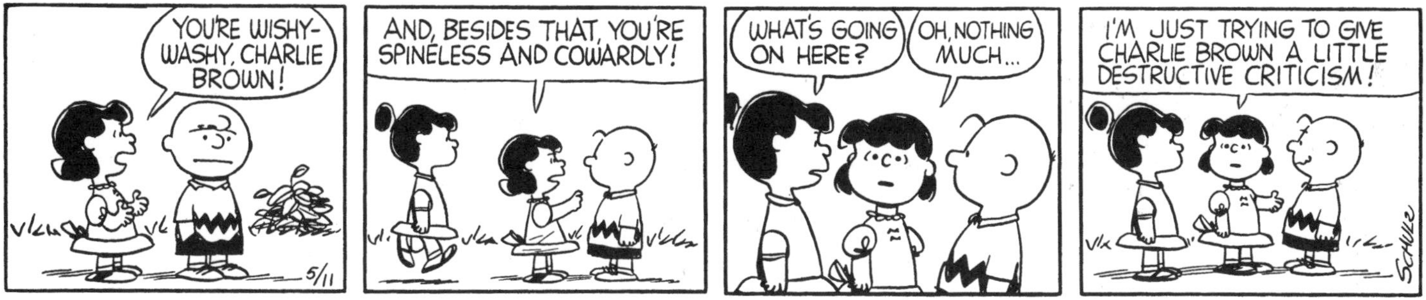
YOU'RE WISHY-WASHY, CHARLIE BROWN!
AND, BESIDES THAT, YOU'RE SPINELESS AND COWARDLY!
WHAT'S GOING ON HERE?
OH, NOTHING MUCH...
I'M JUST TRYING TO GIVE CHARLIE BROWN A LITTLE DESTRUCTIVE CRITICISM!

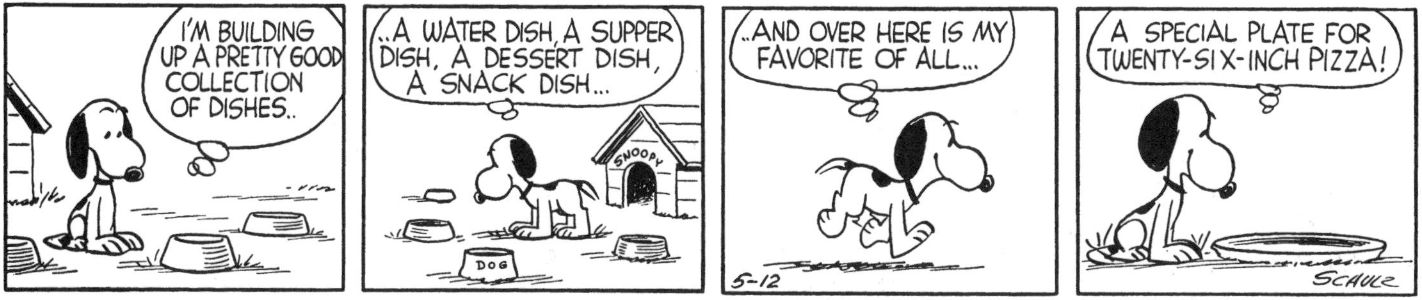
I'M BUILDING UP A PRETTY GOOD COLLECTION OF DISHES..
..A WATER DISH, A SUPPER DISH, A DESSERT DISH, A SNACK DISH...
SNOOPY
DOG
..AND OVER HERE IS MY FAVORITE OF ALL...
A SPECIAL PLATE FOR TWENTY-SIX-INCH PIZZA!

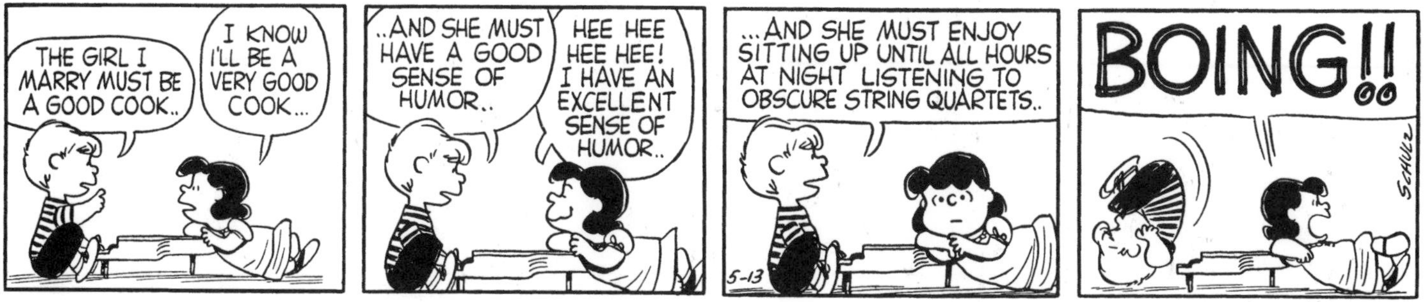
THE GIRL I MARRY MUST BE A GOOD COOK..
I KNOW I'LL BE A VERY GOOD COOK...
..AND SHE MUST HAVE A GOOD SENSE OF HUMOR..
HEE HEE HEE HEE! I HAVE AN EXCELLENT SENSE OF HUMOR..
...AND SHE MUST ENJOY SITTING UP UNTIL ALL HOURS AT NIGHT LISTENING TO OBSCURE STRING QUARTETS..
BOING!!

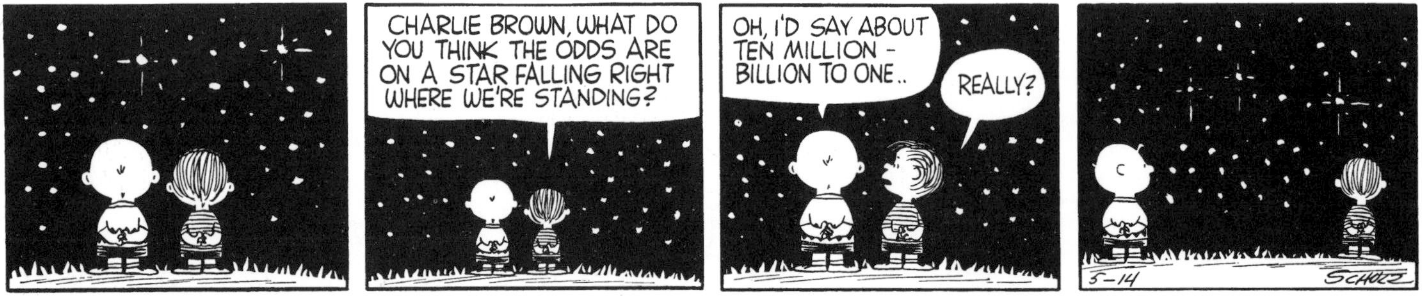
CHARLIE BROWN, WHAT DO YOU THINK THE ODDS ARE ON A STAR FALLING RIGHT WHERE WE'RE STANDING?
OH, I'D SAY ABOUT TEN MILLION - BILLION TO ONE..
REALLY?
5-14
SCHULZ

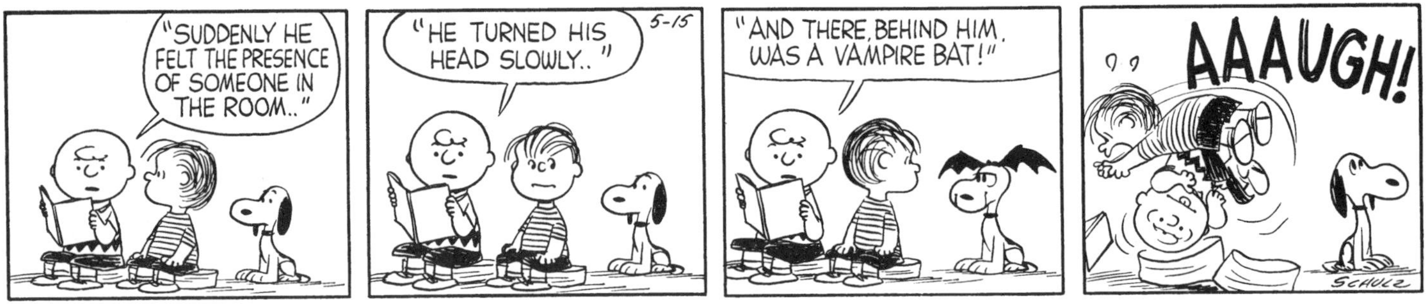
"SUDDENLY HE FELT THE PRESENCE OF SOMEONE IN THE ROOM.."
"HE TURNED HIS HEAD SLOWLY.."
5-15
"AND THERE, BEHIND HIM, WAS A VAMPIRE BAT!"
AAAUGH!
SCHULZ

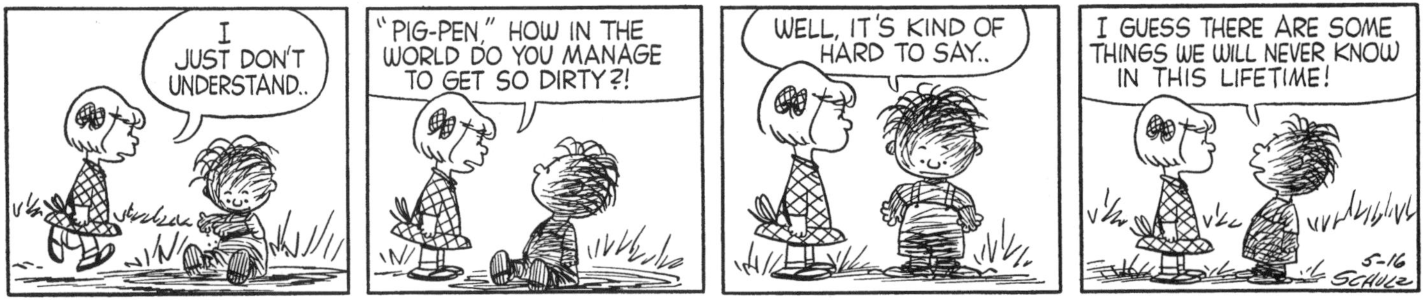
I JUST DON'T UNDERSTAND..
"PIG-PEN," HOW IN THE WORLD DO YOU MANAGE TO GET SO DIRTY?!
WELL, IT'S KIND OF HARD TO SAY..
I GUESS THERE ARE SOME THINGS WE WILL NEVER KNOW IN THIS LIFETIME!
5-16
SCHULZ

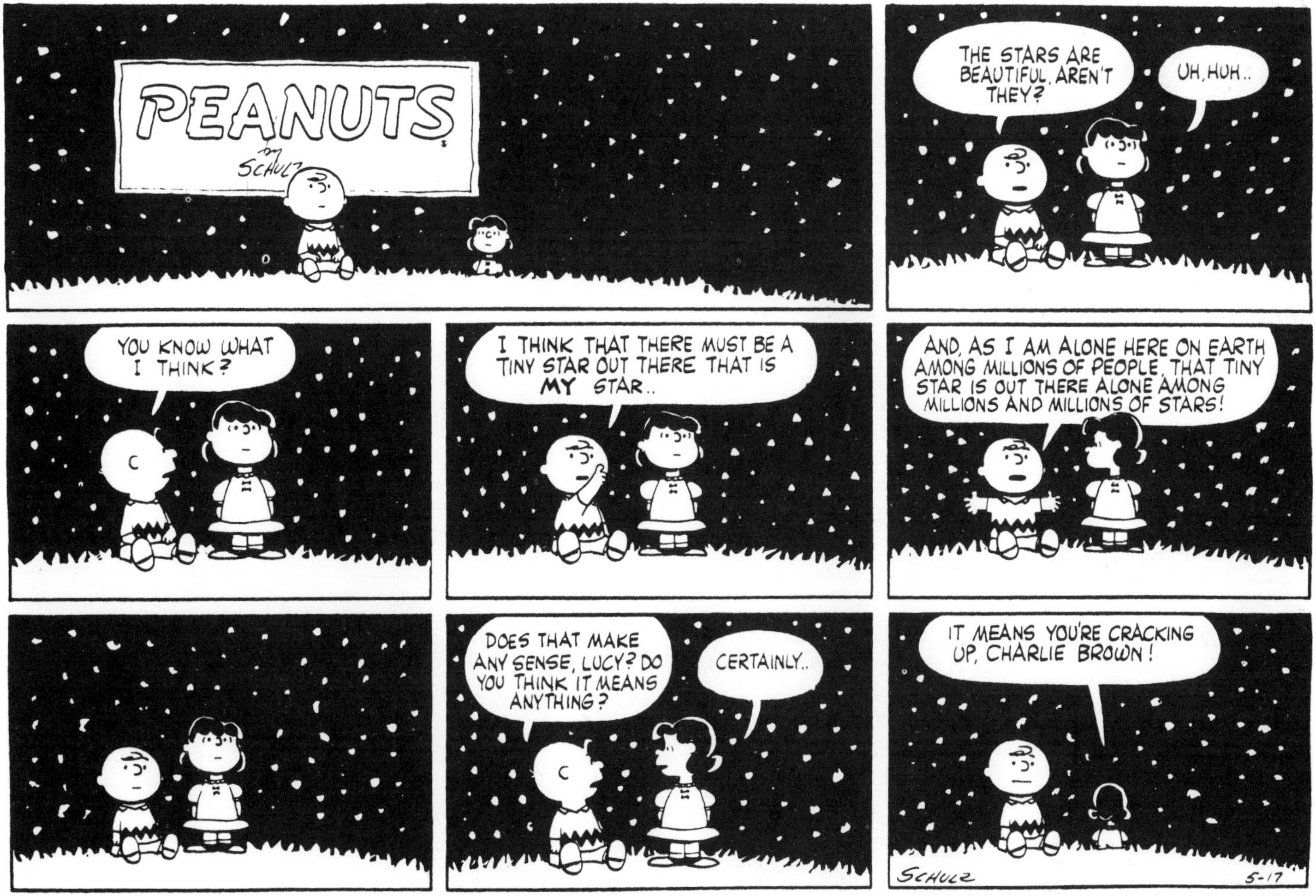
PEANUTS
by SCHULZ
THE STARS ARE BEAUTIFUL, AREN'T THEY?
UH, HUH..
YOU KNOW WHAT I THINK?
I THINK THAT THERE MUST BE A TINY STAR OUT THERE THAT IS MY STAR..
AND, AS I AM ALONE HERE ON EARTH AMONG MILLIONS OF PEOPLE, THAT TINY STAR IS OUT THERE ALONE AMONG MILLIONS AND MILLIONS OF STARS!
DOES THAT MAKE ANY SENSE, LUCY? DO YOU THINK IT MEANS ANYTHING?
CERTAINLY..
IT MEANS YOU'RE CRACKING UP, CHARLIE BROWN!
SCHULZ
5-17

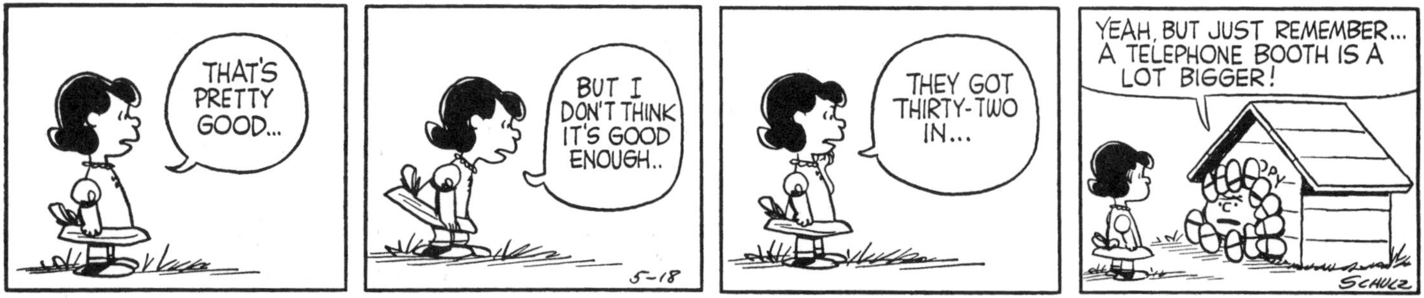
THAT'S PRETTY GOOD...
BUT I DON'T THINK IT'S GOOD ENOUGH..
5-18
THEY GOT THIRTY-TWO IN...
YEAH, BUT JUST REMEMBER... A TELEPHONE BOOTH IS A LOT BIGGER!
SCHULZ

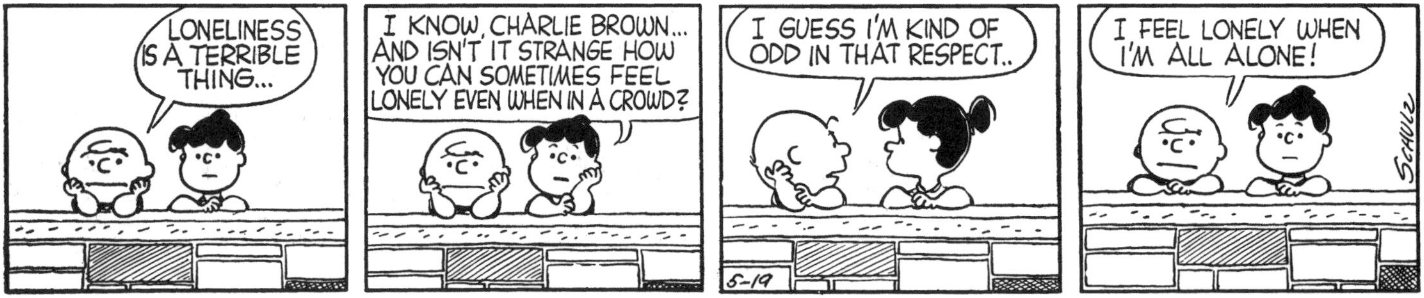
LONELINESS IS A TERRIBLE THING...
I KNOW, CHARLIE BROWN... AND ISN'T IT STRANGE HOW YOU CAN SOMETIMES FEEL LONELY EVEN WHEN IN A CROWD?
I GUESS I'M KIND OF ODD IN THAT RESPECT..
5-19
I FEEL LONELY WHEN I'M ALL ALONE!
SCHULZ

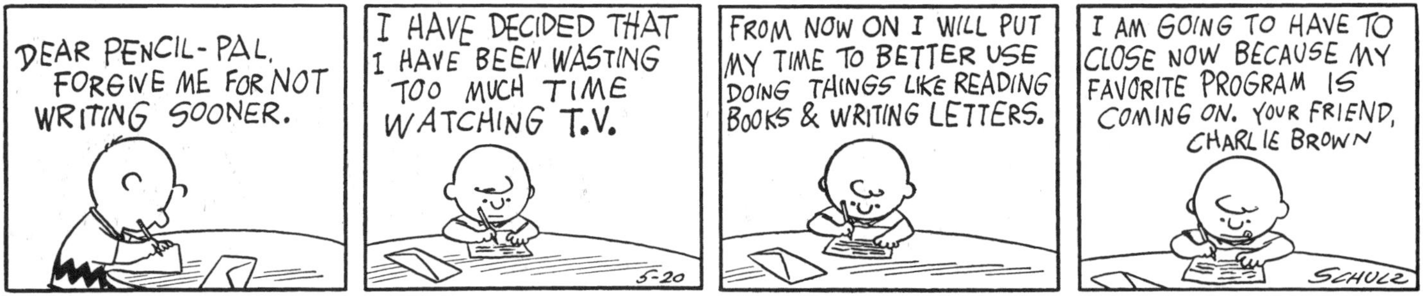
DEAR PENCIL-PAL, FORGIVE ME FOR NOT WRITING SOONER.
I HAVE DECIDED THAT I HAVE BEEN WASTING TOO MUCH TIME WATCHING T.V.
5-20
FROM NOW ON I WILL PUT MY TIME TO BETTER USE DOING THINGS LIKE READING BOOKS & WRITING LETTERS.
I AM GOING TO HAVE TO CLOSE NOW BECAUSE MY FAVORITE PROGRAM IS COMING ON. YOUR FRIEND, CHARLIE BROWN
SCHULZ

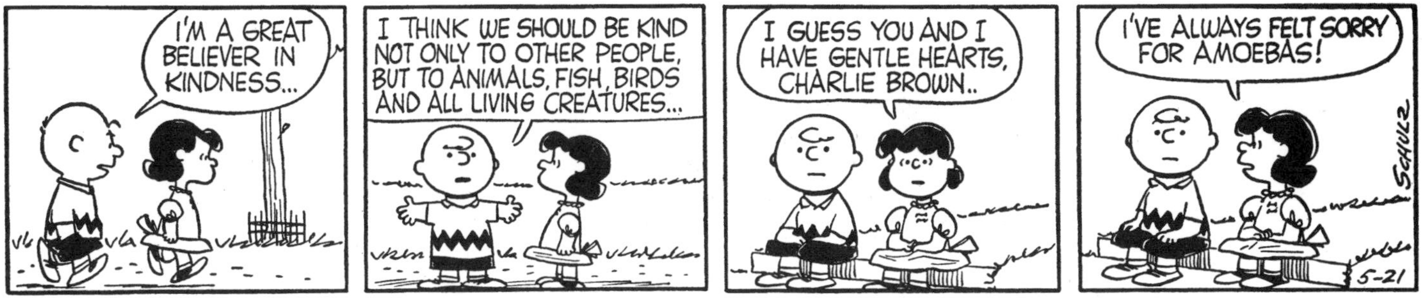
I'M A GREAT BELIEVER IN KINDNESS...
I THINK WE SHOULD BE KIND NOT ONLY TO OTHER PEOPLE, BUT TO ANIMALS, FISH, BIRDS AND ALL LIVING CREATURES...
I GUESS YOU AND I HAVE GENTLE HEARTS, CHARLIE BROWN..
I'VE ALWAYS FELT SORRY FOR AMOEBAS!
SCHULZ
5-21

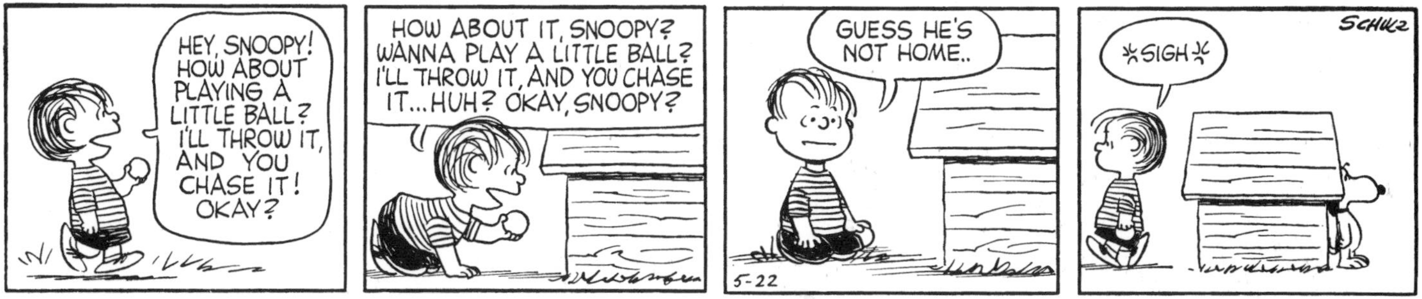
HEY, SNOOPY! HOW ABOUT PLAYING A LITTLE BALL? I'LL THROW IT, AND YOU CHASE IT! OKAY?
HOW ABOUT IT, SNOOPY? WANNA PLAY A LITTLE BALL? I'LL THROW IT, AND YOU CHASE IT... HUH? OKAY, SNOOPY?
GUESS HE'S NOT HOME..
5-22
SCHULZ
SIGH

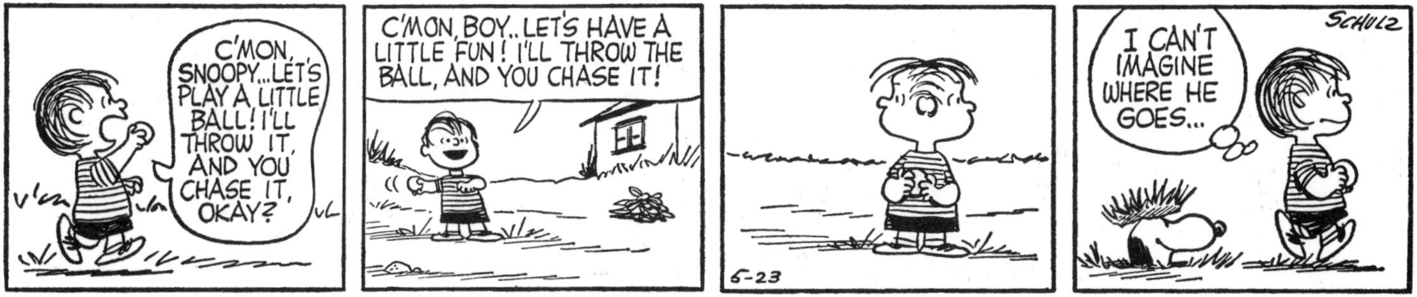
C'MON, SNOOPY...LET'S PLAY A LITTLE BALL! I'LL THROW IT, AND YOU CHASE IT, OKAY?
C'MON, BOY.. LET'S HAVE A LITTLE FUN! I'LL THROW THE BALL, AND YOU CHASE IT!
5-23
SCHULZ
I CAN'T IMAGINE WHERE HE GOES...

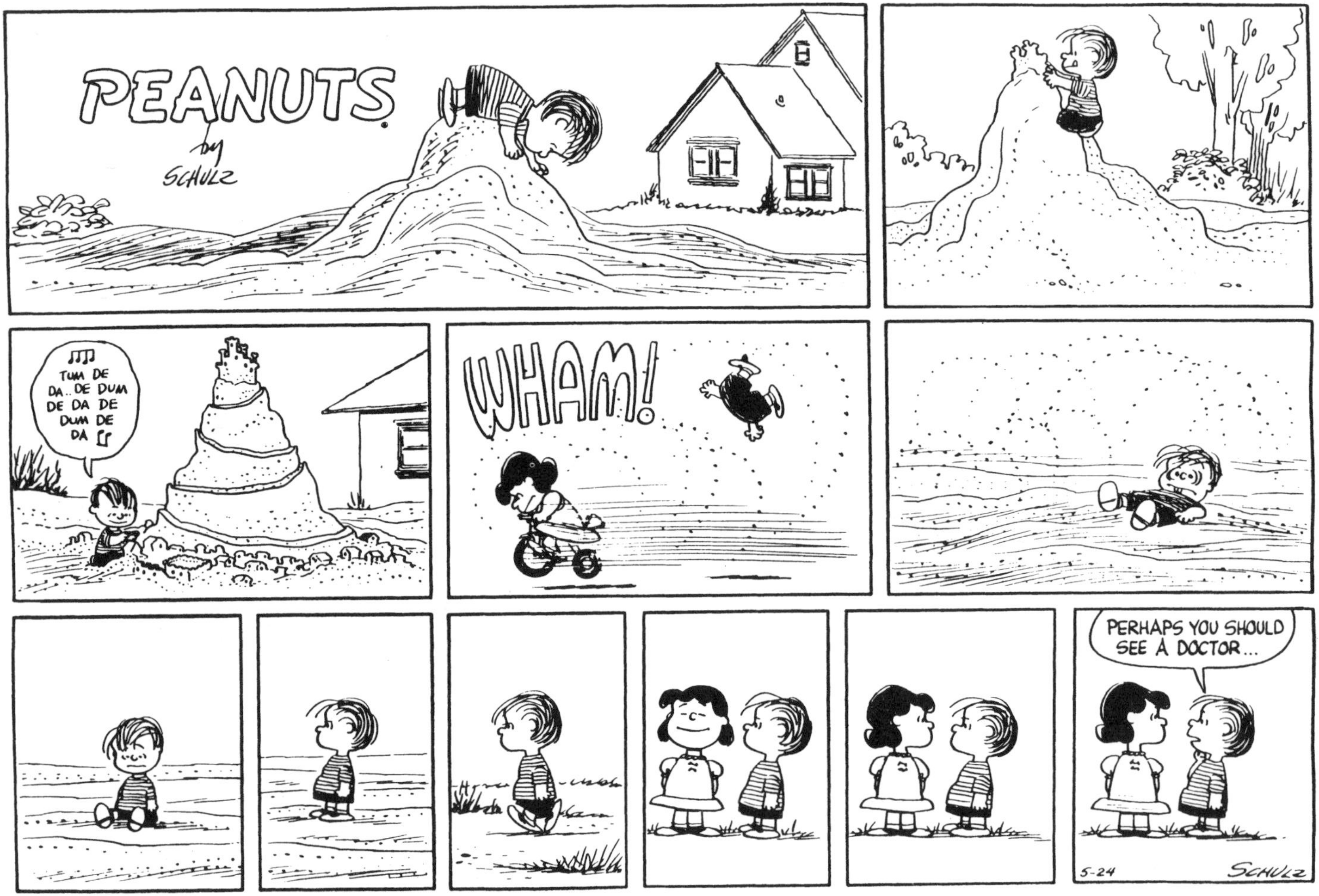
PEANUTS
by SCHULZ
TUM DE DA...DE DUM DE DA DE DUM DE DA
WHAM!
PERHAPS YOU SHOULD SEE A DOCTOR...
5-24
SCHULZ

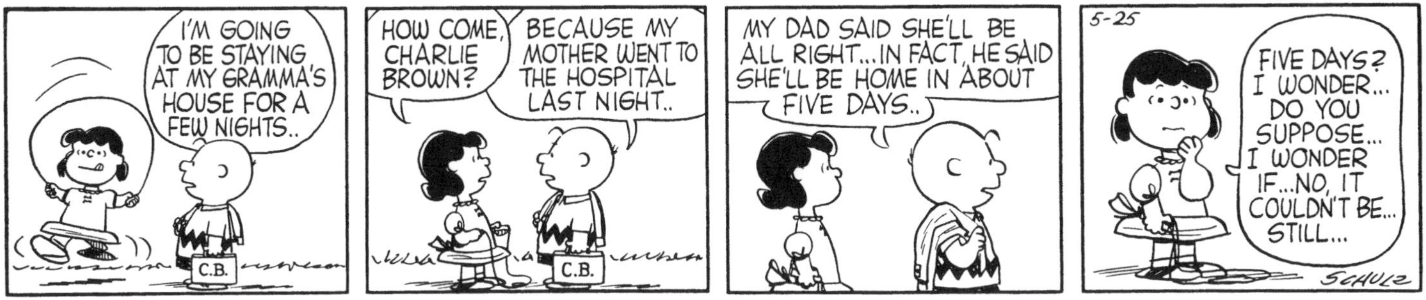
I'M GOING TO BE STAYING AT MY GRAMMA'S HOUSE FOR A FEW NIGHTS..
C.B.
HOW COME, CHARLIE BROWN?
BECAUSE MY MOTHER WENT TO THE HOSPITAL LAST NIGHT..
C.B.
MY DAD SAID SHE'LL BE ALL RIGHT...IN FACT, HE SAID SHE'LL BE HOME IN ABOUT FIVE DAYS..
5-25
FIVE DAYS? I WONDER... DO YOU SUPPOSE... I WONDER IF...NO, IT COULDN'T BE... STILL...
SCHULZ

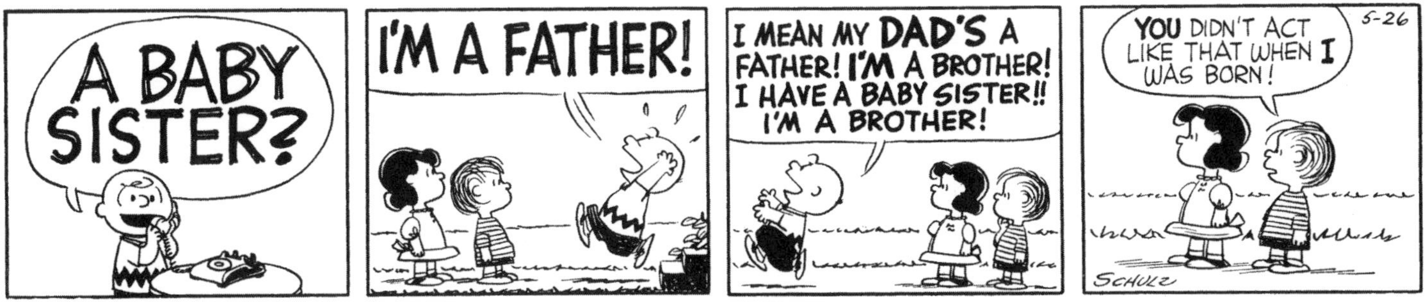
A BABY SISTER?
I'M A FATHER!
I MEAN MY DAD'S A FATHER! I'M A BROTHER! I HAVE A BABY SISTER!! I'M A BROTHER!
5-26
YOU DIDN'T ACT LIKE THAT WHEN I WAS BORN!
SCHULZ

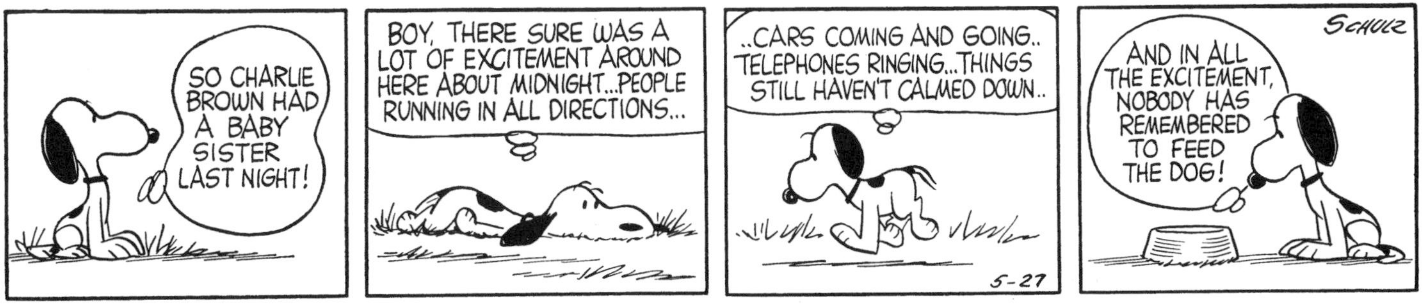
SO CHARLIE BROWN HAD A BABY SISTER LAST NIGHT!
BOY, THERE SURE WAS A LOT OF EXCITEMENT AROUND HERE ABOUT MIDNIGHT...PEOPLE RUNNING IN ALL DIRECTIONS...
..CARS COMING AND GOING.. TELEPHONES RINGING...THINGS STILL HAVEN'T CALMED DOWN..
5-27
SCHULZ
AND IN ALL THE EXCITEMENT, NOBODY HAS REMEMBERED TO FEED THE DOG!

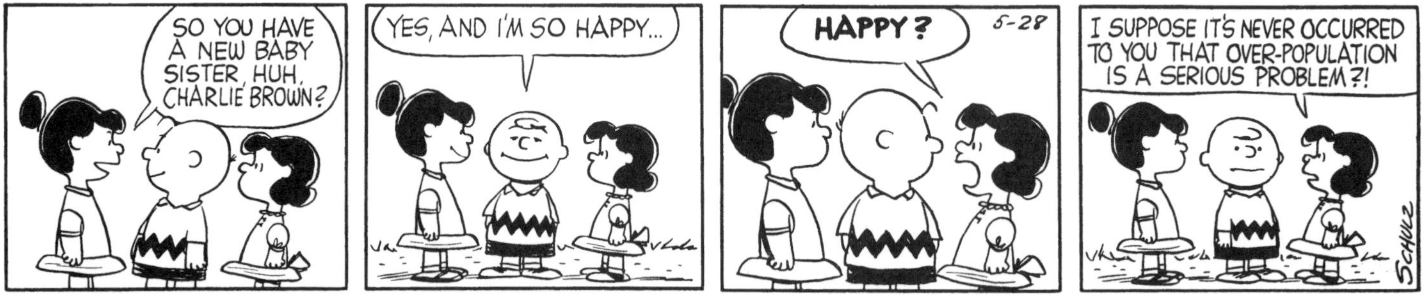
SO YOU HAVE A NEW BABY SISTER, HUH, CHARLIE BROWN?
YES, AND I'M SO HAPPY...
HAPPY?
5-28
I SUPPOSE IT'S NEVER OCCURRED TO YOU THAT OVER-POPULATION IS A SERIOUS PROBLEM?!
SCHULZ

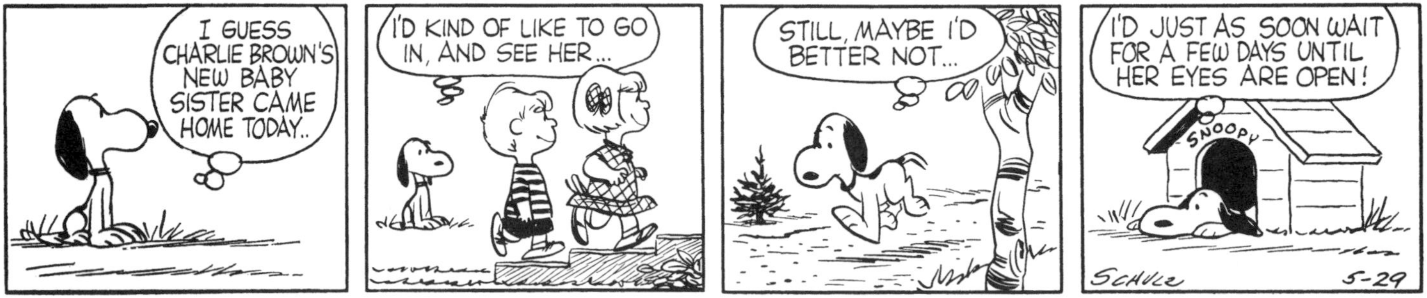
I GUESS CHARLIE BROWN'S NEW BABY SISTER CAME HOME TODAY..
I'D KIND OF LIKE TO GO IN, AND SEE HER...
STILL, MAYBE I'D BETTER NOT...
I'D JUST AS SOON WAIT FOR A FEW DAYS UNTIL HER EYES ARE OPEN!
SNOOPY
SCHULZ
5-29

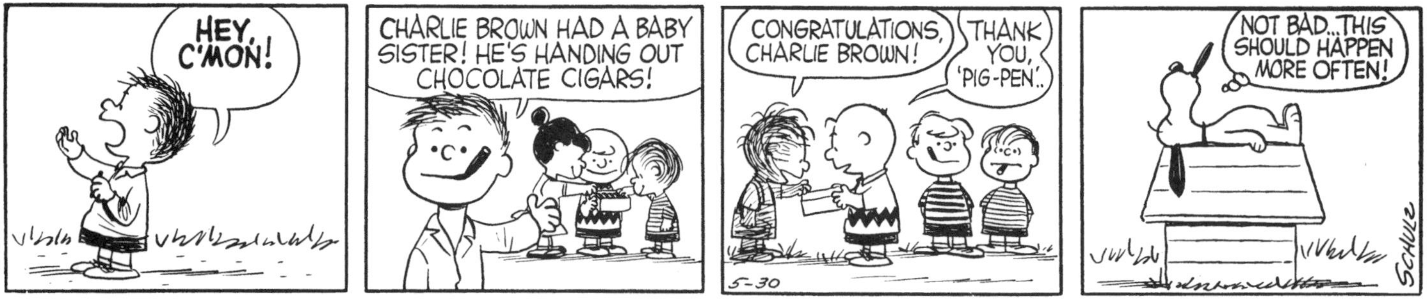
HEY, C'MON!
CHARLIE BROWN HAD A BABY SISTER! HE'S HANDING OUT CHOCOLATE CIGARS!
CONGRATULATIONS, CHARLIE BROWN!
THANK YOU, 'PIG-PEN'..
5-30
NOT BAD...THIS SHOULD HAPPEN MORE OFTEN!
SCHULZ

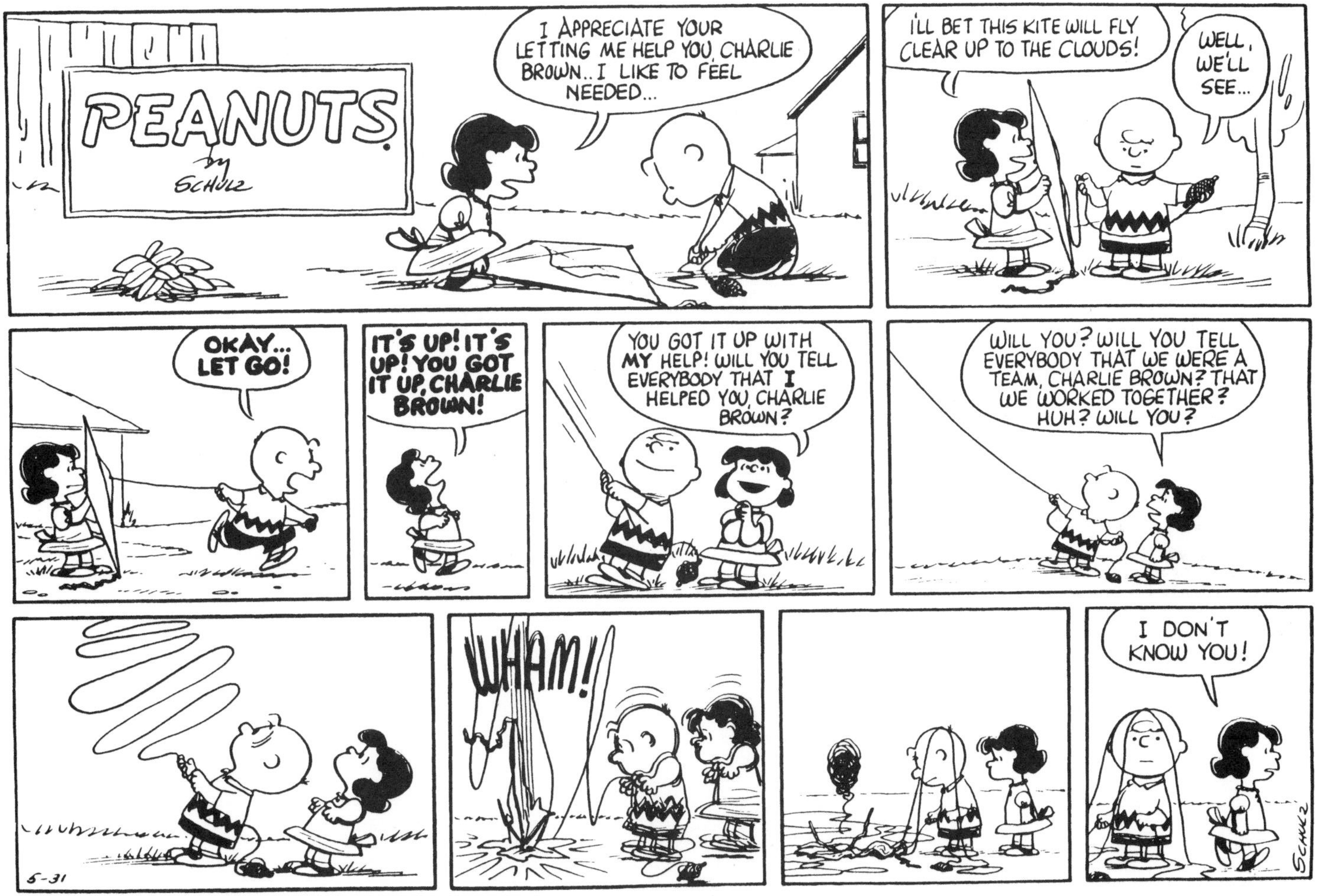
PEANUTS
by SCHULZ
I APPRECIATE YOUR LETTING ME HELP YOU, CHARLIE BROWN.. I LIKE TO FEEL NEEDED...
I'LL BET THIS KITE WILL FLY CLEAR UP TO THE CLOUDS!
WELL, WE'LL SEE...
OKAY... LET GO!
IT'S UP! IT'S UP! YOU GOT IT UP, CHARLIE BROWN!
YOU GOT IT UP WITH MY HELP! WILL YOU TELL EVERYBODY THAT I HELPED YOU, CHARLIE BROWN?
WILL YOU? WILL YOU TELL EVERYBODY THAT WE WERE A TEAM, CHARLIE BROWN? THAT WE WORKED TOGETHER? HUH? WILL YOU?
5-31
WHAM!!
I DON'T KNOW YOU!
SCHULZ

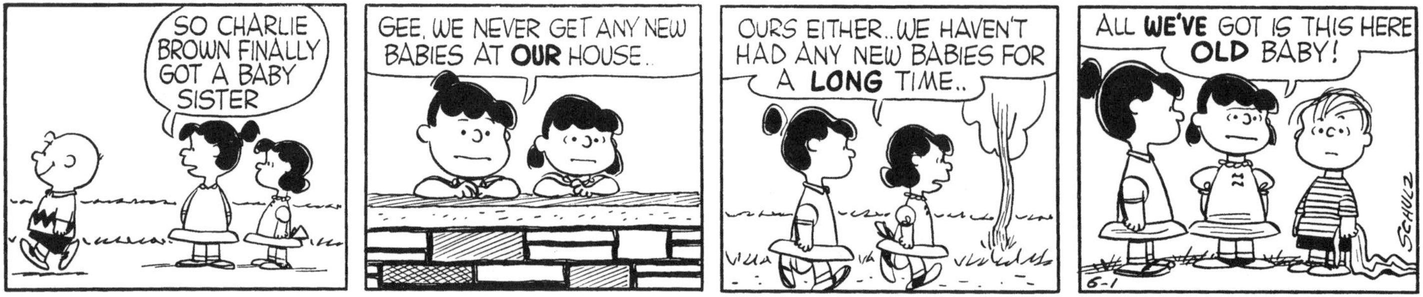
SO CHARLIE BROWN FINALLY GOT A BABY SISTER
GEE, WE NEVER GET ANY NEW BABIES AT **OUR** HOUSE..
OURS EITHER..WE HAVEN'T HAD ANY NEW BABIES FOR A **LONG** TIME..
ALL **WE'VE** GOT IS THIS HERE **OLD** BABY!
6-1

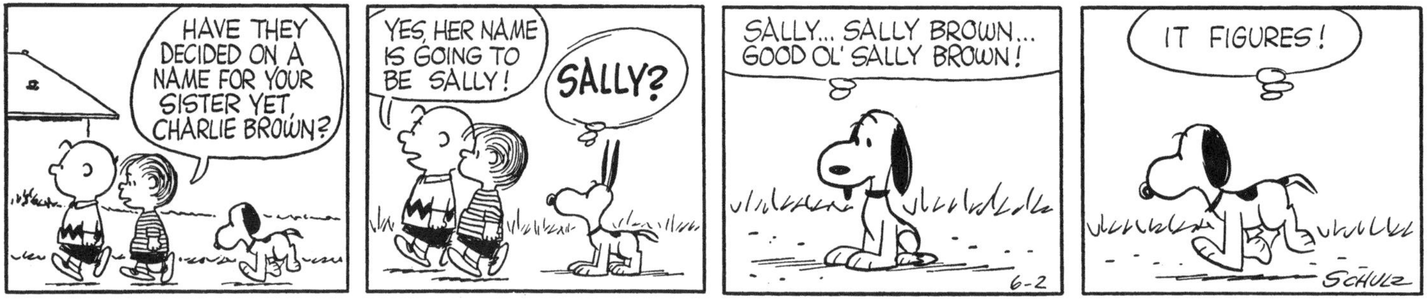
HAVE THEY DECIDED ON A NAME FOR YOUR SISTER YET, CHARLIE BROWN?
YES, HER NAME IS GOING TO BE SALLY!
SALLY?
SALLY... SALLY BROWN... GOOD OL' SALLY BROWN!
6-2
IT FIGURES!

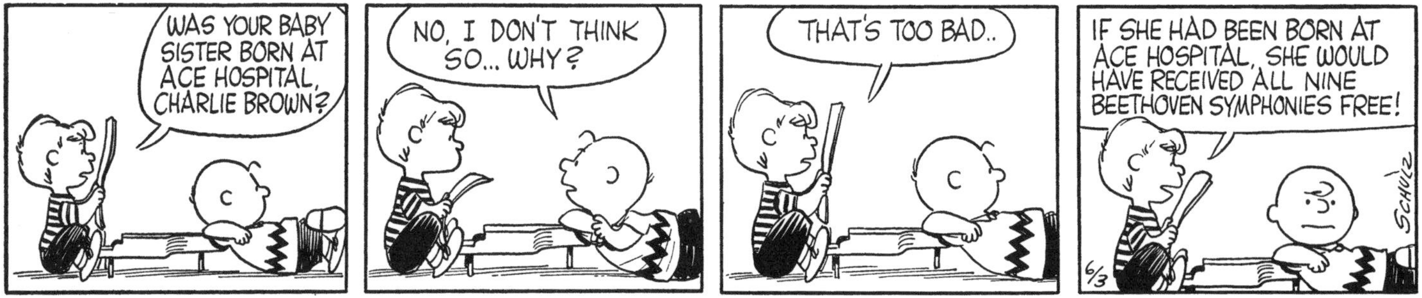
WAS YOUR BABY SISTER BORN AT ACE HOSPITAL, CHARLIE BROWN?
NO, I DON'T THINK SO... WHY?
THAT'S TOO BAD..
IF SHE HAD BEEN BORN AT ACE HOSPITAL, SHE WOULD HAVE RECEIVED ALL NINE BEETHOVEN SYMPHONIES FREE!
6/3

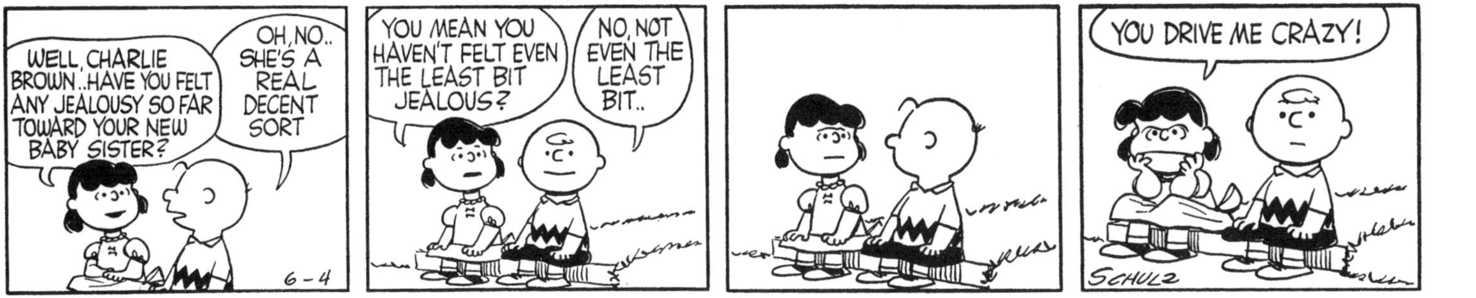
WELL, CHARLIE BROWN..HAVE YOU FELT ANY JEALOUSY SO FAR TOWARD YOUR NEW BABY SISTER?
OH, NO.. SHE'S A REAL DECENT SORT
6-4
YOU MEAN YOU HAVEN'T FELT EVEN THE LEAST BIT JEALOUS?
NO, NOT EVEN THE LEAST BIT..
YOU DRIVE ME CRAZY!
SCHULZ

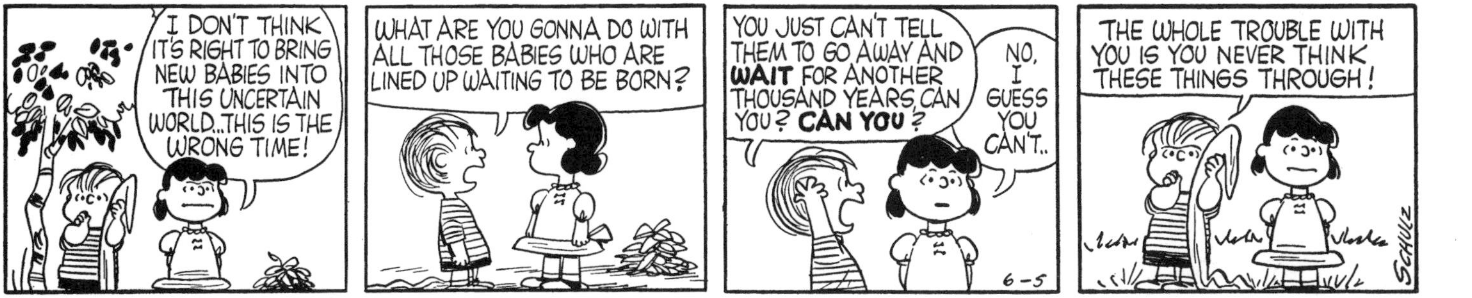
I DON'T THINK IT'S RIGHT TO BRING NEW BABIES INTO THIS UNCERTAIN WORLD..THIS IS THE WRONG TIME!
WHAT ARE YOU GONNA DO WITH ALL THOSE BABIES WHO ARE LINED UP WAITING TO BE BORN?
YOU JUST CAN'T TELL THEM TO GO AWAY AND WAIT FOR ANOTHER THOUSAND YEARS, CAN YOU? CAN YOU?
NO, I GUESS YOU CAN'T..
6-5
THE WHOLE TROUBLE WITH YOU IS YOU NEVER THINK THESE THINGS THROUGH!
SCHULZ

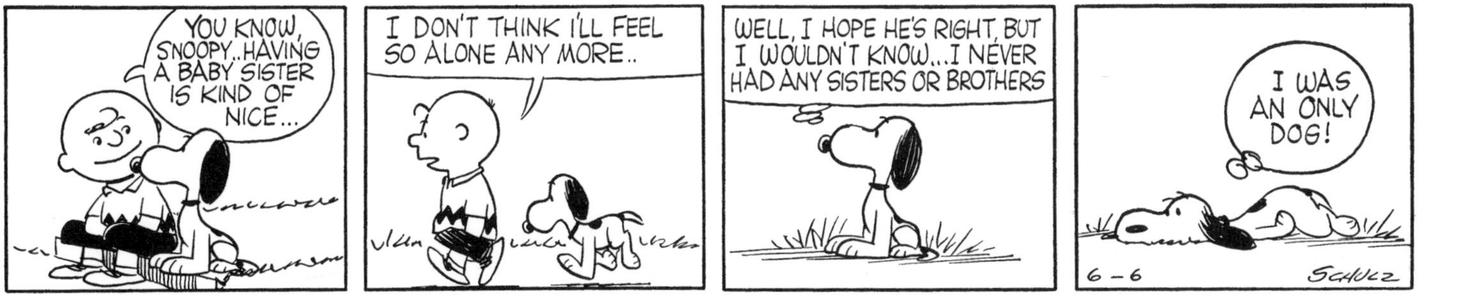
YOU KNOW, SNOOPY..HAVING A BABY SISTER IS KIND OF NICE...
I DON'T THINK I'LL FEEL SO ALONE ANY MORE..
WELL, I HOPE HE'S RIGHT, BUT I WOULDN'T KNOW...I NEVER HAD ANY SISTERS OR BROTHERS
I WAS AN ONLY DOG!
6-6
SCHULZ

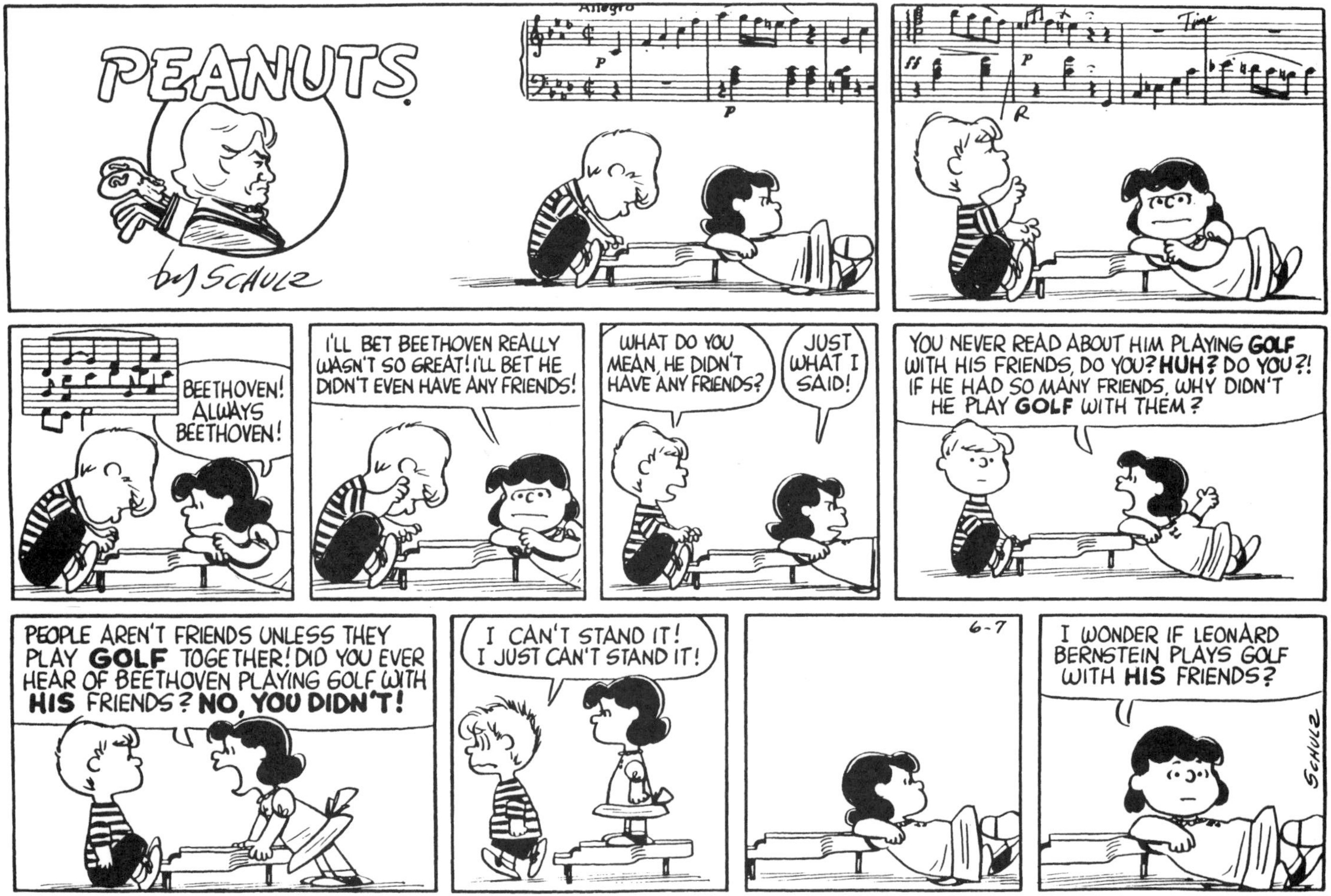
PEANUTS
by SCHULZ
Allegro
BEETHOVEN! ALWAYS BEETHOVEN!
I'LL BET BEETHOVEN REALLY WASN'T SO GREAT! I'LL BET HE DIDN'T EVEN HAVE ANY FRIENDS!
WHAT DO YOU MEAN, HE DIDN'T HAVE ANY FRIENDS?
JUST WHAT I SAID!
YOU NEVER READ ABOUT HIM PLAYING GOLF WITH HIS FRIENDS, DO YOU? HUH? DO YOU?! IF HE HAD SO MANY FRIENDS, WHY DIDN'T HE PLAY GOLF WITH THEM?
PEOPLE AREN'T FRIENDS UNLESS THEY PLAY GOLF TOGETHER! DID YOU EVER HEAR OF BEETHOVEN PLAYING GOLF WITH HIS FRIENDS? NO, YOU DIDN'T!
I CAN'T STAND IT! I JUST CAN'T STAND IT!
6-7
I WONDER IF LEONARD BERNSTEIN PLAYS GOLF WITH HIS FRIENDS?
SCHULZ

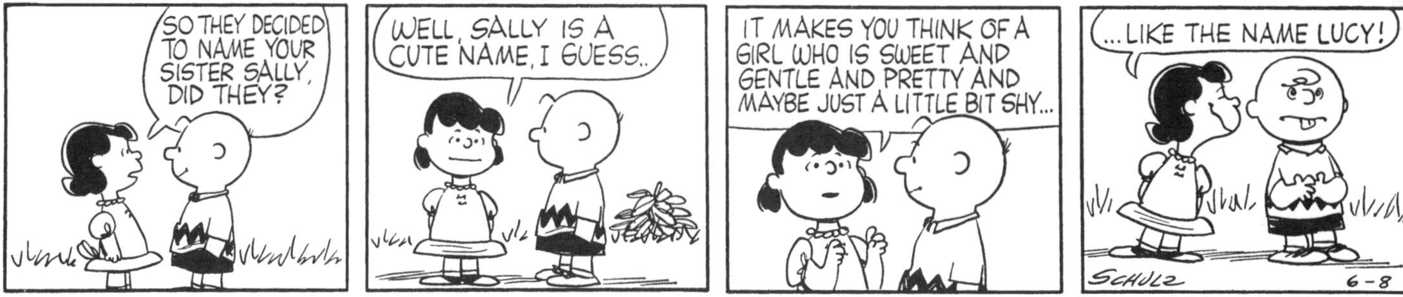
SO THEY DECIDED TO NAME YOUR SISTER SALLY, DID THEY?
WELL, SALLY IS A CUTE NAME, I GUESS..
IT MAKES YOU THINK OF A GIRL WHO IS SWEET AND GENTLE AND PRETTY AND MAYBE JUST A LITTLE BIT SHY...
...LIKE THE NAME LUCY!
SCHULZ
6-8

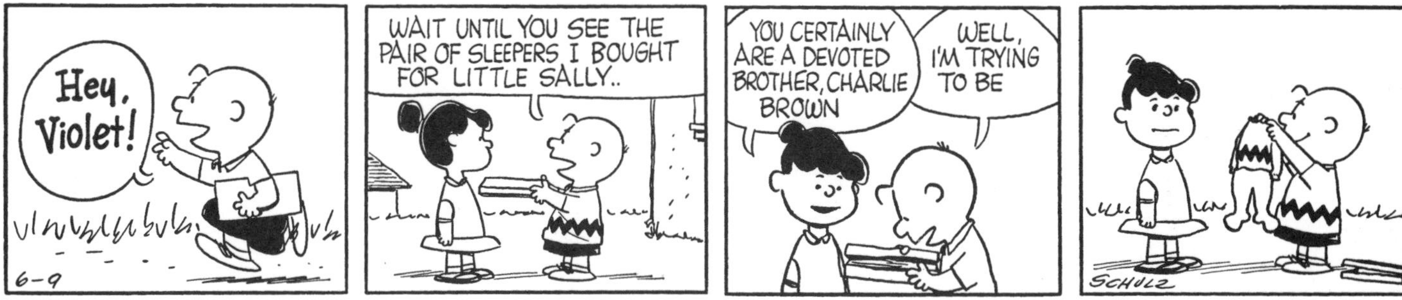
Hey, Violet!
6-9
WAIT UNTIL YOU SEE THE PAIR OF SLEEPERS I BOUGHT FOR LITTLE SALLY..
YOU CERTAINLY ARE A DEVOTED BROTHER, CHARLIE BROWN
WELL, I'M TRYING TO BE
SCHULZ

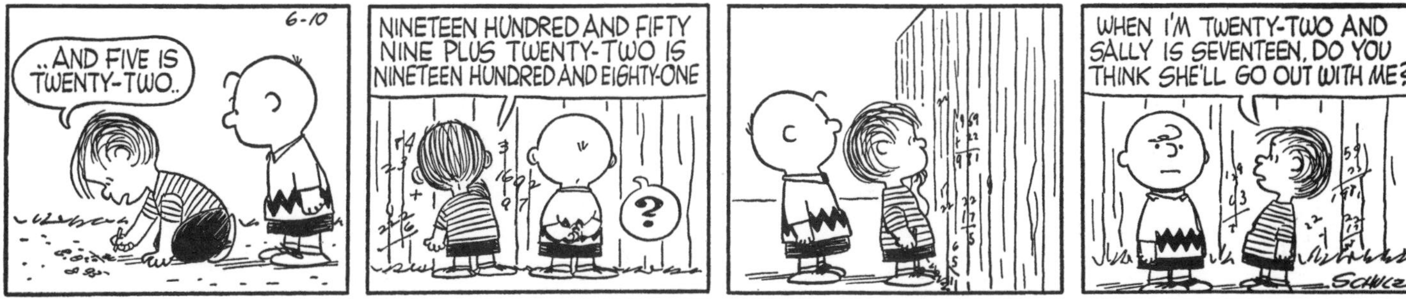
6-10
..AND FIVE IS TWENTY-TWO..
NINETEEN HUNDRED AND FIFTY NINE PLUS TWENTY-TWO IS NINETEEN HUNDRED AND EIGHTY-ONE
?
WHEN I'M TWENTY-TWO AND SALLY IS SEVENTEEN, DO YOU THINK SHE'LL GO OUT WITH ME?
SCHULZ

Panel 1: THIS HAVING A BABY SISTER MAY DO A LOT FOR CHARLIE BROWN..

Panel 2: IT'S JUST LIABLE TO MAKE HIM INTO A NEW PERSON!

Panel 3: THAT'S A FRIGHTENING THOUGHT...

Panel 4: I CAN THINK OF NOTHING IN ALL THIS WORLD MORE OBNOXIOUS THAN A WELL-ADJUSTED CHARLIE BROWN!

6-11 SCHULZ

Panel 5: YOU THINK HAVING A BABY SISTER IS GREAT, DON'T YOU?

Panel 6: FROM NOW ON YOU'RE GOING TO HAVE TO **SHARE** THE AFFECTION OF YOUR MOTHER AND DAD! BUT YOU THINK YOU WON'T MIND THAT, DON'T YOU?

Panel 7: YOU THINK IT'LL BE FIFTY-FIFTY, DON'T YOU? WELL, IT WON'T! WITH A BABY SISTER, IT'LL BE FIFTY ONE-FORTY NINE! MAYBE EVEN **SIXTY-FORTY**!!

6-12

Panel 8: I'LL BET YOU DIDN'T REALIZE THAT FAMILY LIFE WAS SO MATHEMATICAL!

SCHULZ

6-13

Panel 12: SIGH

SCHULZ

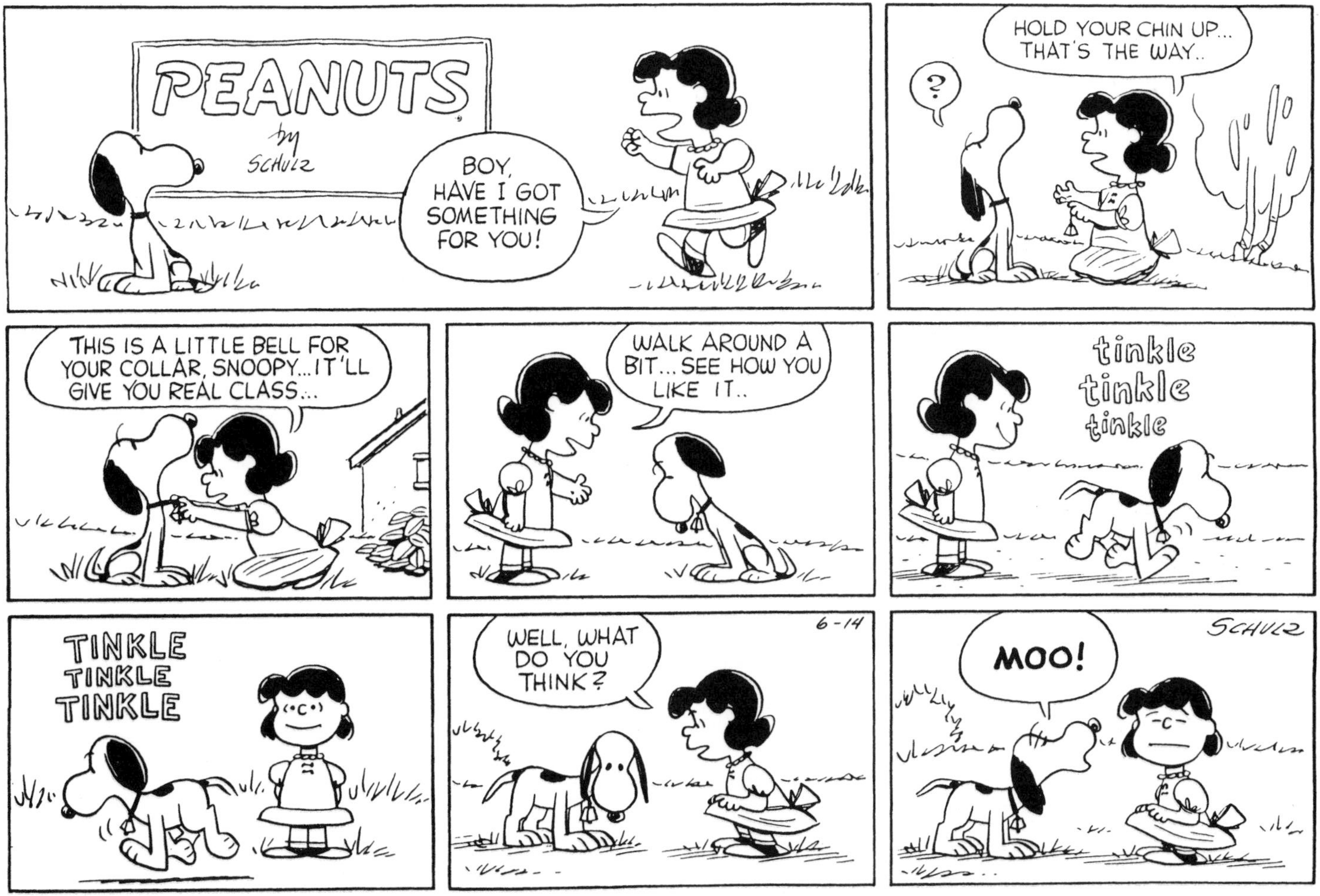
PEANUTS
by SCHULZ
BOY, HAVE I GOT SOMETHING FOR YOU!
?
HOLD YOUR CHIN UP... THAT'S THE WAY..
THIS IS A LITTLE BELL FOR YOUR COLLAR, SNOOPY...IT'LL GIVE YOU REAL CLASS...
WALK AROUND A BIT... SEE HOW YOU LIKE IT..
tinkle tinkle tinkle
TINKLE TINKLE TINKLE
6-14
WELL, WHAT DO YOU THINK?
SCHULZ
MOO!

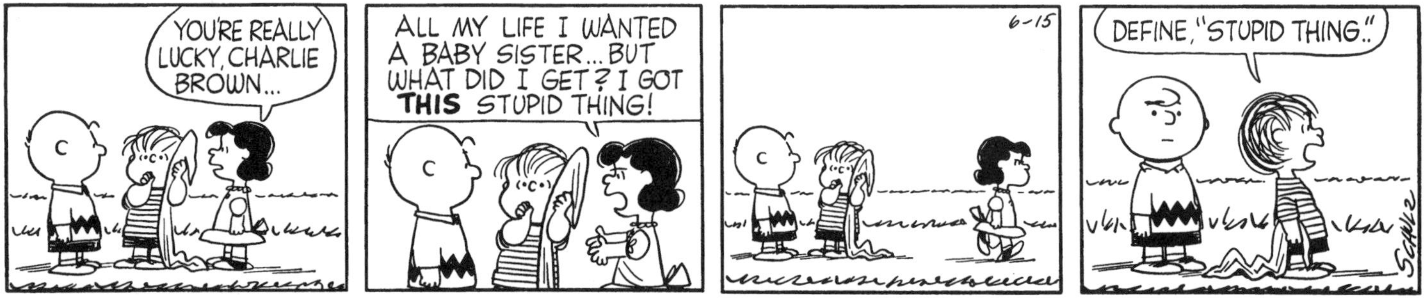
YOU'RE REALLY LUCKY, CHARLIE BROWN...
ALL MY LIFE I WANTED A BABY SISTER... BUT WHAT DID I GET? I GOT **THIS** STUPID THING!
6-15
DEFINE, "STUPID THING."
SCHULZ

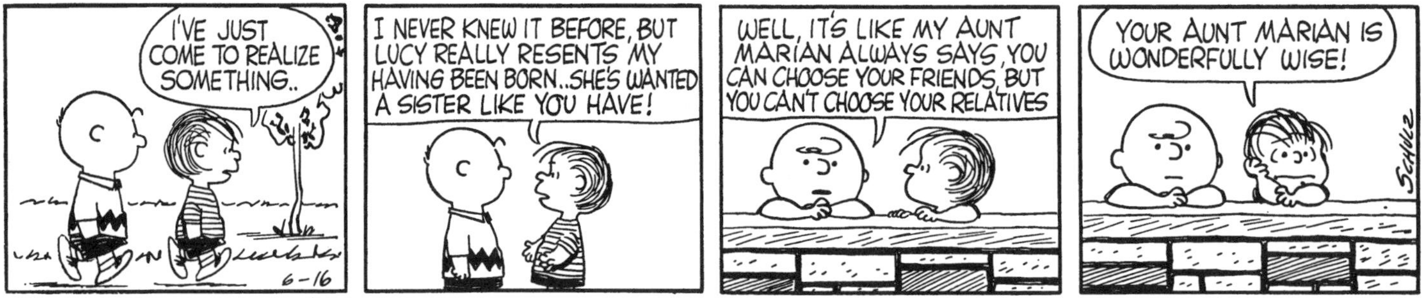
I'VE JUST COME TO REALIZE SOMETHING..
6-16
I NEVER KNEW IT BEFORE, BUT LUCY REALLY RESENTS MY HAVING BEEN BORN..SHE'S WANTED A SISTER LIKE YOU HAVE!
WELL, IT'S LIKE MY AUNT MARIAN ALWAYS SAYS, YOU CAN CHOOSE YOUR FRIENDS, BUT YOU CAN'T CHOOSE YOUR RELATIVES
YOUR AUNT MARIAN IS WONDERFULLY WISE!
SCHULZ

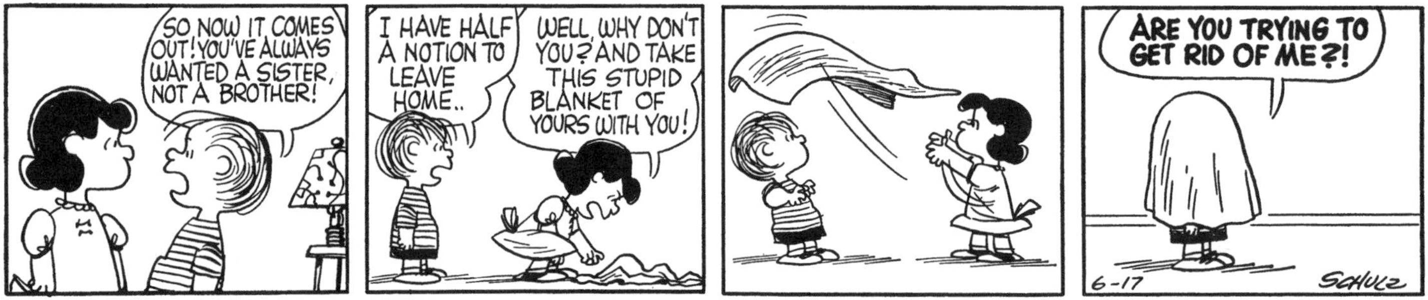
SO NOW IT COMES OUT! YOU'VE ALWAYS WANTED A SISTER, NOT A BROTHER!
I HAVE HALF A NOTION TO LEAVE HOME..
WELL, WHY DON'T YOU? AND TAKE THIS STUPID BLANKET OF YOURS WITH YOU!
ARE YOU TRYING TO GET RID OF ME?!
6-17
SCHULZ

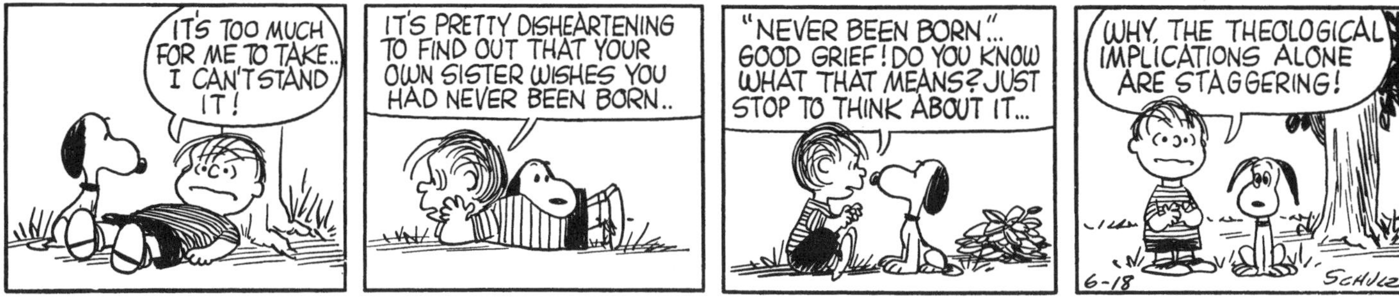
IT'S TOO MUCH FOR ME TO TAKE.. I CAN'T STAND IT!
IT'S PRETTY DISHEARTENING TO FIND OUT THAT YOUR OWN SISTER WISHES YOU HAD NEVER BEEN BORN..
"NEVER BEEN BORN"... GOOD GRIEF! DO YOU KNOW WHAT THAT MEANS? JUST STOP TO THINK ABOUT IT...
WHY, THE THEOLOGICAL IMPLICATIONS ALONE ARE STAGGERING!
6-18
SCHULZ

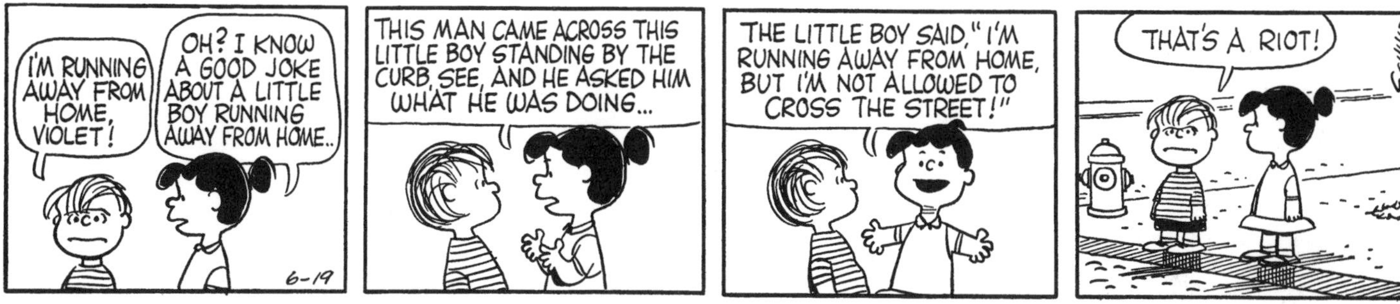
I'M RUNNING AWAY FROM HOME, VIOLET!
OH? I KNOW A GOOD JOKE ABOUT A LITTLE BOY RUNNING AWAY FROM HOME..
6-19
THIS MAN CAME ACROSS THIS LITTLE BOY STANDING BY THE CURB, SEE, AND HE ASKED HIM WHAT HE WAS DOING...
THE LITTLE BOY SAID, "I'M RUNNING AWAY FROM HOME, BUT I'M NOT ALLOWED TO CROSS THE STREET!"
THAT'S A RIOT!
SCHULZ

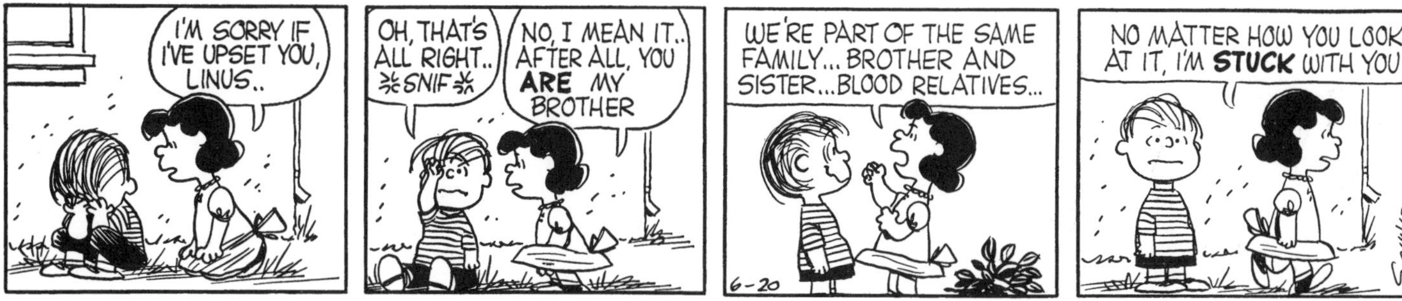
I'M SORRY IF I'VE UPSET YOU, LINUS..
OH, THAT'S ALL RIGHT.. *SNIF*
NO, I MEAN IT.. AFTER ALL, YOU **ARE** MY BROTHER
WE'RE PART OF THE SAME FAMILY... BROTHER AND SISTER...BLOOD RELATIVES...
6-20
NO MATTER HOW YOU LOOK AT IT, I'M **STUCK** WITH YOU!
SCHULZ

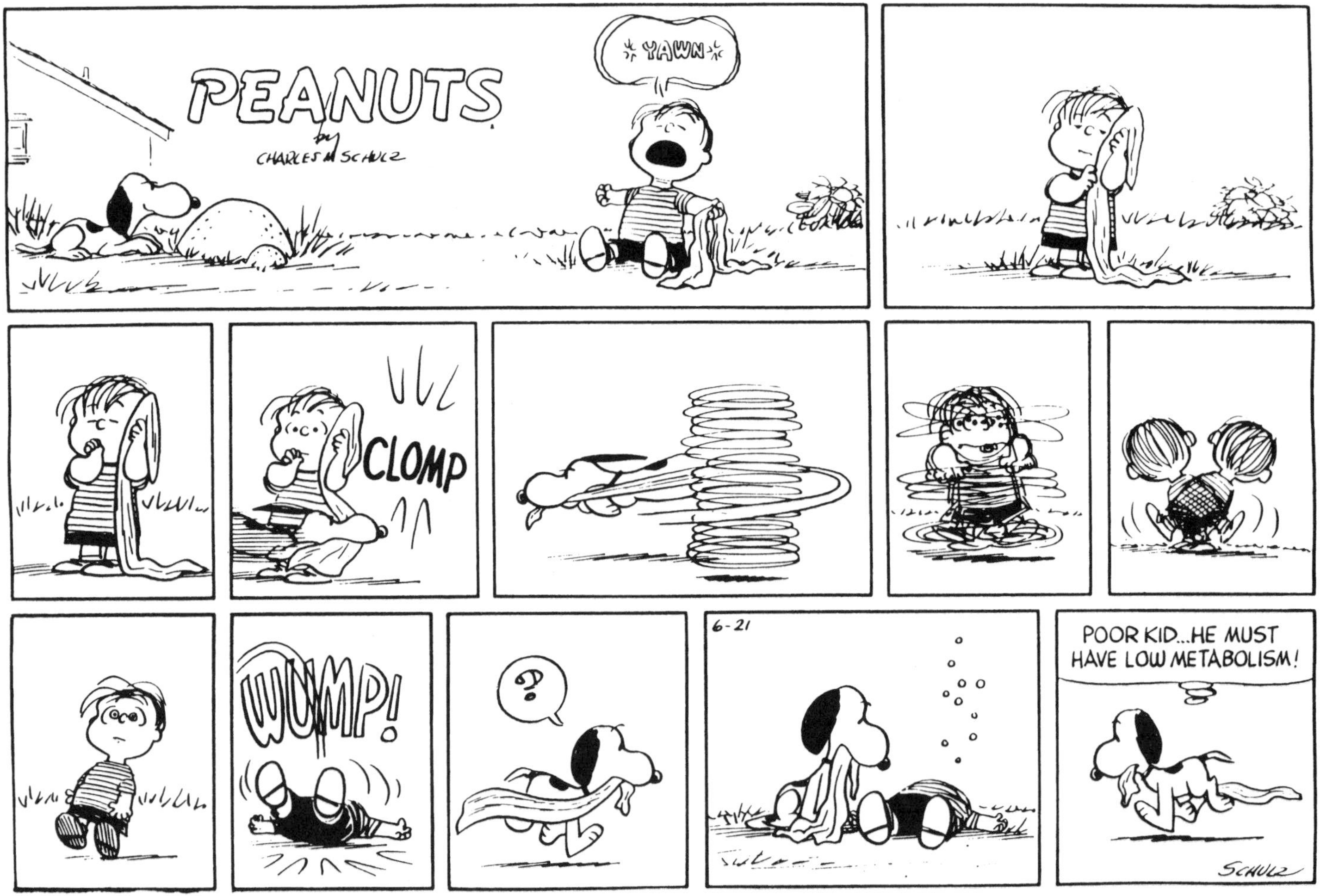
PEANUTS
by
CHARLES M SCHULZ
YAWN
CLOMP
WUMP!
?
6-21
POOR KID...HE MUST HAVE LOW METABOLISM!
SCHULZ

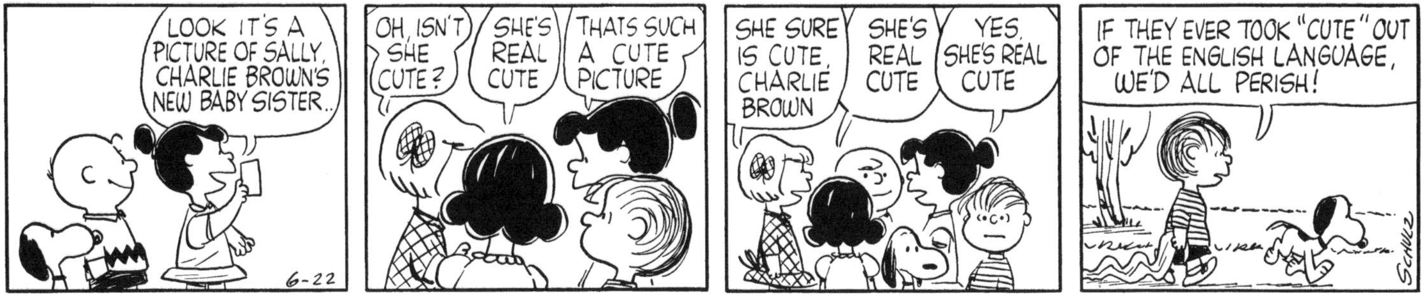
LOOK IT'S A PICTURE OF SALLY, CHARLIE BROWN'S NEW BABY SISTER..
OH, ISN'T SHE CUTE?
SHE'S REAL CUTE
THATS SUCH A CUTE PICTURE
SHE SURE IS CUTE, CHARLIE BROWN
SHE'S REAL CUTE
YES, SHE'S REAL CUTE
IF THEY EVER TOOK "CUTE" OUT OF THE ENGLISH LANGUAGE, WE'D ALL PERISH!
6-22
SCHULZ

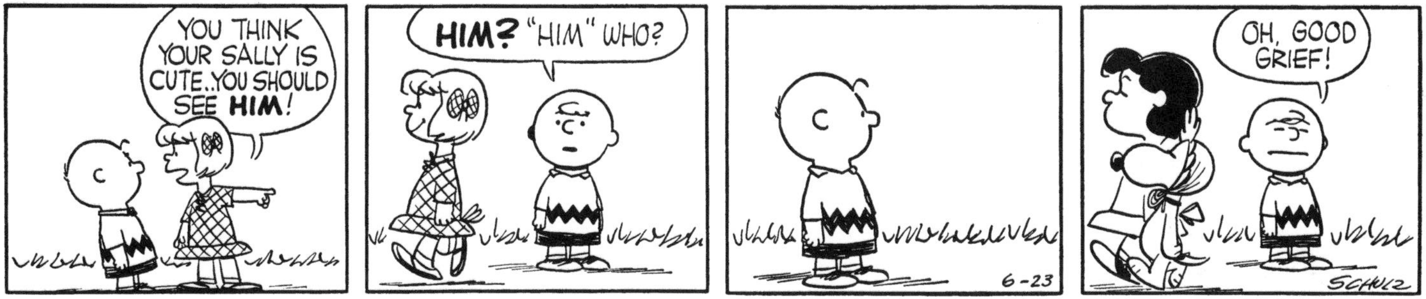
YOU THINK YOUR SALLY IS CUTE..YOU SHOULD SEE **HIM**!
HIM? "HIM" WHO?
6-23
OH, GOOD GRIEF!
SCHULZ

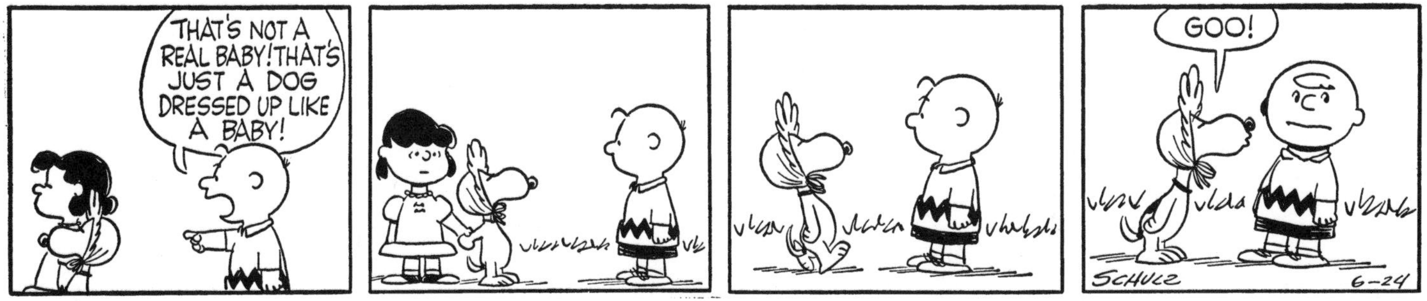
THAT'S NOT A REAL BABY! THAT'S JUST A DOG DRESSED UP LIKE A BABY!
GOO!
SCHULZ
6-24

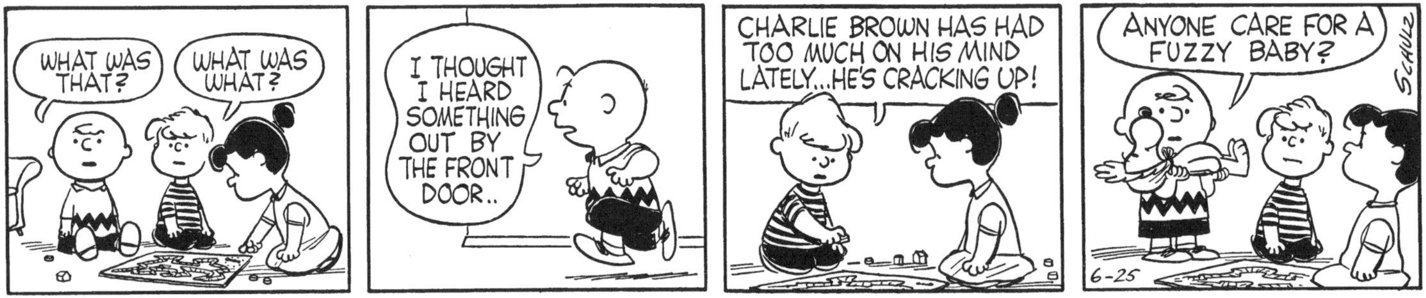
WHAT WAS THAT?
WHAT WAS WHAT?
I THOUGHT I HEARD SOMETHING OUT BY THE FRONT DOOR..
CHARLIE BROWN HAS HAD TOO MUCH ON HIS MIND LATELY...HE'S CRACKING UP!
ANYONE CARE FOR A FUZZY BABY?
SCHULZ
6-25

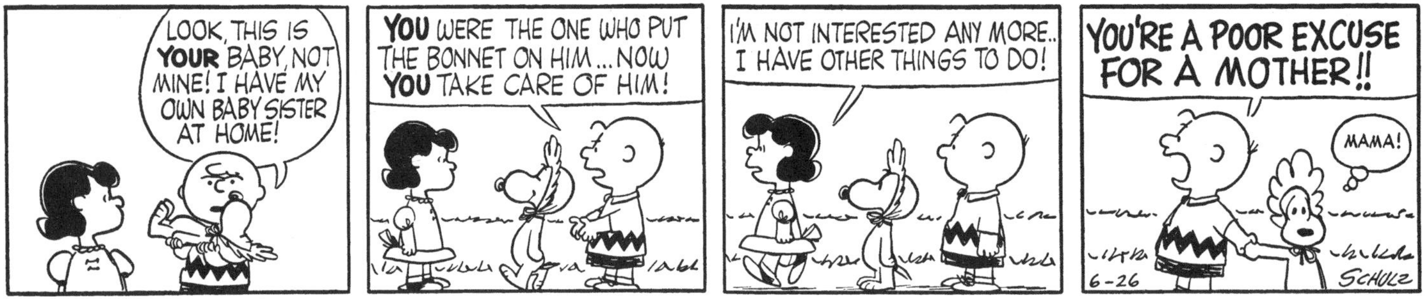
LOOK, THIS IS YOUR BABY, NOT MINE! I HAVE MY OWN BABY SISTER AT HOME!
YOU WERE THE ONE WHO PUT THE BONNET ON HIM ... NOW YOU TAKE CARE OF HIM!
I'M NOT INTERESTED ANY MORE.. I HAVE OTHER THINGS TO DO!
YOU'RE A POOR EXCUSE FOR A MOTHER!!
MAMA!
6-26
SCHULZ

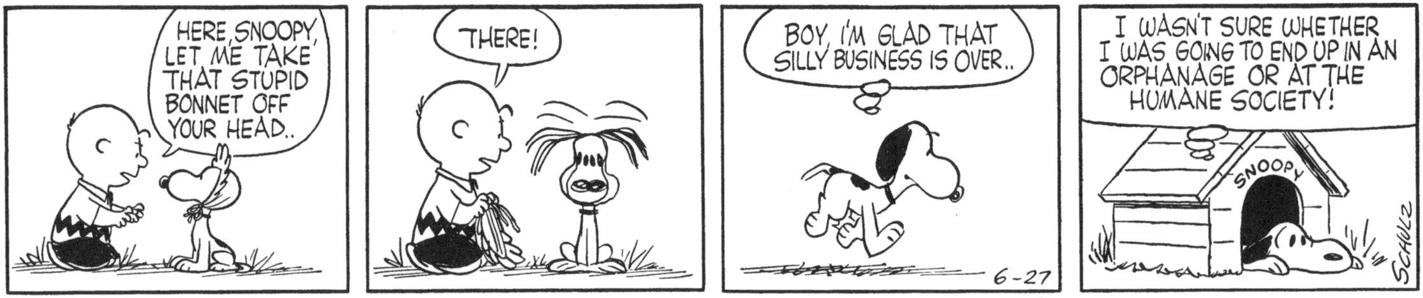
HERE, SNOOPY, LET ME TAKE THAT STUPID BONNET OFF YOUR HEAD..
THERE!
BOY, I'M GLAD THAT SILLY BUSINESS IS OVER..
6-27
I WASN'T SURE WHETHER I WAS GOING TO END UP IN AN ORPHANAGE OR AT THE HUMANE SOCIETY!
SNOOPY
SCHULZ

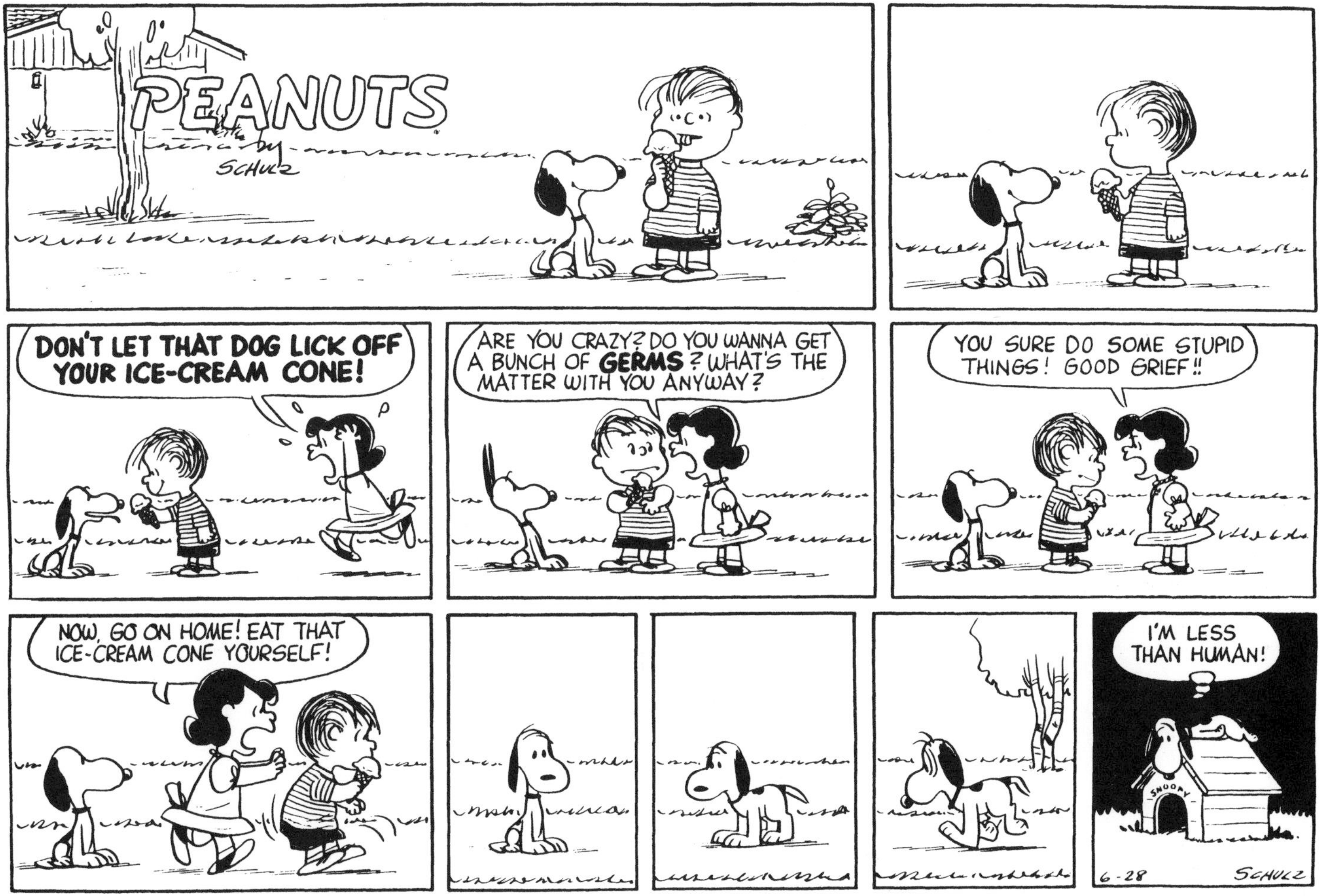
PEANUTS
by SCHULZ
DON'T LET THAT DOG LICK OFF YOUR ICE-CREAM CONE!
ARE YOU CRAZY? DO YOU WANNA GET A BUNCH OF GERMS? WHAT'S THE MATTER WITH YOU ANYWAY?
YOU SURE DO SOME STUPID THINGS! GOOD GRIEF!!
NOW, GO ON HOME! EAT THAT ICE-CREAM CONE YOURSELF!
I'M LESS THAN HUMAN!
SNOOPY
6-28
SCHULZ

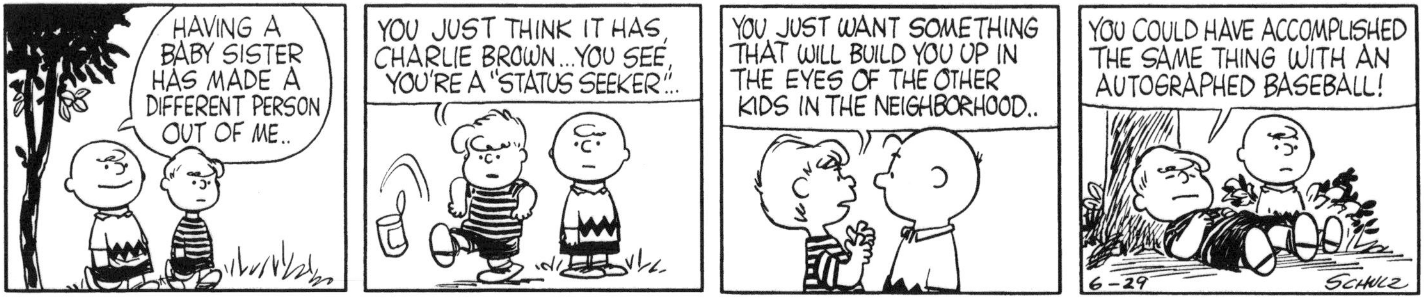
HAVING A BABY SISTER HAS MADE A DIFFERENT PERSON OUT OF ME..
YOU JUST THINK IT HAS, CHARLIE BROWN...YOU SEE, YOU'RE A "STATUS SEEKER"...
YOU JUST WANT SOMETHING THAT WILL BUILD YOU UP IN THE EYES OF THE OTHER KIDS IN THE NEIGHBORHOOD..
YOU COULD HAVE ACCOMPLISHED THE SAME THING WITH AN AUTOGRAPHED BASEBALL!
6-29
SCHULZ

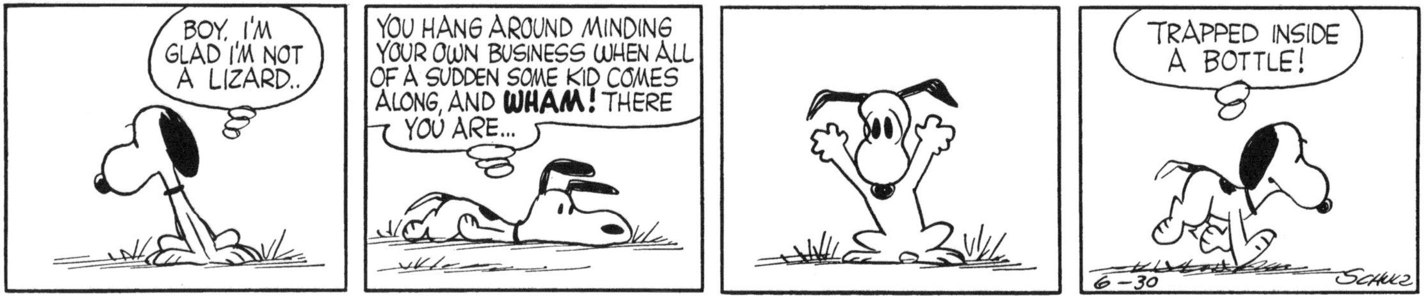
BOY, I'M GLAD I'M NOT A LIZARD..
YOU HANG AROUND MINDING YOUR OWN BUSINESS WHEN ALL OF A SUDDEN SOME KID COMES ALONG, AND **WHAM!** THERE YOU ARE...
TRAPPED INSIDE A BOTTLE!
6-30
SCHULZ

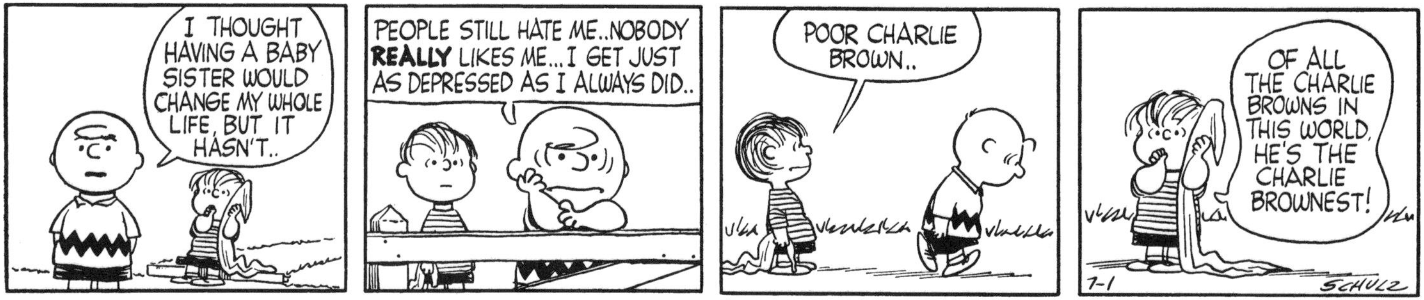
I THOUGHT HAVING A BABY SISTER WOULD CHANGE MY WHOLE LIFE, BUT IT HASN'T..
PEOPLE STILL HATE ME..NOBODY **REALLY** LIKES ME...I GET JUST AS DEPRESSED AS I ALWAYS DID..
POOR CHARLIE BROWN..
OF ALL THE CHARLIE BROWNS IN THIS WORLD, HE'S THE CHARLIE BROWNEST!
7-1
SCHULZ

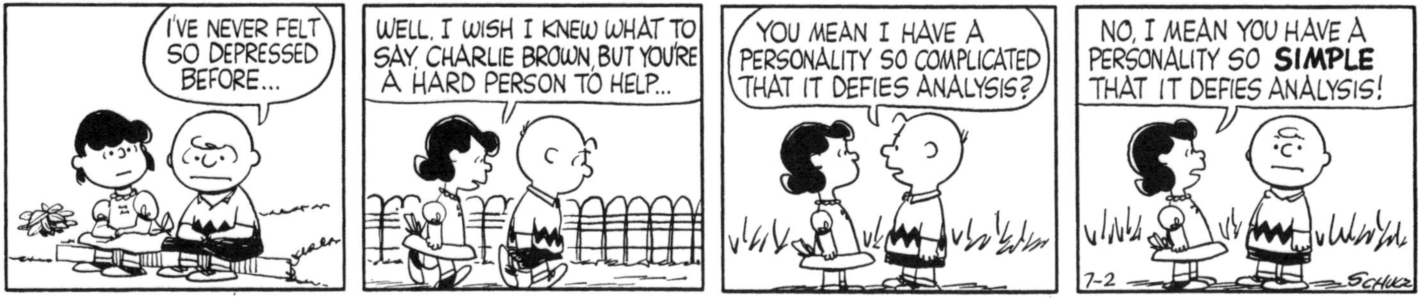
I'VE NEVER FELT SO DEPRESSED BEFORE...
WELL, I WISH I KNEW WHAT TO SAY, CHARLIE BROWN, BUT YOU'RE A HARD PERSON TO HELP...
YOU MEAN I HAVE A PERSONALITY SO COMPLICATED THAT IT DEFIES ANALYSIS?
NO, I MEAN YOU HAVE A PERSONALITY SO **SIMPLE** THAT IT DEFIES ANALYSIS!
7-2
SCHULZ

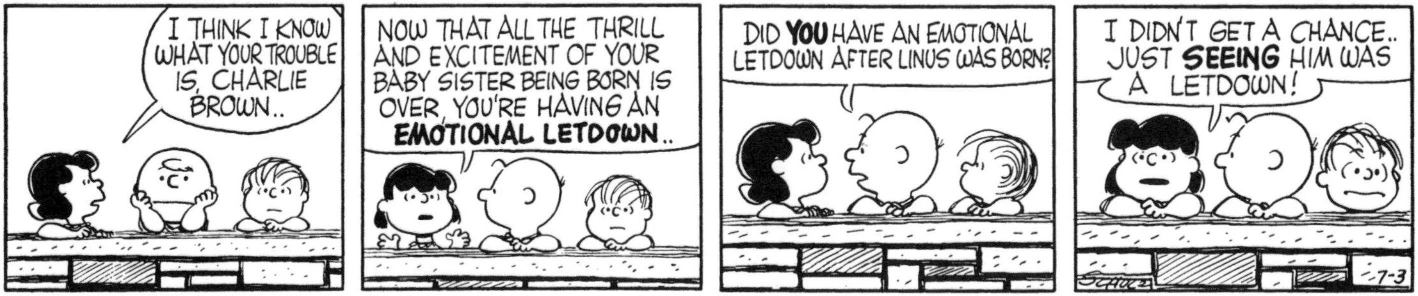
I THINK I KNOW WHAT YOUR TROUBLE IS, CHARLIE BROWN..
NOW THAT ALL THE THRILL AND EXCITEMENT OF YOUR BABY SISTER BEING BORN IS OVER, YOU'RE HAVING AN **EMOTIONAL LETDOWN**..
DID **YOU** HAVE AN EMOTIONAL LETDOWN AFTER LINUS WAS BORN?
I DIDN'T GET A CHANCE.. JUST **SEEING** HIM WAS A LETDOWN!
SCHULZ
7-3

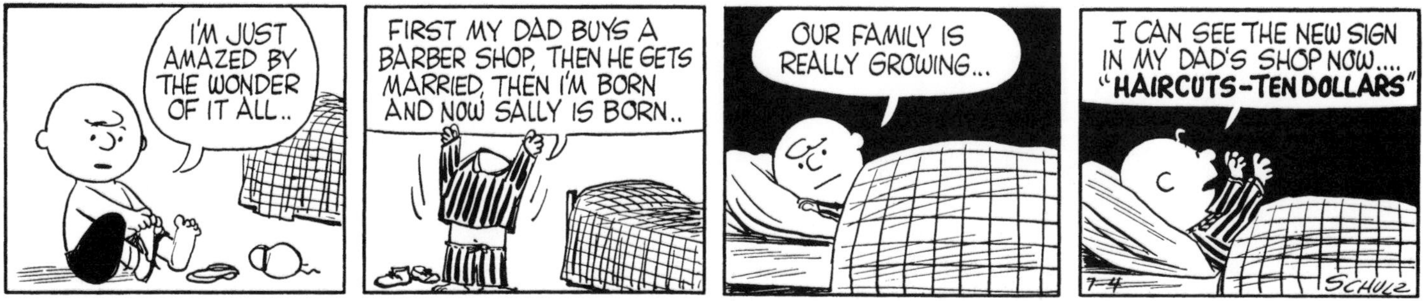
I'M JUST AMAZED BY THE WONDER OF IT ALL..
FIRST MY DAD BUYS A BARBER SHOP, THEN HE GETS MARRIED, THEN I'M BORN AND NOW SALLY IS BORN..
OUR FAMILY IS REALLY GROWING...
I CAN SEE THE NEW SIGN IN MY DAD'S SHOP NOW.... "**HAIRCUTS-TEN DOLLARS**"
7-4
SCHULZ

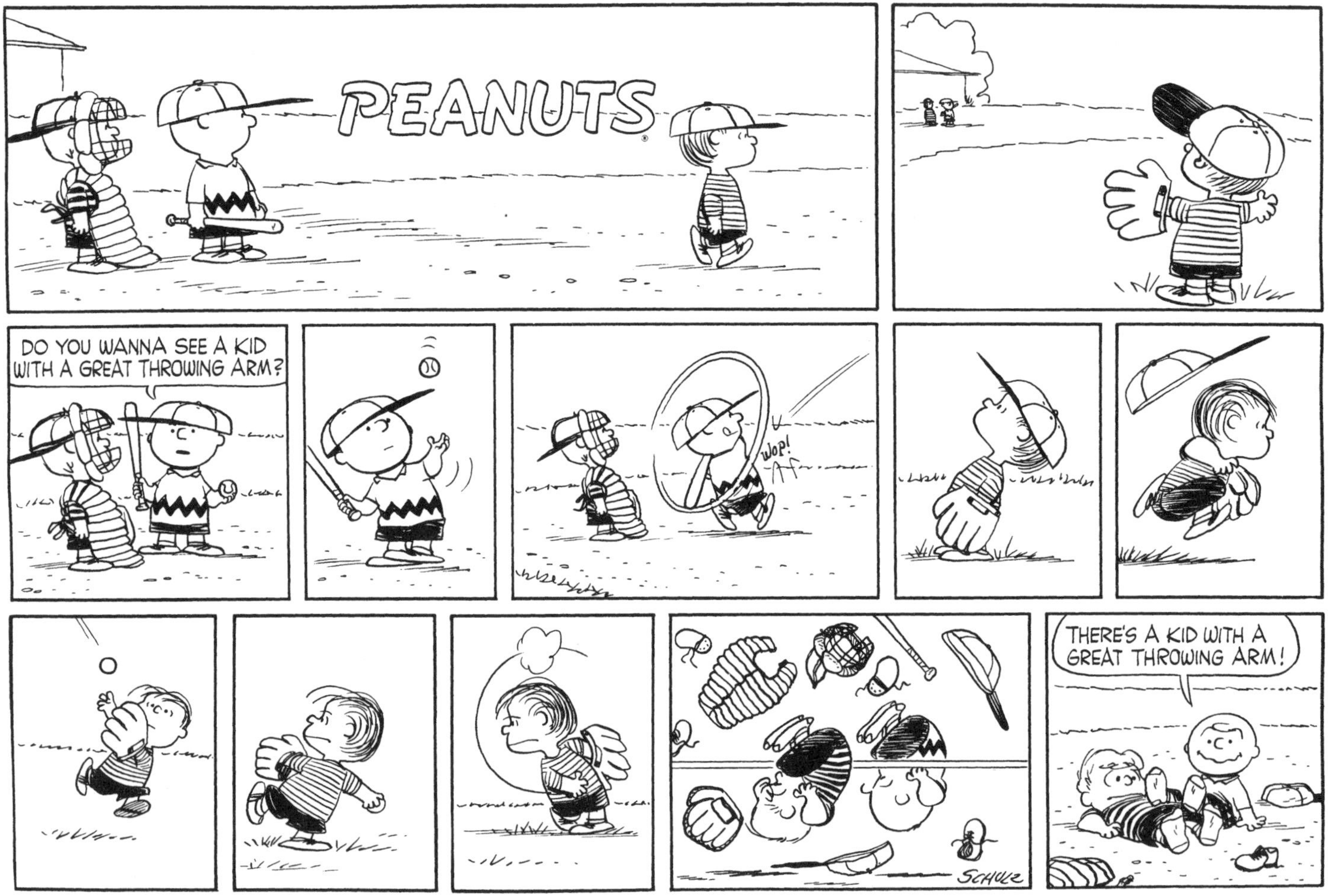
PEANUTS
DO YOU WANNA SEE A KID WITH A GREAT THROWING ARM?
WOP!
THERE'S A KID WITH A GREAT THROWING ARM!
SCHULZ

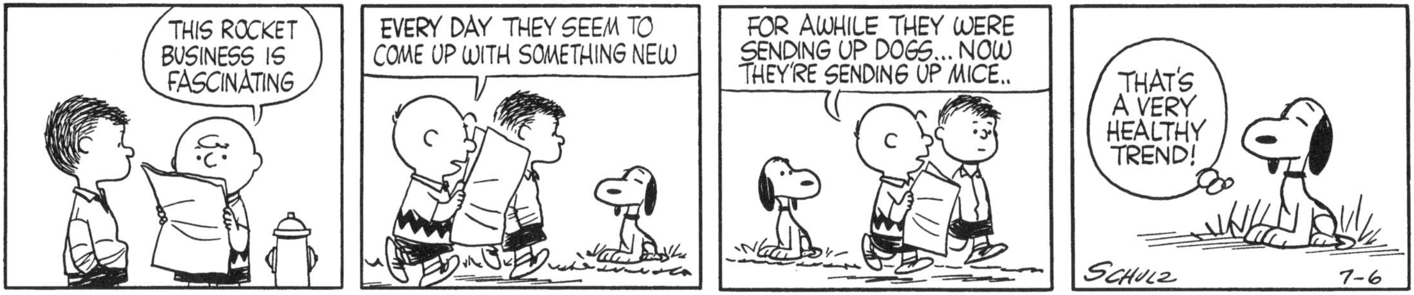
THIS ROCKET BUSINESS IS FASCINATING
EVERY DAY THEY SEEM TO COME UP WITH SOMETHING NEW
FOR AWHILE THEY WERE SENDING UP DOGS... NOW THEY'RE SENDING UP MICE..
THAT'S A VERY HEALTHY TREND!
SCHULZ
7-6

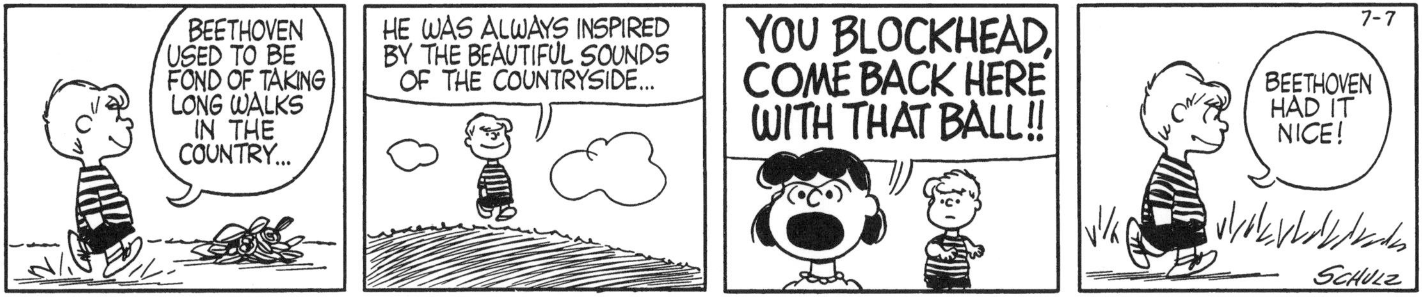
BEETHOVEN USED TO BE FOND OF TAKING LONG WALKS IN THE COUNTRY...
HE WAS ALWAYS INSPIRED BY THE BEAUTIFUL SOUNDS OF THE COUNTRYSIDE...
YOU BLOCKHEAD, COME BACK HERE WITH THAT BALL!!
7-7
BEETHOVEN HAD IT NICE!
SCHULZ

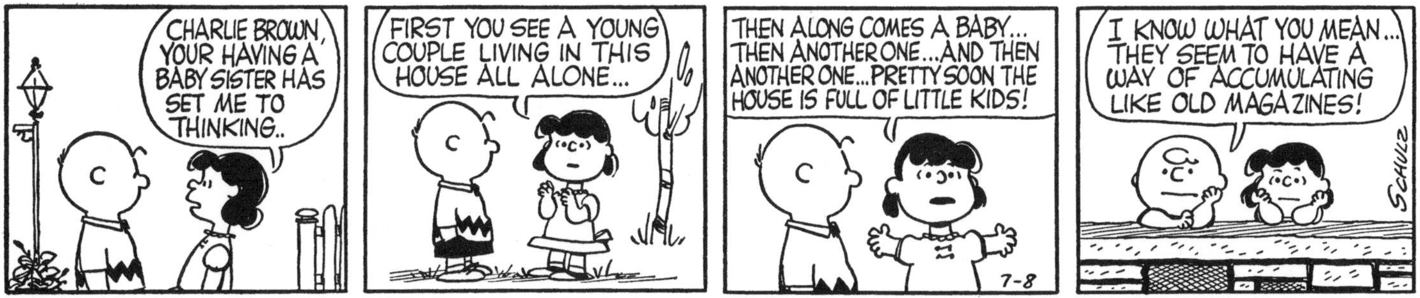
CHARLIE BROWN, YOUR HAVING A BABY SISTER HAS SET ME TO THINKING..
FIRST YOU SEE A YOUNG COUPLE LIVING IN THIS HOUSE ALL ALONE...
THEN ALONG COMES A BABY... THEN ANOTHER ONE...AND THEN ANOTHER ONE...PRETTY SOON THE HOUSE IS FULL OF LITTLE KIDS!
7-8
I KNOW WHAT YOU MEAN... THEY SEEM TO HAVE A WAY OF ACCUMULATING LIKE OLD MAGAZINES!
SCHULZ

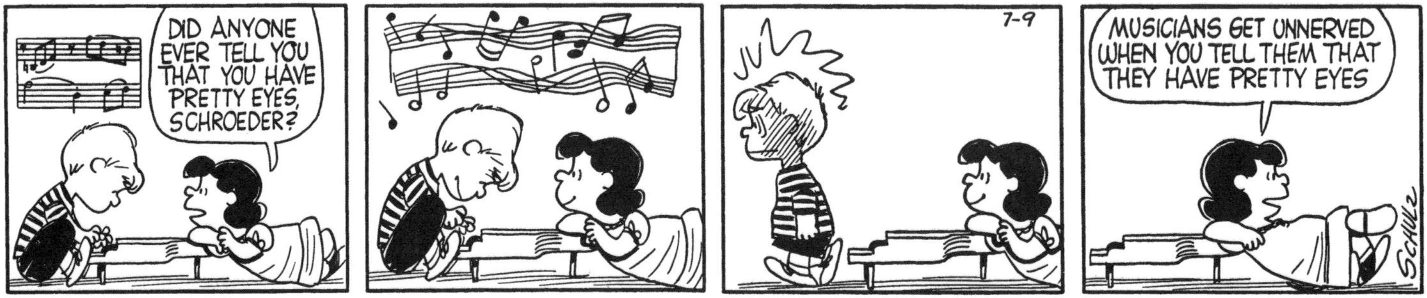
DID ANYONE EVER TELL YOU THAT YOU HAVE PRETTY EYES, SCHROEDER?
7-9
MUSICIANS GET UNNERVED WHEN YOU TELL THEM THAT THEY HAVE PRETTY EYES
SCHULZ

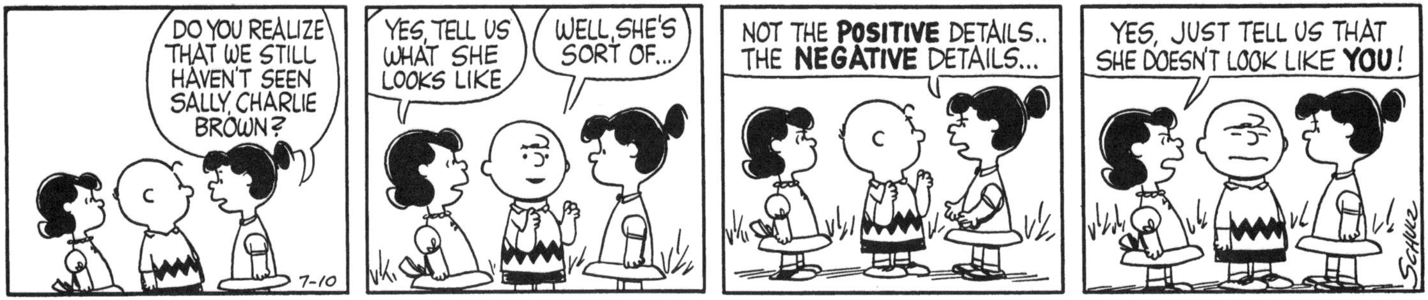
DO YOU REALIZE THAT WE STILL HAVEN'T SEEN SALLY, CHARLIE BROWN?
7-10
YES, TELL US WHAT SHE LOOKS LIKE
WELL, SHE'S SORT OF...
NOT THE **POSITIVE** DETAILS.. THE **NEGATIVE** DETAILS...
YES, JUST TELL US THAT SHE DOESN'T LOOK LIKE **YOU**!
SCHULZ

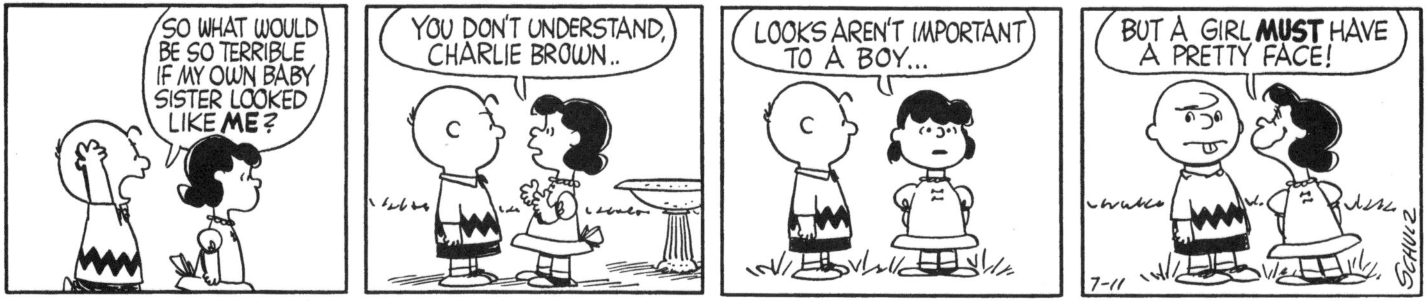
SO WHAT WOULD BE SO TERRIBLE IF MY OWN BABY SISTER LOOKED LIKE **ME**?
YOU DON'T UNDERSTAND, CHARLIE BROWN..
LOOKS AREN'T IMPORTANT TO A BOY...
BUT A GIRL **MUST** HAVE A PRETTY FACE!
7-11
SCHULZ

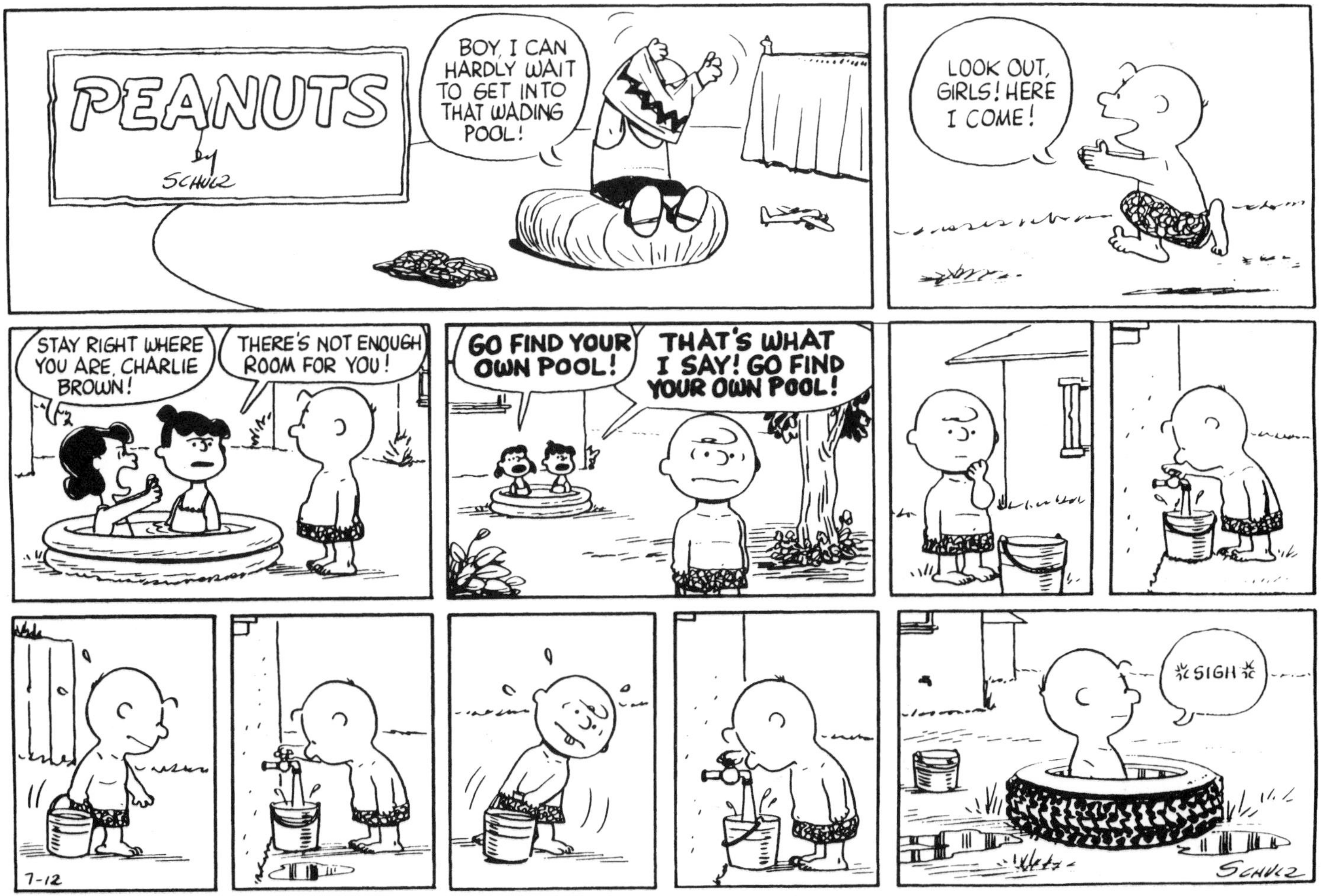
PEANUTS
by SCHULZ
BOY, I CAN HARDLY WAIT TO GET INTO THAT WADING POOL!
LOOK OUT, GIRLS! HERE I COME!
STAY RIGHT WHERE YOU ARE, CHARLIE BROWN!
THERE'S NOT ENOUGH ROOM FOR YOU!
GO FIND YOUR OWN POOL!
THAT'S WHAT I SAY! GO FIND YOUR OWN POOL!
7-12
SIGH
SCHULZ

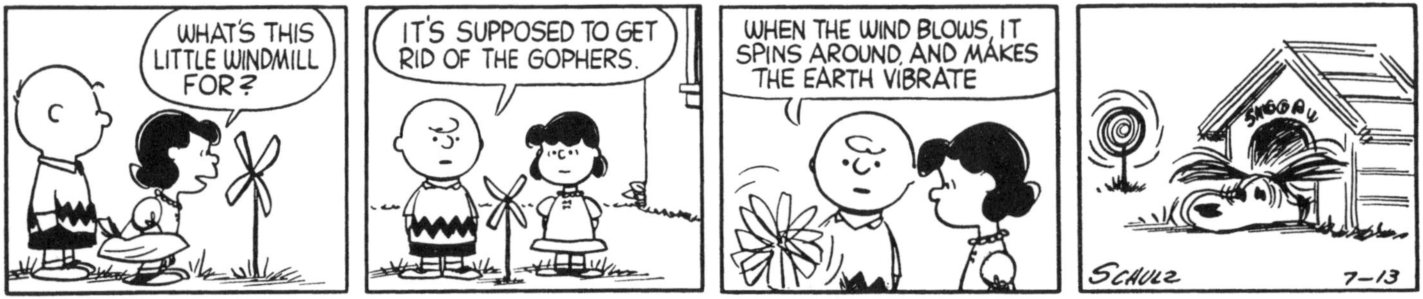
WHAT'S THIS LITTLE WINDMILL FOR?
IT'S SUPPOSED TO GET RID OF THE GOPHERS.
WHEN THE WIND BLOWS, IT SPINS AROUND, AND MAKES THE EARTH VIBRATE
SCHULZ
7-13

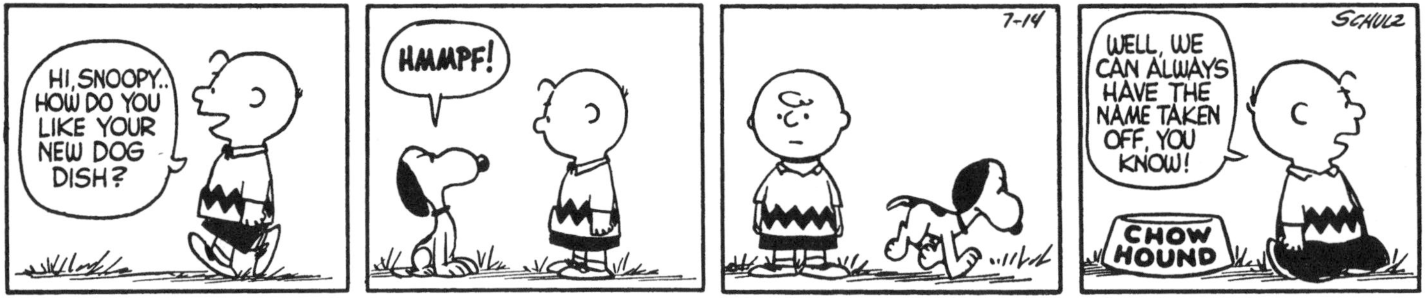
HI, SNOOPY.. HOW DO YOU LIKE YOUR NEW DOG DISH?
HMMPF!
7-14
SCHULZ
WELL, WE CAN ALWAYS HAVE THE NAME TAKEN OFF, YOU KNOW!
CHOW HOUND

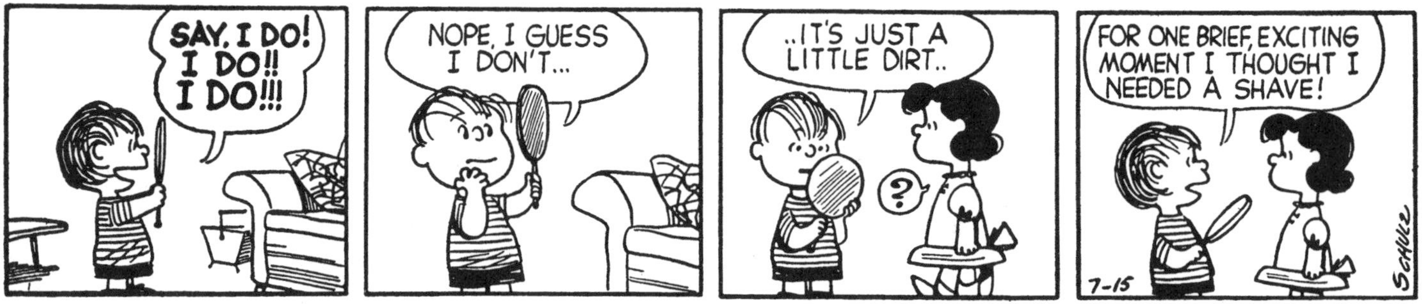
SAY, I DO! I DO!! I DO!!!
NOPE, I GUESS I DON'T...
..IT'S JUST A LITTLE DIRT..
?
FOR ONE BRIEF, EXCITING MOMENT I THOUGHT I NEEDED A SHAVE!
7-15
SCHULZ

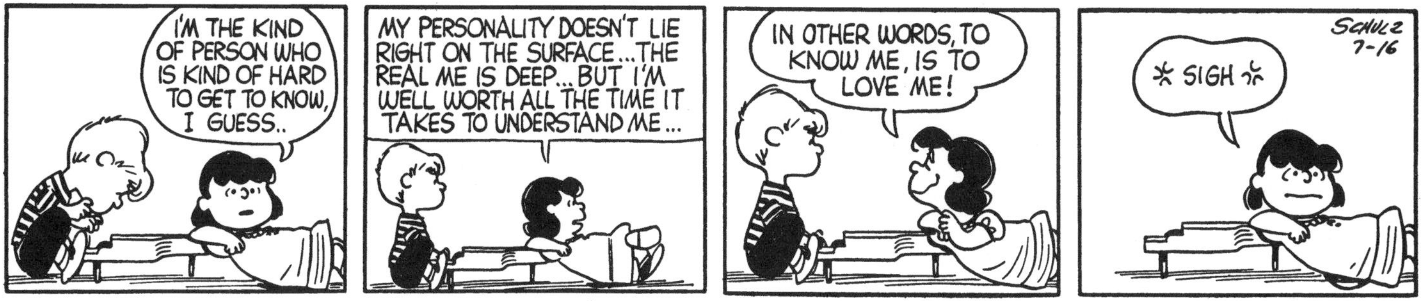

I'M THE KIND OF PERSON WHO IS KIND OF HARD TO GET TO KNOW, I GUESS..
MY PERSONALITY DOESN'T LIE RIGHT ON THE SURFACE...THE REAL ME IS DEEP... BUT I'M WELL WORTH ALL THE TIME IT TAKES TO UNDERSTAND ME...
IN OTHER WORDS, TO KNOW ME, IS TO LOVE ME!
SIGH
SCHULZ 7-16

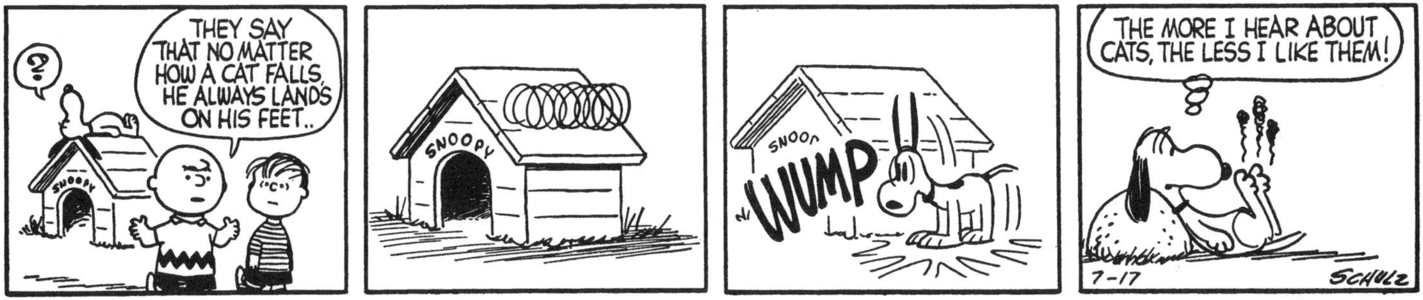

?
THEY SAY THAT NO MATTER HOW A CAT FALLS, HE ALWAYS LANDS ON HIS FEET..
SNOOPY
SNOOPY
SNOOP
WUMP
THE MORE I HEAR ABOUT CATS, THE LESS I LIKE THEM!
7-17
SCHULZ

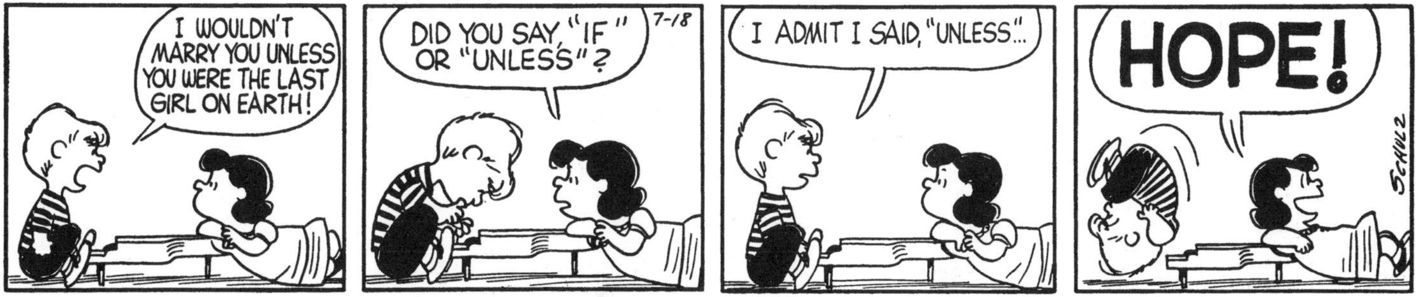

I WOULDN'T MARRY YOU UNLESS YOU WERE THE LAST GIRL ON EARTH!
DID YOU SAY, "IF" OR "UNLESS"?
7-18
I ADMIT I SAID, "UNLESS"...
HOPE!
SCHULZ

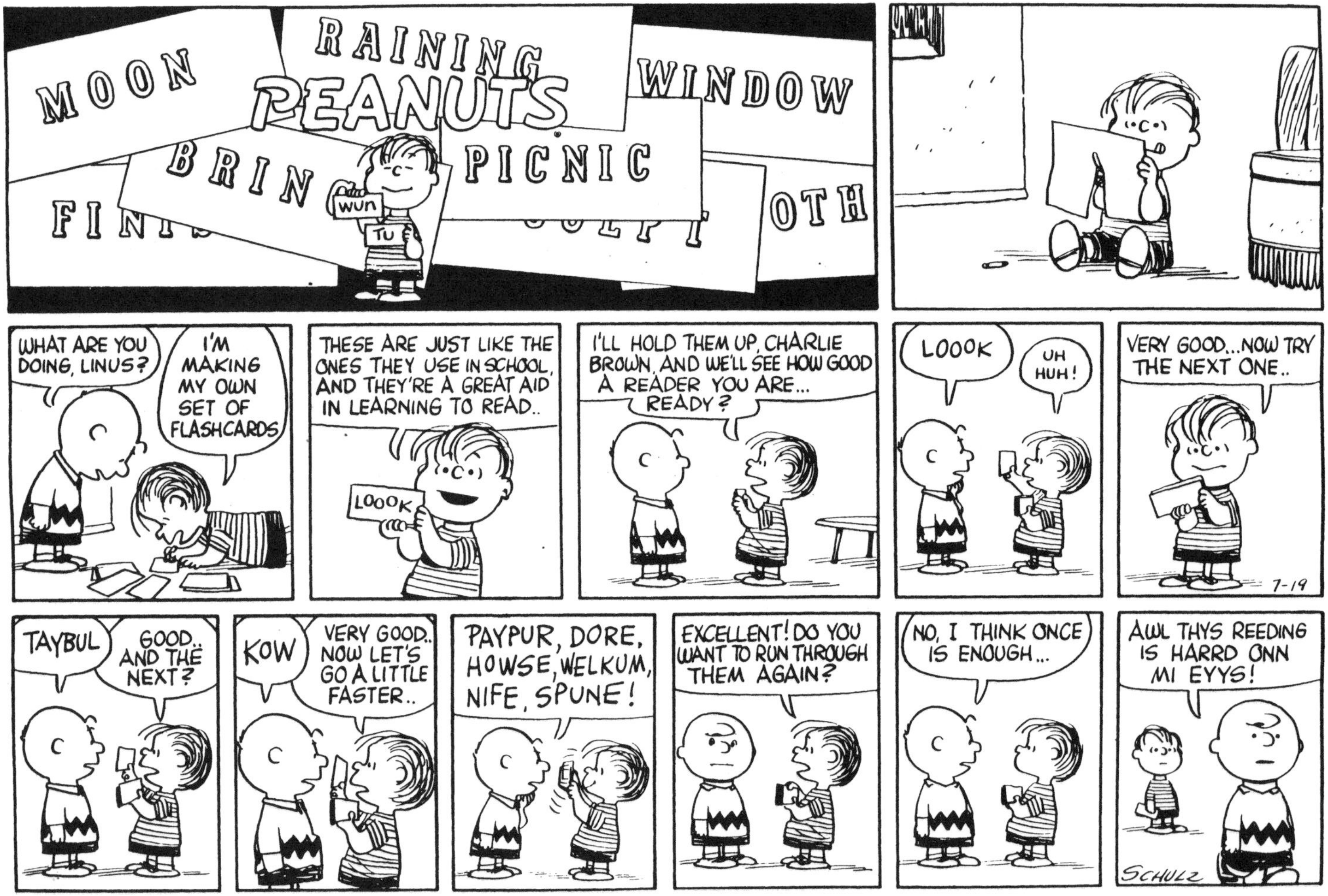
MOON
RAINING
WINDOW
PEANUTS
BRING
PICNIC
FINI
WUN
TU
OTH
WHAT ARE YOU DOING, LINUS?
I'M MAKING MY OWN SET OF FLASHCARDS
THESE ARE JUST LIKE THE ONES THEY USE IN SCHOOL, AND THEY'RE A GREAT AID IN LEARNING TO READ..
LOOOK
I'LL HOLD THEM UP, CHARLIE BROWN, AND WE'LL SEE HOW GOOD A READER YOU ARE... READY?
LOOOK
UH HUH!
VERY GOOD...NOW TRY THE NEXT ONE..
7-19
TAYBUL
GOOD.. AND THE NEXT?
KOW
VERY GOOD.. NOW LET'S GO A LITTLE FASTER..
PAYPUR, DORE, HOWSE, WELKUM, NIFE, SPUNE!
EXCELLENT! DO YOU WANT TO RUN THROUGH THEM AGAIN?
NO, I THINK ONCE IS ENOUGH...
AWL THYS REEDING IS HARRD ONN MI EYYS!
SCHULZ

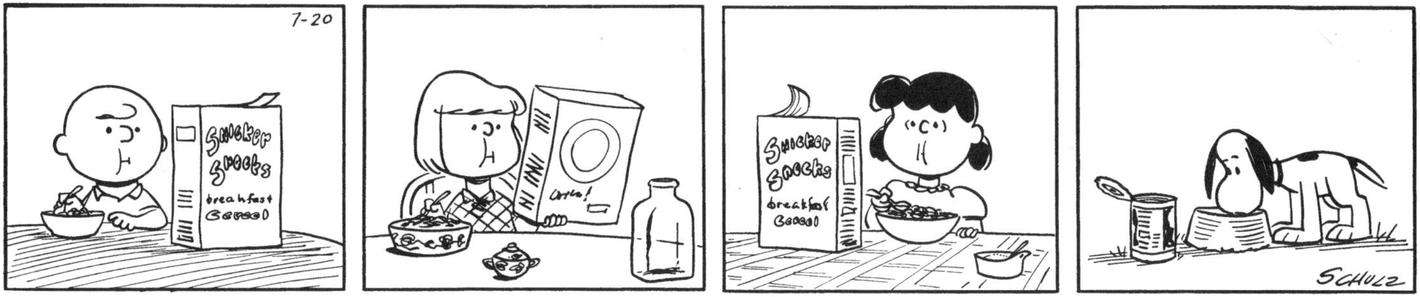
7-20
SCHULZ

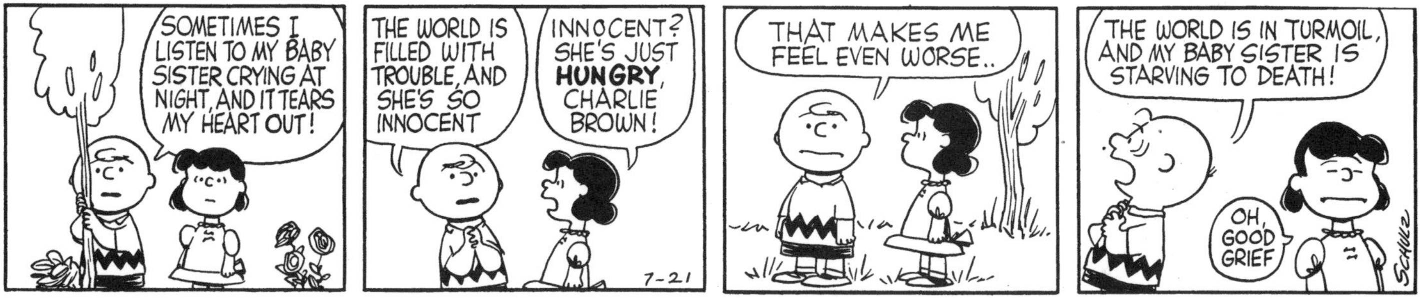
SOMETIMES I LISTEN TO MY BABY SISTER CRYING AT NIGHT, AND IT TEARS MY HEART OUT!
THE WORLD IS FILLED WITH TROUBLE, AND SHE'S SO INNOCENT
INNOCENT? SHE'S JUST **HUNGRY**, CHARLIE BROWN!
7-21
THAT MAKES ME FEEL EVEN WORSE..
THE WORLD IS IN TURMOIL, AND MY BABY SISTER IS STARVING TO DEATH!
OH, GOOD GRIEF
SCHULZ

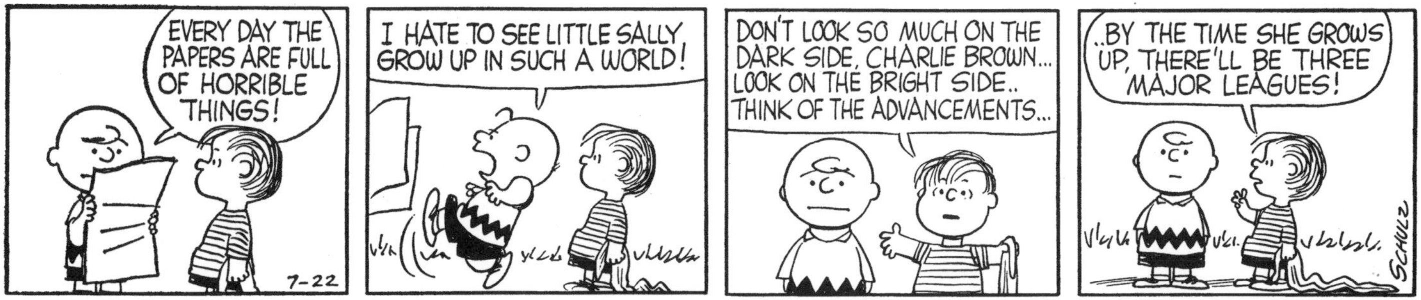
EVERY DAY THE PAPERS ARE FULL OF HORRIBLE THINGS!
7-22
I HATE TO SEE LITTLE SALLY GROW UP IN SUCH A WORLD!
DON'T LOOK SO MUCH ON THE DARK SIDE, CHARLIE BROWN... LOOK ON THE BRIGHT SIDE.. THINK OF THE ADVANCEMENTS...
..BY THE TIME SHE GROWS UP, THERE'LL BE THREE MAJOR LEAGUES!
SCHULZ

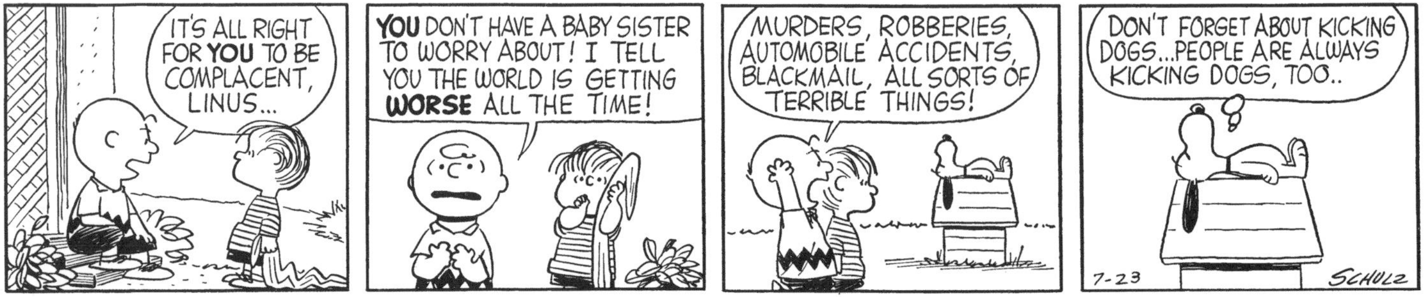
IT'S ALL RIGHT FOR YOU TO BE COMPLACENT, LINUS...
YOU DON'T HAVE A BABY SISTER TO WORRY ABOUT! I TELL YOU THE WORLD IS GETTING WORSE ALL THE TIME!
MURDERS, ROBBERIES, AUTOMOBILE ACCIDENTS, BLACKMAIL, ALL SORTS OF TERRIBLE THINGS!
DON'T FORGET ABOUT KICKING DOGS...PEOPLE ARE ALWAYS KICKING DOGS, TOO..
7-23
SCHULZ

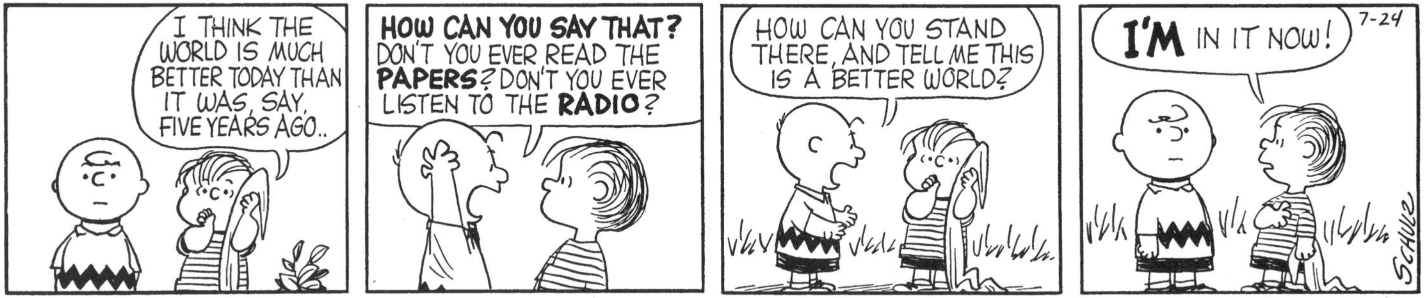
I THINK THE WORLD IS MUCH BETTER TODAY THAN IT WAS, SAY, FIVE YEARS AGO..
HOW CAN YOU SAY THAT? DON'T YOU EVER READ THE PAPERS? DON'T YOU EVER LISTEN TO THE RADIO?
HOW CAN YOU STAND THERE, AND TELL ME THIS IS A BETTER WORLD?
I'M IN IT NOW!
7-24
SCHULZ

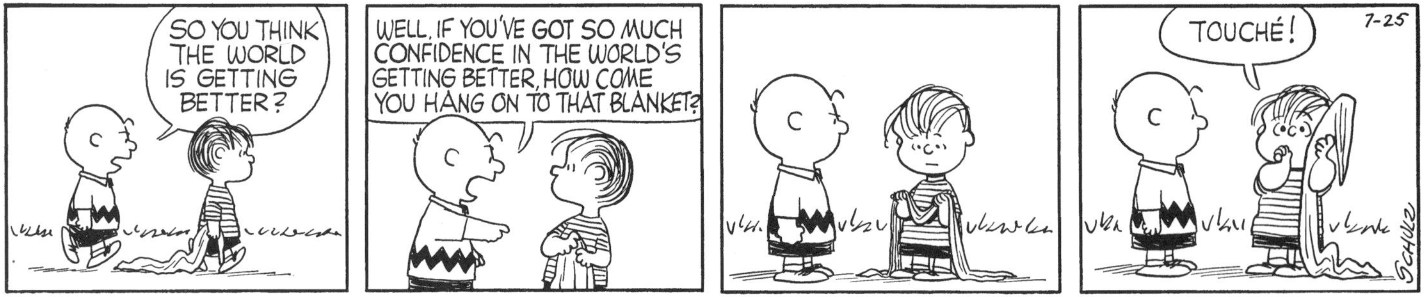
SO YOU THINK THE WORLD IS GETTING BETTER?
WELL, IF YOU'VE GOT SO MUCH CONFIDENCE IN THE WORLD'S GETTING BETTER, HOW COME YOU HANG ON TO THAT BLANKET?
TOUCHÉ!
7-25
SCHULZ

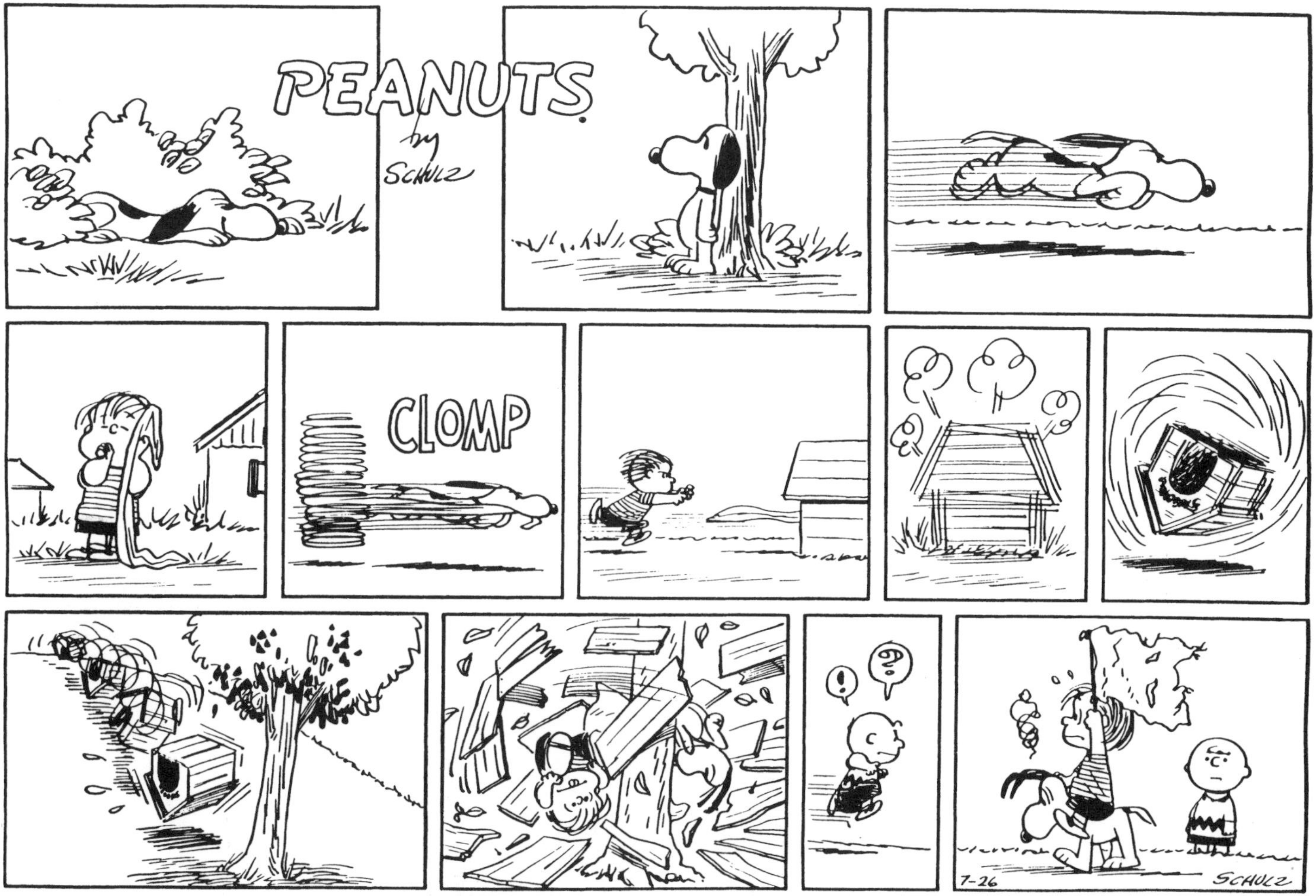
PEANUTS
by SCHULZ
CLOMP
!
?
7-26
SCHULZ

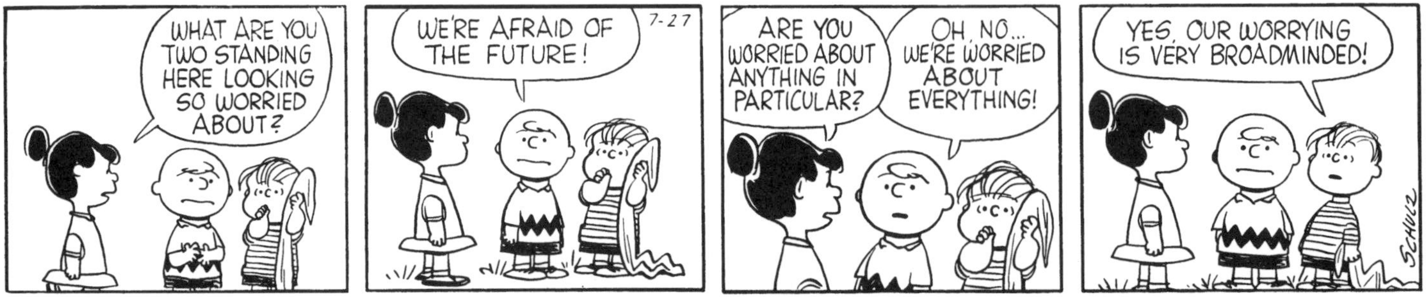
WHAT ARE YOU TWO STANDING HERE LOOKING SO WORRIED ABOUT?
WE'RE AFRAID OF THE FUTURE!
7-27
ARE YOU WORRIED ABOUT ANYTHING IN PARTICULAR?
OH, NO... WE'RE WORRIED ABOUT EVERYTHING!
YES, OUR WORRYING IS VERY BROADMINDED!
SCHULZ

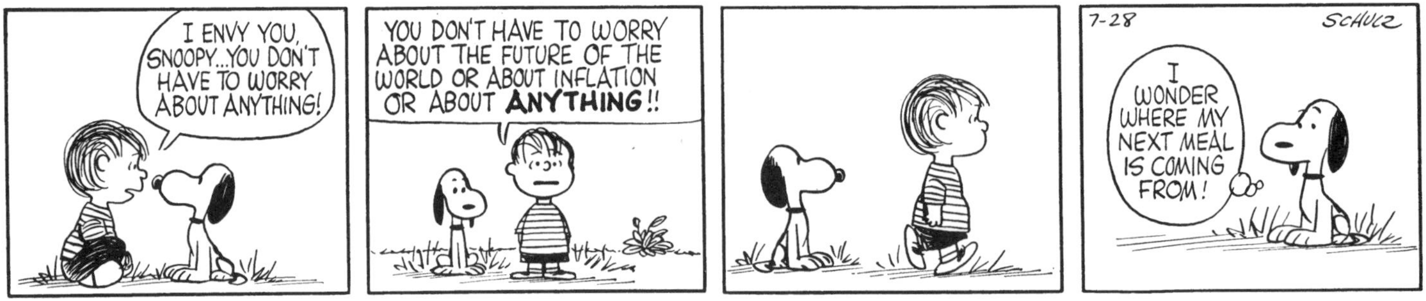
I ENVY YOU, SNOOPY...YOU DON'T HAVE TO WORRY ABOUT ANYTHING!
YOU DON'T HAVE TO WORRY ABOUT THE FUTURE OF THE WORLD OR ABOUT INFLATION OR ABOUT **ANYTHING**!!
7-28
SCHULZ
I WONDER WHERE MY NEXT MEAL IS COMING FROM!

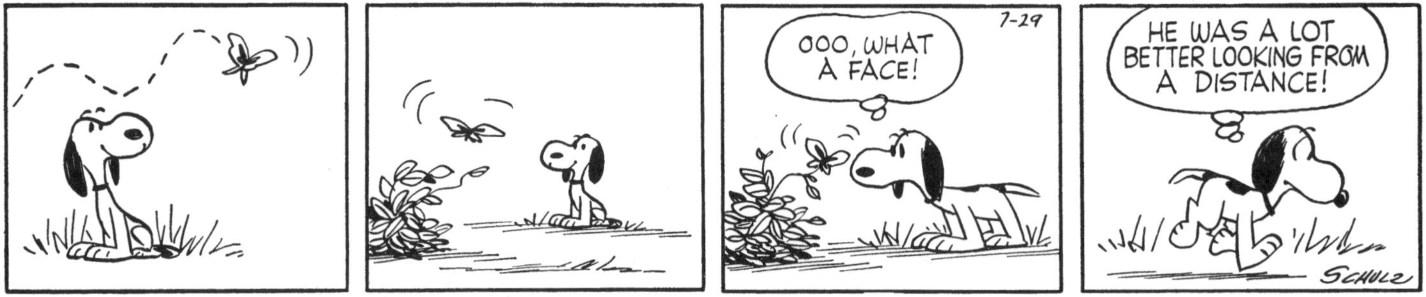
7-29
OOO, WHAT A FACE!
HE WAS A LOT BETTER LOOKING FROM A DISTANCE!
SCHULZ

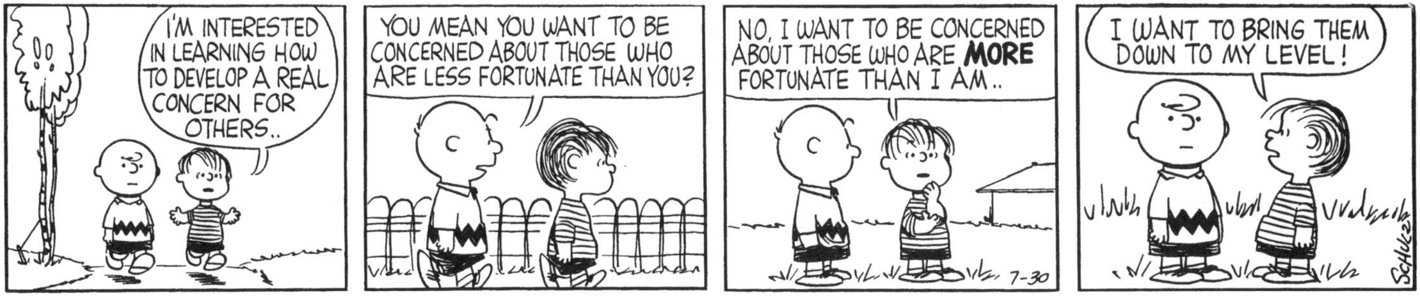
I'M INTERESTED IN LEARNING HOW TO DEVELOP A REAL CONCERN FOR OTHERS..
YOU MEAN YOU WANT TO BE CONCERNED ABOUT THOSE WHO ARE LESS FORTUNATE THAN YOU?
NO, I WANT TO BE CONCERNED ABOUT THOSE WHO ARE **MORE** FORTUNATE THAN I AM..
7-30
I WANT TO BRING THEM DOWN TO MY LEVEL!
SCHULZ

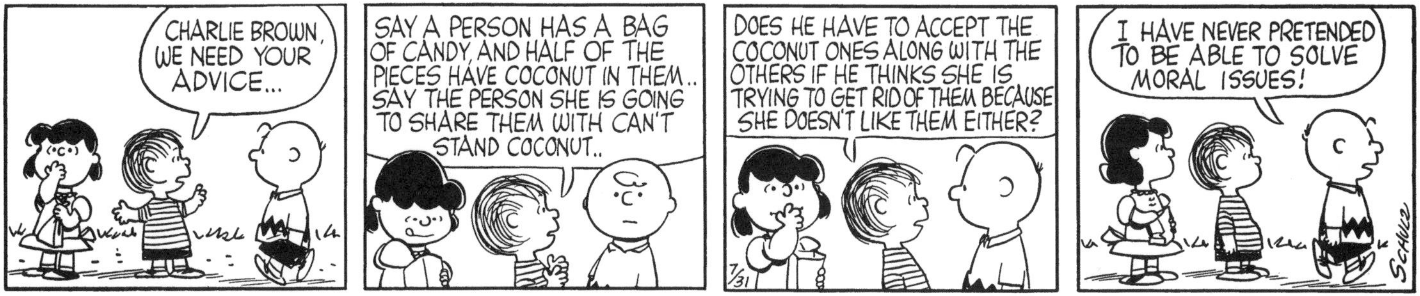
CHARLIE BROWN, WE NEED YOUR ADVICE...
SAY A PERSON HAS A BAG OF CANDY, AND HALF OF THE PIECES HAVE COCONUT IN THEM.. SAY THE PERSON SHE IS GOING TO SHARE THEM WITH CAN'T STAND COCONUT..
DOES HE HAVE TO ACCEPT THE COCONUT ONES ALONG WITH THE OTHERS IF HE THINKS SHE IS TRYING TO GET RID OF THEM BECAUSE SHE DOESN'T LIKE THEM EITHER?
7/31
I HAVE NEVER PRETENDED TO BE ABLE TO SOLVE MORAL ISSUES!
SCHULZ

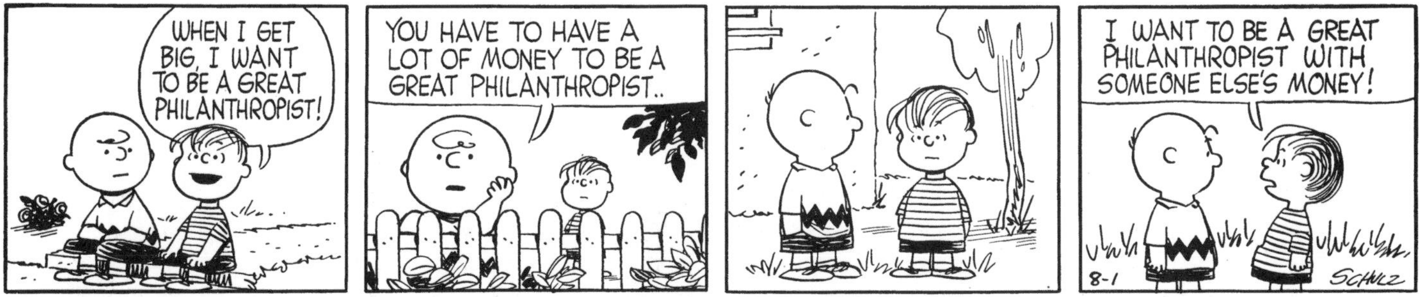
WHEN I GET BIG, I WANT TO BE A GREAT PHILANTHROPIST!
YOU HAVE TO HAVE A LOT OF MONEY TO BE A GREAT PHILANTHROPIST..
I WANT TO BE A GREAT PHILANTHROPIST WITH SOMEONE ELSE'S MONEY!
8-1
SCHULZ

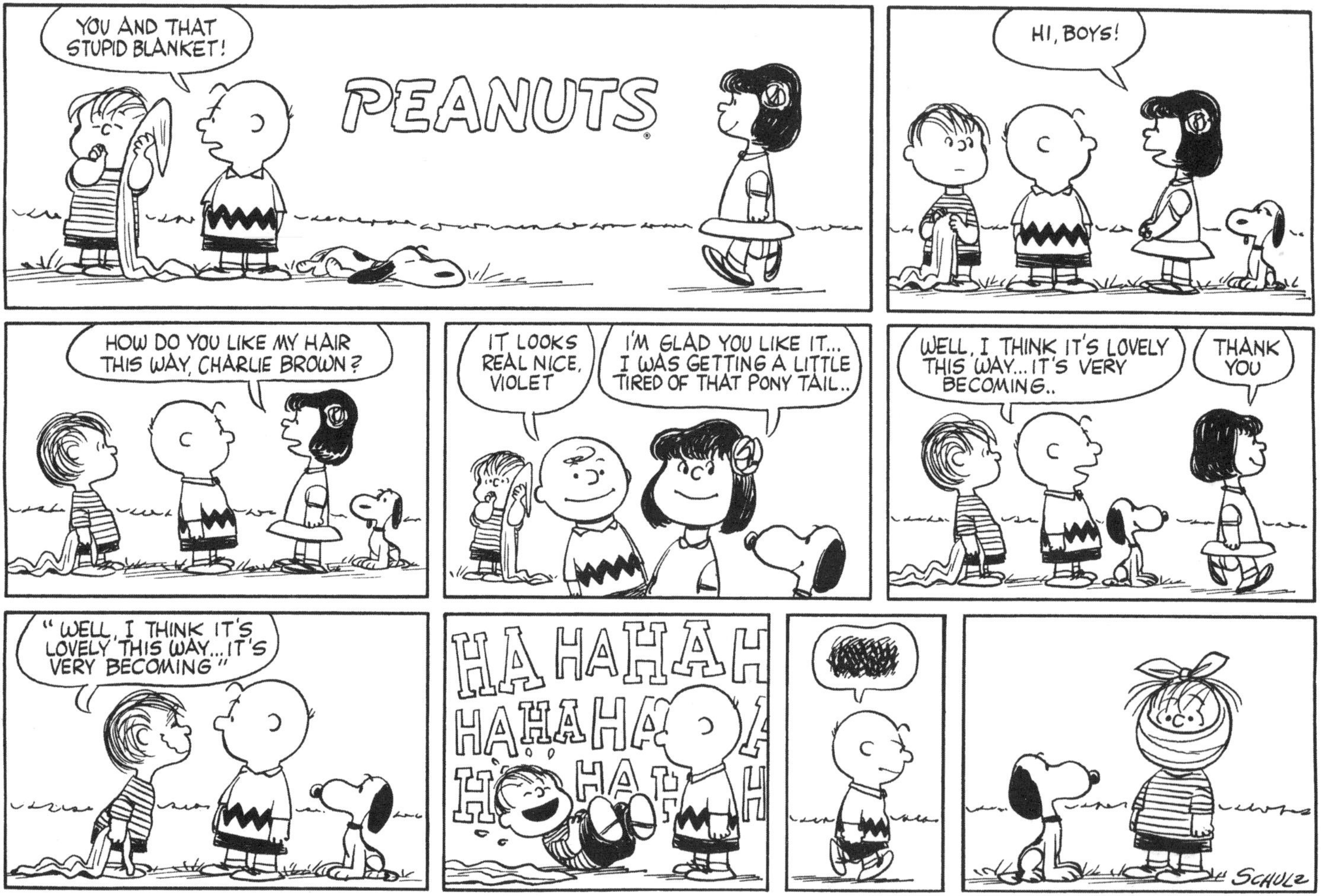

YOU AND THAT STUPID BLANKET!
PEANUTS
HI, BOYS!
HOW DO YOU LIKE MY HAIR THIS WAY, CHARLIE BROWN?
IT LOOKS REAL NICE, VIOLET
I'M GLAD YOU LIKE IT... I WAS GETTING A LITTLE TIRED OF THAT PONY TAIL..
WELL, I THINK IT'S LOVELY THIS WAY...IT'S VERY BECOMING..
THANK YOU
"WELL, I THINK IT'S LOVELY THIS WAY...IT'S VERY BECOMING"
HA HAHAH
HAHAHA
H HA H
SCHULZ

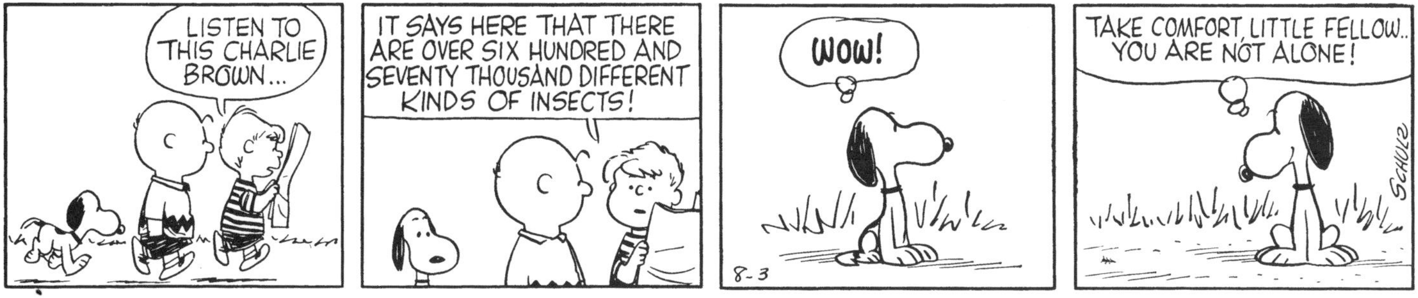
LISTEN TO THIS CHARLIE BROWN...
IT SAYS HERE THAT THERE ARE OVER SIX HUNDRED AND SEVENTY THOUSAND DIFFERENT KINDS OF INSECTS!
WOW!
8-3
TAKE COMFORT, LITTLE FELLOW.. YOU ARE NOT ALONE!
SCHULZ

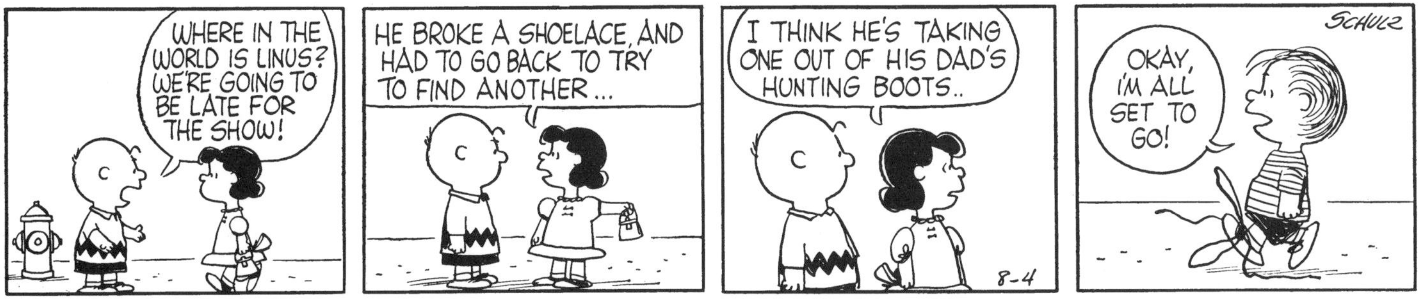
WHERE IN THE WORLD IS LINUS? WE'RE GOING TO BE LATE FOR THE SHOW!
HE BROKE A SHOELACE, AND HAD TO GO BACK TO TRY TO FIND ANOTHER...
I THINK HE'S TAKING ONE OUT OF HIS DAD'S HUNTING BOOTS..
8-4
SCHULZ
OKAY, I'M ALL SET TO GO!

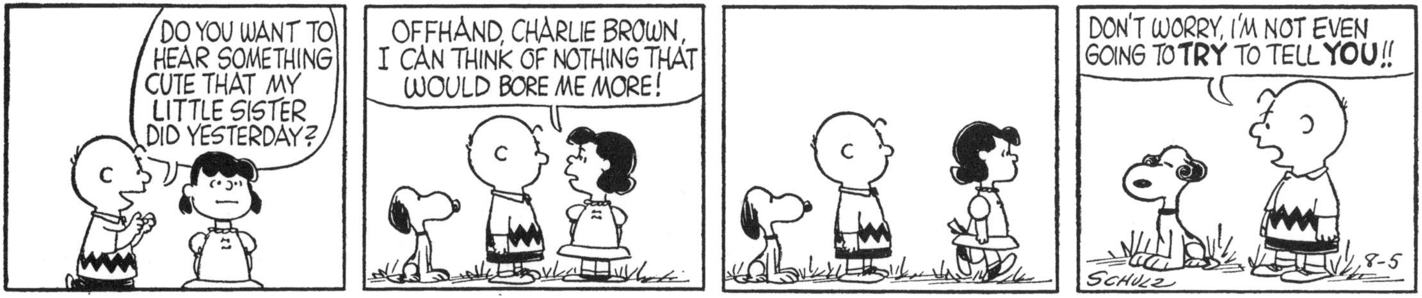
DO YOU WANT TO HEAR SOMETHING CUTE THAT MY LITTLE SISTER DID YESTERDAY?
OFFHAND, CHARLIE BROWN, I CAN THINK OF NOTHING THAT WOULD BORE ME MORE!
DON'T WORRY, I'M NOT EVEN GOING TO TRY TO TELL YOU!!
8-5
SCHULZ

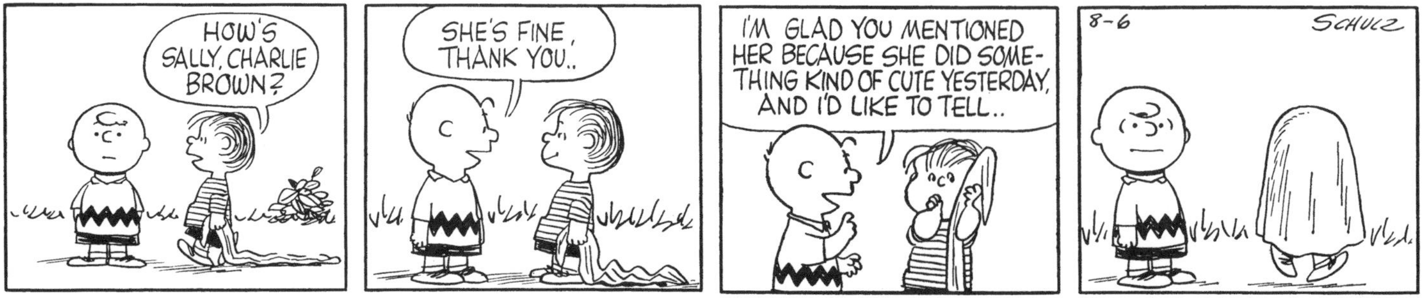
HOW'S SALLY, CHARLIE BROWN?
SHE'S FINE, THANK YOU..
I'M GLAD YOU MENTIONED HER BECAUSE SHE DID SOMETHING KIND OF CUTE YESTERDAY, AND I'D LIKE TO TELL..
8-6
SCHULZ

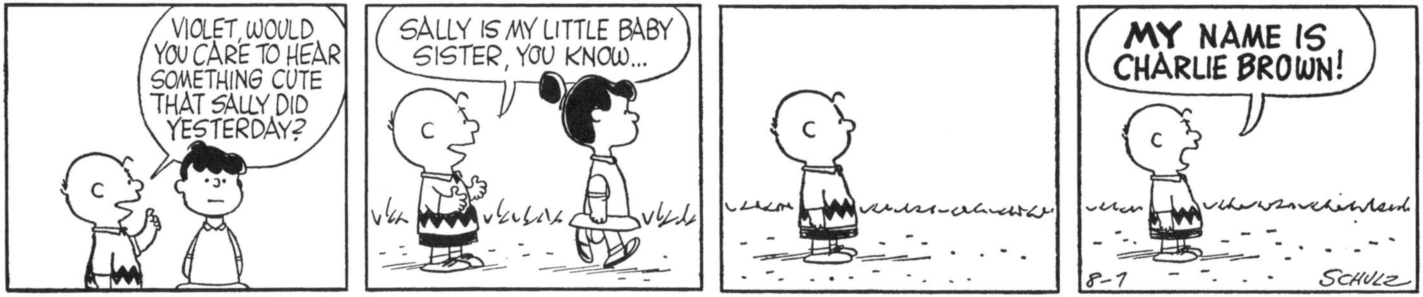
VIOLET, WOULD YOU CARE TO HEAR SOMETHING CUTE THAT SALLY DID YESTERDAY?
SALLY IS MY LITTLE BABY SISTER, YOU KNOW...
MY NAME IS CHARLIE BROWN!
8-7
SCHULZ

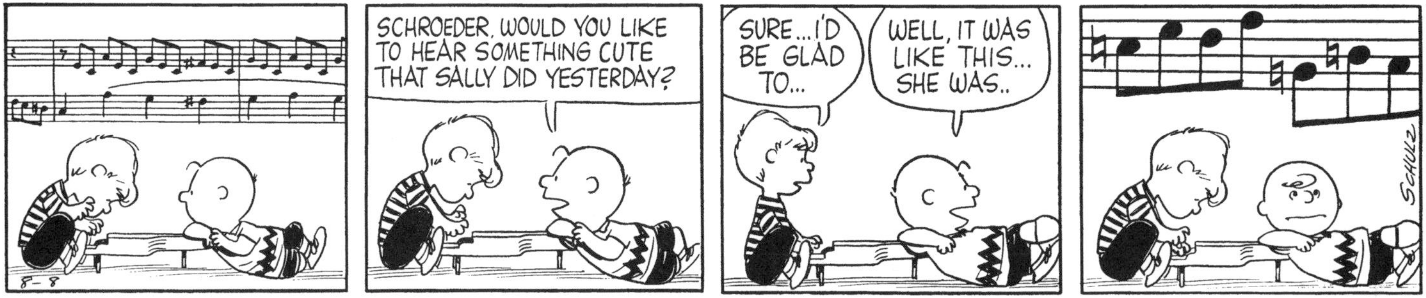
8-8
SCHROEDER, WOULD YOU LIKE TO HEAR SOMETHING CUTE THAT SALLY DID YESTERDAY?
SURE...I'D BE GLAD TO...
WELL, IT WAS LIKE THIS... SHE WAS..
SCHULZ

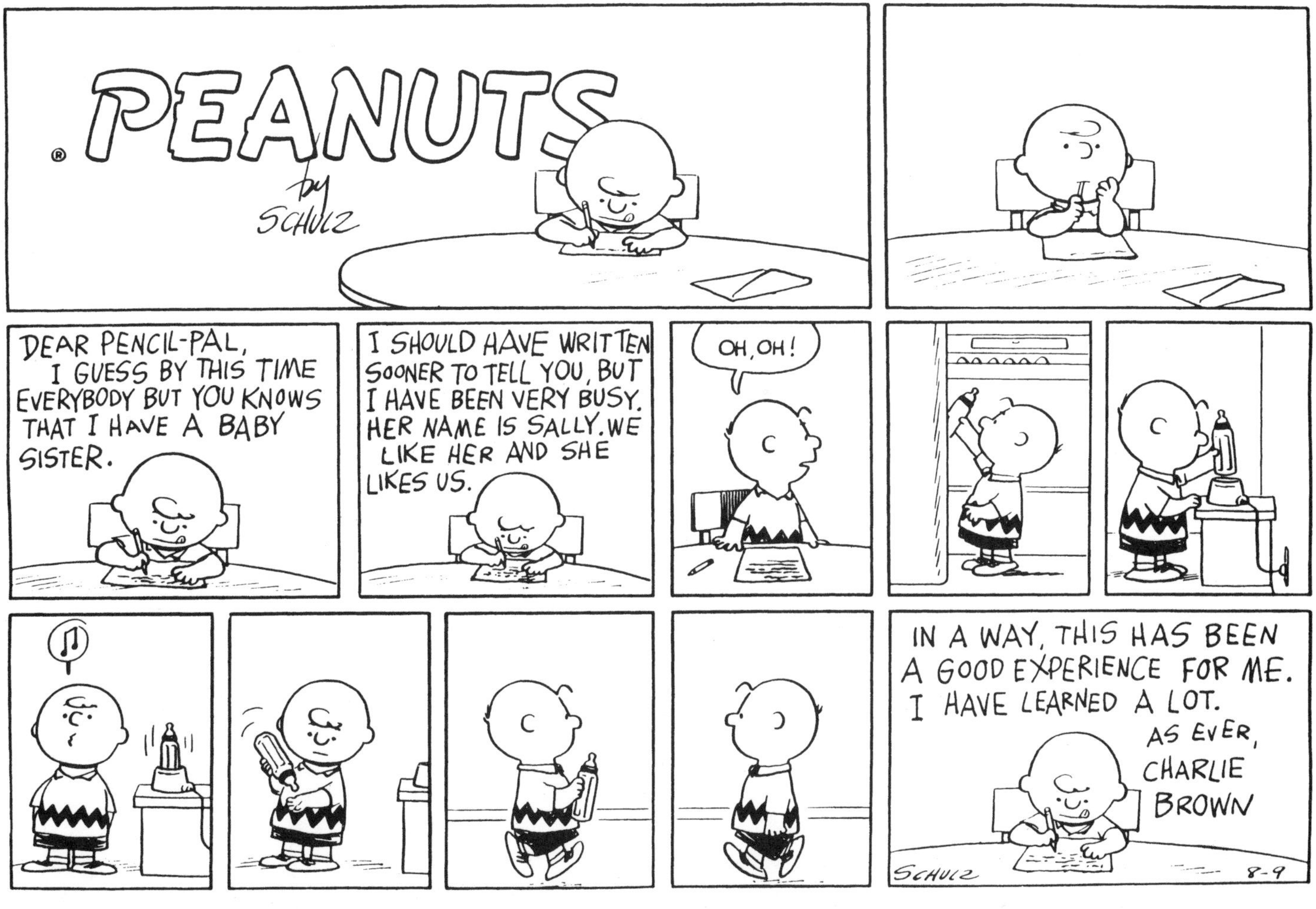
PEANUTS
by SCHULZ
DEAR PENCIL-PAL,
I GUESS BY THIS TIME EVERYBODY BUT YOU KNOWS THAT I HAVE A BABY SISTER.
I SHOULD HAVE WRITTEN SOONER TO TELL YOU, BUT I HAVE BEEN VERY BUSY. HER NAME IS SALLY. WE LIKE HER AND SHE LIKES US.
OH, OH!
IN A WAY, THIS HAS BEEN A GOOD EXPERIENCE FOR ME. I HAVE LEARNED A LOT.
AS EVER, CHARLIE BROWN
SCHULZ
8-9

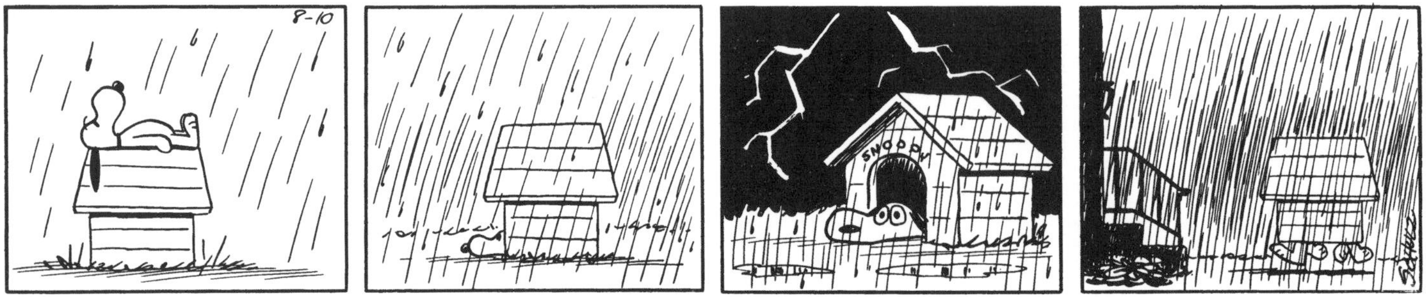
8-10
SNOOPY
SCHULZ

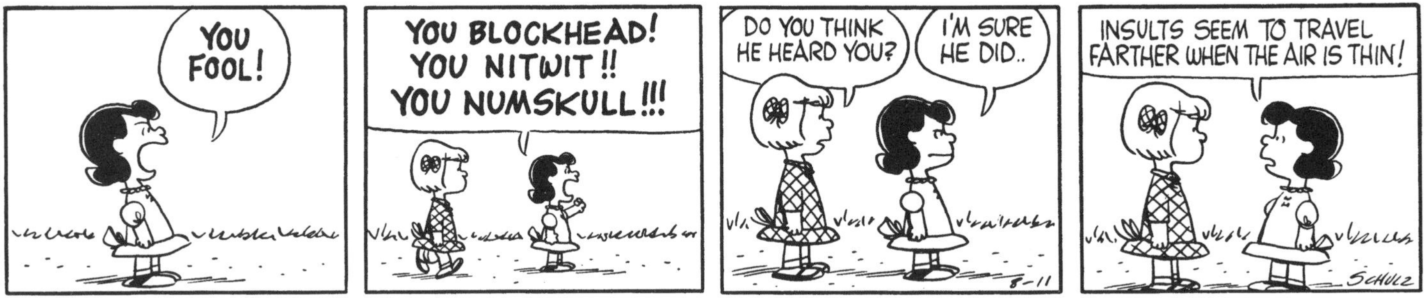
YOU FOOL!
YOU BLOCKHEAD! YOU NITWIT!! YOU NUMSKULL!!!
DO YOU THINK HE HEARD YOU?
I'M SURE HE DID..
8-11
INSULTS SEEM TO TRAVEL FARTHER WHEN THE AIR IS THIN!
SCHULZ

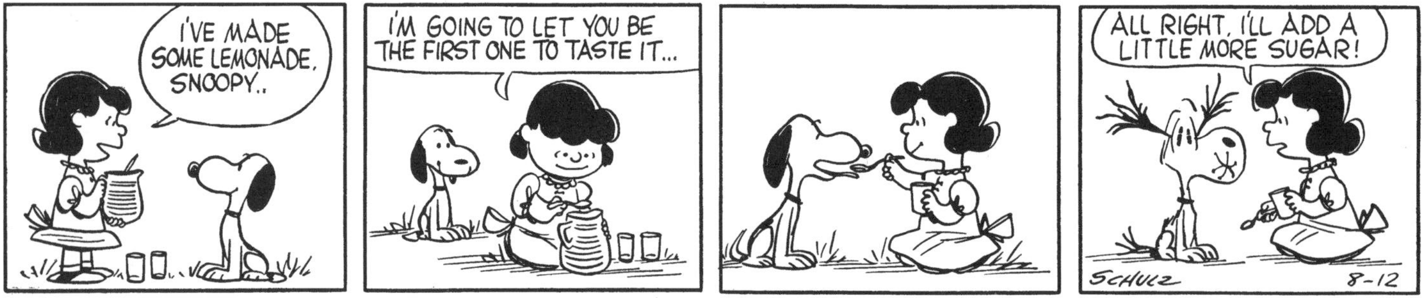
I'VE MADE SOME LEMONADE, SNOOPY..
I'M GOING TO LET YOU BE THE FIRST ONE TO TASTE IT...
ALL RIGHT, I'LL ADD A LITTLE MORE SUGAR!
SCHULZ
8-12

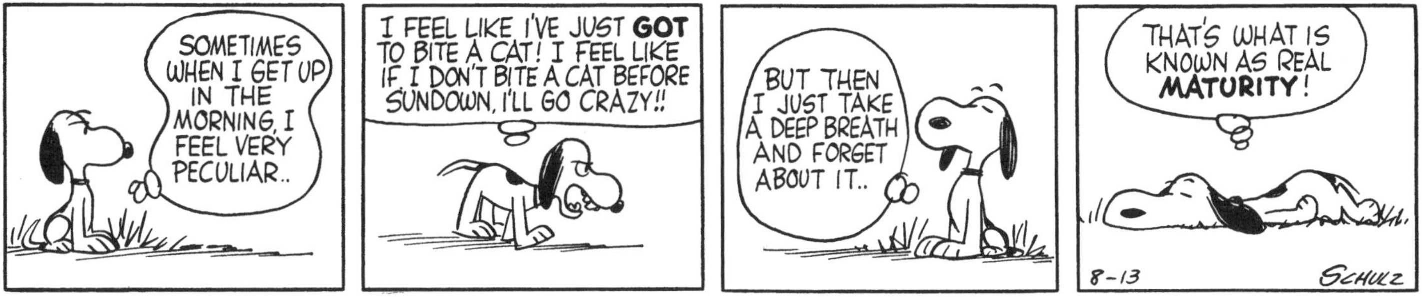
SOMETIMES WHEN I GET UP IN THE MORNING, I FEEL VERY PECULIAR..
I FEEL LIKE I'VE JUST **GOT** TO BITE A CAT! I FEEL LIKE IF I DON'T BITE A CAT BEFORE SUNDOWN, I'LL GO CRAZY!!
BUT THEN I JUST TAKE A DEEP BREATH AND FORGET ABOUT IT..
THAT'S WHAT IS KNOWN AS REAL **MATURITY**!
8-13
SCHULZ

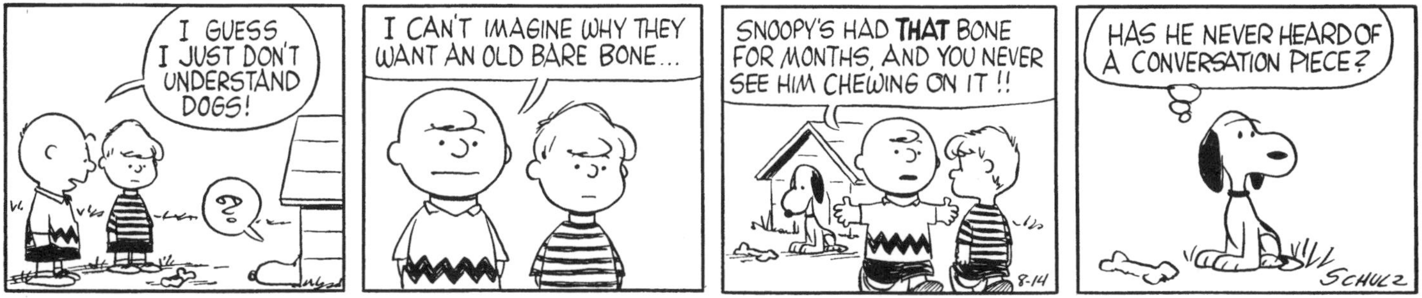
I GUESS I JUST DON'T UNDERSTAND DOGS!
?
I CAN'T IMAGINE WHY THEY WANT AN OLD BARE BONE...
SNOOPY'S HAD **THAT** BONE FOR MONTHS, AND YOU NEVER SEE HIM CHEWING ON IT !!
8-14
HAS HE NEVER HEARD OF A CONVERSATION PIECE?
SCHULZ

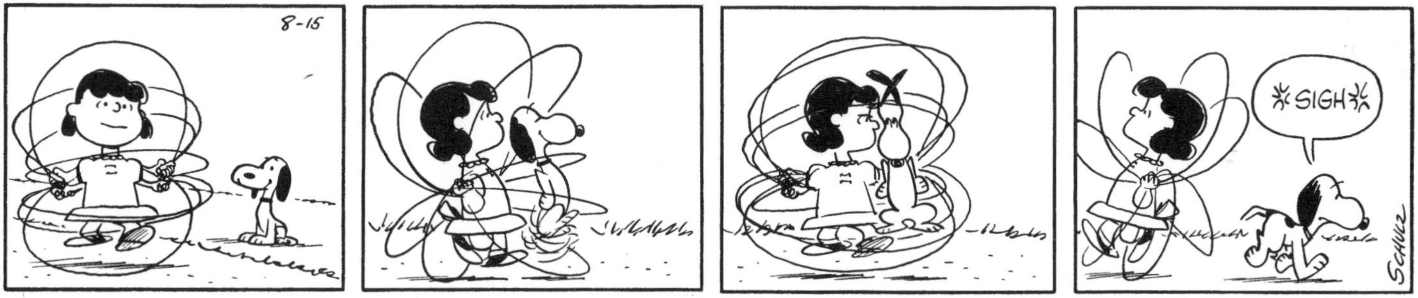
8-15
SIGH
SCHULZ

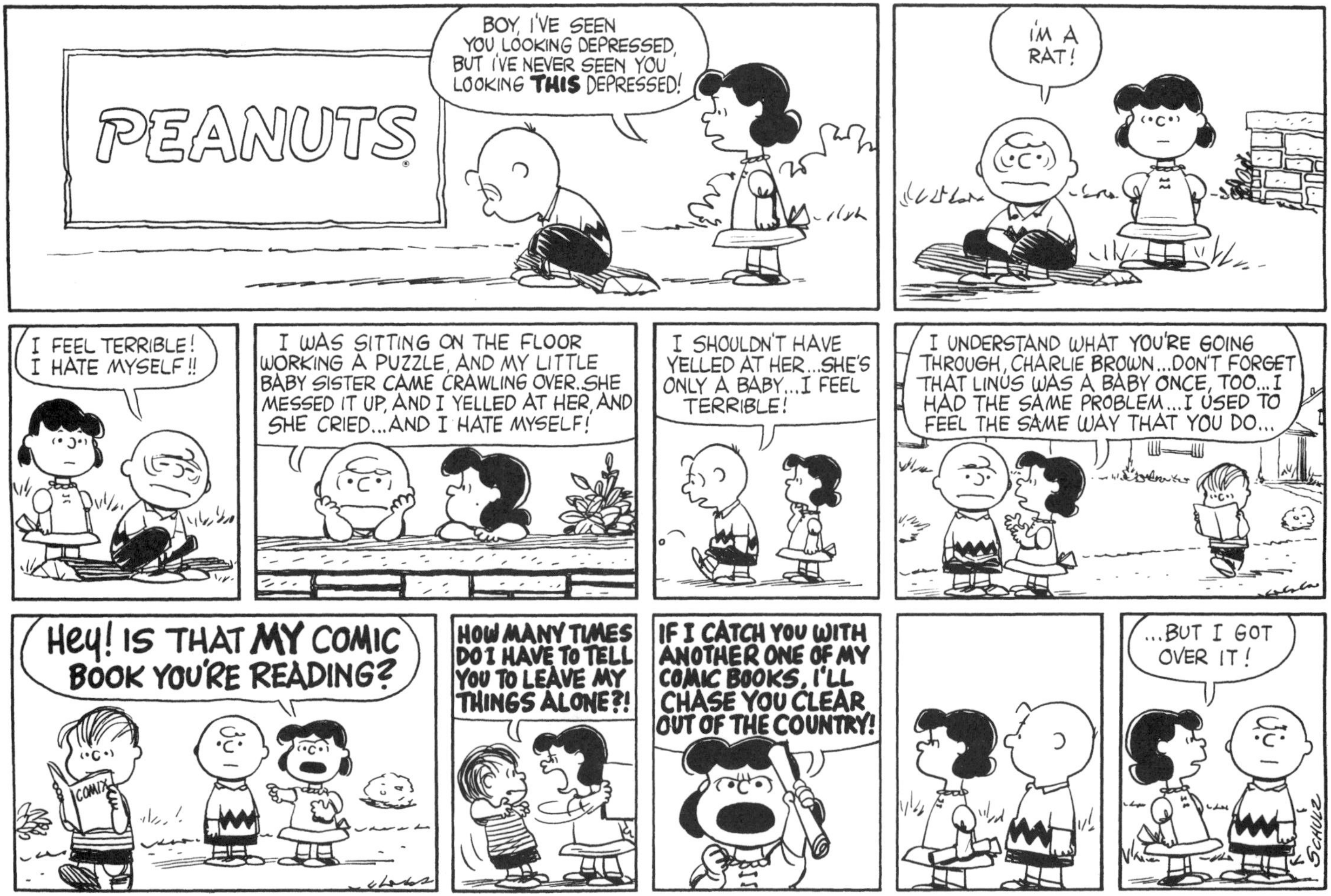
PEANUTS
BOY, I'VE SEEN YOU LOOKING DEPRESSED, BUT I'VE NEVER SEEN YOU LOOKING THIS DEPRESSED!
I'M A RAT!
I FEEL TERRIBLE! I HATE MYSELF!!
I WAS SITTING ON THE FLOOR WORKING A PUZZLE, AND MY LITTLE BABY SISTER CAME CRAWLING OVER..SHE MESSED IT UP, AND I YELLED AT HER, AND SHE CRIED...AND I HATE MYSELF!
I SHOULDN'T HAVE YELLED AT HER...SHE'S ONLY A BABY...I FEEL TERRIBLE!
I UNDERSTAND WHAT YOU'RE GOING THROUGH, CHARLIE BROWN...DON'T FORGET THAT LINUS WAS A BABY ONCE, TOO...I HAD THE SAME PROBLEM...I USED TO FEEL THE SAME WAY THAT YOU DO...
HEY! IS THAT MY COMIC BOOK YOU'RE READING?
COMIX
HOW MANY TIMES DO I HAVE TO TELL YOU TO LEAVE MY THINGS ALONE?!
IF I CATCH YOU WITH ANOTHER ONE OF MY COMIC BOOKS, I'LL CHASE YOU CLEAR OUT OF THE COUNTRY!
...BUT I GOT OVER IT!
SCHULZ

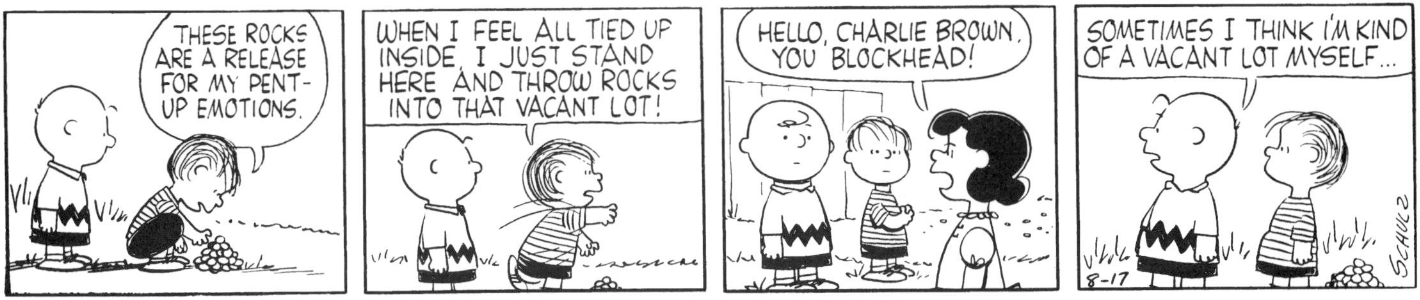
THESE ROCKS ARE A RELEASE FOR MY PENT-UP EMOTIONS.
WHEN I FEEL ALL TIED UP INSIDE, I JUST STAND HERE AND THROW ROCKS INTO THAT VACANT LOT!
HELLO, CHARLIE BROWN, YOU BLOCKHEAD!
SOMETIMES I THINK I'M KIND OF A VACANT LOT MYSELF...
8-17
SCHULZ

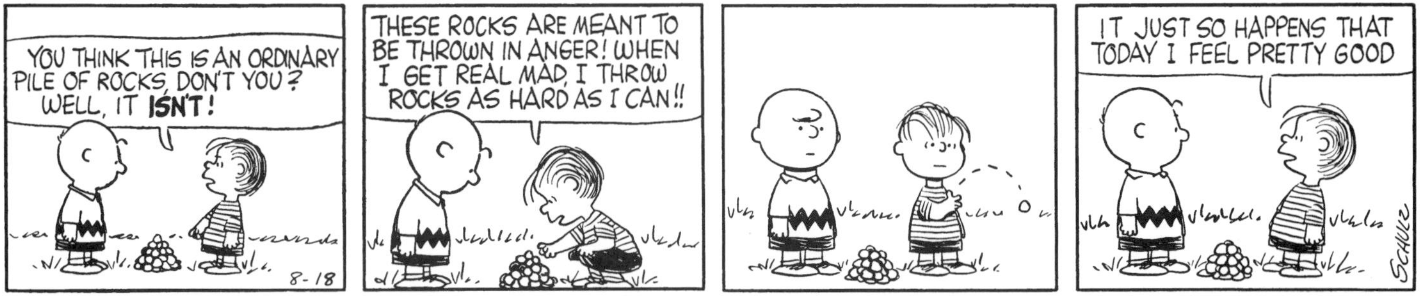
YOU THINK THIS IS AN ORDINARY PILE OF ROCKS, DON'T YOU? WELL, IT **ISN'T**!
8-18
THESE ROCKS ARE MEANT TO BE THROWN IN ANGER! WHEN I GET REAL MAD, I THROW ROCKS AS HARD AS I CAN!!
IT JUST SO HAPPENS THAT TODAY I FEEL PRETTY GOOD
SCHULZ

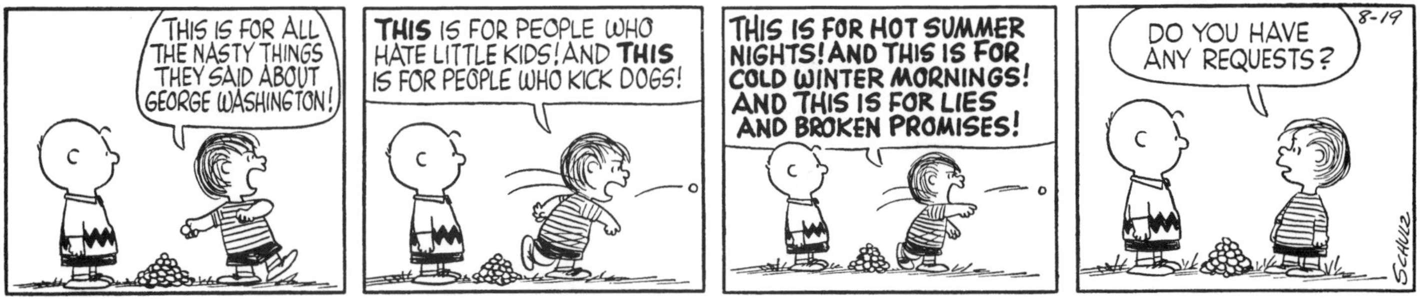
THIS IS FOR ALL THE NASTY THINGS THEY SAID ABOUT GEORGE WASHINGTON!
THIS IS FOR PEOPLE WHO HATE LITTLE KIDS! AND **THIS** IS FOR PEOPLE WHO KICK DOGS!
THIS IS FOR HOT SUMMER NIGHTS! AND THIS IS FOR COLD WINTER MORNINGS! AND THIS IS FOR LIES AND BROKEN PROMISES!
SCHULZ
8-19
DO YOU HAVE ANY REQUESTS?
SCHULZ

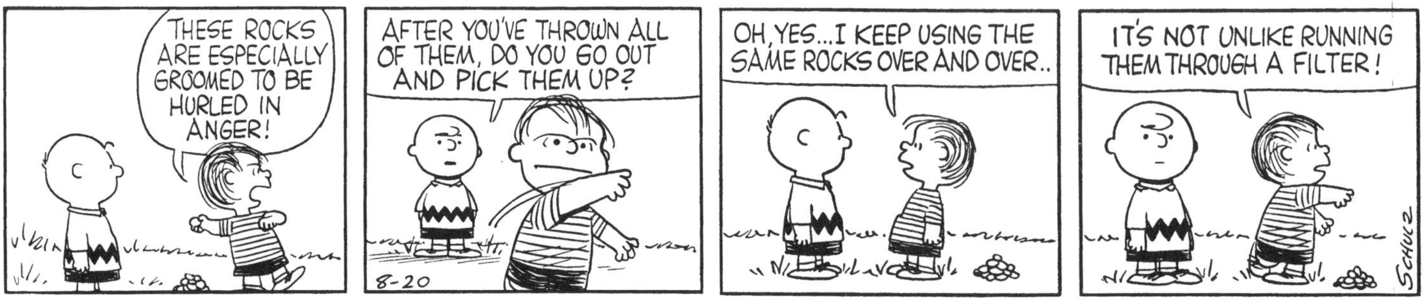
THESE ROCKS ARE ESPECIALLY GROOMED TO BE HURLED IN ANGER!
AFTER YOU'VE THROWN ALL OF THEM, DO YOU GO OUT AND PICK THEM UP?
8-20
OH, YES...I KEEP USING THE SAME ROCKS OVER AND OVER..
IT'S NOT UNLIKE RUNNING THEM THROUGH A FILTER!
SCHULZ

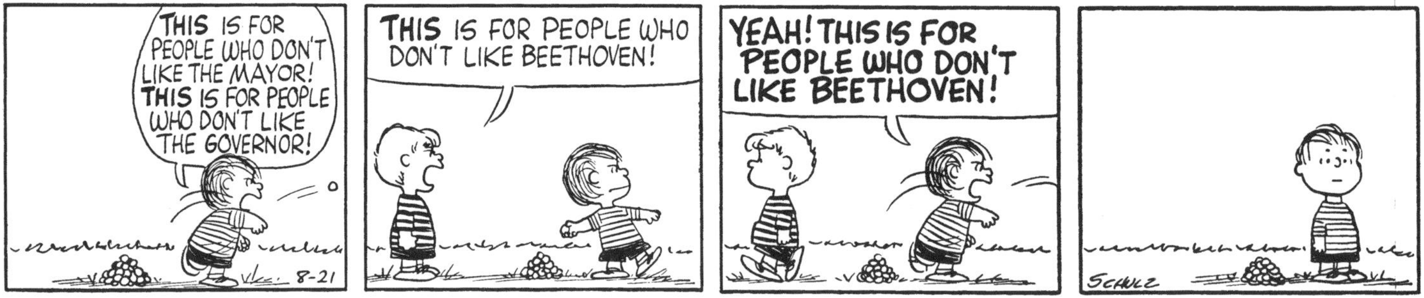
THIS IS FOR PEOPLE WHO DON'T LIKE THE MAYOR! THIS IS FOR PEOPLE WHO DON'T LIKE THE GOVERNOR!
8-21
THIS IS FOR PEOPLE WHO DON'T LIKE BEETHOVEN!
YEAH! THIS IS FOR PEOPLE WHO DON'T LIKE BEETHOVEN!
SCHULZ

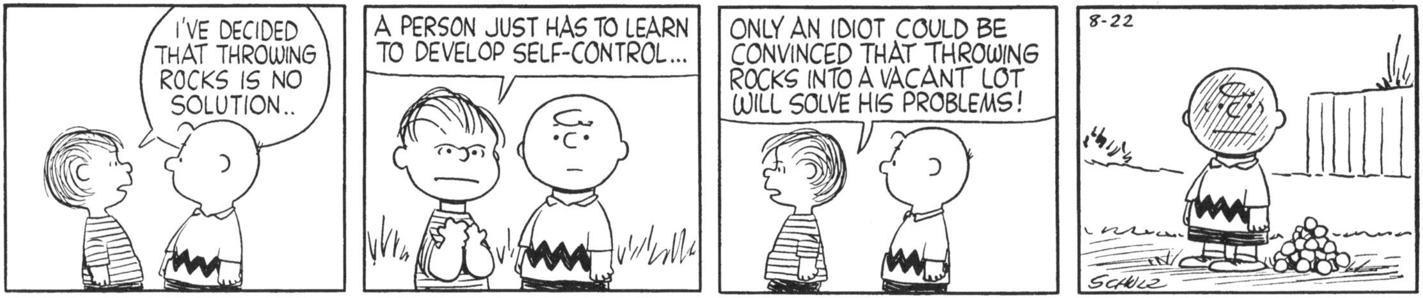
I'VE DECIDED THAT THROWING ROCKS IS NO SOLUTION..
A PERSON JUST HAS TO LEARN TO DEVELOP SELF-CONTROL...
ONLY AN IDIOT COULD BE CONVINCED THAT THROWING ROCKS INTO A VACANT LOT WILL SOLVE HIS PROBLEMS!
8-22
SCHULZ

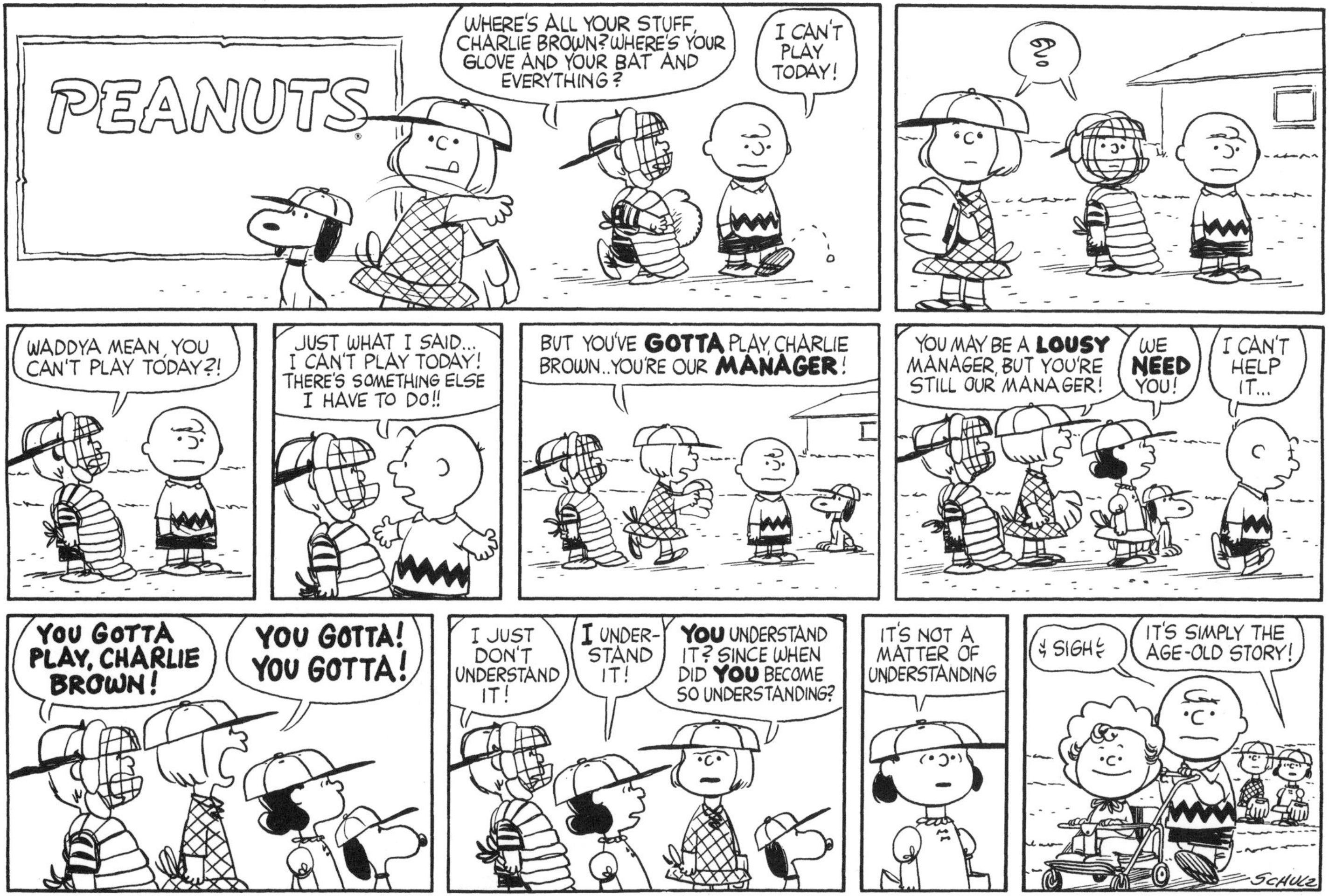
PEANUTS
WHERE'S ALL YOUR STUFF, CHARLIE BROWN? WHERE'S YOUR GLOVE AND YOUR BAT AND EVERYTHING?
I CAN'T PLAY TODAY!
WADDYA MEAN, YOU CAN'T PLAY TODAY?!
JUST WHAT I SAID... I CAN'T PLAY TODAY! THERE'S SOMETHING ELSE I HAVE TO DO!!
BUT YOU'VE GOTTA PLAY, CHARLIE BROWN.. YOU'RE OUR MANAGER!
YOU MAY BE A LOUSY MANAGER, BUT YOU'RE STILL OUR MANAGER!
WE NEED YOU!
I CAN'T HELP IT...
YOU GOTTA PLAY, CHARLIE BROWN!
YOU GOTTA! YOU GOTTA!
I JUST DON'T UNDERSTAND IT!
I UNDERSTAND IT!
YOU UNDERSTAND IT? SINCE WHEN DID YOU BECOME SO UNDERSTANDING?
IT'S NOT A MATTER OF UNDERSTANDING
SIGH
IT'S SIMPLY THE AGE-OLD STORY!
SCHULZ

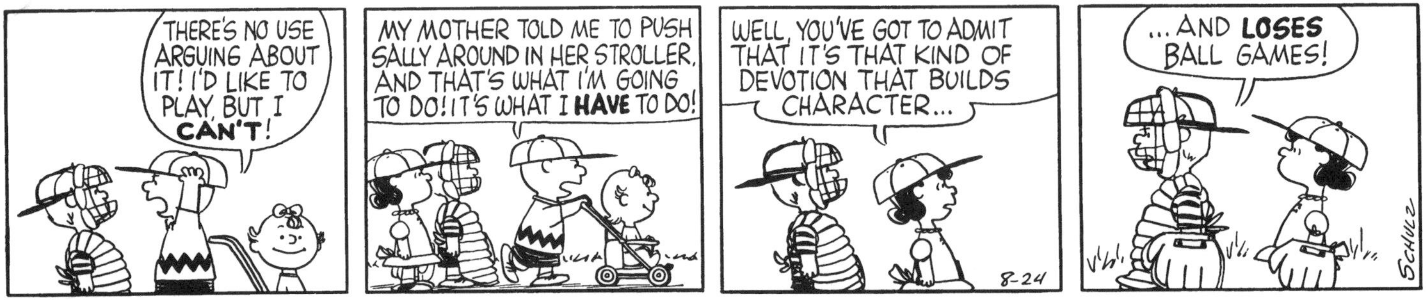
THERE'S NO USE ARGUING ABOUT IT! I'D LIKE TO PLAY, BUT I **CAN'T**!
MY MOTHER TOLD ME TO PUSH SALLY AROUND IN HER STROLLER, AND THAT'S WHAT I'M GOING TO DO! IT'S WHAT I **HAVE** TO DO!
WELL, YOU'VE GOT TO ADMIT THAT IT'S THAT KIND OF DEVOTION THAT BUILDS CHARACTER...
...AND **LOSES** BALL GAMES!
8-24
SCHULZ

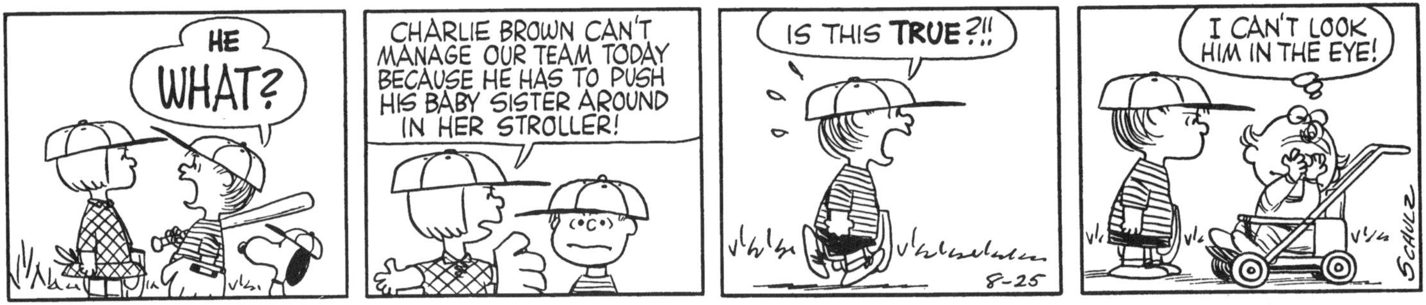
HE WHAT?
CHARLIE BROWN CAN'T MANAGE OUR TEAM TODAY BECAUSE HE HAS TO PUSH HIS BABY SISTER AROUND IN HER STROLLER!
IS THIS **TRUE**?!!
I CAN'T LOOK HIM IN THE EYE!
8-25
SCHULZ

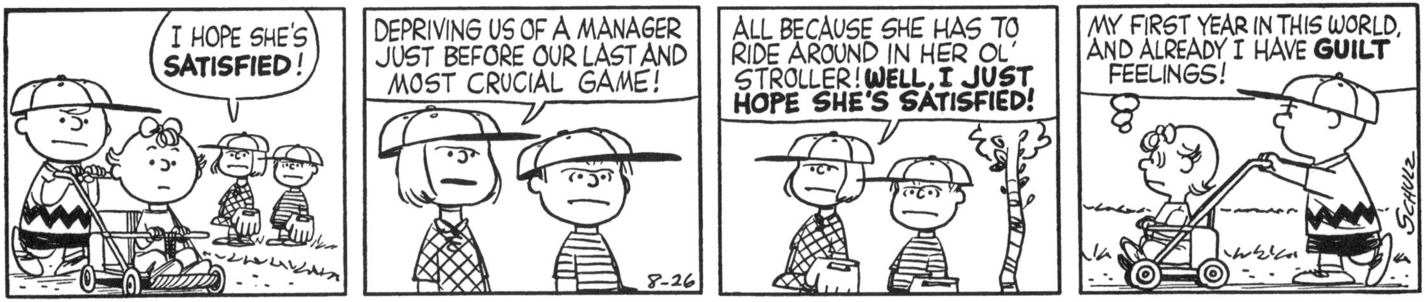
I HOPE SHE'S **SATISFIED**!
DEPRIVING US OF A MANAGER JUST BEFORE OUR LAST AND MOST CRUCIAL GAME!
ALL BECAUSE SHE HAS TO RIDE AROUND IN HER OL' STROLLER! **WELL, I JUST HOPE SHE'S SATISFIED!**
MY FIRST YEAR IN THIS WORLD, AND ALREADY I HAVE **GUILT** FEELINGS!
8-26
SCHULZ

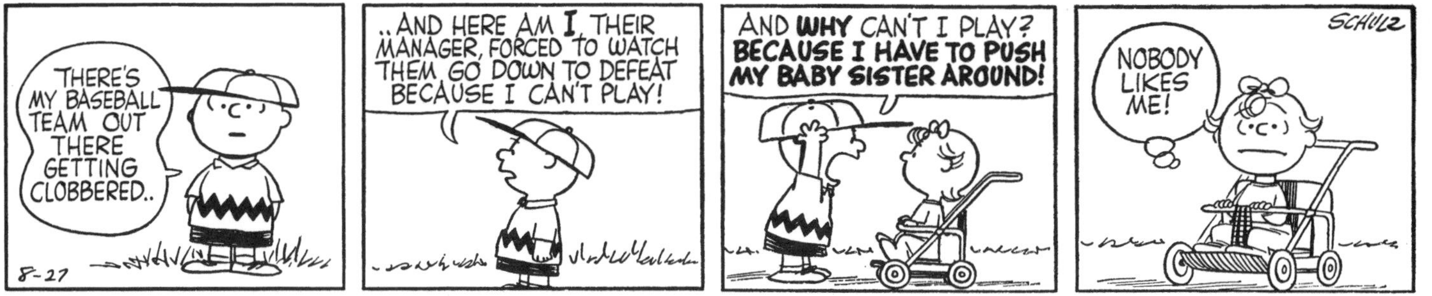
8-27
THERE'S MY BASEBALL TEAM OUT THERE GETTING CLOBBERED..
..AND HERE AM I, THEIR MANAGER, FORCED TO WATCH THEM GO DOWN TO DEFEAT BECAUSE I CAN'T PLAY!
AND WHY CAN'T I PLAY? BECAUSE I HAVE TO PUSH MY BABY SISTER AROUND!
SCHULZ
NOBODY LIKES ME!

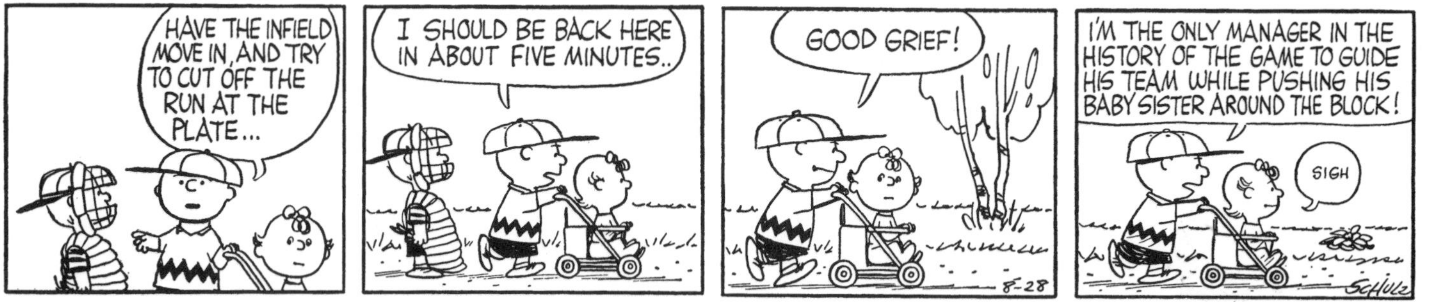
HAVE THE INFIELD MOVE IN, AND TRY TO CUT OFF THE RUN AT THE PLATE...
I SHOULD BE BACK HERE IN ABOUT FIVE MINUTES..
GOOD GRIEF!
8-28
I'M THE ONLY MANAGER IN THE HISTORY OF THE GAME TO GUIDE HIS TEAM WHILE PUSHING HIS BABY SISTER AROUND THE BLOCK!
SIGH
SCHULZ

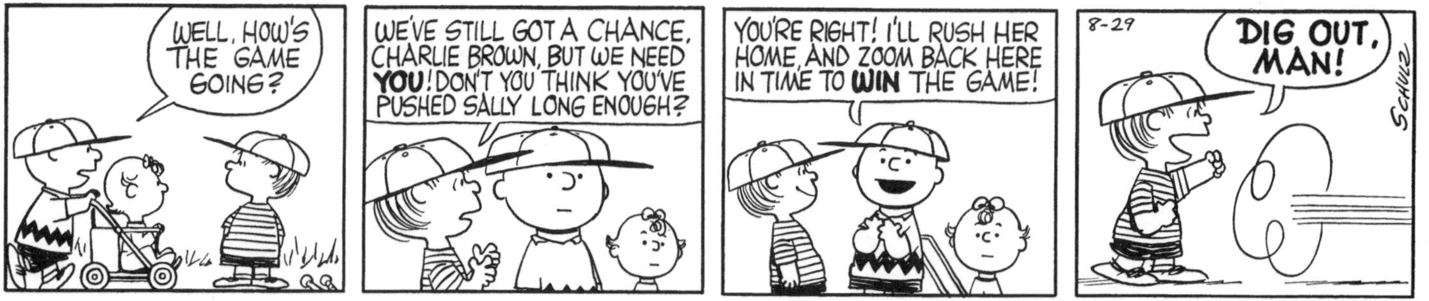
WELL, HOW'S THE GAME GOING?
WE'VE STILL GOT A CHANCE, CHARLIE BROWN, BUT WE NEED YOU! DON'T YOU THINK YOU'VE PUSHED SALLY LONG ENOUGH?
YOU'RE RIGHT! I'LL RUSH HER HOME, AND ZOOM BACK HERE IN TIME TO WIN THE GAME!
8-29
DIG OUT, MAN!
SCHULZ

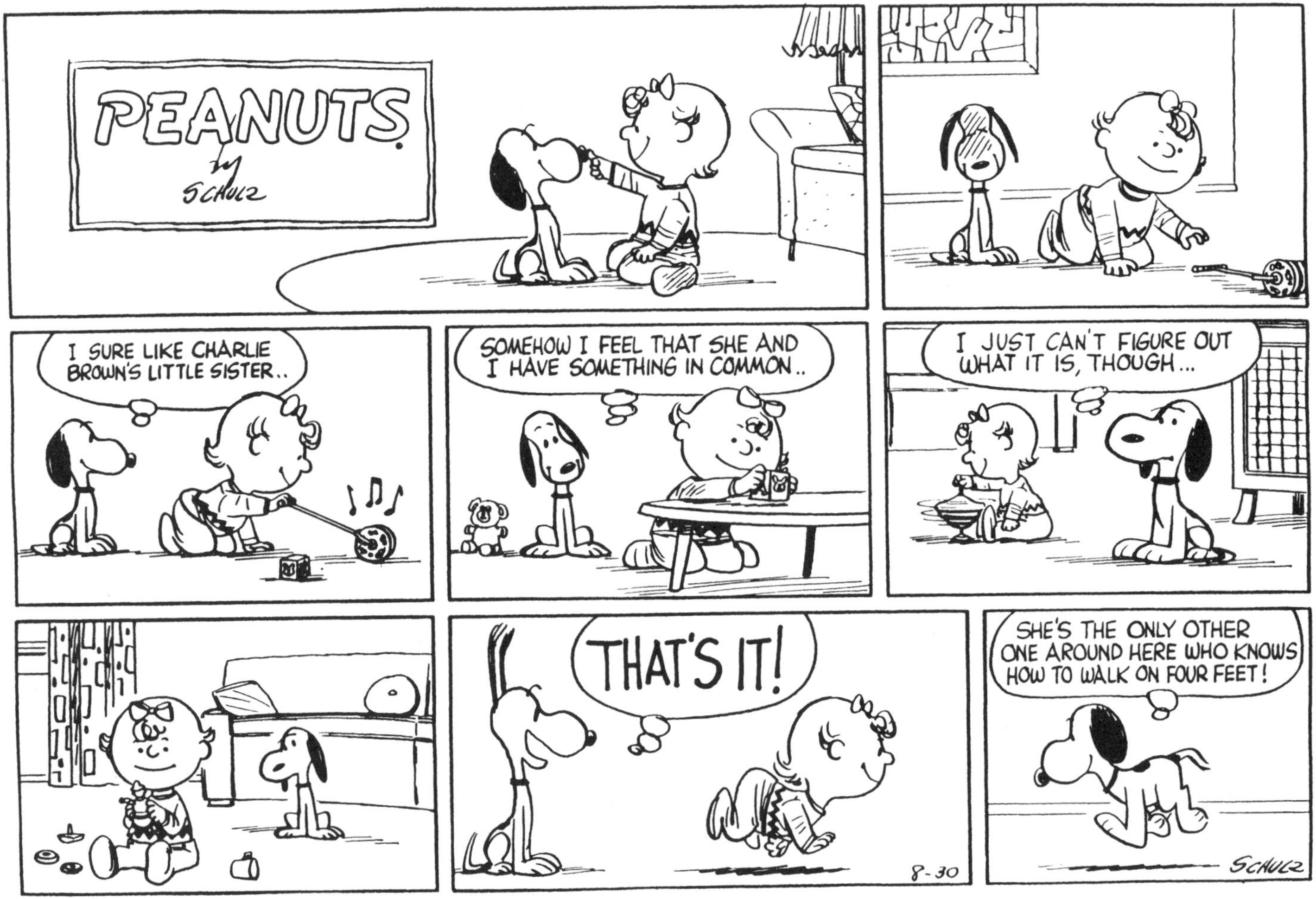
PEANUTS
by SCHULZ
I SURE LIKE CHARLIE BROWN'S LITTLE SISTER..
SOMEHOW I FEEL THAT SHE AND I HAVE SOMETHING IN COMMON..
I JUST CAN'T FIGURE OUT WHAT IT IS, THOUGH...
THAT'S IT!
8-30
SHE'S THE ONLY OTHER ONE AROUND HERE WHO KNOWS HOW TO WALK ON FOUR FEET!
SCHULZ

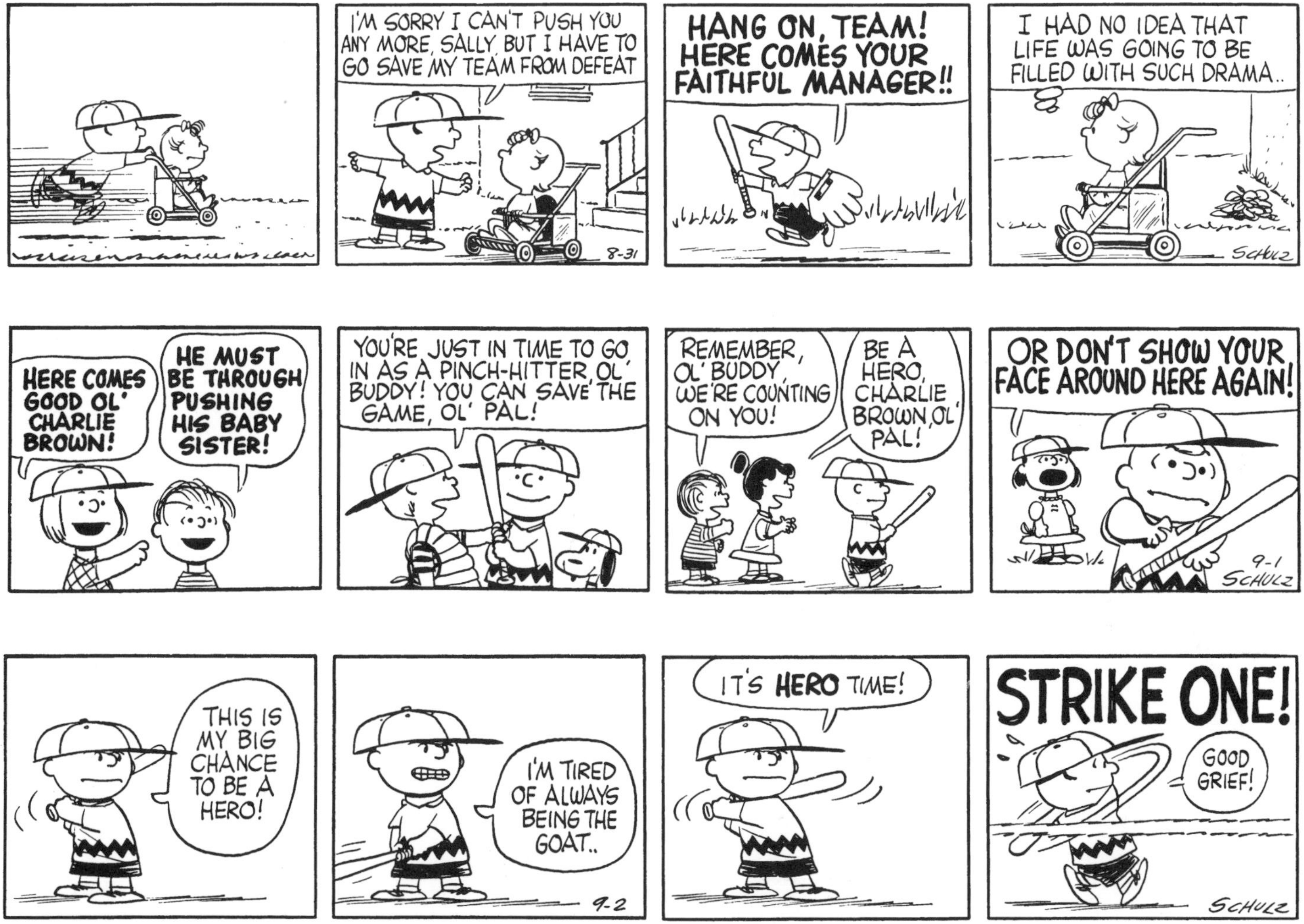
I'M SORRY I CAN'T PUSH YOU ANY MORE, SALLY, BUT I HAVE TO GO SAVE MY TEAM FROM DEFEAT
8-31
HANG ON, TEAM! HERE COMES YOUR FAITHFUL MANAGER!!
I HAD NO IDEA THAT LIFE WAS GOING TO BE FILLED WITH SUCH DRAMA..
SCHULZ
HERE COMES GOOD OL' CHARLIE BROWN!
HE MUST BE THROUGH PUSHING HIS BABY SISTER!
YOU'RE JUST IN TIME TO GO IN AS A PINCH-HITTER, OL' BUDDY! YOU CAN SAVE THE GAME, OL' PAL!
REMEMBER, OL' BUDDY, WE'RE COUNTING ON YOU!
BE A HERO, CHARLIE BROWN, OL' PAL!
OR DON'T SHOW YOUR FACE AROUND HERE AGAIN!
9-1
SCHULZ
THIS IS MY BIG CHANCE TO BE A HERO!
I'M TIRED OF ALWAYS BEING THE GOAT..
9-2
IT'S HERO TIME!
STRIKE ONE!
GOOD GRIEF!
SCHULZ

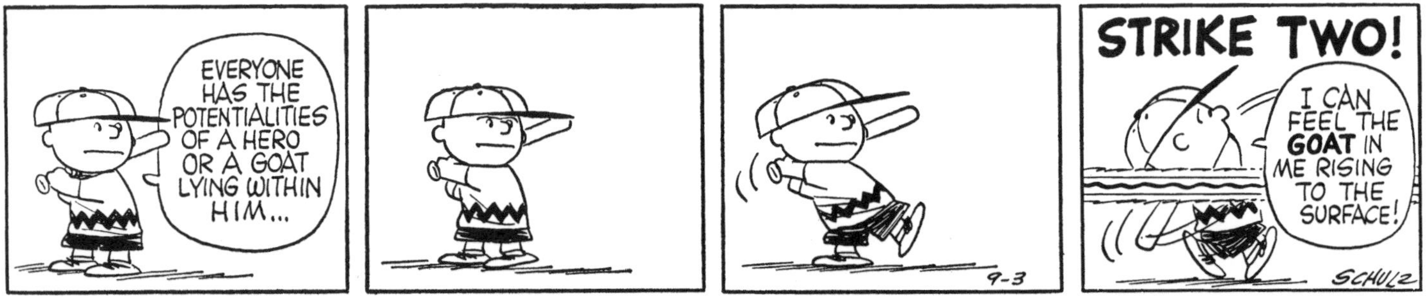
EVERYONE HAS THE POTENTIALITIES OF A HERO OR A GOAT LYING WITHIN HIM...
9-3
STRIKE TWO!
I CAN FEEL THE **GOAT** IN ME RISING TO THE SURFACE!
SCHULZ

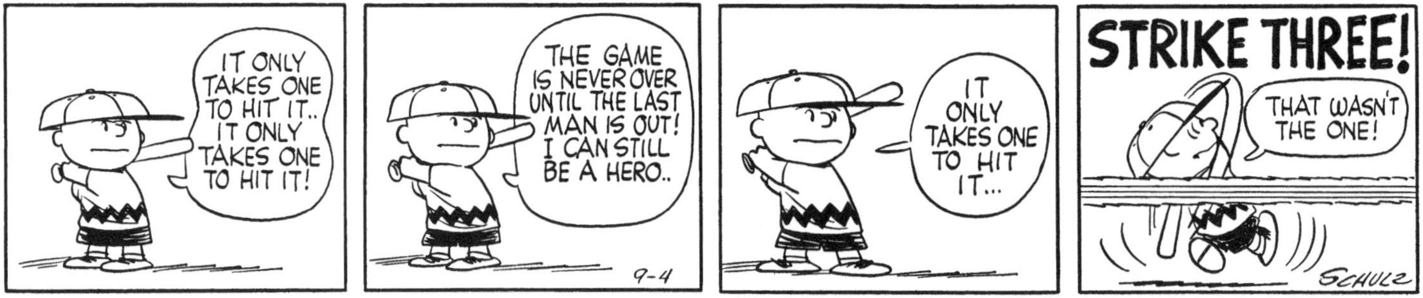
IT ONLY TAKES ONE TO HIT IT.. IT ONLY TAKES ONE TO HIT IT!
THE GAME IS NEVER OVER UNTIL THE LAST MAN IS OUT! I CAN STILL BE A HERO..
9-4
IT ONLY TAKES ONE TO HIT IT...
STRIKE THREE!
THAT WASN'T THE ONE!
SCHULZ

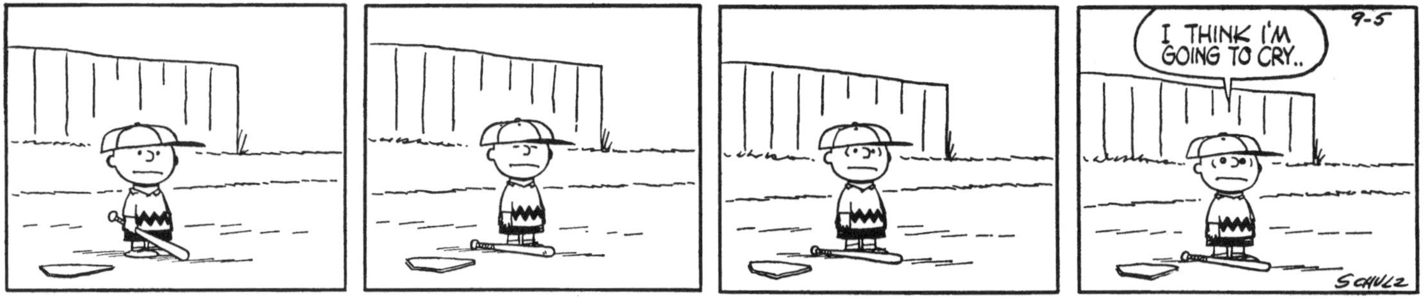
9-5
I THINK I'M GOING TO CRY..
SCHULZ

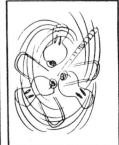

THUS ENDETH THE CROQUET GAME!

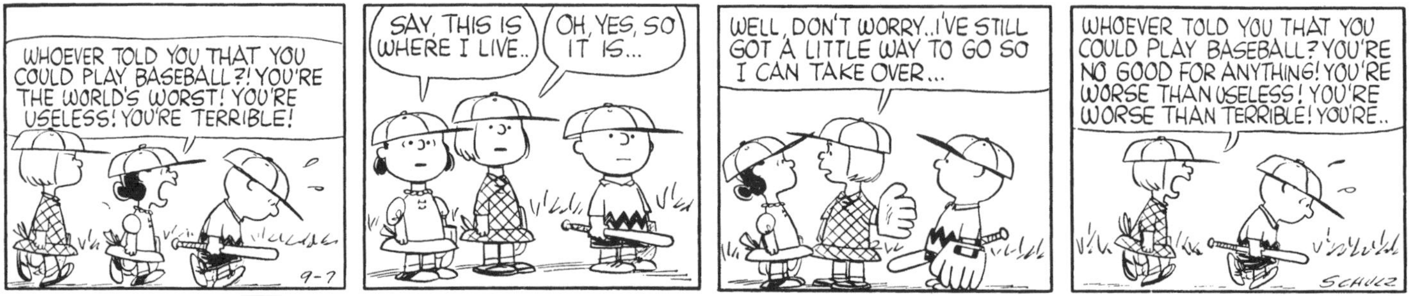
WHOEVER TOLD YOU THAT YOU COULD PLAY BASEBALL?! YOU'RE THE WORLD'S WORST! YOU'RE USELESS! YOU'RE TERRIBLE!
9-7
SAY, THIS IS WHERE I LIVE..
OH, YES, SO IT IS...
WELL, DON'T WORRY..I'VE STILL GOT A LITTLE WAY TO GO SO I CAN TAKE OVER...
WHOEVER TOLD YOU THAT YOU COULD PLAY BASEBALL? YOU'RE NO GOOD FOR ANYTHING! YOU'RE WORSE THAN USELESS! YOU'RE WORSE THAN TERRIBLE! YOU'RE..
SCHULZ

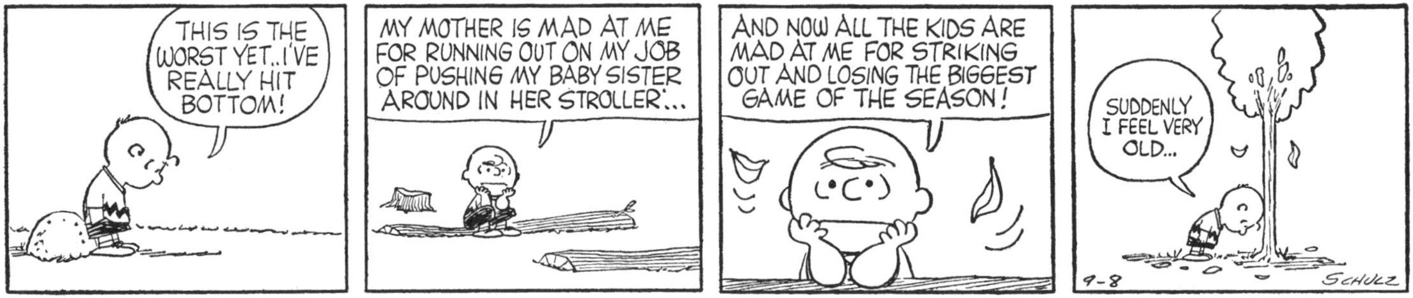
THIS IS THE WORST YET..I'VE REALLY HIT BOTTOM!
MY MOTHER IS MAD AT ME FOR RUNNING OUT ON MY JOB OF PUSHING MY BABY SISTER AROUND IN HER STROLLER...
AND NOW ALL THE KIDS ARE MAD AT ME FOR STRIKING OUT AND LOSING THE BIGGEST GAME OF THE SEASON!
SUDDENLY I FEEL VERY OLD...
9-8
SCHULZ

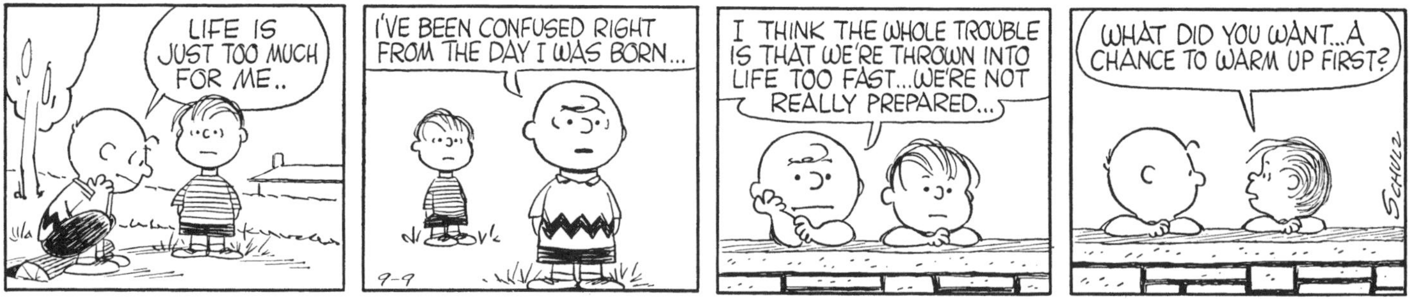
LIFE IS JUST TOO MUCH FOR ME..
I'VE BEEN CONFUSED RIGHT FROM THE DAY I WAS BORN...
9-9
I THINK THE WHOLE TROUBLE IS THAT WE'RE THROWN INTO LIFE TOO FAST...WE'RE NOT REALLY PREPARED...
WHAT DID YOU WANT...A CHANCE TO WARM UP FIRST?
SCHULZ

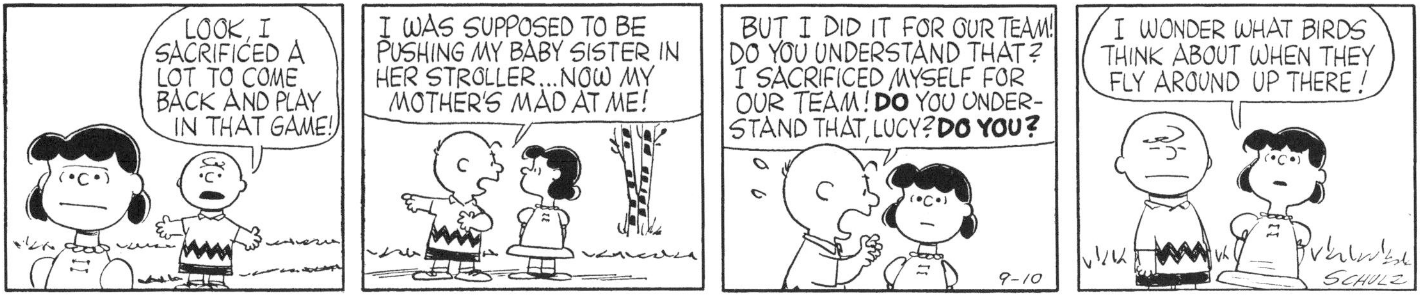
LOOK, I SACRIFICED A LOT TO COME BACK AND PLAY IN THAT GAME!
I WAS SUPPOSED TO BE PUSHING MY BABY SISTER IN HER STROLLER...NOW MY MOTHER'S MAD AT ME!
BUT I DID IT FOR OUR TEAM! DO YOU UNDERSTAND THAT? I SACRIFICED MYSELF FOR OUR TEAM! DO YOU UNDERSTAND THAT, LUCY? DO YOU?
9-10
I WONDER WHAT BIRDS THINK ABOUT WHEN THEY FLY AROUND UP THERE!
SCHULZ

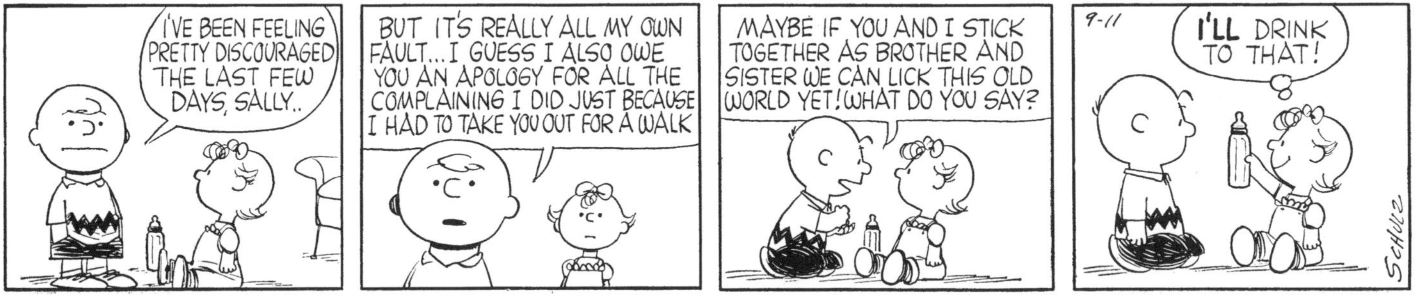
I'VE BEEN FEELING PRETTY DISCOURAGED THE LAST FEW DAYS, SALLY..
BUT IT'S REALLY ALL MY OWN FAULT...I GUESS I ALSO OWE YOU AN APOLOGY FOR ALL THE COMPLAINING I DID JUST BECAUSE I HAD TO TAKE YOU OUT FOR A WALK
MAYBE IF YOU AND I STICK TOGETHER AS BROTHER AND SISTER WE CAN LICK THIS OLD WORLD YET! WHAT DO YOU SAY?
9-11
I'LL DRINK TO THAT!
SCHULZ

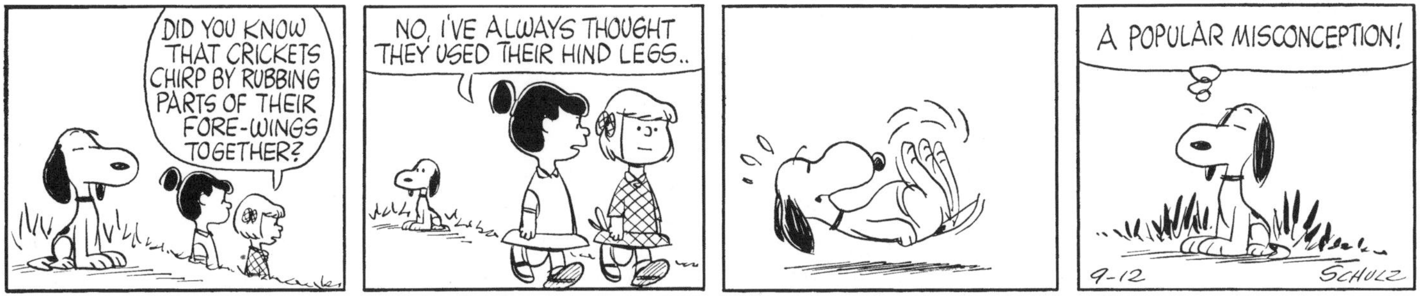
DID YOU KNOW THAT CRICKETS CHIRP BY RUBBING PARTS OF THEIR FORE-WINGS TOGETHER?
NO, I'VE ALWAYS THOUGHT THEY USED THEIR HIND LEGS..
A POPULAR MISCONCEPTION!
9-12
SCHULZ

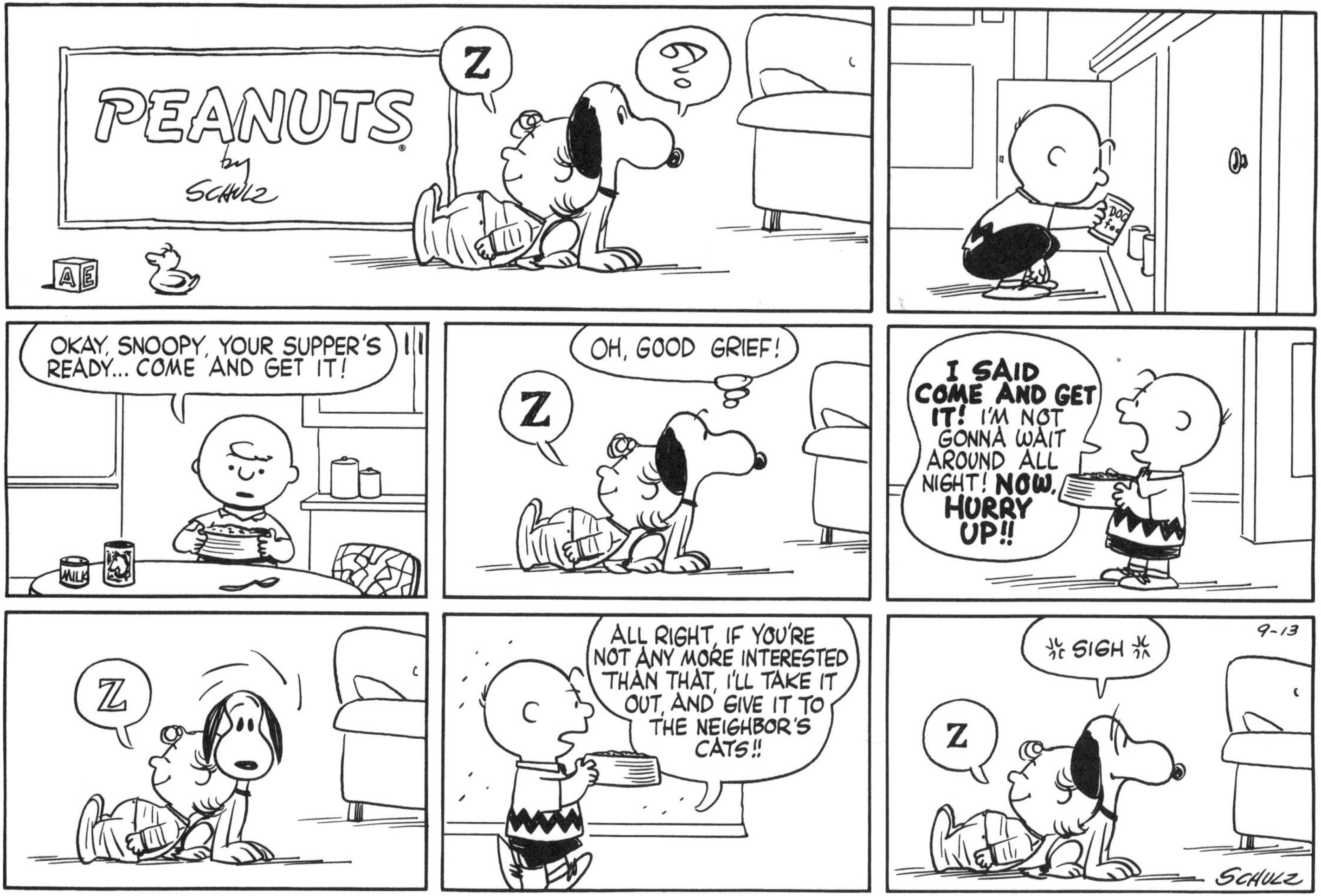
PEANUTS
by SCHULZ
Z
A E
DOG FOOD
OKAY, SNOOPY, YOUR SUPPER'S READY... COME AND GET IT!
MILK
Z
OH, GOOD GRIEF!
I SAID COME AND GET IT! I'M NOT GONNA WAIT AROUND ALL NIGHT! NOW, HURRY UP!!
Z
ALL RIGHT, IF YOU'RE NOT ANY MORE INTERESTED THAN THAT, I'LL TAKE IT OUT, AND GIVE IT TO THE NEIGHBOR'S CATS!!
9-13
SIGH
Z
SCHULZ

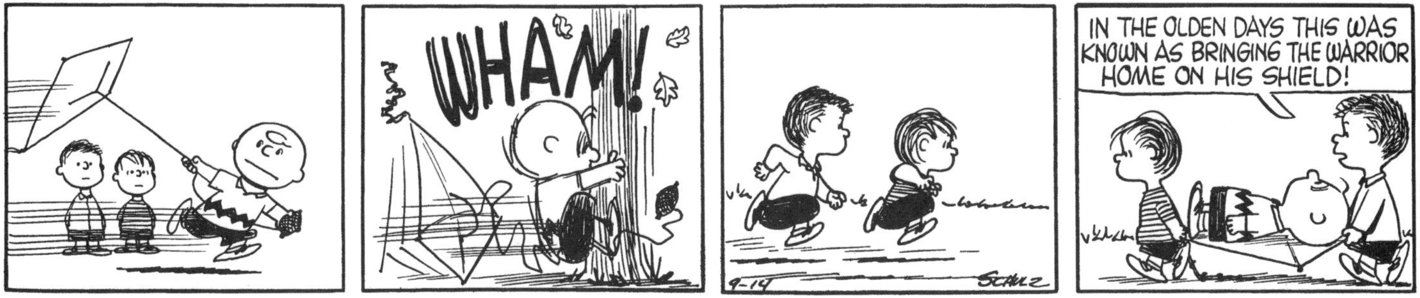
WHAM!
9-14
SCHULZ
IN THE OLDEN DAYS THIS WAS KNOWN AS BRINGING THE WARRIOR HOME ON HIS SHIELD!

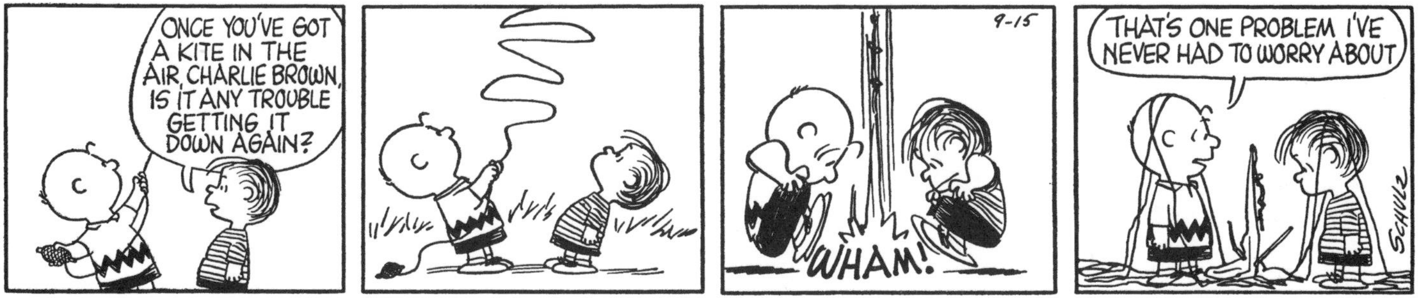
ONCE YOU'VE GOT A KITE IN THE AIR, CHARLIE BROWN, IS IT ANY TROUBLE GETTING IT DOWN AGAIN?
9-15
WHAM!
THAT'S ONE PROBLEM I'VE NEVER HAD TO WORRY ABOUT
SCHULZ

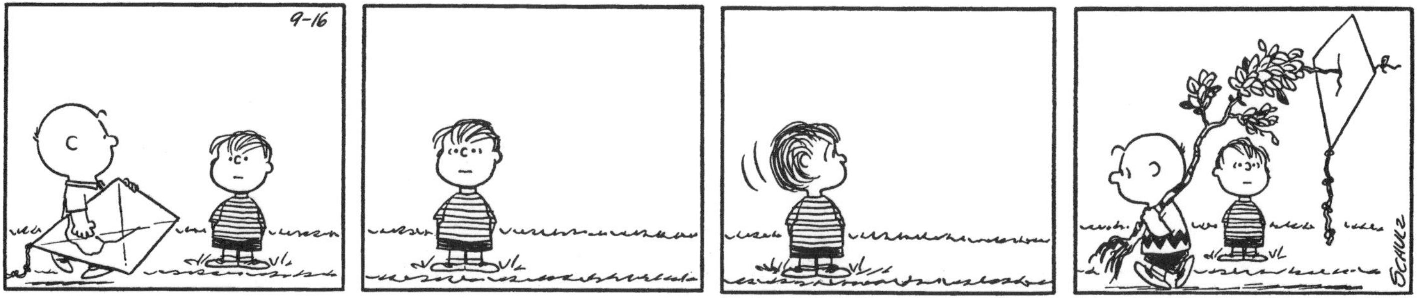
9-16
SCHULZ

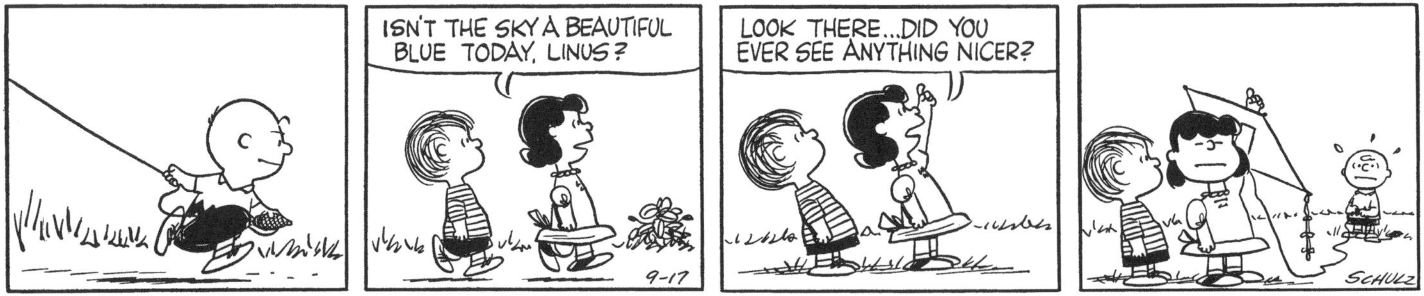
ISN'T THE SKY A BEAUTIFUL BLUE TODAY, LINUS?
LOOK THERE...DID YOU EVER SEE ANYTHING NICER?

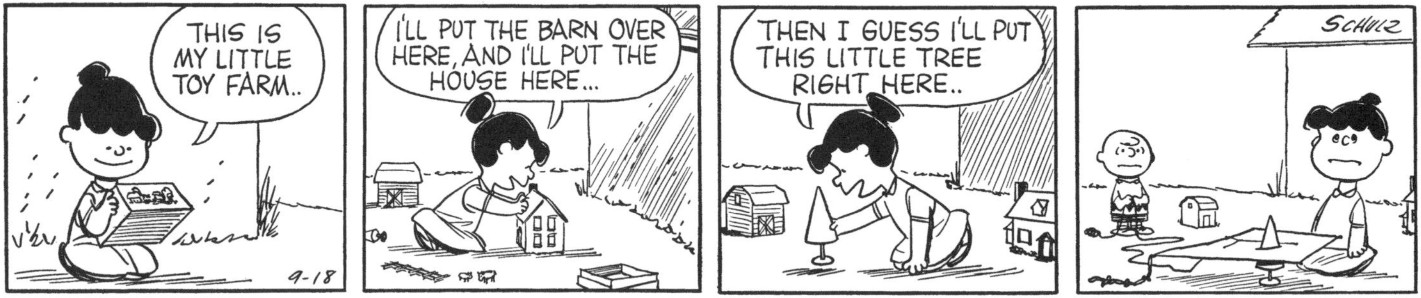
THIS IS MY LITTLE TOY FARM..
I'LL PUT THE BARN OVER HERE, AND I'LL PUT THE HOUSE HERE...
THEN I GUESS I'LL PUT THIS LITTLE TREE RIGHT HERE..

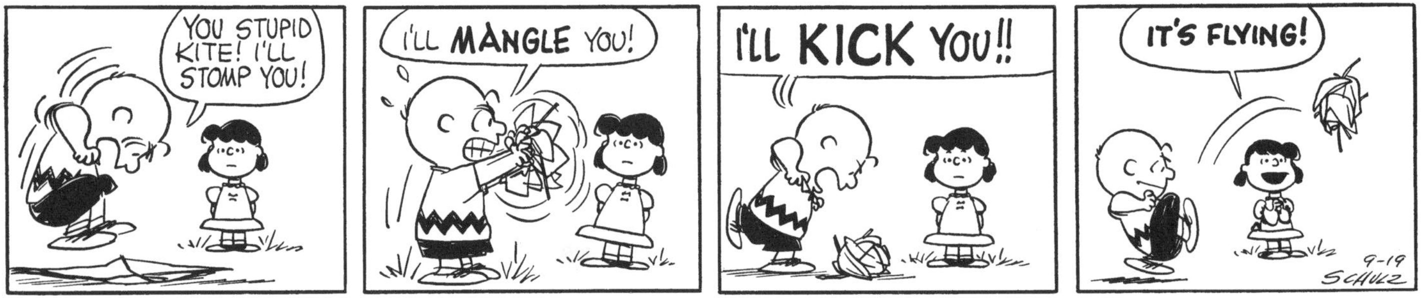
YOU STUPID KITE! I'LL STOMP YOU!
I'LL MANGLE YOU!
I'LL KICK YOU!!
IT'S FLYING!

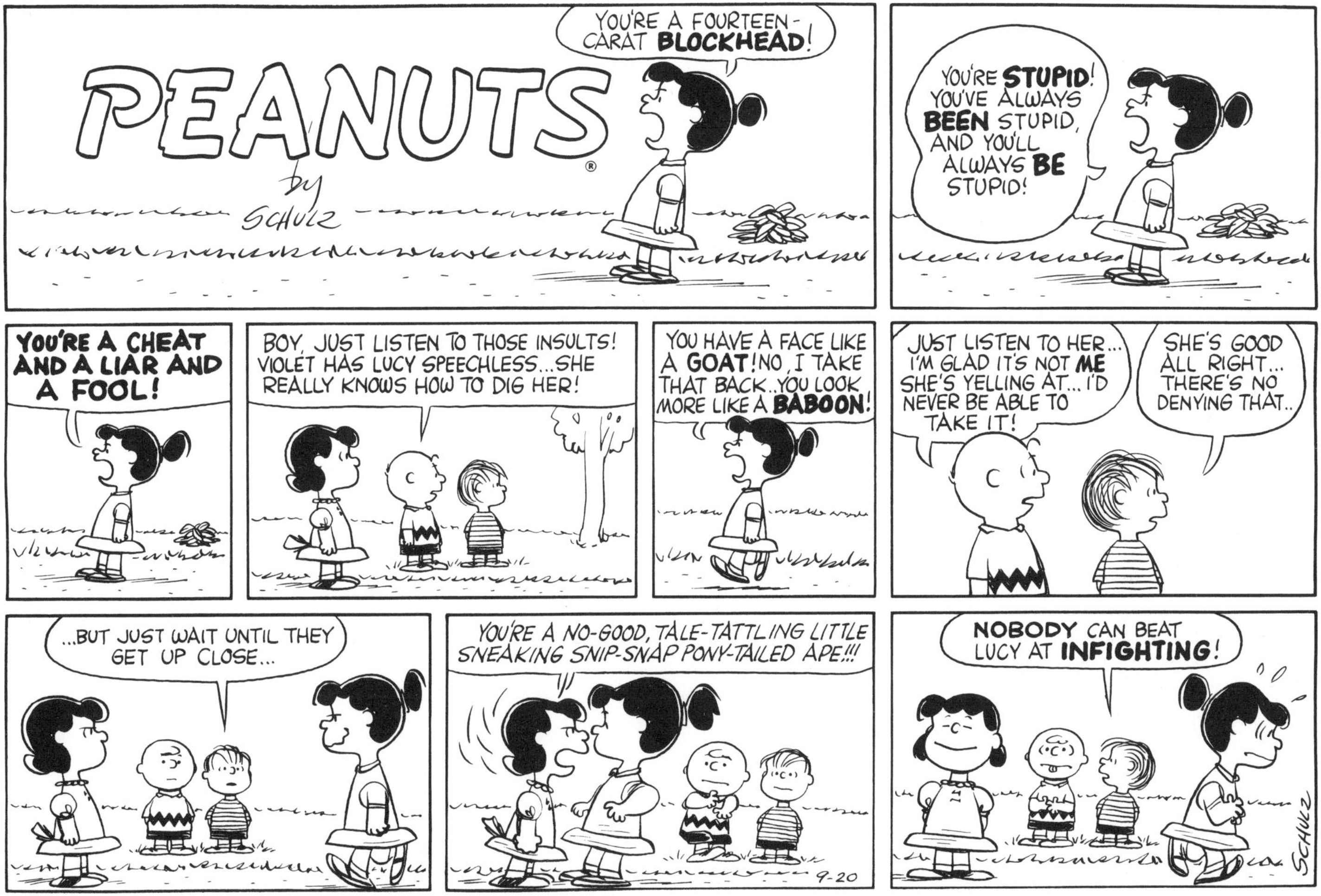
PEANUTS
by SCHULZ
YOU'RE A FOURTEEN-CARAT BLOCKHEAD!
YOU'RE STUPID! YOU'VE ALWAYS BEEN STUPID, AND YOU'LL ALWAYS BE STUPID!
YOU'RE A CHEAT AND A LIAR AND A FOOL!
BOY, JUST LISTEN TO THOSE INSULTS! VIOLET HAS LUCY SPEECHLESS...SHE REALLY KNOWS HOW TO DIG HER!
YOU HAVE A FACE LIKE A GOAT! NO, I TAKE THAT BACK..YOU LOOK MORE LIKE A BABOON!
JUST LISTEN TO HER... I'M GLAD IT'S NOT ME SHE'S YELLING AT... I'D NEVER BE ABLE TO TAKE IT!
SHE'S GOOD ALL RIGHT... THERE'S NO DENYING THAT..
...BUT JUST WAIT UNTIL THEY GET UP CLOSE...
YOU'RE A NO-GOOD, TALE-TATTLING LITTLE SNEAKING SNIP-SNAP PONY-TAILED APE!!!
9-20
NOBODY CAN BEAT LUCY AT INFIGHTING!
SCHULZ

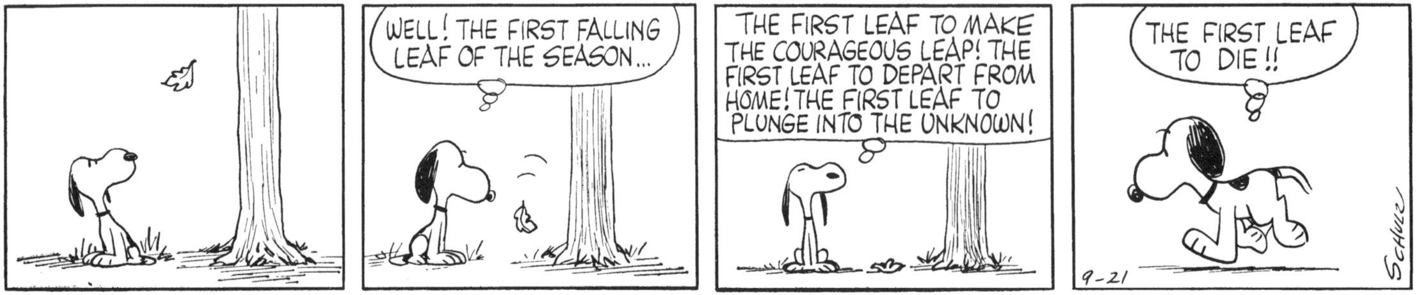
WELL! THE FIRST FALLING LEAF OF THE SEASON...
THE FIRST LEAF TO MAKE THE COURAGEOUS LEAP! THE FIRST LEAF TO DEPART FROM HOME! THE FIRST LEAF TO PLUNGE INTO THE UNKNOWN!
THE FIRST LEAF TO DIE!!
9-21
SCHULZ

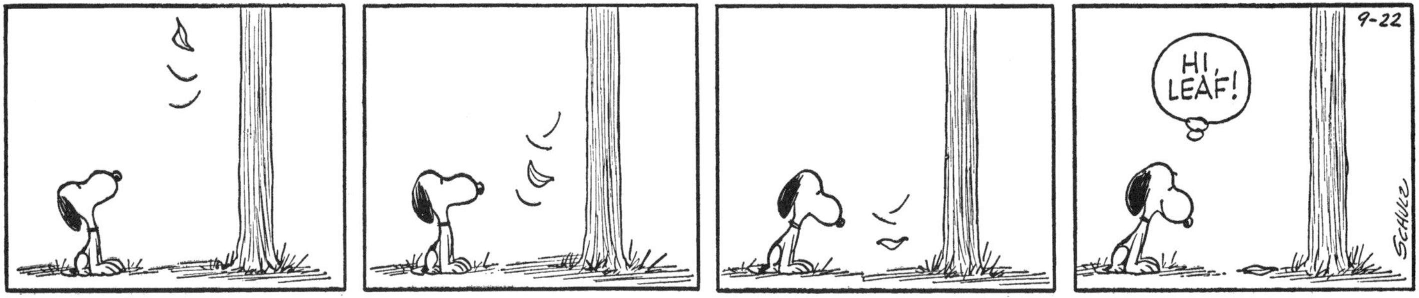
9-22
HI, LEAF!
SCHULZ

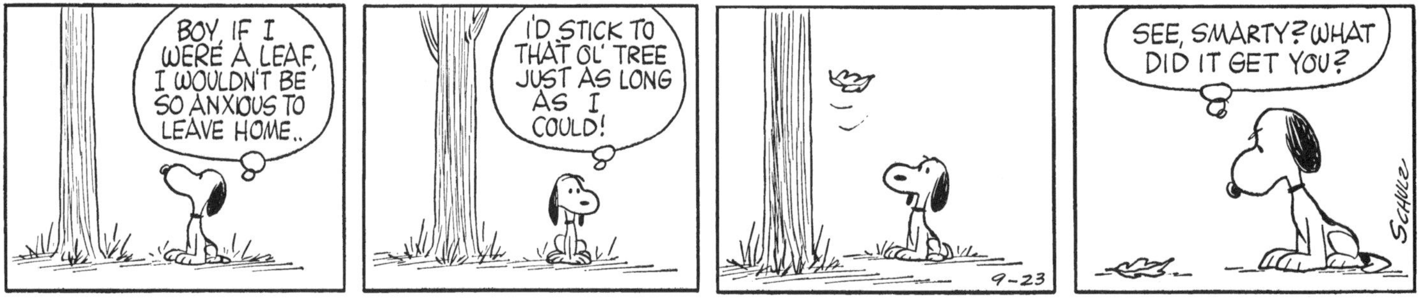
BOY, IF I WERE A LEAF, I WOULDN'T BE SO ANXIOUS TO LEAVE HOME..
I'D STICK TO THAT OL' TREE JUST AS LONG AS I COULD!
9-23
SEE, SMARTY? WHAT DID IT GET YOU?
SCHULZ

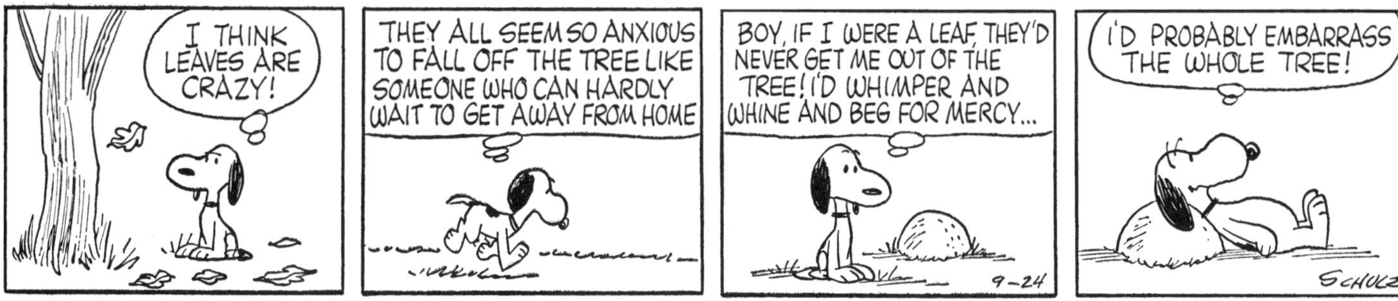
I THINK LEAVES ARE CRAZY!
THEY ALL SEEM SO ANXIOUS TO FALL OFF THE TREE LIKE SOMEONE WHO CAN HARDLY WAIT TO GET AWAY FROM HOME
BOY, IF I WERE A LEAF, THEY'D NEVER GET ME OUT OF THE TREE! I'D WHIMPER AND WHINE AND BEG FOR MERCY...
9-24
I'D PROBABLY EMBARRASS THE WHOLE TREE!
SCHULZ

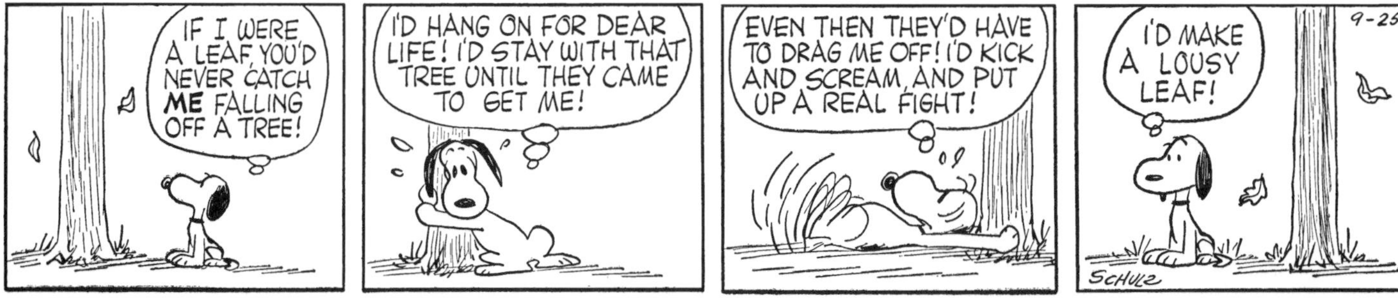
IF I WERE A LEAF, YOU'D NEVER CATCH **ME** FALLING OFF A TREE!
I'D HANG ON FOR DEAR LIFE! I'D STAY WITH THAT TREE UNTIL THEY CAME TO GET ME!
EVEN THEN THEY'D HAVE TO DRAG ME OFF! I'D KICK AND SCREAM, AND PUT UP A REAL FIGHT!
9-25
I'D MAKE A LOUSY LEAF!
SCHULZ

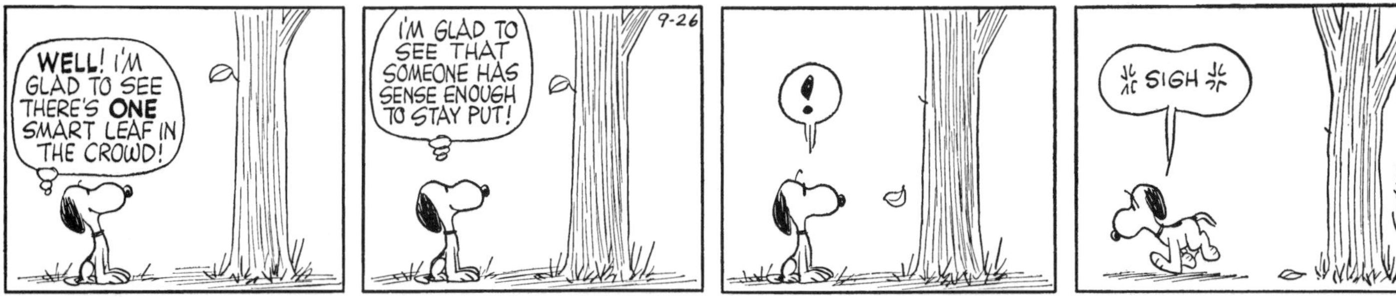
WELL! I'M GLAD TO SEE THERE'S **ONE** SMART LEAF IN THE CROWD!
9-26
I'M GLAD TO SEE THAT SOMEONE HAS SENSE ENOUGH TO STAY PUT!
!
SIGH
SCHULZ

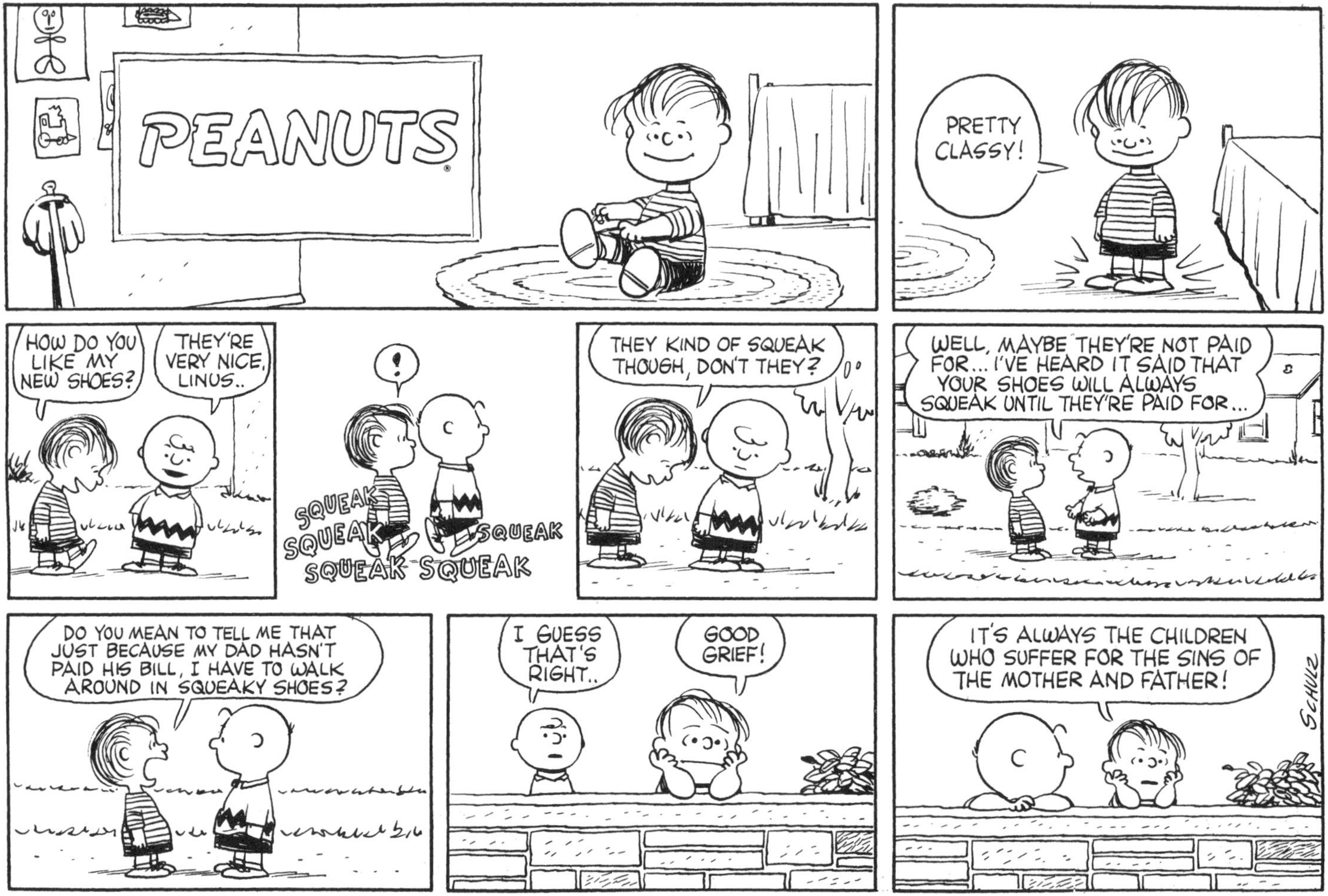
PEANUTS
PRETTY CLASSY!
HOW DO YOU LIKE MY NEW SHOES?
THEY'RE VERY NICE, LINUS..
!
SQUEAK SQUEAK SQUEAK SQUEAK SQUEAK
THEY KIND OF SQUEAK THOUGH, DON'T THEY?
WELL, MAYBE THEY'RE NOT PAID FOR... I'VE HEARD IT SAID THAT YOUR SHOES WILL ALWAYS SQUEAK UNTIL THEY'RE PAID FOR...
DO YOU MEAN TO TELL ME THAT JUST BECAUSE MY DAD HASN'T PAID HIS BILL, I HAVE TO WALK AROUND IN SQUEAKY SHOES?
I GUESS THAT'S RIGHT..
GOOD GRIEF!
IT'S ALWAYS THE CHILDREN WHO SUFFER FOR THE SINS OF THE MOTHER AND FATHER!
SCHULZ

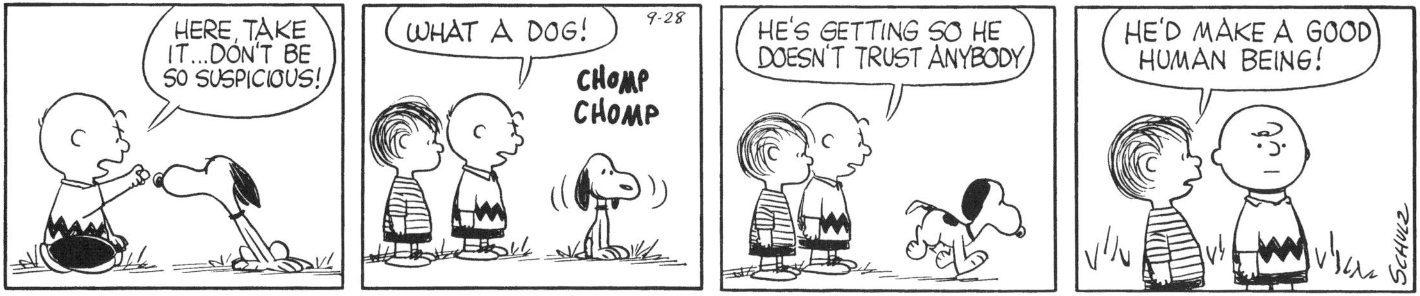
HERE, TAKE IT...DON'T BE SO SUSPICIOUS!
WHAT A DOG!
9-28
CHOMP CHOMP
HE'S GETTING SO HE DOESN'T TRUST ANYBODY
HE'D MAKE A GOOD HUMAN BEING!
SCHULZ

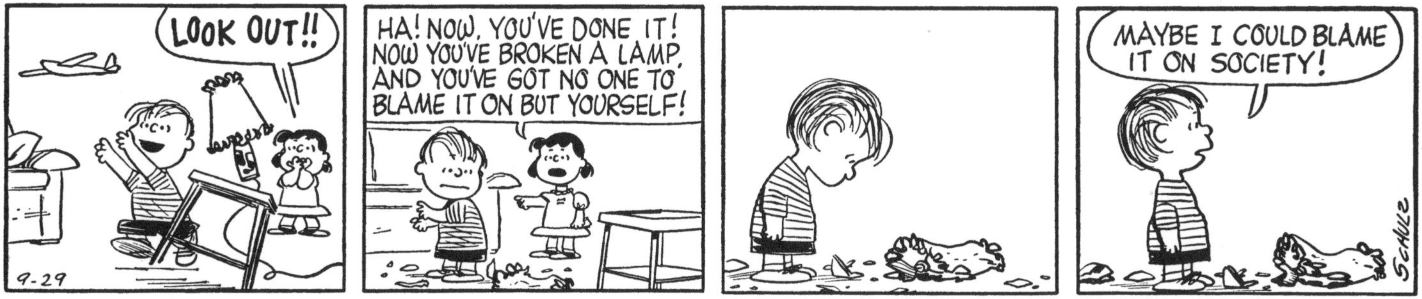
LOOK OUT!!
9-29
HA! NOW, YOU'VE DONE IT! NOW YOU'VE BROKEN A LAMP, AND YOU'VE GOT NO ONE TO BLAME IT ON BUT YOURSELF!
MAYBE I COULD BLAME IT ON SOCIETY!
SCHULZ

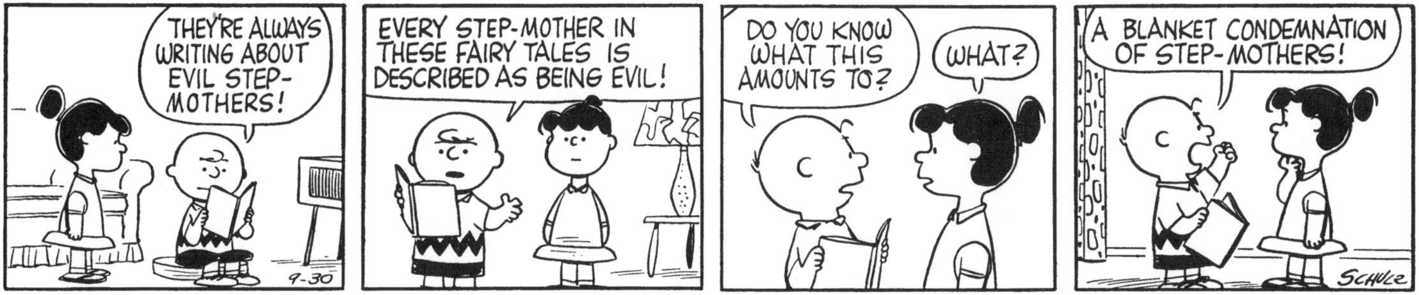
THEY'RE ALWAYS WRITING ABOUT EVIL STEP-MOTHERS!
9-30
EVERY STEP-MOTHER IN THESE FAIRY TALES IS DESCRIBED AS BEING EVIL!
DO YOU KNOW WHAT THIS AMOUNTS TO?
WHAT?
A BLANKET CONDEMNATION OF STEP-MOTHERS!
SCHULZ

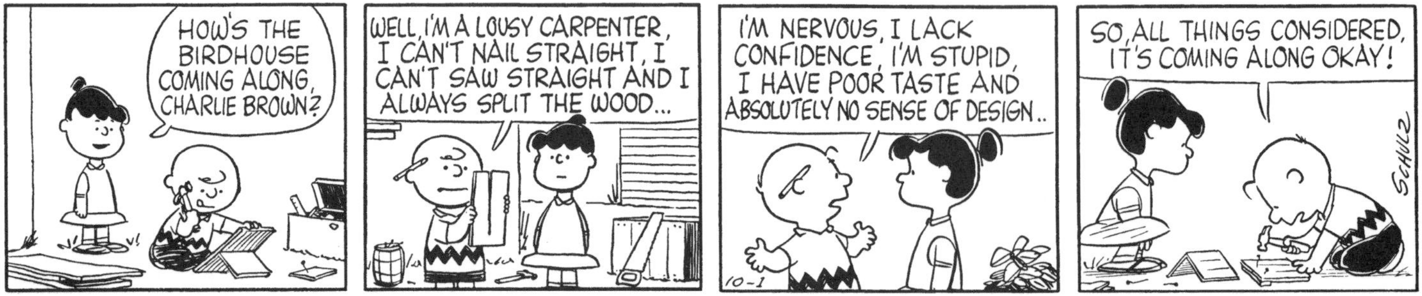
HOW'S THE BIRDHOUSE COMING ALONG, CHARLIE BROWN?
WELL, I'M A LOUSY CARPENTER, I CAN'T NAIL STRAIGHT, I CAN'T SAW STRAIGHT AND I ALWAYS SPLIT THE WOOD...
I'M NERVOUS, I LACK CONFIDENCE, I'M STUPID, I HAVE POOR TASTE AND ABSOLUTELY NO SENSE OF DESIGN..
10-1
SO, ALL THINGS CONSIDERED, IT'S COMING ALONG OKAY!
SCHULZ

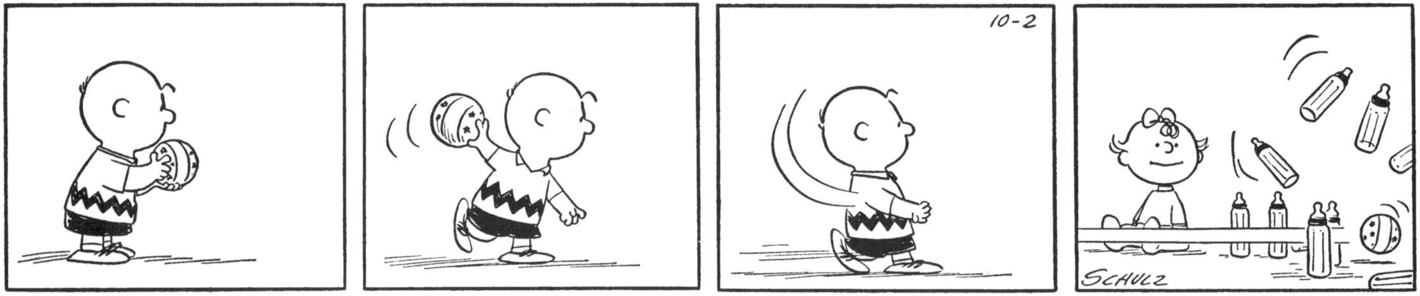
10-2
SCHULZ

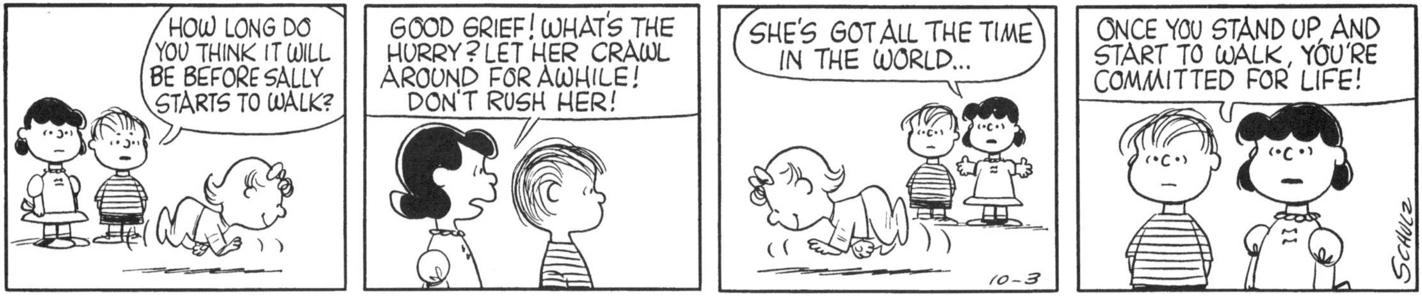
HOW LONG DO YOU THINK IT WILL BE BEFORE SALLY STARTS TO WALK?
GOOD GRIEF! WHAT'S THE HURRY? LET HER CRAWL AROUND FOR AWHILE! DON'T RUSH HER!
SHE'S GOT ALL THE TIME IN THE WORLD...
10-3
ONCE YOU STAND UP, AND START TO WALK, YOU'RE COMMITTED FOR LIFE!
SCHULZ

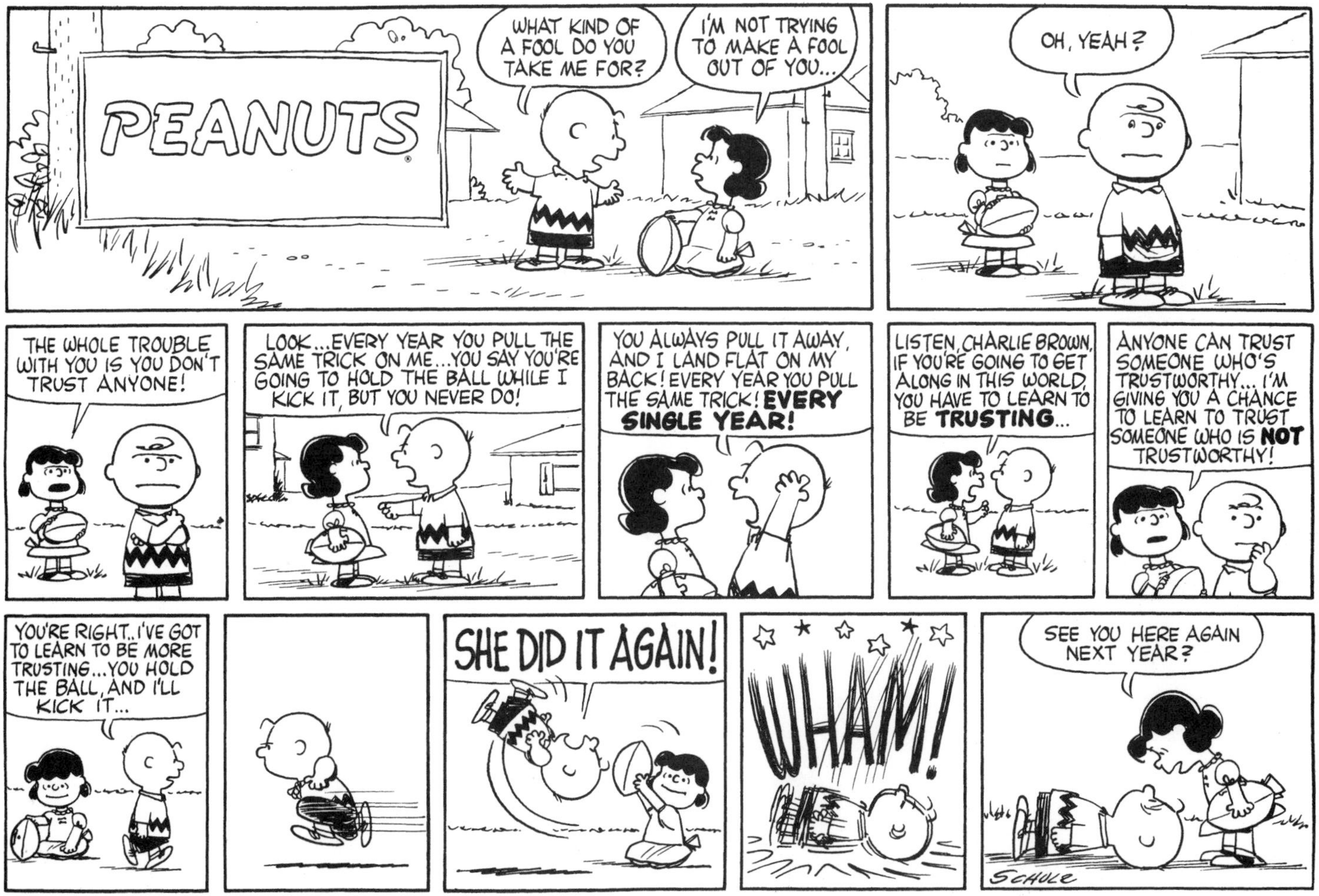
PEANUTS
WHAT KIND OF A FOOL DO YOU TAKE ME FOR?
I'M NOT TRYING TO MAKE A FOOL OUT OF YOU...
OH, YEAH?
THE WHOLE TROUBLE WITH YOU IS YOU DON'T TRUST ANYONE!
LOOK...EVERY YEAR YOU PULL THE SAME TRICK ON ME...YOU SAY YOU'RE GOING TO HOLD THE BALL WHILE I KICK IT, BUT YOU NEVER DO!
YOU ALWAYS PULL IT AWAY, AND I LAND FLAT ON MY BACK! EVERY YEAR YOU PULL THE SAME TRICK! EVERY SINGLE YEAR!
LISTEN, CHARLIE BROWN, IF YOU'RE GOING TO GET ALONG IN THIS WORLD, YOU HAVE TO LEARN TO BE TRUSTING...
ANYONE CAN TRUST SOMEONE WHO'S TRUSTWORTHY... I'M GIVING YOU A CHANCE TO LEARN TO TRUST SOMEONE WHO IS NOT TRUSTWORTHY!
YOU'RE RIGHT..I'VE GOT TO LEARN TO BE MORE TRUSTING...YOU HOLD THE BALL, AND I'LL KICK IT...
SHE DID IT AGAIN!
WHAM!
SEE YOU HERE AGAIN NEXT YEAR?
SCHULZ

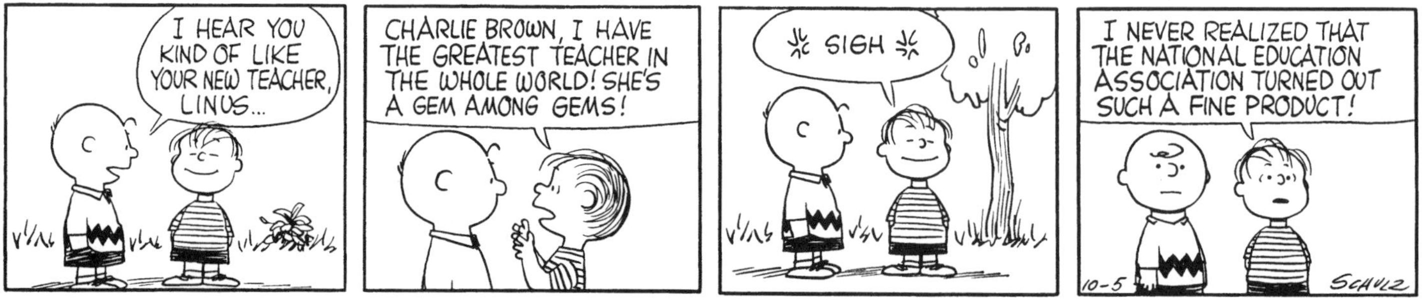
I HEAR YOU KIND OF LIKE YOUR NEW TEACHER, LINUS...
CHARLIE BROWN, I HAVE THE GREATEST TEACHER IN THE WHOLE WORLD! SHE'S A GEM AMONG GEMS!
SIGH
I NEVER REALIZED THAT THE NATIONAL EDUCATION ASSOCIATION TURNED OUT SUCH A FINE PRODUCT!
10-5
SCHULZ

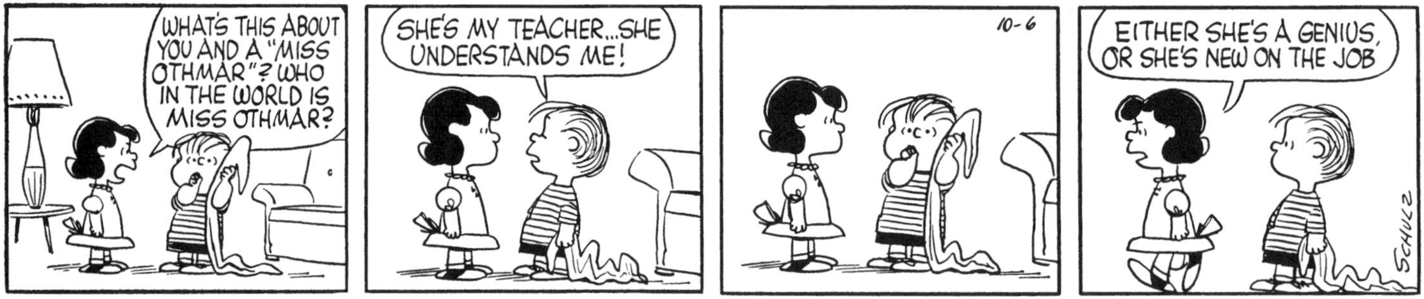
WHAT'S THIS ABOUT YOU AND A "MISS OTHMAR"? WHO IN THE WORLD IS MISS OTHMAR?
SHE'S MY TEACHER...SHE UNDERSTANDS ME!
10-6
EITHER SHE'S A GENIUS, OR SHE'S NEW ON THE JOB
SCHULZ

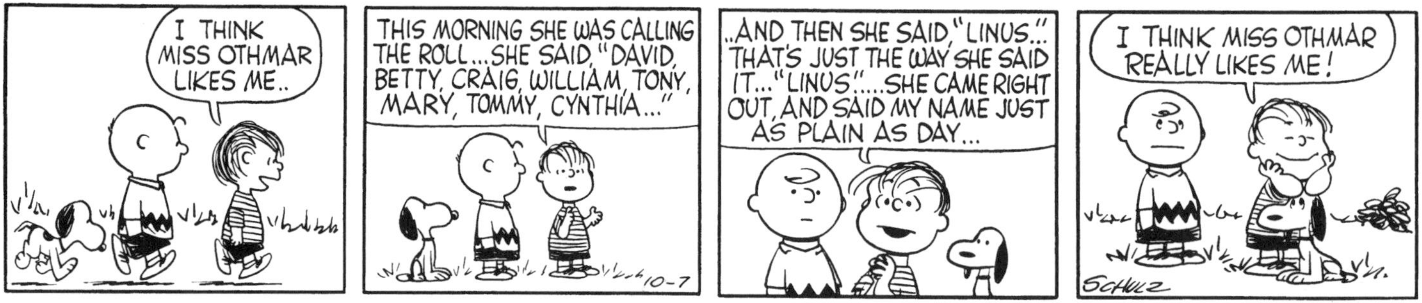
I THINK MISS OTHMAR LIKES ME..
THIS MORNING SHE WAS CALLING THE ROLL...SHE SAID, "DAVID, BETTY, CRAIG, WILLIAM, TONY, MARY, TOMMY, CYNTHIA..."
10-7
..AND THEN SHE SAID, "LINUS.." THAT'S JUST THE WAY SHE SAID IT..."LINUS"....SHE CAME RIGHT OUT, AND SAID MY NAME JUST AS PLAIN AS DAY...
I THINK MISS OTHMAR REALLY LIKES ME!
SCHULZ

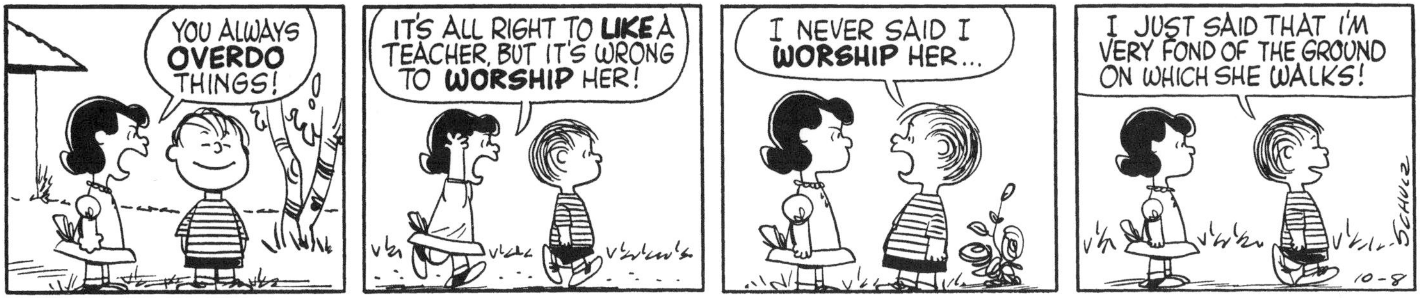
YOU ALWAYS **OVERDO** THINGS!
IT'S ALL RIGHT TO **LIKE** A TEACHER, BUT IT'S WRONG TO **WORSHIP** HER!
I NEVER SAID I **WORSHIP** HER...
I JUST SAID THAT I'M VERY FOND OF THE GROUND ON WHICH SHE WALKS!
SCHULZ
10-8

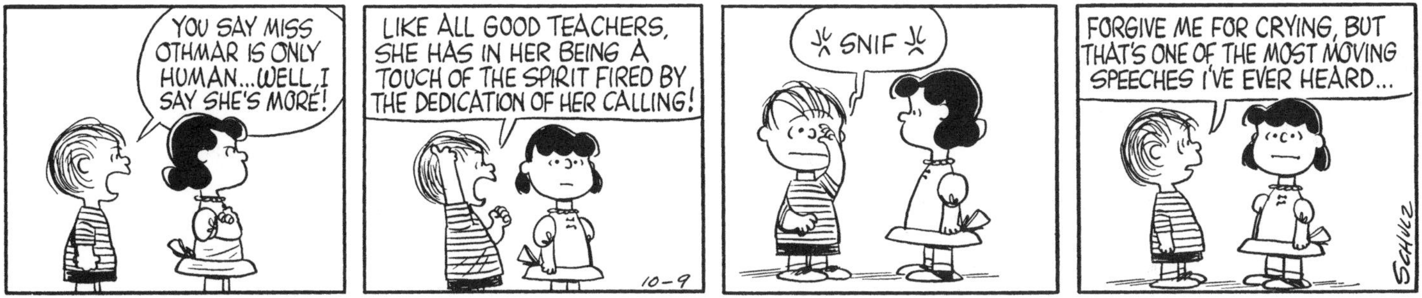
YOU SAY MISS OTHMAR IS ONLY HUMAN...WELL, I SAY SHE'S MORE!
LIKE ALL GOOD TEACHERS, SHE HAS IN HER BEING A TOUCH OF THE SPIRIT FIRED BY THE DEDICATION OF HER CALLING!
10-9
SNIF
FORGIVE ME FOR CRYING, BUT THAT'S ONE OF THE MOST MOVING SPEECHES I'VE EVER HEARD...
SCHULZ

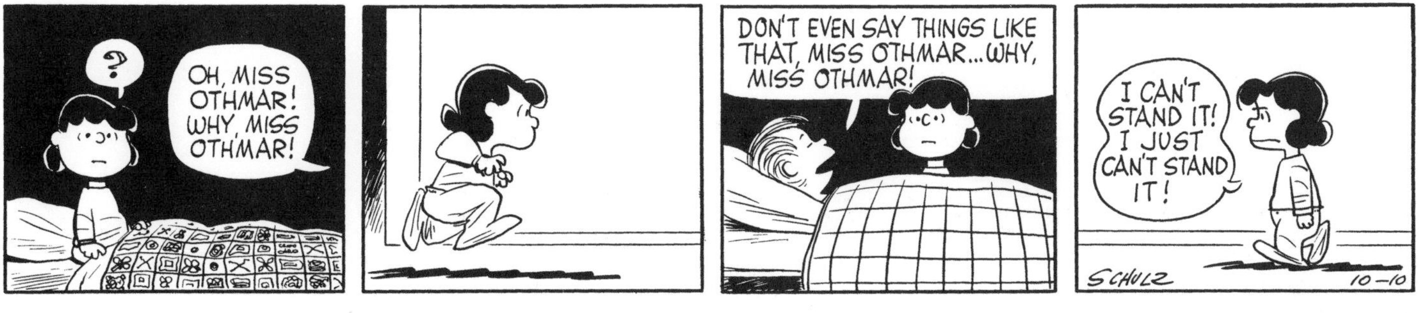
?
OH, MISS OTHMAR! WHY, MISS OTHMAR!
DON'T EVEN SAY THINGS LIKE THAT, MISS OTHMAR...WHY, MISS OTHMAR!
I CAN'T STAND IT! I JUST CAN'T STAND IT!
SCHULZ
10-10

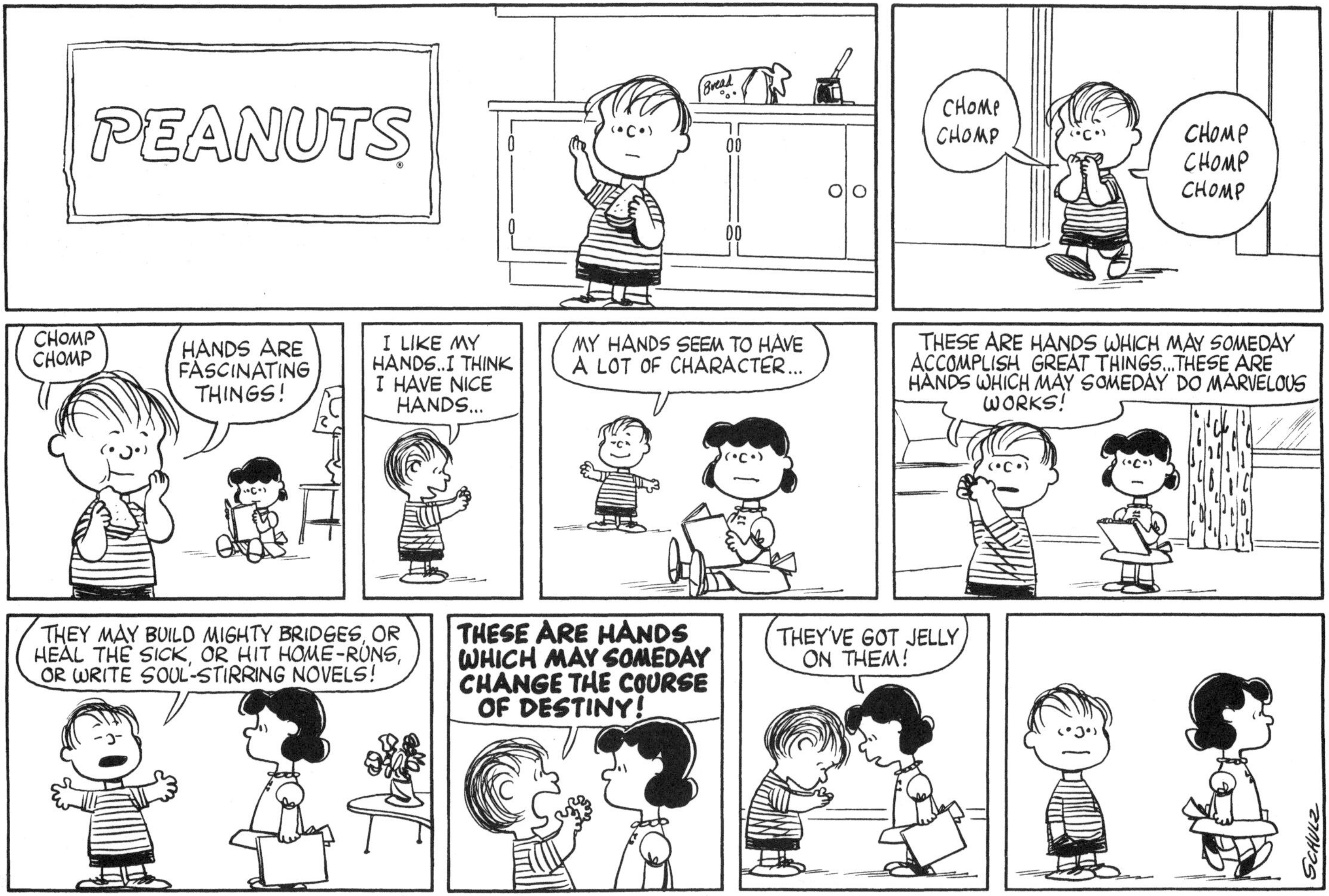
PEANUTS
Bread
CHOMP CHOMP
CHOMP CHOMP CHOMP
CHOMP CHOMP
HANDS ARE FASCINATING THINGS!
I LIKE MY HANDS..I THINK I HAVE NICE HANDS...
MY HANDS SEEM TO HAVE A LOT OF CHARACTER...
THESE ARE HANDS WHICH MAY SOMEDAY ACCOMPLISH GREAT THINGS...THESE ARE HANDS WHICH MAY SOMEDAY DO MARVELOUS WORKS!
THEY MAY BUILD MIGHTY BRIDGES, OR HEAL THE SICK, OR HIT HOME-RUNS, OR WRITE SOUL-STIRRING NOVELS!
THESE ARE HANDS WHICH MAY SOMEDAY CHANGE THE COURSE OF DESTINY!
THEY'VE GOT JELLY ON THEM!
SCHULZ

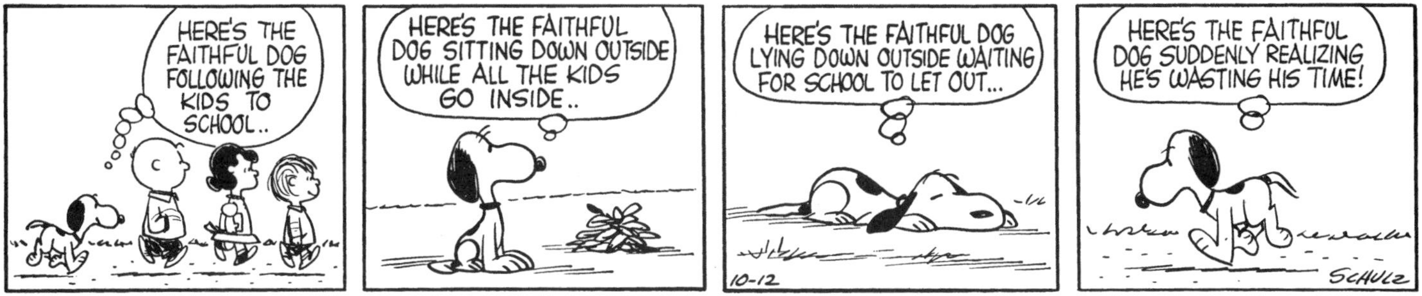
HERE'S THE FAITHFUL DOG FOLLOWING THE KIDS TO SCHOOL..
HERE'S THE FAITHFUL DOG SITTING DOWN OUTSIDE WHILE ALL THE KIDS GO INSIDE..
HERE'S THE FAITHFUL DOG LYING DOWN OUTSIDE WAITING FOR SCHOOL TO LET OUT...
10-12
HERE'S THE FAITHFUL DOG SUDDENLY REALIZING HE'S WASTING HIS TIME!
SCHULZ

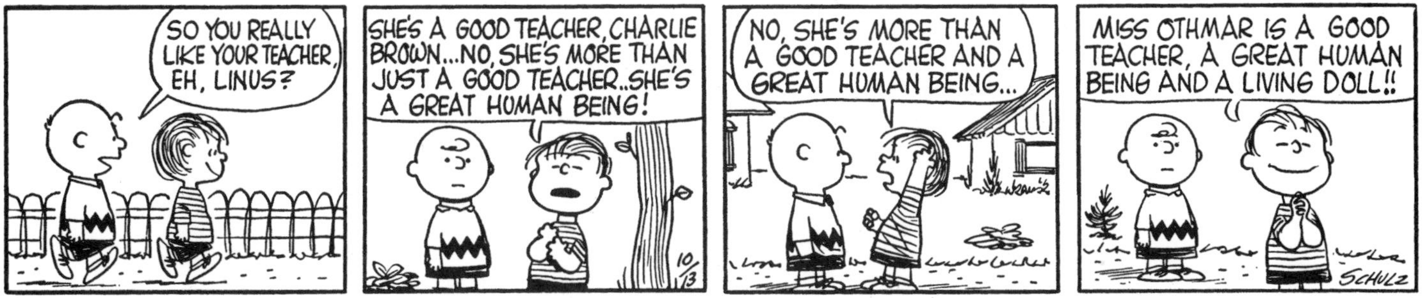
SO YOU REALLY LIKE YOUR TEACHER, EH, LINUS?
SHE'S A GOOD TEACHER, CHARLIE BROWN...NO, SHE'S MORE THAN JUST A GOOD TEACHER..SHE'S A GREAT HUMAN BEING!
10/13
NO, SHE'S MORE THAN A GOOD TEACHER AND A GREAT HUMAN BEING...
MISS OTHMAR IS A GOOD TEACHER, A GREAT HUMAN BEING AND A LIVING DOLL!!
SCHULZ

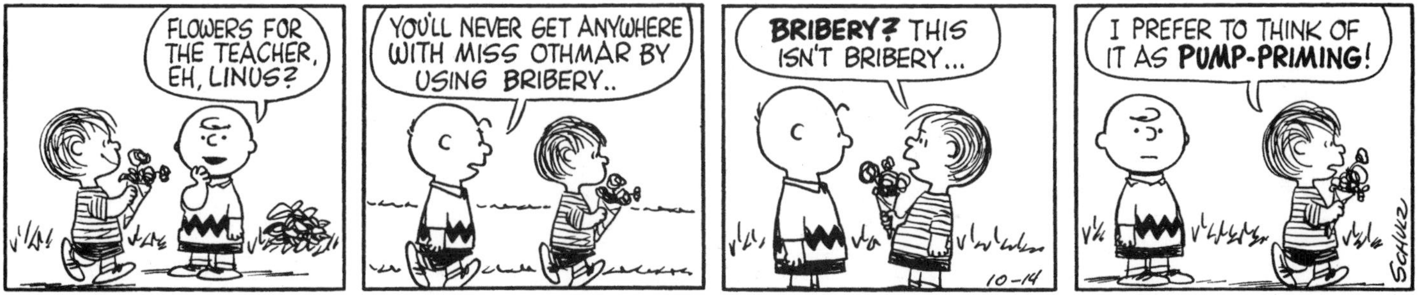
FLOWERS FOR THE TEACHER, EH, LINUS?
YOU'LL NEVER GET ANYWHERE WITH MISS OTHMAR BY USING BRIBERY..
BRIBERY? THIS ISN'T BRIBERY...
10-14
I PREFER TO THINK OF IT AS PUMP-PRIMING!
SCHULZ

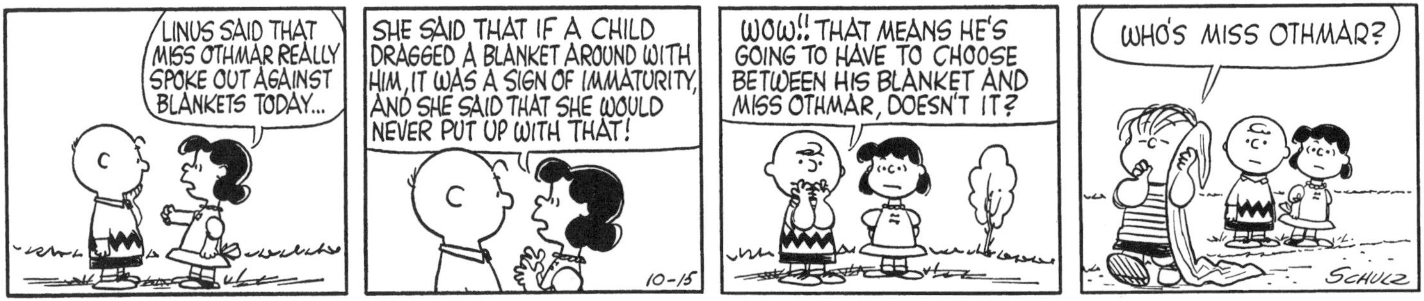
LINUS SAID THAT MISS OTHMAR REALLY SPOKE OUT AGAINST BLANKETS TODAY...
SHE SAID THAT IF A CHILD DRAGGED A BLANKET AROUND WITH HIM, IT WAS A SIGN OF IMMATURITY, AND SHE SAID THAT SHE WOULD NEVER PUT UP WITH THAT!
10-15
WOW!! THAT MEANS HE'S GOING TO HAVE TO CHOOSE BETWEEN HIS BLANKET AND MISS OTHMAR, DOESN'T IT?
WHO'S MISS OTHMAR?
SCHULZ

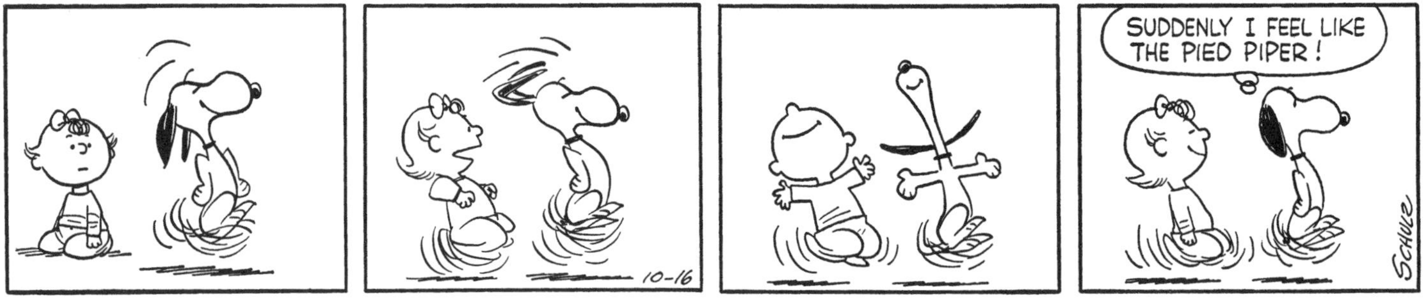
10-16
SUDDENLY I FEEL LIKE THE PIED PIPER!
SCHULZ

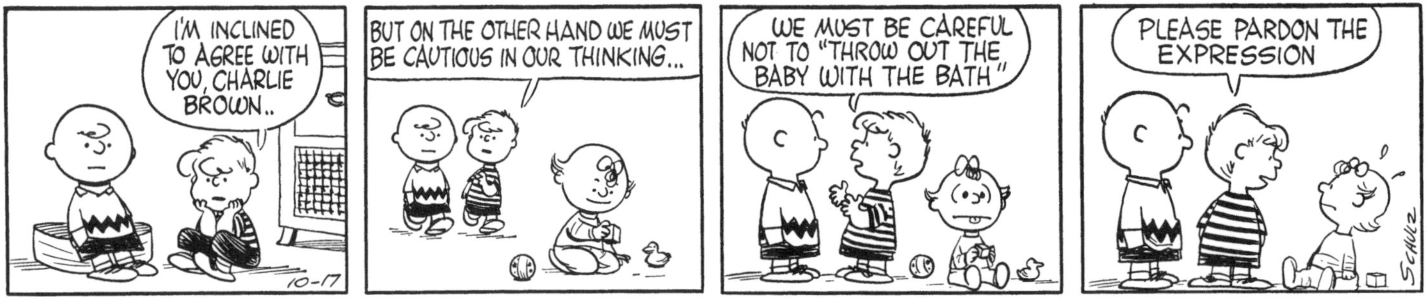
I'M INCLINED TO AGREE WITH YOU, CHARLIE BROWN..
10-17
BUT ON THE OTHER HAND WE MUST BE CAUTIOUS IN OUR THINKING...
WE MUST BE CAREFUL NOT TO "THROW OUT THE BABY WITH THE BATH"
PLEASE PARDON THE EXPRESSION
SCHULZ

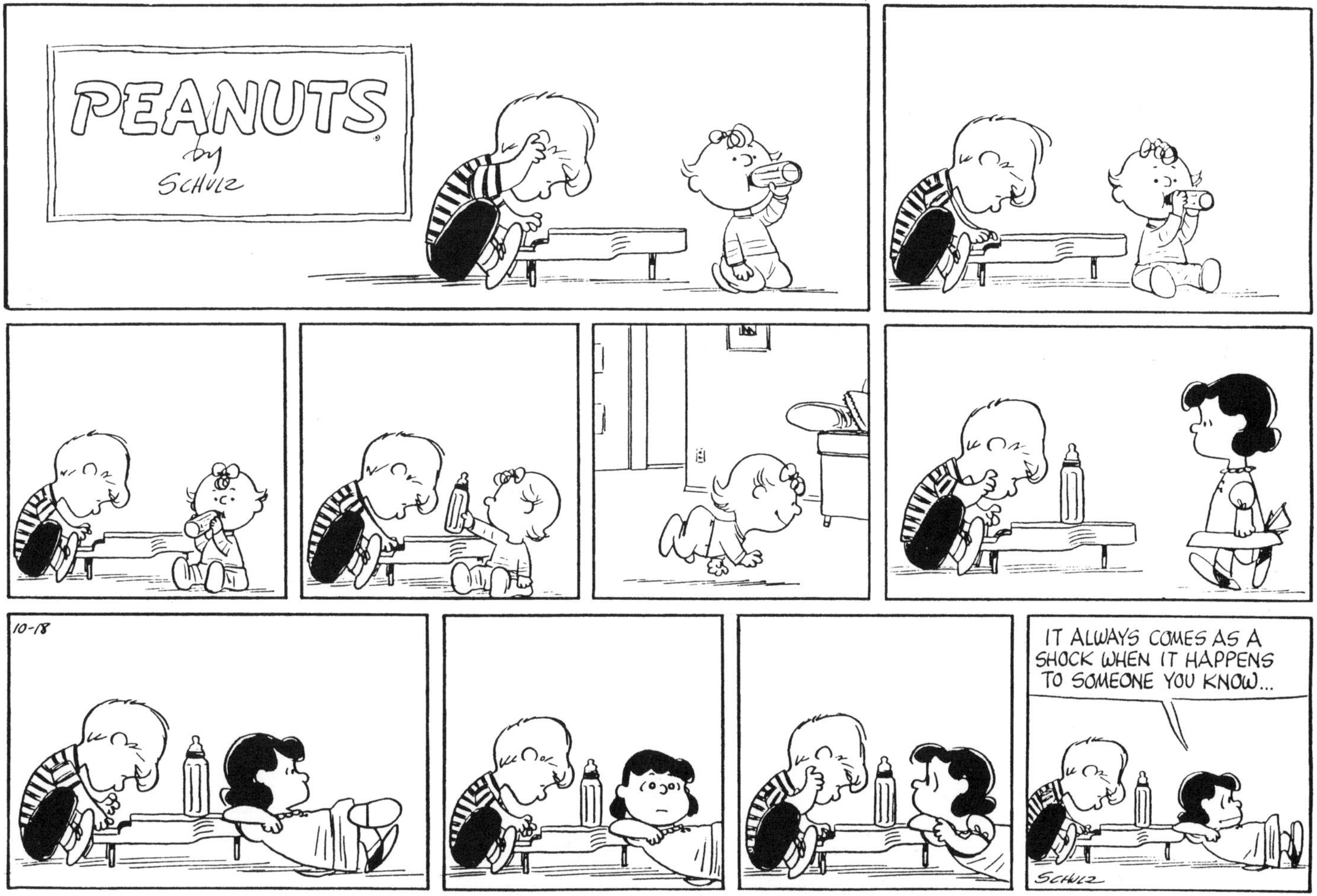
PEANUTS
by
SCHULZ
10-18
IT ALWAYS COMES AS A SHOCK WHEN IT HAPPENS TO SOMEONE YOU KNOW...
SCHULZ

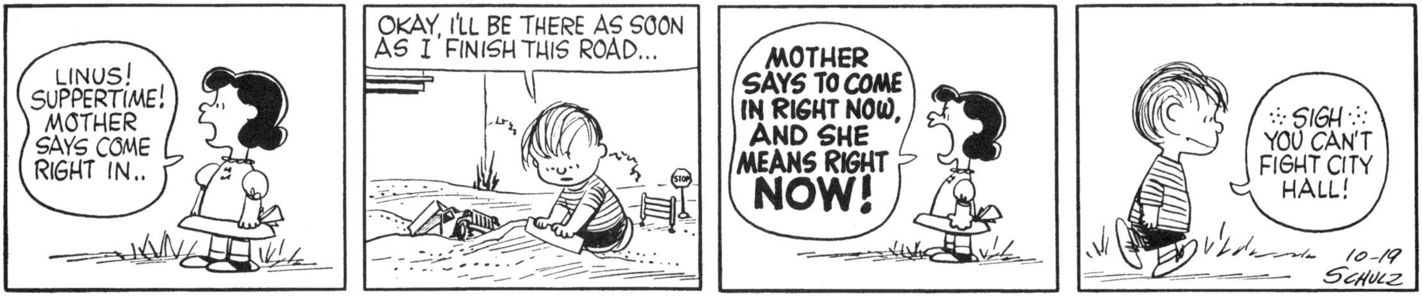
LINUS! SUPPERTIME! MOTHER SAYS COME RIGHT IN..
OKAY, I'LL BE THERE AS SOON AS I FINISH THIS ROAD...
STOP
MOTHER SAYS TO COME IN RIGHT NOW, AND SHE MEANS RIGHT NOW!
SIGH YOU CAN'T FIGHT CITY HALL!
10-19
SCHULZ

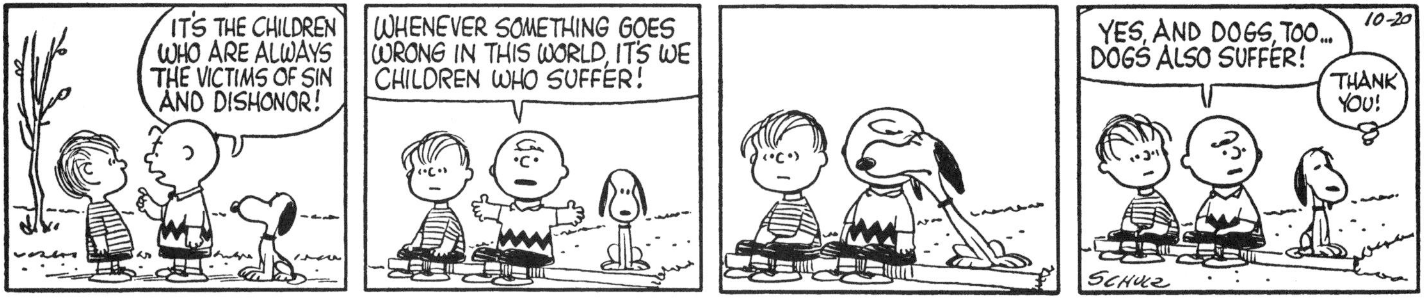
IT'S THE CHILDREN WHO ARE ALWAYS THE VICTIMS OF SIN AND DISHONOR!
WHENEVER SOMETHING GOES WRONG IN THIS WORLD, IT'S WE CHILDREN WHO SUFFER!
YES, AND DOGS, TOO... DOGS ALSO SUFFER!
THANK YOU!
10-20
SCHULZ

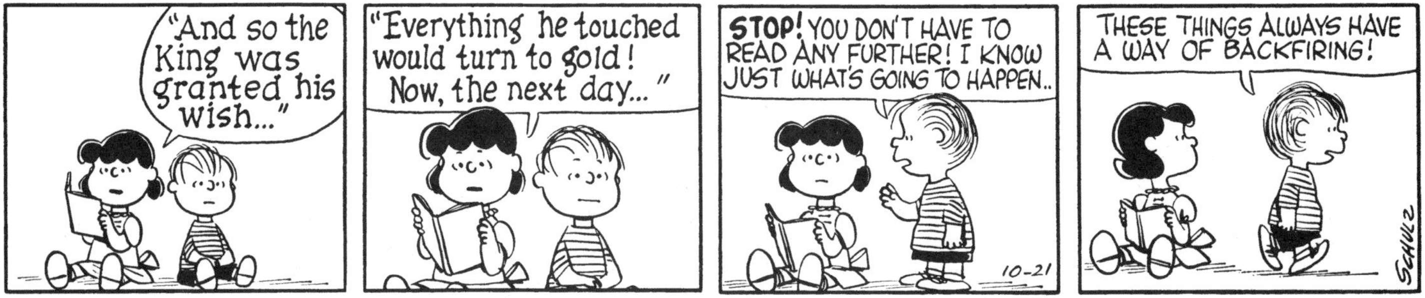
"And so the King was granted his wish..."
"Everything he touched would turn to gold! Now, the next day..."
STOP! YOU DON'T HAVE TO READ ANY FURTHER! I KNOW JUST WHAT'S GOING TO HAPPEN..
10-21
THESE THINGS ALWAYS HAVE A WAY OF BACKFIRING!
SCHULZ

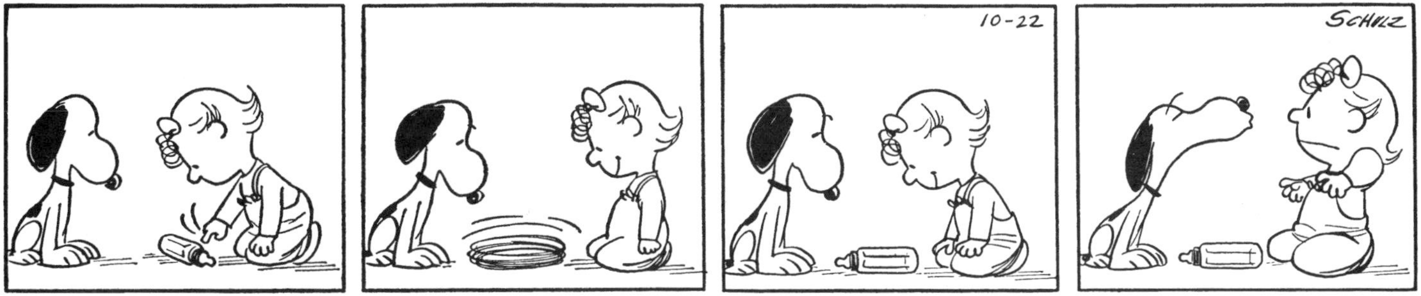
10-22
SCHULZ

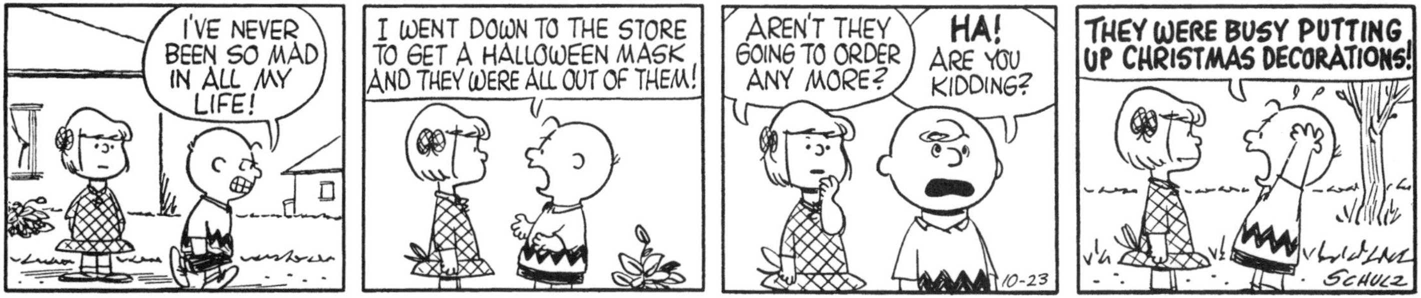
I'VE NEVER BEEN SO MAD IN ALL MY LIFE!
I WENT DOWN TO THE STORE TO GET A HALLOWEEN MASK AND THEY WERE ALL OUT OF THEM!
AREN'T THEY GOING TO ORDER ANY MORE?
HA! ARE YOU KIDDING?
10-23
THEY WERE BUSY PUTTING UP CHRISTMAS DECORATIONS!
SCHULZ

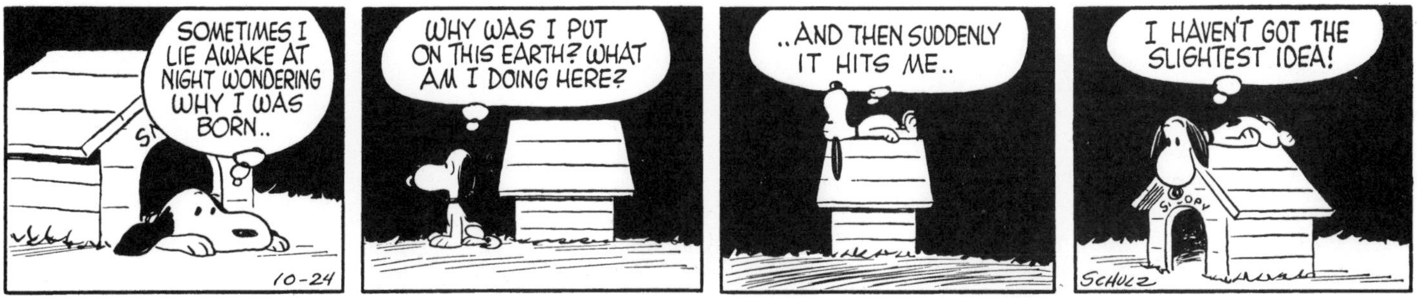
SOMETIMES I LIE AWAKE AT NIGHT WONDERING WHY I WAS BORN..
10-24
WHY WAS I PUT ON THIS EARTH? WHAT AM I DOING HERE?
..AND THEN SUDDENLY IT HITS ME..
I HAVEN'T GOT THE SLIGHTEST IDEA!
SCHULZ

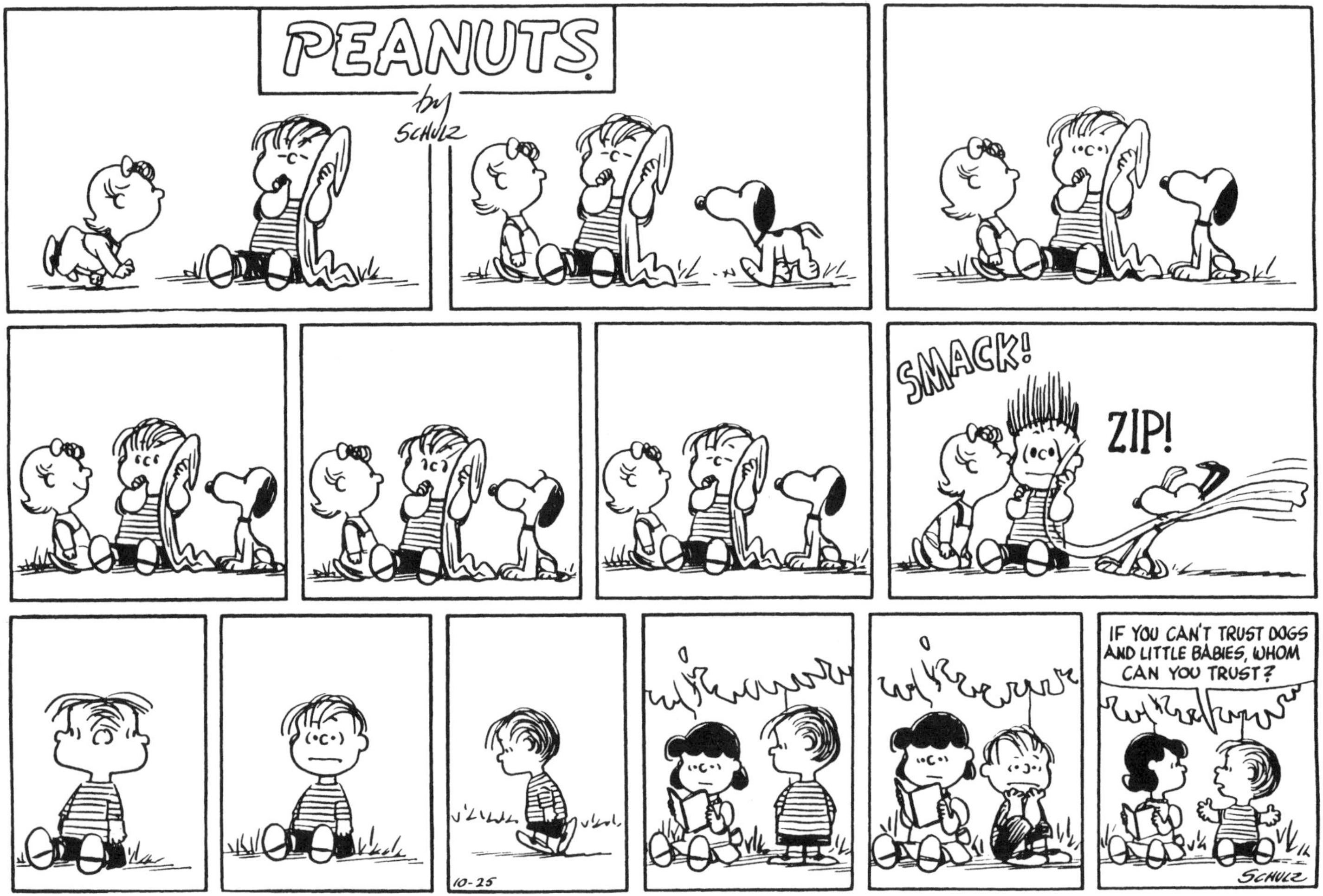
PEANUTS
by SCHULZ
SMACK!
ZIP!
10-25
IF YOU CAN'T TRUST DOGS AND LITTLE BABIES, WHOM CAN YOU TRUST?
SCHULZ

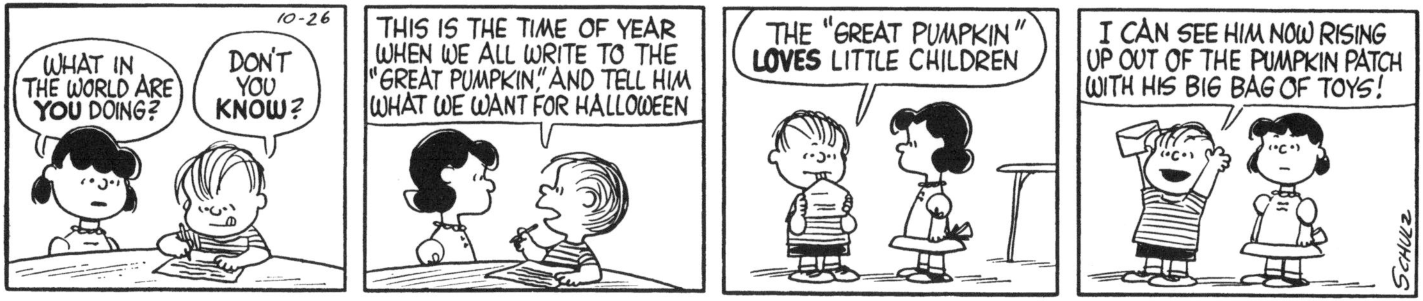
10-26
WHAT IN THE WORLD ARE YOU DOING?
DON'T YOU KNOW?
THIS IS THE TIME OF YEAR WHEN WE ALL WRITE TO THE "GREAT PUMPKIN," AND TELL HIM WHAT WE WANT FOR HALLOWEEN
THE "GREAT PUMPKIN" LOVES LITTLE CHILDREN
I CAN SEE HIM NOW RISING UP OUT OF THE PUMPKIN PATCH WITH HIS BIG BAG OF TOYS!
SCHULZ

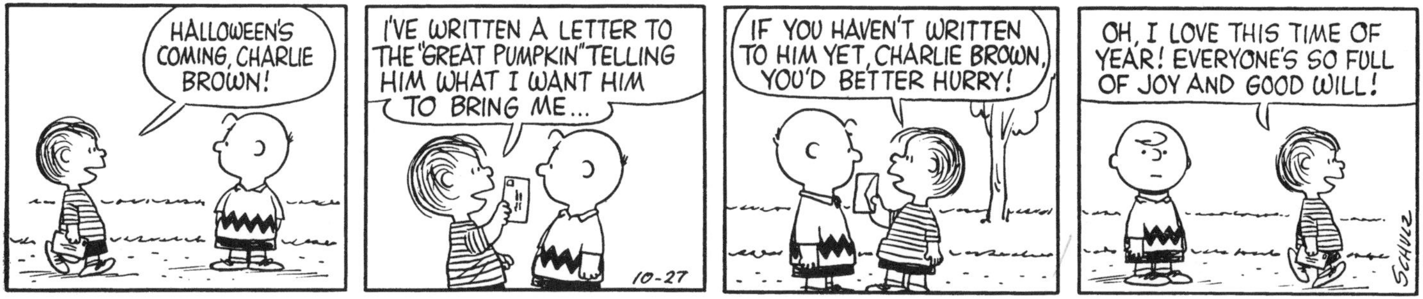
HALLOWEEN'S COMING, CHARLIE BROWN!
I'VE WRITTEN A LETTER TO THE "GREAT PUMPKIN" TELLING HIM WHAT I WANT HIM TO BRING ME...
10-27
IF YOU HAVEN'T WRITTEN TO HIM YET, CHARLIE BROWN, YOU'D BETTER HURRY!
OH, I LOVE THIS TIME OF YEAR! EVERYONE'S SO FULL OF JOY AND GOOD WILL!
SCHULZ

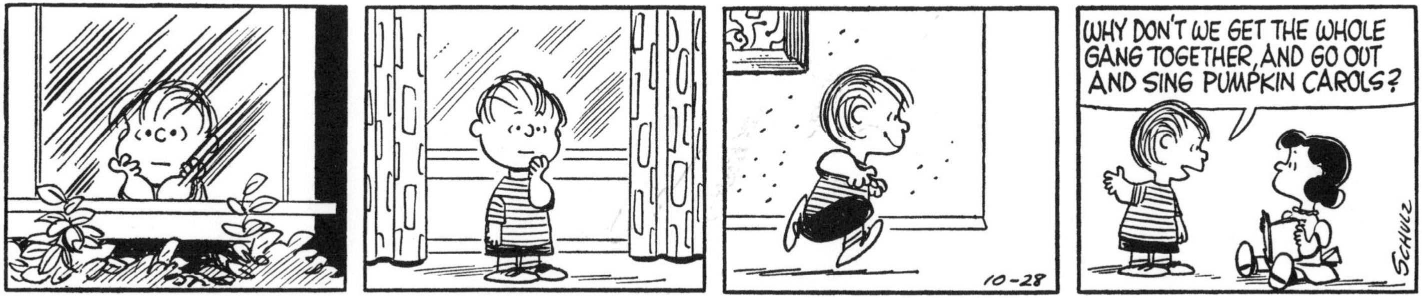
10-28
WHY DON'T WE GET THE WHOLE GANG TOGETHER, AND GO OUT AND SING PUMPKIN CAROLS?
SCHULZ

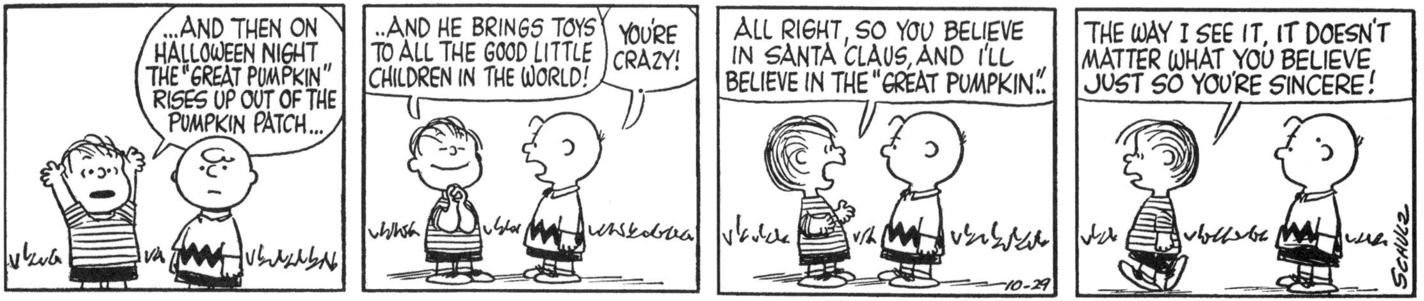
...AND THEN ON HALLOWEEN NIGHT THE "GREAT PUMPKIN" RISES UP OUT OF THE PUMPKIN PATCH...
..AND HE BRINGS TOYS TO ALL THE GOOD LITTLE CHILDREN IN THE WORLD!
YOU'RE CRAZY!
ALL RIGHT, SO YOU BELIEVE IN SANTA CLAUS, AND I'LL BELIEVE IN THE "GREAT PUMPKIN"..
10-29
THE WAY I SEE IT, IT DOESN'T MATTER WHAT YOU BELIEVE JUST SO YOU'RE SINCERE!
SCHULZ

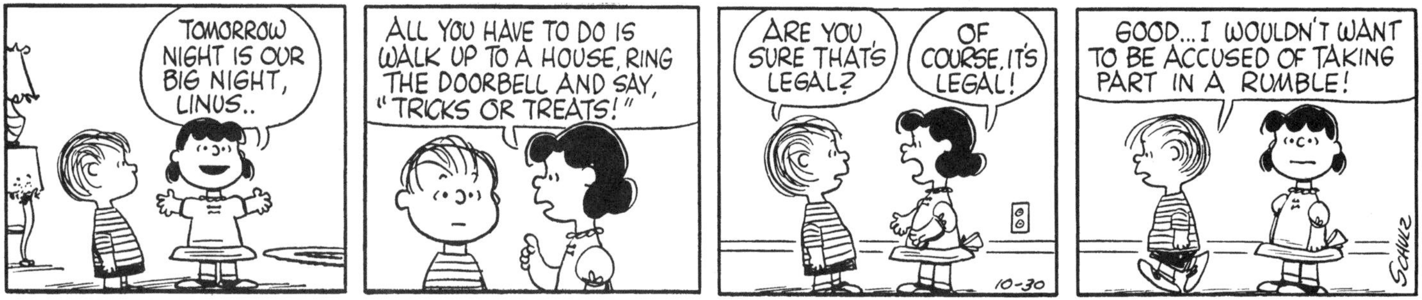
TOMORROW NIGHT IS OUR BIG NIGHT, LINUS..
ALL YOU HAVE TO DO IS WALK UP TO A HOUSE, RING THE DOORBELL AND SAY, "TRICKS OR TREATS!"
ARE YOU SURE THAT'S LEGAL?
OF COURSE, IT'S LEGAL!
10-30
GOOD...I WOULDN'T WANT TO BE ACCUSED OF TAKING PART IN A RUMBLE!
SCHULZ

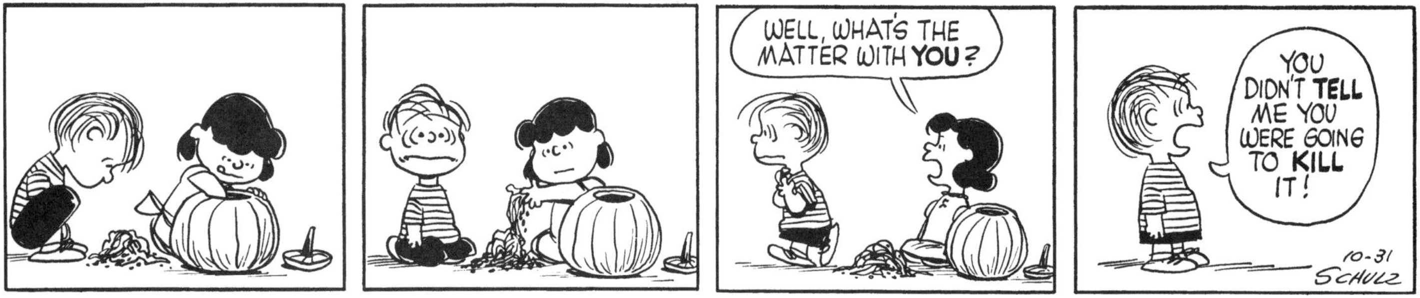
WELL, WHAT'S THE MATTER WITH YOU?
YOU DIDN'T TELL ME YOU WERE GOING TO KILL IT!
10-31
SCHULZ

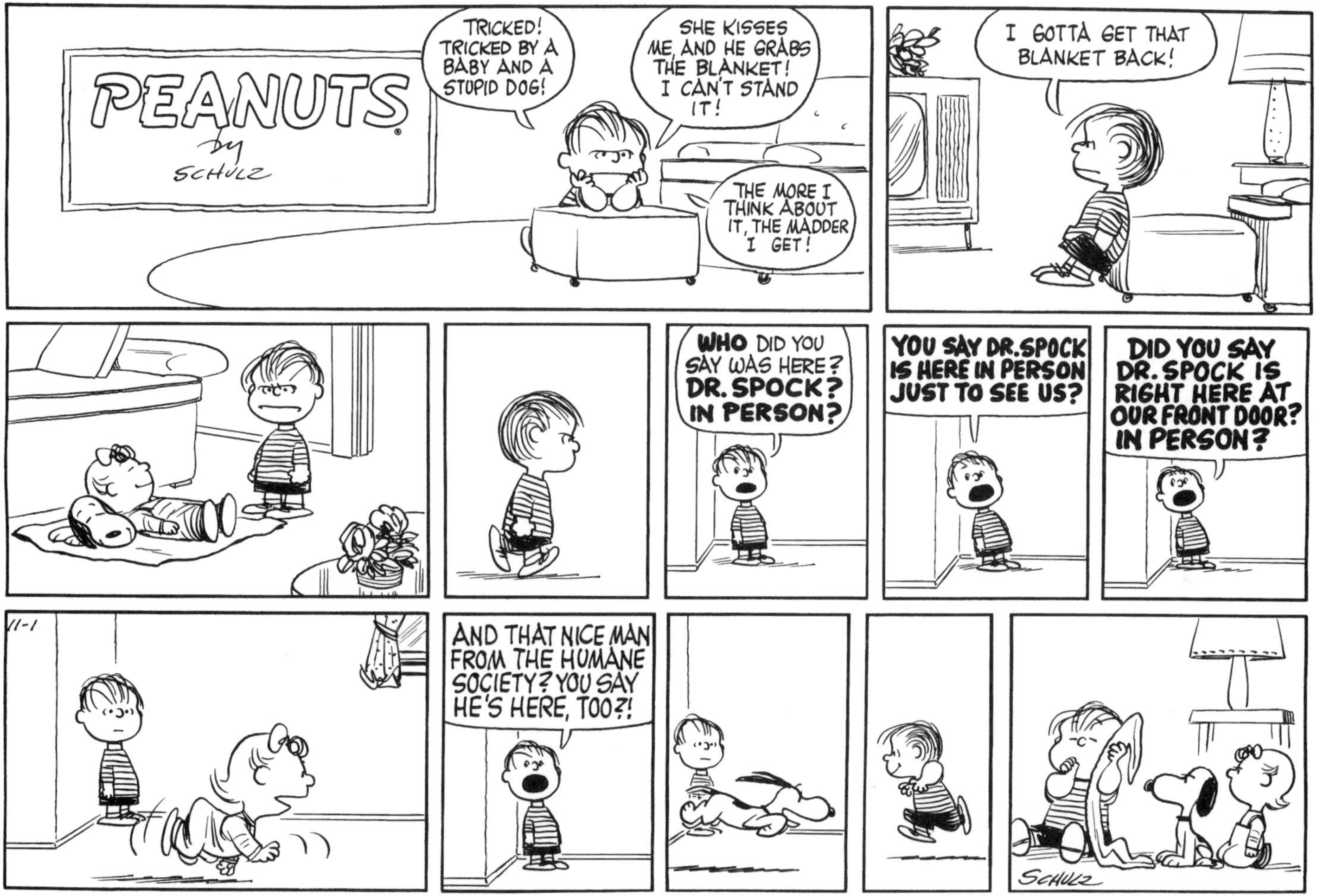
PEANUTS
by SCHULZ
TRICKED! TRICKED BY A BABY AND A STUPID DOG!
SHE KISSES ME, AND HE GRABS THE BLANKET! I CAN'T STAND IT!
THE MORE I THINK ABOUT IT, THE MADDER I GET!
I GOTTA GET THAT BLANKET BACK!
WHO DID YOU SAY WAS HERE? DR. SPOCK? IN PERSON?
YOU SAY DR. SPOCK IS HERE IN PERSON JUST TO SEE US?
DID YOU SAY DR. SPOCK IS RIGHT HERE AT OUR FRONT DOOR? IN PERSON?
11-1
AND THAT NICE MAN FROM THE HUMANE SOCIETY? YOU SAY HE'S HERE, TOO?!
SCHULZ

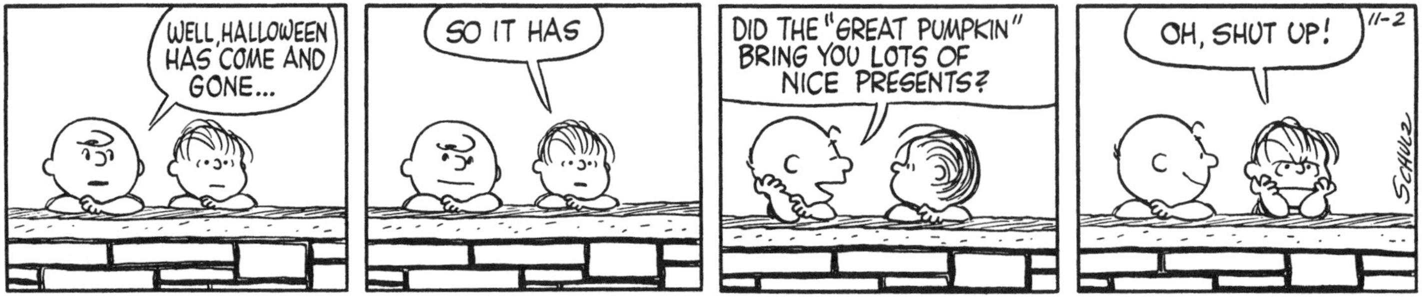
WELL, HALLOWEEN HAS COME AND GONE...
SO IT HAS
DID THE "GREAT PUMPKIN" BRING YOU LOTS OF NICE PRESENTS?
OH, SHUT UP!
11-2
SCHULZ

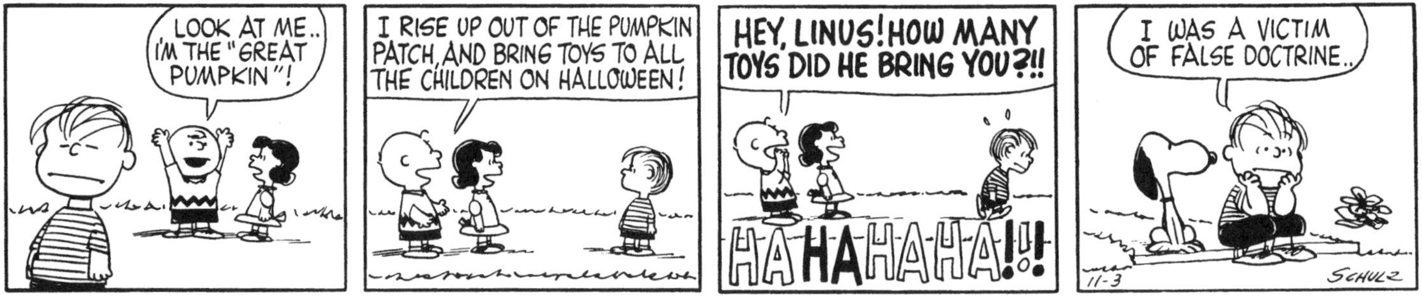
LOOK AT ME.. I'M THE "GREAT PUMPKIN"!
I RISE UP OUT OF THE PUMPKIN PATCH, AND BRING TOYS TO ALL THE CHILDREN ON HALLOWEEN!
HEY, LINUS! HOW MANY TOYS DID HE BRING YOU?!!
HAHAHAHAHA!!!
I WAS A VICTIM OF FALSE DOCTRINE..
11-3
SCHULZ

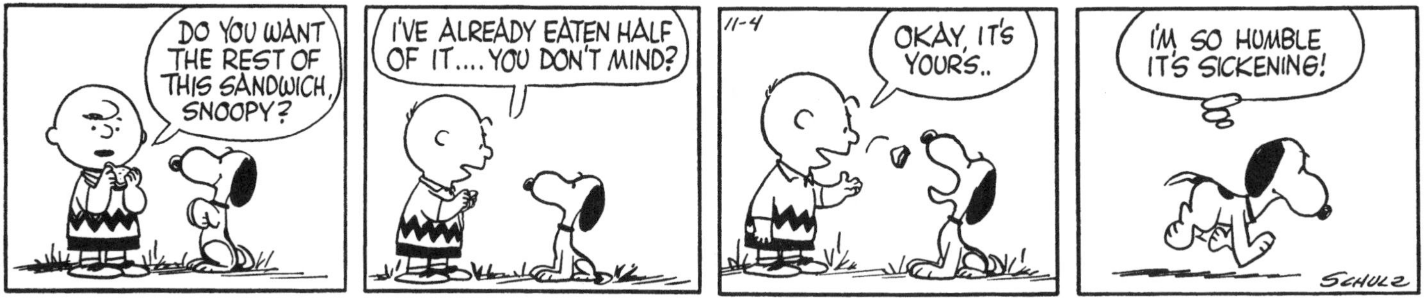
DO YOU WANT THE REST OF THIS SANDWICH, SNOOPY?
I'VE ALREADY EATEN HALF OF IT.... YOU DON'T MIND?
11-4
OKAY, IT'S YOURS..
I'M SO HUMBLE IT'S SICKENING!
SCHULZ

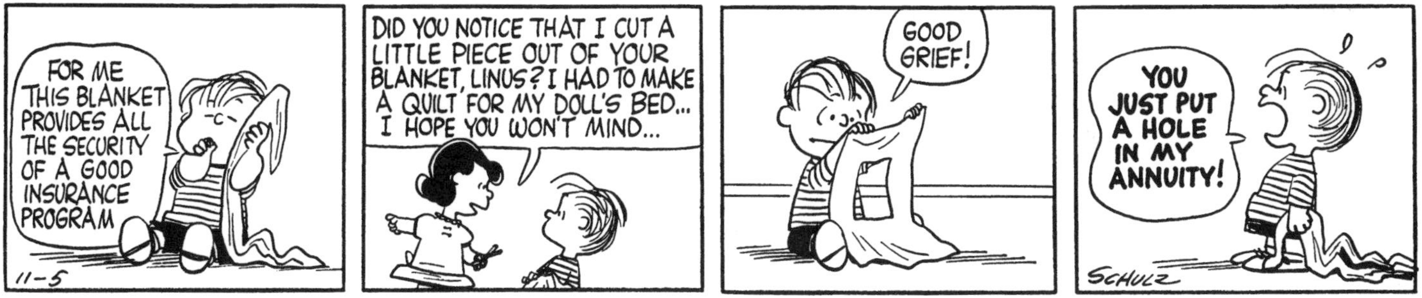
FOR ME THIS BLANKET PROVIDES ALL THE SECURITY OF A GOOD INSURANCE PROGRAM
11-5
DID YOU NOTICE THAT I CUT A LITTLE PIECE OUT OF YOUR BLANKET, LINUS? I HAD TO MAKE A QUILT FOR MY DOLL'S BED... I HOPE YOU WON'T MIND...
GOOD GRIEF!
YOU JUST PUT A HOLE IN MY ANNUITY!
SCHULZ

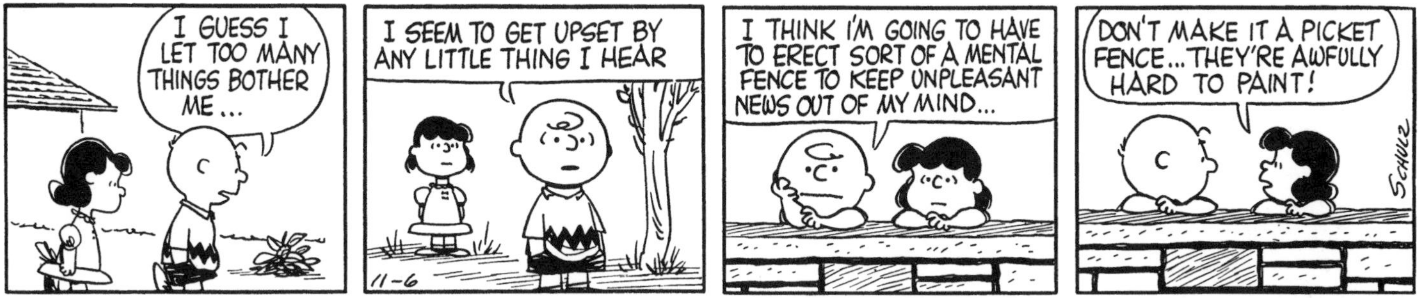
I GUESS I LET TOO MANY THINGS BOTHER ME...
I SEEM TO GET UPSET BY ANY LITTLE THING I HEAR
11-6
I THINK I'M GOING TO HAVE TO ERECT SORT OF A MENTAL FENCE TO KEEP UNPLEASANT NEWS OUT OF MY MIND...
DON'T MAKE IT A PICKET FENCE... THEY'RE AWFULLY HARD TO PAINT!
SCHULZ

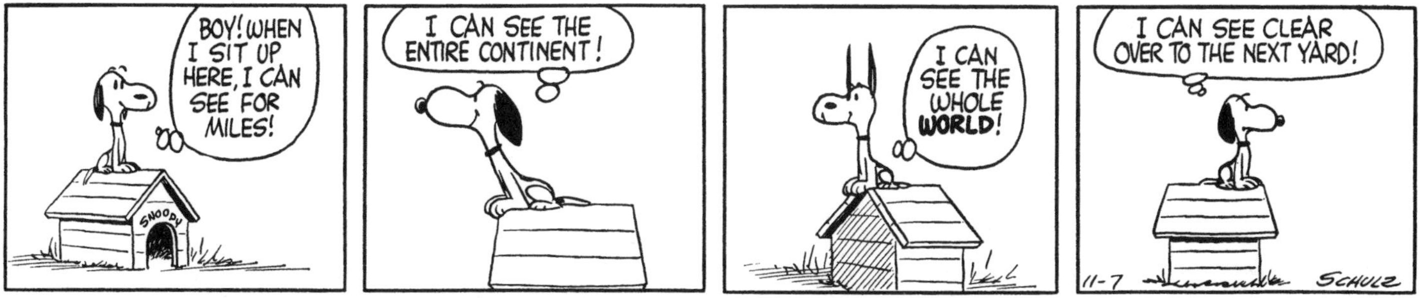
BOY! WHEN I SIT UP HERE, I CAN SEE FOR MILES!
SNOOPY
I CAN SEE THE ENTIRE CONTINENT!
I CAN SEE THE WHOLE WORLD!
I CAN SEE CLEAR OVER TO THE NEXT YARD!
11-7
SCHULZ

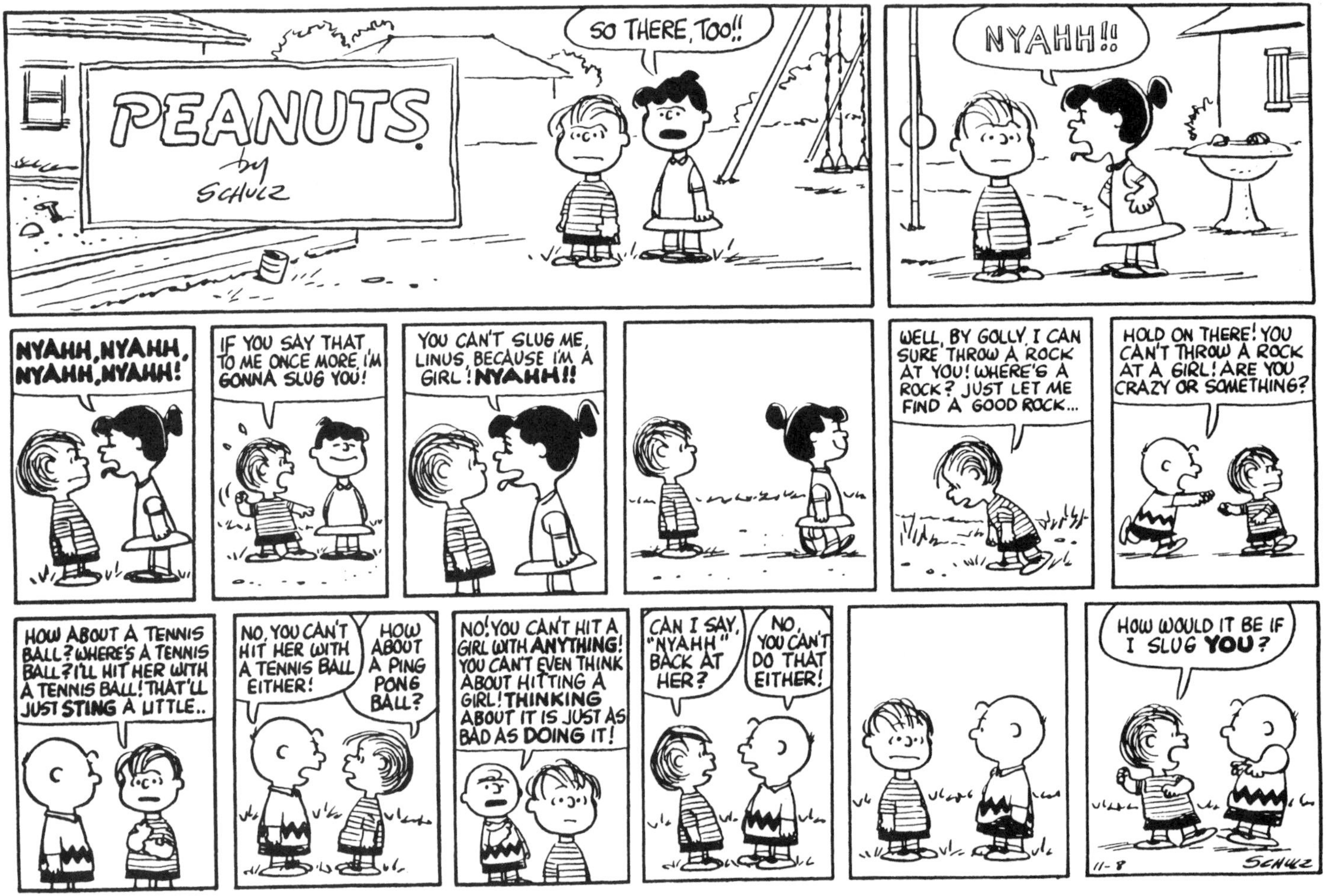
PEANUTS
by SCHULZ
SO THERE, TOO!!
NYAHH!!
NYAHH, NYAHH, NYAHH, NYAHH!
IF YOU SAY THAT TO ME ONCE MORE, I'M GONNA SLUG YOU!
YOU CAN'T SLUG ME, LINUS, BECAUSE I'M A GIRL! NYAHH!!
WELL, BY GOLLY, I CAN SURE THROW A ROCK AT YOU! WHERE'S A ROCK? JUST LET ME FIND A GOOD ROCK...
HOLD ON THERE! YOU CAN'T THROW A ROCK AT A GIRL! ARE YOU CRAZY OR SOMETHING?
HOW ABOUT A TENNIS BALL? WHERE'S A TENNIS BALL? I'LL HIT HER WITH A TENNIS BALL! THAT'LL JUST STING A LITTLE..
NO, YOU CAN'T HIT HER WITH A TENNIS BALL EITHER!
HOW ABOUT A PING PONG BALL?
NO! YOU CAN'T HIT A GIRL WITH ANYTHING! YOU CAN'T EVEN THINK ABOUT HITTING A GIRL! THINKING ABOUT IT IS JUST AS BAD AS DOING IT!
CAN I SAY, "NYAHH" BACK AT HER?
NO, YOU CAN'T DO THAT EITHER!
HOW WOULD IT BE IF I SLUG YOU?
11-8
SCHULZ

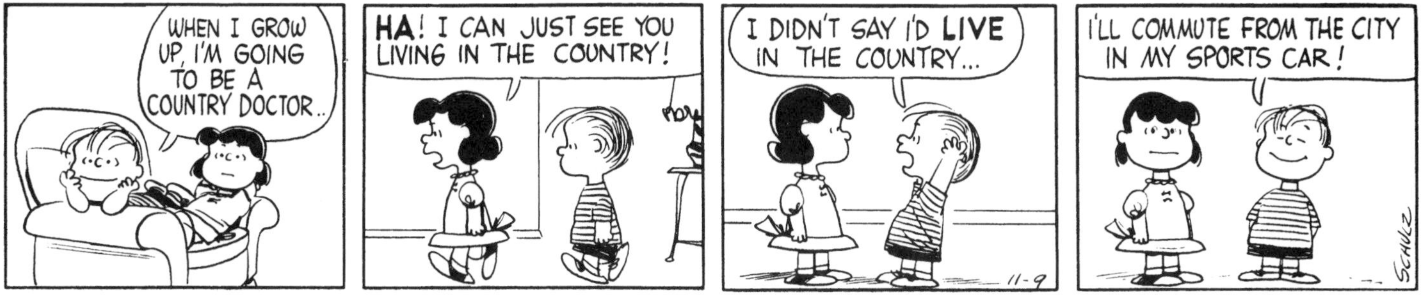
WHEN I GROW UP, I'M GOING TO BE A COUNTRY DOCTOR..
HA! I CAN JUST SEE YOU LIVING IN THE COUNTRY!
I DIDN'T SAY I'D LIVE IN THE COUNTRY...
I'LL COMMUTE FROM THE CITY IN MY SPORTS CAR!
11-9
SCHULZ

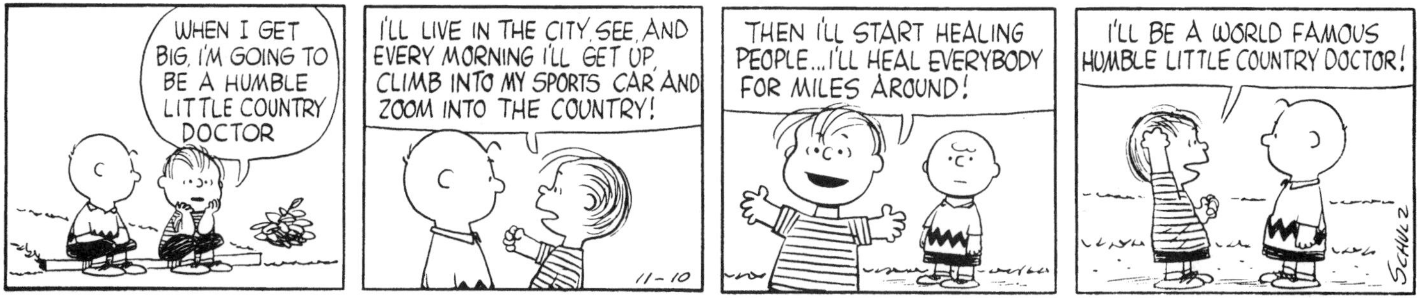
WHEN I GET BIG, I'M GOING TO BE A HUMBLE LITTLE COUNTRY DOCTOR
I'LL LIVE IN THE CITY, SEE, AND EVERY MORNING I'LL GET UP, CLIMB INTO MY SPORTS CAR AND ZOOM INTO THE COUNTRY!
11-10
THEN I'LL START HEALING PEOPLE...I'LL HEAL EVERYBODY FOR MILES AROUND!
I'LL BE A WORLD FAMOUS HUMBLE LITTLE COUNTRY DOCTOR!
SCHULZ

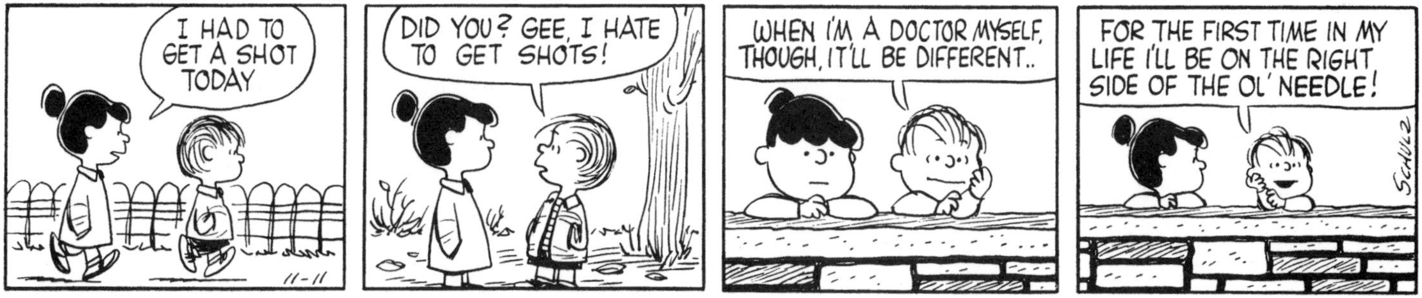
I HAD TO GET A SHOT TODAY
11-11
DID YOU? GEE, I HATE TO GET SHOTS!
WHEN I'M A DOCTOR MYSELF, THOUGH, IT'LL BE DIFFERENT..
FOR THE FIRST TIME IN MY LIFE I'LL BE ON THE RIGHT SIDE OF THE OL' NEEDLE!
SCHULZ

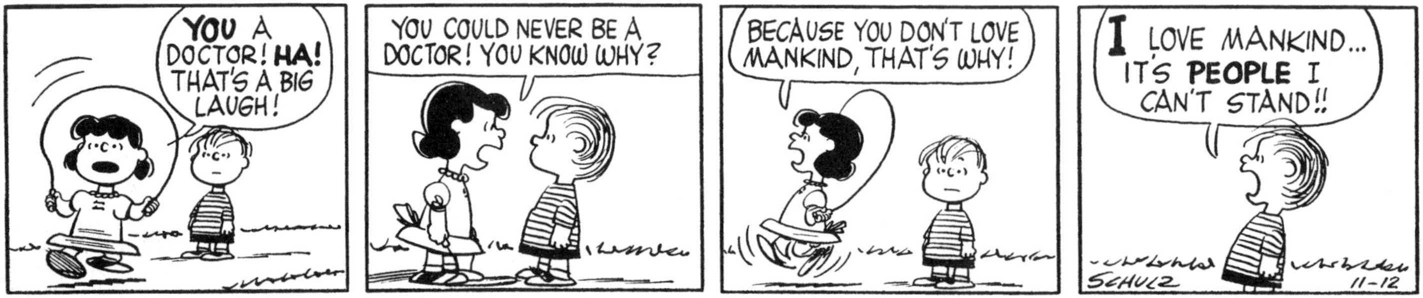
YOU A DOCTOR! HA! THAT'S A BIG LAUGH!
YOU COULD NEVER BE A DOCTOR! YOU KNOW WHY?
BECAUSE YOU DON'T LOVE MANKIND, THAT'S WHY!
I LOVE MANKIND... IT'S PEOPLE I CAN'T STAND!!
SCHULZ
11-12

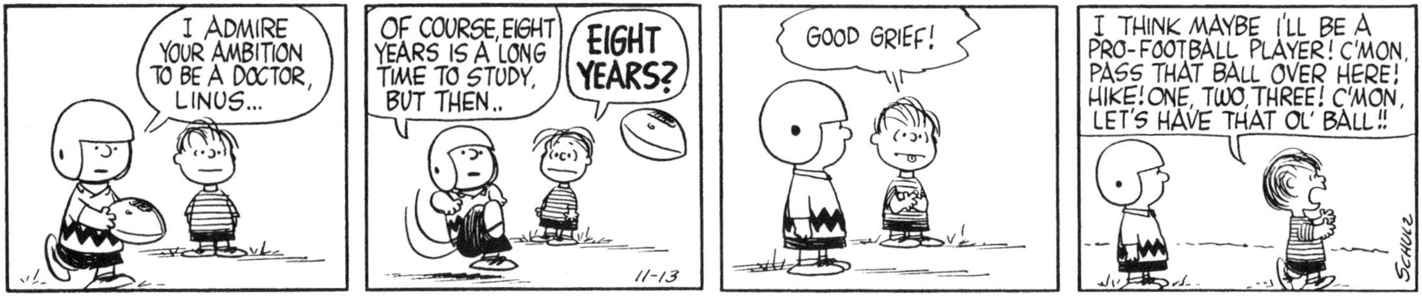
I ADMIRE YOUR AMBITION TO BE A DOCTOR, LINUS...
OF COURSE, EIGHT YEARS IS A LONG TIME TO STUDY, BUT THEN..
EIGHT YEARS?
11-13
GOOD GRIEF!
I THINK MAYBE I'LL BE A PRO-FOOTBALL PLAYER! C'MON, PASS THAT BALL OVER HERE! HIKE! ONE, TWO, THREE! C'MON, LET'S HAVE THAT OL' BALL!!
SCHULZ

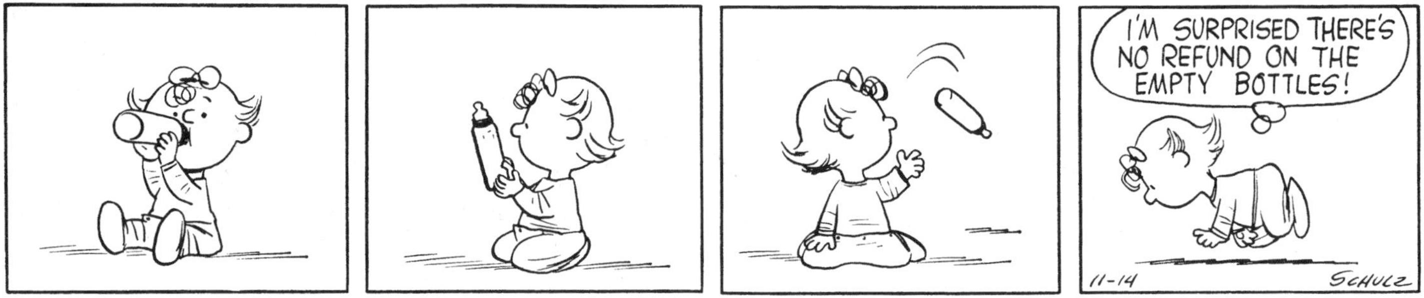
I'M SURPRISED THERE'S NO REFUND ON THE EMPTY BOTTLES!
11-14
SCHULZ

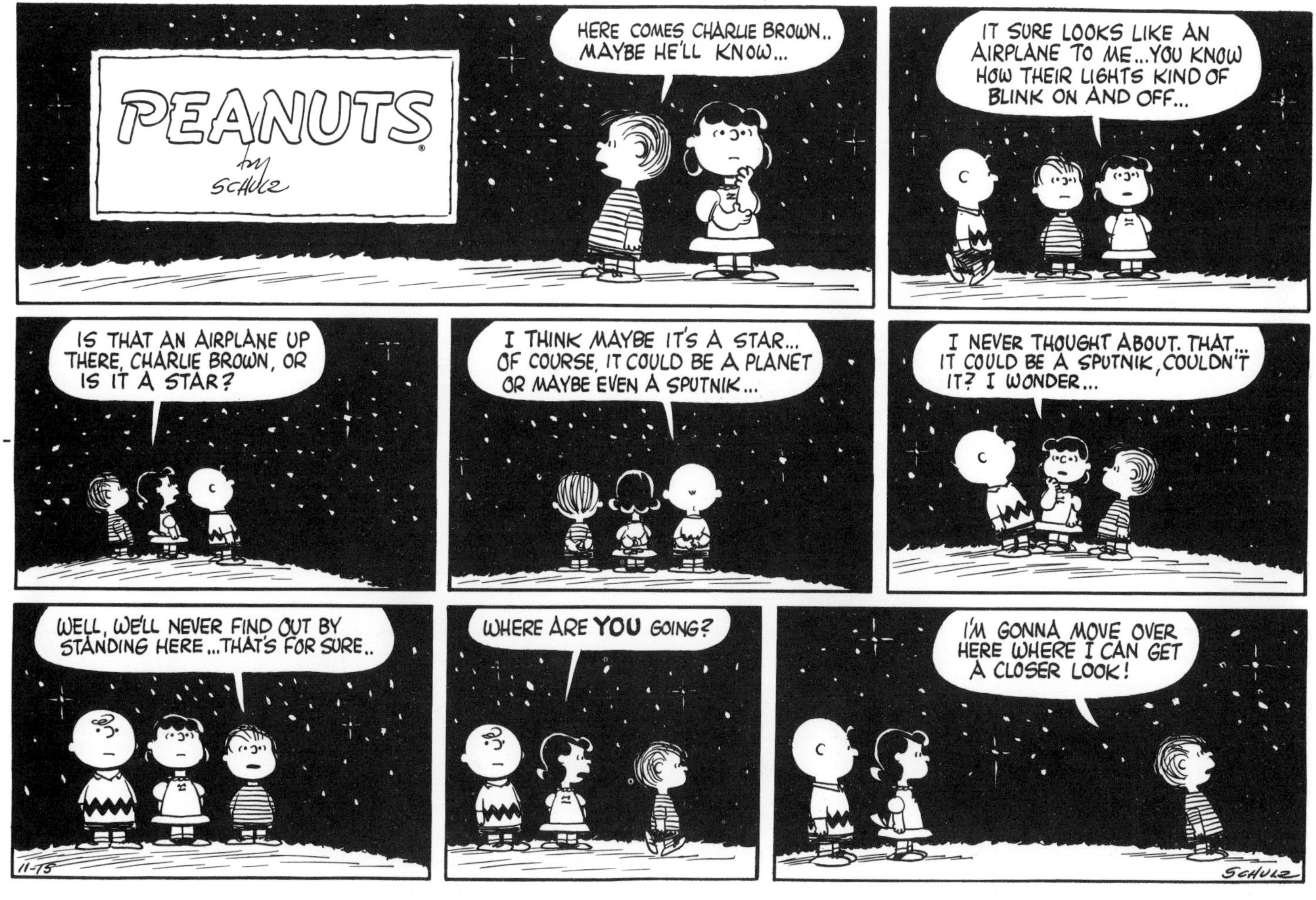
PEANUTS
by SCHULZ
HERE COMES CHARLIE BROWN.. MAYBE HE'LL KNOW...
IT SURE LOOKS LIKE AN AIRPLANE TO ME...YOU KNOW HOW THEIR LIGHTS KIND OF BLINK ON AND OFF...
IS THAT AN AIRPLANE UP THERE, CHARLIE BROWN, OR IS IT A STAR?
I THINK MAYBE IT'S A STAR... OF COURSE, IT COULD BE A PLANET OR MAYBE EVEN A SPUTNIK...
I NEVER THOUGHT ABOUT. THAT... IT COULD BE A SPUTNIK, COULDN'T IT? I WONDER...
WELL, WE'LL NEVER FIND OUT BY STANDING HERE...THAT'S FOR SURE..
11-15
WHERE ARE YOU GOING?
I'M GONNA MOVE OVER HERE WHERE I CAN GET A CLOSER LOOK!
SCHULZ

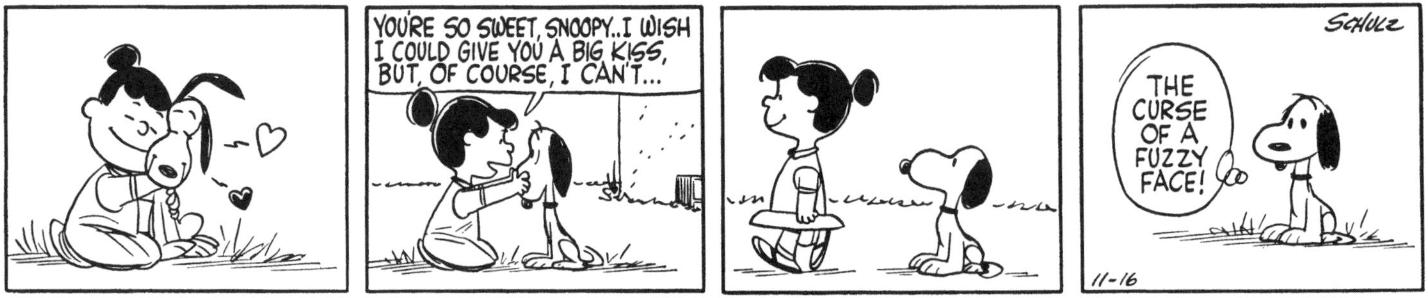
YOU'RE SO SWEET, SNOOPY..I WISH I COULD GIVE YOU A BIG KISS, BUT, OF COURSE, I CAN'T...
SCHULZ
THE CURSE OF A FUZZY FACE!
11-16

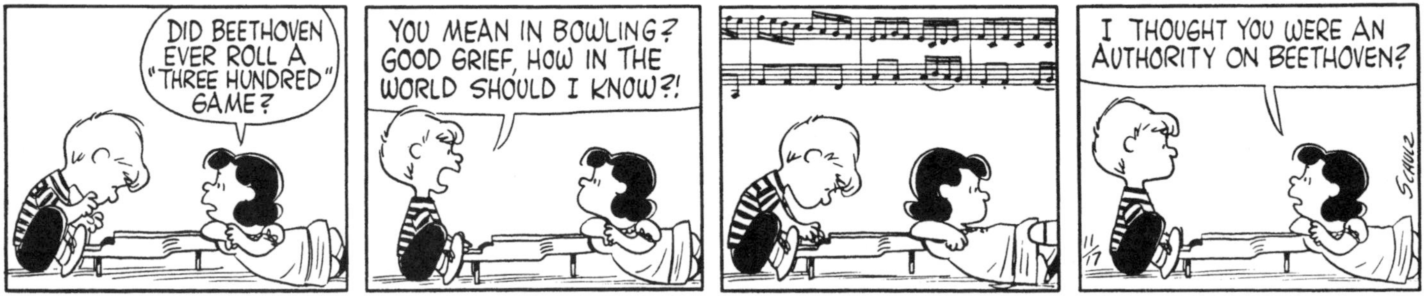
DID BEETHOVEN EVER ROLL A "THREE HUNDRED" GAME?
YOU MEAN IN BOWLING? GOOD GRIEF, HOW IN THE WORLD SHOULD I KNOW?!
I THOUGHT YOU WERE AN AUTHORITY ON BEETHOVEN?
SCHULZ
11/17

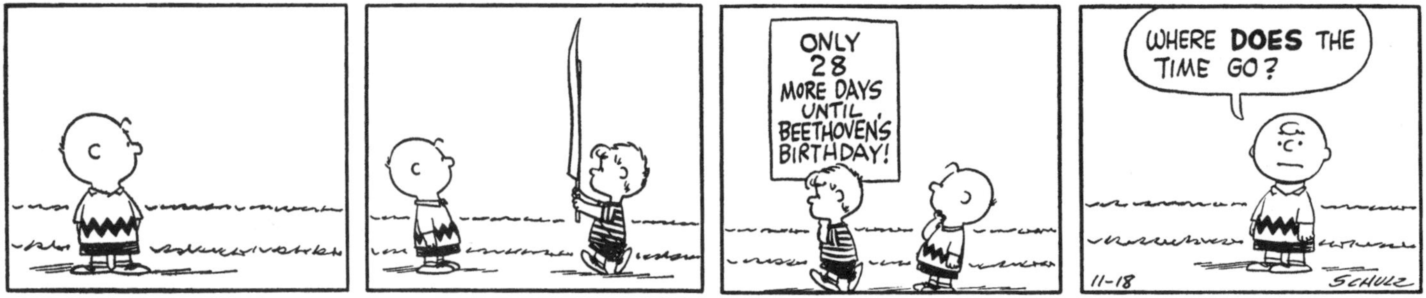
ONLY 28 MORE DAYS UNTIL BEETHOVEN'S BIRTHDAY!
WHERE **DOES** THE TIME GO?
11-18
SCHULZ

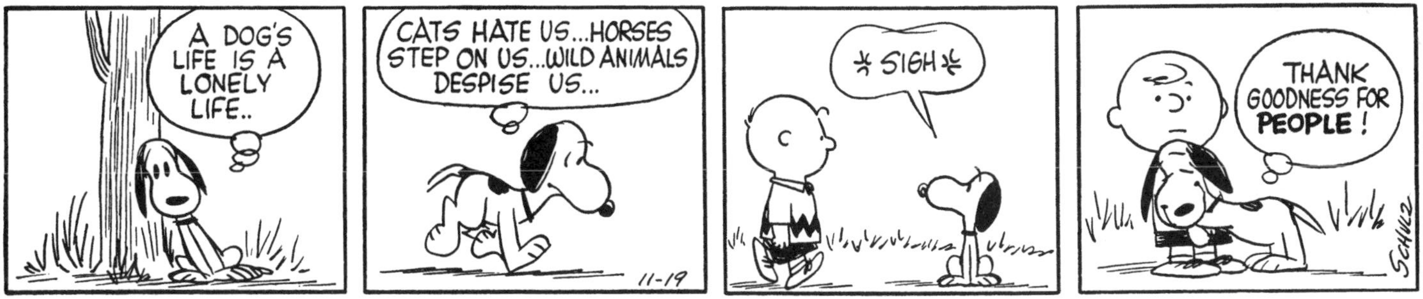
A DOG'S LIFE IS A LONELY LIFE..
CATS HATE US...HORSES STEP ON US...WILD ANIMALS DESPISE US...
11-19
* SIGH *
THANK GOODNESS FOR PEOPLE!
SCHULZ

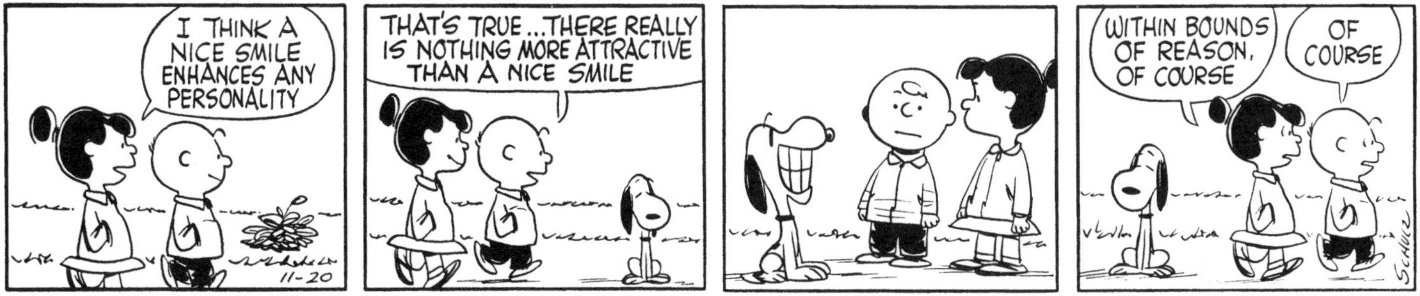
I THINK A NICE SMILE ENHANCES ANY PERSONALITY
11-20
THAT'S TRUE...THERE REALLY IS NOTHING MORE ATTRACTIVE THAN A NICE SMILE
WITHIN BOUNDS OF REASON, OF COURSE
OF COURSE
SCHULZ

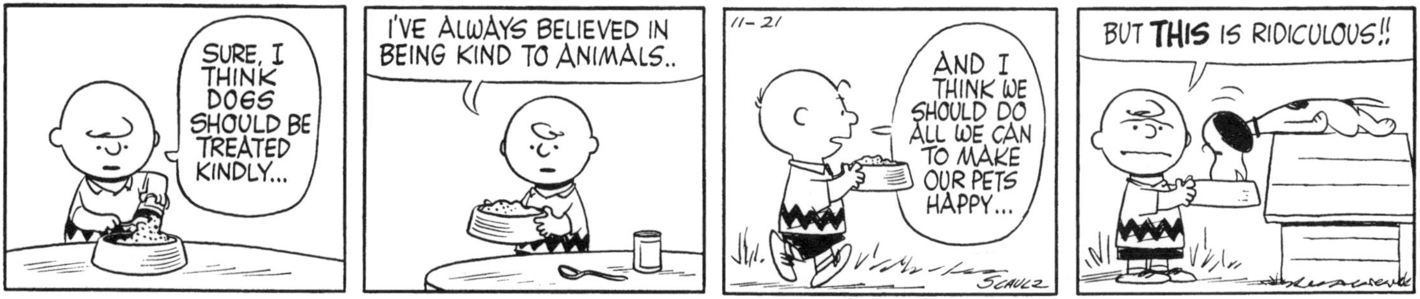
SURE, I THINK DOGS SHOULD BE TREATED KINDLY...
I'VE ALWAYS BELIEVED IN BEING KIND TO ANIMALS..
11-21
AND I THINK WE SHOULD DO ALL WE CAN TO MAKE OUR PETS HAPPY...
SCHULZ
BUT THIS IS RIDICULOUS!!

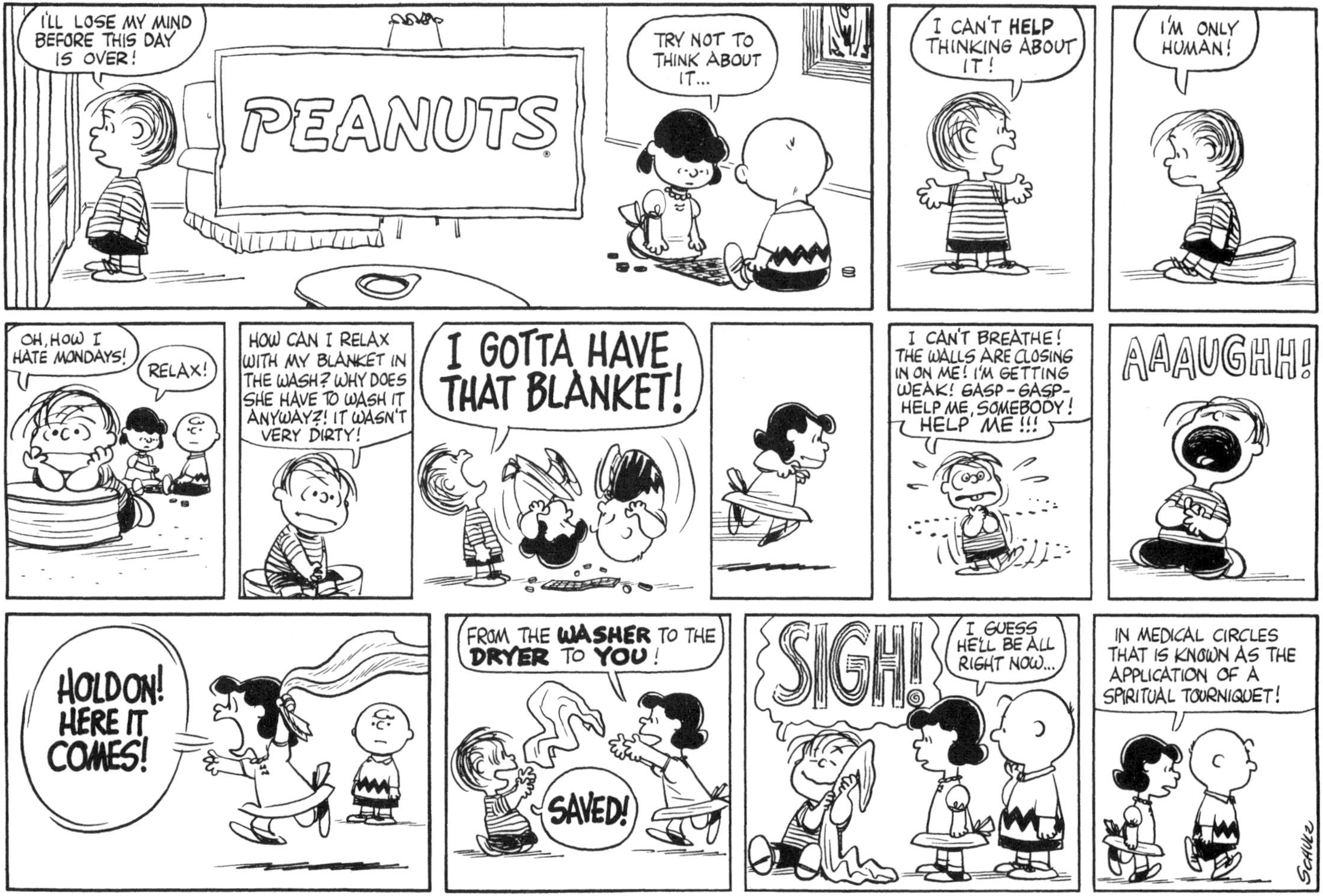
I'LL LOSE MY MIND BEFORE THIS DAY IS OVER!
PEANUTS
TRY NOT TO THINK ABOUT IT...
I CAN'T HELP THINKING ABOUT IT!
I'M ONLY HUMAN!
OH, HOW I HATE MONDAYS!
RELAX!
HOW CAN I RELAX WITH MY BLANKET IN THE WASH? WHY DOES SHE HAVE TO WASH IT ANYWAY?! IT WASN'T VERY DIRTY!
I GOTTA HAVE THAT BLANKET!
I CAN'T BREATHE! THE WALLS ARE CLOSING IN ON ME! I'M GETTING WEAK! GASP-GASP-HELP ME, SOMEBODY! HELP ME!!!
AAAUGHH!
HOLD ON! HERE IT COMES!
FROM THE WASHER TO THE DRYER TO YOU!
SAVED!
SIGH!
I GUESS HE'LL BE ALL RIGHT NOW...
IN MEDICAL CIRCLES THAT IS KNOWN AS THE APPLICATION OF A SPIRITUAL TOURNIQUET!
SCHULZ

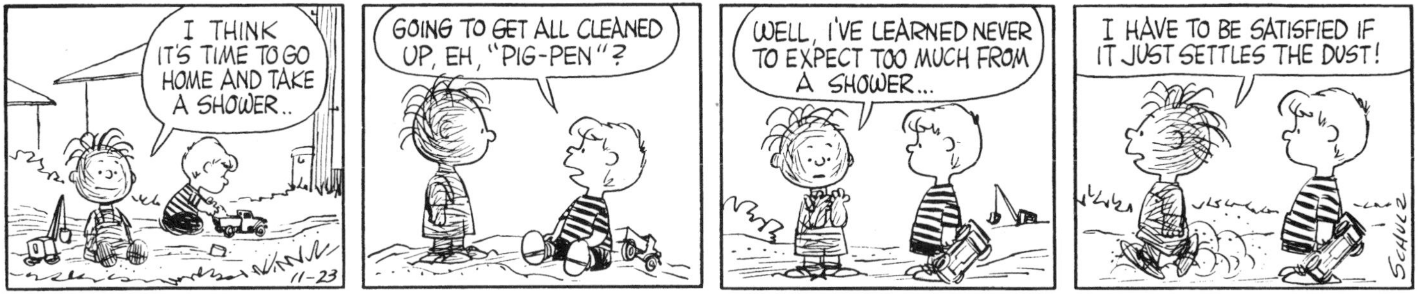
I THINK IT'S TIME TO GO HOME AND TAKE A SHOWER..
GOING TO GET ALL CLEANED UP, EH, "PIG-PEN"?
WELL, I'VE LEARNED NEVER TO EXPECT TOO MUCH FROM A SHOWER...
I HAVE TO BE SATISFIED IF IT JUST SETTLES THE DUST!
11-23
SCHULZ

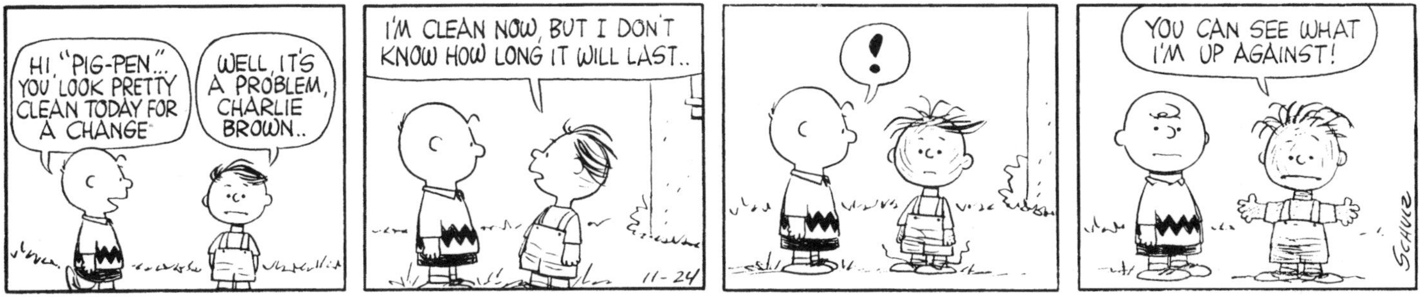
HI, "PIG-PEN"... YOU LOOK PRETTY CLEAN TODAY FOR A CHANGE
WELL, IT'S A PROBLEM, CHARLIE BROWN..
I'M CLEAN NOW, BUT I DON'T KNOW HOW LONG IT WILL LAST..
11-24
!
YOU CAN SEE WHAT I'M UP AGAINST!
SCHULZ

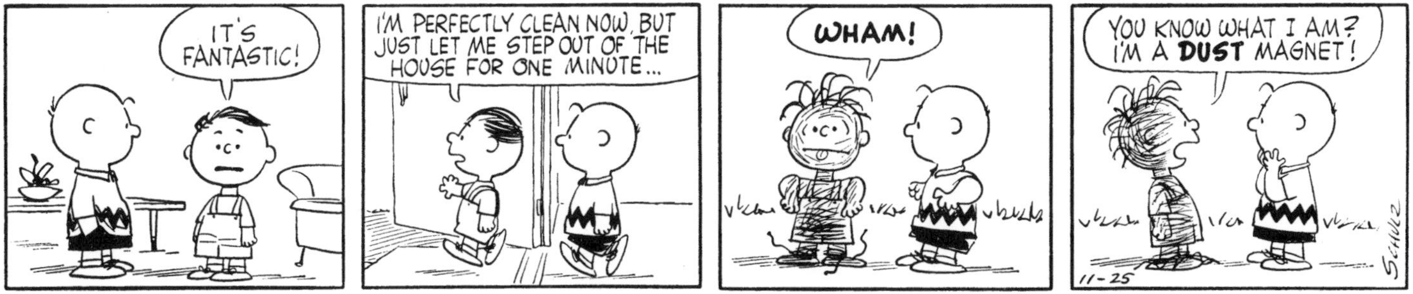
IT'S FANTASTIC!
I'M PERFECTLY CLEAN NOW, BUT JUST LET ME STEP OUT OF THE HOUSE FOR ONE MINUTE...
WHAM!
YOU KNOW WHAT I AM? I'M A **DUST** MAGNET!
11-25
SCHULZ

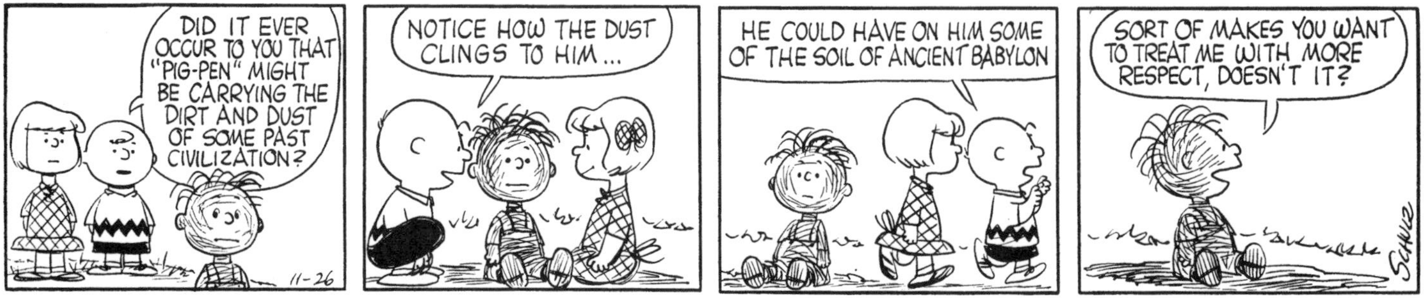
DID IT EVER OCCUR TO YOU THAT "PIG-PEN" MIGHT BE CARRYING THE DIRT AND DUST OF SOME PAST CIVILIZATION?
11-26
NOTICE HOW THE DUST CLINGS TO HIM...
HE COULD HAVE ON HIM SOME OF THE SOIL OF ANCIENT BABYLON
SORT OF MAKES YOU WANT TO TREAT ME WITH MORE RESPECT, DOESN'T IT?
SCHULZ

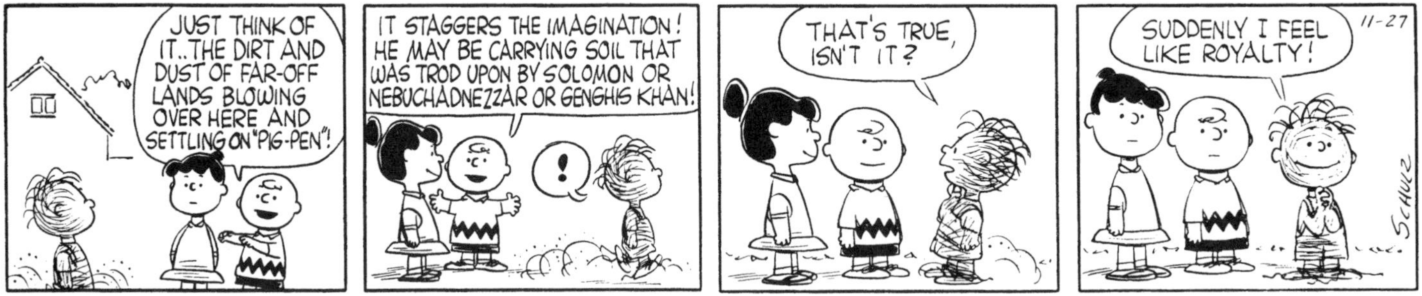
JUST THINK OF IT..THE DIRT AND DUST OF FAR-OFF LANDS BLOWING OVER HERE AND SETTLING ON "PIG-PEN"!
IT STAGGERS THE IMAGINATION! HE MAY BE CARRYING SOIL THAT WAS TROD UPON BY SOLOMON OR NEBUCHADNEZZAR OR GENGHIS KHAN!
!
THAT'S TRUE, ISN'T IT?
11-27
SUDDENLY I FEEL LIKE ROYALTY!
SCHULZ

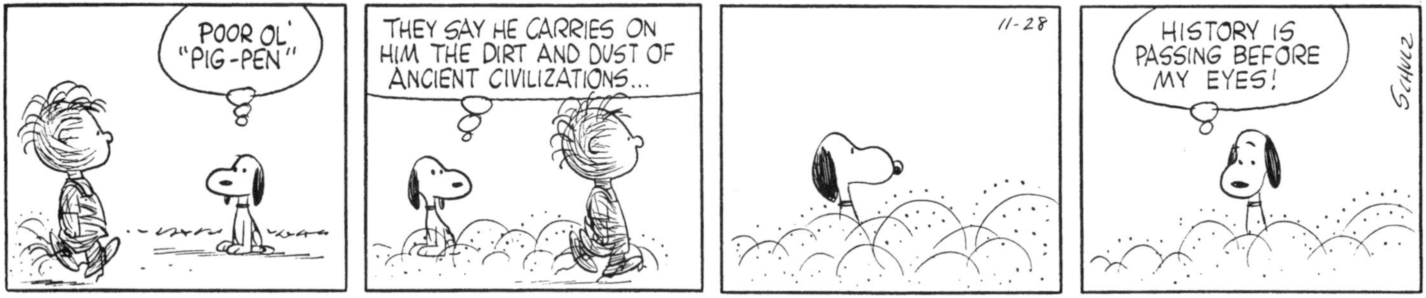
POOR OL' "PIG-PEN"
THEY SAY HE CARRIES ON HIM THE DIRT AND DUST OF ANCIENT CIVILIZATIONS...
11-28
HISTORY IS PASSING BEFORE MY EYES!
SCHULZ

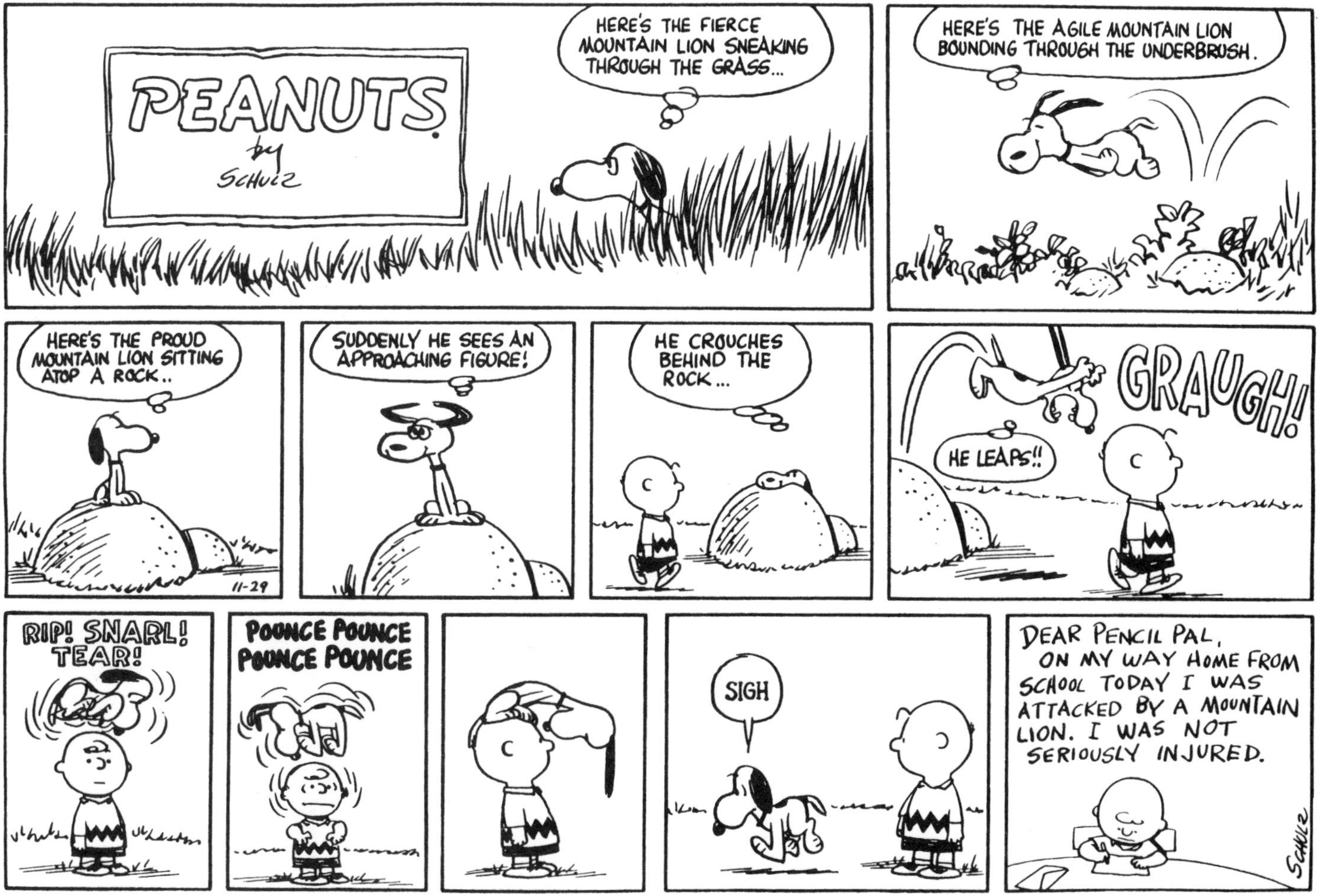
PEANUTS
by SCHULZ
HERE'S THE FIERCE MOUNTAIN LION SNEAKING THROUGH THE GRASS...
HERE'S THE AGILE MOUNTAIN LION BOUNDING THROUGH THE UNDERBRUSH.
HERE'S THE PROUD MOUNTAIN LION SITTING ATOP A ROCK..
11-29
SUDDENLY HE SEES AN APPROACHING FIGURE!
HE CROUCHES BEHIND THE ROCK...
HE LEAPS!!
GRAUGH!
RIP! SNARL! TEAR!
POUNCE POUNCE POUNCE POUNCE
SIGH
DEAR PENCIL PAL, ON MY WAY HOME FROM SCHOOL TODAY I WAS ATTACKED BY A MOUNTAIN LION. I WAS NOT SERIOUSLY INJURED.
SCHULZ

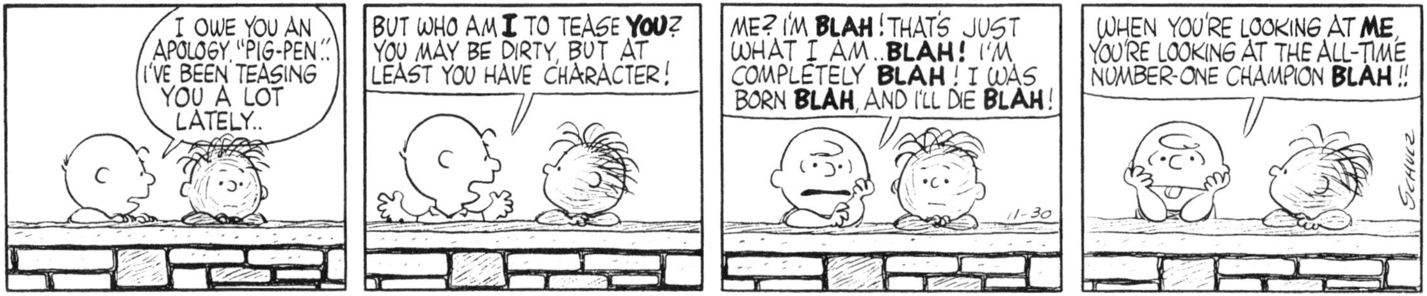
I OWE YOU AN APOLOGY, "PIG-PEN".. I'VE BEEN TEASING YOU A LOT LATELY..
BUT WHO AM **I** TO TEASE **YOU**? YOU MAY BE DIRTY, BUT AT LEAST YOU HAVE CHARACTER!
ME? I'M **BLAH**! THAT'S JUST WHAT I AM..**BLAH!** I'M COMPLETELY **BLAH**! I WAS BORN **BLAH**, AND I'LL DIE **BLAH**!
11-30
WHEN YOU'RE LOOKING AT **ME**, YOU'RE LOOKING AT THE ALL-TIME NUMBER-ONE CHAMPION **BLAH**!!
SCHULZ

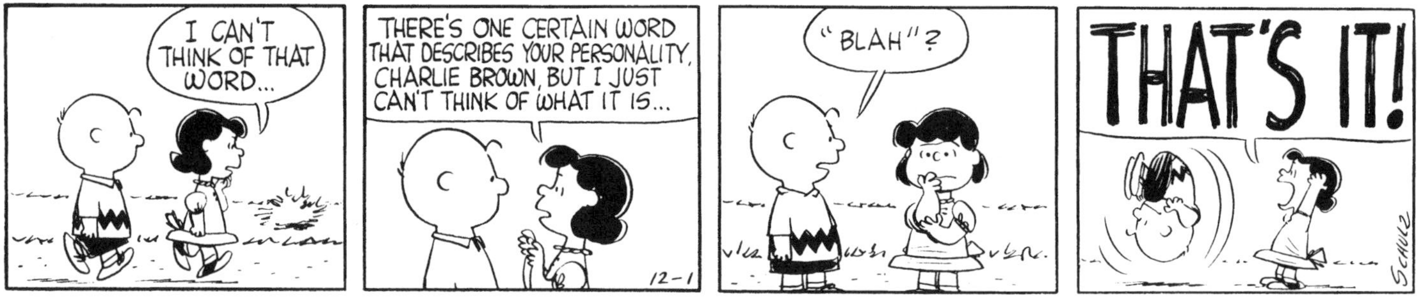
I CAN'T THINK OF THAT WORD...
THERE'S ONE CERTAIN WORD THAT DESCRIBES YOUR PERSONALITY, CHARLIE BROWN, BUT I JUST CAN'T THINK OF WHAT IT IS...
12-1
"BLAH"?
THAT'S IT!
SCHULZ

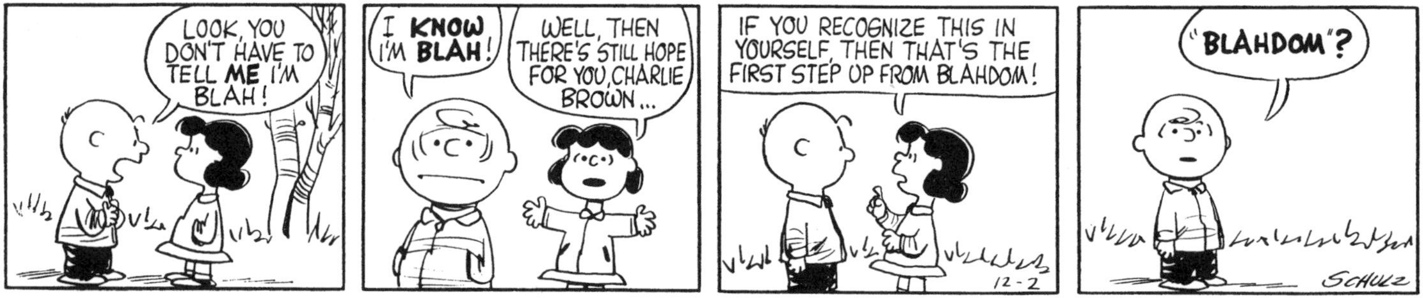
LOOK, YOU DON'T HAVE TO TELL **ME** I'M BLAH!
I **KNOW** I'M **BLAH**!
WELL, THEN THERE'S STILL HOPE FOR YOU, CHARLIE BROWN...
IF YOU RECOGNIZE THIS IN YOURSELF, THEN THAT'S THE FIRST STEP UP FROM BLAHDOM!
12-2
"**BLAHDOM**"?
SCHULZ

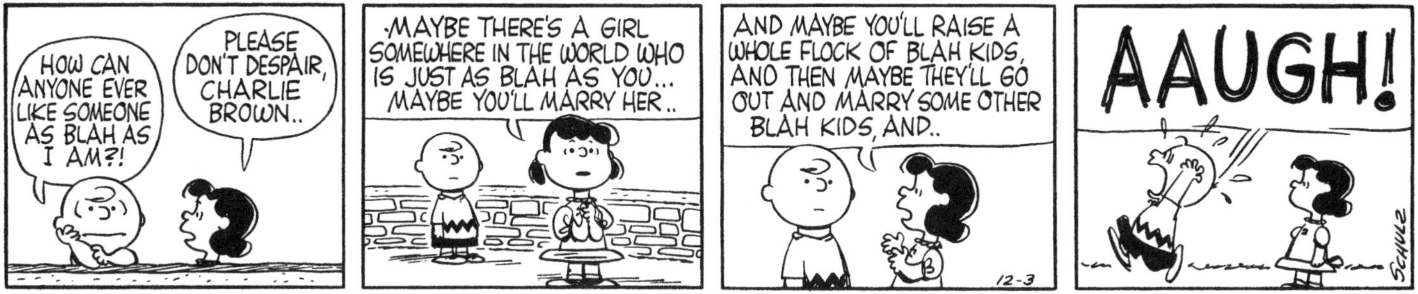
HOW CAN ANYONE EVER LIKE SOMEONE AS BLAH AS I AM?!
PLEASE DON'T DESPAIR, CHARLIE BROWN..
MAYBE THERE'S A GIRL SOMEWHERE IN THE WORLD WHO IS JUST AS BLAH AS YOU... MAYBE YOU'LL MARRY HER..
AND MAYBE YOU'LL RAISE A WHOLE FLOCK OF BLAH KIDS, AND THEN MAYBE THEY'LL GO OUT AND MARRY SOME OTHER BLAH KIDS, AND..
12-3
AAUGH!
SCHULZ

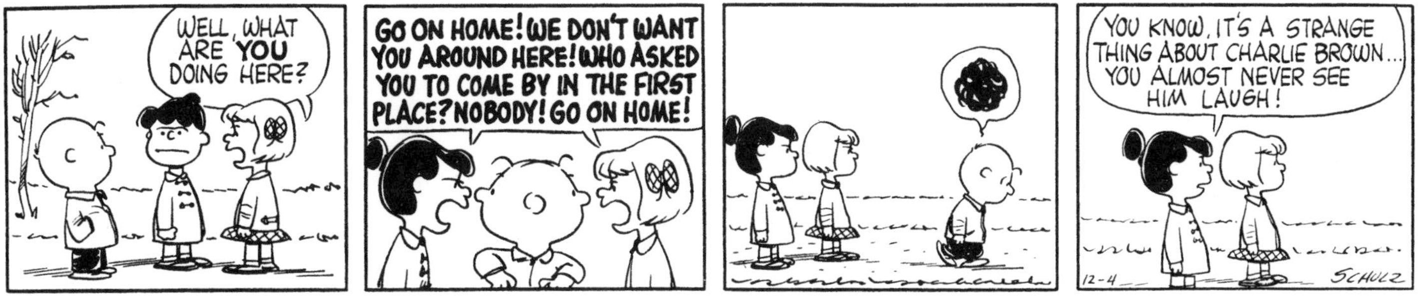
WELL, WHAT ARE **YOU** DOING HERE?
GO ON HOME! WE DON'T WANT YOU AROUND HERE! WHO ASKED YOU TO COME BY IN THE FIRST PLACE? NOBODY! GO ON HOME!
YOU KNOW, IT'S A STRANGE THING ABOUT CHARLIE BROWN... YOU ALMOST NEVER SEE HIM LAUGH!
12-4
SCHULZ

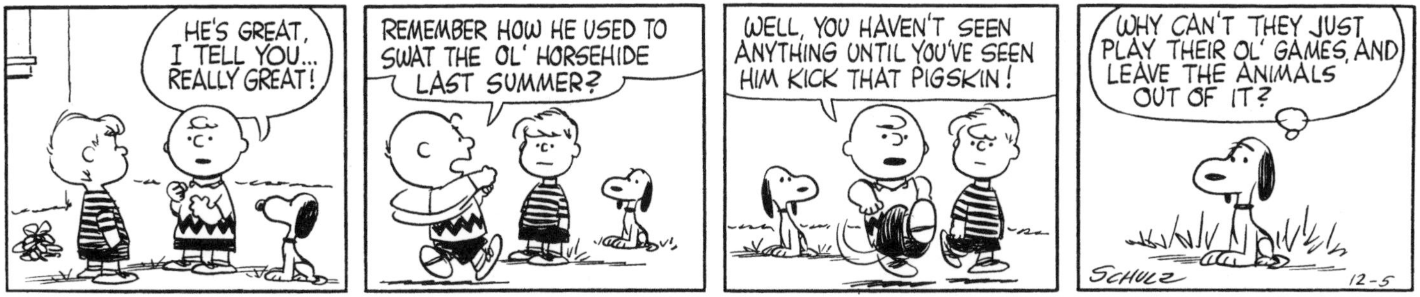
HE'S GREAT, I TELL YOU... REALLY GREAT!
REMEMBER HOW HE USED TO SWAT THE OL' HORSEHIDE LAST SUMMER?
WELL, YOU HAVEN'T SEEN ANYTHING UNTIL YOU'VE SEEN HIM KICK THAT PIGSKIN!
WHY CAN'T THEY JUST PLAY THEIR OL' GAMES, AND LEAVE THE ANIMALS OUT OF IT?
SCHULZ
12-5

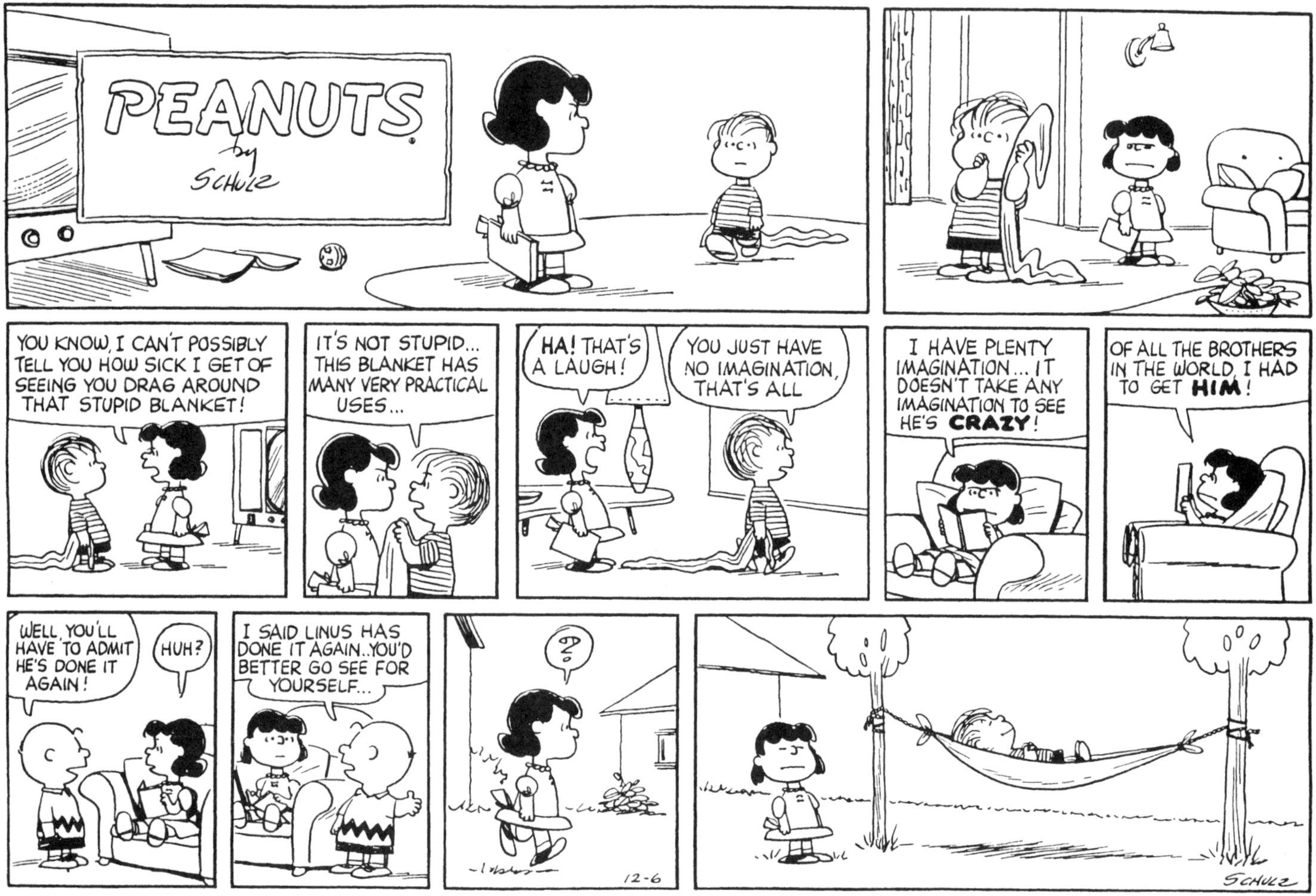
PEANUTS
by SCHULZ
YOU KNOW, I CAN'T POSSIBLY TELL YOU HOW SICK I GET OF SEEING YOU DRAG AROUND THAT STUPID BLANKET!
IT'S NOT STUPID... THIS BLANKET HAS MANY VERY PRACTICAL USES...
HA! THAT'S A LAUGH!
YOU JUST HAVE NO IMAGINATION, THAT'S ALL
I HAVE PLENTY IMAGINATION... IT DOESN'T TAKE ANY IMAGINATION TO SEE HE'S CRAZY!
OF ALL THE BROTHERS IN THE WORLD, I HAD TO GET HIM!
WELL, YOU'LL HAVE TO ADMIT HE'S DONE IT AGAIN!
HUH?
I SAID LINUS HAS DONE IT AGAIN..YOU'D BETTER GO SEE FOR YOURSELF...
?
12-6
SCHULZ

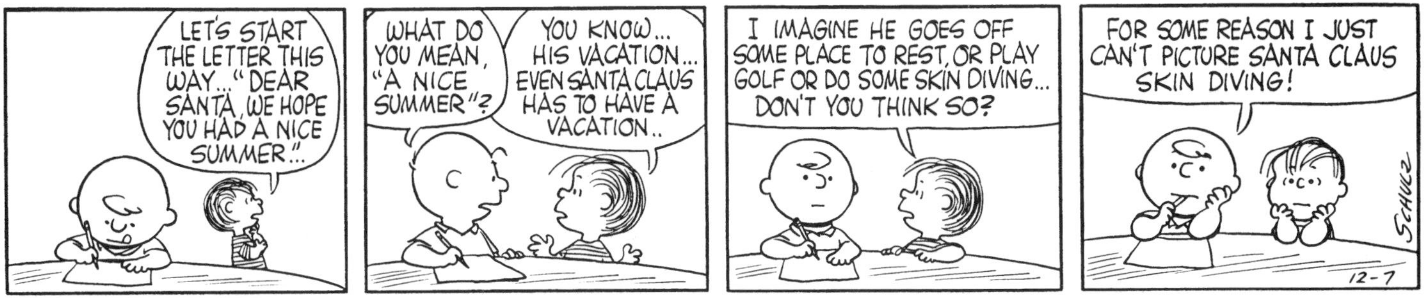
LET'S START THE LETTER THIS WAY..."DEAR SANTA, WE HOPE YOU HAD A NICE SUMMER."
WHAT DO YOU MEAN, "A NICE SUMMER"?
YOU KNOW... HIS VACATION... EVEN SANTA CLAUS HAS TO HAVE A VACATION..
I IMAGINE HE GOES OFF SOME PLACE TO REST, OR PLAY GOLF OR DO SOME SKIN DIVING... DON'T YOU THINK SO?
FOR SOME REASON I JUST CAN'T PICTURE SANTA CLAUS SKIN DIVING!
SCHULZ
12-7

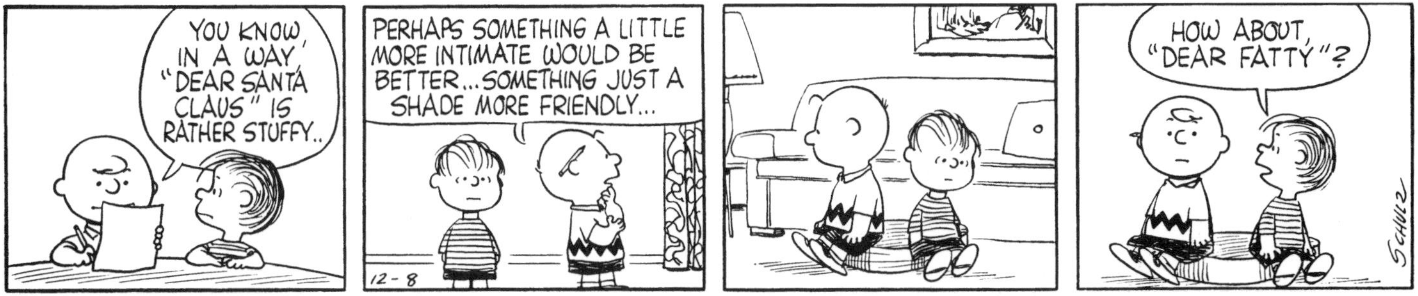
YOU KNOW, IN A WAY "DEAR SANTA CLAUS" IS RATHER STUFFY..
PERHAPS SOMETHING A LITTLE MORE INTIMATE WOULD BE BETTER...SOMETHING JUST A SHADE MORE FRIENDLY...
12-8
HOW ABOUT, "DEAR FATTY"?
SCHULZ

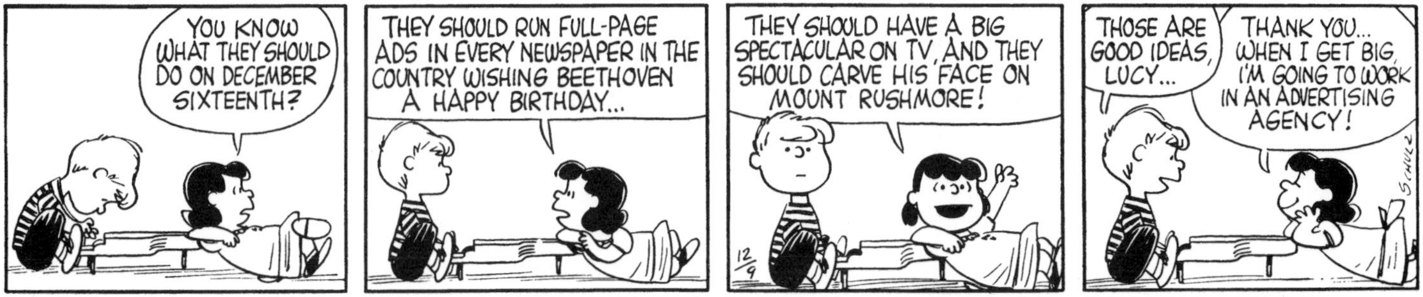
YOU KNOW WHAT THEY SHOULD DO ON DECEMBER SIXTEENTH?
THEY SHOULD RUN FULL-PAGE ADS IN EVERY NEWSPAPER IN THE COUNTRY WISHING BEETHOVEN A HAPPY BIRTHDAY...
THEY SHOULD HAVE A BIG SPECTACULAR ON TV, AND THEY SHOULD CARVE HIS FACE ON MOUNT RUSHMORE!
12/9
THOSE ARE GOOD IDEAS, LUCY...
THANK YOU... WHEN I GET BIG, I'M GOING TO WORK IN AN ADVERTISING AGENCY!
SCHULZ

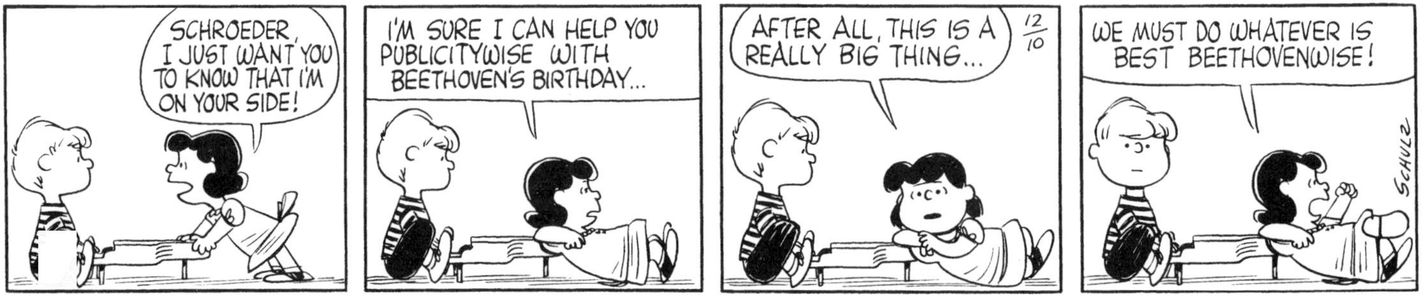
SCHROEDER, I JUST WANT YOU TO KNOW THAT I'M ON YOUR SIDE!
I'M SURE I CAN HELP YOU PUBLICITYWISE WITH BEETHOVEN'S BIRTHDAY...
AFTER ALL, THIS IS A REALLY BIG THING...
12/10
WE MUST DO WHATEVER IS BEST BEETHOVENWISE!
SCHULZ

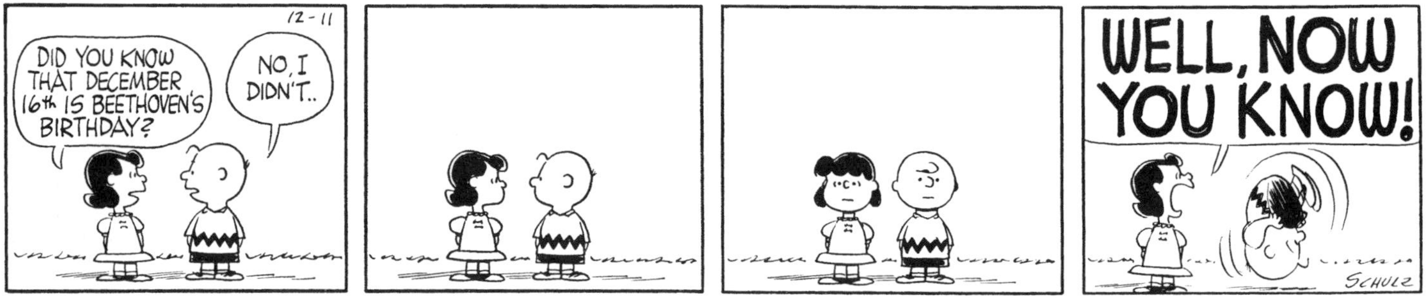
12-11
DID YOU KNOW THAT DECEMBER 16th IS BEETHOVEN'S BIRTHDAY?
NO, I DIDN'T..
WELL, NOW YOU KNOW!
SCHULZ

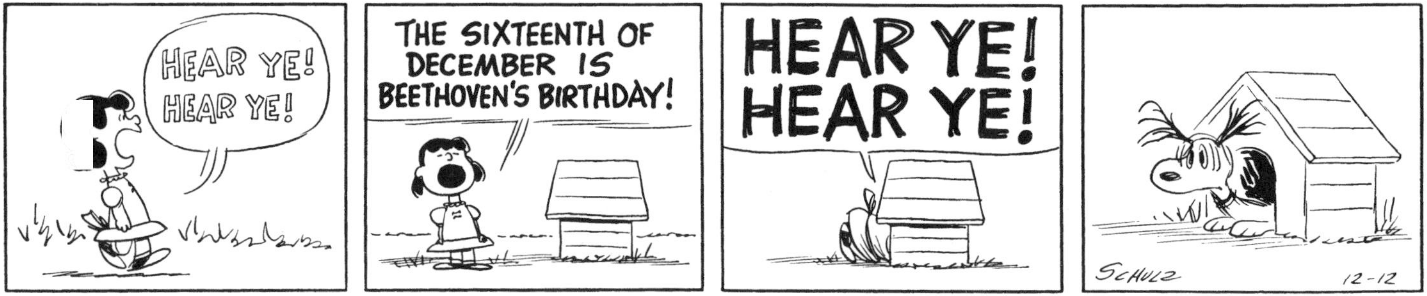
HEAR YE! HEAR YE!
THE SIXTEENTH OF DECEMBER IS BEETHOVEN'S BIRTHDAY!
HEAR YE! HEAR YE!
SCHULZ
12-12

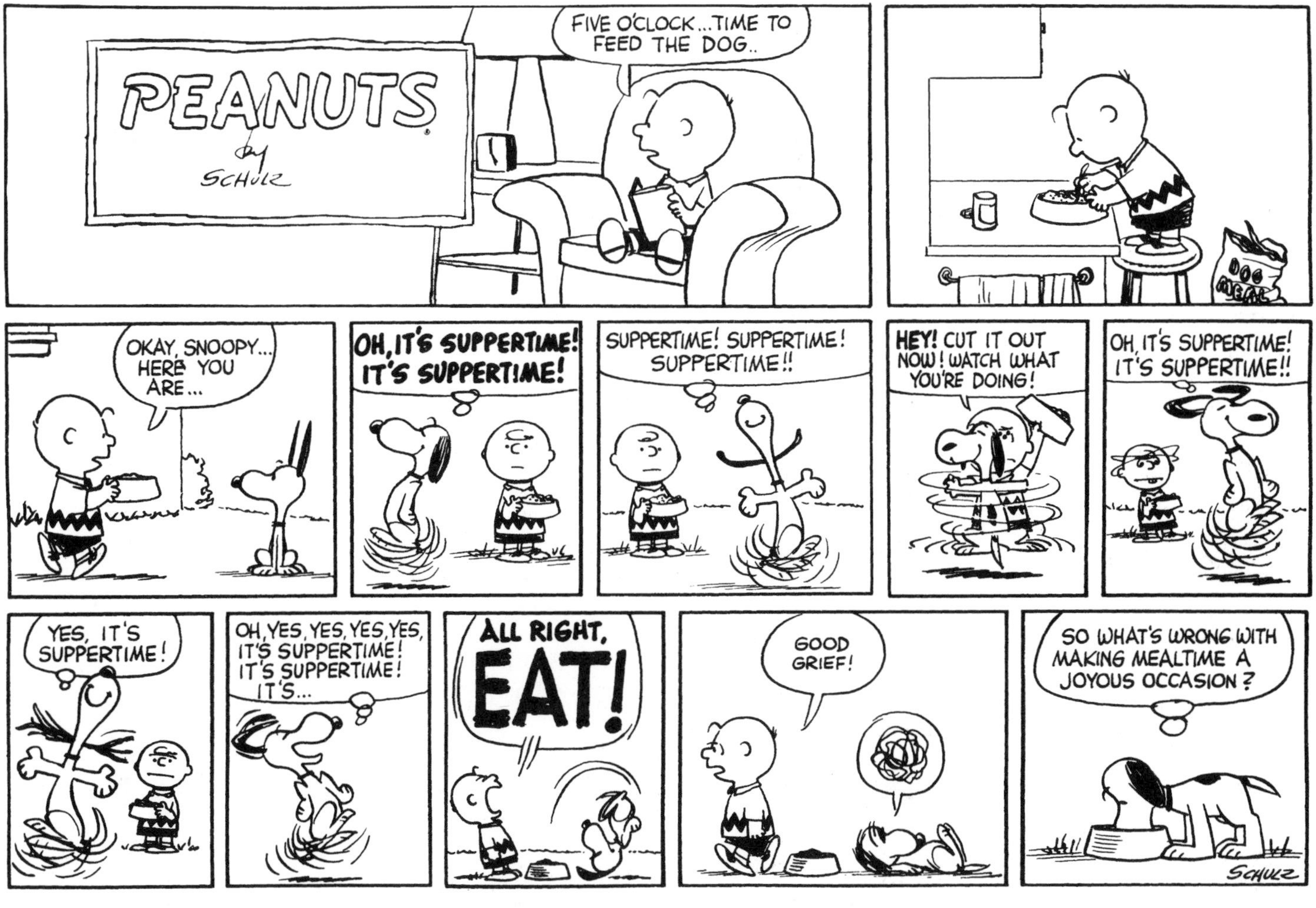
PEANUTS
by SCHULZ
FIVE O'CLOCK...TIME TO FEED THE DOG..
DOG MEAL
OKAY, SNOOPY... HERE YOU ARE...
OH, IT'S SUPPERTIME! IT'S SUPPERTIME!
SUPPERTIME! SUPPERTIME! SUPPERTIME!!
HEY! CUT IT OUT NOW! WATCH WHAT YOU'RE DOING!
OH, IT'S SUPPERTIME! IT'S SUPPERTIME!!
YES, IT'S SUPPERTIME!
OH, YES, YES, YES, YES, IT'S SUPPERTIME! IT'S SUPPERTIME! IT'S...
ALL RIGHT, EAT!
GOOD GRIEF!
SO WHAT'S WRONG WITH MAKING MEALTIME A JOYOUS OCCASION?
SCHULZ

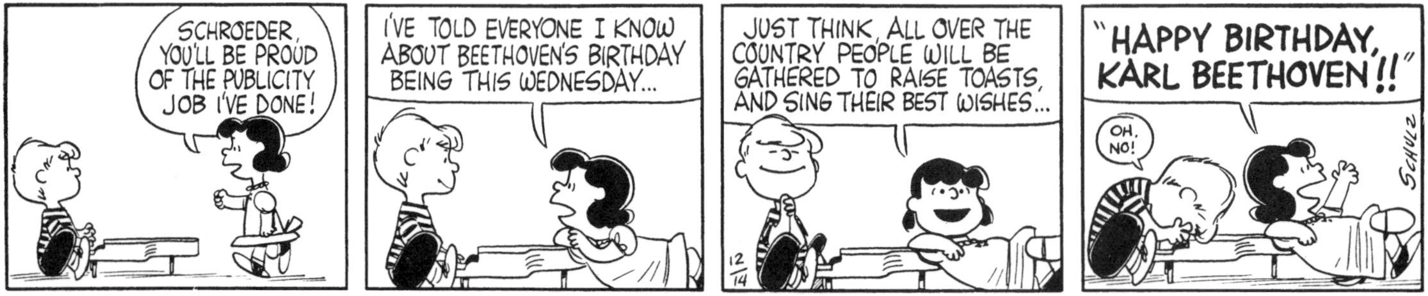
SCHROEDER, YOU'LL BE PROUD OF THE PUBLICITY JOB I'VE DONE!
I'VE TOLD EVERYONE I KNOW ABOUT BEETHOVEN'S BIRTHDAY BEING THIS WEDNESDAY...
JUST THINK, ALL OVER THE COUNTRY PEOPLE WILL BE GATHERED TO RAISE TOASTS, AND SING THEIR BEST WISHES...
12/14
"HAPPY BIRTHDAY, KARL BEETHOVEN!!"
OH, NO!
SCHULZ

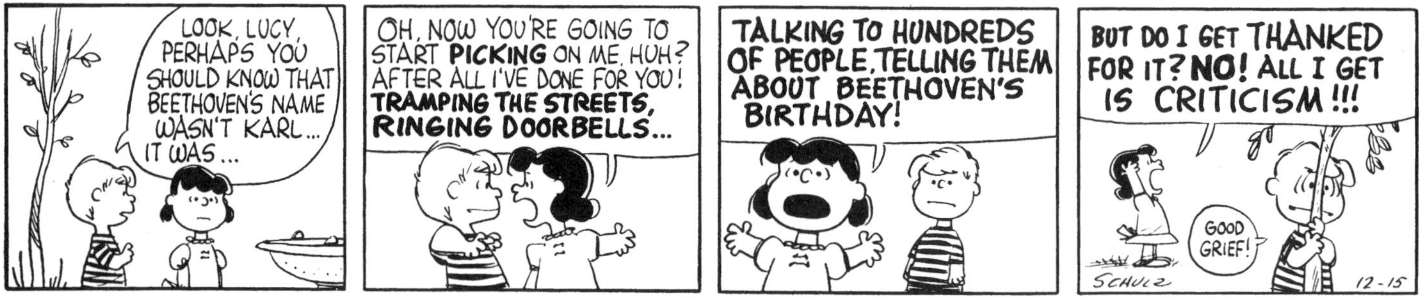
LOOK, LUCY, PERHAPS YOU SHOULD KNOW THAT BEETHOVEN'S NAME WASN'T KARL... IT WAS...
OH, NOW YOU'RE GOING TO START **PICKING** ON ME, HUH? AFTER ALL I'VE DONE FOR YOU! **TRAMPING THE STREETS, RINGING DOORBELLS...**
TALKING TO HUNDREDS OF PEOPLE, TELLING THEM ABOUT BEETHOVEN'S BIRTHDAY!
BUT DO I GET THANKED FOR IT? **NO!** ALL I GET IS CRITICISM!!!
GOOD GRIEF!
SCHULZ
12-15

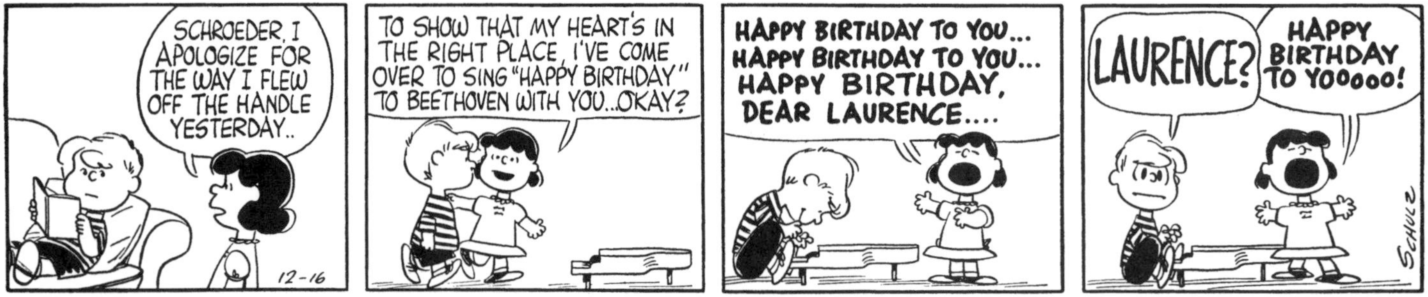
SCHROEDER, I APOLOGIZE FOR THE WAY I FLEW OFF THE HANDLE YESTERDAY..
12-16
TO SHOW THAT MY HEART'S IN THE RIGHT PLACE, I'VE COME OVER TO SING "HAPPY BIRTHDAY" TO BEETHOVEN WITH YOU...OKAY?
HAPPY BIRTHDAY TO YOU... HAPPY BIRTHDAY TO YOU... HAPPY BIRTHDAY, DEAR LAURENCE....
LAURENCE?
HAPPY BIRTHDAY TO YOooooo!
SCHULZ

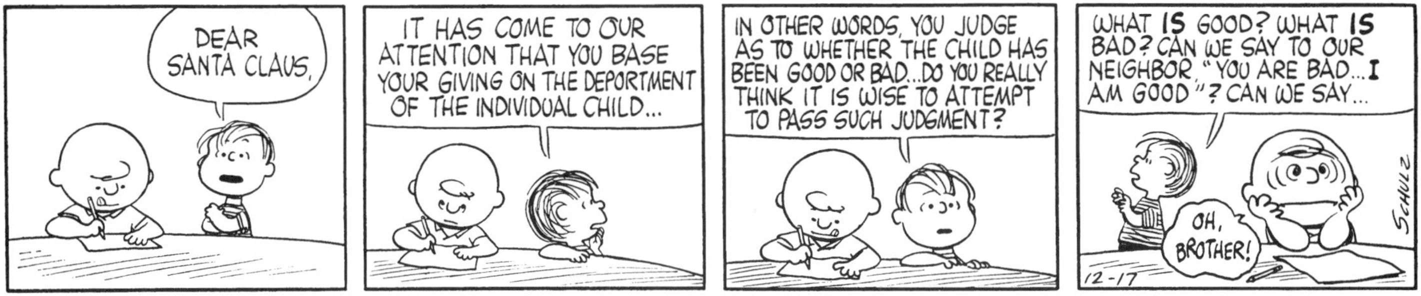
DEAR SANTA CLAUS,
IT HAS COME TO OUR ATTENTION THAT YOU BASE YOUR GIVING ON THE DEPORTMENT OF THE INDIVIDUAL CHILD...
IN OTHER WORDS, YOU JUDGE AS TO WHETHER THE CHILD HAS BEEN GOOD OR BAD...DO YOU REALLY THINK IT IS WISE TO ATTEMPT TO PASS SUCH JUDGMENT?
WHAT IS GOOD? WHAT IS BAD? CAN WE SAY TO OUR NEIGHBOR, "YOU ARE BAD...I AM GOOD"? CAN WE SAY...
OH, BROTHER!
SCHULZ
12-17

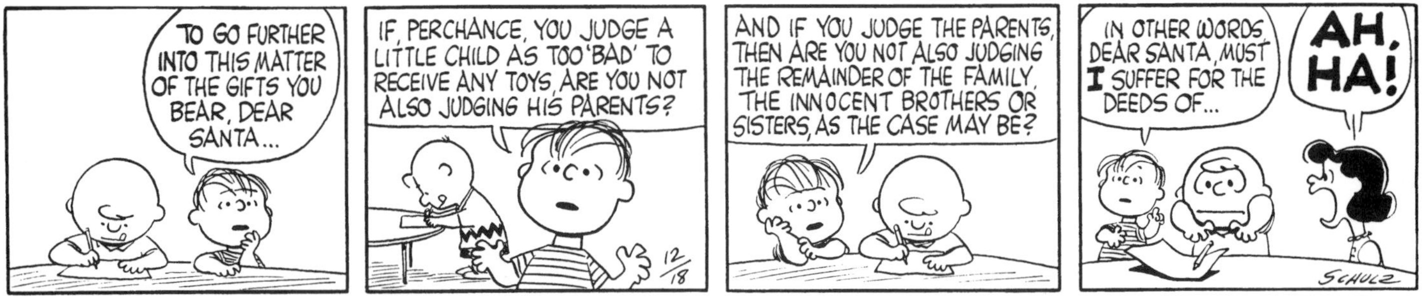
TO GO FURTHER INTO THIS MATTER OF THE GIFTS YOU BEAR, DEAR SANTA...
IF, PERCHANCE, YOU JUDGE A LITTLE CHILD AS TOO 'BAD' TO RECEIVE ANY TOYS, ARE YOU NOT ALSO JUDGING HIS PARENTS?
12/18
AND IF YOU JUDGE THE PARENTS, THEN ARE YOU NOT ALSO JUDGING THE REMAINDER OF THE FAMILY, THE INNOCENT BROTHERS OR SISTERS, AS THE CASE MAY BE?
IN OTHER WORDS DEAR SANTA, MUST I SUFFER FOR THE DEEDS OF...
AH, HA!
SCHULZ

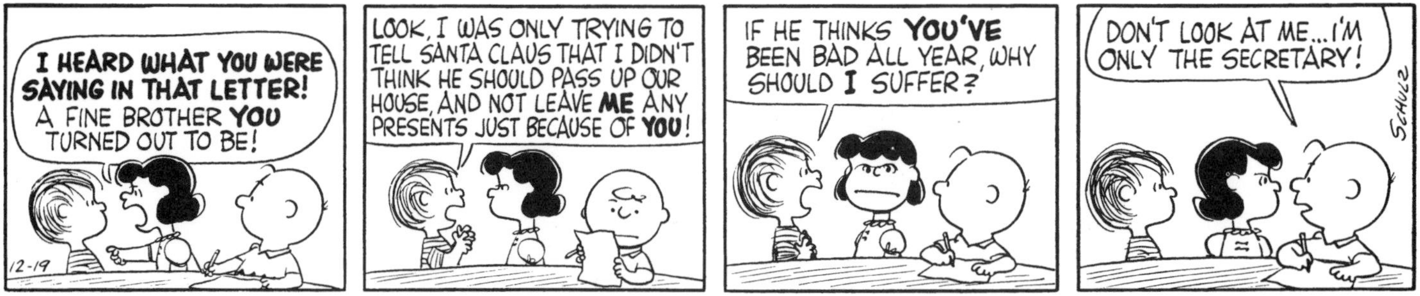
I HEARD WHAT YOU WERE SAYING IN THAT LETTER! A FINE BROTHER YOU TURNED OUT TO BE!
12-19
LOOK, I WAS ONLY TRYING TO TELL SANTA CLAUS THAT I DIDN'T THINK HE SHOULD PASS UP OUR HOUSE, AND NOT LEAVE ME ANY PRESENTS JUST BECAUSE OF YOU!
IF HE THINKS YOU'VE BEEN BAD ALL YEAR, WHY SHOULD I SUFFER?
DON'T LOOK AT ME...I'M ONLY THE SECRETARY!
SCHULZ

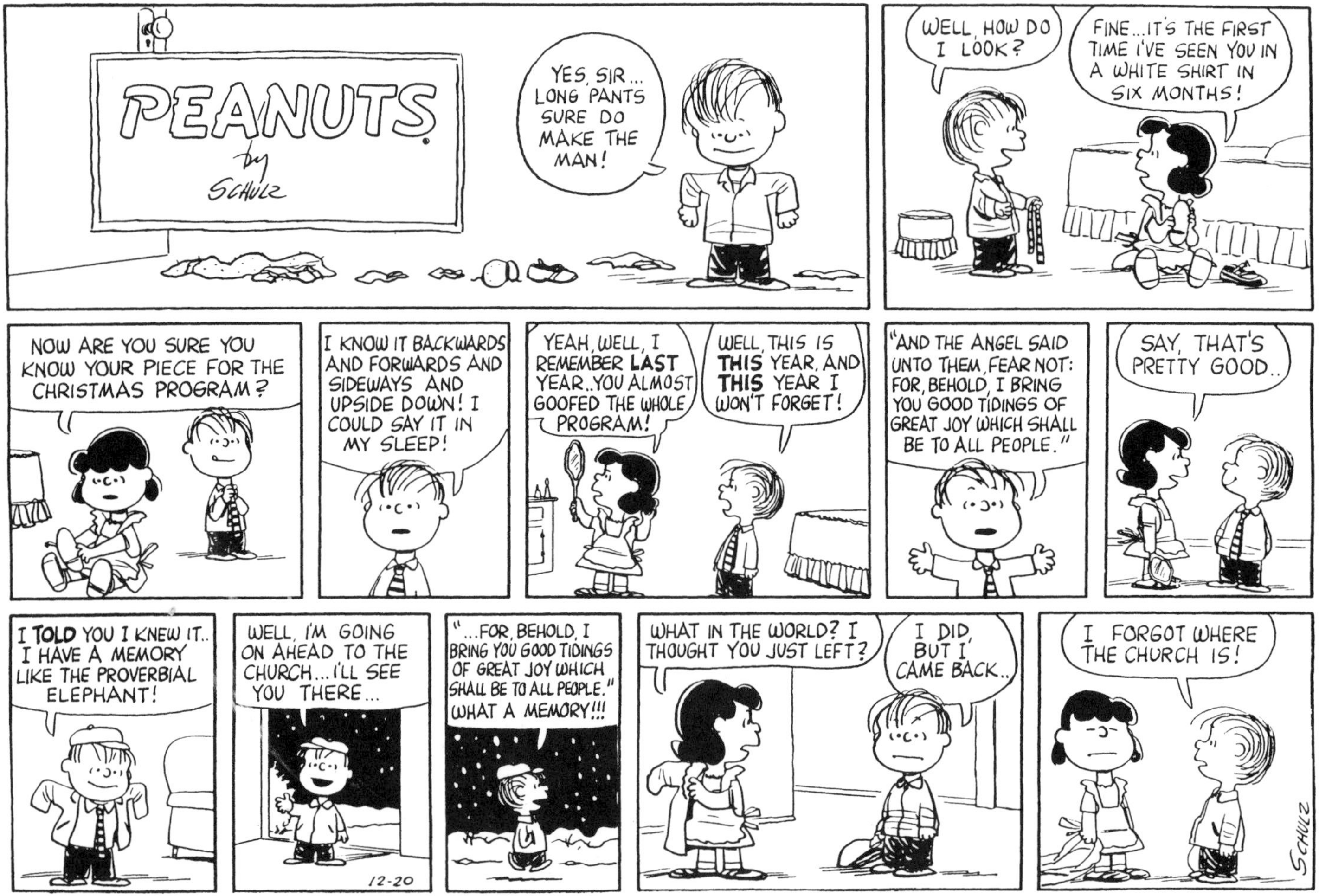
PEANUTS
by SCHULZ
YES, SIR... LONG PANTS SURE DO MAKE THE MAN!
WELL, HOW DO I LOOK?
FINE... IT'S THE FIRST TIME I'VE SEEN YOU IN A WHITE SHIRT IN SIX MONTHS!
NOW ARE YOU SURE YOU KNOW YOUR PIECE FOR THE CHRISTMAS PROGRAM?
I KNOW IT BACKWARDS AND FORWARDS AND SIDEWAYS AND UPSIDE DOWN! I COULD SAY IT IN MY SLEEP!
YEAH, WELL, I REMEMBER LAST YEAR..YOU ALMOST GOOFED THE WHOLE PROGRAM!
WELL, THIS IS THIS YEAR, AND THIS YEAR I WON'T FORGET!
"AND THE ANGEL SAID UNTO THEM, FEAR NOT: FOR, BEHOLD, I BRING YOU GOOD TIDINGS OF GREAT JOY WHICH SHALL BE TO ALL PEOPLE."
SAY, THAT'S PRETTY GOOD..
I TOLD YOU I KNEW IT.. I HAVE A MEMORY LIKE THE PROVERBIAL ELEPHANT!
WELL, I'M GOING ON AHEAD TO THE CHURCH... I'LL SEE YOU THERE...
12-20
"...FOR, BEHOLD, I BRING YOU GOOD TIDINGS OF GREAT JOY WHICH SHALL BE TO ALL PEOPLE." WHAT A MEMORY!!!
WHAT IN THE WORLD? I THOUGHT YOU JUST LEFT?
I DID, BUT I CAME BACK..
I FORGOT WHERE THE CHURCH IS!
SCHULZ

YOU AND YOUR LETTERS TO SANTA CLAUS!

YOU THINK YOU CAN GET ME IN BAD WITH HIM, BUT YOU CAN'T! SANTA IS VERY FORGIVING WITH LITTLE GIRLS!

OH, YEAH?

12-21

YEAH! LITTLE GIRLS CAN GET AWAY WITH A LOT MORE THAN LITTLE BOYS!

WHAT MAKES YOU THINK SO?

BECAUSE WE'RE SO CUTE!

CHARLIE BROWN, DO YOU THINK THAT SANTA CLAUS REALLY KNOWS HIS JOB?

12-22

OH, YES... AFTER ALL, HE'S BEEN AT IT FOR A LONG TIME..

THAT'S JUST WHAT HAS ME WORRIED...

PERHAPS IT'S TIME FOR A **YOUNGER** MAN TO TAKE OVER!

ARE YOU AND LINUS STILL FIGHTING?

NO, I HAVE A PHILOSOPHY THAT PREVENTS THAT SORT OF THING

I HAVE A PROFOUND PHILOSOPHY THAT HAS STOOD THE TEST OF TIME DIFFICULT AS IT MAY BE FOR THE LAYMAN TO UNDERSTAND..

I HAVE A PHILOSOPHY THAT HAS BEEN REFINED IN THE FIRES OF HARDSHIP AND STRUGGLE...

12-23

"LIVE AND LET LIVE!"

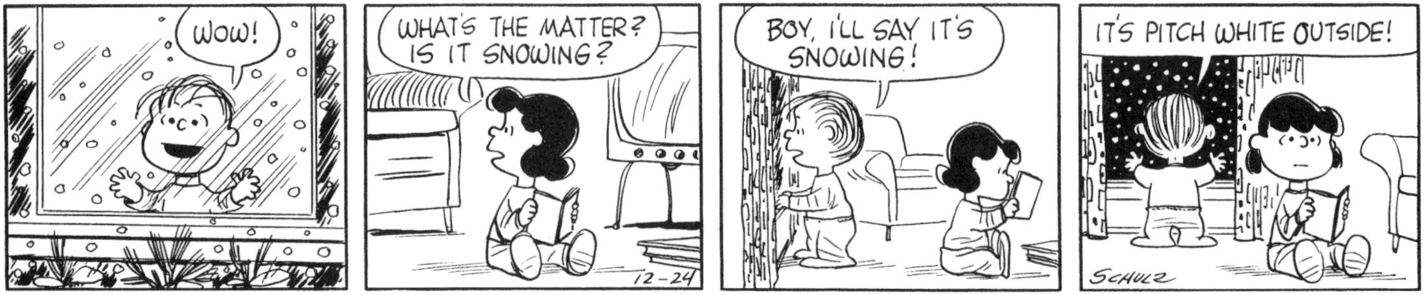
WOW!
WHAT'S THE MATTER? IS IT SNOWING?
12-24
BOY, I'LL SAY IT'S SNOWING!
IT'S PITCH WHITE OUTSIDE!
SCHULZ

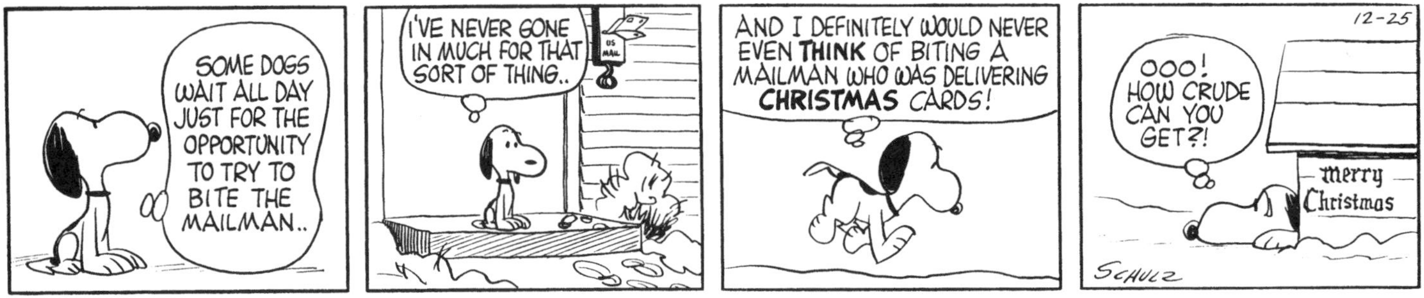
SOME DOGS WAIT ALL DAY JUST FOR THE OPPORTUNITY TO TRY TO BITE THE MAILMAN..
I'VE NEVER GONE IN MUCH FOR THAT SORT OF THING..
US MAIL
AND I DEFINITELY WOULD NEVER EVEN THINK OF BITING A MAILMAN WHO WAS DELIVERING CHRISTMAS CARDS!
12-25
OOO! HOW CRUDE CAN YOU GET?!
Merry Christmas
SCHULZ

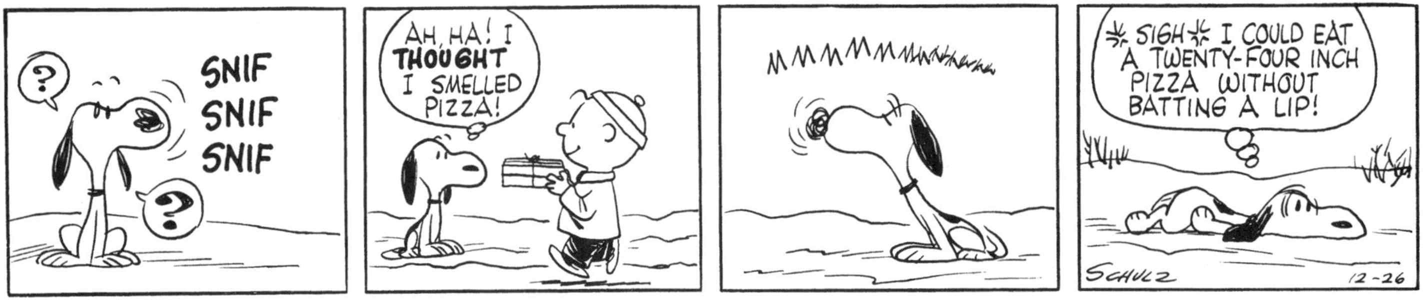
?
SNIF SNIF SNIF
?
AH, HA! I THOUGHT I SMELLED PIZZA!
MMMMMMMMMM
SIGH I COULD EAT A TWENTY-FOUR INCH PIZZA WITHOUT BATTING A LIP!
SCHULZ
12-26

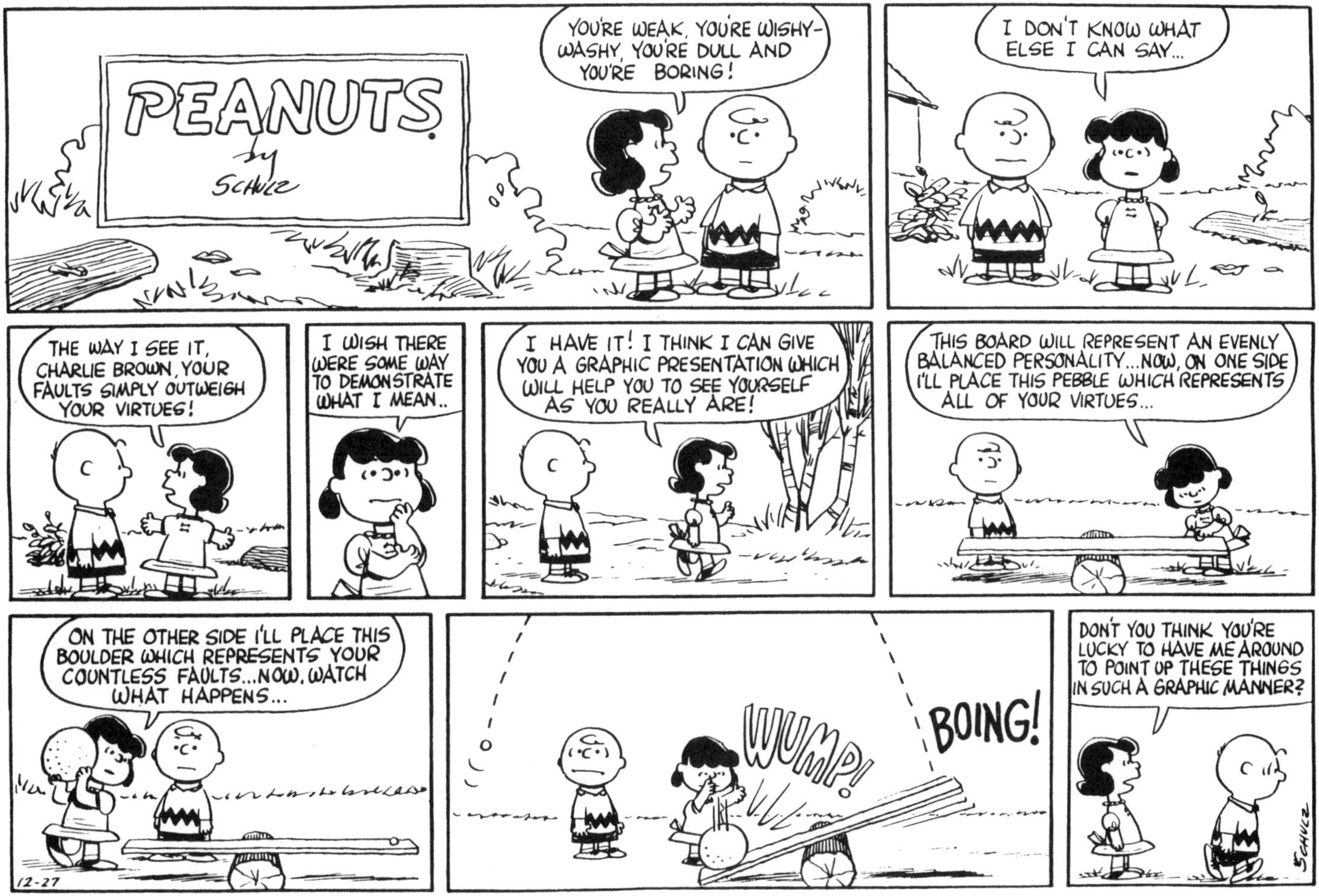
PEANUTS
by
SCHULZ
YOU'RE WEAK, YOU'RE WISHY-WASHY, YOU'RE DULL AND YOU'RE BORING!
I DON'T KNOW WHAT ELSE I CAN SAY...
THE WAY I SEE IT, CHARLIE BROWN, YOUR FAULTS SIMPLY OUTWEIGH YOUR VIRTUES!
I WISH THERE WERE SOME WAY TO DEMONSTRATE WHAT I MEAN..
I HAVE IT! I THINK I CAN GIVE YOU A GRAPHIC PRESENTATION WHICH WILL HELP YOU TO SEE YOURSELF AS YOU REALLY ARE!
THIS BOARD WILL REPRESENT AN EVENLY BALANCED PERSONALITY...NOW, ON ONE SIDE I'LL PLACE THIS PEBBLE WHICH REPRESENTS ALL OF YOUR VIRTUES...
ON THE OTHER SIDE I'LL PLACE THIS BOULDER WHICH REPRESENTS YOUR COUNTLESS FAULTS...NOW, WATCH WHAT HAPPENS...
12-27
WUMP!
BOING!
DON'T YOU THINK YOU'RE LUCKY TO HAVE ME AROUND TO POINT UP THESE THINGS IN SUCH A GRAPHIC MANNER?
SCHULZ

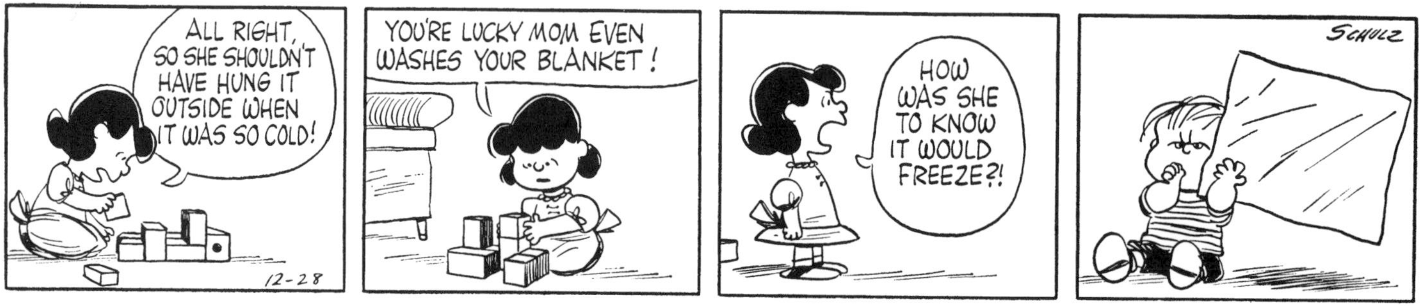
ALL RIGHT, SO SHE SHOULDN'T HAVE HUNG IT OUTSIDE WHEN IT WAS SO COLD!
YOU'RE LUCKY MOM EVEN WASHES YOUR BLANKET!
HOW WAS SHE TO KNOW IT WOULD FREEZE?!
12-28
SCHULZ

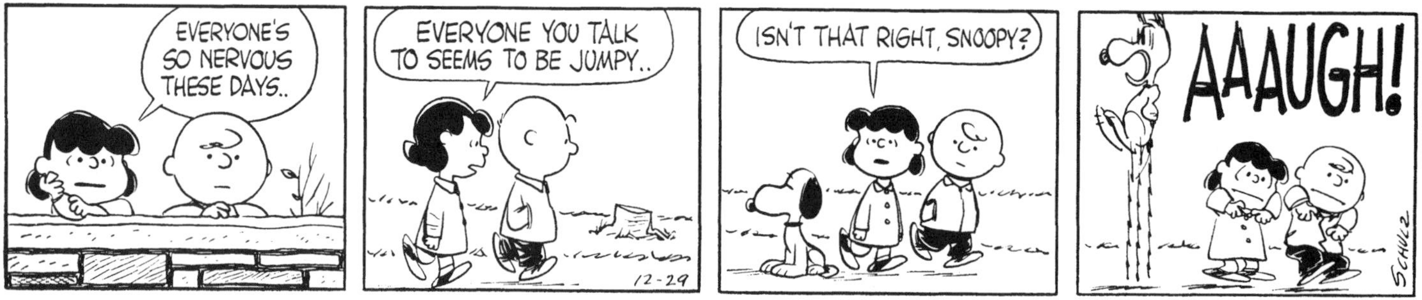
EVERYONE'S SO NERVOUS THESE DAYS..
EVERYONE YOU TALK TO SEEMS TO BE JUMPY..
12-29
ISN'T THAT RIGHT, SNOOPY?
AAAUGH!
SCHULZ

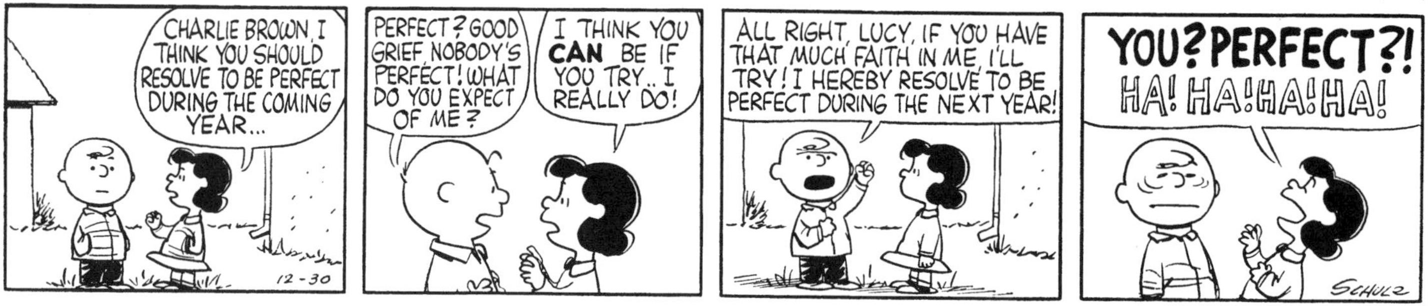
CHARLIE BROWN, I THINK YOU SHOULD RESOLVE TO BE PERFECT DURING THE COMING YEAR...
12-30
PERFECT? GOOD GRIEF, NOBODY'S PERFECT! WHAT DO YOU EXPECT OF ME?
I THINK YOU CAN BE IF YOU TRY.. I REALLY DO!
ALL RIGHT, LUCY, IF YOU HAVE THAT MUCH FAITH IN ME, I'LL TRY! I HEREBY RESOLVE TO BE PERFECT DURING THE NEXT YEAR!
YOU? PERFECT?!
HA! HA! HA! HA!
SCHULZ

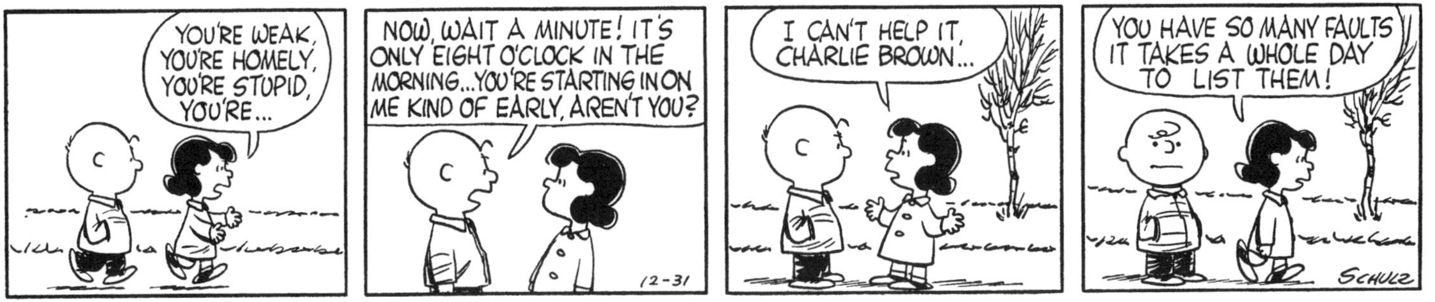
YOU'RE WEAK, YOU'RE HOMELY, YOU'RE STUPID, YOU'RE...
NOW, WAIT A MINUTE! IT'S ONLY EIGHT O'CLOCK IN THE MORNING...YOU'RE STARTING IN ON ME KIND OF EARLY, AREN'T YOU?
12-31
I CAN'T HELP IT, CHARLIE BROWN...
YOU HAVE SO MANY FAULTS IT TAKES A WHOLE DAY TO LIST THEM!
SCHULZ

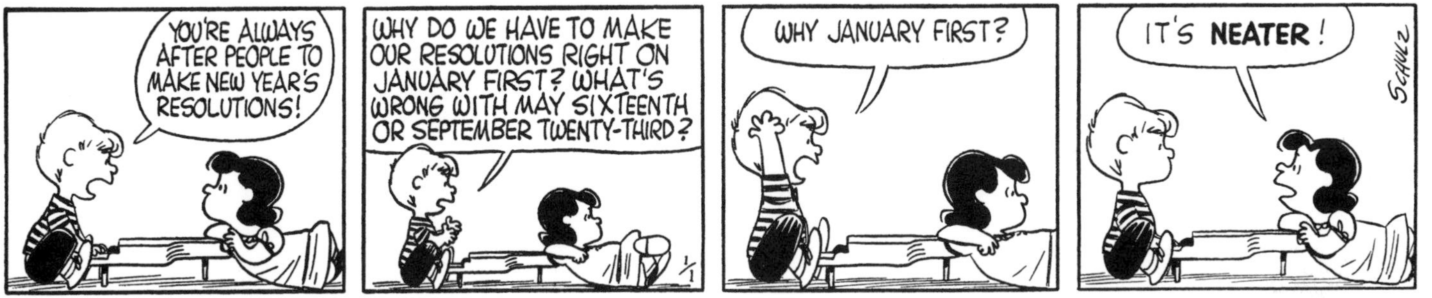
YOU'RE ALWAYS AFTER PEOPLE TO MAKE NEW YEAR'S RESOLUTIONS!
WHY DO WE HAVE TO MAKE OUR RESOLUTIONS RIGHT ON JANUARY FIRST? WHAT'S WRONG WITH MAY SIXTEENTH OR SEPTEMBER TWENTY-THIRD?
1/1
WHY JANUARY FIRST?
IT'S **NEATER**!
SCHULZ

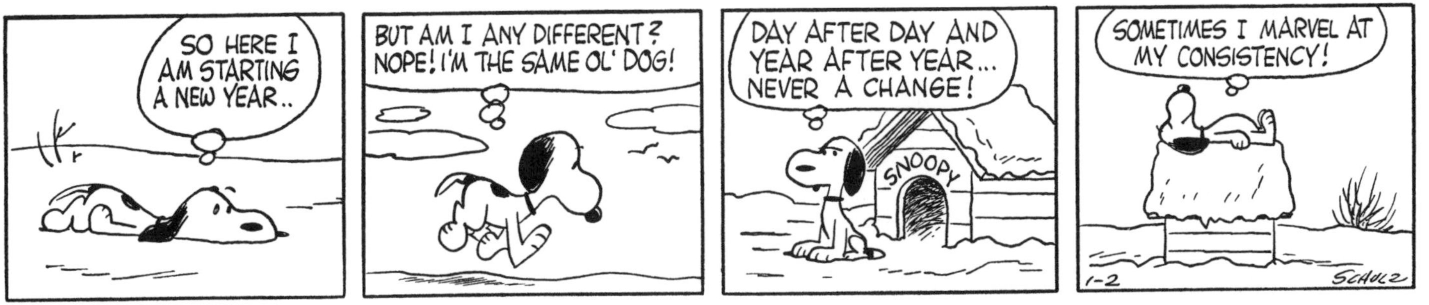
SO HERE I AM STARTING A NEW YEAR..
BUT AM I ANY DIFFERENT? NOPE! I'M THE SAME OL' DOG!
DAY AFTER DAY AND YEAR AFTER YEAR... NEVER A CHANGE!
SNOOPY
SOMETIMES I MARVEL AT MY CONSISTENCY!
1-2
SCHULZ

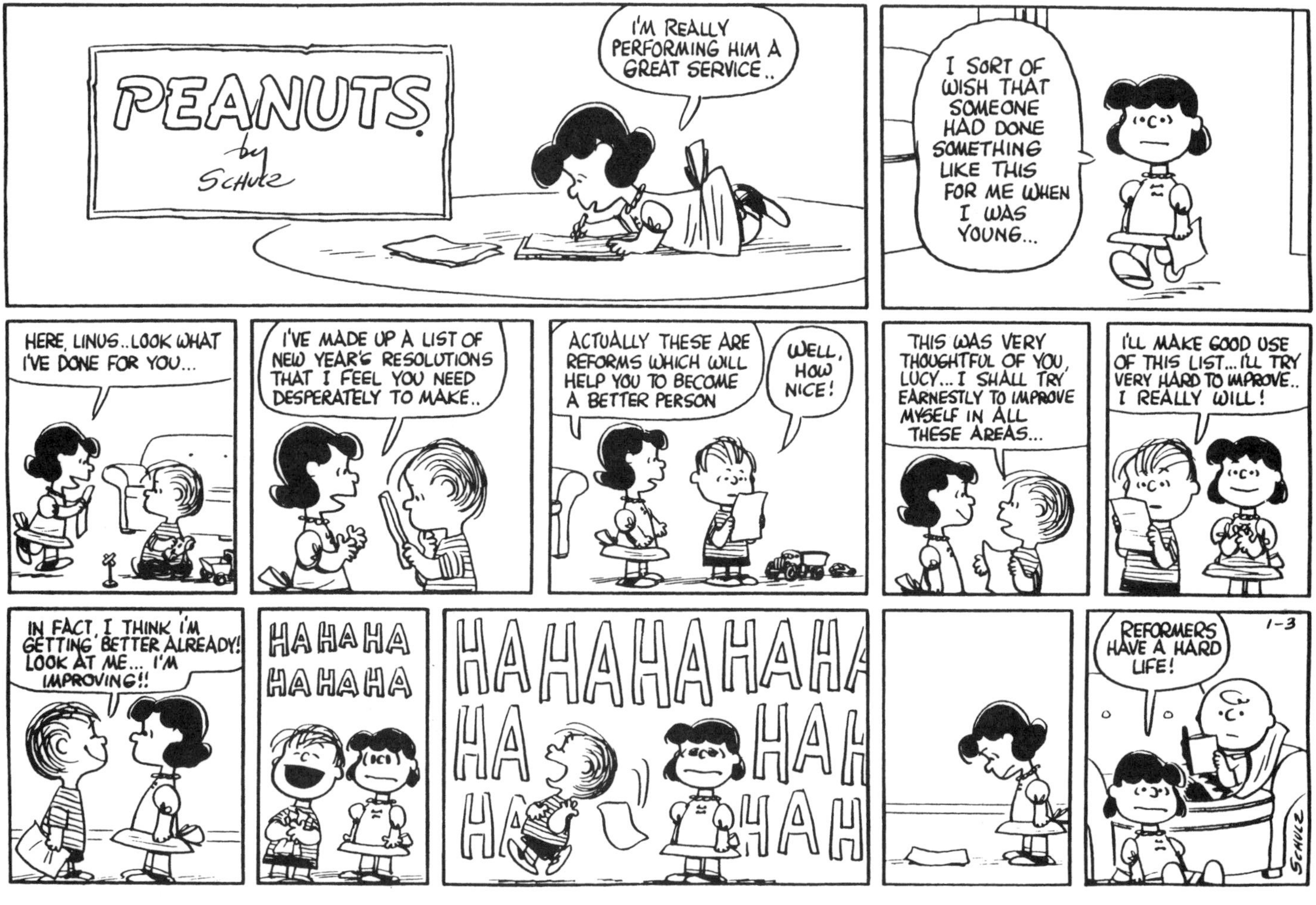
PEANUTS
by SCHULZ
I'M REALLY PERFORMING HIM A GREAT SERVICE..
I SORT OF WISH THAT SOMEONE HAD DONE SOMETHING LIKE THIS FOR ME WHEN I WAS YOUNG...
HERE, LINUS..LOOK WHAT I'VE DONE FOR YOU...
I'VE MADE UP A LIST OF NEW YEAR'S RESOLUTIONS THAT I FEEL YOU NEED DESPERATELY TO MAKE..
ACTUALLY THESE ARE REFORMS WHICH WILL HELP YOU TO BECOME A BETTER PERSON
WELL, HOW NICE!
THIS WAS VERY THOUGHTFUL OF YOU, LUCY... I SHALL TRY EARNESTLY TO IMPROVE MYSELF IN ALL THESE AREAS...
I'LL MAKE GOOD USE OF THIS LIST... I'LL TRY VERY HARD TO IMPROVE.. I REALLY WILL!
IN FACT, I THINK I'M GETTING BETTER ALREADY! LOOK AT ME... I'M IMPROVING!!
HA HA HA HA HA HA
HAHAHAHAHAHAHA HA HAH HA HAH
1-3
REFORMERS HAVE A HARD LIFE!
SCHULZ

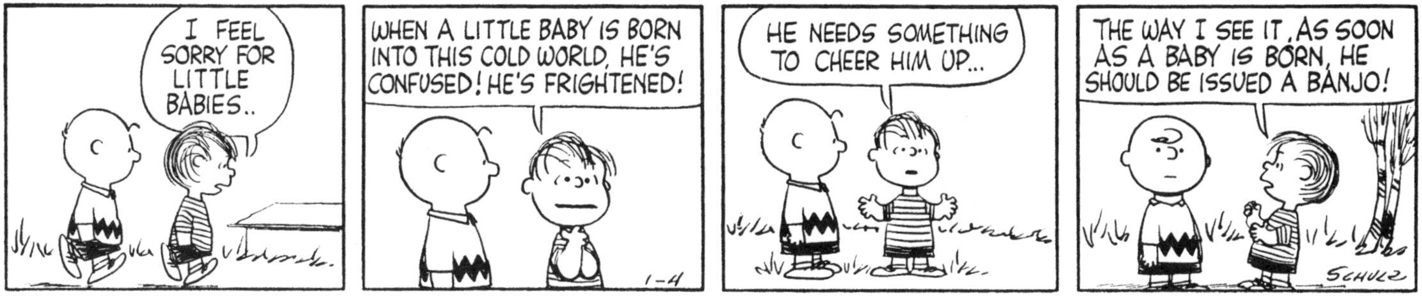
I FEEL SORRY FOR LITTLE BABIES..
WHEN A LITTLE BABY IS BORN INTO THIS COLD WORLD, HE'S CONFUSED! HE'S FRIGHTENED!
1-4
HE NEEDS SOMETHING TO CHEER HIM UP...
THE WAY I SEE IT, AS SOON AS A BABY IS BORN, HE SHOULD BE ISSUED A BANJO!
SCHULZ

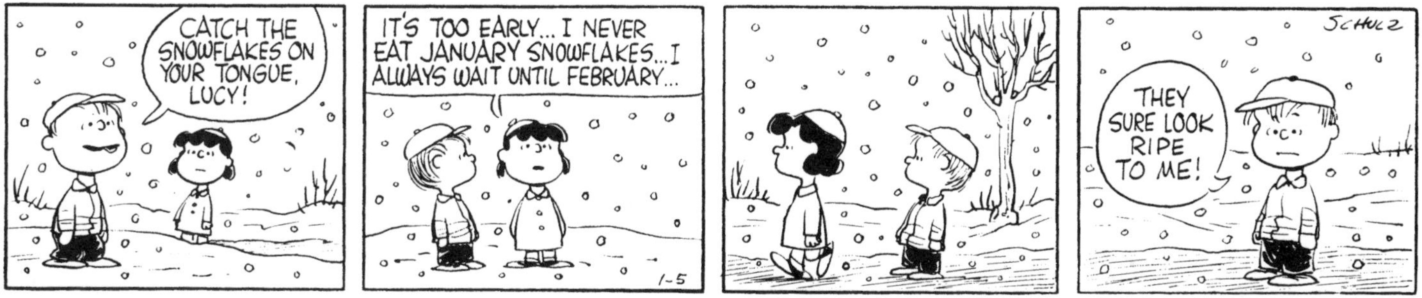
CATCH THE SNOWFLAKES ON YOUR TONGUE, LUCY!
IT'S TOO EARLY... I NEVER EAT JANUARY SNOWFLAKES... I ALWAYS WAIT UNTIL FEBRUARY...
1-5
SCHULZ
THEY SURE LOOK RIPE TO ME!

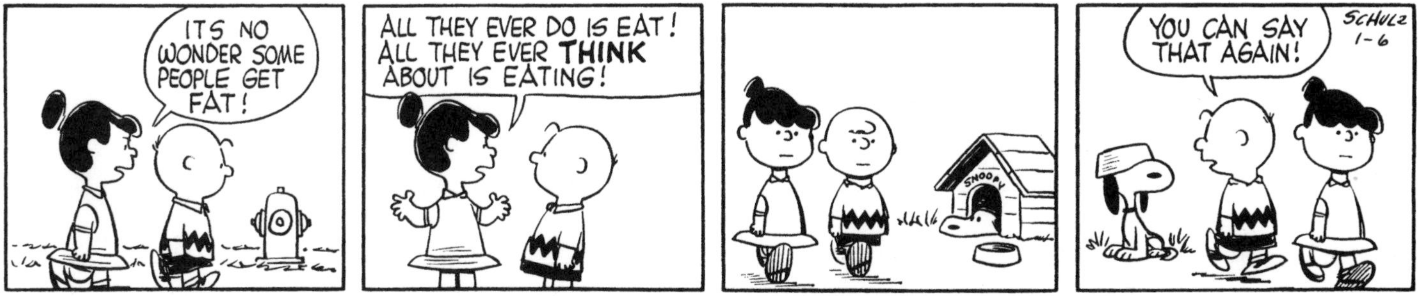
ITS NO WONDER SOME PEOPLE GET FAT!
ALL THEY EVER DO IS EAT! ALL THEY EVER **THINK** ABOUT IS EATING!
SNOOPY
YOU CAN SAY THAT AGAIN!
SCHULZ 1-6

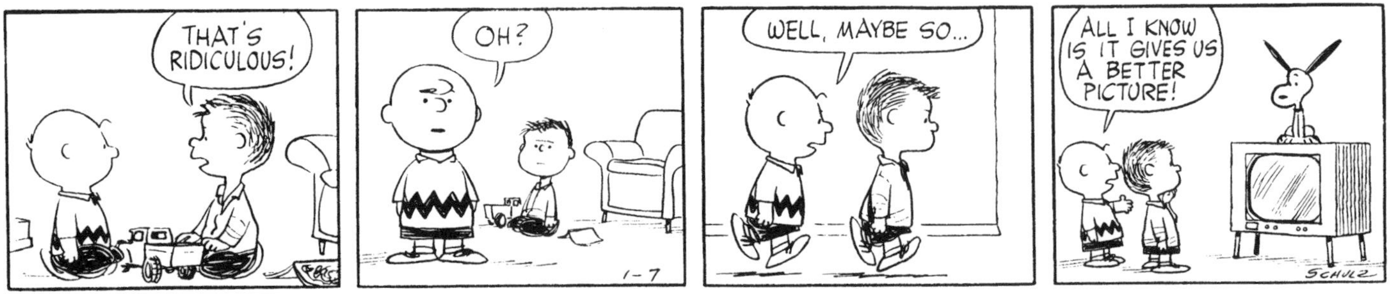
THAT'S RIDICULOUS!
OH?
WELL, MAYBE SO...
ALL I KNOW IS IT GIVES US A BETTER PICTURE!

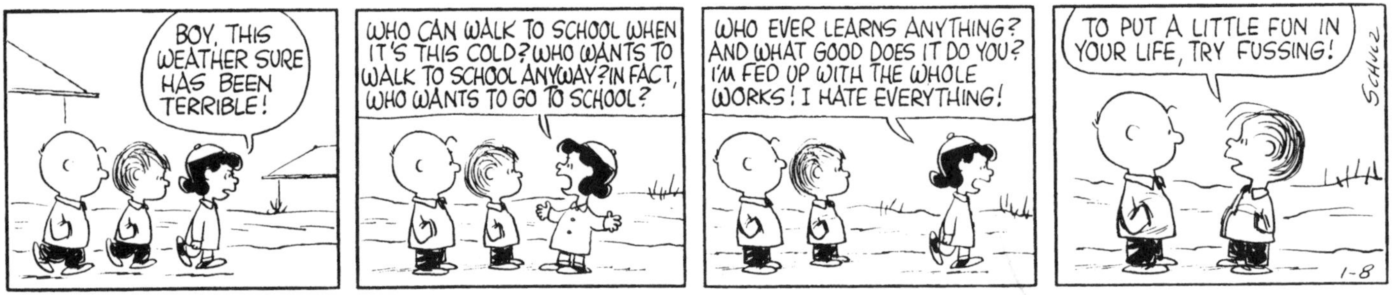
BOY, THIS WEATHER SURE HAS BEEN TERRIBLE!
WHO CAN WALK TO SCHOOL WHEN IT'S THIS COLD? WHO WANTS TO WALK TO SCHOOL ANYWAY? IN FACT, WHO WANTS TO GO TO SCHOOL?
WHO EVER LEARNS ANYTHING? AND WHAT GOOD DOES IT DO YOU? I'M FED UP WITH THE WHOLE WORKS! I HATE EVERYTHING!
TO PUT A LITTLE FUN IN YOUR LIFE, TRY FUSSING!

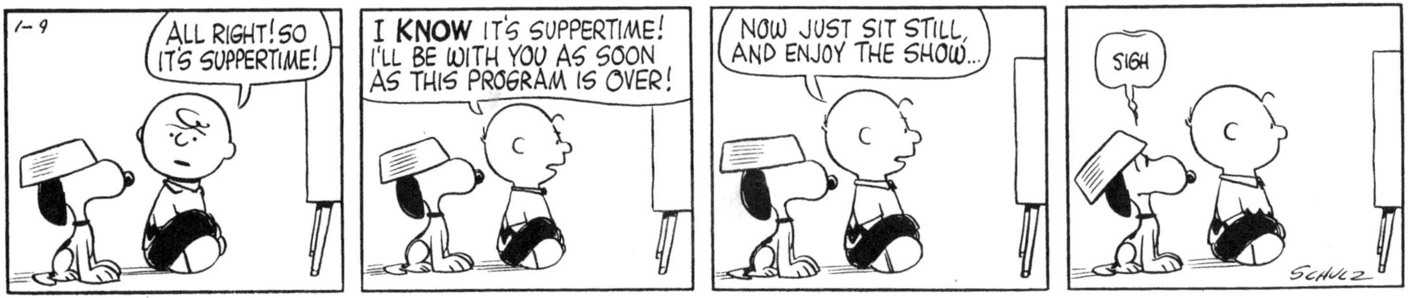
ALL RIGHT! SO IT'S SUPPERTIME!
I **KNOW** IT'S SUPPERTIME! I'LL BE WITH YOU AS SOON AS THIS PROGRAM IS OVER!
NOW JUST SIT STILL, AND ENJOY THE SHOW...
SIGH

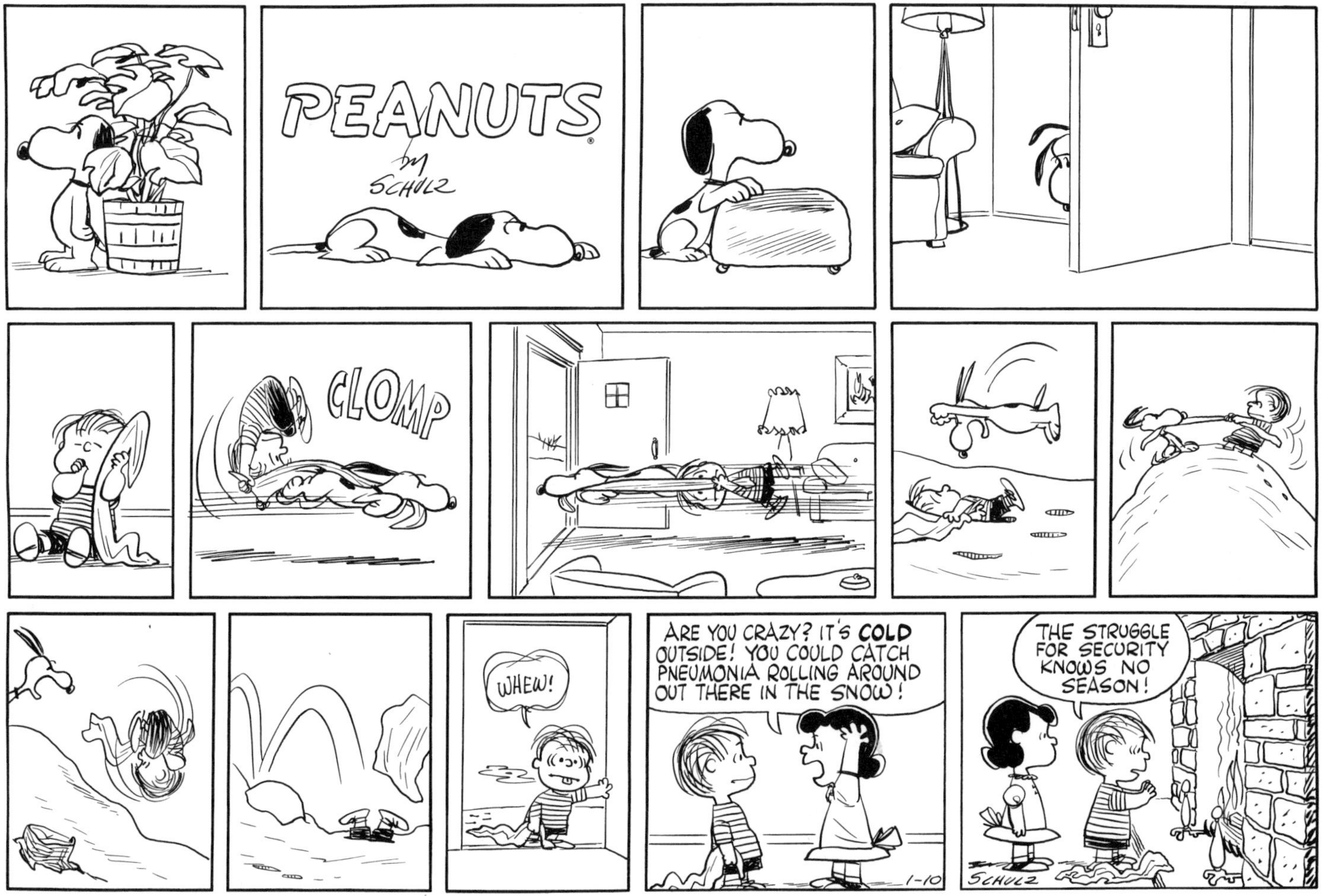
PEANUTS
by SCHULZ
CLOMP
WHEW!
ARE YOU CRAZY? IT'S COLD OUTSIDE! YOU COULD CATCH PNEUMONIA ROLLING AROUND OUT THERE IN THE SNOW!
1-10
THE STRUGGLE FOR SECURITY KNOWS NO SEASON!
SCHULZ

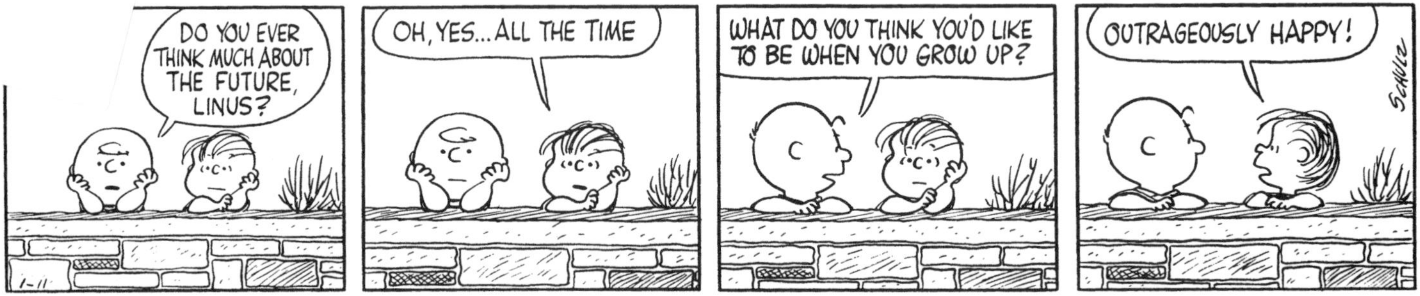
DO YOU EVER THINK MUCH ABOUT THE FUTURE, LINUS?
OH, YES... ALL THE TIME
WHAT DO YOU THINK YOU'D LIKE TO BE WHEN YOU GROW UP?
OUTRAGEOUSLY HAPPY!

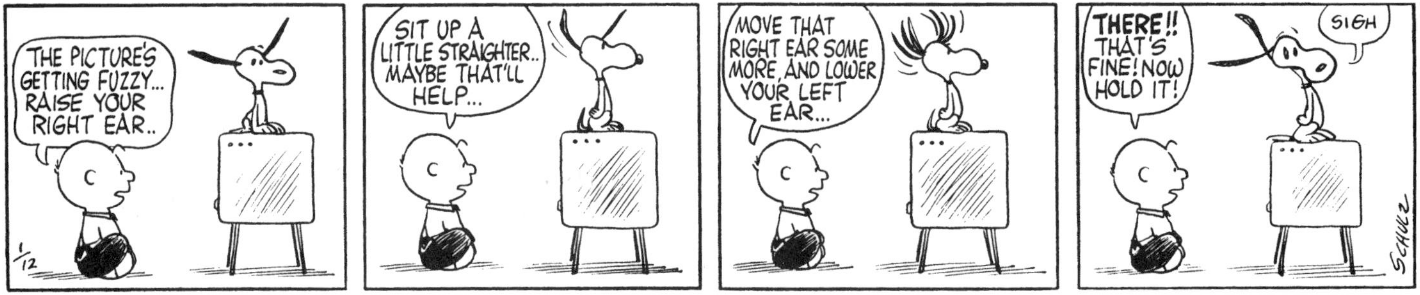
THE PICTURE'S GETTING FUZZY... RAISE YOUR RIGHT EAR..
SIT UP A LITTLE STRAIGHTER.. MAYBE THAT'LL HELP...
MOVE THAT RIGHT EAR SOME MORE, AND LOWER YOUR LEFT EAR...
THERE!! THAT'S FINE! NOW HOLD IT!
SIGH

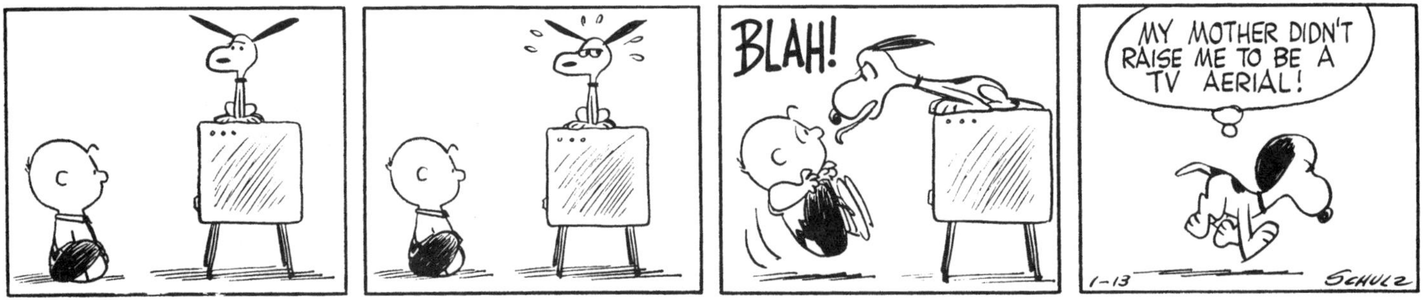
BLAH!
MY MOTHER DIDN'T RAISE ME TO BE A TV AERIAL!

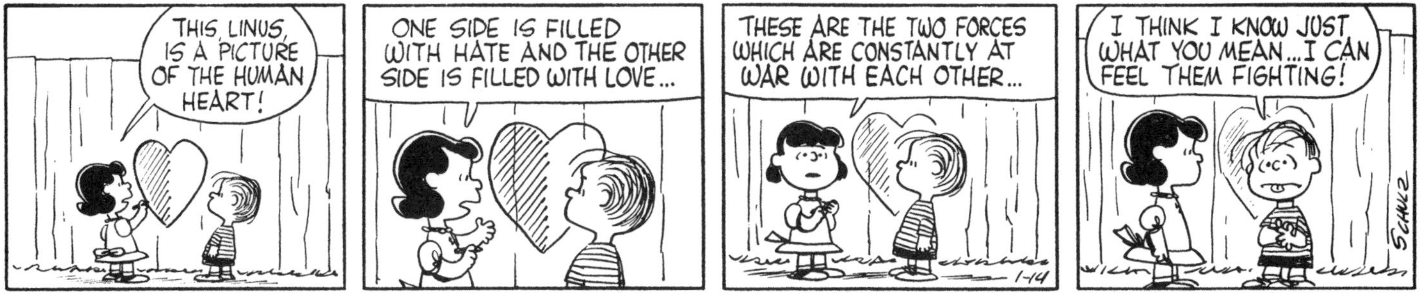
THIS, LINUS, IS A PICTURE OF THE HUMAN HEART!
ONE SIDE IS FILLED WITH HATE AND THE OTHER SIDE IS FILLED WITH LOVE...
THESE ARE THE TWO FORCES WHICH ARE CONSTANTLY AT WAR WITH EACH OTHER...
1-14
I THINK I KNOW JUST WHAT YOU MEAN...I CAN FEEL THEM FIGHTING!
SCHULZ

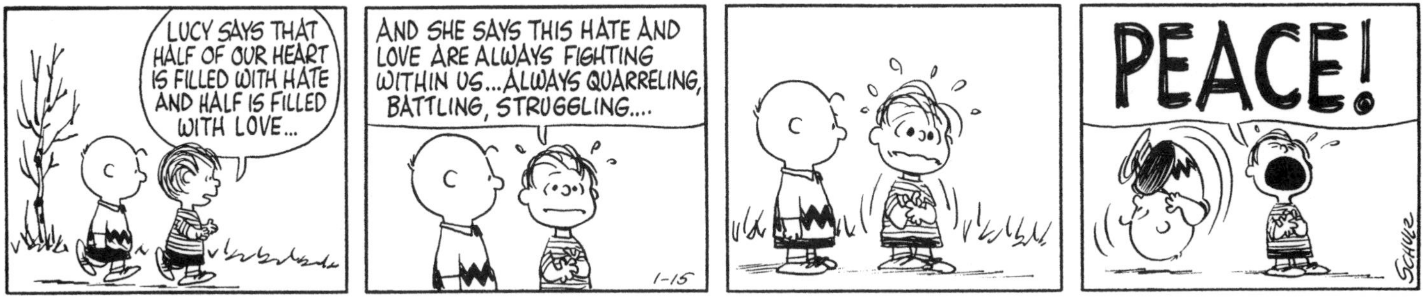
LUCY SAYS THAT HALF OF OUR HEART IS FILLED WITH HATE AND HALF IS FILLED WITH LOVE...
AND SHE SAYS THIS HATE AND LOVE ARE ALWAYS FIGHTING WITHIN US...ALWAYS QUARRELING, BATTLING, STRUGGLING....
1-15
PEACE!
SCHULZ

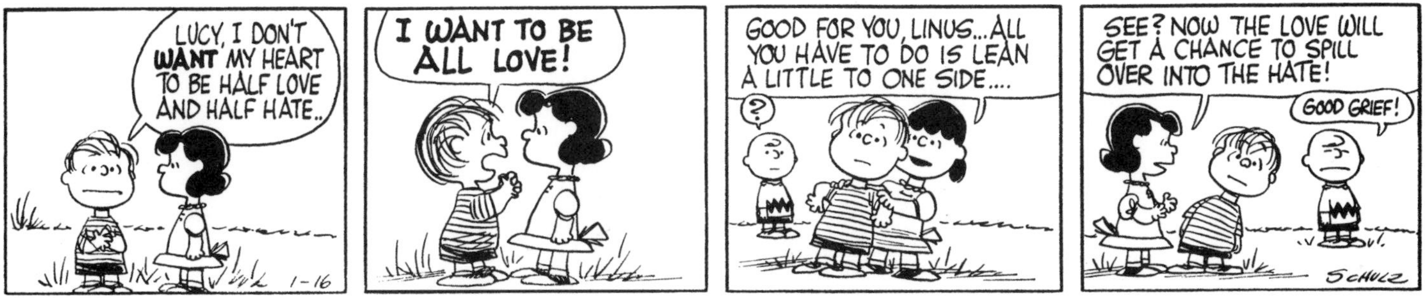
LUCY, I DON'T **WANT** MY HEART TO BE HALF LOVE AND HALF HATE..
1-16
I WANT TO BE ALL LOVE!
GOOD FOR YOU, LINUS...ALL YOU HAVE TO DO IS LEAN A LITTLE TO ONE SIDE....
?
SEE? NOW THE LOVE WILL GET A CHANCE TO SPILL OVER INTO THE HATE!
GOOD GRIEF!
SCHULZ

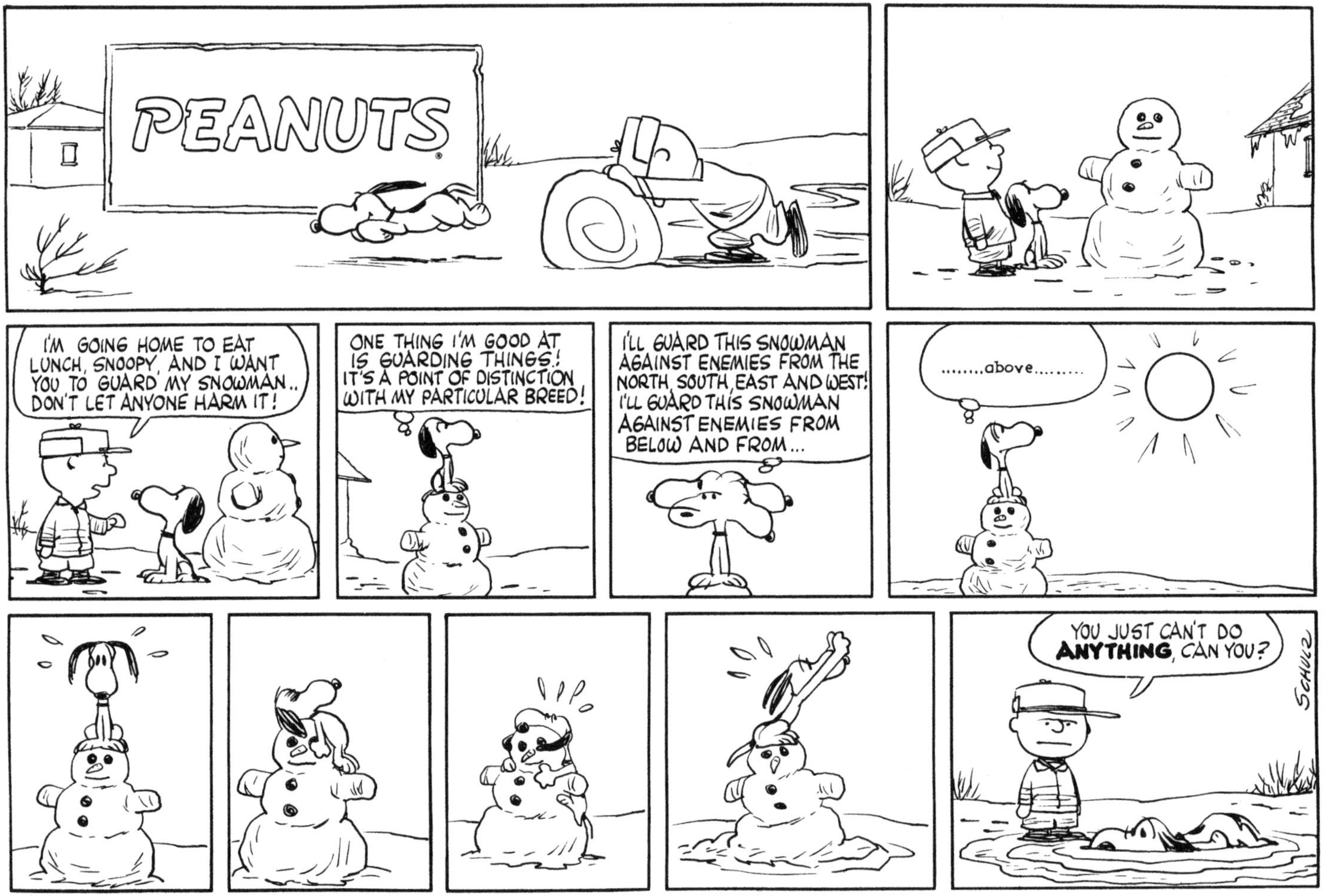
PEANUTS
I'M GOING HOME TO EAT LUNCH, SNOOPY, AND I WANT YOU TO GUARD MY SNOWMAN.. DON'T LET ANYONE HARM IT!
ONE THING I'M GOOD AT IS GUARDING THINGS! IT'S A POINT OF DISTINCTION WITH MY PARTICULAR BREED!
I'LL GUARD THIS SNOWMAN AGAINST ENEMIES FROM THE NORTH, SOUTH, EAST AND WEST! I'LL GUARD THIS SNOWMAN AGAINST ENEMIES FROM BELOW AND FROM...
........above.........
YOU JUST CAN'T DO **ANYTHING**, CAN YOU?
SCHULZ

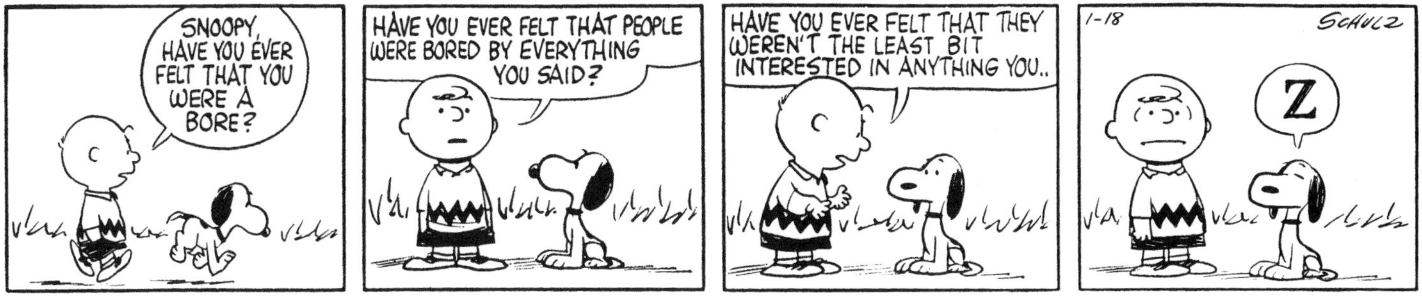
SNOOPY, HAVE YOU EVER FELT THAT YOU WERE A BORE?
HAVE YOU EVER FELT THAT PEOPLE WERE BORED BY EVERYTHING YOU SAID?
HAVE YOU EVER FELT THAT THEY WEREN'T THE LEAST BIT INTERESTED IN ANYTHING YOU..
1-18
SCHULZ
Z

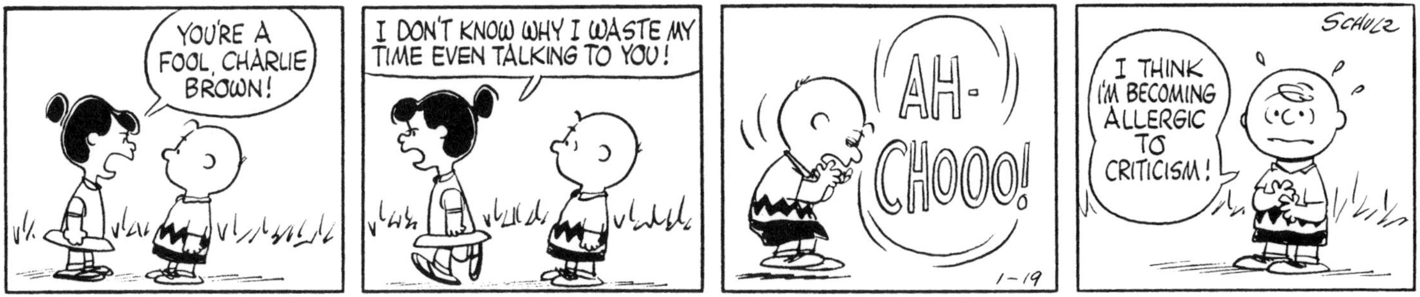
YOU'RE A FOOL, CHARLIE BROWN!
I DON'T KNOW WHY I WASTE MY TIME EVEN TALKING TO YOU!
AH-CHOOO!
1-19
SCHULZ
I THINK I'M BECOMING ALLERGIC TO CRITICISM!

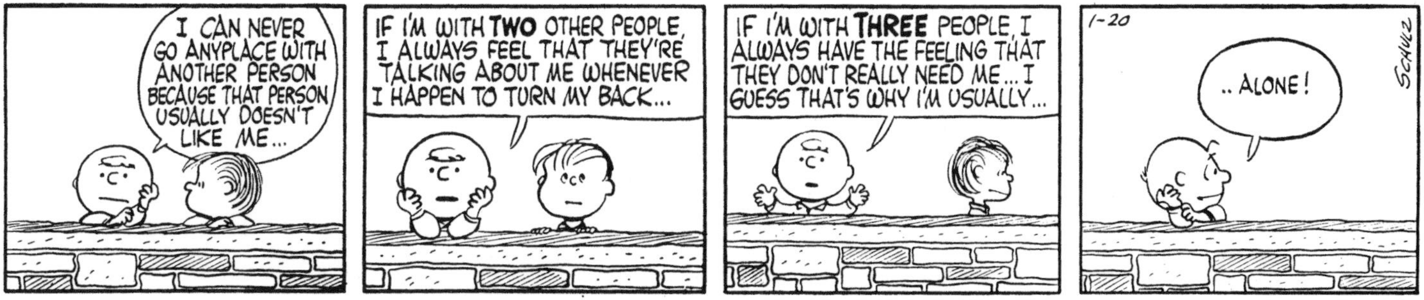
I CAN NEVER GO ANYPLACE WITH ANOTHER PERSON BECAUSE THAT PERSON USUALLY DOESN'T LIKE ME...
IF I'M WITH **TWO** OTHER PEOPLE, I ALWAYS FEEL THAT THEY'RE TALKING ABOUT ME WHENEVER I HAPPEN TO TURN MY BACK...
IF I'M WITH **THREE** PEOPLE, I ALWAYS HAVE THE FEELING THAT THEY DON'T REALLY NEED ME... I GUESS THAT'S WHY I'M USUALLY...
1-20
SCHULZ
..ALONE!

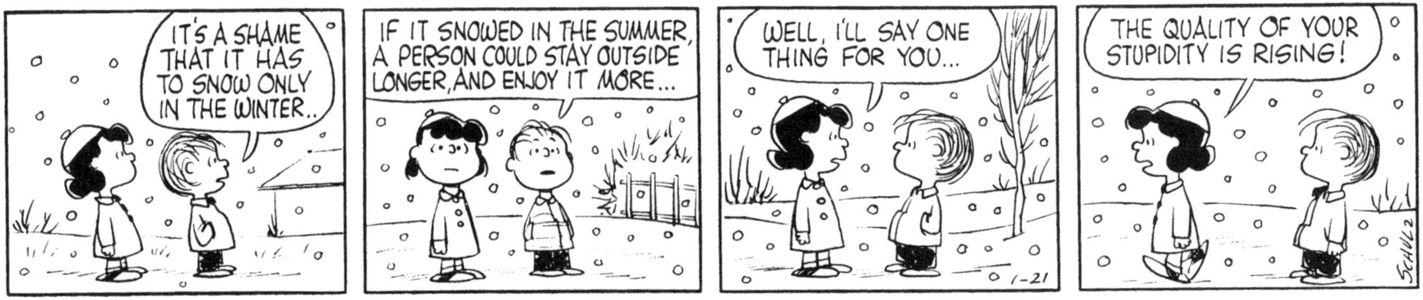
IT'S A SHAME THAT IT HAS TO SNOW ONLY IN THE WINTER..
IF IT SNOWED IN THE SUMMER, A PERSON COULD STAY OUTSIDE LONGER, AND ENJOY IT MORE...
WELL, I'LL SAY ONE THING FOR YOU...
1-21
THE QUALITY OF YOUR STUPIDITY IS RISING!
SCHULZ

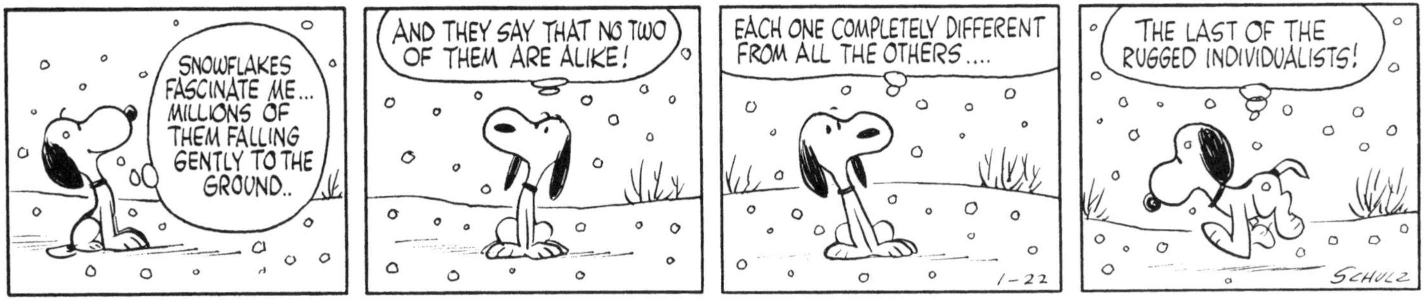
SNOWFLAKES FASCINATE ME... MILLIONS OF THEM FALLING GENTLY TO THE GROUND..
AND THEY SAY THAT NO TWO OF THEM ARE ALIKE!
EACH ONE COMPLETELY DIFFERENT FROM ALL THE OTHERS....
1-22
THE LAST OF THE RUGGED INDIVIDUALISTS!
SCHULZ

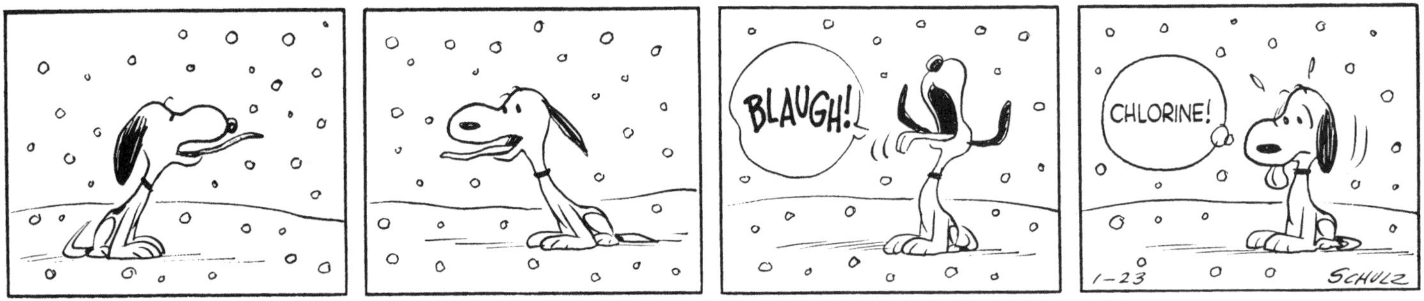
BLAUGH!
CHLORINE!
1-23
SCHULZ

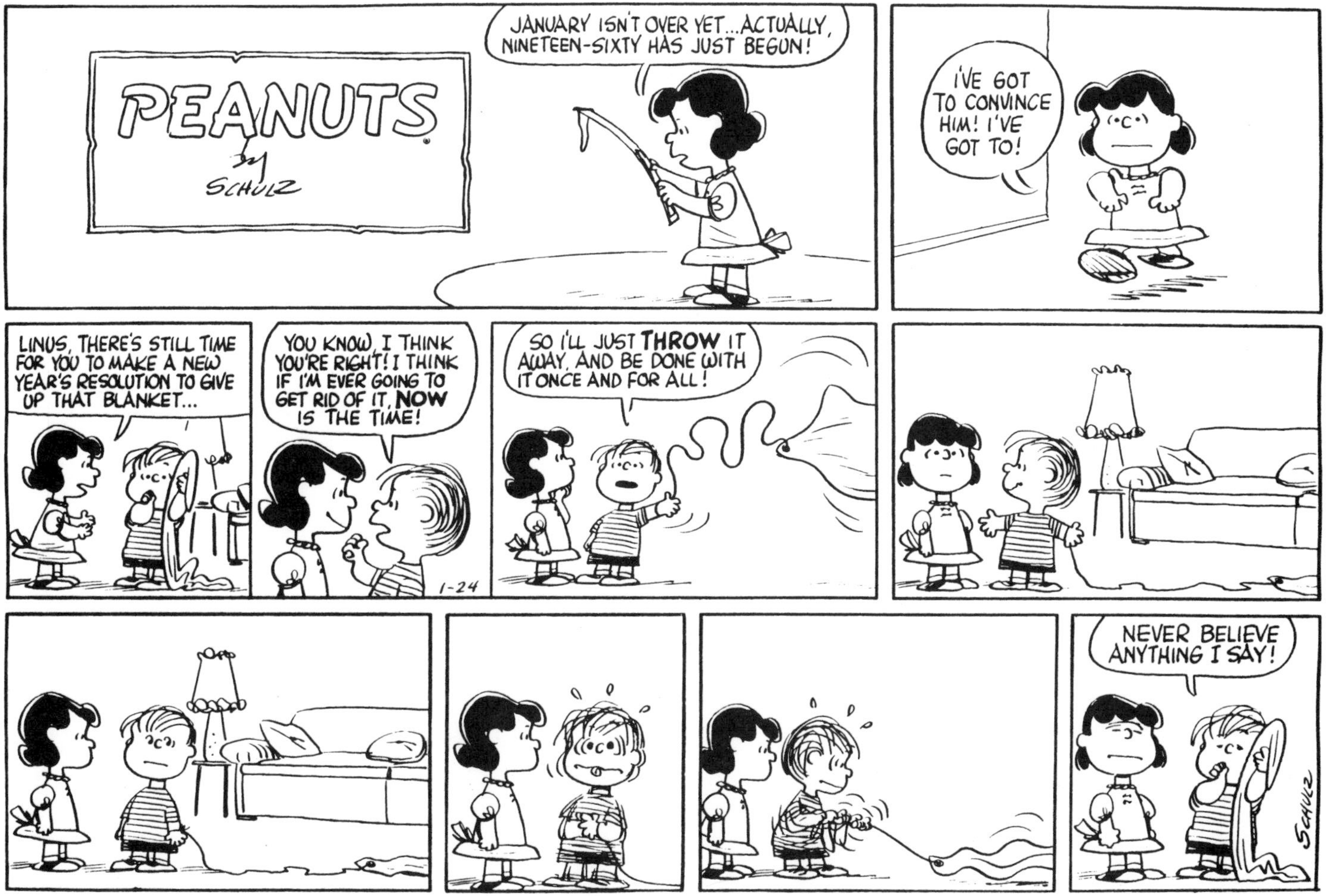
PEANUTS
by
SCHULZ
JANUARY ISN'T OVER YET...ACTUALLY, NINETEEN-SIXTY HAS JUST BEGUN!
I'VE GOT TO CONVINCE HIM! I'VE GOT TO!
LINUS, THERE'S STILL TIME FOR YOU TO MAKE A NEW YEAR'S RESOLUTION TO GIVE UP THAT BLANKET...
YOU KNOW, I THINK YOU'RE RIGHT! I THINK IF I'M EVER GOING TO GET RID OF IT, NOW IS THE TIME!
1-24
SO I'LL JUST THROW IT AWAY, AND BE DONE WITH IT ONCE AND FOR ALL!
NEVER BELIEVE ANYTHING I SAY!
SCHULZ

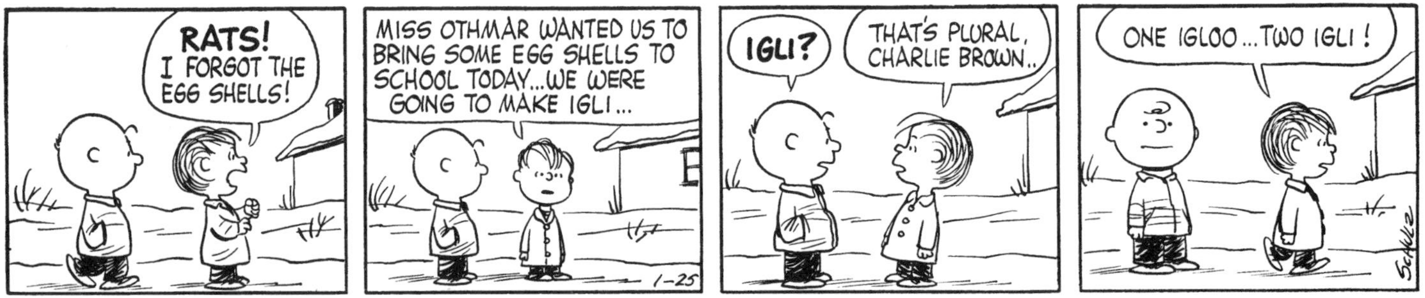
RATS! I FORGOT THE EGG SHELLS!
MISS OTHMAR WANTED US TO BRING SOME EGG SHELLS TO SCHOOL TODAY...WE WERE GOING TO MAKE IGLI...
1-25
IGLI?
THAT'S PLURAL, CHARLIE BROWN..
ONE IGLOO...TWO IGLI!
SCHULZ

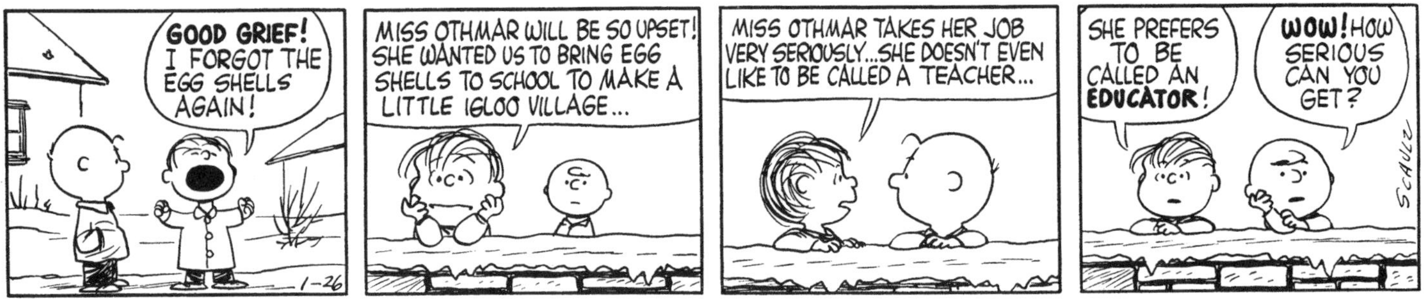
GOOD GRIEF! I FORGOT THE EGG SHELLS AGAIN!
1-26
MISS OTHMAR WILL BE SO UPSET! SHE WANTED US TO BRING EGG SHELLS TO SCHOOL TO MAKE A LITTLE IGLOO VILLAGE...
MISS OTHMAR TAKES HER JOB VERY SERIOUSLY...SHE DOESN'T EVEN LIKE TO BE CALLED A TEACHER...
SHE PREFERS TO BE CALLED AN EDUCATOR!
WOW! HOW SERIOUS CAN YOU GET?
SCHULZ

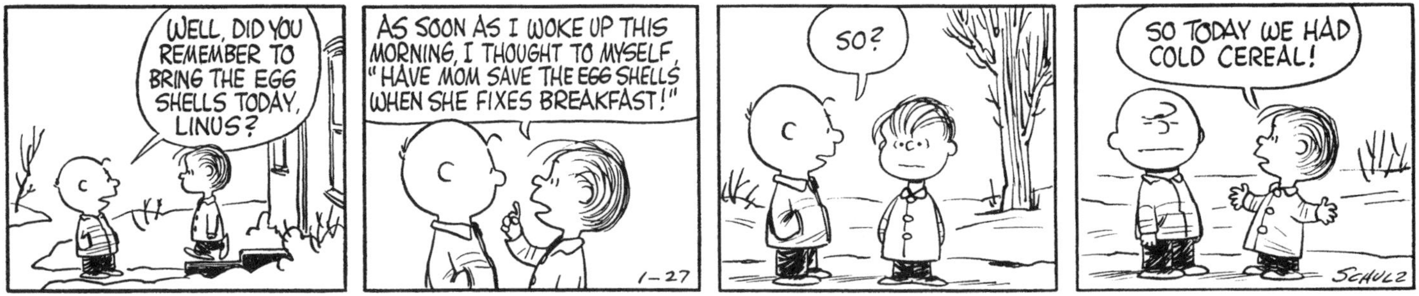
WELL, DID YOU REMEMBER TO BRING THE EGG SHELLS TODAY, LINUS?
AS SOON AS I WOKE UP THIS MORNING, I THOUGHT TO MYSELF, "HAVE MOM SAVE THE EGG SHELLS WHEN SHE FIXES BREAKFAST!"
1-27
SO?
SO TODAY WE HAD COLD CEREAL!
SCHULZ

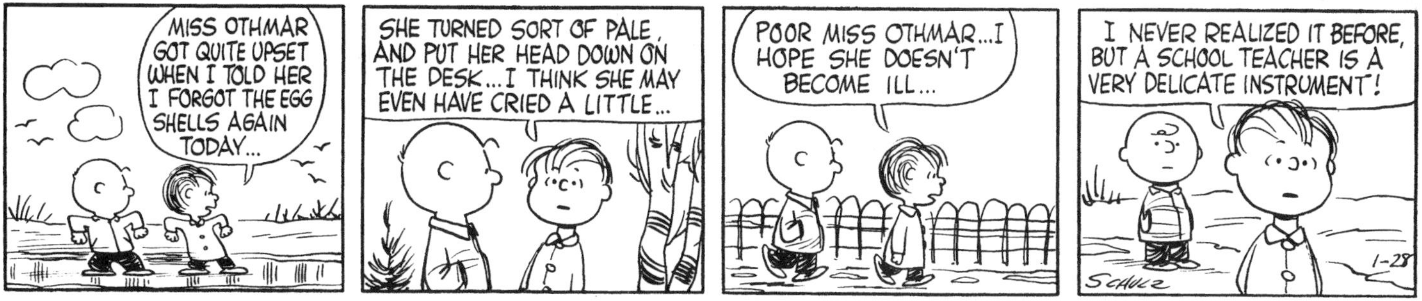
MISS OTHMAR GOT QUITE UPSET WHEN I TOLD HER I FORGOT THE EGG SHELLS AGAIN TODAY...
SHE TURNED SORT OF PALE, AND PUT HER HEAD DOWN ON THE DESK...I THINK SHE MAY EVEN HAVE CRIED A LITTLE...
POOR MISS OTHMAR...I HOPE SHE DOESN'T BECOME ILL...
I NEVER REALIZED IT BEFORE, BUT A SCHOOL TEACHER IS A VERY DELICATE INSTRUMENT!
1-28
SCHULZ

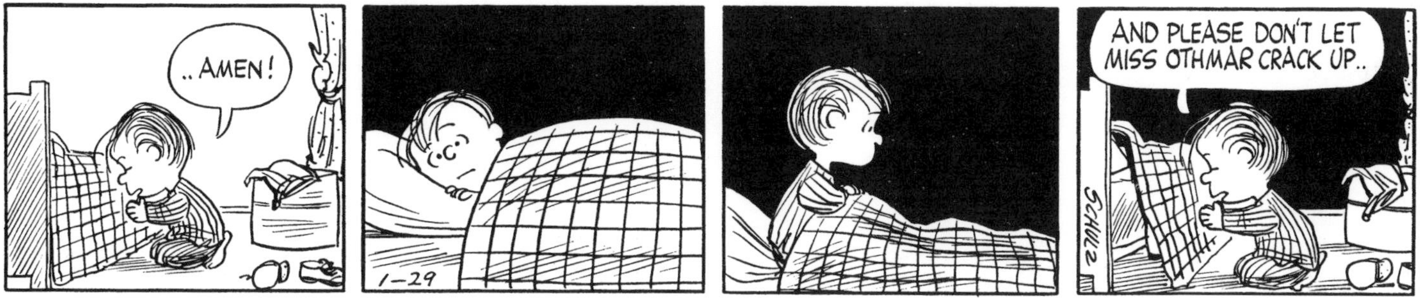
..AMEN!
1-29
AND PLEASE DON'T LET MISS OTHMAR CRACK UP..
SCHULZ

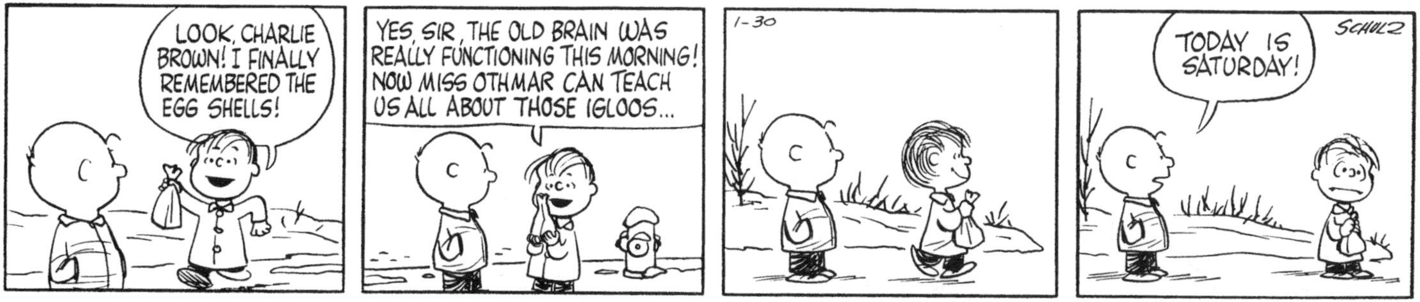
LOOK, CHARLIE BROWN! I FINALLY REMEMBERED THE EGG SHELLS!
YES, SIR, THE OLD BRAIN WAS REALLY FUNCTIONING THIS MORNING! NOW MISS OTHMAR CAN TEACH US ALL ABOUT THOSE IGLOOS...
1-30
SCHULZ
TODAY IS SATURDAY!

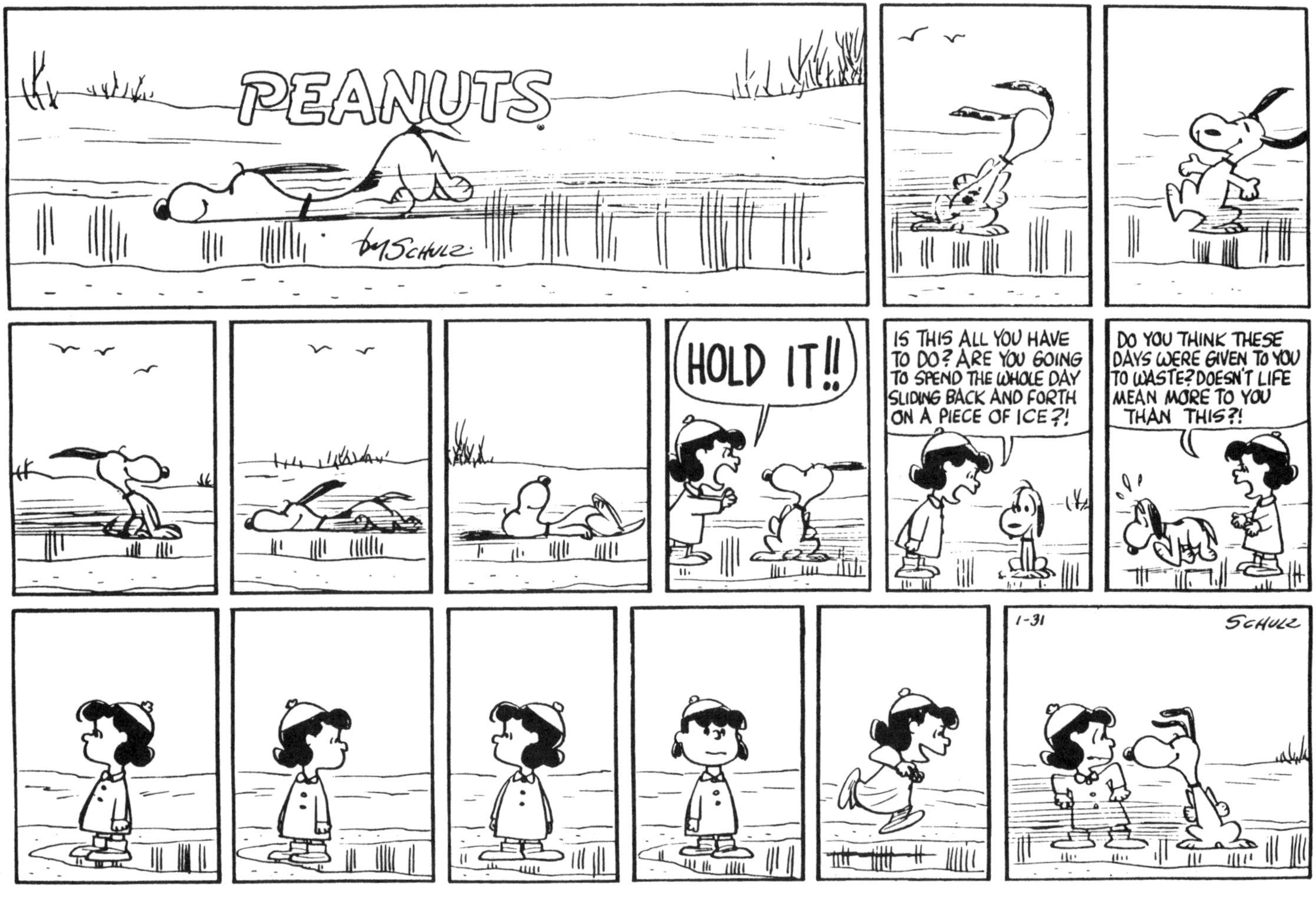
PEANUTS
by SCHULZ
HOLD IT!!
IS THIS ALL YOU HAVE TO DO? ARE YOU GOING TO SPEND THE WHOLE DAY SLIDING BACK AND FORTH ON A PIECE OF ICE?!
DO YOU THINK THESE DAYS WERE GIVEN TO YOU TO WASTE? DOESN'T LIFE MEAN MORE TO YOU THAN THIS?!
1-31
SCHULZ

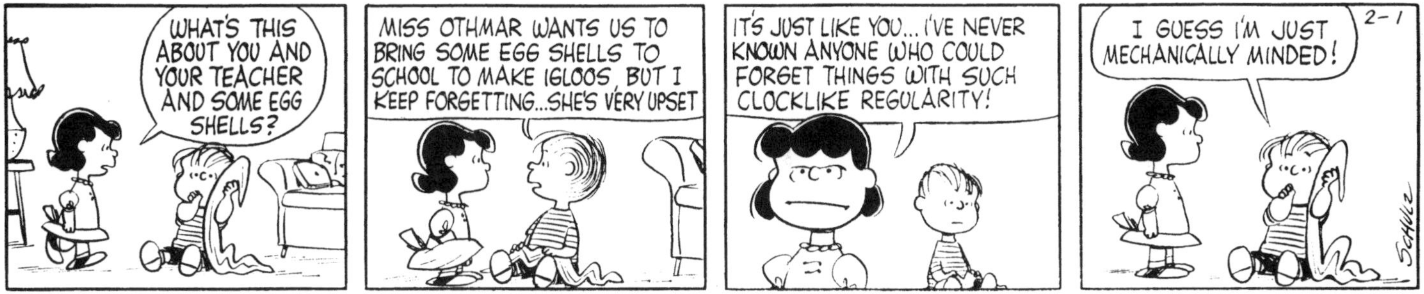
WHAT'S THIS ABOUT YOU AND YOUR TEACHER AND SOME EGG SHELLS?
MISS OTHMAR WANTS US TO BRING SOME EGG SHELLS TO SCHOOL TO MAKE IGLOOS, BUT I KEEP FORGETTING...SHE'S VERY UPSET
IT'S JUST LIKE YOU... I'VE NEVER KNOWN ANYONE WHO COULD FORGET THINGS WITH SUCH CLOCKLIKE REGULARITY!
I GUESS I'M JUST MECHANICALLY MINDED!
2-1
SCHULZ

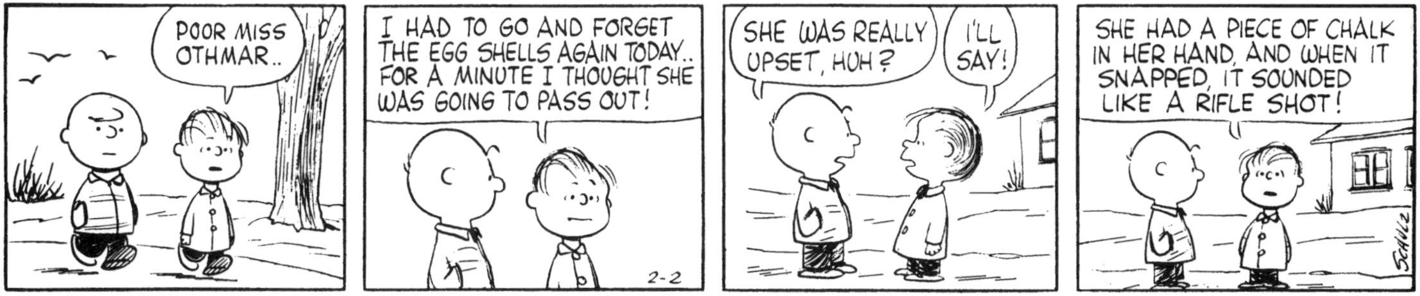
POOR MISS OTHMAR..
I HAD TO GO AND FORGET THE EGG SHELLS AGAIN TODAY.. FOR A MINUTE I THOUGHT SHE WAS GOING TO PASS OUT!
2-2
SHE WAS REALLY UPSET, HUH?
I'LL SAY!
SHE HAD A PIECE OF CHALK IN HER HAND, AND WHEN IT SNAPPED, IT SOUNDED LIKE A RIFLE SHOT!
SCHULZ

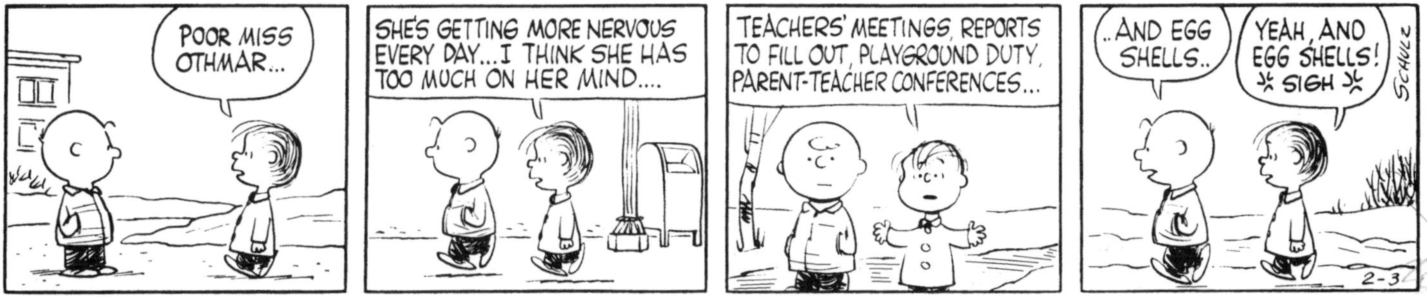
POOR MISS OTHMAR...
SHE'S GETTING MORE NERVOUS EVERY DAY...I THINK SHE HAS TOO MUCH ON HER MIND....
TEACHERS' MEETINGS, REPORTS TO FILL OUT, PLAYGROUND DUTY, PARENT-TEACHER CONFERENCES...
..AND EGG SHELLS..
YEAH, AND EGG SHELLS! SIGH
SCHULZ
2-3

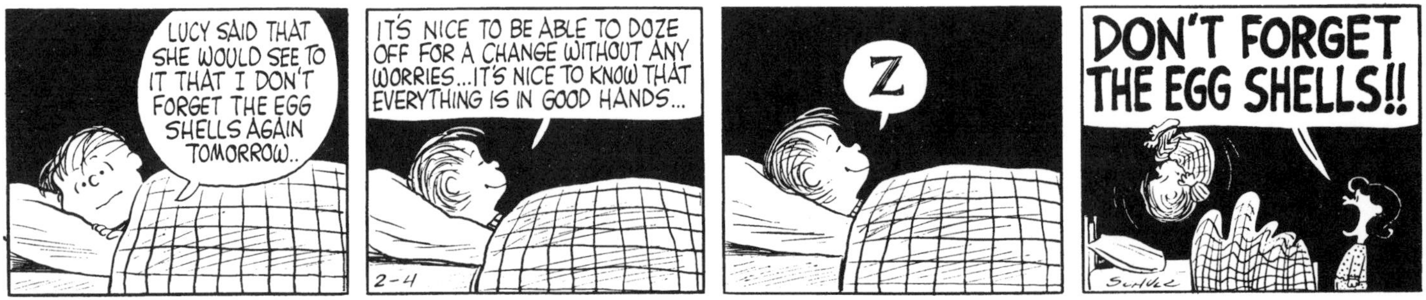
LUCY SAID THAT SHE WOULD SEE TO IT THAT I DON'T FORGET THE EGG SHELLS AGAIN TOMORROW..
IT'S NICE TO BE ABLE TO DOZE OFF FOR A CHANGE WITHOUT ANY WORRIES...IT'S NICE TO KNOW THAT EVERYTHING IS IN GOOD HANDS...
2-4
Z
DON'T FORGET THE EGG SHELLS!!
SCHULZ

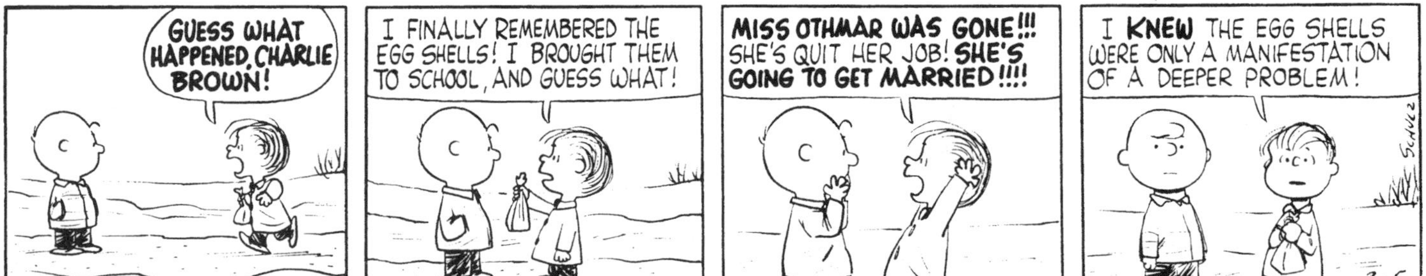
GUESS WHAT HAPPENED, CHARLIE BROWN!
I FINALLY REMEMBERED THE EGG SHELLS! I BROUGHT THEM TO SCHOOL, AND GUESS WHAT!
MISS OTHMAR WAS GONE!!! SHE'S QUIT HER JOB! SHE'S GOING TO GET MARRIED!!!!
I KNEW THE EGG SHELLS WERE ONLY A MANIFESTATION OF A DEEPER PROBLEM!
SCHULZ
2-5

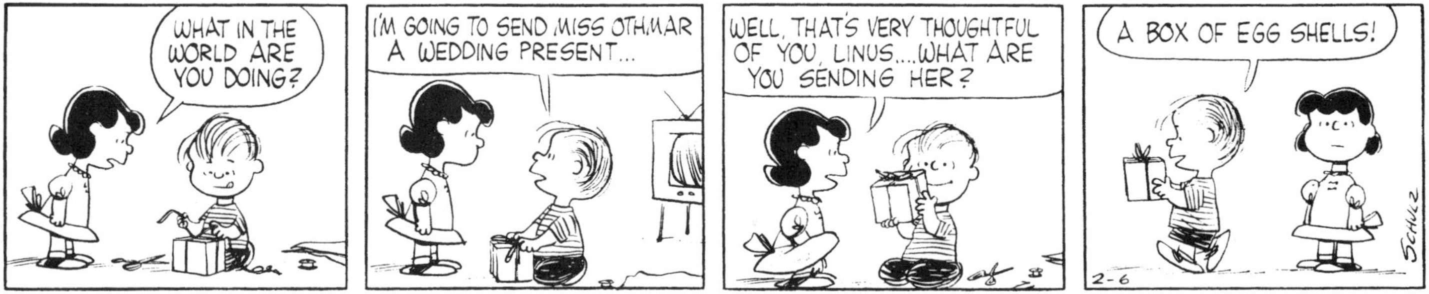
WHAT IN THE WORLD ARE YOU DOING?
I'M GOING TO SEND MISS OTHMAR A WEDDING PRESENT...
WELL, THAT'S VERY THOUGHTFUL OF YOU, LINUS....WHAT ARE YOU SENDING HER?
A BOX OF EGG SHELLS!
SCHULZ
2-6

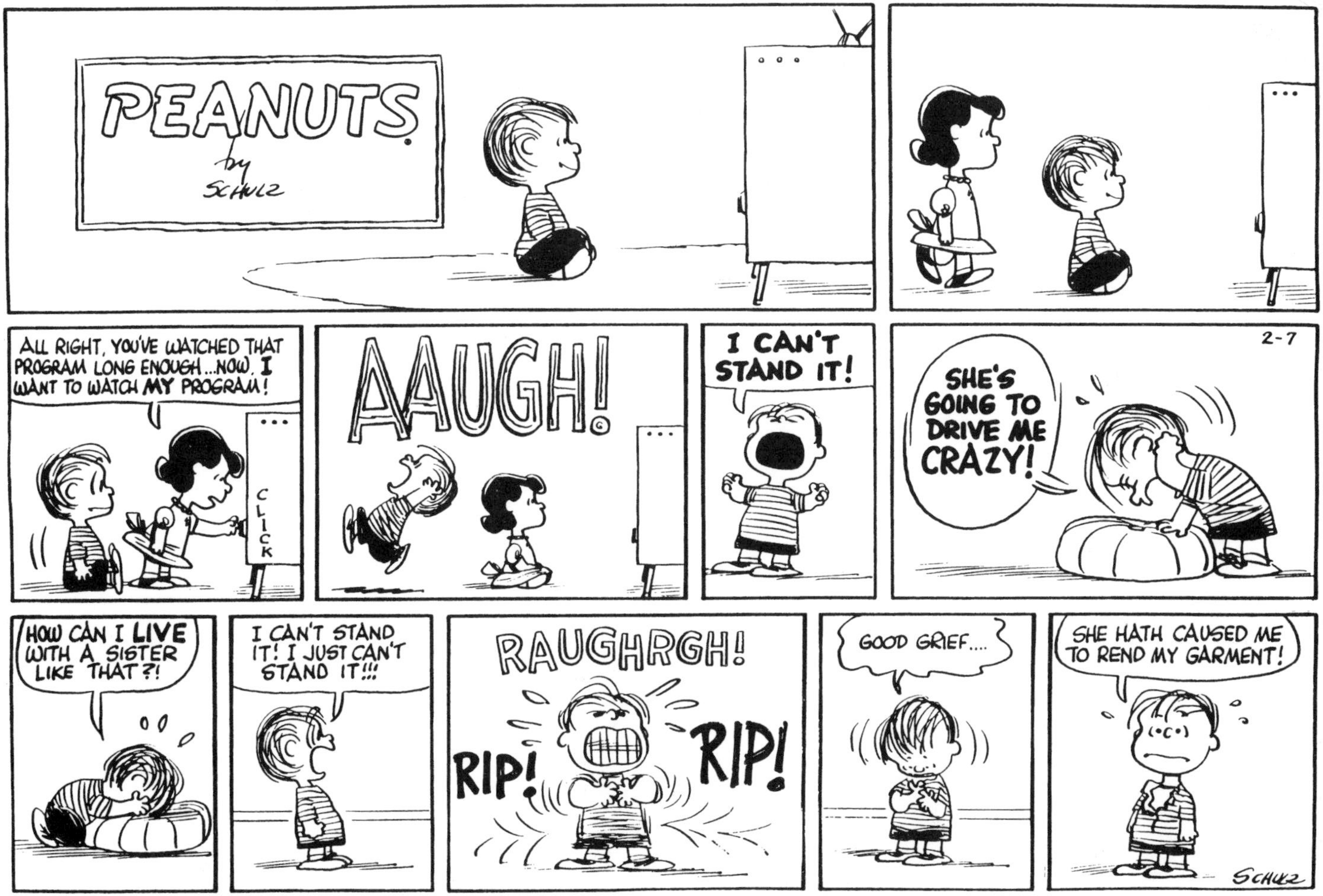
PEANUTS
by SCHULZ
ALL RIGHT, YOU'VE WATCHED THAT PROGRAM LONG ENOUGH...NOW, I WANT TO WATCH MY PROGRAM!
CLICK
AAUGH!
I CAN'T STAND IT!
2-7
SHE'S GOING TO DRIVE ME CRAZY!
HOW CAN I LIVE WITH A SISTER LIKE THAT?!
I CAN'T STAND IT! I JUST CAN'T STAND IT!!!
RAUGHRGH!
RIP!
RIP!
GOOD GRIEF....
SHE HATH CAUSED ME TO REND MY GARMENT!
SCHULZ

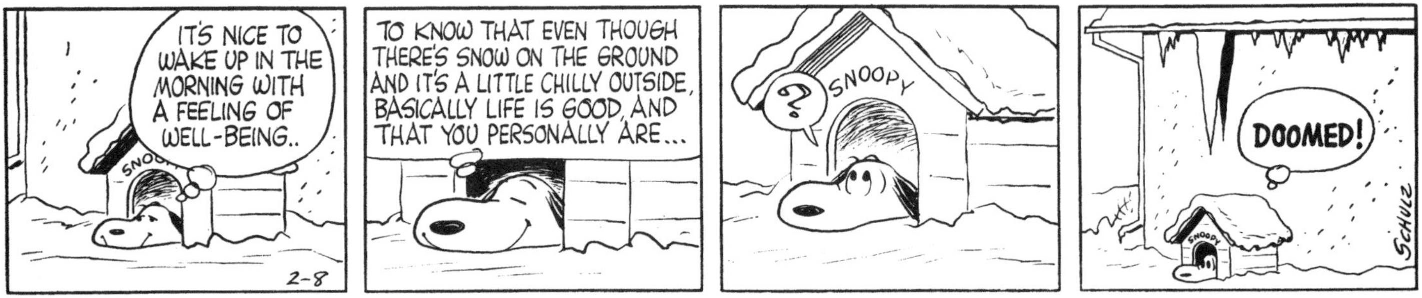
IT'S NICE TO WAKE UP IN THE MORNING WITH A FEELING OF WELL-BEING..
2-8
TO KNOW THAT EVEN THOUGH THERE'S SNOW ON THE GROUND AND IT'S A LITTLE CHILLY OUTSIDE, BASICALLY LIFE IS GOOD, AND THAT YOU PERSONALLY ARE...
SNOOPY
?
DOOMED!
SCHULZ

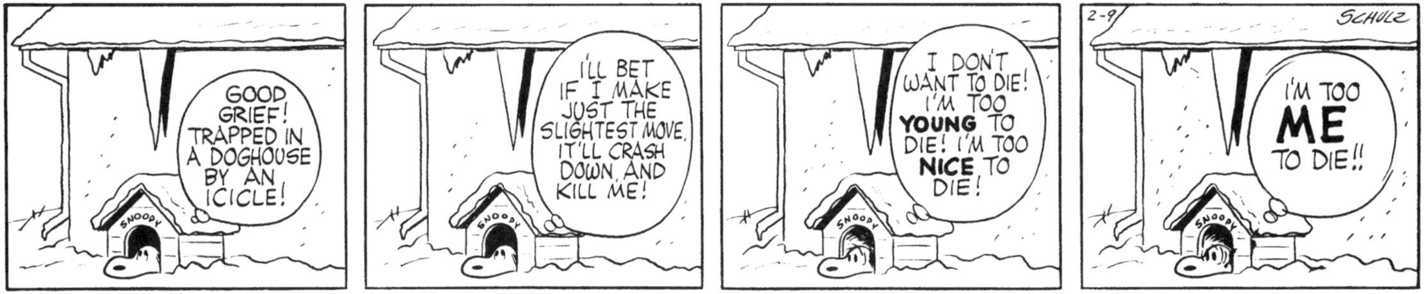
GOOD GRIEF! TRAPPED IN A DOGHOUSE BY AN ICICLE!
I'LL BET IF I MAKE JUST THE SLIGHTEST MOVE, IT'LL CRASH DOWN, AND KILL ME!
I DON'T WANT TO DIE! I'M TOO YOUNG TO DIE! I'M TOO NICE TO DIE!
2-9
SCHULZ
I'M TOO ME TO DIE!!

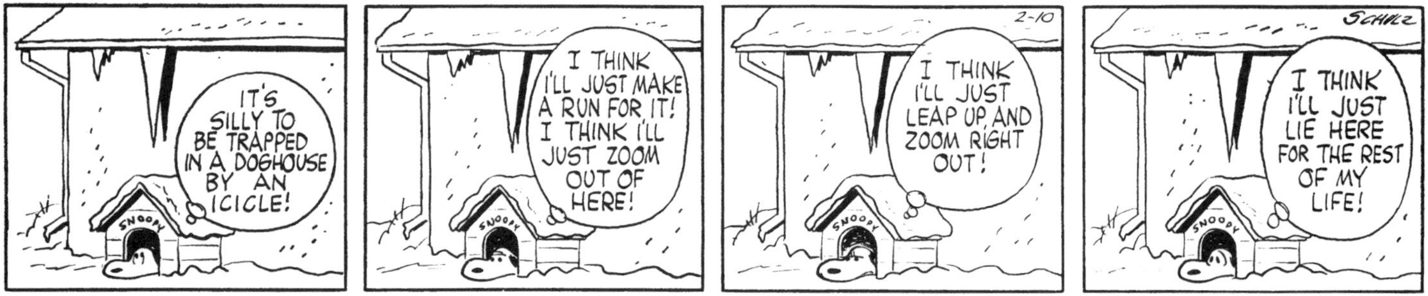
IT'S SILLY TO BE TRAPPED IN A DOGHOUSE BY AN ICICLE!
I THINK I'LL JUST MAKE A RUN FOR IT! I THINK I'LL JUST ZOOM OUT OF HERE!
2-10
I THINK I'LL JUST LEAP UP, AND ZOOM RIGHT OUT!
SCHULZ
I THINK I'LL JUST LIE HERE FOR THE REST OF MY LIFE!

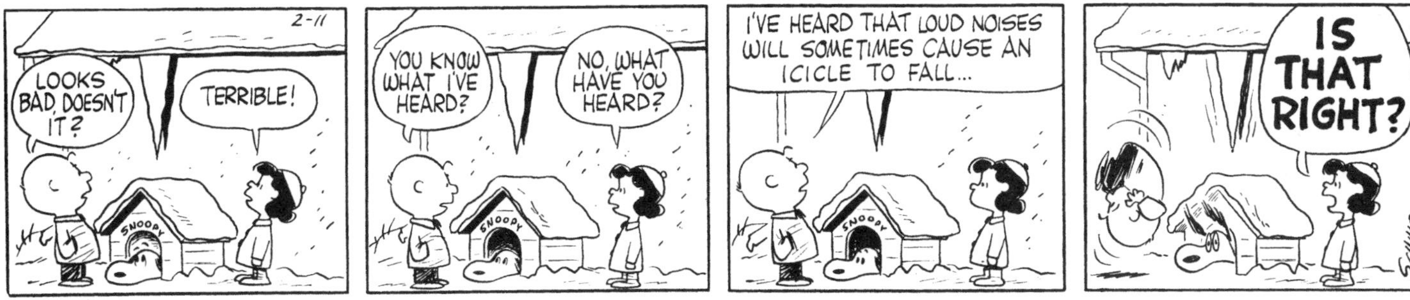
2-11
LOOKS BAD, DOESN'T IT?
TERRIBLE!
YOU KNOW WHAT I'VE HEARD?
NO, WHAT HAVE YOU HEARD?
I'VE HEARD THAT LOUD NOISES WILL SOMETIMES CAUSE AN ICICLE TO FALL...
IS THAT RIGHT?
SNOOPY
SCHULZ

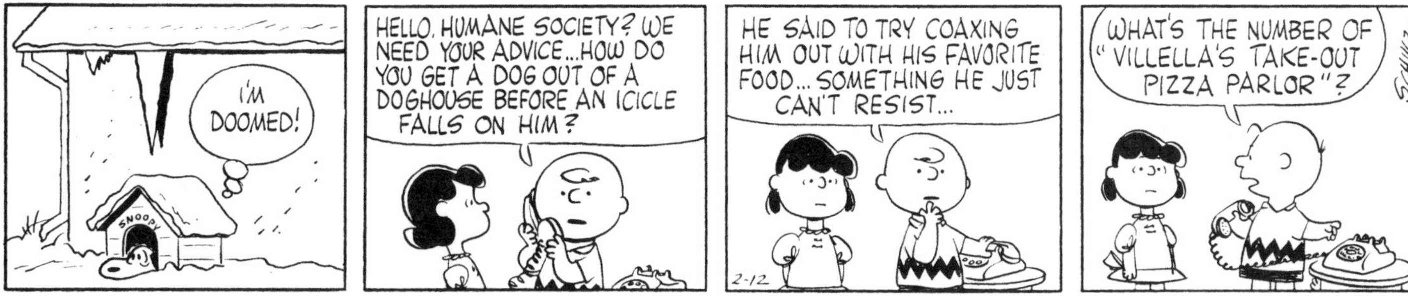
I'M DOOMED!
HELLO, HUMANE SOCIETY? WE NEED YOUR ADVICE...HOW DO YOU GET A DOG OUT OF A DOGHOUSE BEFORE AN ICICLE FALLS ON HIM?
HE SAID TO TRY COAXING HIM OUT WITH HIS FAVORITE FOOD... SOMETHING HE JUST CAN'T RESIST...
2-12
WHAT'S THE NUMBER OF "VILLELLA'S TAKE-OUT PIZZA PARLOR"?
SCHULZ

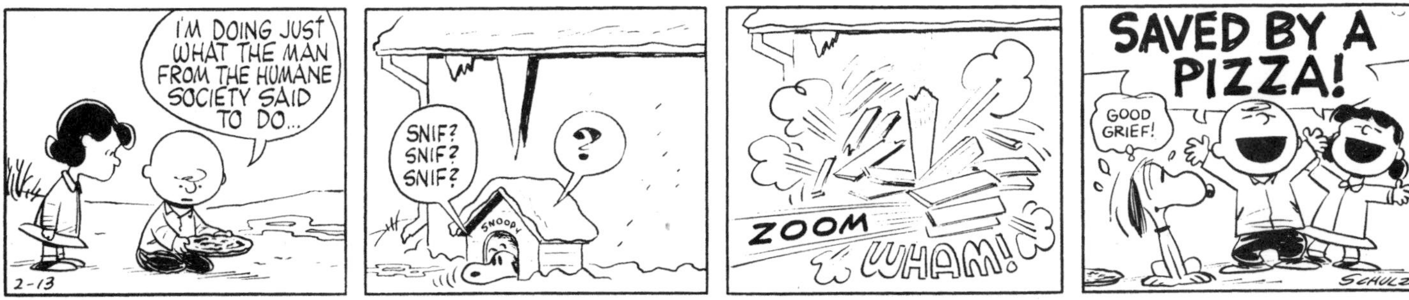
I'M DOING JUST WHAT THE MAN FROM THE HUMANE SOCIETY SAID TO DO...
2-13
SNIF? SNIF? SNIF?
?
ZOOM
WHAM!
SAVED BY A PIZZA!
GOOD GRIEF!
SCHULZ

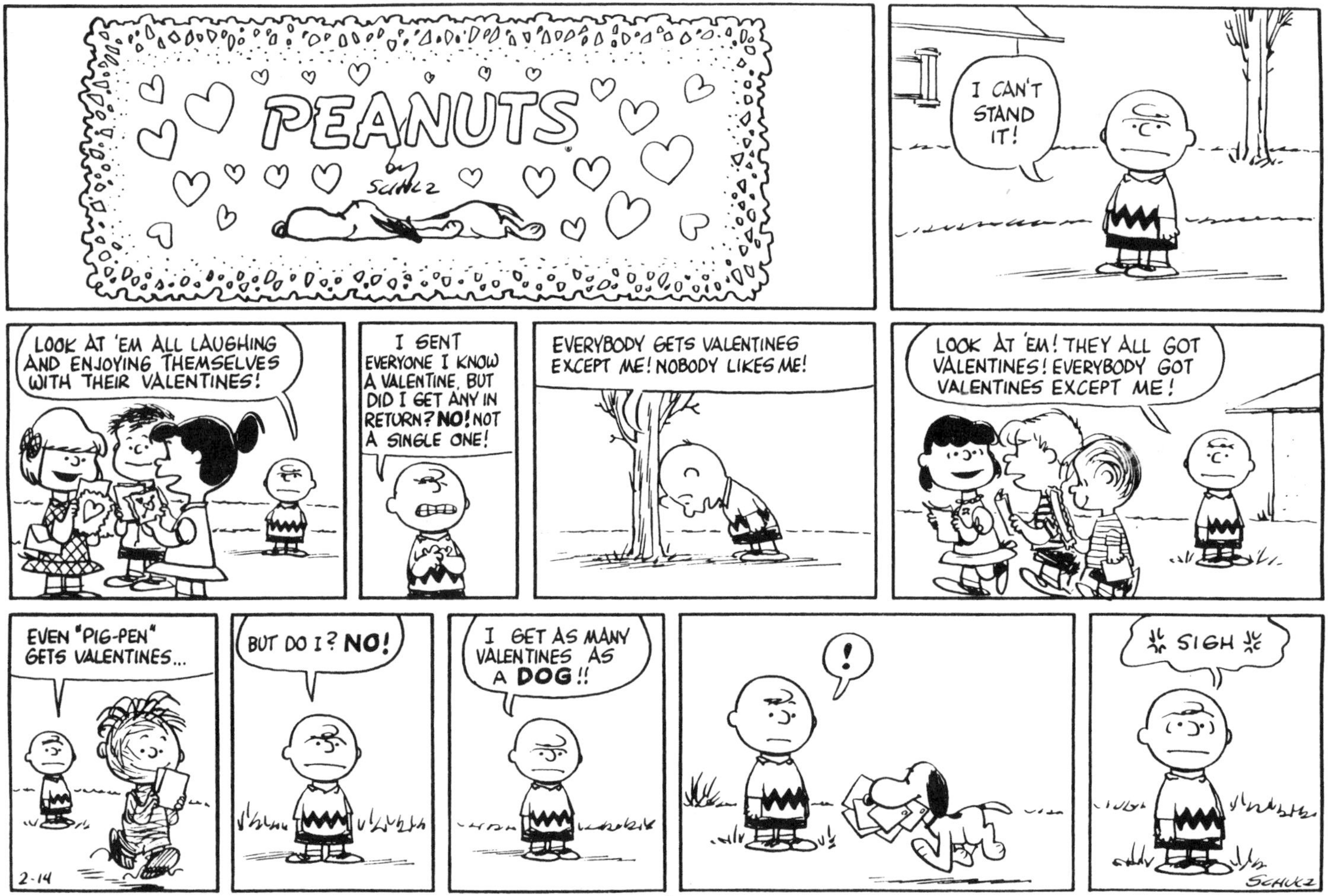
PEANUTS
by SCHULZ
I CAN'T STAND IT!
LOOK AT 'EM ALL LAUGHING AND ENJOYING THEMSELVES WITH THEIR VALENTINES!
I SENT EVERYONE I KNOW A VALENTINE, BUT DID I GET ANY IN RETURN? NO! NOT A SINGLE ONE!
EVERYBODY GETS VALENTINES EXCEPT ME! NOBODY LIKES ME!
LOOK AT 'EM! THEY ALL GOT VALENTINES! EVERYBODY GOT VALENTINES EXCEPT ME!
EVEN "PIG-PEN" GETS VALENTINES...
2-14
BUT DO I? NO!
I GET AS MANY VALENTINES AS A DOG!!
!
SIGH
SCHULZ

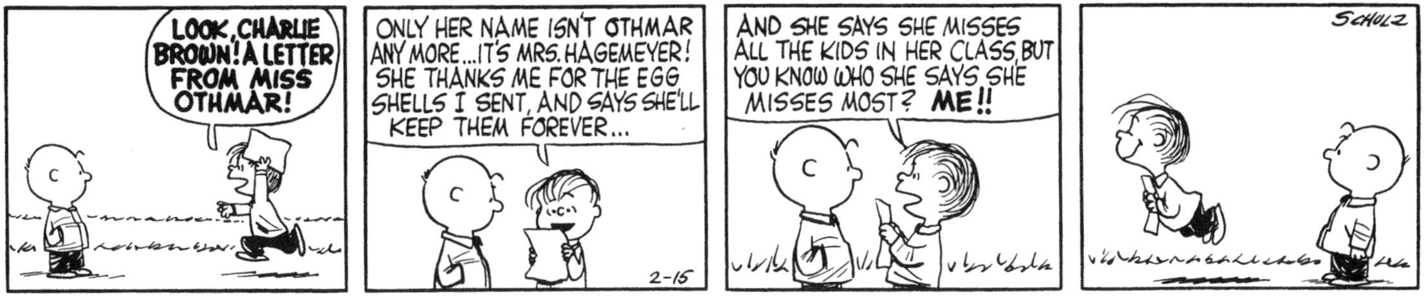
LOOK, CHARLIE BROWN! A LETTER FROM MISS OTHMAR!
ONLY HER NAME ISN'T OTHMAR ANY MORE...IT'S MRS. HAGEMEYER! SHE THANKS ME FOR THE EGG SHELLS I SENT, AND SAYS SHE'LL KEEP THEM FOREVER...
2-15
AND SHE SAYS SHE MISSES ALL THE KIDS IN HER CLASS, BUT YOU KNOW WHO SHE SAYS SHE MISSES MOST? ME!!
SCHULZ

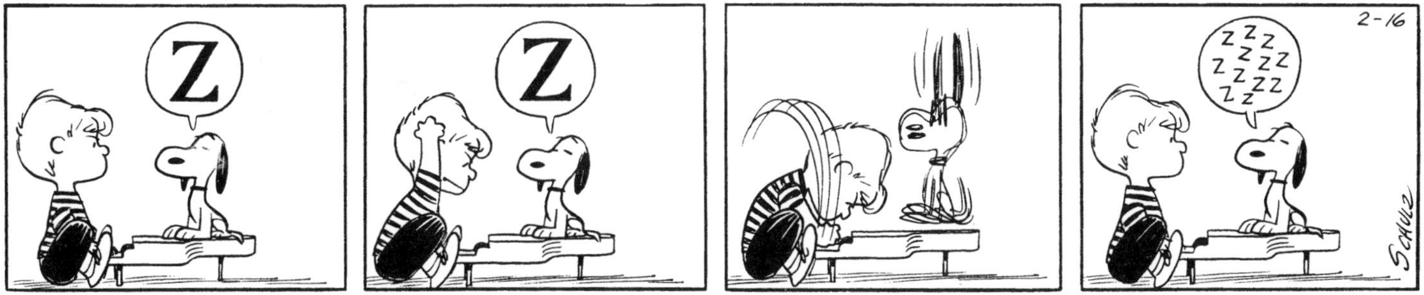
Z
Z
2-16
Z Z Z Z Z Z Z Z Z Z Z Z
SCHULZ

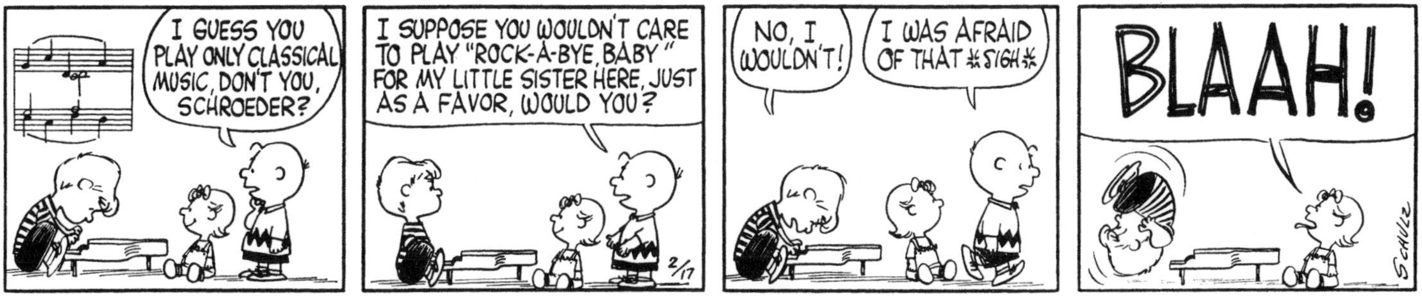
I GUESS YOU PLAY ONLY CLASSICAL MUSIC, DON'T YOU, SCHROEDER?
I SUPPOSE YOU WOULDN'T CARE TO PLAY "ROCK-A-BYE, BABY" FOR MY LITTLE SISTER HERE, JUST AS A FAVOR, WOULD YOU?
2/17
NO, I WOULDN'T!
I WAS AFRAID OF THAT *SIGH*
BLAAH!
SCHULZ

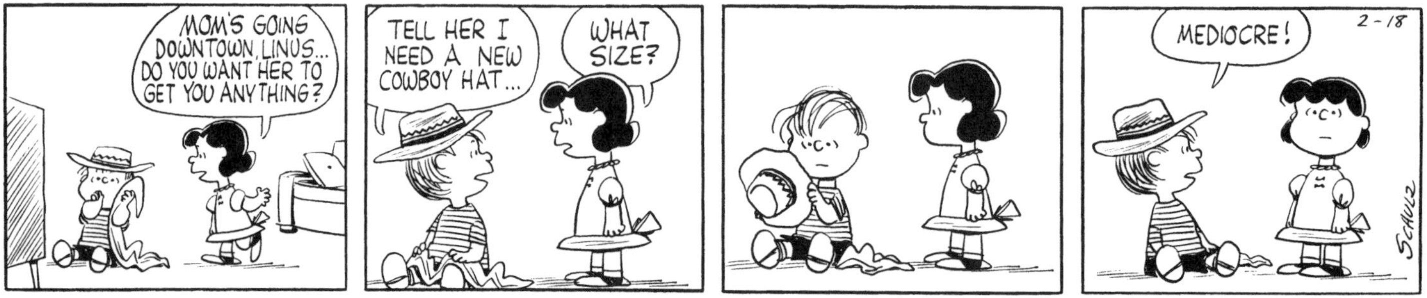
MOM'S GOING DOWNTOWN, LINUS... DO YOU WANT HER TO GET YOU ANYTHING?
TELL HER I NEED A NEW COWBOY HAT...
WHAT SIZE?
MEDIOCRE!
2-18
SCHULZ

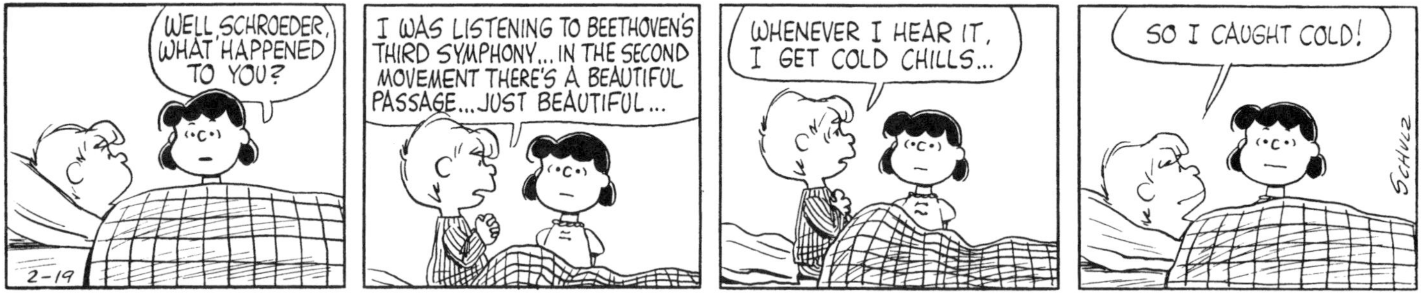
WELL, SCHROEDER, WHAT HAPPENED TO YOU?
2-19
I WAS LISTENING TO BEETHOVEN'S THIRD SYMPHONY... IN THE SECOND MOVEMENT THERE'S A BEAUTIFUL PASSAGE... JUST BEAUTIFUL...
WHENEVER I HEAR IT, I GET COLD CHILLS...
SO I CAUGHT COLD!
SCHULZ

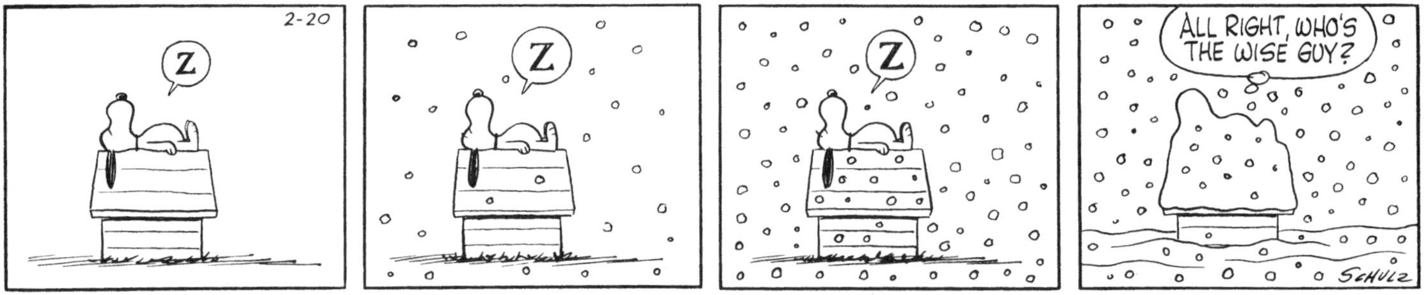
2-20
Z
Z
Z
ALL RIGHT, WHO'S THE WISE GUY?
SCHULZ

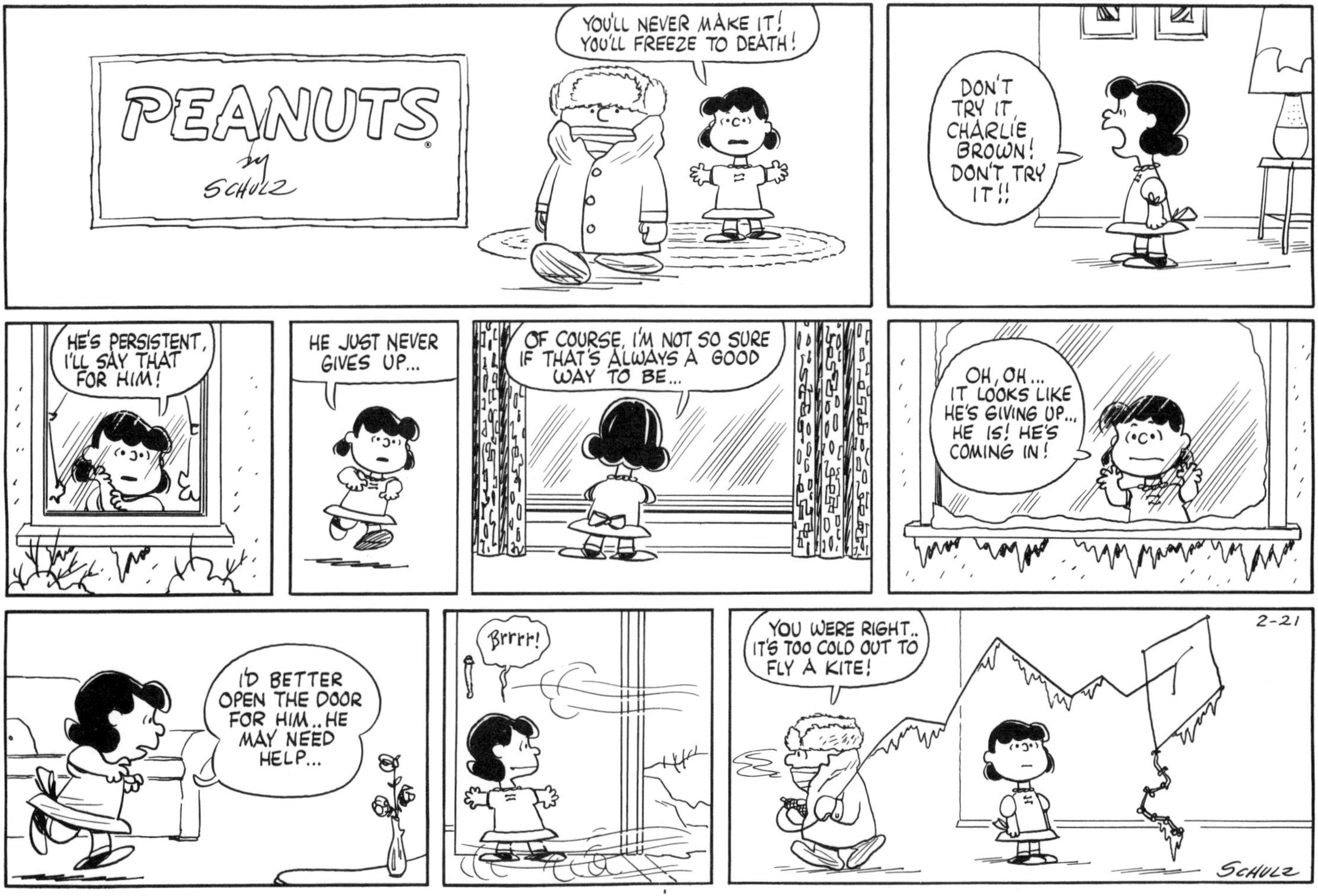
PEANUTS
by SCHULZ
YOU'LL NEVER MAKE IT! YOU'LL FREEZE TO DEATH!
DON'T TRY IT, CHARLIE BROWN! DON'T TRY IT!!
HE'S PERSISTENT, I'LL SAY THAT FOR HIM!
HE JUST NEVER GIVES UP...
OF COURSE, I'M NOT SO SURE IF THAT'S ALWAYS A GOOD WAY TO BE...
OH, OH... IT LOOKS LIKE HE'S GIVING UP... HE IS! HE'S COMING IN!
I'D BETTER OPEN THE DOOR FOR HIM.. HE MAY NEED HELP...
Brrrr!
2-21
YOU WERE RIGHT.. IT'S TOO COLD OUT TO FLY A KITE!
SCHULZ

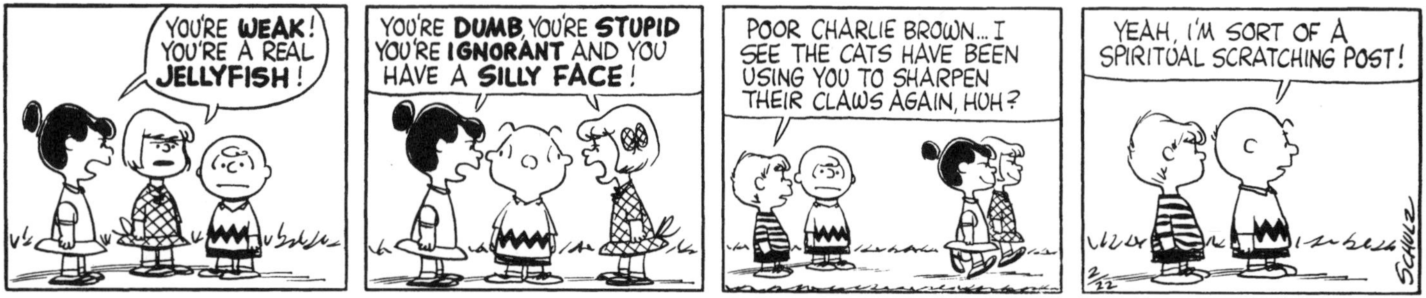
YOU'RE **WEAK**! YOU'RE A REAL **JELLYFISH**!
YOU'RE **DUMB**, YOU'RE **STUPID** YOU'RE **IGNORANT** AND YOU HAVE A **SILLY FACE**!
POOR CHARLIE BROWN... I SEE THE CATS HAVE BEEN USING YOU TO SHARPEN THEIR CLAWS AGAIN, HUH?
YEAH, I'M SORT OF A SPIRITUAL SCRATCHING POST!
2/22
SCHULZ

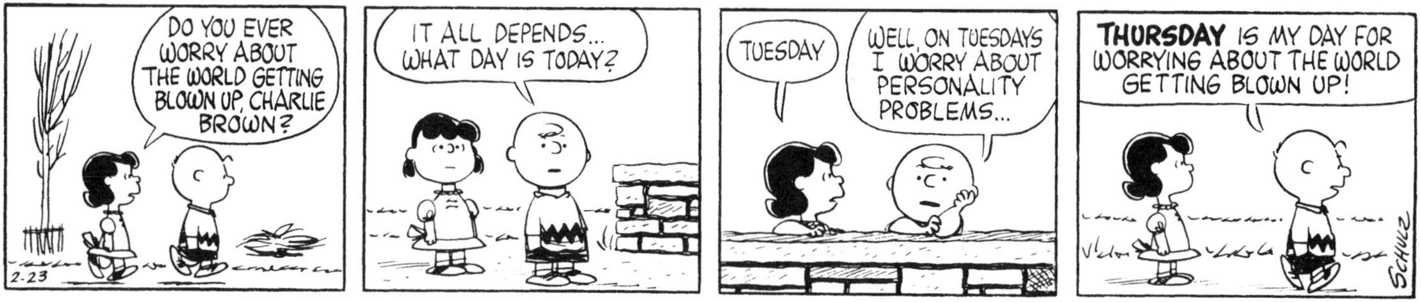
2-23
DO YOU EVER WORRY ABOUT THE WORLD GETTING BLOWN UP, CHARLIE BROWN?
IT ALL DEPENDS... WHAT DAY IS TODAY?
TUESDAY
WELL, ON TUESDAYS I WORRY ABOUT PERSONALITY PROBLEMS...
THURSDAY IS MY DAY FOR WORRYING ABOUT THE WORLD GETTING BLOWN UP!
SCHULZ

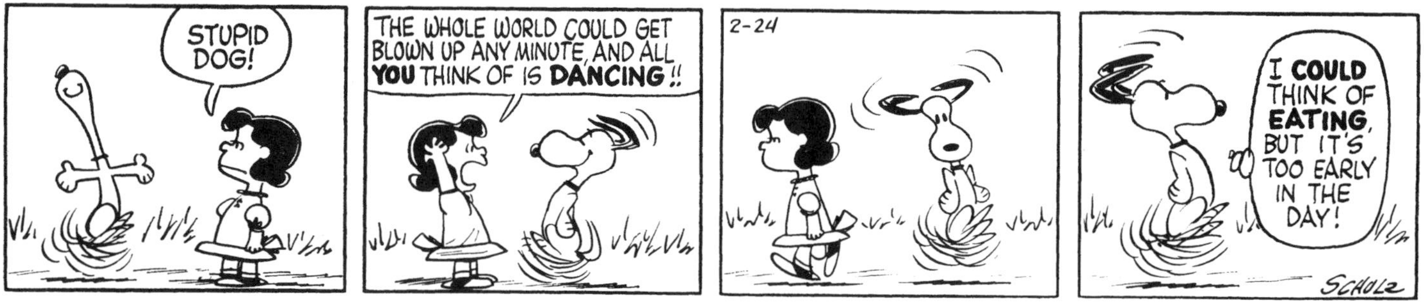
STUPID DOG!
THE WHOLE WORLD COULD GET BLOWN UP ANY MINUTE, AND ALL **YOU** THINK OF IS **DANCING**!!
2-24
I **COULD** THINK OF **EATING**, BUT IT'S TOO EARLY IN THE DAY!
SCHULZ

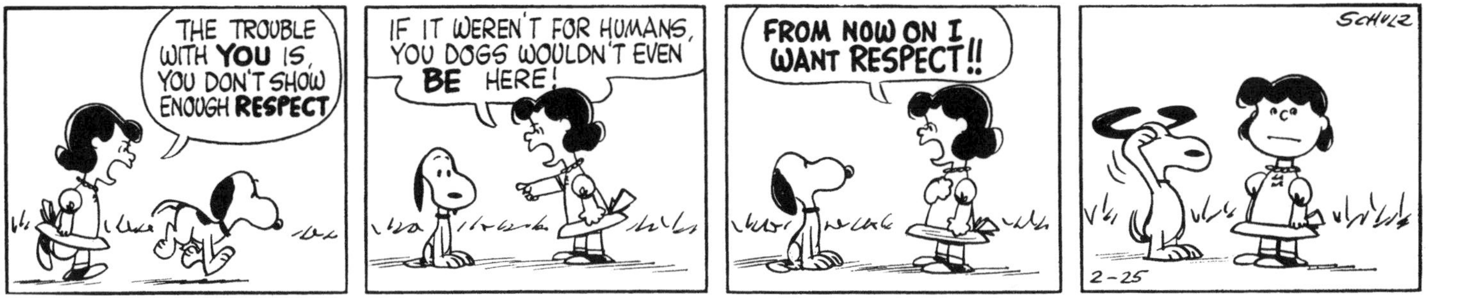
THE TROUBLE WITH YOU IS, YOU DON'T SHOW ENOUGH RESPECT
IF IT WEREN'T FOR HUMANS, YOU DOGS WOULDN'T EVEN BE HERE!
FROM NOW ON I WANT RESPECT!!
SCHULZ
2-25

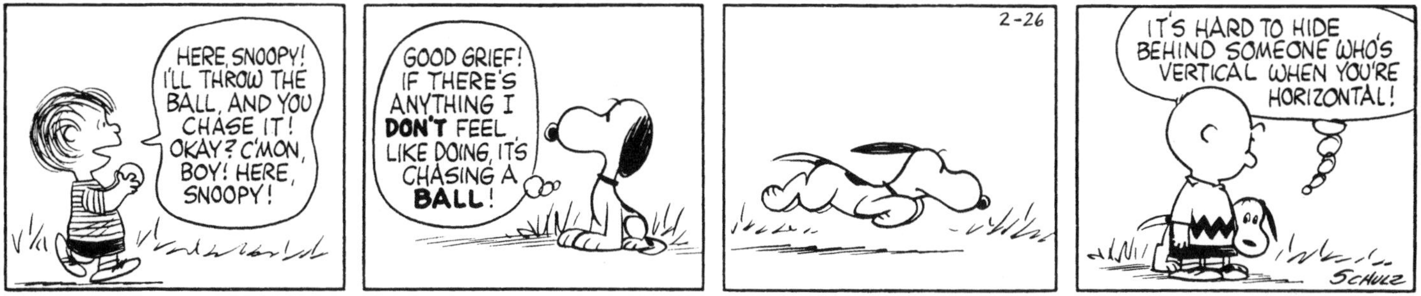
HERE, SNOOPY! I'LL THROW THE BALL, AND YOU CHASE IT! OKAY? C'MON, BOY! HERE, SNOOPY!
GOOD GRIEF! IF THERE'S ANYTHING I DON'T FEEL LIKE DOING, IT'S CHASING A BALL!
2-26
IT'S HARD TO HIDE BEHIND SOMEONE WHO'S VERTICAL WHEN YOU'RE HORIZONTAL!
SCHULZ

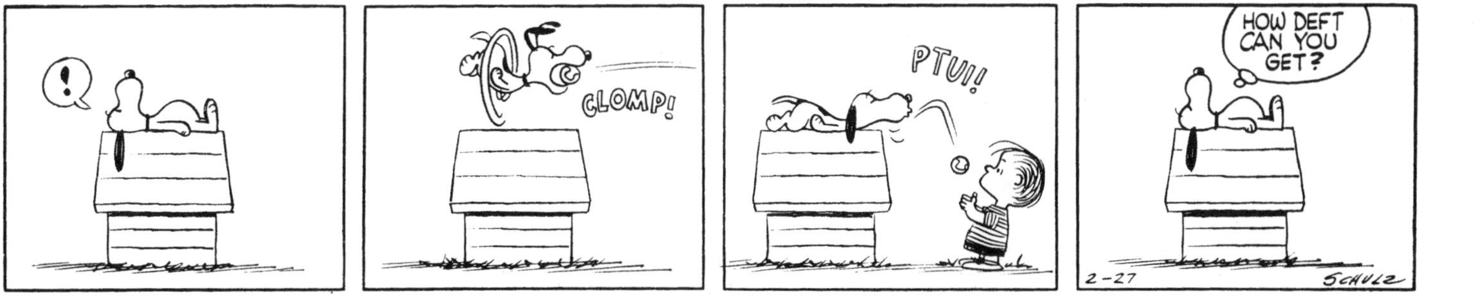
!
CLOMP!
PTUI!
HOW DEFT CAN YOU GET?
2-27
SCHULZ

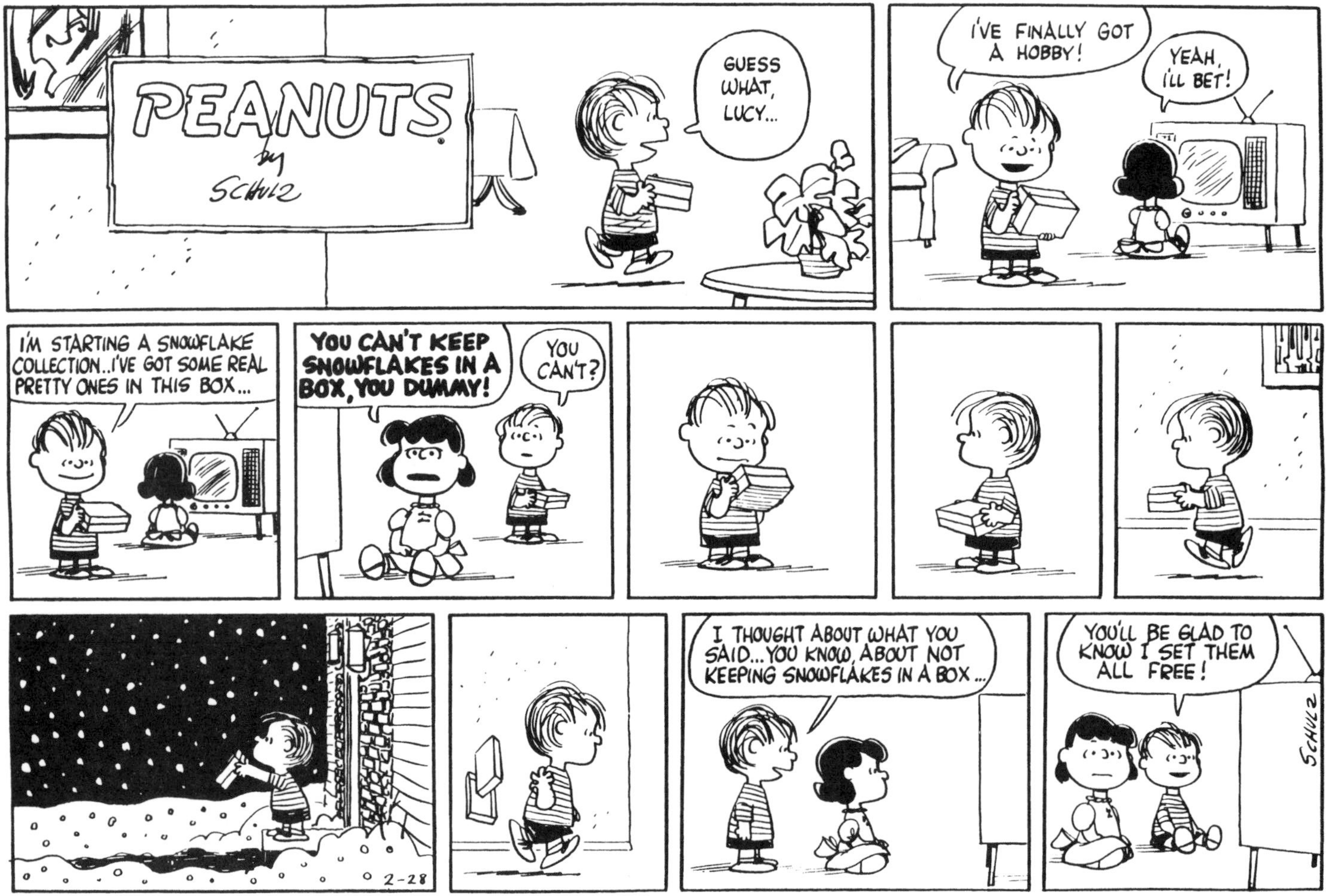
PEANUTS
by SCHULZ
GUESS WHAT, LUCY...
I'VE FINALLY GOT A HOBBY!
YEAH, I'LL BET!
I'M STARTING A SNOWFLAKE COLLECTION..I'VE GOT SOME REAL PRETTY ONES IN THIS BOX...
YOU CAN'T KEEP SNOWFLAKES IN A BOX, YOU DUMMY!
YOU CAN'T?
2-28
I THOUGHT ABOUT WHAT YOU SAID...YOU KNOW, ABOUT NOT KEEPING SNOWFLAKES IN A BOX...
YOU'LL BE GLAD TO KNOW I SET THEM ALL FREE!
SCHULZ

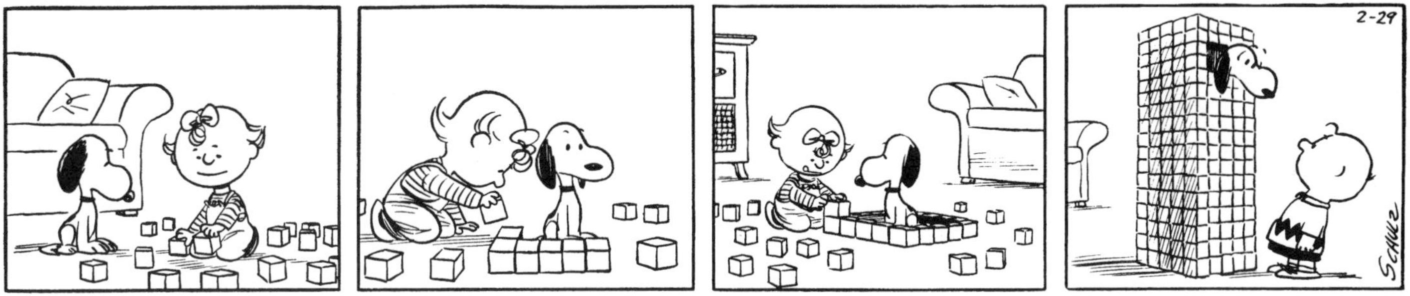
2-29
SCHULZ

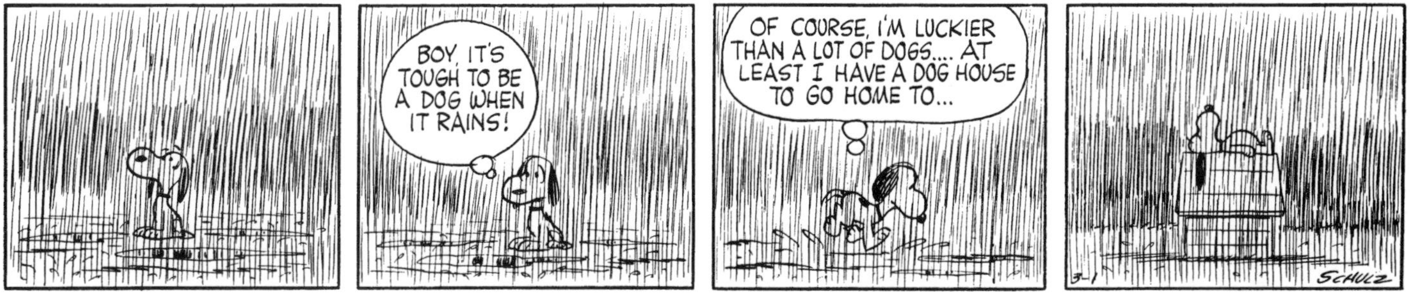
BOY, IT'S TOUGH TO BE A DOG WHEN IT RAINS!
OF COURSE, I'M LUCKIER THAN A LOT OF DOGS.... AT LEAST I HAVE A DOG HOUSE TO GO HOME TO...
3-1
SCHULZ

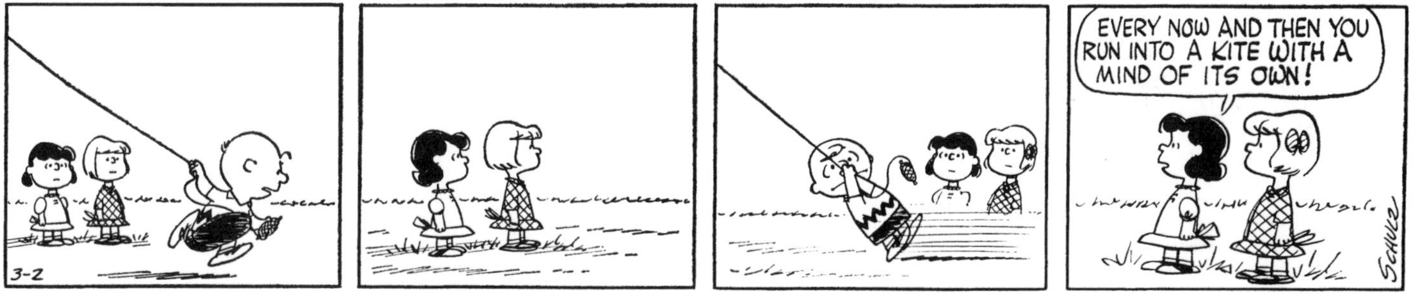
3-2
EVERY NOW AND THEN YOU RUN INTO A KITE WITH A MIND OF ITS OWN!
SCHULZ

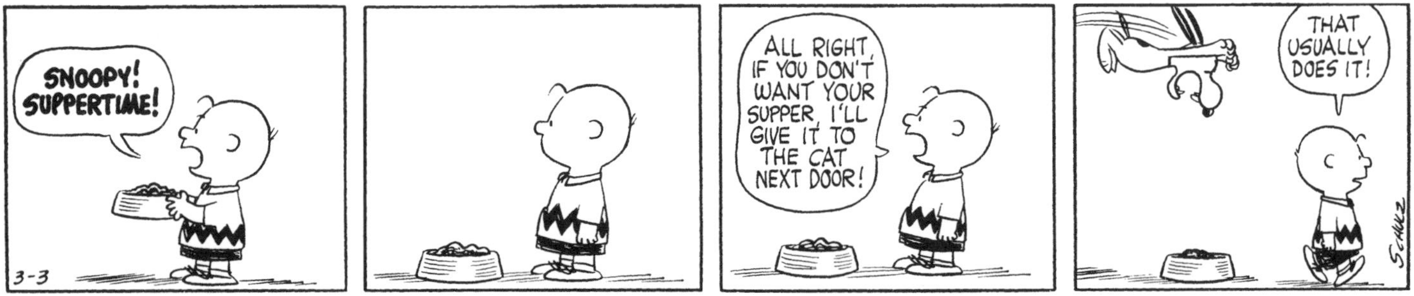
SNOOPY! SUPPERTIME!
3-3
ALL RIGHT, IF YOU DON'T WANT YOUR SUPPER, I'LL GIVE IT TO THE CAT NEXT DOOR!
THAT USUALLY DOES IT!
SCHULZ

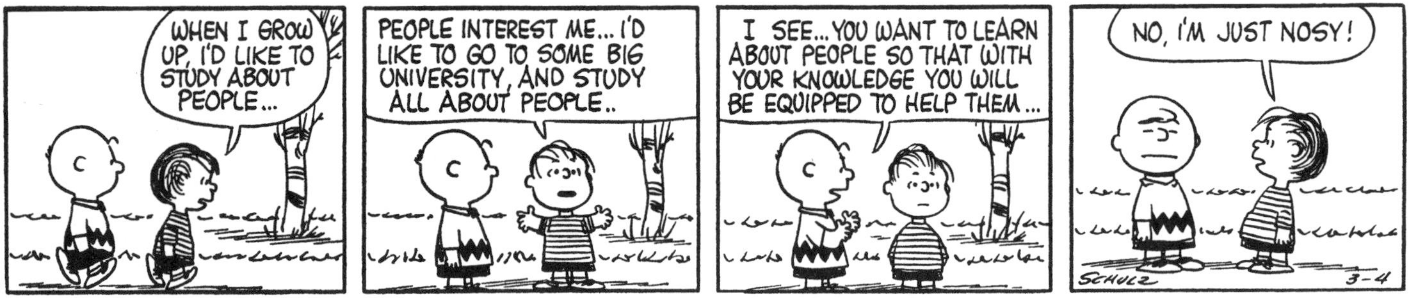
WHEN I GROW UP, I'D LIKE TO STUDY ABOUT PEOPLE...
PEOPLE INTEREST ME... I'D LIKE TO GO TO SOME BIG UNIVERSITY, AND STUDY ALL ABOUT PEOPLE..
I SEE... YOU WANT TO LEARN ABOUT PEOPLE SO THAT WITH YOUR KNOWLEDGE YOU WILL BE EQUIPPED TO HELP THEM...
NO, I'M JUST NOSY!
SCHULZ
3-4

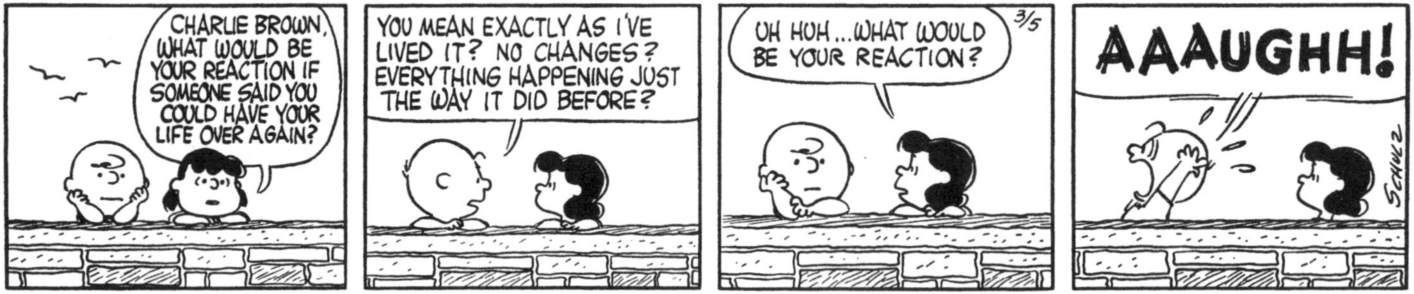
CHARLIE BROWN, WHAT WOULD BE YOUR REACTION IF SOMEONE SAID YOU COULD HAVE YOUR LIFE OVER AGAIN?
YOU MEAN EXACTLY AS I'VE LIVED IT? NO CHANGES? EVERYTHING HAPPENING JUST THE WAY IT DID BEFORE?
3/5
UH HUH... WHAT WOULD BE YOUR REACTION?
AAAUGHH!
SCHULZ

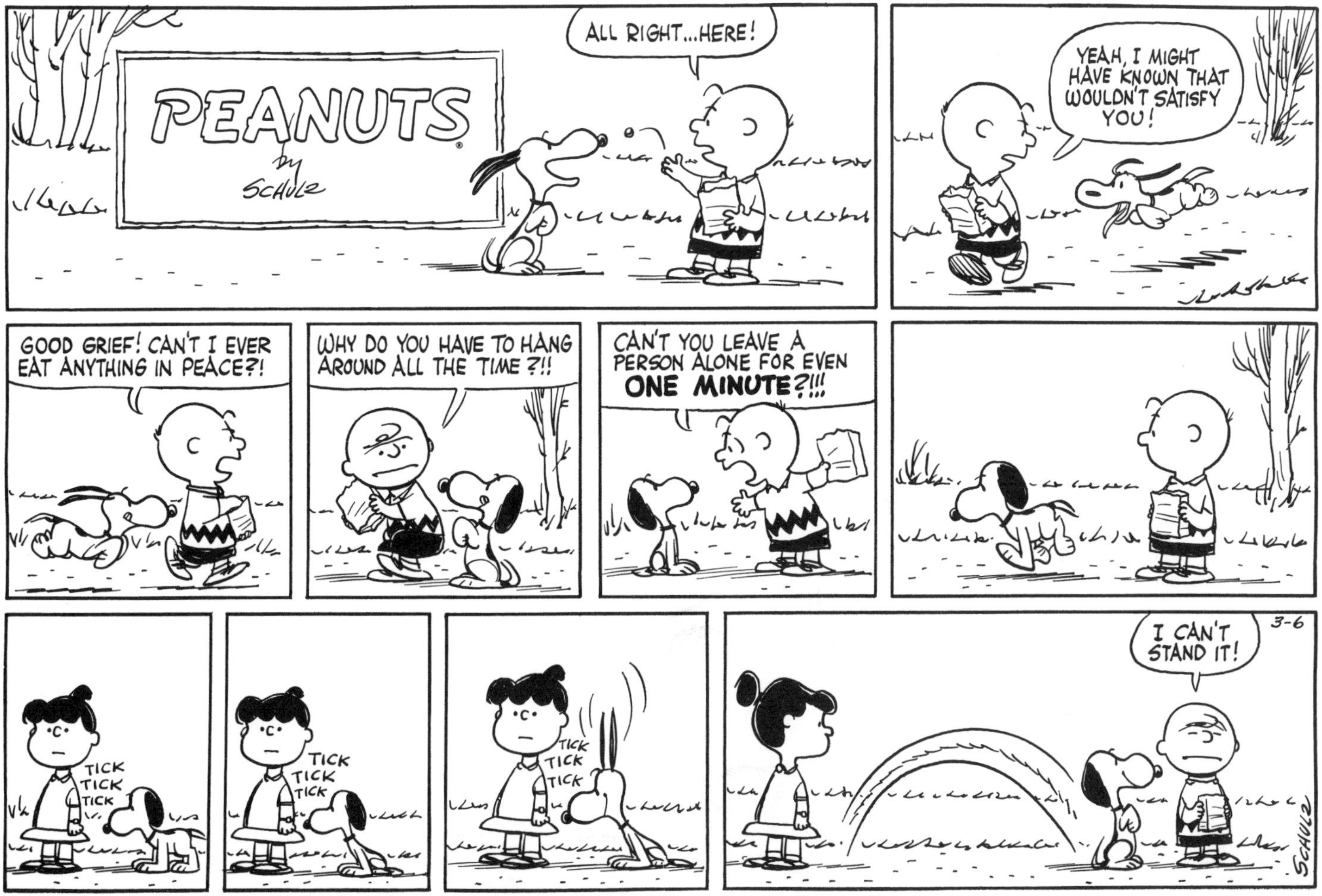
PEANUTS
by SCHULZ
ALL RIGHT...HERE!
YEAH, I MIGHT HAVE KNOWN THAT WOULDN'T SATISFY YOU!
GOOD GRIEF! CAN'T I EVER EAT ANYTHING IN PEACE?!
WHY DO YOU HAVE TO HANG AROUND ALL THE TIME?!!
CAN'T YOU LEAVE A PERSON ALONE FOR EVEN ONE MINUTE?!!!
TICK TICK TICK
TICK TICK TICK
TICK TICK TICK
I CAN'T STAND IT!
3-6
SCHULZ

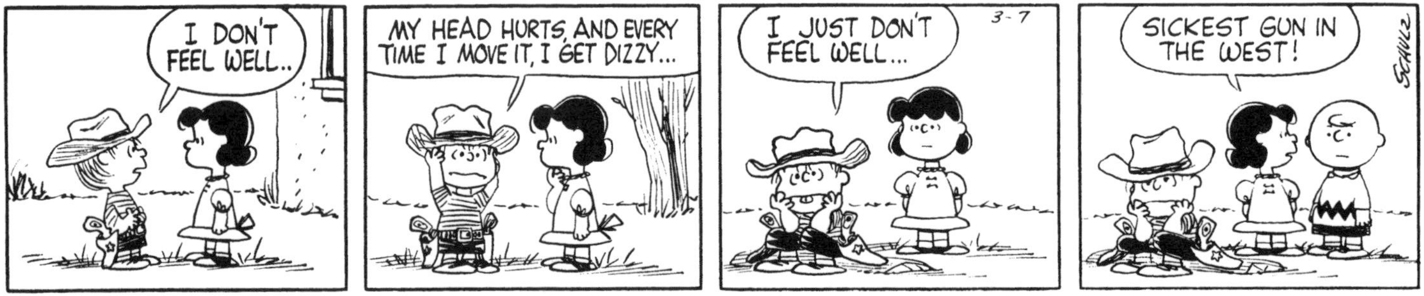
I DON'T FEEL WELL..
MY HEAD HURTS, AND EVERY TIME I MOVE IT, I GET DIZZY...
I JUST DON'T FEEL WELL...
3-7
SICKEST GUN IN THE WEST!
SCHULZ

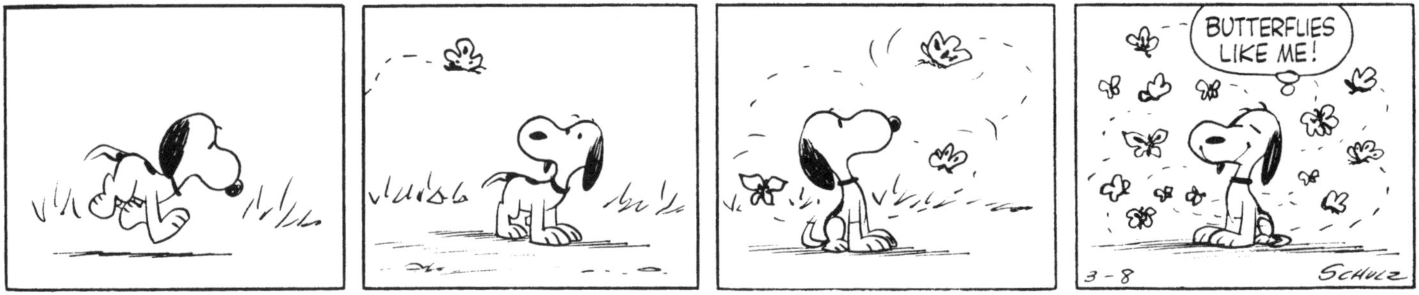
BUTTERFLIES LIKE ME!
3-8
SCHULZ

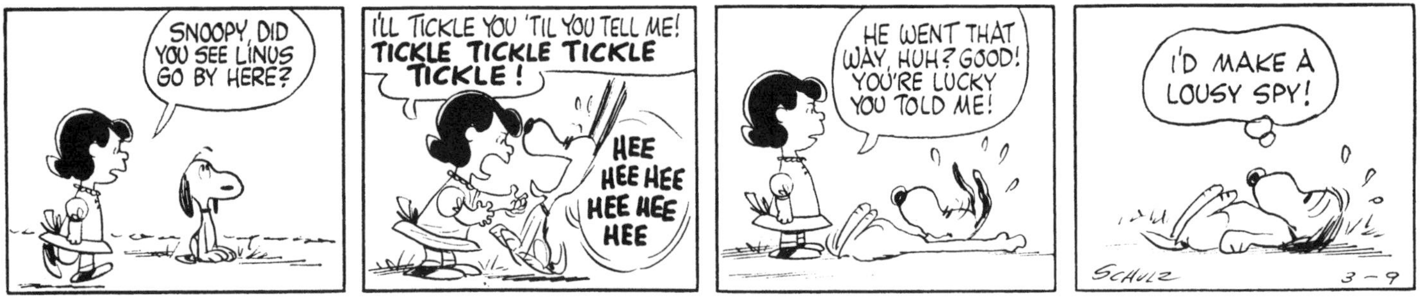
SNOOPY, DID YOU SEE LINUS GO BY HERE?
I'LL TICKLE YOU 'TIL YOU TELL ME! TICKLE TICKLE TICKLE TICKLE!
HEE HEE HEE HEE HEE HEE
HE WENT THAT WAY, HUH? GOOD! YOU'RE LUCKY YOU TOLD ME!
I'D MAKE A LOUSY SPY!
SCHULZ
3-9

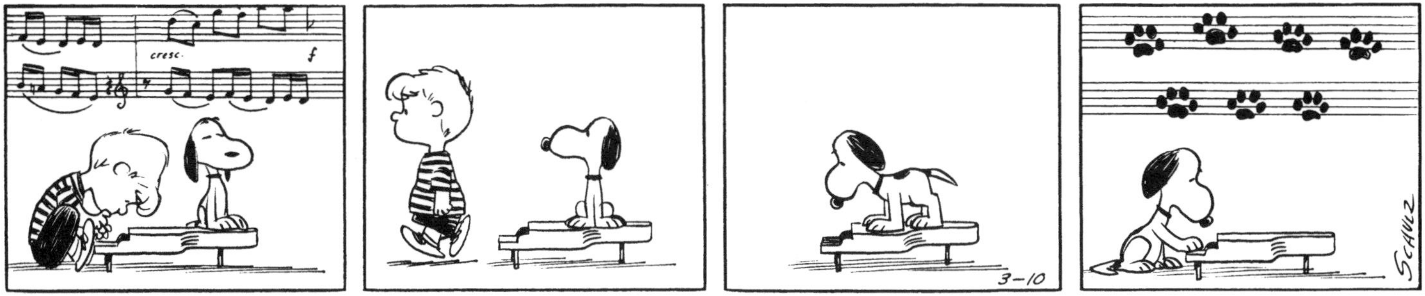
cresc.
f
3-10
SCHULZ

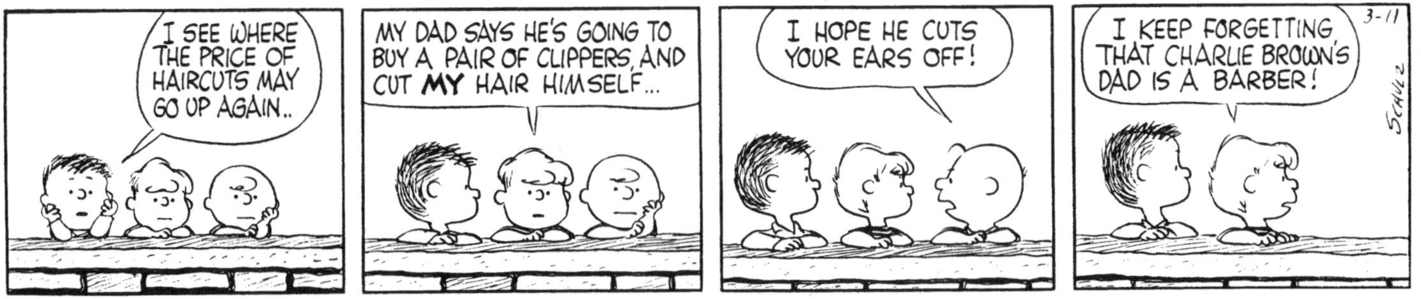
I SEE WHERE THE PRICE OF HAIRCUTS MAY GO UP AGAIN..
MY DAD SAYS HE'S GOING TO BUY A PAIR OF CLIPPERS, AND CUT **MY** HAIR HIMSELF...
I HOPE HE CUTS YOUR EARS OFF!
I KEEP FORGETTING THAT CHARLIE BROWN'S DAD IS A BARBER!
3-11
SCHULZ

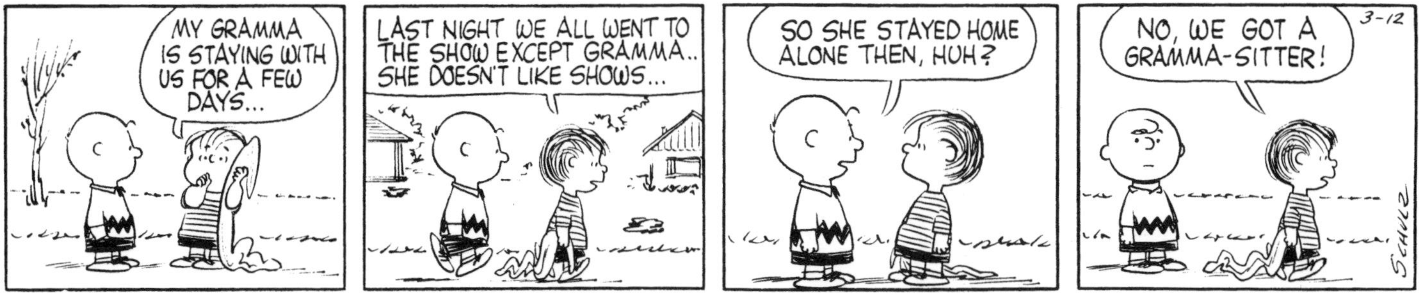
MY GRAMMA IS STAYING WITH US FOR A FEW DAYS...
LAST NIGHT WE ALL WENT TO THE SHOW EXCEPT GRAMMA.. SHE DOESN'T LIKE SHOWS...
SO SHE STAYED HOME ALONE THEN, HUH?
NO, WE GOT A GRAMMA-SITTER!
3-12
SCHULZ

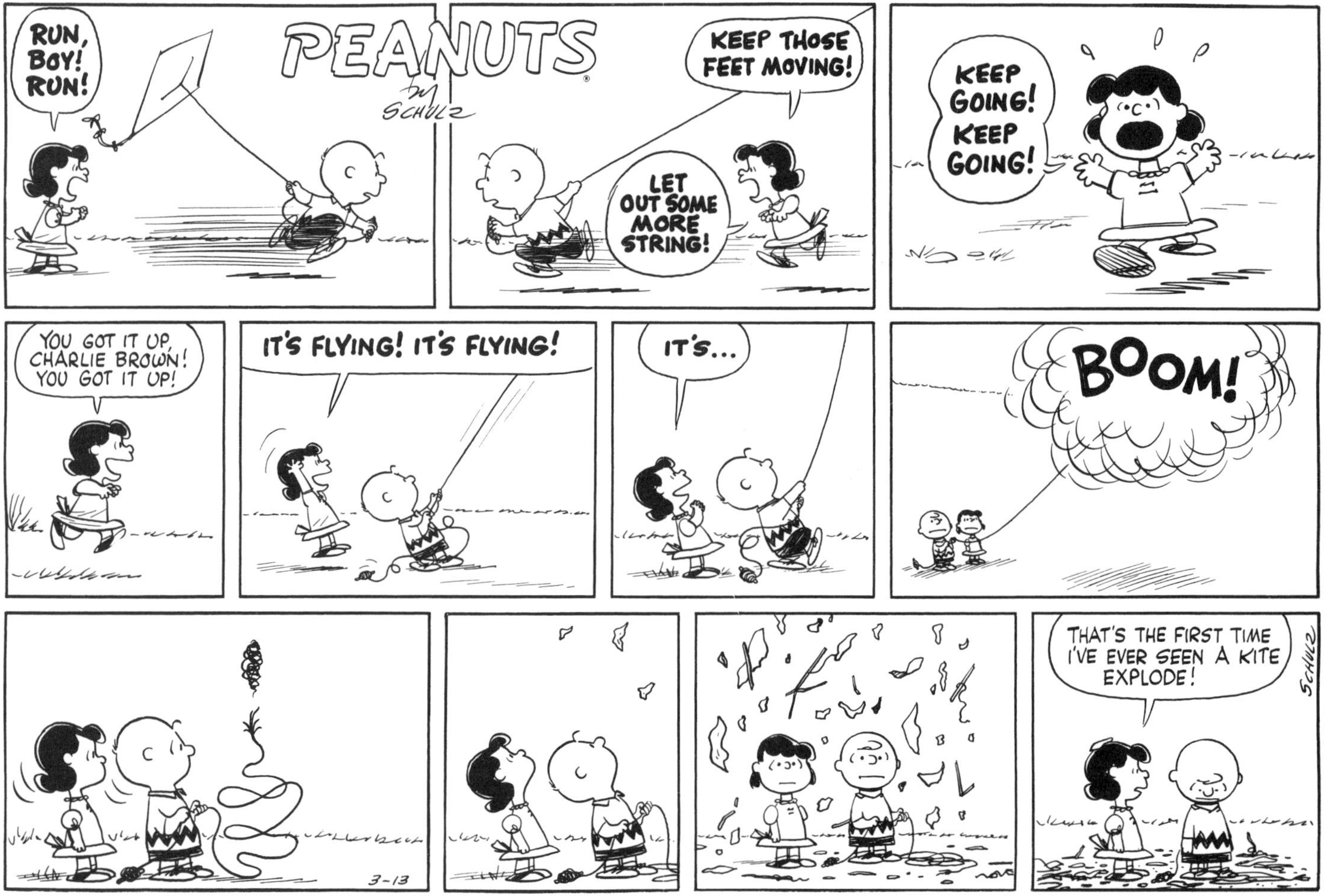
RUN, BOY! RUN!
PEANUTS
by SCHULZ
KEEP THOSE FEET MOVING!
LET OUT SOME MORE STRING!
KEEP GOING! KEEP GOING!
YOU GOT IT UP, CHARLIE BROWN! YOU GOT IT UP!
IT'S FLYING! IT'S FLYING!
IT'S...
BOOM!
3-13
THAT'S THE FIRST TIME I'VE EVER SEEN A KITE EXPLODE!
SCHULZ

Lucy: THAT'S THE FIRST TIME IN MY LIFE I'VE EVER SEEN A WHIRLYDOG!

Lucy: NOT WHIRLYDOG... WHIRLYBIRD!

3-14

Lucy: I THINK IF I HAD **MEANT** WHIRLYBIRD, I WOULD HAVE **SAID** WHIRLYBIRD!

Charlie Brown: I DON'T THINK I'M GOING TO BE ABLE TO STAND THESE NEXT FEW DAYS!

3-15

Charlie Brown: SNOOPY! SUPPERTIME!

3-16

CLOMP!

♡— SMACK —♡

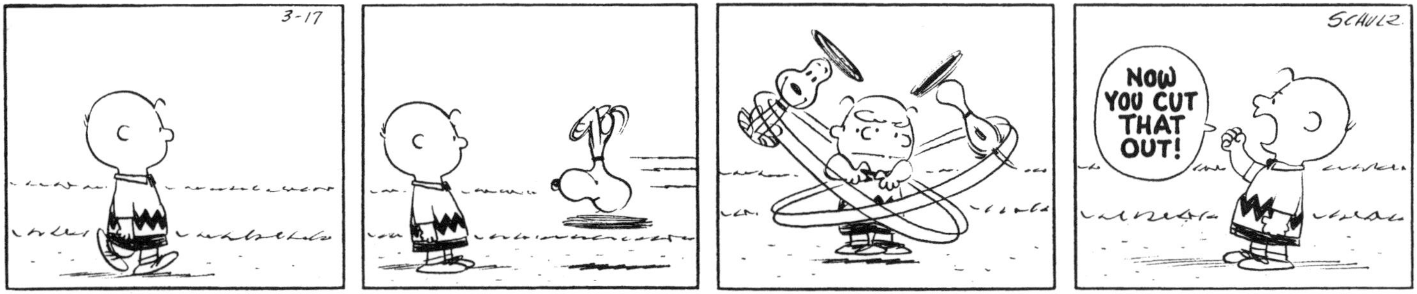
3-17
SCHULZ
NOW YOU CUT THAT OUT!

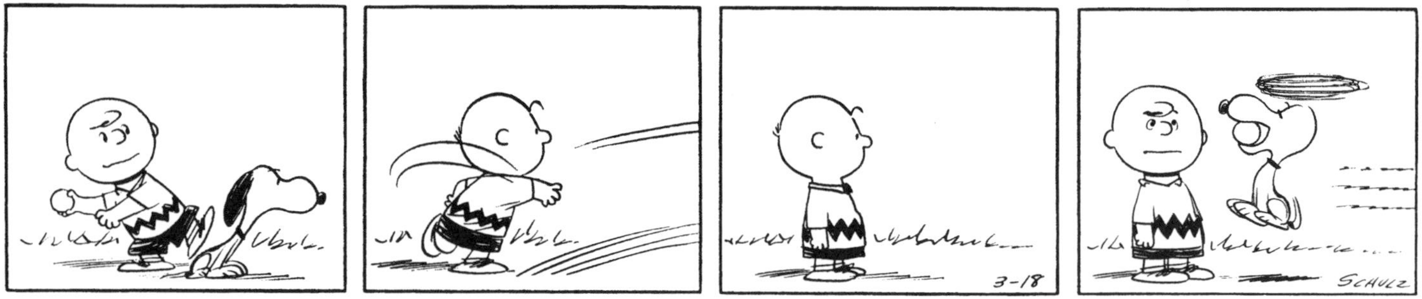
3-18
SCHULZ

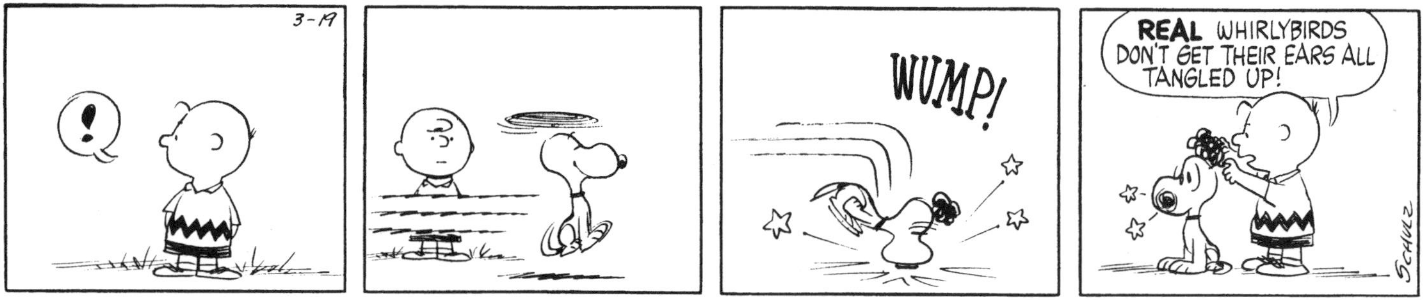
3-19
!
WUMP!
REAL WHIRLYBIRDS DON'T GET THEIR EARS ALL TANGLED UP!
SCHULZ

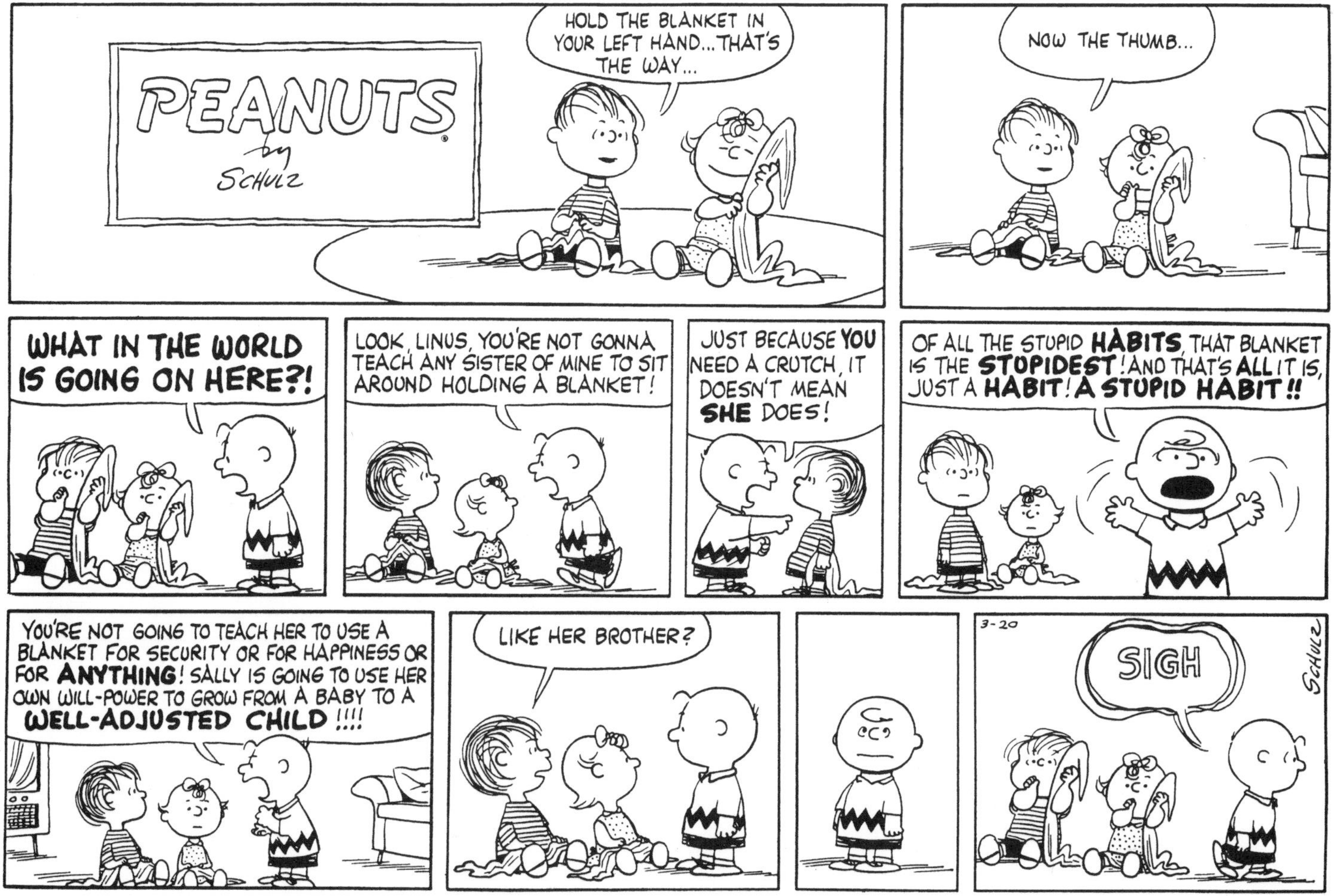
PEANUTS
by SCHULZ
HOLD THE BLANKET IN YOUR LEFT HAND... THAT'S THE WAY...
NOW THE THUMB...
WHAT IN THE WORLD IS GOING ON HERE?!
LOOK, LINUS, YOU'RE NOT GONNA TEACH ANY SISTER OF MINE TO SIT AROUND HOLDING A BLANKET!
JUST BECAUSE YOU NEED A CRUTCH, IT DOESN'T MEAN SHE DOES!
OF ALL THE STUPID HABITS, THAT BLANKET IS THE STUPIDEST! AND THAT'S ALL IT IS, JUST A HABIT! A STUPID HABIT!!
YOU'RE NOT GOING TO TEACH HER TO USE A BLANKET FOR SECURITY OR FOR HAPPINESS OR FOR ANYTHING! SALLY IS GOING TO USE HER OWN WILL-POWER TO GROW FROM A BABY TO A WELL-ADJUSTED CHILD!!!!
LIKE HER BROTHER?
3-20
SIGH
SCHULZ

Panel 1: WELL, I'VE DISCOVERED A NEW TRUTH..

Panel 2: THERE ARE TWO CLASSES OF PEOPLE IN THIS WORLD WHICH ARE VIOLENTLY OPPOSED TO THUMB-SUCKING...

Panel 3: ONE OF THEM IS DENTISTS AND ONE OF THEM IS GRANDMOTHERS... 3-21

Panel 4: INTERFERING GRANDMOTHERS!!

Panel 5: WHAT IN THE WORLD ARE YOU DOING?

Panel 6: MY GRAMMA IS GIVING ME TROUBLE AGAIN...SHE KEEPS HIDING MY BLANKET! 3-22

Panel 7: SO?

Panel 8: SO I'M LAYING OUT DECOYS!

Panel 9: MY GRAMMA KEEPS TRYING TO HIDE MY BLANKET...

Panel 10: I HAVE TO BE PRETTY SHARP TO OUTWIT HER..

Panel 11: ISN'T THIS YOUR GRAMMA COMING NOW?

Panel 12: 3-23

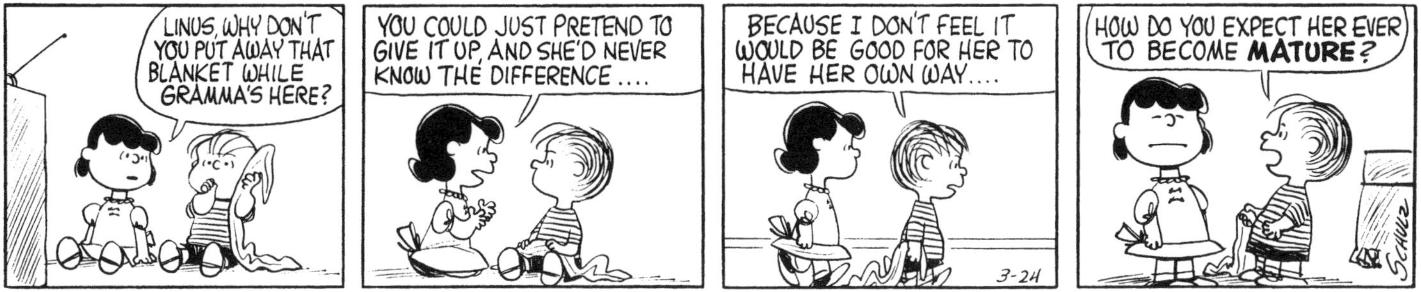
LINUS, WHY DON'T YOU PUT AWAY THAT BLANKET WHILE GRAMMA'S HERE?
YOU COULD JUST PRETEND TO GIVE IT UP, AND SHE'D NEVER KNOW THE DIFFERENCE....
BECAUSE I DON'T FEEL IT WOULD BE GOOD FOR HER TO HAVE HER OWN WAY....
3-24
HOW DO YOU EXPECT HER EVER TO BECOME **MATURE**?
SCHULZ

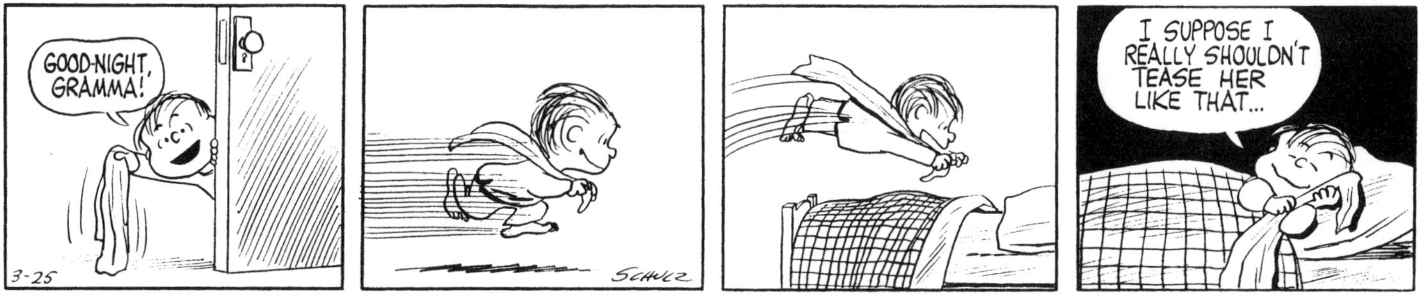
GOOD-NIGHT, GRAMMA!
3-25
SCHULZ
I SUPPOSE I REALLY SHOULDN'T TEASE HER LIKE THAT...

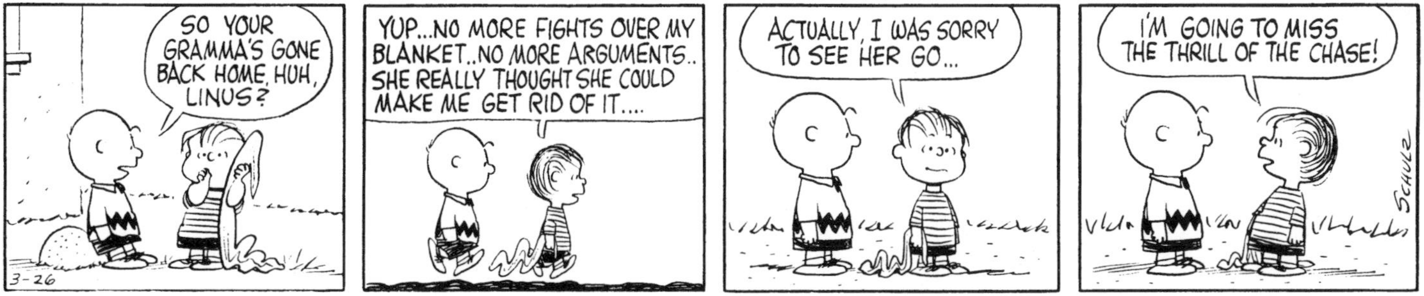
SO YOUR GRAMMA'S GONE BACK HOME, HUH, LINUS?
3-26
YUP...NO MORE FIGHTS OVER MY BLANKET..NO MORE ARGUMENTS.. SHE REALLY THOUGHT SHE COULD MAKE ME GET RID OF IT....
ACTUALLY, I WAS SORRY TO SEE HER GO...
I'M GOING TO MISS THE THRILL OF THE CHASE!
SCHULZ

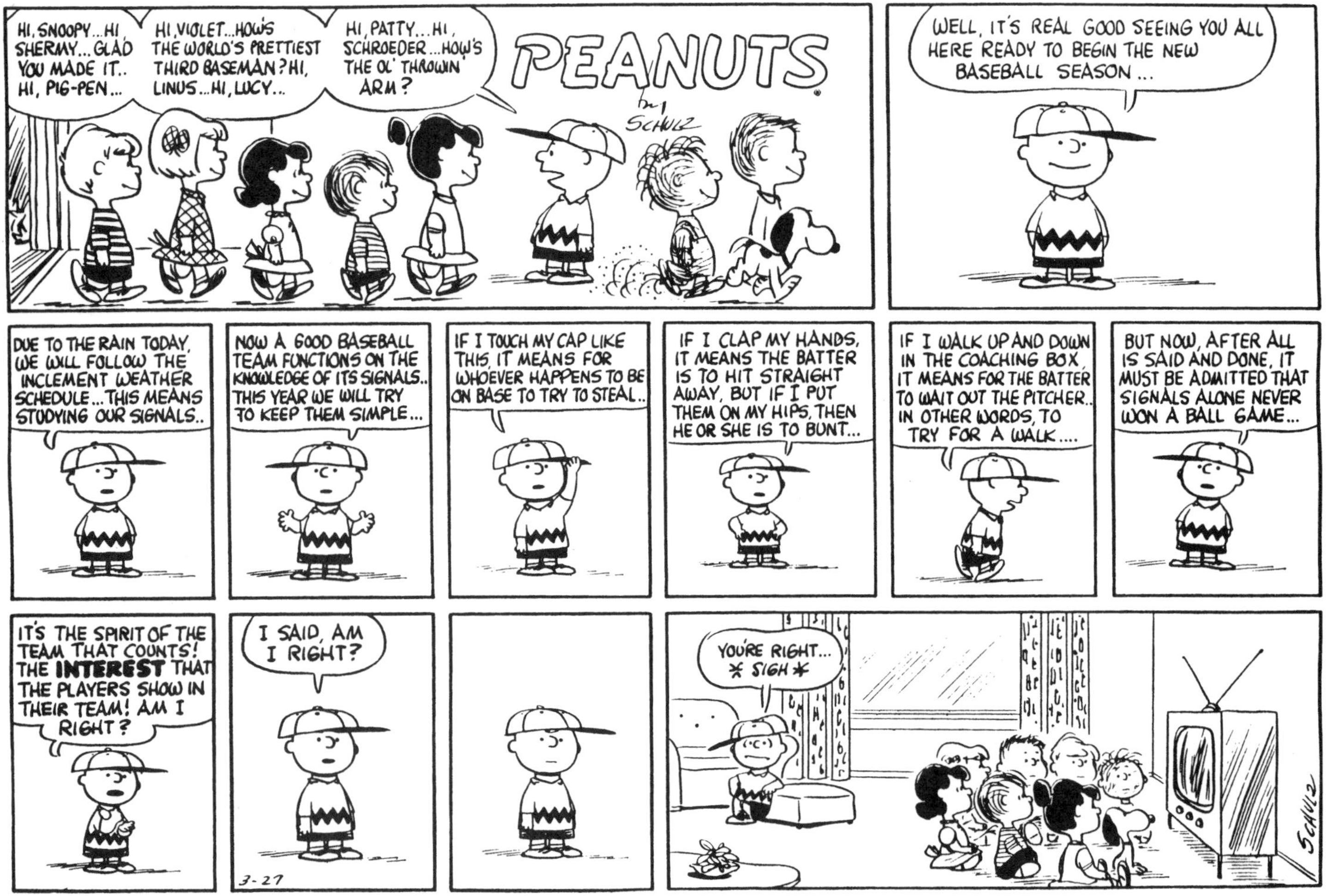
HI, SNOOPY...HI, SHERMY... GLAD YOU MADE IT.. HI, PIG-PEN...
HI, VIOLET...HOW'S THE WORLD'S PRETTIEST THIRD BASEMAN? HI, LINUS...HI, LUCY...
HI, PATTY... HI, SCHROEDER...HOW'S THE OL' THROWIN' ARM?
PEANUTS
by SCHULZ
WELL, IT'S REAL GOOD SEEING YOU ALL HERE READY TO BEGIN THE NEW BASEBALL SEASON...
DUE TO THE RAIN TODAY, WE WILL FOLLOW THE INCLEMENT WEATHER SCHEDULE...THIS MEANS STUDYING OUR SIGNALS..
NOW A GOOD BASEBALL TEAM FUNCTIONS ON THE KNOWLEDGE OF ITS SIGNALS.. THIS YEAR WE WILL TRY TO KEEP THEM SIMPLE...
IF I TOUCH MY CAP LIKE THIS, IT MEANS FOR WHOEVER HAPPENS TO BE ON BASE TO TRY TO STEAL..
IF I CLAP MY HANDS, IT MEANS THE BATTER IS TO HIT STRAIGHT AWAY, BUT IF I PUT THEM ON MY HIPS, THEN HE OR SHE IS TO BUNT...
IF I WALK UP AND DOWN IN THE COACHING BOX, IT MEANS FOR THE BATTER TO WAIT OUT THE PITCHER.. IN OTHER WORDS, TO TRY FOR A WALK....
BUT NOW, AFTER ALL IS SAID AND DONE, IT MUST BE ADMITTED THAT SIGNALS ALONE NEVER WON A BALL GAME...
IT'S THE SPIRIT OF THE TEAM THAT COUNTS! THE INTEREST THAT THE PLAYERS SHOW IN THEIR TEAM! AM I RIGHT?
I SAID, AM I RIGHT?
3-27
YOU'RE RIGHT... * SIGH *
SCHULZ

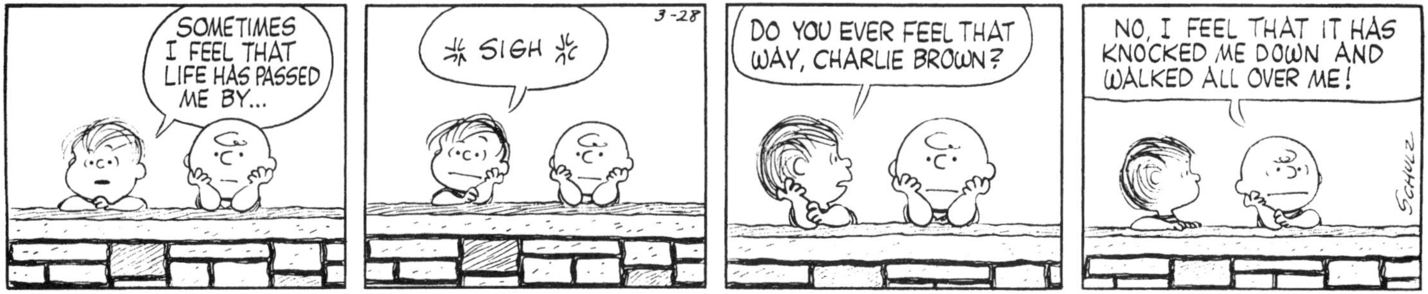
SOMETIMES I FEEL THAT LIFE HAS PASSED ME BY...
3-28
SIGH
DO YOU EVER FEEL THAT WAY, CHARLIE BROWN?
NO, I FEEL THAT IT HAS KNOCKED ME DOWN AND WALKED ALL OVER ME!
SCHULZ

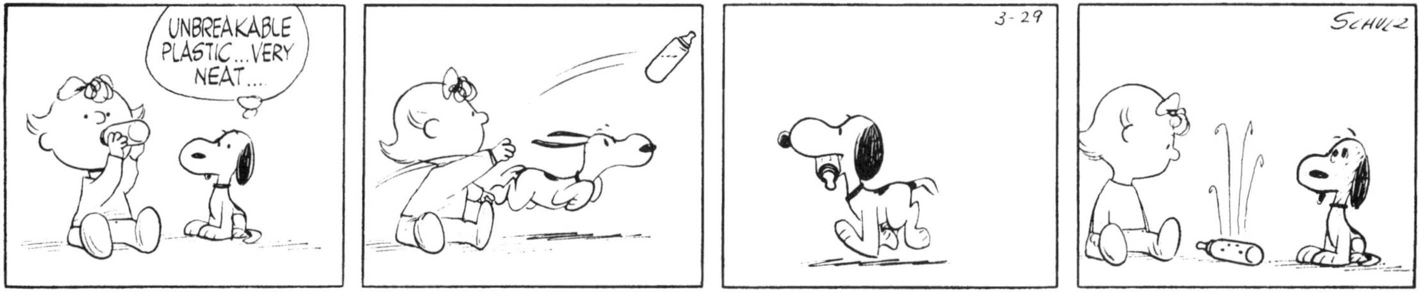
UNBREAKABLE PLASTIC...VERY NEAT....
3-29
SCHULZ

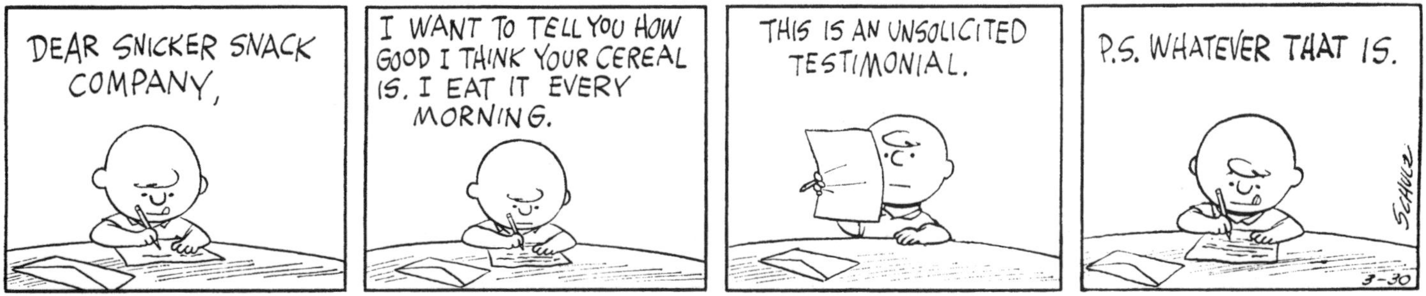
DEAR SNICKER SNACK COMPANY,
I WANT TO TELL YOU HOW GOOD I THINK YOUR CEREAL IS. I EAT IT EVERY MORNING.
THIS IS AN UNSOLICITED TESTIMONIAL.
P.S. WHATEVER THAT IS.
SCHULZ
3-30

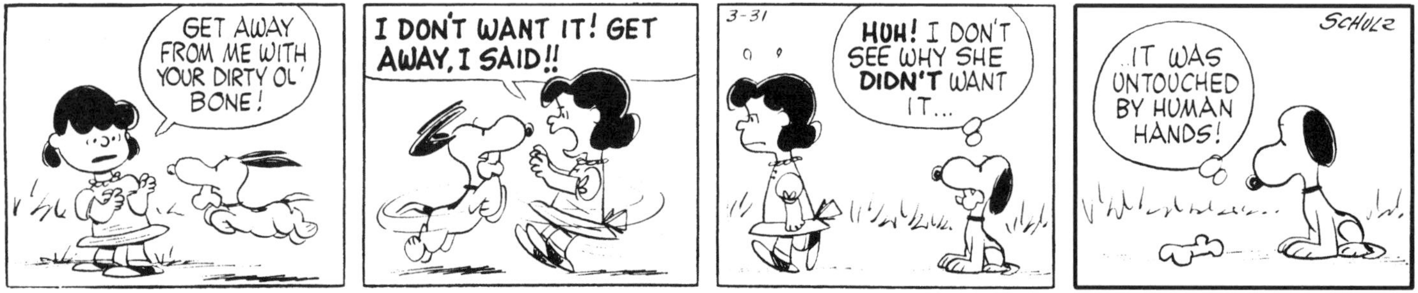
GET AWAY FROM ME WITH YOUR DIRTY OL' BONE!
I DON'T WANT IT! GET AWAY, I SAID!!
3-31
HUH! I DON'T SEE WHY SHE DIDN'T WANT IT...
SCHULZ
..IT WAS UNTOUCHED BY HUMAN HANDS!

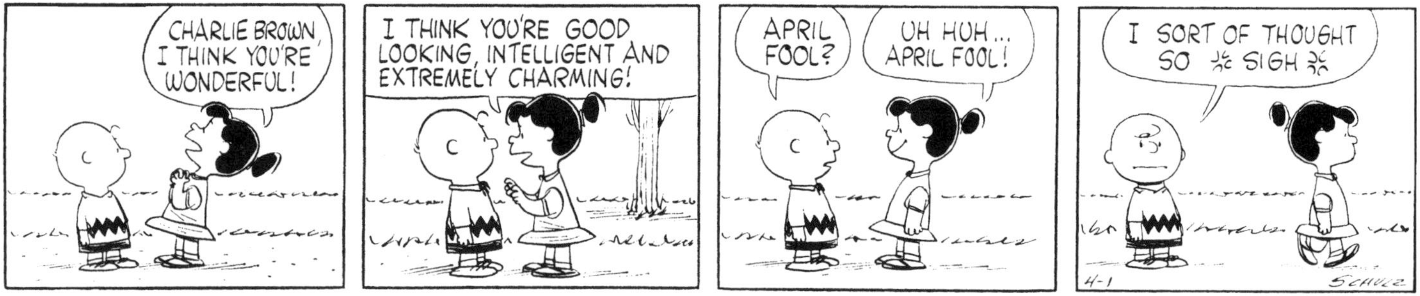
CHARLIE BROWN, I THINK YOU'RE WONDERFUL!
I THINK YOU'RE GOOD LOOKING, INTELLIGENT AND EXTREMELY CHARMING!
APRIL FOOL?
UH HUH... APRIL FOOL!
I SORT OF THOUGHT SO ※ SIGH ※
4-1
SCHULZ

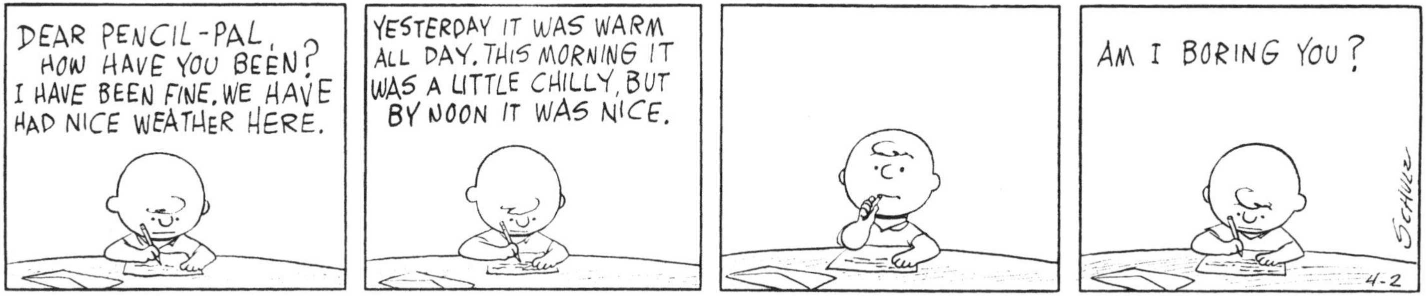
DEAR PENCIL-PAL, HOW HAVE YOU BEEN? I HAVE BEEN FINE. WE HAVE HAD NICE WEATHER HERE.
YESTERDAY IT WAS WARM ALL DAY. THIS MORNING IT WAS A LITTLE CHILLY, BUT BY NOON IT WAS NICE.
AM I BORING YOU?
SCHULZ
4-2

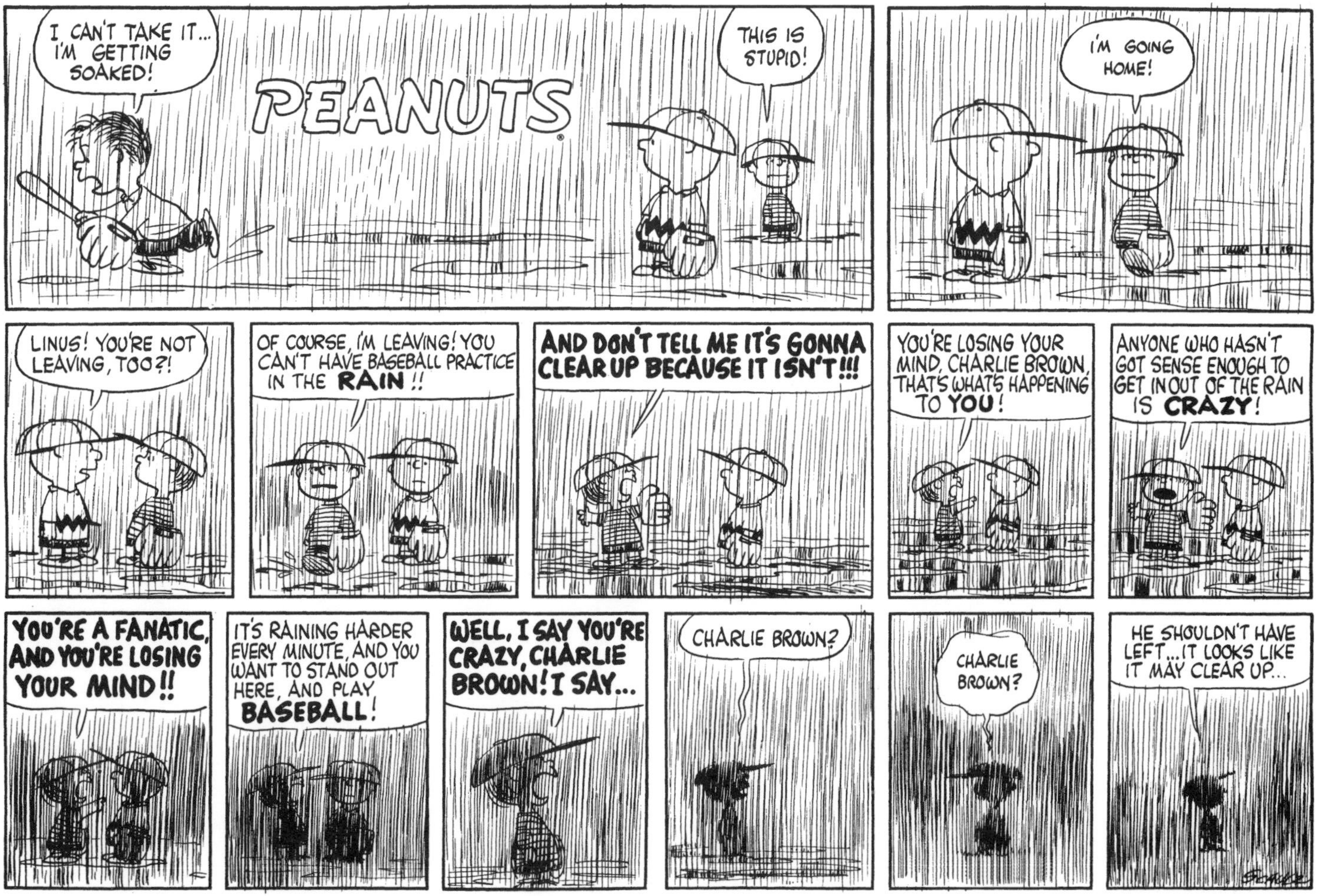
I CAN'T TAKE IT... I'M GETTING SOAKED!
PEANUTS
THIS IS STUPID!
I'M GOING HOME!
LINUS! YOU'RE NOT LEAVING, TOO?!
OF COURSE, I'M LEAVING! YOU CAN'T HAVE BASEBALL PRACTICE IN THE RAIN!!
AND DON'T TELL ME IT'S GONNA CLEAR UP BECAUSE IT ISN'T!!!
YOU'RE LOSING YOUR MIND, CHARLIE BROWN, THAT'S WHAT'S HAPPENING TO YOU!
ANYONE WHO HASN'T GOT SENSE ENOUGH TO GET IN OUT OF THE RAIN IS CRAZY!
YOU'RE A FANATIC, AND YOU'RE LOSING YOUR MIND!!
IT'S RAINING HARDER EVERY MINUTE, AND YOU WANT TO STAND OUT HERE, AND PLAY BASEBALL!
WELL, I SAY YOU'RE CRAZY, CHARLIE BROWN! I SAY...
CHARLIE BROWN?
CHARLIE BROWN?
HE SHOULDN'T HAVE LEFT...IT LOOKS LIKE IT MAY CLEAR UP...

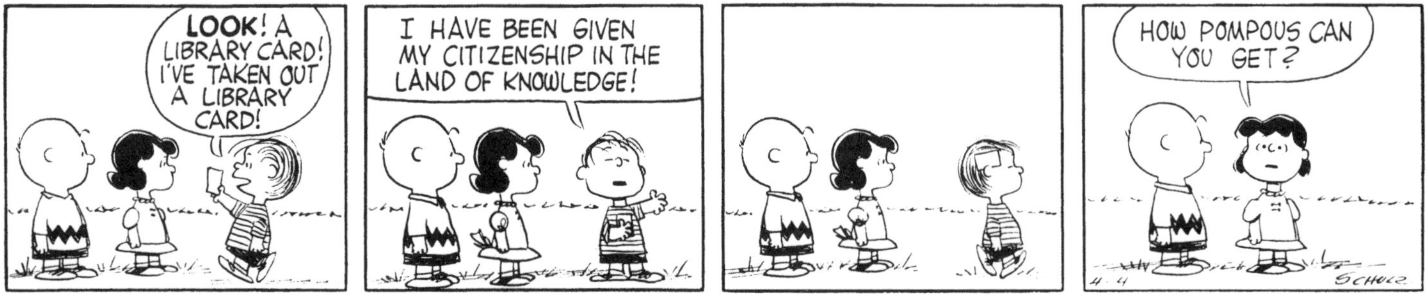
LOOK! A LIBRARY CARD! I'VE TAKEN OUT A LIBRARY CARD!
I HAVE BEEN GIVEN MY CITIZENSHIP IN THE LAND OF KNOWLEDGE!
HOW POMPOUS CAN YOU GET?
4-4
SCHULZ

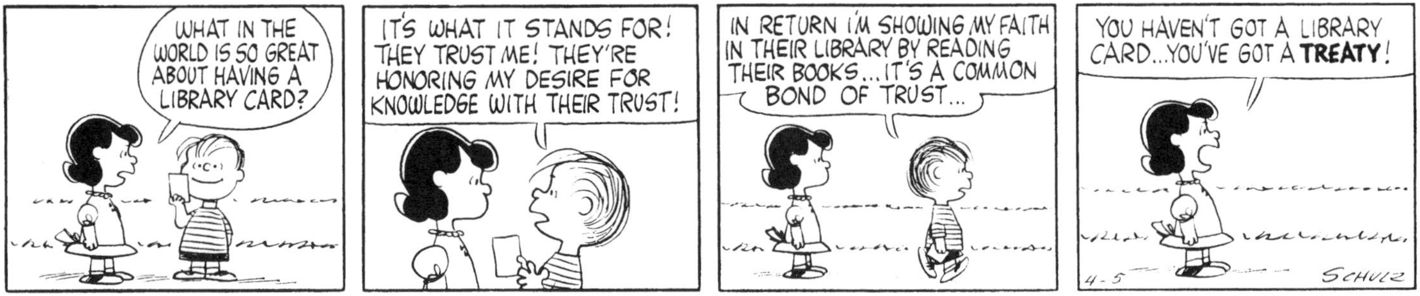
WHAT IN THE WORLD IS SO GREAT ABOUT HAVING A LIBRARY CARD?
IT'S WHAT IT STANDS FOR! THEY TRUST ME! THEY'RE HONORING MY DESIRE FOR KNOWLEDGE WITH THEIR TRUST!
IN RETURN I'M SHOWING MY FAITH IN THEIR LIBRARY BY READING THEIR BOOKS...IT'S A COMMON BOND OF TRUST...
YOU HAVEN'T GOT A LIBRARY CARD...YOU'VE GOT A **TREATY**!
4-5
SCHULZ

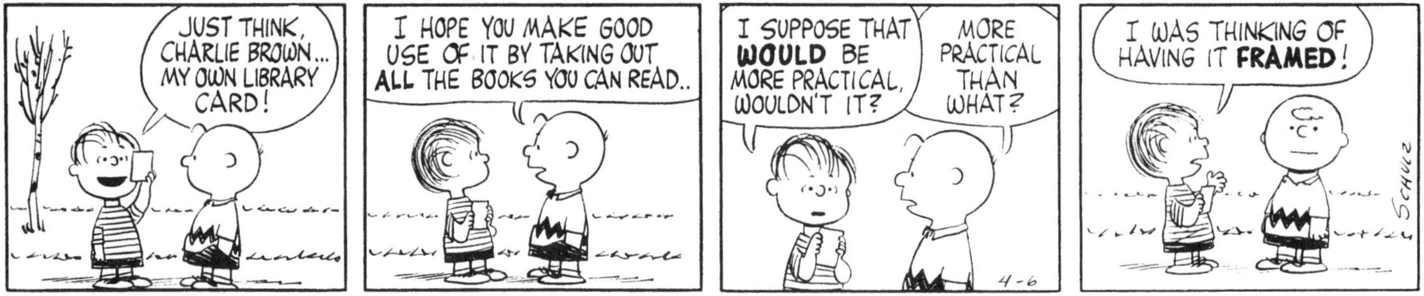
JUST THINK, CHARLIE BROWN... MY OWN LIBRARY CARD!
I HOPE YOU MAKE GOOD USE OF IT BY TAKING OUT **ALL** THE BOOKS YOU CAN READ..
I SUPPOSE THAT **WOULD** BE MORE PRACTICAL, WOULDN'T IT?
MORE PRACTICAL THAN WHAT?
4-6
I WAS THINKING OF HAVING IT **FRAMED**!
SCHULZ

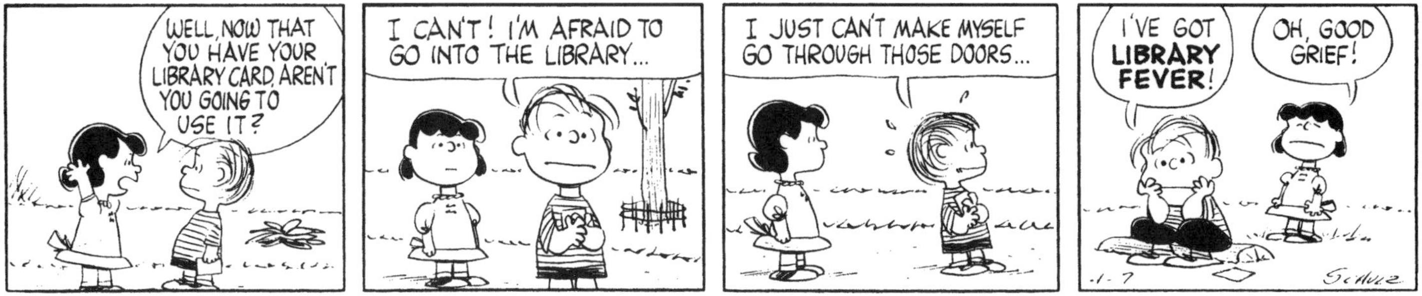
WELL, NOW THAT YOU HAVE YOUR LIBRARY CARD, AREN'T YOU GOING TO USE IT?
I CAN'T! I'M AFRAID TO GO INTO THE LIBRARY...
I JUST CAN'T MAKE MYSELF GO THROUGH THOSE DOORS...
I'VE GOT **LIBRARY FEVER**!
OH, GOOD GRIEF!
4-7
SCHULZ

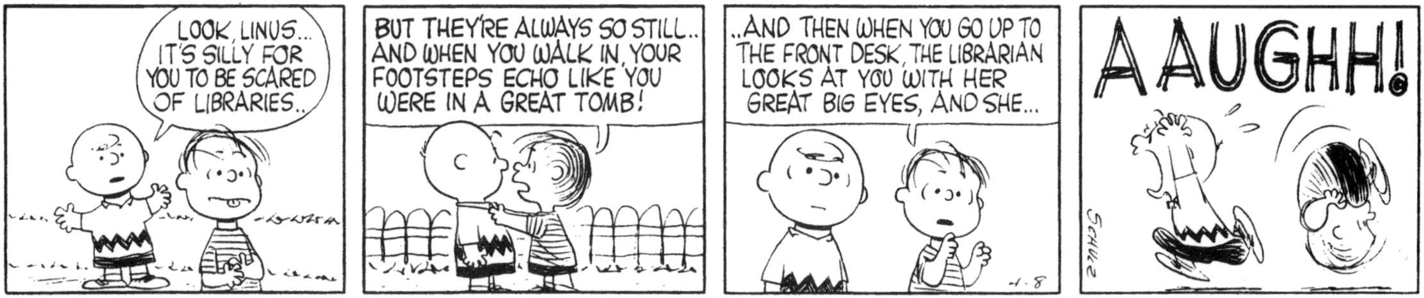
LOOK, LINUS... IT'S SILLY FOR YOU TO BE SCARED OF LIBRARIES..
BUT THEY'RE ALWAYS SO STILL.. AND WHEN YOU WALK IN, YOUR FOOTSTEPS ECHO LIKE YOU WERE IN A GREAT TOMB!
..AND THEN WHEN YOU GO UP TO THE FRONT DESK, THE LIBRARIAN LOOKS AT YOU WITH HER GREAT BIG EYES, AND SHE...
4-8
AAUGHH!
SCHULZ

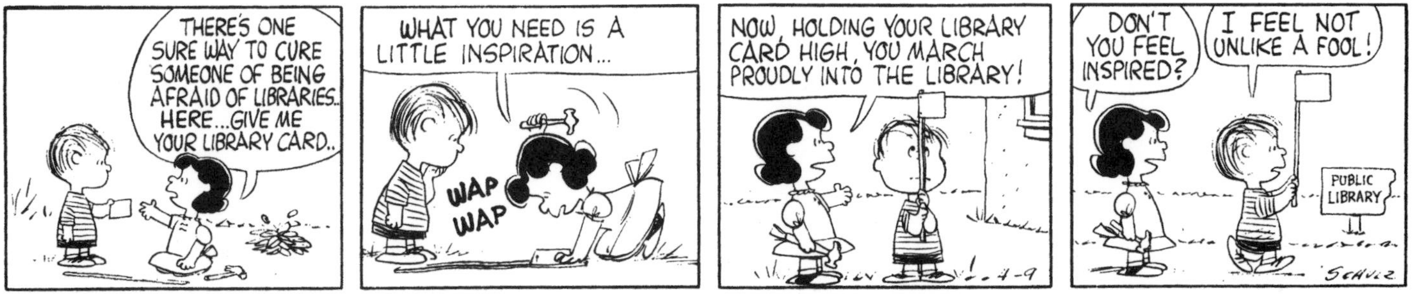
THERE'S ONE SURE WAY TO CURE SOMEONE OF BEING AFRAID OF LIBRARIES.. HERE...GIVE ME YOUR LIBRARY CARD..
WHAT YOU NEED IS A LITTLE INSPIRATION...
WAP WAP
NOW, HOLDING YOUR LIBRARY CARD HIGH, YOU MARCH PROUDLY INTO THE LIBRARY!
4-9
DON'T YOU FEEL INSPIRED?
I FEEL NOT UNLIKE A FOOL!
PUBLIC LIBRARY
SCHULZ

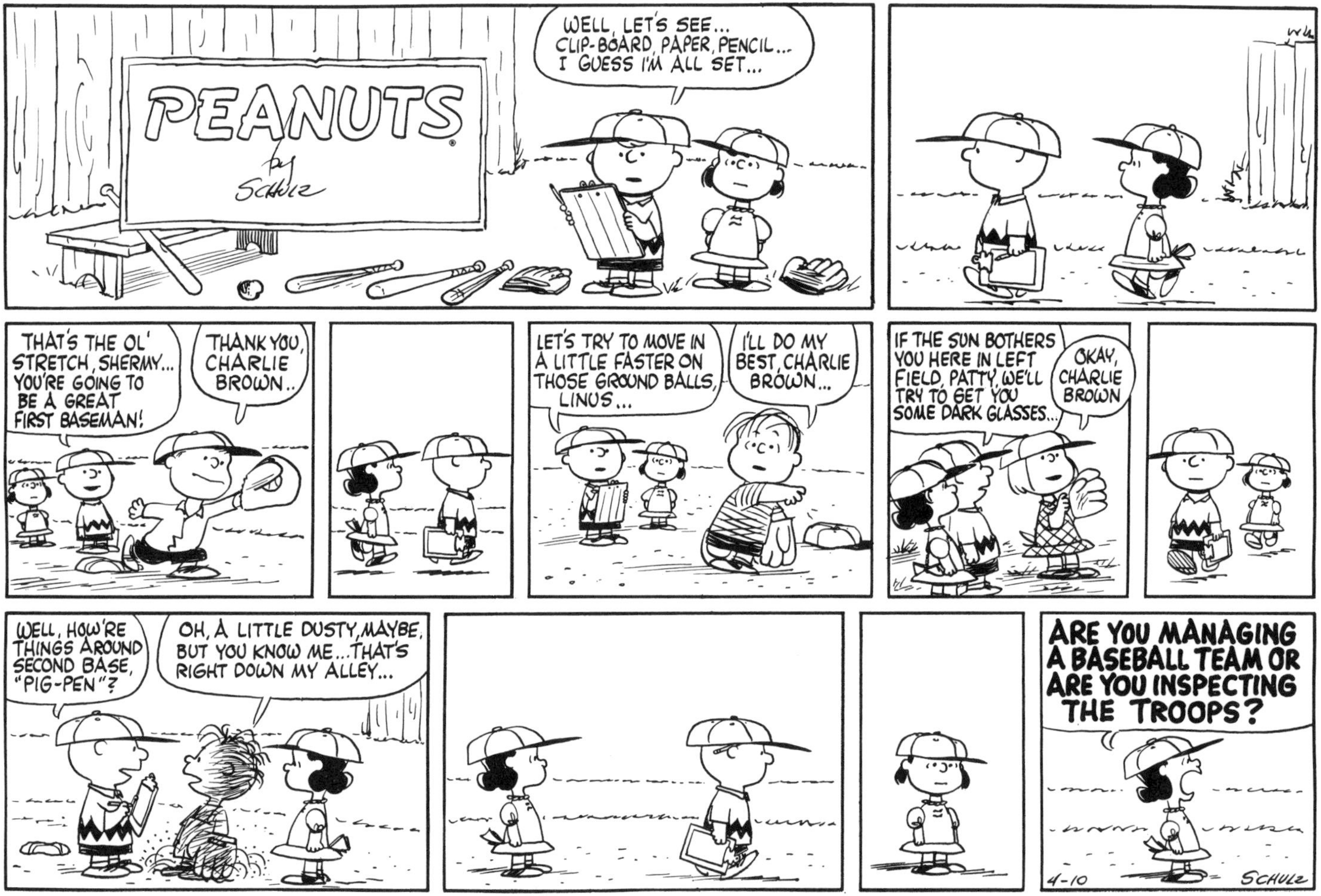
PEANUTS
by Schulz
WELL, LET'S SEE... CLIP-BOARD, PAPER, PENCIL... I GUESS I'M ALL SET...
THAT'S THE OL' STRETCH, SHERMY... YOU'RE GOING TO BE A GREAT FIRST BASEMAN!
THANK YOU, CHARLIE BROWN..
LET'S TRY TO MOVE IN A LITTLE FASTER ON THOSE GROUND BALLS, LINUS...
I'LL DO MY BEST, CHARLIE BROWN...
IF THE SUN BOTHERS YOU HERE IN LEFT FIELD, PATTY, WE'LL TRY TO GET YOU SOME DARK GLASSES...
OKAY, CHARLIE BROWN
WELL, HOW'RE THINGS AROUND SECOND BASE, "PIG-PEN"?
OH, A LITTLE DUSTY, MAYBE, BUT YOU KNOW ME...THAT'S RIGHT DOWN MY ALLEY...
ARE YOU MANAGING A BASEBALL TEAM OR ARE YOU INSPECTING THE TROOPS?
4-10
SCHULZ

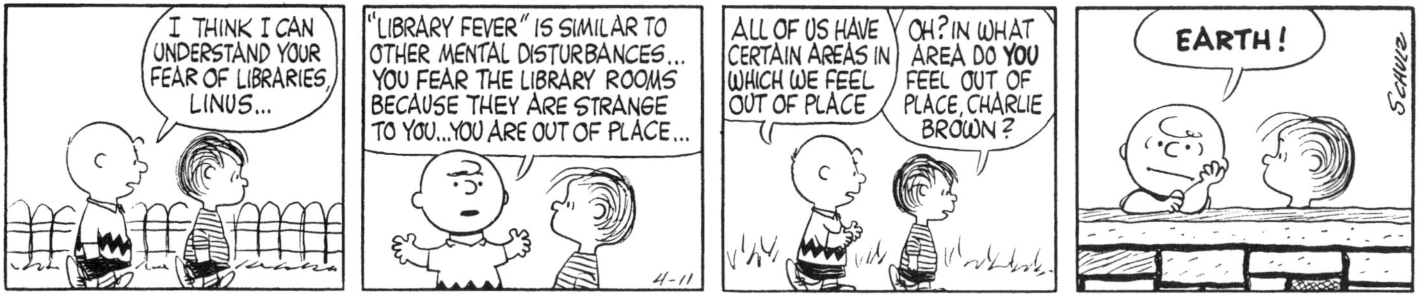
I THINK I CAN UNDERSTAND YOUR FEAR OF LIBRARIES, LINUS...
"LIBRARY FEVER" IS SIMILAR TO OTHER MENTAL DISTURBANCES... YOU FEAR THE LIBRARY ROOMS BECAUSE THEY ARE STRANGE TO YOU...YOU ARE OUT OF PLACE...
ALL OF US HAVE CERTAIN AREAS IN WHICH WE FEEL OUT OF PLACE
OH? IN WHAT AREA DO **YOU** FEEL OUT OF PLACE, CHARLIE BROWN?
EARTH!

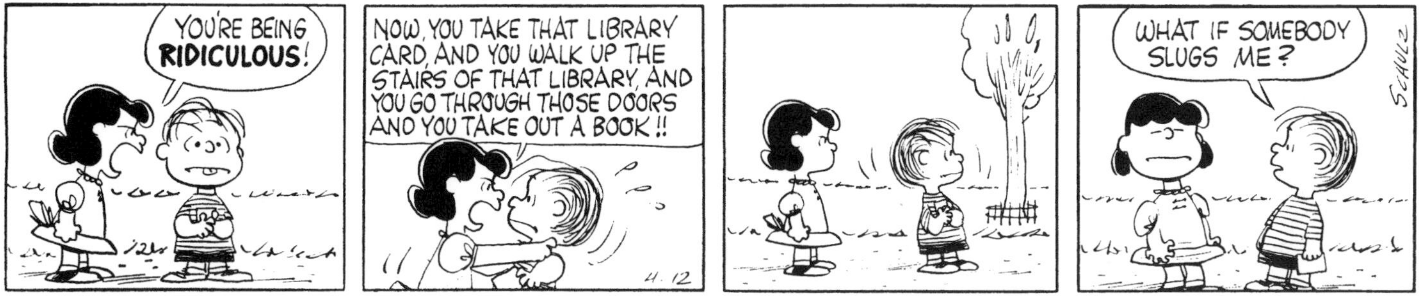
YOU'RE BEING **RIDICULOUS**!
NOW, YOU TAKE THAT LIBRARY CARD, AND YOU WALK UP THE STAIRS OF THAT LIBRARY, AND YOU GO THROUGH THOSE DOORS AND YOU TAKE OUT A BOOK!!
WHAT IF SOMEBODY SLUGS ME?

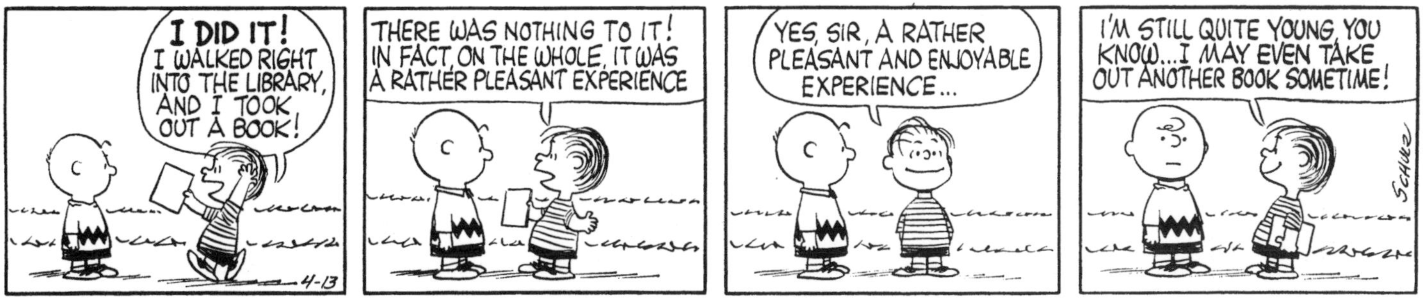
I DID IT! I WALKED RIGHT INTO THE LIBRARY, AND I TOOK OUT A BOOK!
THERE WAS NOTHING TO IT! IN FACT, ON THE WHOLE, IT WAS A RATHER PLEASANT EXPERIENCE
YES, SIR, A RATHER PLEASANT AND ENJOYABLE EXPERIENCE...
I'M STILL QUITE YOUNG, YOU KNOW...I MAY EVEN TAKE OUT ANOTHER BOOK SOMETIME!

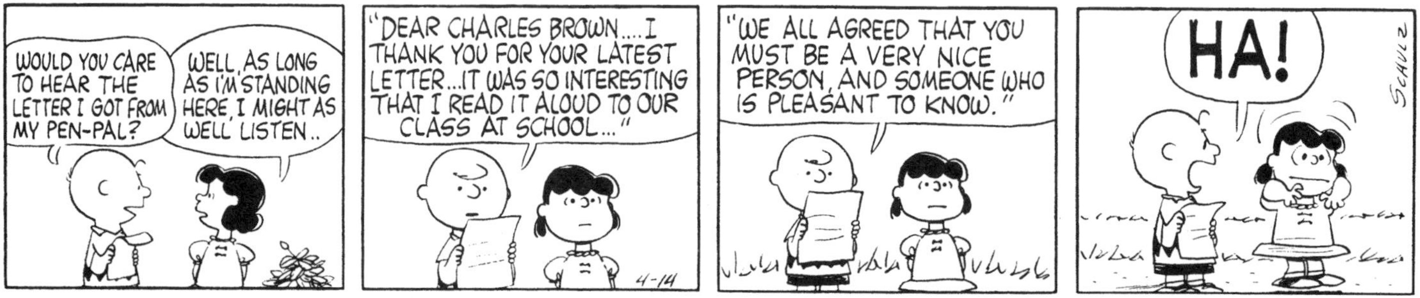
WOULD YOU CARE TO HEAR THE LETTER I GOT FROM MY PEN-PAL?
WELL, AS LONG AS I'M STANDING HERE, I MIGHT AS WELL LISTEN..
"DEAR CHARLES BROWN....I THANK YOU FOR YOUR LATEST LETTER...IT WAS SO INTERESTING THAT I READ IT ALOUD TO OUR CLASS AT SCHOOL..."
4-14
"WE ALL AGREED THAT YOU MUST BE A VERY NICE PERSON, AND SOMEONE WHO IS PLEASANT TO KNOW."
HA!
SCHULZ

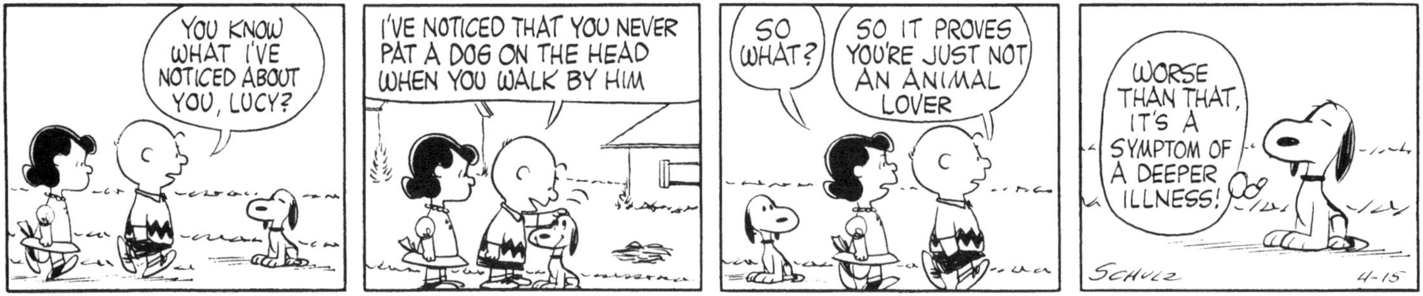
YOU KNOW WHAT I'VE NOTICED ABOUT YOU, LUCY?
I'VE NOTICED THAT YOU NEVER PAT A DOG ON THE HEAD WHEN YOU WALK BY HIM
SO WHAT?
SO IT PROVES YOU'RE JUST NOT AN ANIMAL LOVER
WORSE THAN THAT, IT'S A SYMPTOM OF A DEEPER ILLNESS!
SCHULZ
4-15

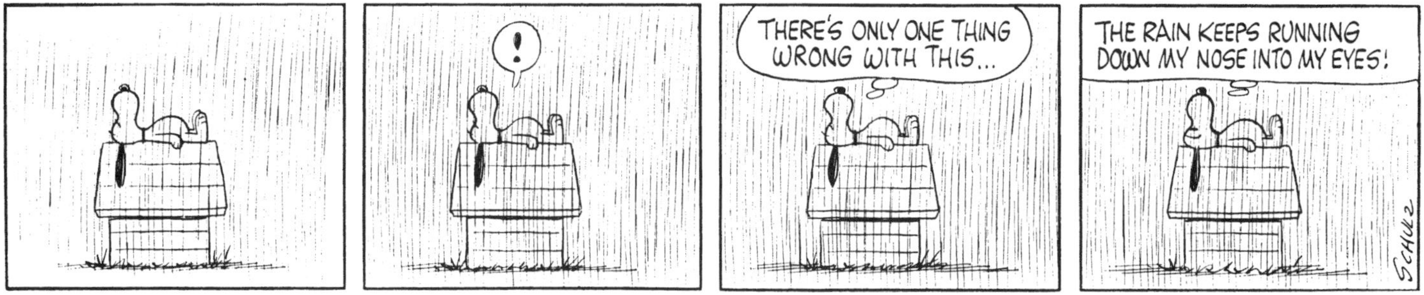
!
THERE'S ONLY ONE THING WRONG WITH THIS...
THE RAIN KEEPS RUNNING DOWN MY NOSE INTO MY EYES!
SCHULZ

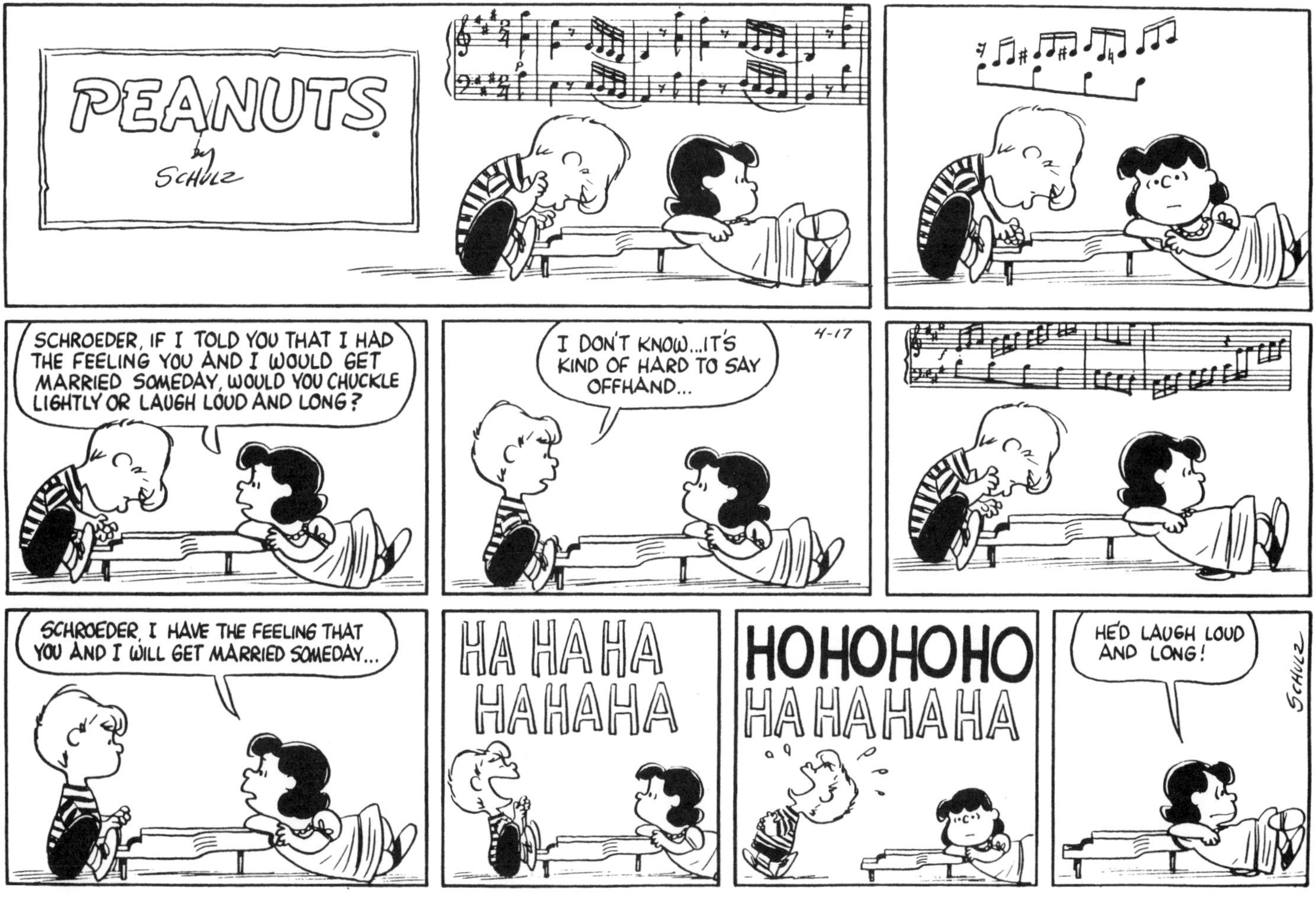
PEANUTS
by SCHULZ
SCHROEDER, IF I TOLD YOU THAT I HAD THE FEELING YOU AND I WOULD GET MARRIED SOMEDAY, WOULD YOU CHUCKLE LIGHTLY OR LAUGH LOUD AND LONG?
I DON'T KNOW...IT'S KIND OF HARD TO SAY OFFHAND...
4-17
SCHROEDER, I HAVE THE FEELING THAT YOU AND I WILL GET MARRIED SOMEDAY...
HA HAHA HAHAHA
HOHOHOHO HAHAHAHA
HE'D LAUGH LOUD AND LONG!
SCHULZ

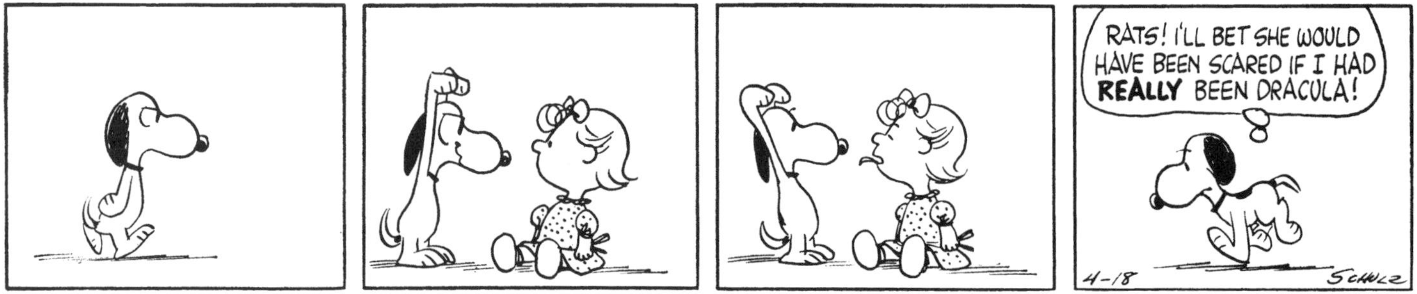
RATS! I'LL BET SHE WOULD HAVE BEEN SCARED IF I HAD **REALLY** BEEN DRACULA!
4-18
SCHULZ

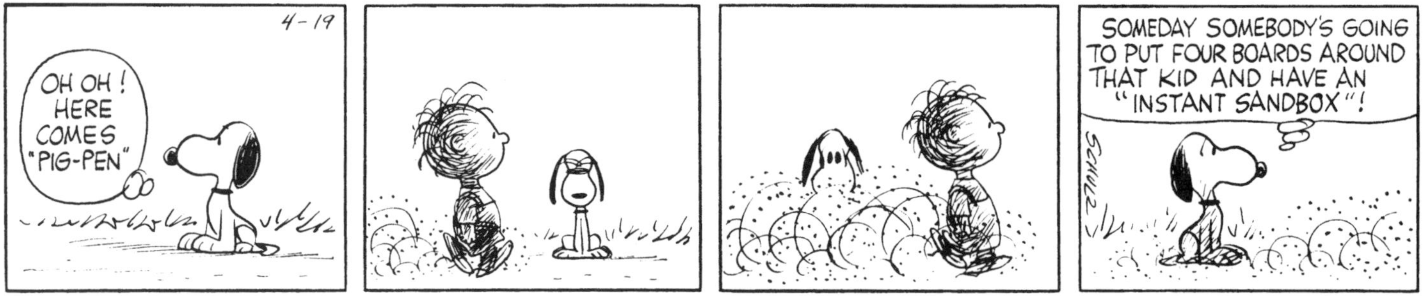
4-19
OH OH! HERE COMES "PIG-PEN"
SCHULZ
SOMEDAY SOMEBODY'S GOING TO PUT FOUR BOARDS AROUND THAT KID AND HAVE AN "INSTANT SANDBOX"!

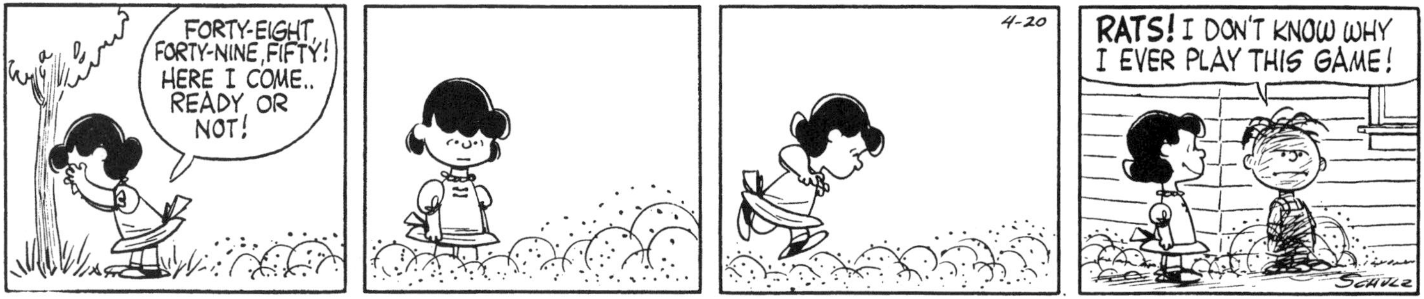
FORTY-EIGHT, FORTY-NINE, FIFTY! HERE I COME.. READY OR NOT!
4-20
RATS! I DON'T KNOW WHY I EVER PLAY THIS GAME!
SCHULZ

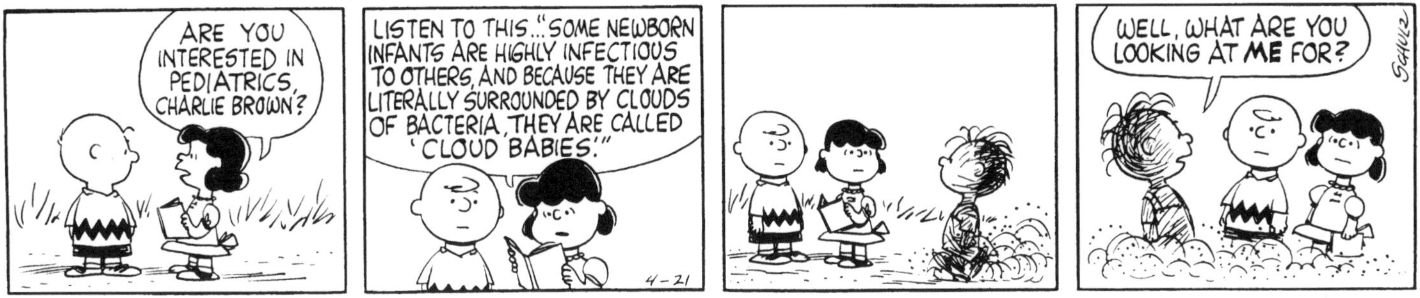
ARE YOU INTERESTED IN PEDIATRICS, CHARLIE BROWN?
LISTEN TO THIS..."SOME NEWBORN INFANTS ARE HIGHLY INFECTIOUS TO OTHERS, AND BECAUSE THEY ARE LITERALLY SURROUNDED BY CLOUDS OF BACTERIA, THEY ARE CALLED 'CLOUD BABIES.'"
4-21
WELL, WHAT ARE YOU LOOKING AT **ME** FOR?
SCHULZ

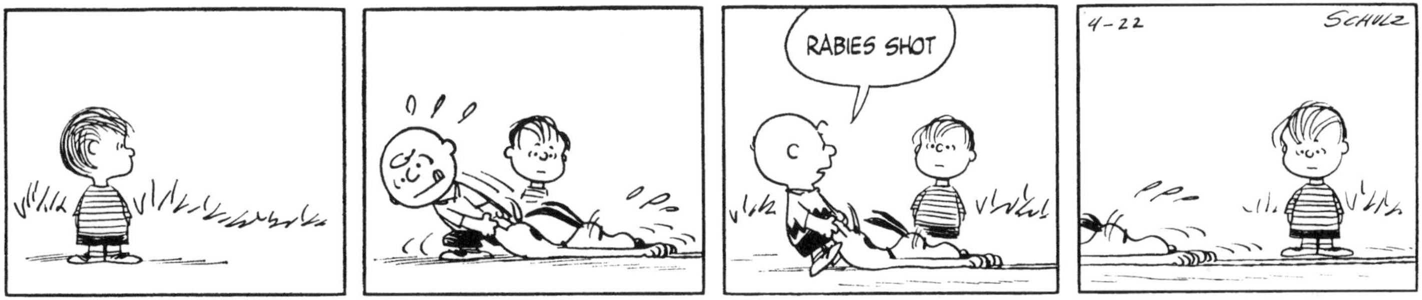
RABIES SHOT
4-22
SCHULZ

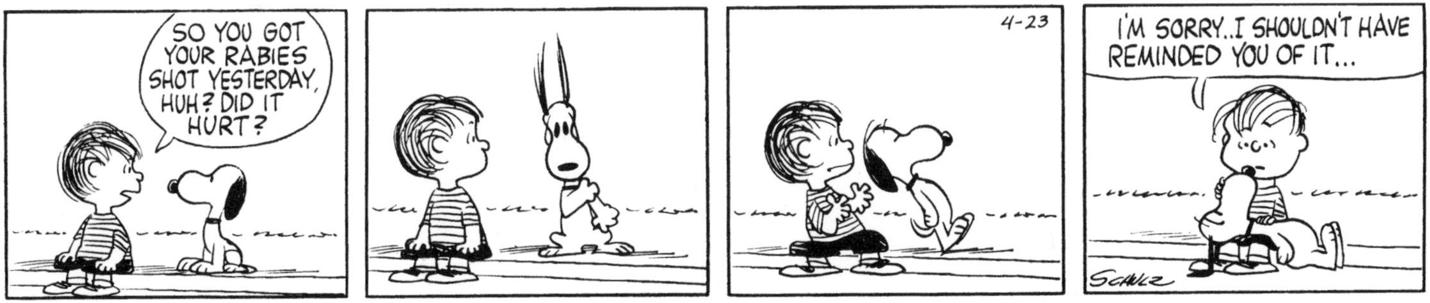
SO YOU GOT YOUR RABIES SHOT YESTERDAY, HUH? DID IT HURT?
4-23
I'M SORRY..I SHOULDN'T HAVE REMINDED YOU OF IT...
SCHULZ

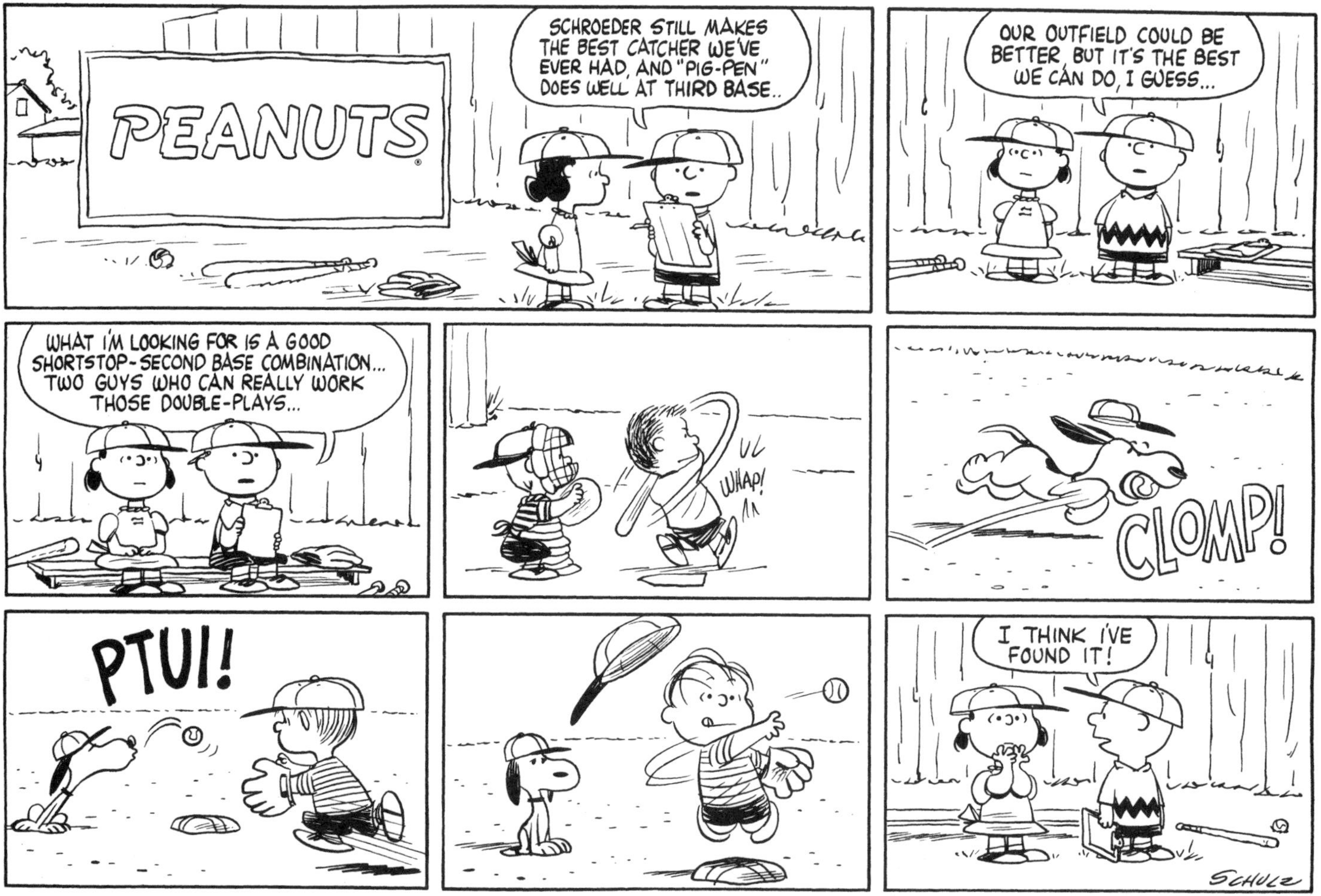
PEANUTS
SCHROEDER STILL MAKES THE BEST CATCHER WE'VE EVER HAD, AND "PIG-PEN" DOES WELL AT THIRD BASE..
OUR OUTFIELD COULD BE BETTER, BUT IT'S THE BEST WE CAN DO, I GUESS...
WHAT I'M LOOKING FOR IS A GOOD SHORTSTOP-SECOND BASE COMBINATION... TWO GUYS WHO CAN REALLY WORK THOSE DOUBLE-PLAYS...
WHAP!
CLOMP!
PTUI!
I THINK I'VE FOUND IT!
SCHULZ

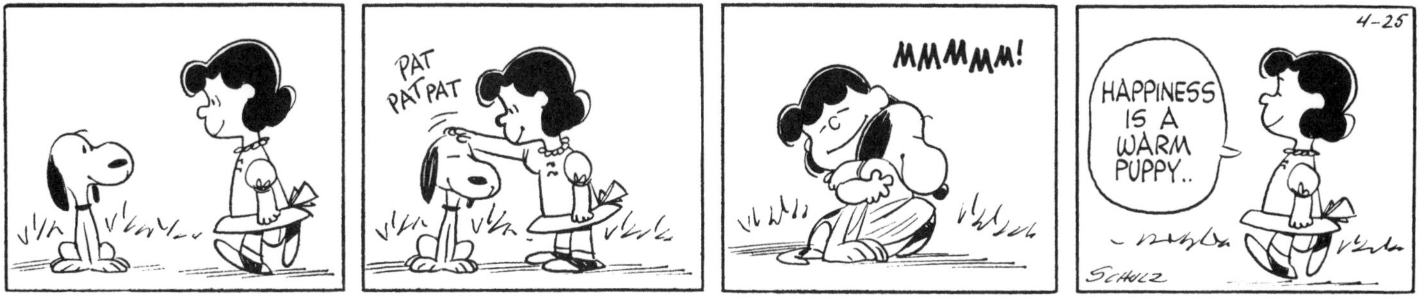
PAT
PAT PAT
MMMMM!
4-25
HAPPINESS IS A WARM PUPPY..
SCHULZ

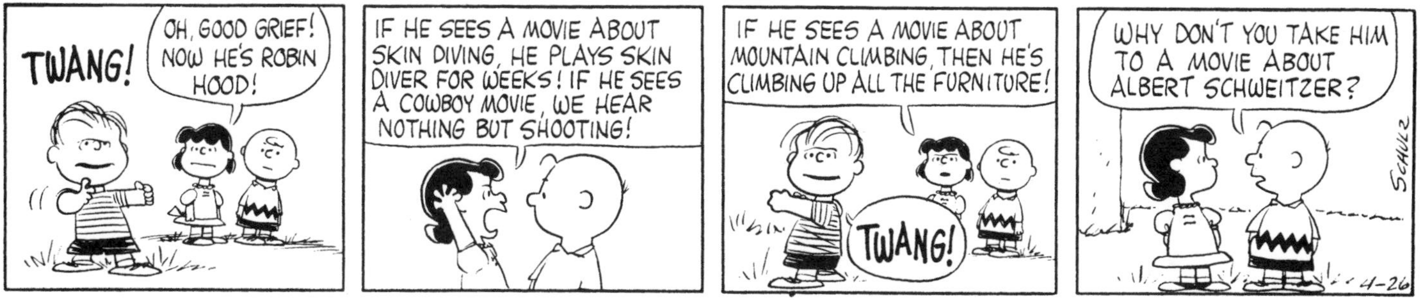
TWANG!
OH, GOOD GRIEF! NOW HE'S ROBIN HOOD!
IF HE SEES A MOVIE ABOUT SKIN DIVING, HE PLAYS SKIN DIVER FOR WEEKS! IF HE SEES A COWBOY MOVIE, WE HEAR NOTHING BUT SHOOTING!
IF HE SEES A MOVIE ABOUT MOUNTAIN CLIMBING, THEN HE'S CLIMBING UP ALL THE FURNITURE!
TWANG!
WHY DON'T YOU TAKE HIM TO A MOVIE ABOUT ALBERT SCHWEITZER?
SCHULZ
4-26

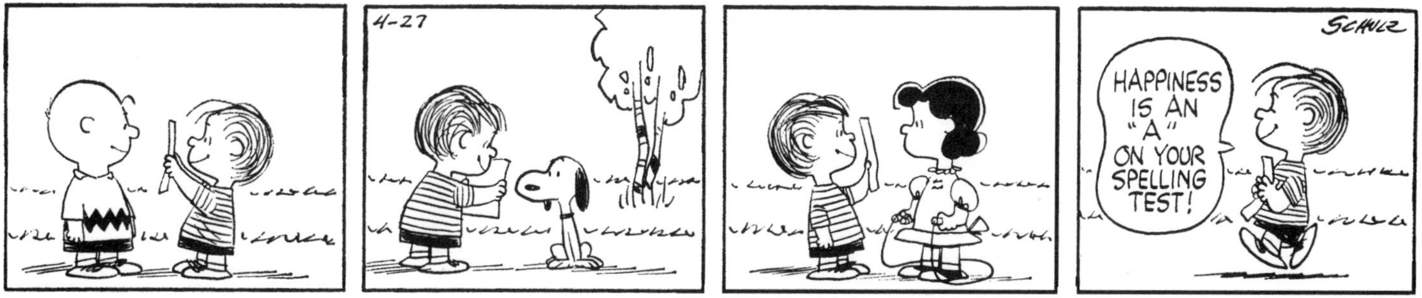
4-27
SCHULZ
HAPPINESS IS AN "A" ON YOUR SPELLING TEST!

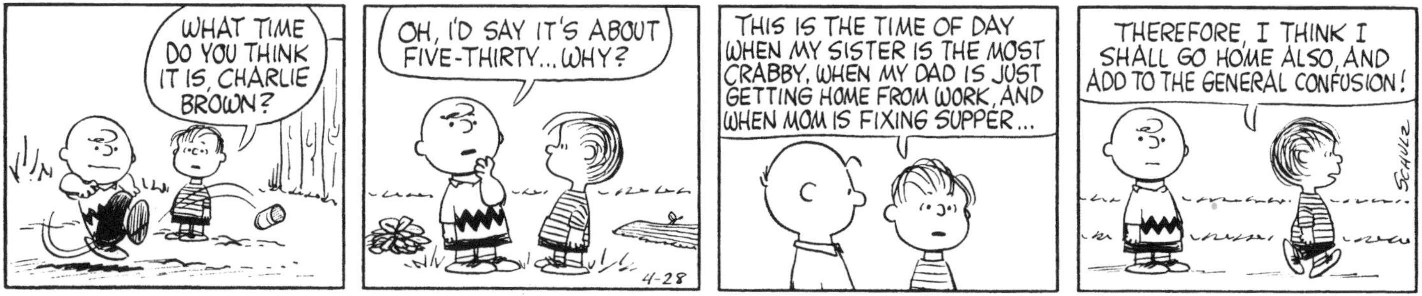
WHAT TIME DO YOU THINK IT IS, CHARLIE BROWN?
OH, I'D SAY IT'S ABOUT FIVE-THIRTY... WHY?
4-28
THIS IS THE TIME OF DAY WHEN MY SISTER IS THE MOST CRABBY, WHEN MY DAD IS JUST GETTING HOME FROM WORK, AND WHEN MOM IS FIXING SUPPER...
THEREFORE, I THINK I SHALL GO HOME ALSO, AND ADD TO THE GENERAL CONFUSION!
SCHULZ

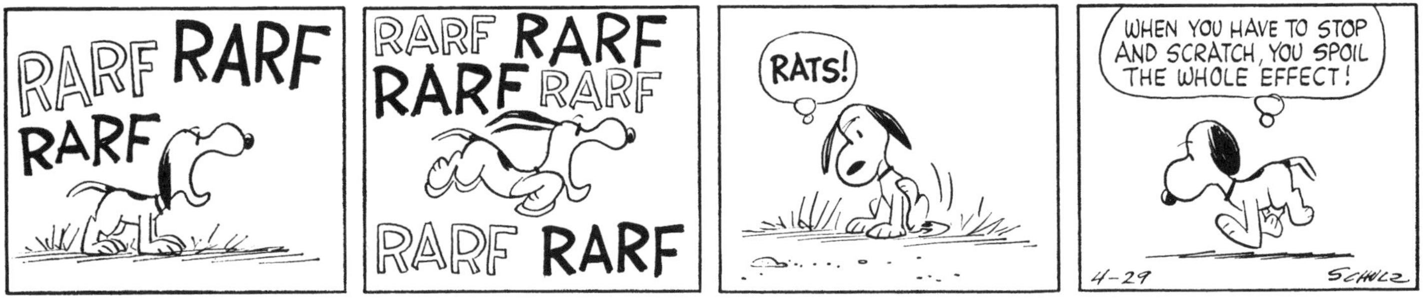
RARF RARF
RARF
RARF RARF
RARF RARF
RARF RARF
RATS!
WHEN YOU HAVE TO STOP AND SCRATCH, YOU SPOIL THE WHOLE EFFECT!
4-29
SCHULZ

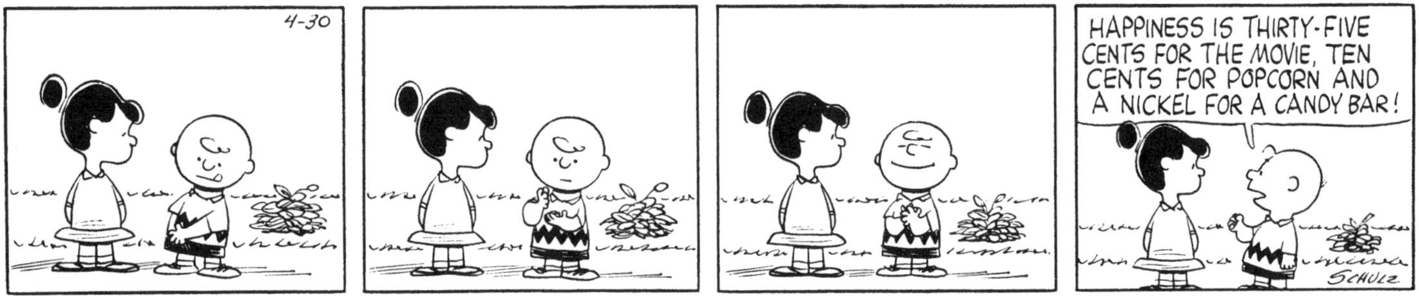
4-30
HAPPINESS IS THIRTY-FIVE CENTS FOR THE MOVIE, TEN CENTS FOR POPCORN AND A NICKEL FOR A CANDY BAR!
SCHULZ

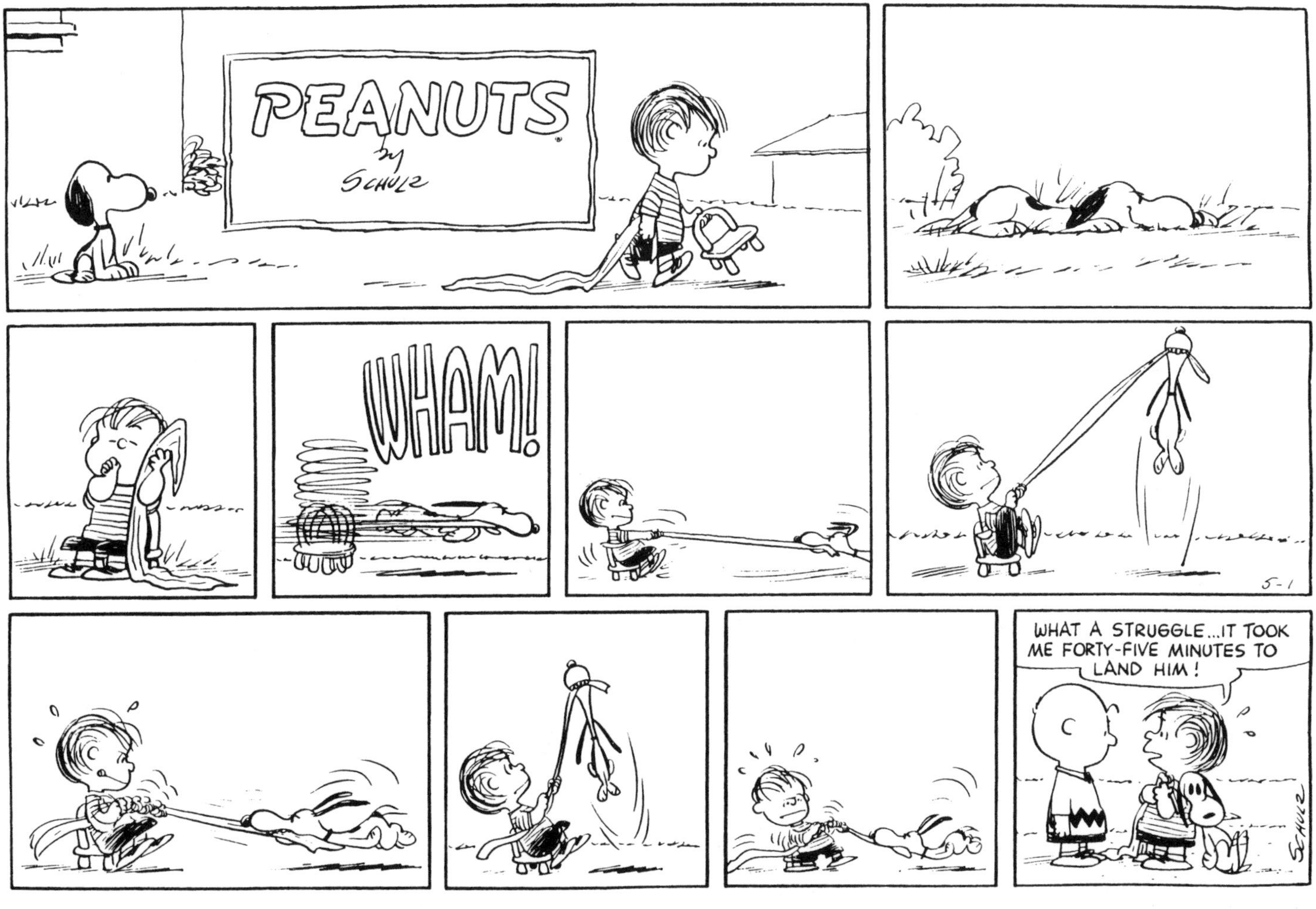
PEANUTS
by
SCHULZ
WHAM!
5-1
WHAT A STRUGGLE...IT TOOK ME FORTY-FIVE MINUTES TO LAND HIM!
SCHULZ

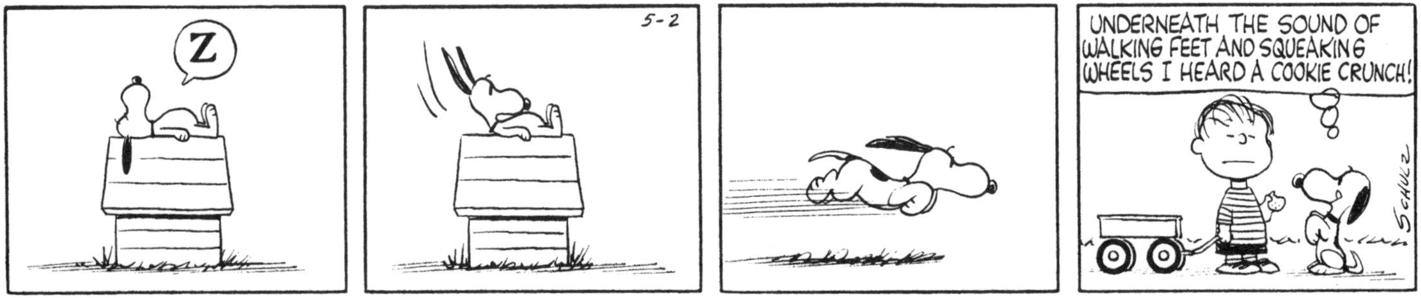
Z
5-2
UNDERNEATH THE SOUND OF WALKING FEET AND SQUEAKING WHEELS I HEARD A COOKIE CRUNCH!
SCHULZ

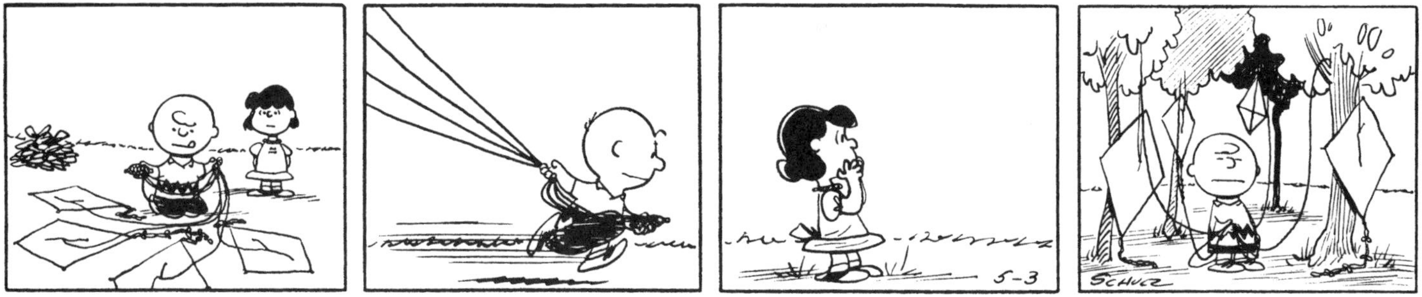
5-3
SCHULZ

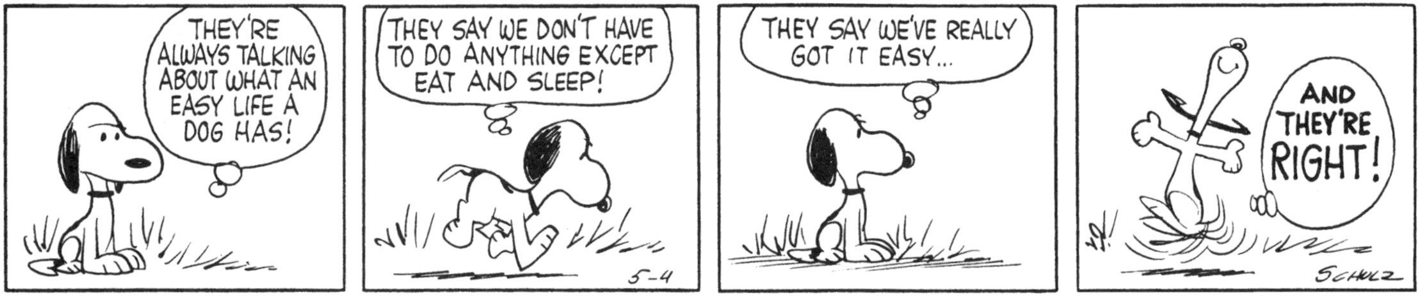
THEY'RE ALWAYS TALKING ABOUT WHAT AN EASY LIFE A DOG HAS!
THEY SAY WE DON'T HAVE TO DO ANYTHING EXCEPT EAT AND SLEEP!
5-4
THEY SAY WE'VE REALLY GOT IT EASY...
AND THEY'RE RIGHT!
SCHULZ

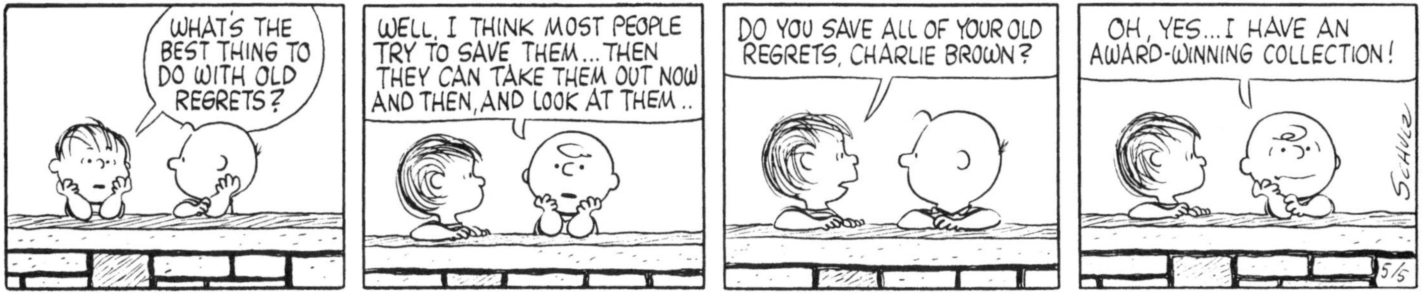
WHAT'S THE BEST THING TO DO WITH OLD REGRETS?
WELL, I THINK MOST PEOPLE TRY TO SAVE THEM... THEN THEY CAN TAKE THEM OUT NOW AND THEN, AND LOOK AT THEM..
DO YOU SAVE ALL OF YOUR OLD REGRETS, CHARLIE BROWN?
OH, YES... I HAVE AN AWARD-WINNING COLLECTION!
SCHULZ
5/5

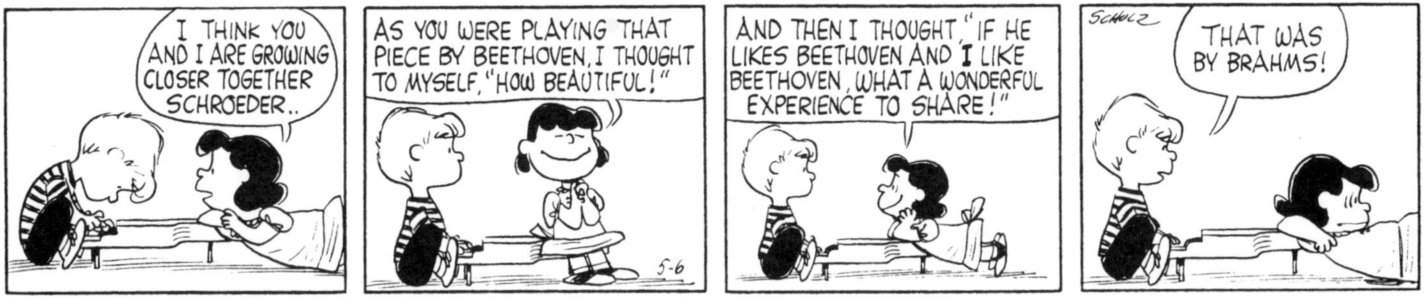
I THINK YOU AND I ARE GROWING CLOSER TOGETHER SCHROEDER..
AS YOU WERE PLAYING THAT PIECE BY BEETHOVEN, I THOUGHT TO MYSELF, "HOW BEAUTIFUL!"
5-6
AND THEN I THOUGHT, "IF HE LIKES BEETHOVEN AND I LIKE BEETHOVEN, WHAT A WONDERFUL EXPERIENCE TO SHARE!"
SCHULZ
THAT WAS BY BRAHMS!

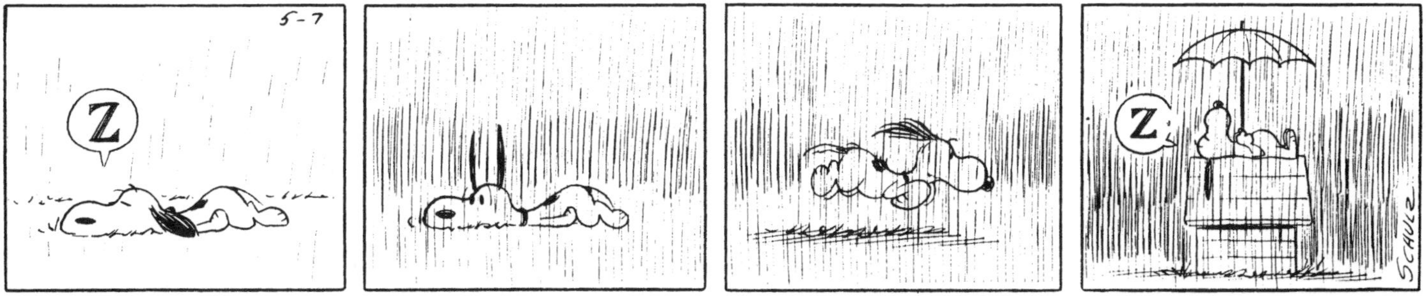
5-7
Z
Z
SCHULZ

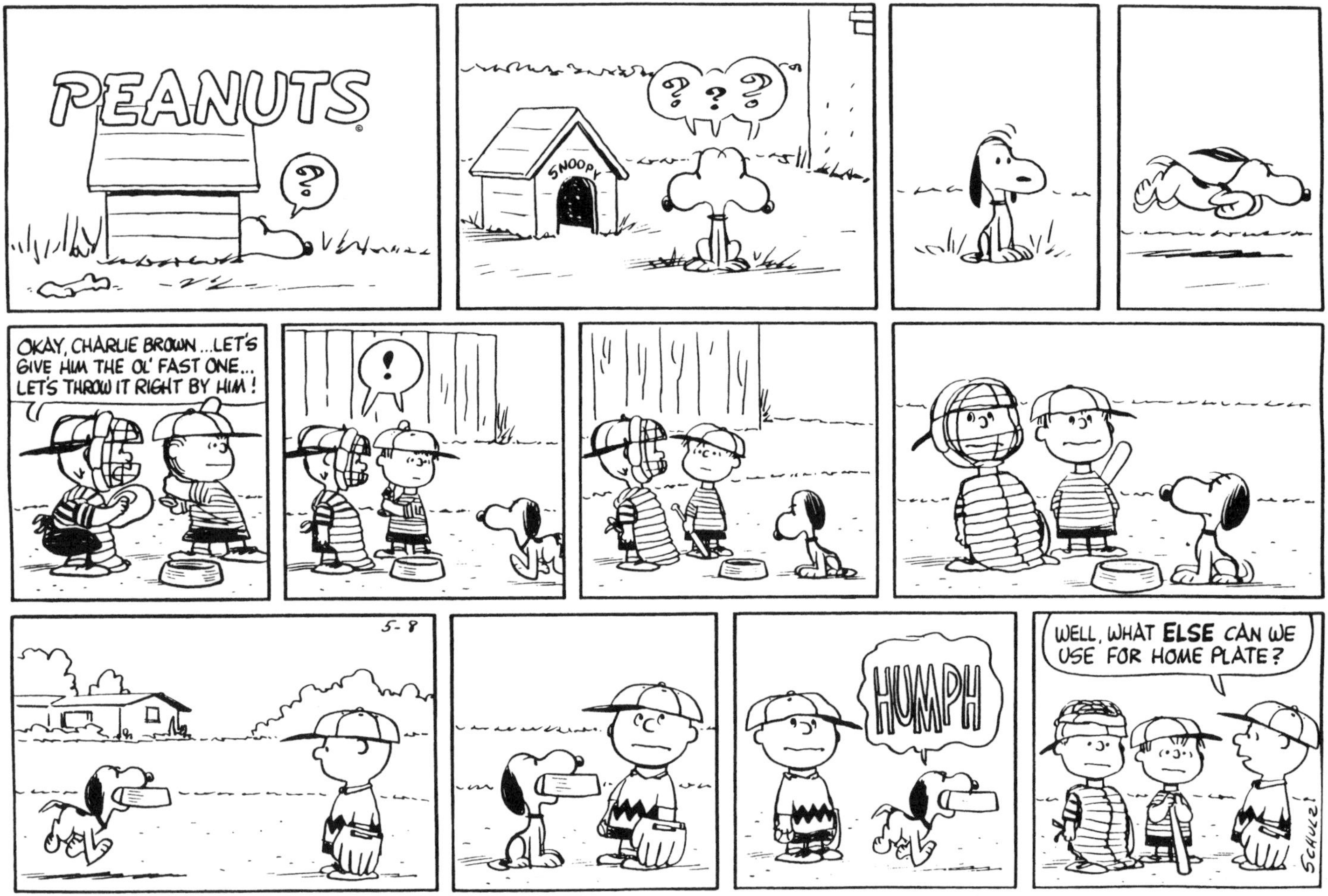
PEANUTS
?
SNOOPY
? ? ?
OKAY, CHARLIE BROWN...LET'S GIVE HIM THE OL' FAST ONE... LET'S THROW IT RIGHT BY HIM!
!
5-8
HUMPH
WELL, WHAT ELSE CAN WE USE FOR HOME PLATE?
SCHULZ

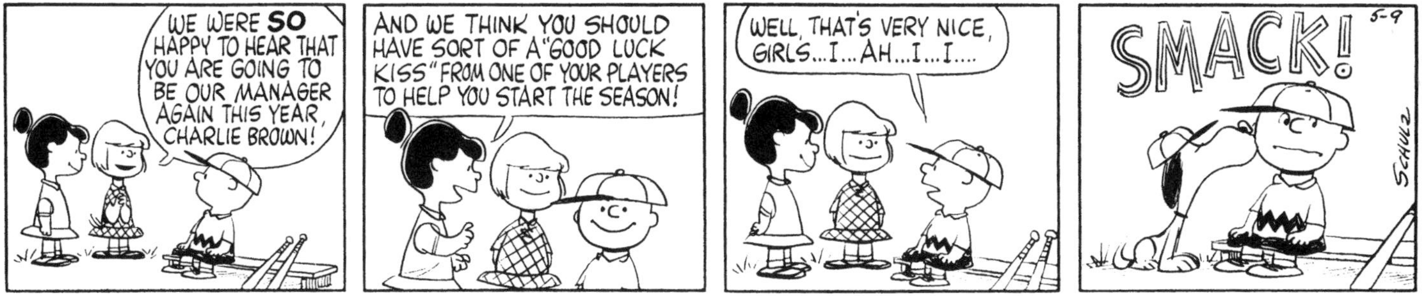
WE WERE SO HAPPY TO HEAR THAT YOU ARE GOING TO BE OUR MANAGER AGAIN THIS YEAR, CHARLIE BROWN!
AND WE THINK YOU SHOULD HAVE SORT OF A "GOOD LUCK KISS" FROM ONE OF YOUR PLAYERS TO HELP YOU START THE SEASON!
WELL, THAT'S VERY NICE, GIRLS...I...AH...I...I....
SMACK!
5-9
SCHULZ

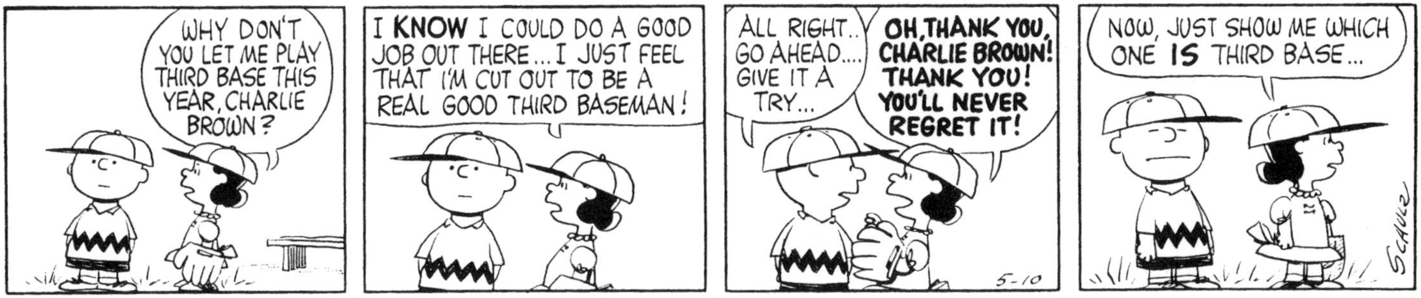
WHY DON'T YOU LET ME PLAY THIRD BASE THIS YEAR, CHARLIE BROWN?
I KNOW I COULD DO A GOOD JOB OUT THERE... I JUST FEEL THAT I'M CUT OUT TO BE A REAL GOOD THIRD BASEMAN!
ALL RIGHT.. GO AHEAD.... GIVE IT A TRY...
OH, THANK YOU, CHARLIE BROWN! THANK YOU! YOU'LL NEVER REGRET IT!
5-10
NOW, JUST SHOW ME WHICH ONE IS THIRD BASE...
SCHULZ

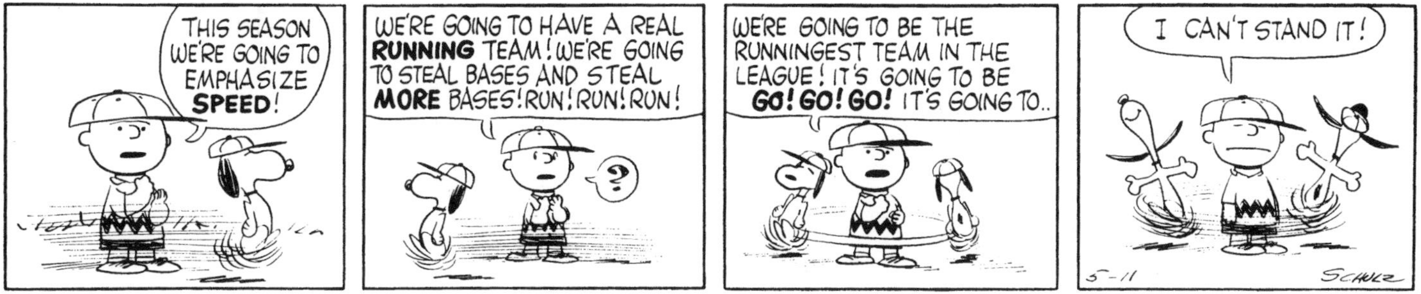
THIS SEASON WE'RE GOING TO EMPHASIZE SPEED!
WE'RE GOING TO HAVE A REAL RUNNING TEAM! WE'RE GOING TO STEAL BASES AND STEAL MORE BASES! RUN! RUN! RUN!
?
WE'RE GOING TO BE THE RUNNINGEST TEAM IN THE LEAGUE! IT'S GOING TO BE GO! GO! GO! IT'S GOING TO..
I CAN'T STAND IT!
5-11
SCHULZ

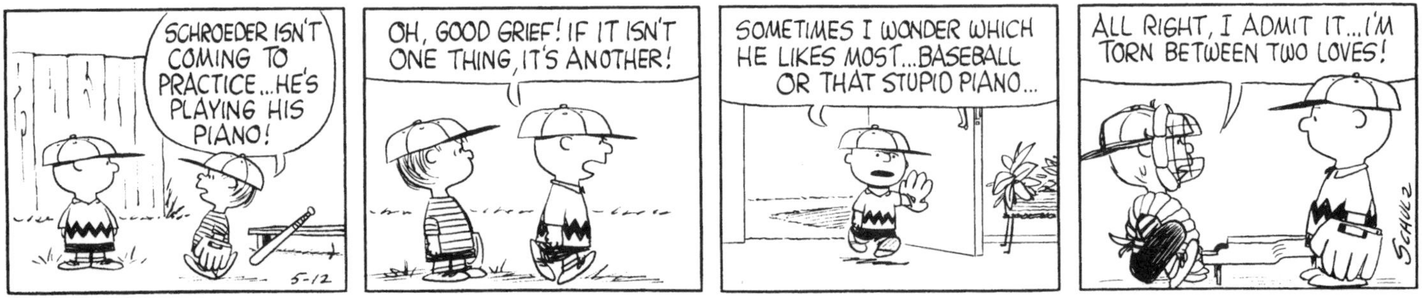
SCHROEDER ISN'T COMING TO PRACTICE...HE'S PLAYING HIS PIANO!
OH, GOOD GRIEF! IF IT ISN'T ONE THING, IT'S ANOTHER!
SOMETIMES I WONDER WHICH HE LIKES MOST...BASEBALL OR THAT STUPID PIANO...
ALL RIGHT, I ADMIT IT...I'M TORN BETWEEN TWO LOVES!
SCHULZ
5-12

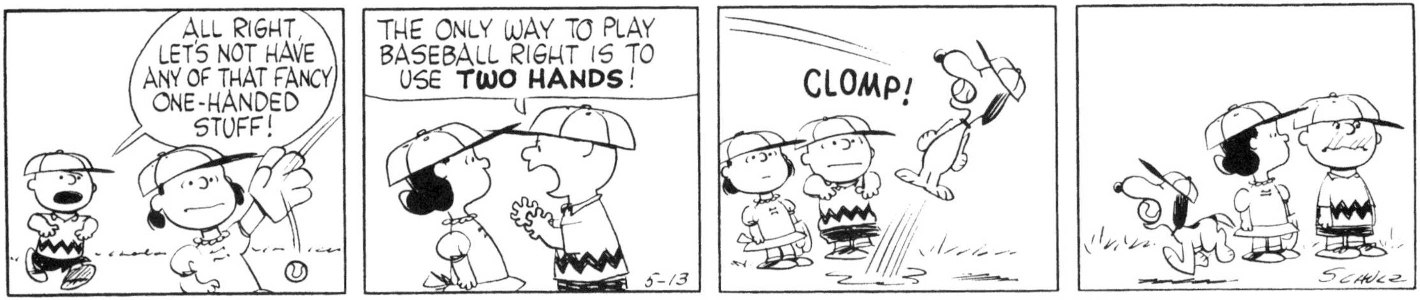
ALL RIGHT, LET'S NOT HAVE ANY OF THAT FANCY ONE-HANDED STUFF!
THE ONLY WAY TO PLAY BASEBALL RIGHT IS TO USE **TWO HANDS**!
5-13
CLOMP!
SCHULZ

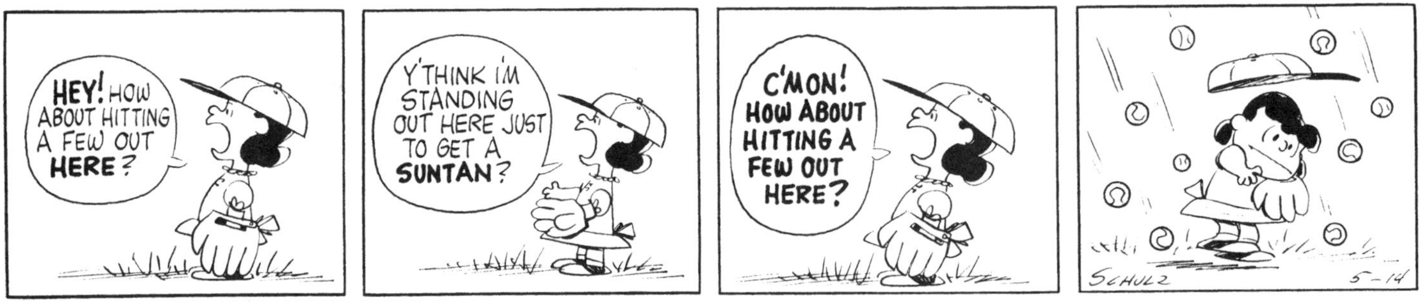
HEY! HOW ABOUT HITTING A FEW OUT **HERE**?
Y'THINK I'M STANDING OUT HERE JUST TO GET A **SUNTAN**?
C'MON! HOW ABOUT HITTING A FEW OUT HERE?
SCHULZ
5-14

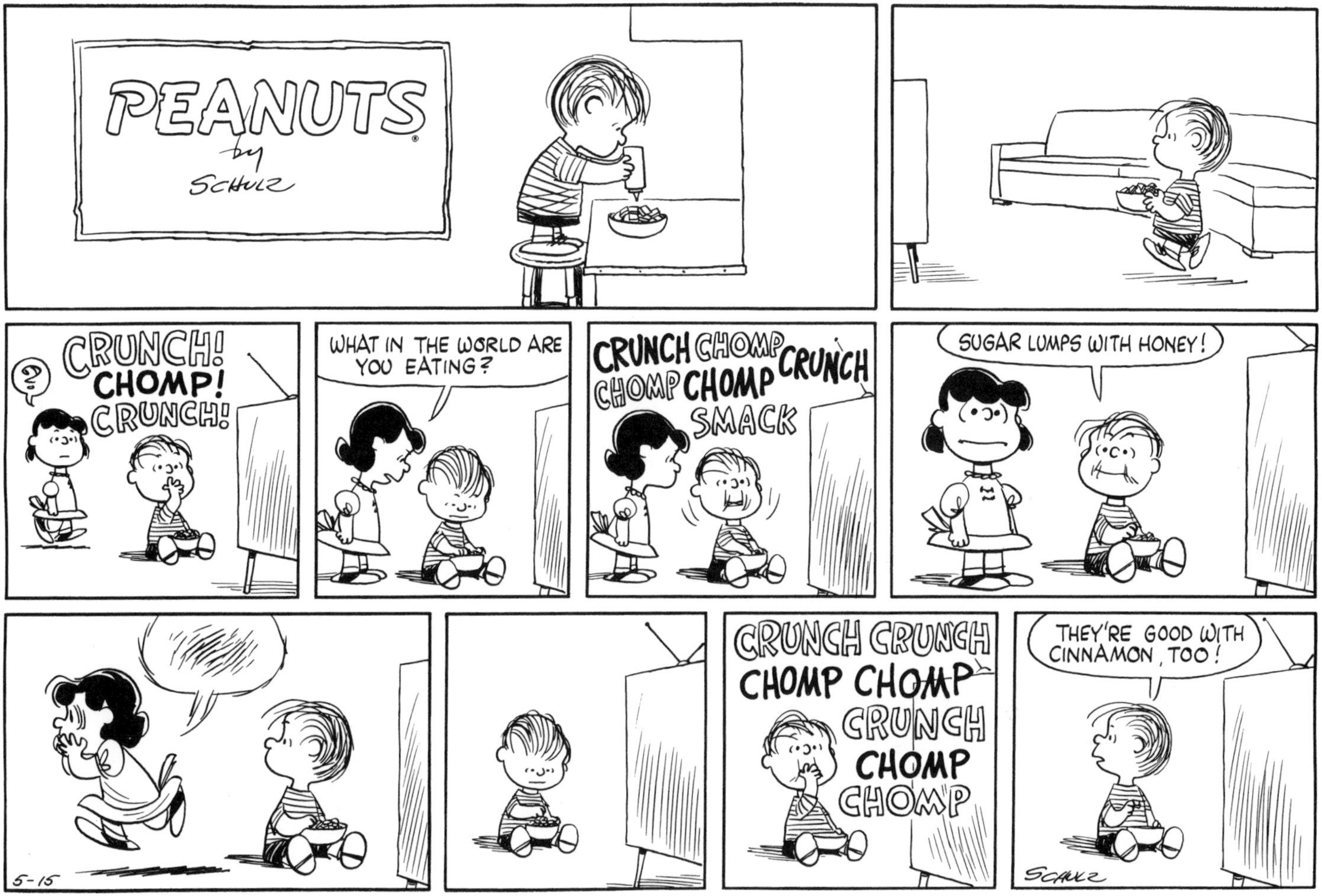
PEANUTS
by
SCHULZ
?
CRUNCH!
CHOMP!
CRUNCH!
WHAT IN THE WORLD ARE YOU EATING?
CRUNCH CHOMP CRUNCH
CHOMP CHOMP
SMACK
SUGAR LUMPS WITH HONEY!
5-15
CRUNCH CRUNCH
CHOMP CHOMP
CRUNCH
CHOMP
CHOMP
THEY'RE GOOD WITH CINNAMON, TOO!
SCHULZ

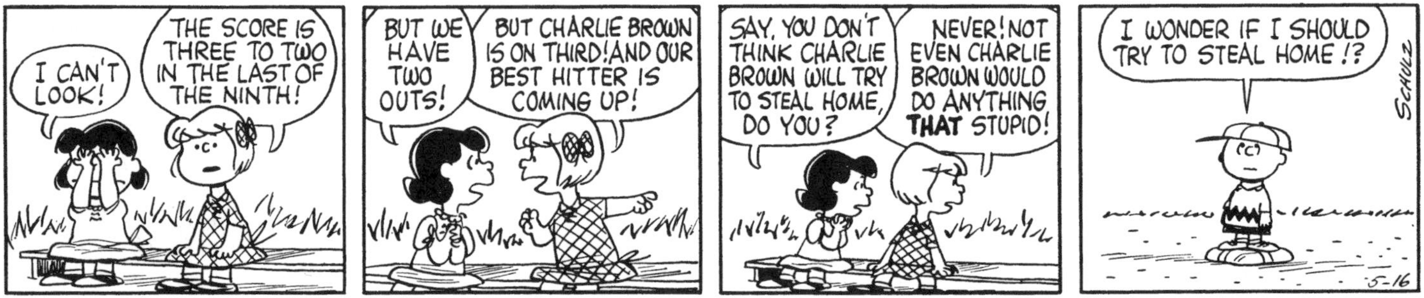
I CAN'T LOOK!
THE SCORE IS THREE TO TWO IN THE LAST OF THE NINTH!
BUT WE HAVE TWO OUTS!
BUT CHARLIE BROWN IS ON THIRD! AND OUR BEST HITTER IS COMING UP!
SAY, YOU DON'T THINK CHARLIE BROWN WILL TRY TO STEAL HOME, DO YOU?
NEVER! NOT EVEN CHARLIE BROWN WOULD DO ANYTHING **THAT** STUPID!
I WONDER IF I SHOULD TRY TO STEAL HOME !?
SCHULZ
5-16

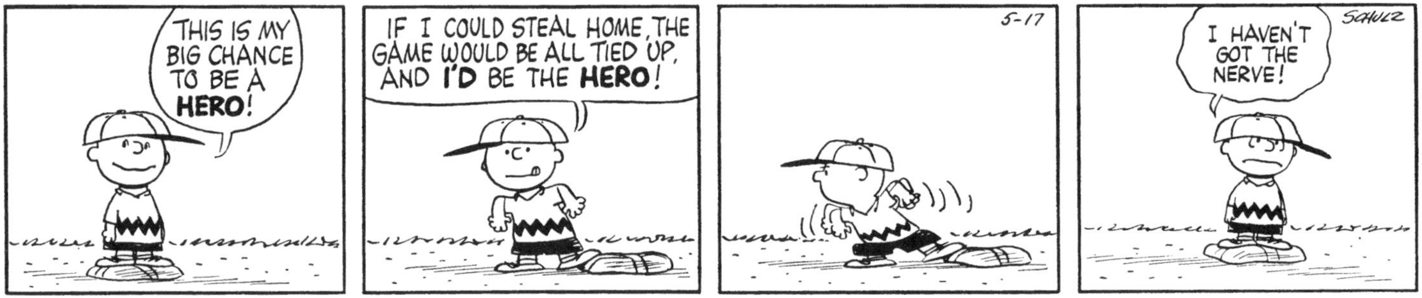
THIS IS MY BIG CHANCE TO BE A **HERO**!
IF I COULD STEAL HOME, THE GAME WOULD BE ALL TIED UP, AND **I'D** BE THE **HERO**!
5-17
SCHULZ
I HAVEN'T GOT THE NERVE!

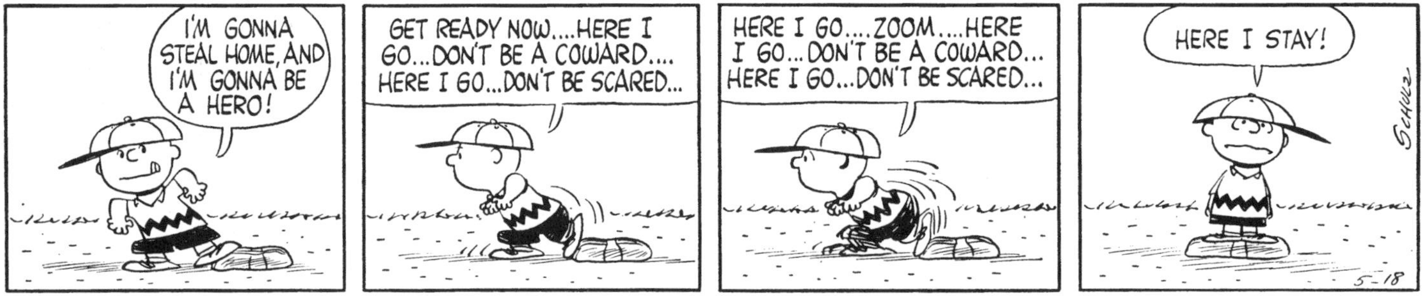
I'M GONNA STEAL HOME, AND I'M GONNA BE A HERO!
GET READY NOW....HERE I GO...DON'T BE A COWARD.... HERE I GO...DON'T BE SCARED...
HERE I GO....ZOOM....HERE I GO...DON'T BE A COWARD... HERE I GO...DON'T BE SCARED...
HERE I STAY!
SCHULZ
5-18

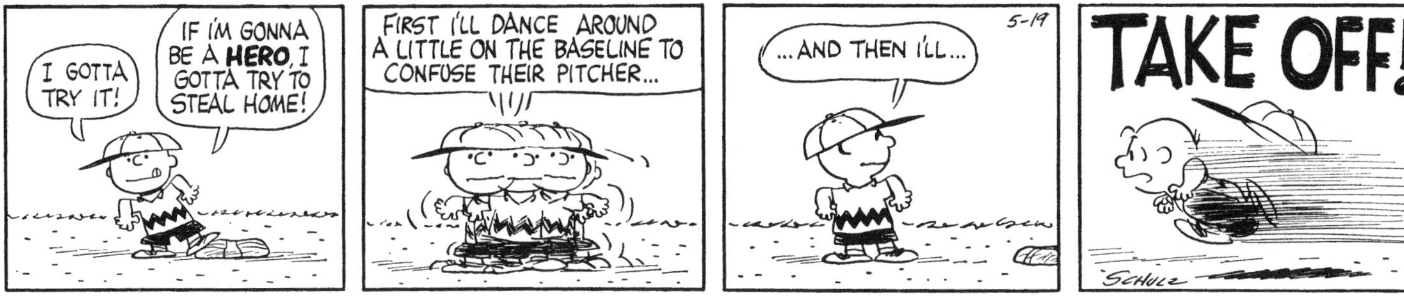
I GOTTA TRY IT!
IF I'M GONNA BE A **HERO**, I GOTTA TRY TO STEAL HOME!
FIRST I'LL DANCE AROUND A LITTLE ON THE BASELINE TO CONFUSE THEIR PITCHER...
5-19
...AND THEN I'LL...
TAKE OFF!
SCHULZ

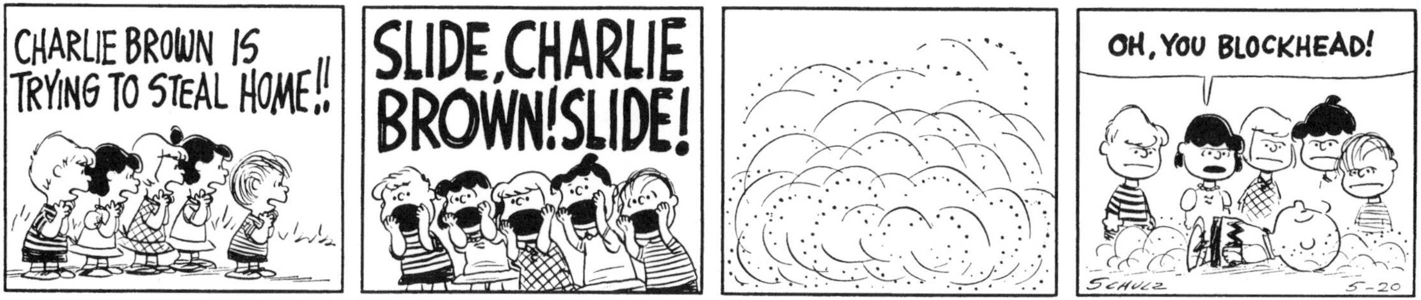
CHARLIE BROWN IS TRYING TO STEAL HOME!!
SLIDE, CHARLIE BROWN! SLIDE!
OH, YOU BLOCKHEAD!
SCHULZ
5-20

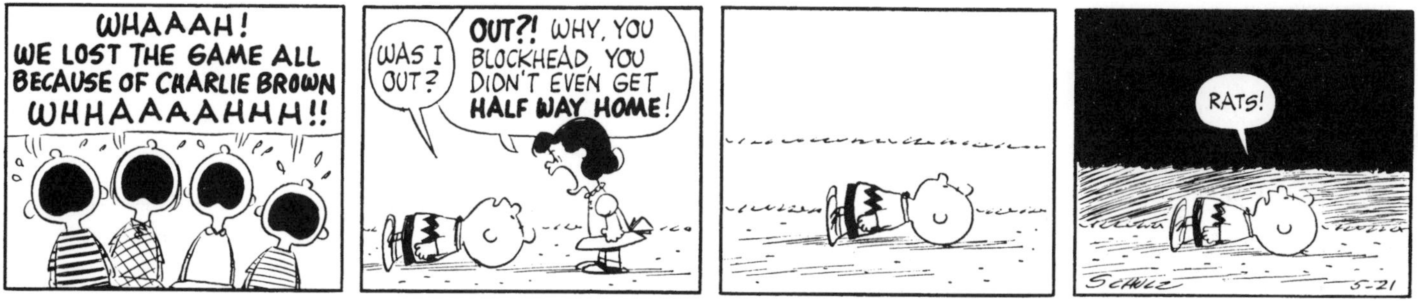
WHAAAH! WE LOST THE GAME ALL BECAUSE OF CHARLIE BROWN WHHAAAAAHHH!!
WAS I OUT?
OUT?! WHY, YOU BLOCKHEAD, YOU DIDN'T EVEN GET **HALF WAY HOME**!
RATS!
SCHULZ
5-21

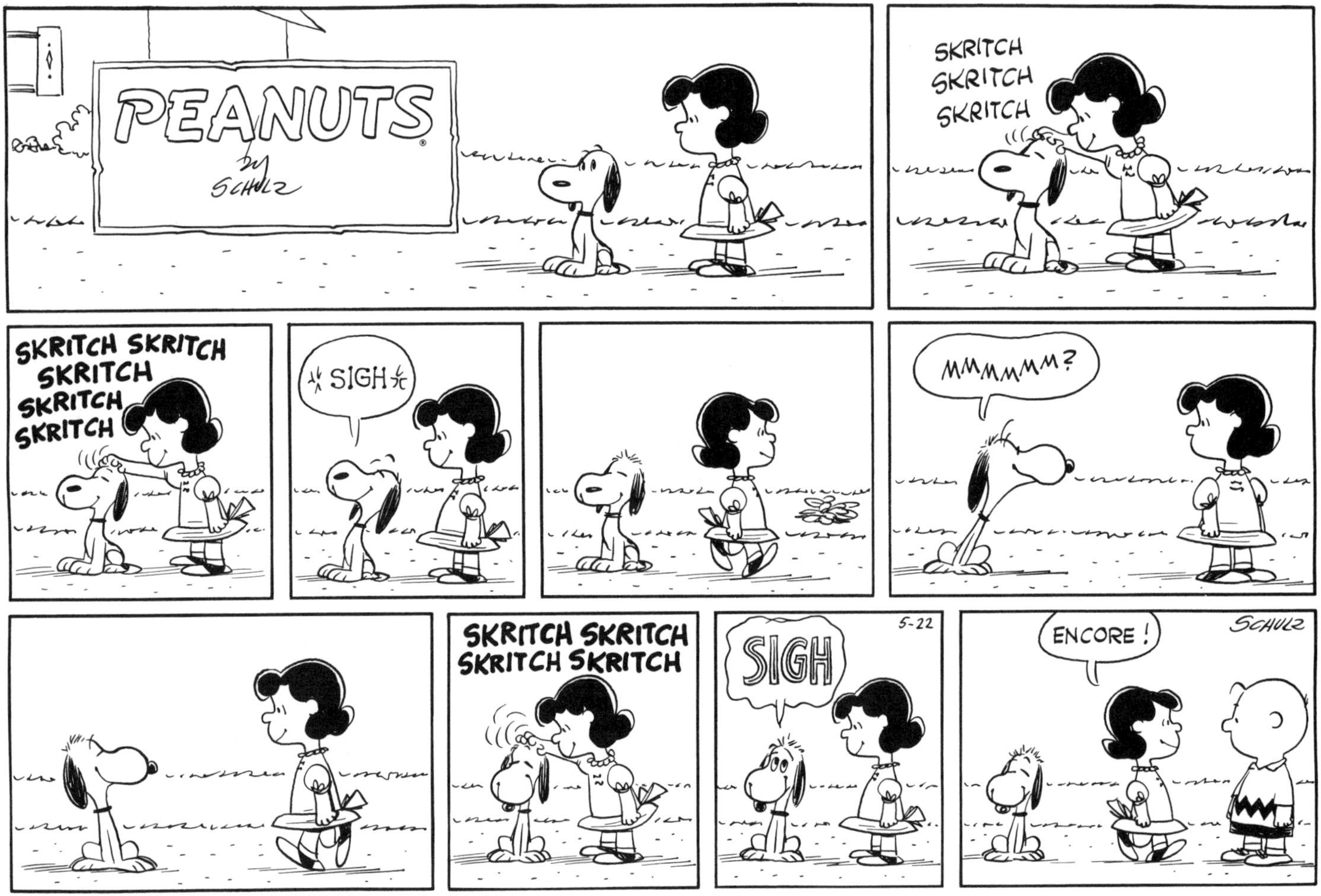
PEANUTS
by SCHULZ
SKRITCH
SKRITCH
SKRITCH
SKRITCH SKRITCH
SKRITCH
SKRITCH
SKRITCH
SIGH
MMMMMM?
SKRITCH SKRITCH
SKRITCH SKRITCH
SIGH
5-22
SCHULZ
ENCORE!

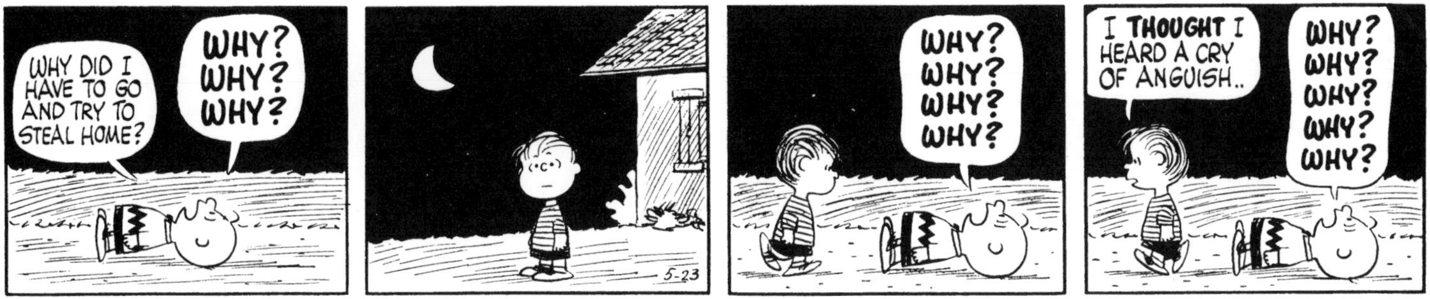
WHY DID I HAVE TO GO AND TRY TO STEAL HOME?
WHY? WHY? WHY?
5-23
WHY? WHY? WHY? WHY?
I **THOUGHT** I HEARD A CRY OF ANGUISH..
WHY? WHY? WHY? WHY? WHY?

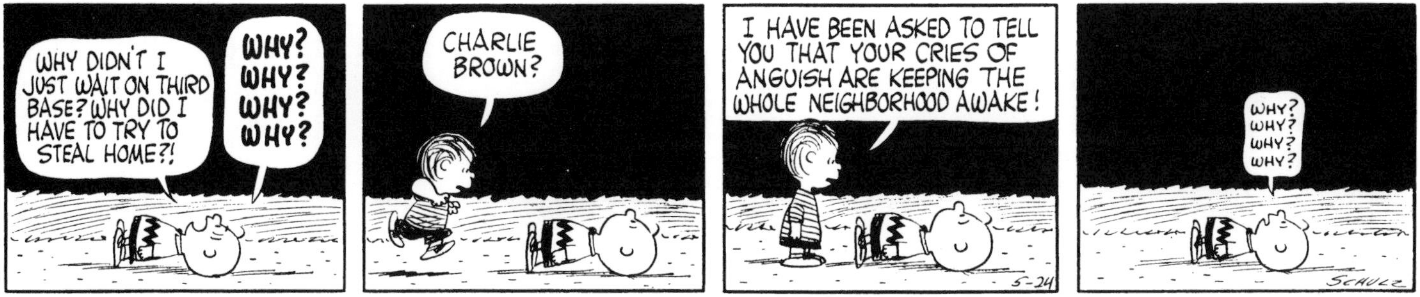
WHY DIDN'T I JUST WAIT ON THIRD BASE? WHY DID I HAVE TO TRY TO STEAL HOME?!
WHY? WHY? WHY? WHY?
CHARLIE BROWN?
I HAVE BEEN ASKED TO TELL YOU THAT YOUR CRIES OF ANGUISH ARE KEEPING THE WHOLE NEIGHBORHOOD AWAKE!
5-24
WHY? WHY? WHY? WHY?
SCHULZ

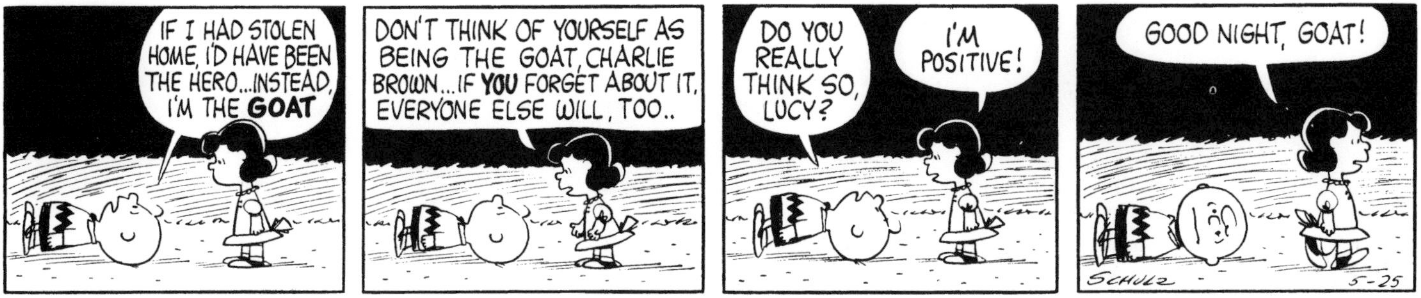
IF I HAD STOLEN HOME, I'D HAVE BEEN THE HERO...INSTEAD, I'M THE **GOAT**
DON'T THINK OF YOURSELF AS BEING THE GOAT, CHARLIE BROWN...IF **YOU** FORGET ABOUT IT, EVERYONE ELSE WILL, TOO..
DO YOU REALLY THINK SO, LUCY?
I'M POSITIVE!
GOOD NIGHT, GOAT!
SCHULZ
5-25

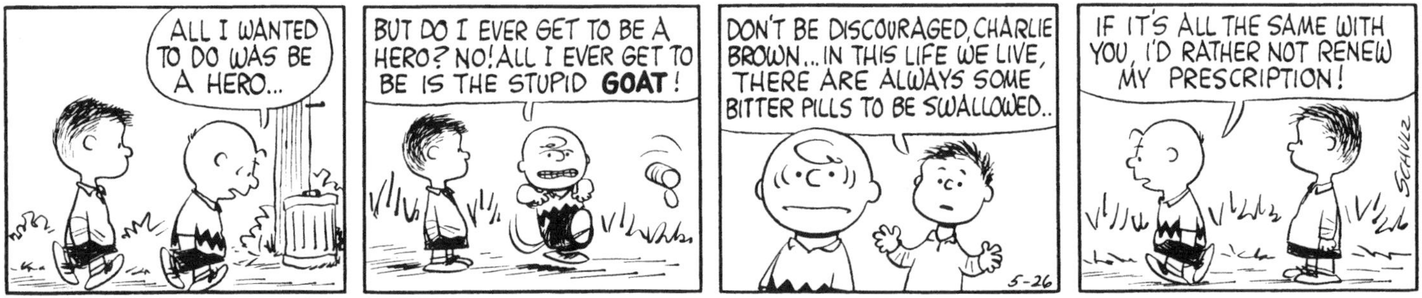
ALL I WANTED TO DO WAS BE A HERO...
BUT DO I EVER GET TO BE A HERO? NO! ALL I EVER GET TO BE IS THE STUPID GOAT!
DON'T BE DISCOURAGED, CHARLIE BROWN... IN THIS LIFE WE LIVE, THERE ARE ALWAYS SOME BITTER PILLS TO BE SWALLOWED..
5-26
IF IT'S ALL THE SAME WITH YOU, I'D RATHER NOT RENEW MY PRESCRIPTION!
SCHULZ

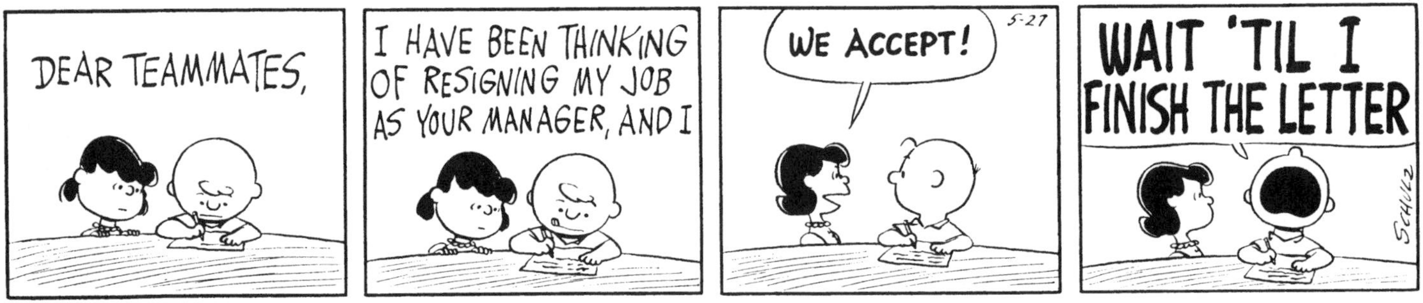
DEAR TEAMMATES,
I HAVE BEEN THINKING OF RESIGNING MY JOB AS YOUR MANAGER, AND I
5-27
WE ACCEPT!
WAIT 'TIL I FINISH THE LETTER
SCHULZ

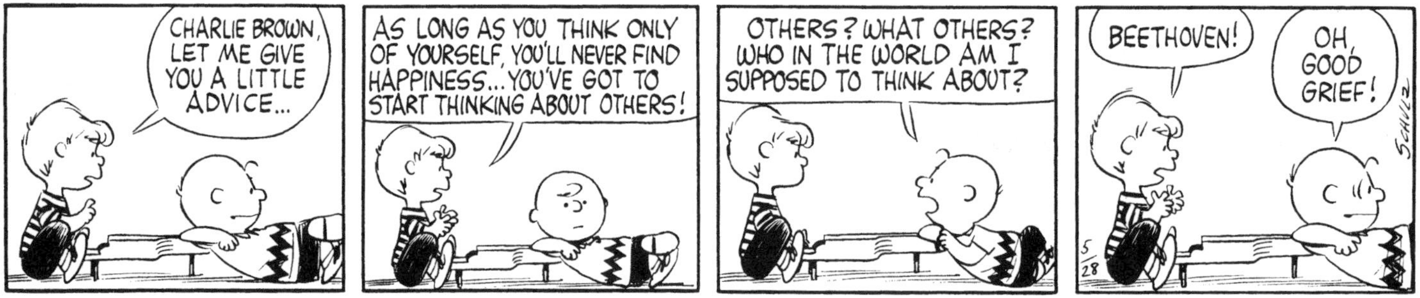
CHARLIE BROWN, LET ME GIVE YOU A LITTLE ADVICE...
AS LONG AS YOU THINK ONLY OF YOURSELF, YOU'LL NEVER FIND HAPPINESS... YOU'VE GOT TO START THINKING ABOUT OTHERS!
OTHERS? WHAT OTHERS? WHO IN THE WORLD AM I SUPPOSED TO THINK ABOUT?
BEETHOVEN!
OH, GOOD GRIEF!
5/28
SCHULZ

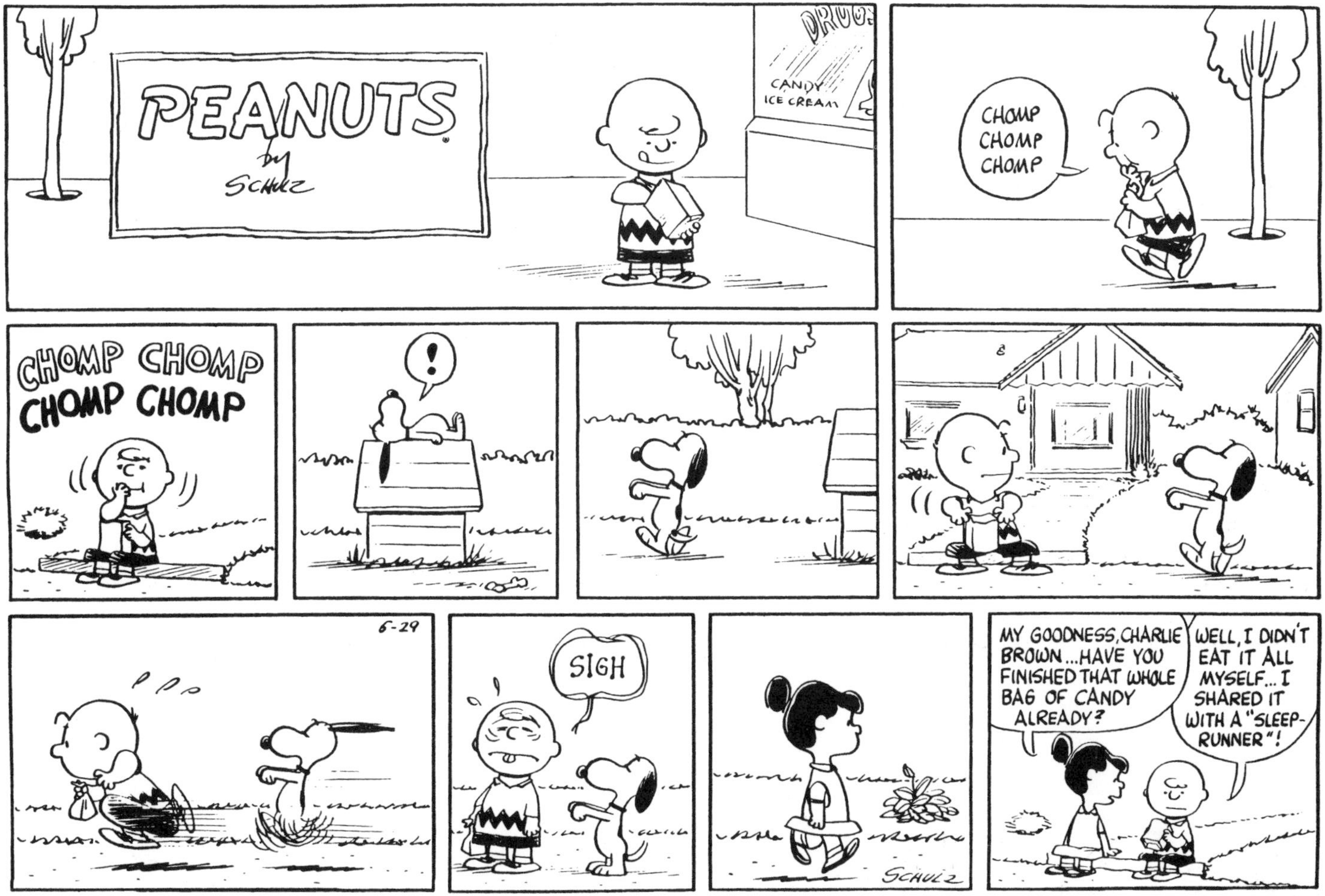
PEANUTS
by SCHULZ
DRUGS
CANDY
ICE CREAM
CHOMP CHOMP CHOMP
CHOMP CHOMP CHOMP CHOMP
!
6-29
SIGH
SCHULZ
MY GOODNESS, CHARLIE BROWN...HAVE YOU FINISHED THAT WHOLE BAG OF CANDY ALREADY?
WELL, I DIDN'T EAT IT ALL MYSELF... I SHARED IT WITH A "SLEEP-RUNNER"!

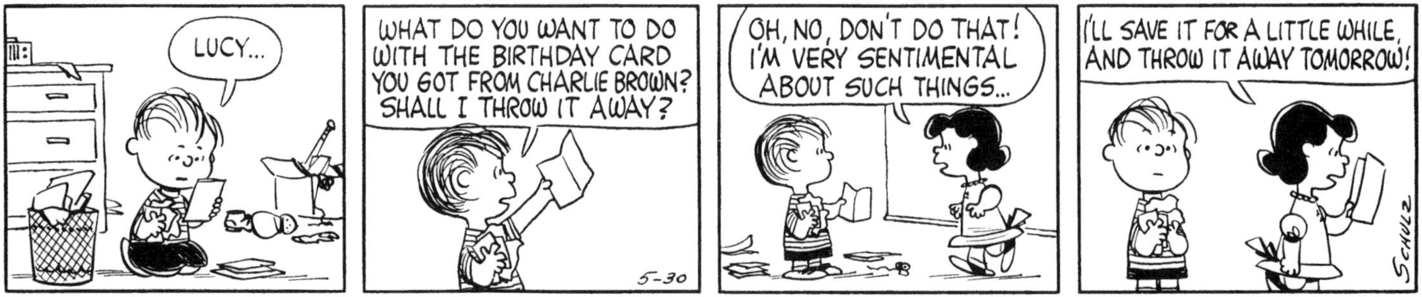
LUCY...
WHAT DO YOU WANT TO DO WITH THE BIRTHDAY CARD YOU GOT FROM CHARLIE BROWN? SHALL I THROW IT AWAY?
5-30
OH, NO, DON'T DO THAT! I'M VERY SENTIMENTAL ABOUT SUCH THINGS...
I'LL SAVE IT FOR A LITTLE WHILE, AND THROW IT AWAY TOMORROW!
SCHULZ

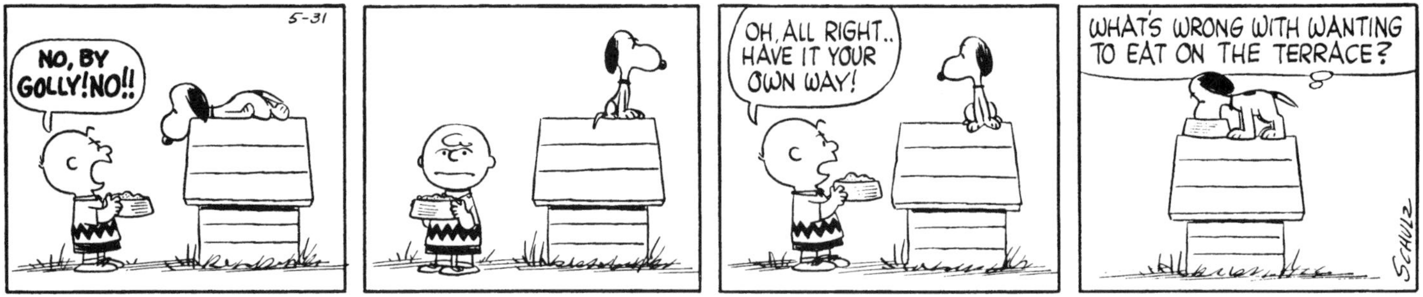
5-31
NO, BY GOLLY! NO!!
OH, ALL RIGHT.. HAVE IT YOUR OWN WAY!
WHAT'S WRONG WITH WANTING TO EAT ON THE TERRACE?
SCHULZ

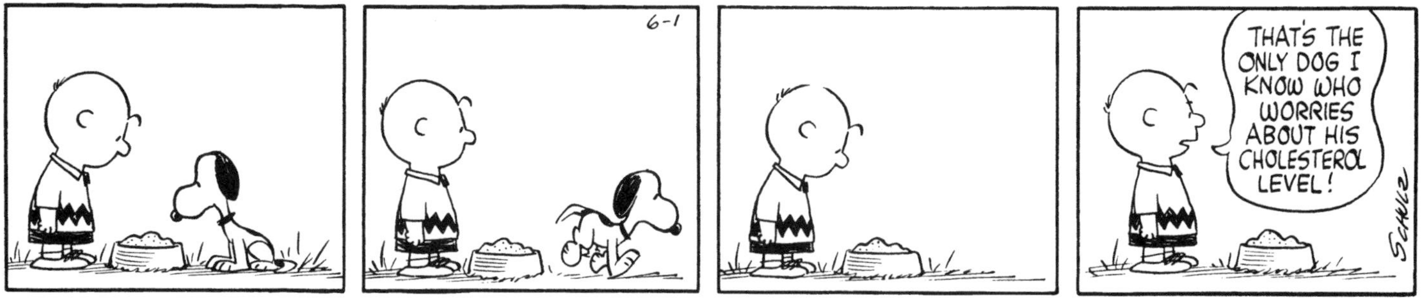
6-1
THAT'S THE ONLY DOG I KNOW WHO WORRIES ABOUT HIS CHOLESTEROL LEVEL!
SCHULZ

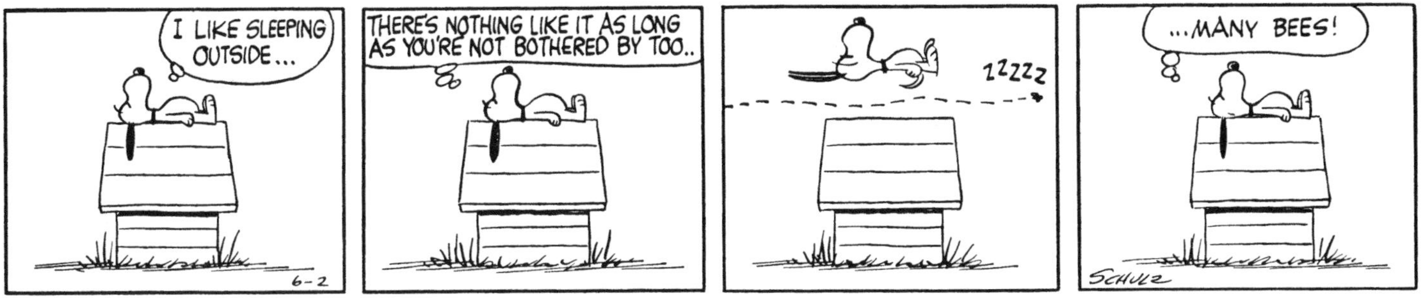
I LIKE SLEEPING OUTSIDE...
THERE'S NOTHING LIKE IT AS LONG AS YOU'RE NOT BOTHERED BY TOO..
ZZZZZ
...MANY BEES!
6-2
SCHULZ

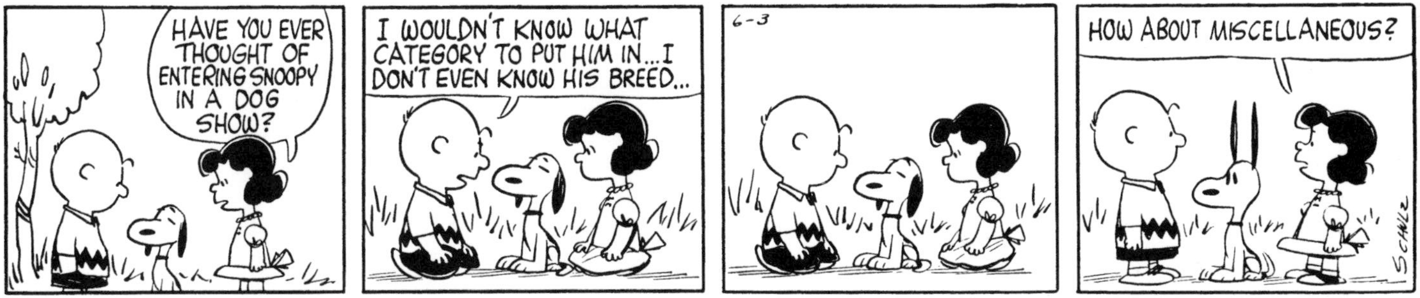
HAVE YOU EVER THOUGHT OF ENTERING SNOOPY IN A DOG SHOW?
I WOULDN'T KNOW WHAT CATEGORY TO PUT HIM IN...I DON'T EVEN KNOW HIS BREED...
6-3
HOW ABOUT MISCELLANEOUS?
SCHULZ

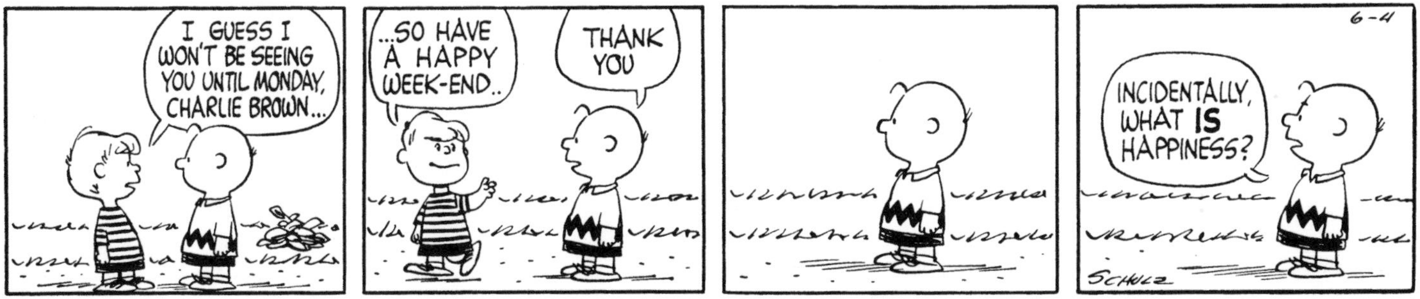
I GUESS I WON'T BE SEEING YOU UNTIL MONDAY, CHARLIE BROWN...
...SO HAVE A HAPPY WEEK-END..
THANK YOU
6-4
INCIDENTALLY, WHAT **IS** HAPPINESS?
SCHULZ

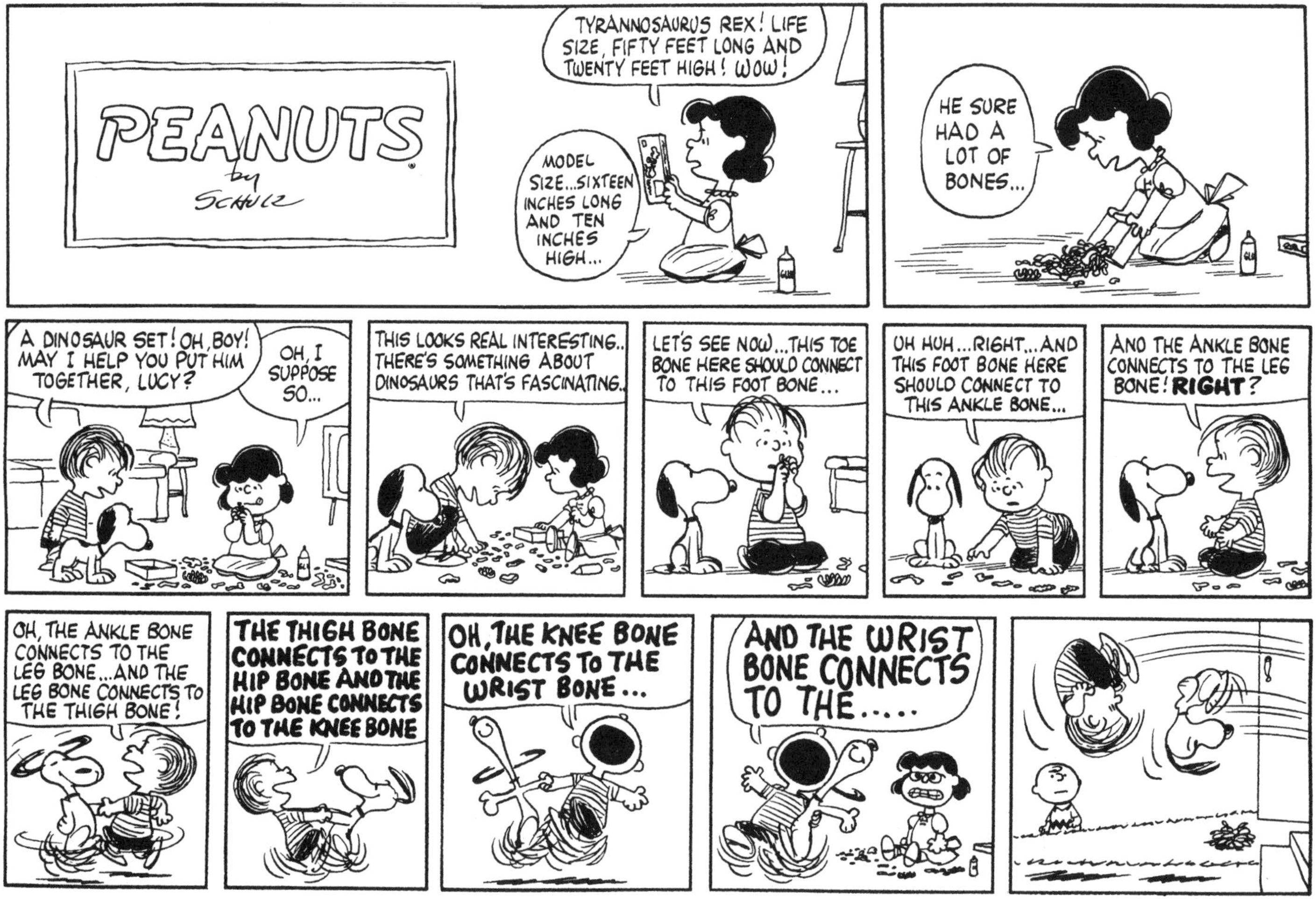
PEANUTS
by SCHULZ
TYRANNOSAURUS REX! LIFE SIZE, FIFTY FEET LONG AND TWENTY FEET HIGH! WOW!
MODEL SIZE...SIXTEEN INCHES LONG AND TEN INCHES HIGH...
HE SURE HAD A LOT OF BONES...
A DINOSAUR SET! OH, BOY! MAY I HELP YOU PUT HIM TOGETHER, LUCY?
OH, I SUPPOSE SO...
THIS LOOKS REAL INTERESTING.. THERE'S SOMETHING ABOUT DINOSAURS THAT'S FASCINATING..
LET'S SEE NOW...THIS TOE BONE HERE SHOULD CONNECT TO THIS FOOT BONE...
UH HUH...RIGHT...AND THIS FOOT BONE HERE SHOULD CONNECT TO THIS ANKLE BONE...
AND THE ANKLE BONE CONNECTS TO THE LEG BONE! RIGHT?
OH, THE ANKLE BONE CONNECTS TO THE LEG BONE...AND THE LEG BONE CONNECTS TO THE THIGH BONE!
THE THIGH BONE CONNECTS TO THE HIP BONE AND THE HIP BONE CONNECTS TO THE KNEE BONE
OH, THE KNEE BONE CONNECTS TO THE WRIST BONE...
AND THE WRIST BONE CONNECTS TO THE.....
!

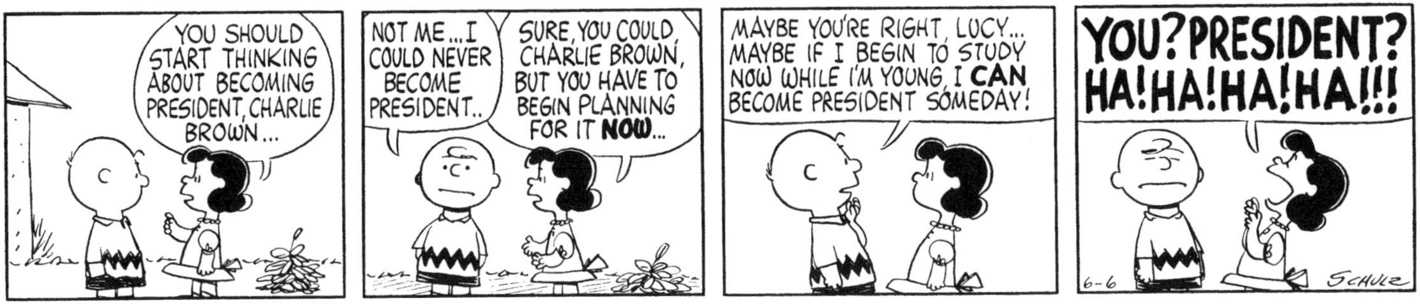
YOU SHOULD START THINKING ABOUT BECOMING PRESIDENT, CHARLIE BROWN...
NOT ME...I COULD NEVER BECOME PRESIDENT..
SURE, YOU COULD, CHARLIE BROWN, BUT YOU HAVE TO BEGIN PLANNING FOR IT **NOW**...
MAYBE YOU'RE RIGHT, LUCY... MAYBE IF I BEGIN TO STUDY NOW WHILE I'M YOUNG, I **CAN** BECOME PRESIDENT SOMEDAY!
YOU? PRESIDENT? HA! HA! HA! HA!!!
6-6
SCHULZ

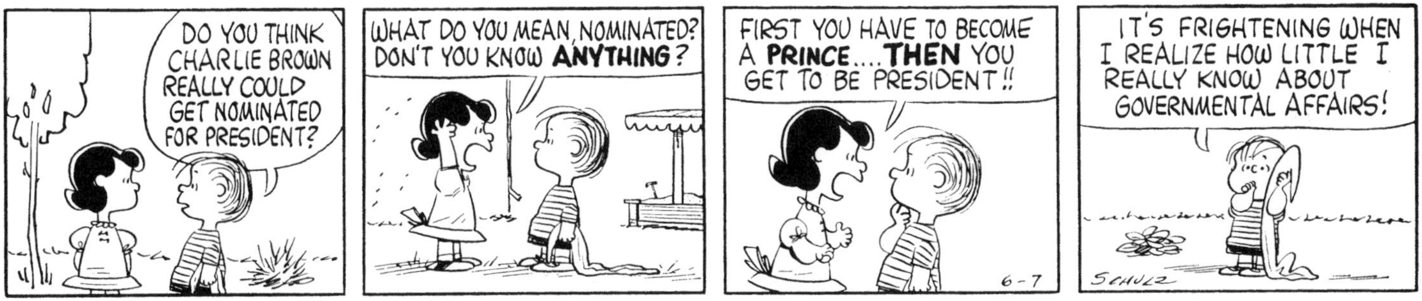
DO YOU THINK CHARLIE BROWN REALLY COULD GET NOMINATED FOR PRESIDENT?
WHAT DO YOU MEAN, NOMINATED? DON'T YOU KNOW **ANYTHING**?
FIRST YOU HAVE TO BECOME A **PRINCE**....**THEN** YOU GET TO BE PRESIDENT!!
6-7
IT'S FRIGHTENING WHEN I REALIZE HOW LITTLE I REALLY KNOW ABOUT GOVERNMENTAL AFFAIRS!
SCHULZ

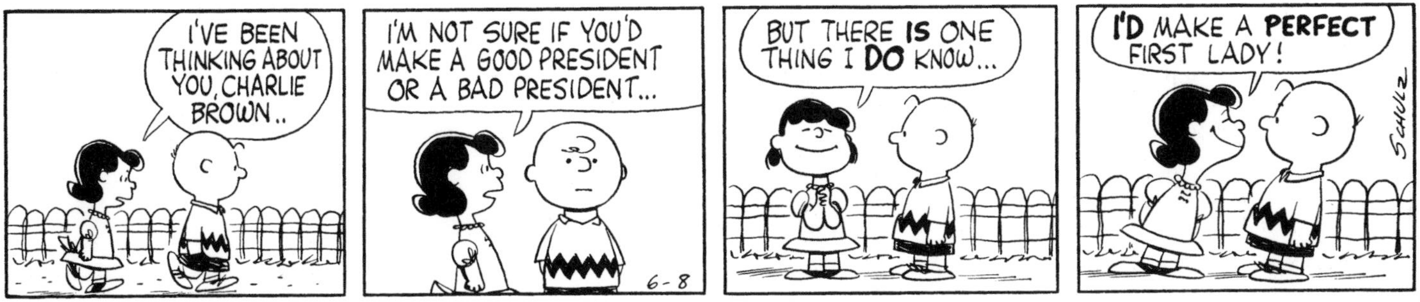
I'VE BEEN THINKING ABOUT YOU, CHARLIE BROWN..
I'M NOT SURE IF YOU'D MAKE A GOOD PRESIDENT OR A BAD PRESIDENT...
6-8
BUT THERE **IS** ONE THING I **DO** KNOW...
I'D MAKE A **PERFECT** FIRST LADY!
SCHULZ

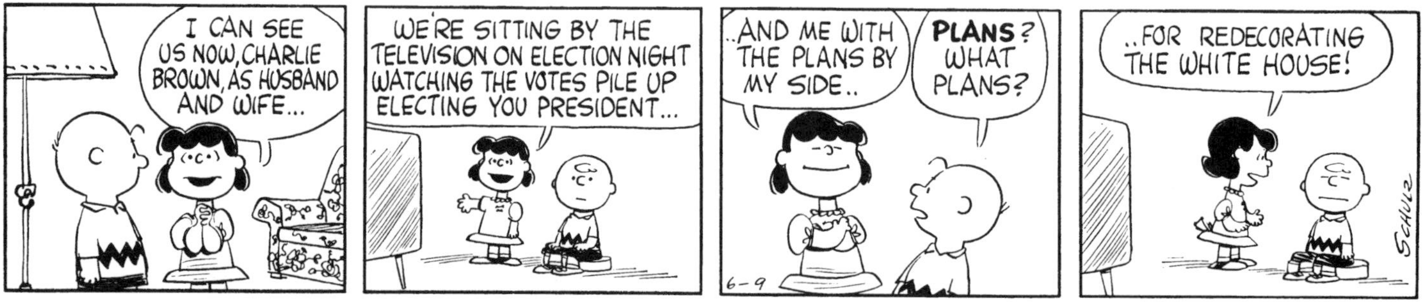
I CAN SEE US NOW, CHARLIE BROWN, AS HUSBAND AND WIFE...
WE'RE SITTING BY THE TELEVISION ON ELECTION NIGHT WATCHING THE VOTES PILE UP ELECTING YOU PRESIDENT...
..AND ME WITH THE PLANS BY MY SIDE..
PLANS? WHAT PLANS?
6-9
..FOR REDECORATING THE WHITE HOUSE!
SCHULZ

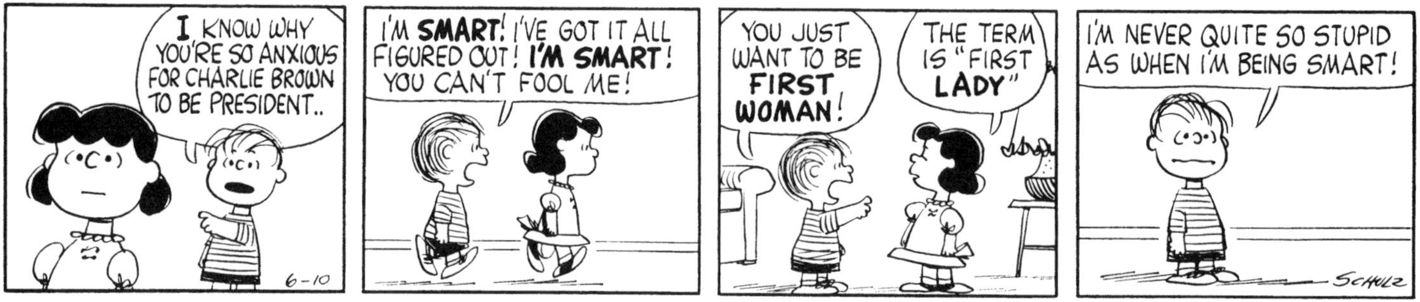
I KNOW WHY YOU'RE SO ANXIOUS FOR CHARLIE BROWN TO BE PRESIDENT..
6-10
I'M SMART! I'VE GOT IT ALL FIGURED OUT! I'M SMART! YOU CAN'T FOOL ME!
YOU JUST WANT TO BE FIRST WOMAN!
THE TERM IS "FIRST LADY"
I'M NEVER QUITE SO STUPID AS WHEN I'M BEING SMART!
SCHULZ

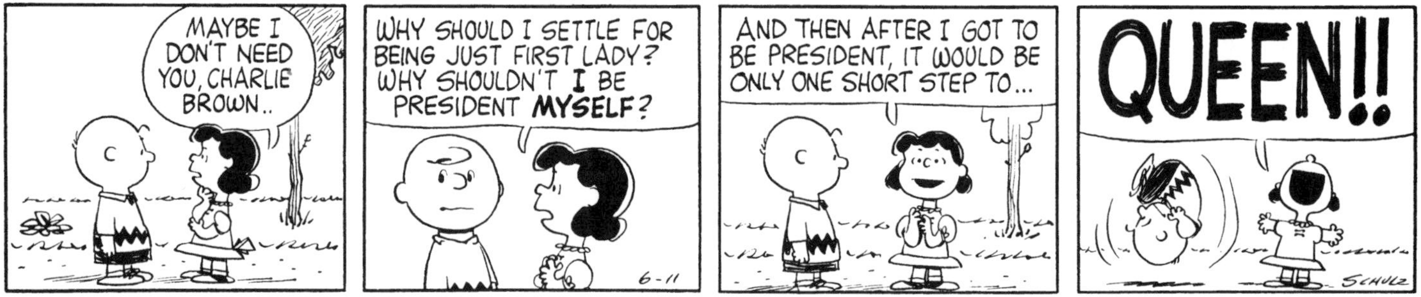
MAYBE I DON'T NEED YOU, CHARLIE BROWN..
WHY SHOULD I SETTLE FOR BEING JUST FIRST LADY? WHY SHOULDN'T I BE PRESIDENT MYSELF?
6-11
AND THEN AFTER I GOT TO BE PRESIDENT, IT WOULD BE ONLY ONE SHORT STEP TO...
QUEEN!!
SCHULZ

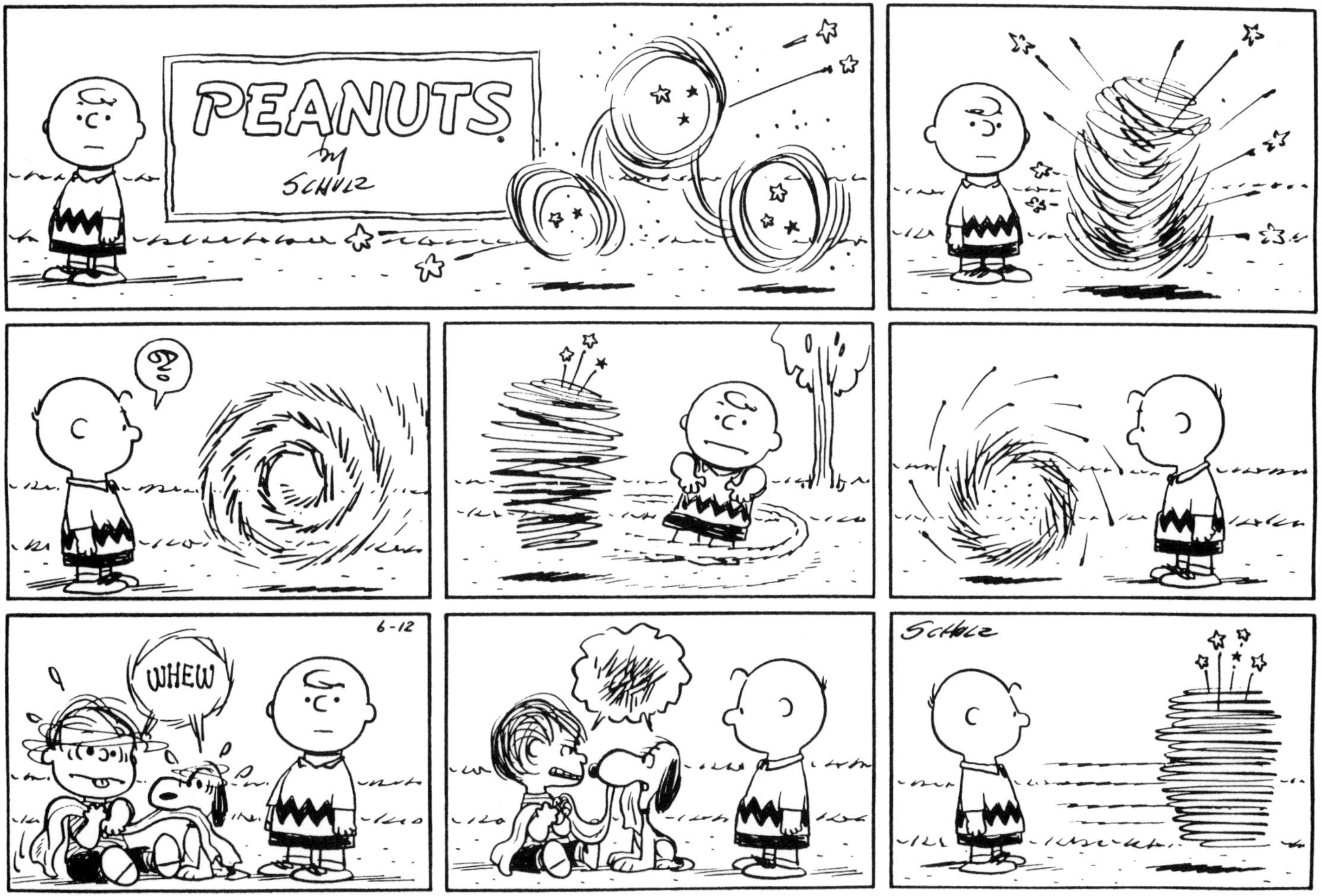
PEANUTS
by
SCHULZ
6-12
WHEW
SCHULZ

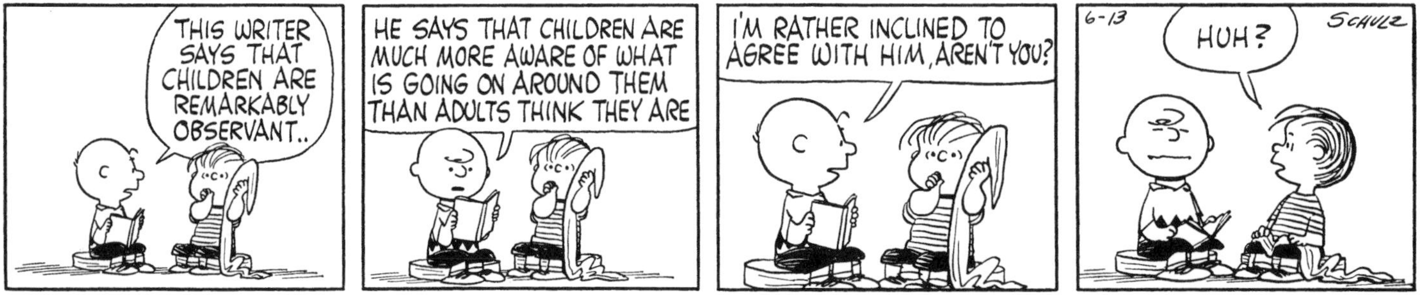
THIS WRITER SAYS THAT CHILDREN ARE REMARKABLY OBSERVANT..
HE SAYS THAT CHILDREN ARE MUCH MORE AWARE OF WHAT IS GOING ON AROUND THEM THAN ADULTS THINK THEY ARE
I'M RATHER INCLINED TO AGREE WITH HIM, AREN'T YOU?
6-13
HUH?
SCHULZ

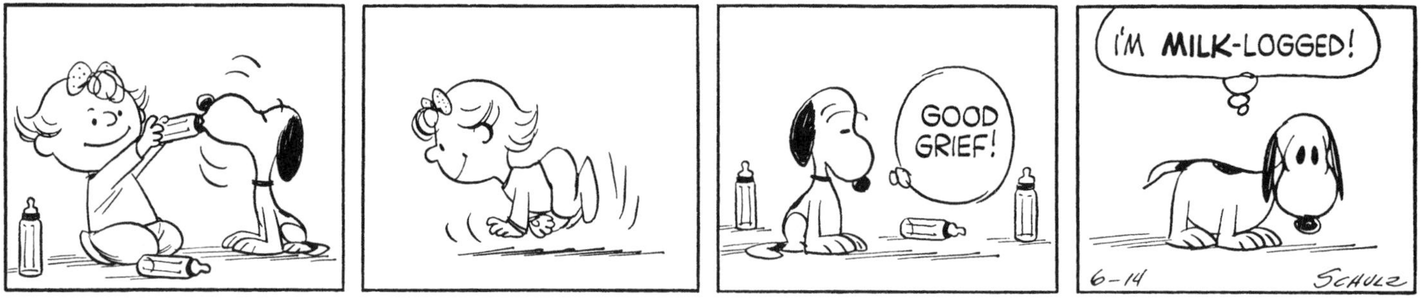
GOOD GRIEF!
I'M MILK-LOGGED!
6-14
SCHULZ

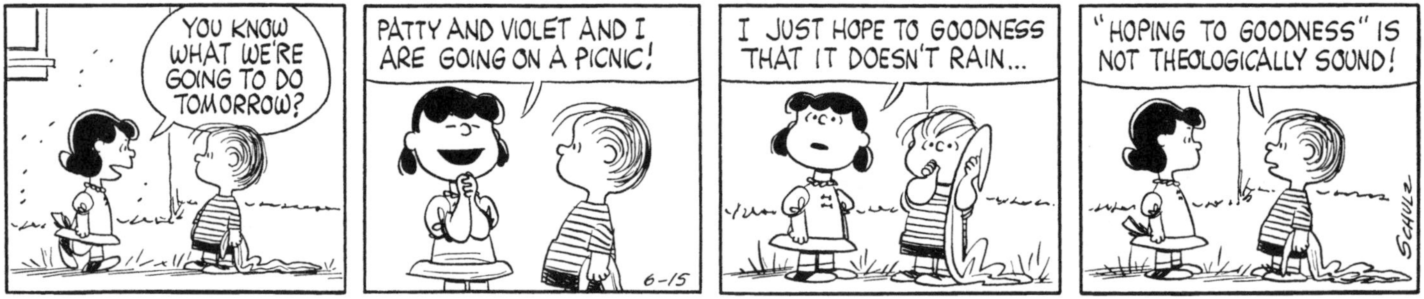
YOU KNOW WHAT WE'RE GOING TO DO TOMORROW?
PATTY AND VIOLET AND I ARE GOING ON A PICNIC!
6-15
I JUST HOPE TO GOODNESS THAT IT DOESN'T RAIN...
"HOPING TO GOODNESS" IS NOT THEOLOGICALLY SOUND!
SCHULZ

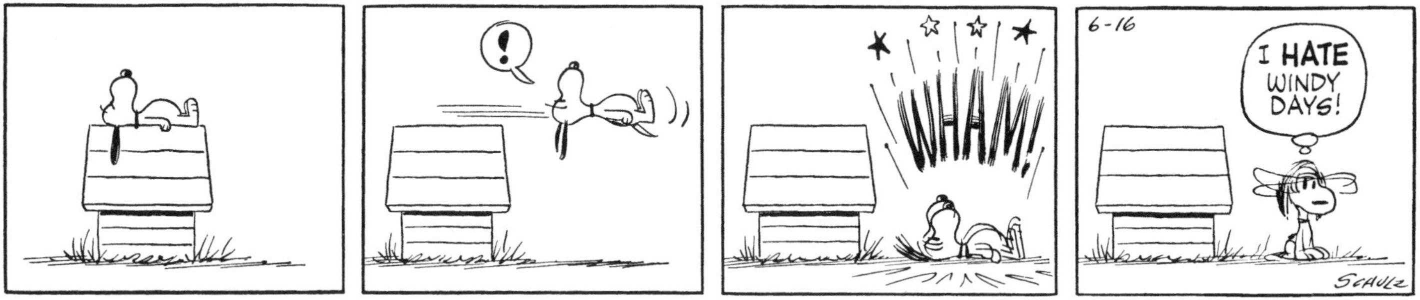
!
WHAM!
6-16
I HATE WINDY DAYS!
SCHULZ

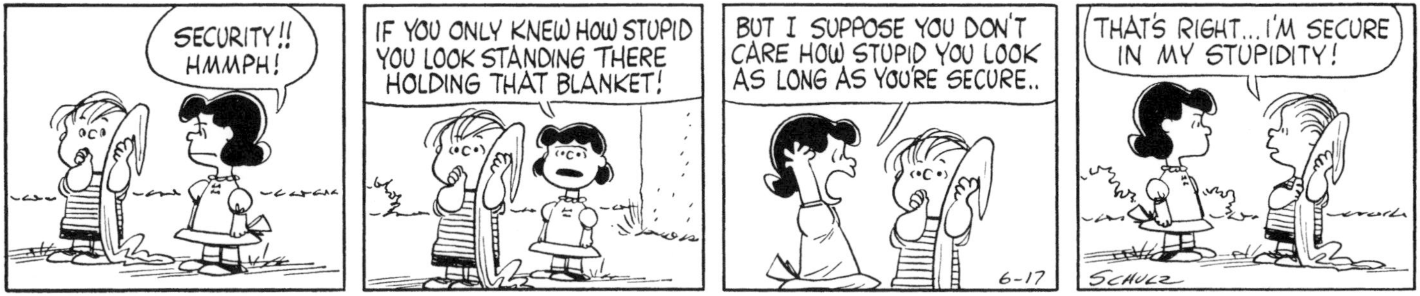
SECURITY!! HMMPH!
IF YOU ONLY KNEW HOW STUPID YOU LOOK STANDING THERE HOLDING THAT BLANKET!
BUT I SUPPOSE YOU DON'T CARE HOW STUPID YOU LOOK AS LONG AS YOU'RE SECURE..
6-17
THAT'S RIGHT... I'M SECURE IN MY STUPIDITY!
SCHULZ

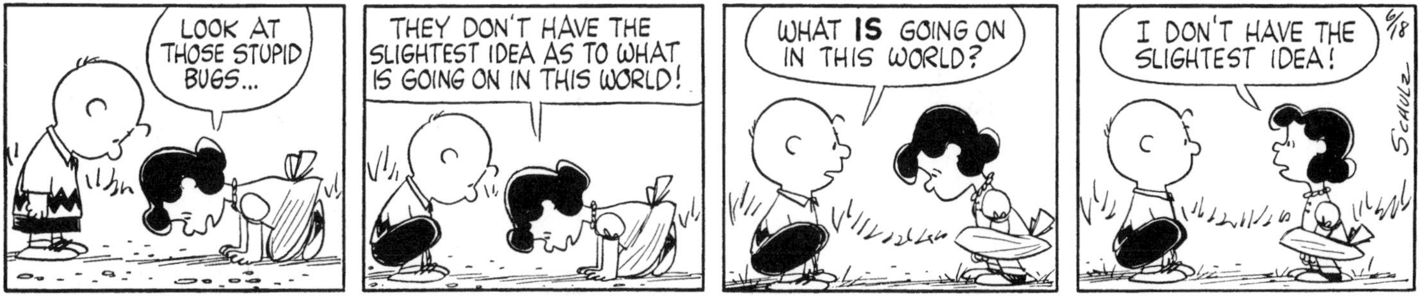
LOOK AT THOSE STUPID BUGS...
THEY DON'T HAVE THE SLIGHTEST IDEA AS TO WHAT IS GOING ON IN THIS WORLD!
WHAT IS GOING ON IN THIS WORLD?
I DON'T HAVE THE SLIGHTEST IDEA!
6/18
SCHULZ

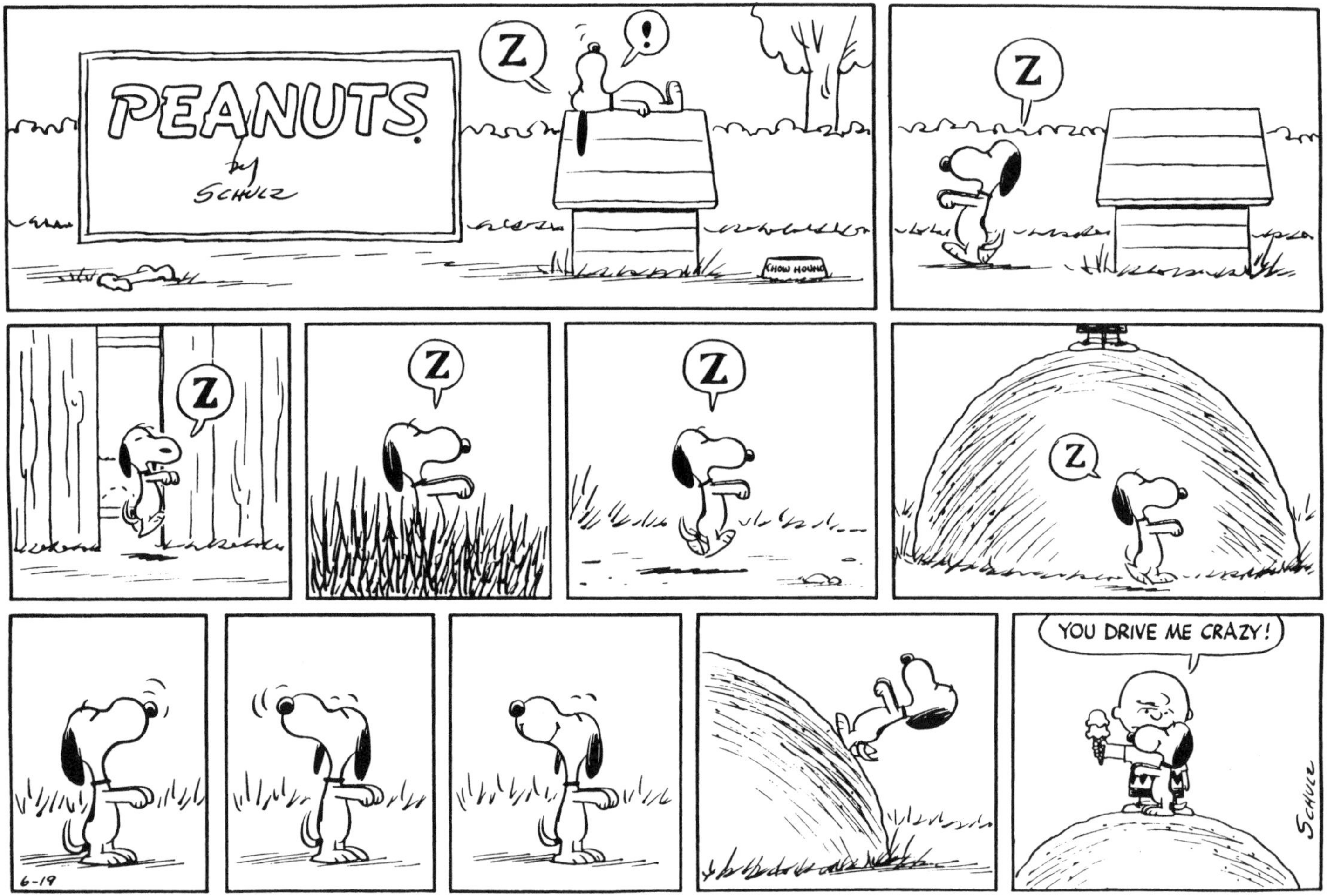
PEANUTS
by SCHULZ
Z
!
Z
Z
Z
Z
Z
6-19
YOU DRIVE ME CRAZY!
SCHULZ

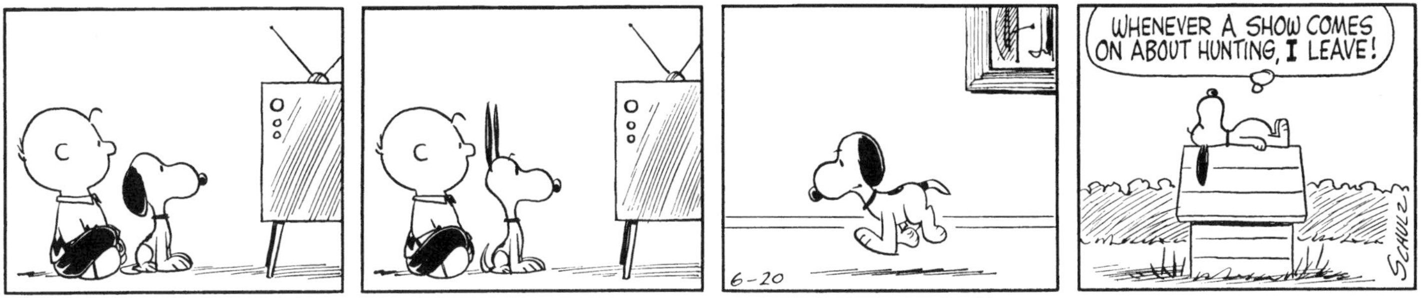
6-20
WHENEVER A SHOW COMES ON ABOUT HUNTING, I LEAVE!
SCHULZ

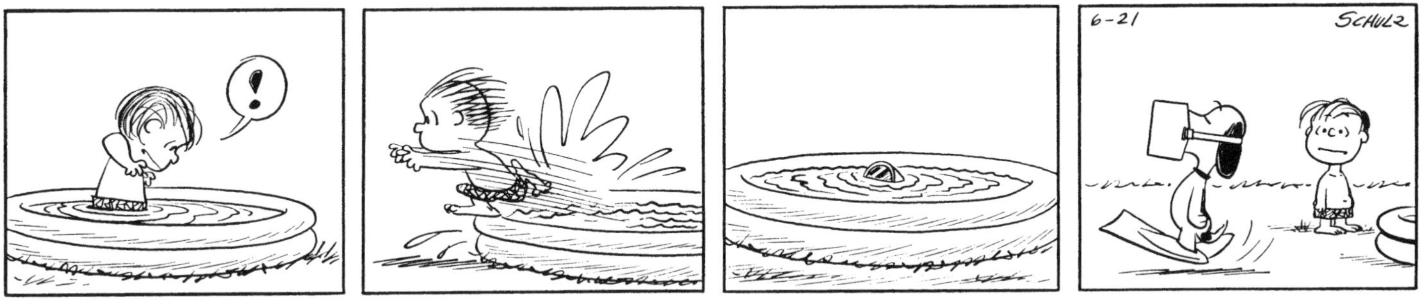
!
6-21
SCHULZ

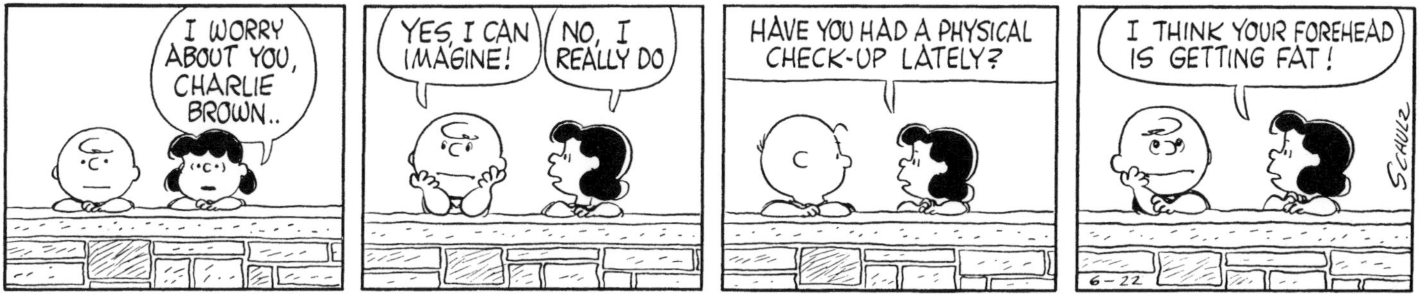
I WORRY ABOUT YOU, CHARLIE BROWN..
YES, I CAN IMAGINE!
NO, I REALLY DO
HAVE YOU HAD A PHYSICAL CHECK-UP LATELY?
I THINK YOUR FOREHEAD IS GETTING FAT!
SCHULZ
6-22

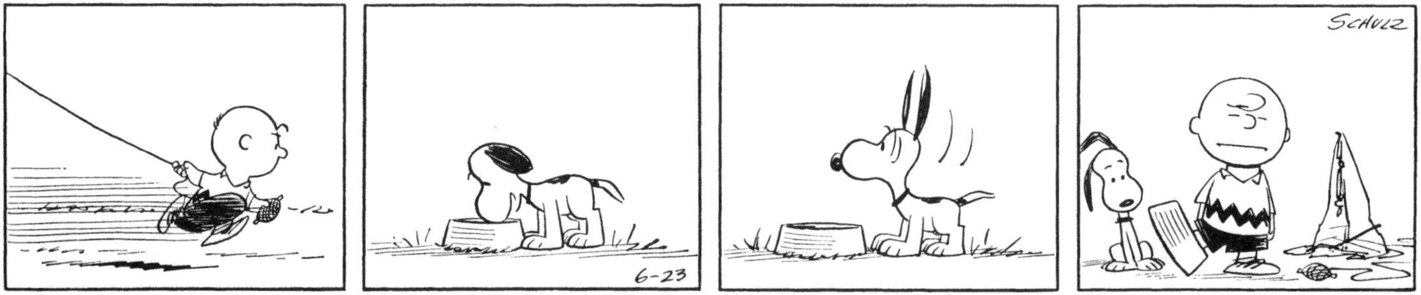
6-23
SCHULZ

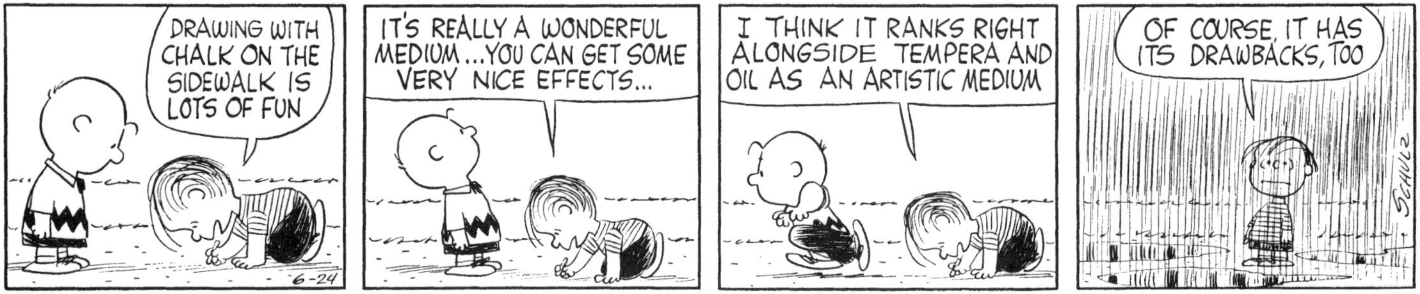
DRAWING WITH CHALK ON THE SIDEWALK IS LOTS OF FUN
6-24
IT'S REALLY A WONDERFUL MEDIUM...YOU CAN GET SOME VERY NICE EFFECTS...
I THINK IT RANKS RIGHT ALONGSIDE TEMPERA AND OIL AS AN ARTISTIC MEDIUM
OF COURSE, IT HAS ITS DRAWBACKS, TOO
SCHULZ

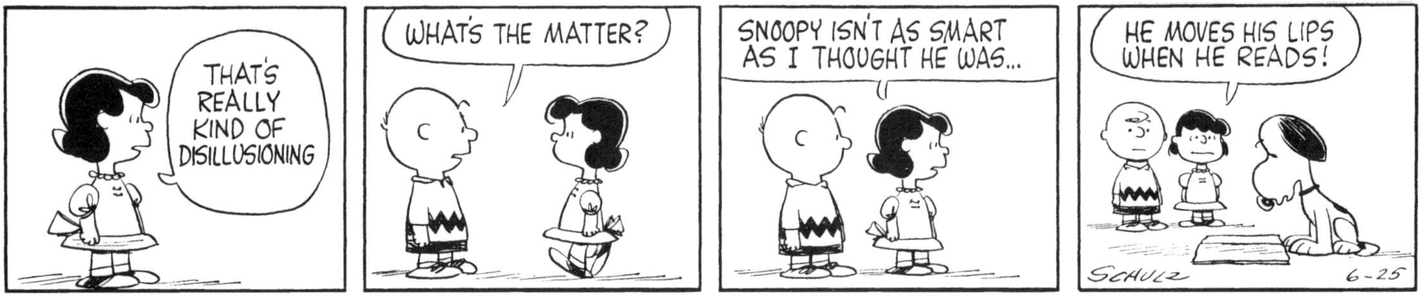
THAT'S REALLY KIND OF DISILLUSIONING
WHAT'S THE MATTER?
SNOOPY ISN'T AS SMART AS I THOUGHT HE WAS...
HE MOVES HIS LIPS WHEN HE READS!
SCHULZ
6-25

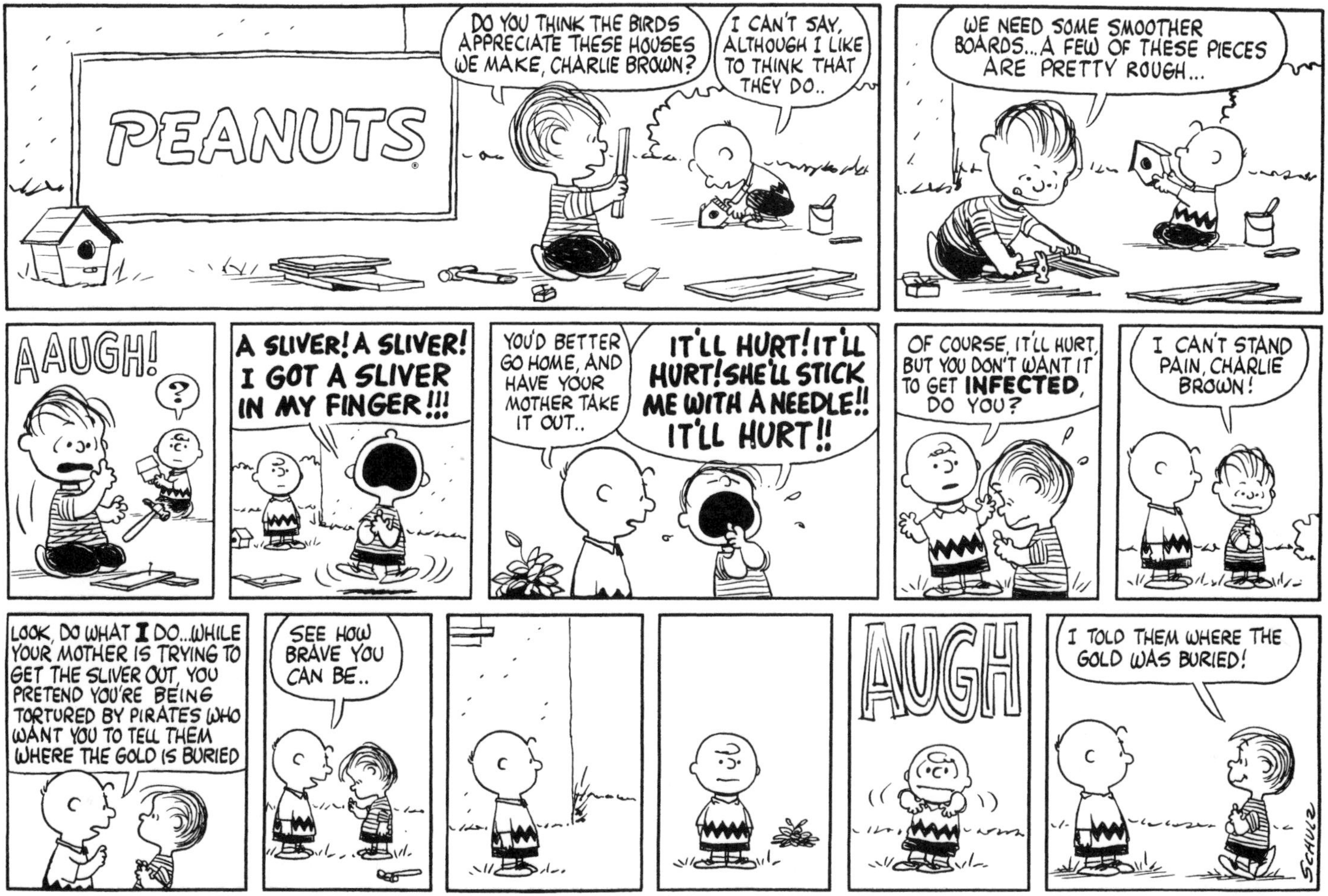
PEANUTS
DO YOU THINK THE BIRDS APPRECIATE THESE HOUSES WE MAKE, CHARLIE BROWN?
I CAN'T SAY, ALTHOUGH I LIKE TO THINK THAT THEY DO..
WE NEED SOME SMOOTHER BOARDS...A FEW OF THESE PIECES ARE PRETTY ROUGH...
AAUGH!
?
A SLIVER! A SLIVER! I GOT A SLIVER IN MY FINGER!!!
YOU'D BETTER GO HOME, AND HAVE YOUR MOTHER TAKE IT OUT..
IT'LL HURT! IT'LL HURT! SHE'LL STICK ME WITH A NEEDLE!! IT'LL HURT!!
OF COURSE, IT'LL HURT, BUT YOU DON'T WANT IT TO GET INFECTED, DO YOU?
I CAN'T STAND PAIN, CHARLIE BROWN!
LOOK, DO WHAT I DO...WHILE YOUR MOTHER IS TRYING TO GET THE SLIVER OUT, YOU PRETEND YOU'RE BEING TORTURED BY PIRATES WHO WANT YOU TO TELL THEM WHERE THE GOLD IS BURIED
SEE HOW BRAVE YOU CAN BE..
AUGH
I TOLD THEM WHERE THE GOLD WAS BURIED!
SCHULZ

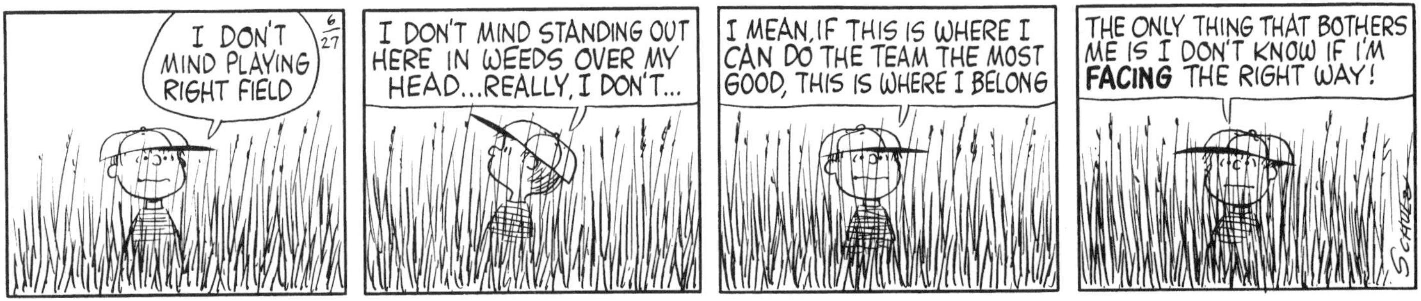
6/27
I DON'T MIND PLAYING RIGHT FIELD
I DON'T MIND STANDING OUT HERE IN WEEDS OVER MY HEAD...REALLY, I DON'T...
I MEAN, IF THIS IS WHERE I CAN DO THE TEAM THE MOST GOOD, THIS IS WHERE I BELONG
THE ONLY THING THAT BOTHERS ME IS I DON'T KNOW IF I'M **FACING** THE RIGHT WAY!
SCHULZ

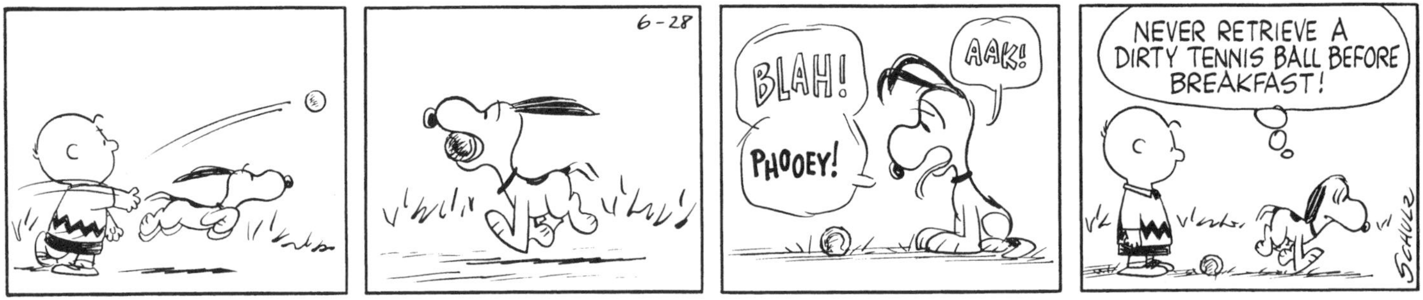
6-28
BLAH!
PHOOEY!
AAK!
NEVER RETRIEVE A DIRTY TENNIS BALL BEFORE BREAKFAST!
SCHULZ

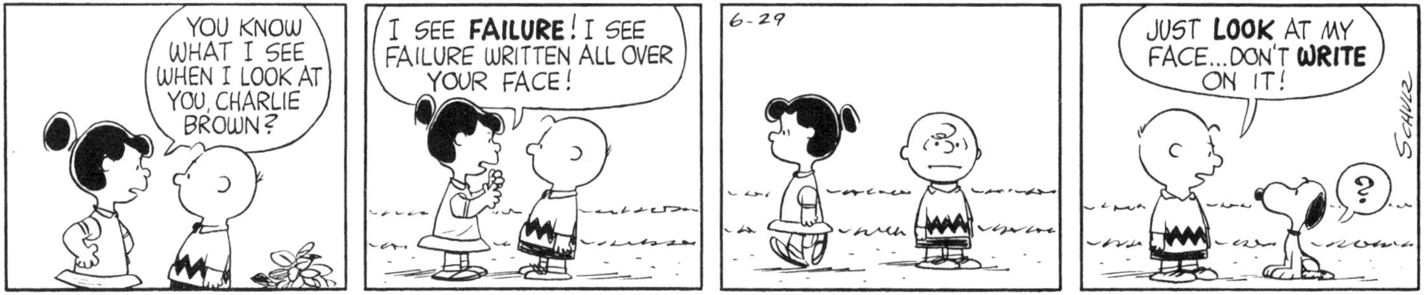
YOU KNOW WHAT I SEE WHEN I LOOK AT YOU, CHARLIE BROWN?
I SEE **FAILURE**! I SEE FAILURE WRITTEN ALL OVER YOUR FACE!
6-29
JUST **LOOK** AT MY FACE...DON'T **WRITE** ON IT!
SCHULZ
?

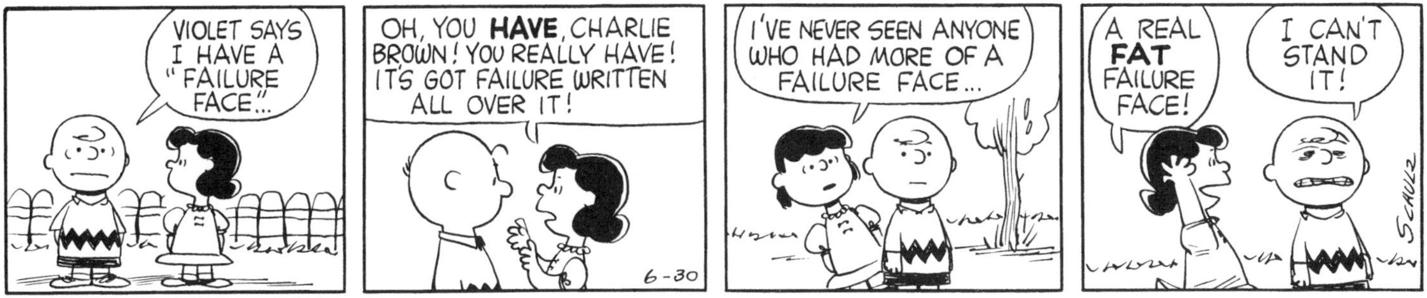
VIOLET SAYS I HAVE A "FAILURE FACE"...
OH, YOU **HAVE**, CHARLIE BROWN! YOU REALLY HAVE! IT'S GOT FAILURE WRITTEN ALL OVER IT!
6-30
I'VE NEVER SEEN ANYONE WHO HAD MORE OF A FAILURE FACE...
A REAL **FAT** FAILURE FACE!
I CAN'T STAND IT!
SCHULZ

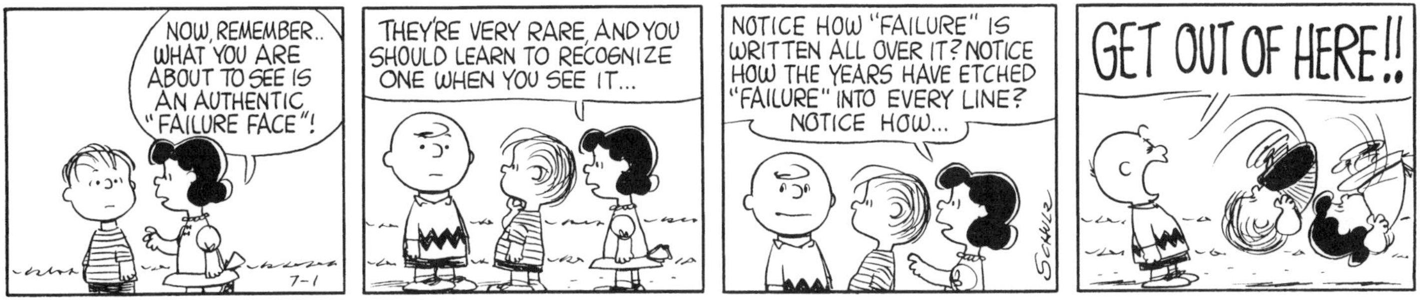
NOW, REMEMBER.. WHAT YOU ARE ABOUT TO SEE IS AN AUTHENTIC "FAILURE FACE"!
7-1
THEY'RE VERY RARE, AND YOU SHOULD LEARN TO RECOGNIZE ONE WHEN YOU SEE IT...
NOTICE HOW "FAILURE" IS WRITTEN ALL OVER IT? NOTICE HOW THE YEARS HAVE ETCHED "FAILURE" INTO EVERY LINE? NOTICE HOW...
SCHULZ
GET OUT OF HERE!!

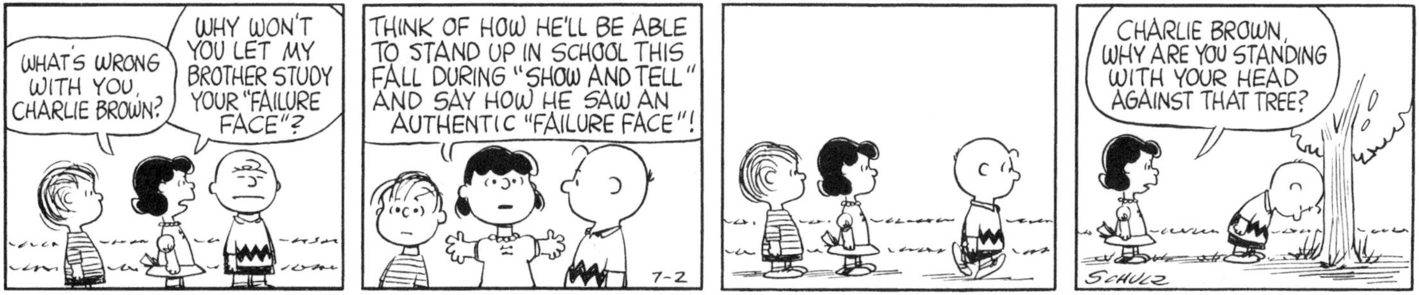
WHAT'S WRONG WITH YOU, CHARLIE BROWN?
WHY WON'T YOU LET MY BROTHER STUDY YOUR "FAILURE FACE"?
THINK OF HOW HE'LL BE ABLE TO STAND UP IN SCHOOL THIS FALL DURING "SHOW AND TELL" AND SAY HOW HE SAW AN AUTHENTIC "FAILURE FACE"!
7-2
CHARLIE BROWN, WHY ARE YOU STANDING WITH YOUR HEAD AGAINST THAT TREE?
SCHULZ

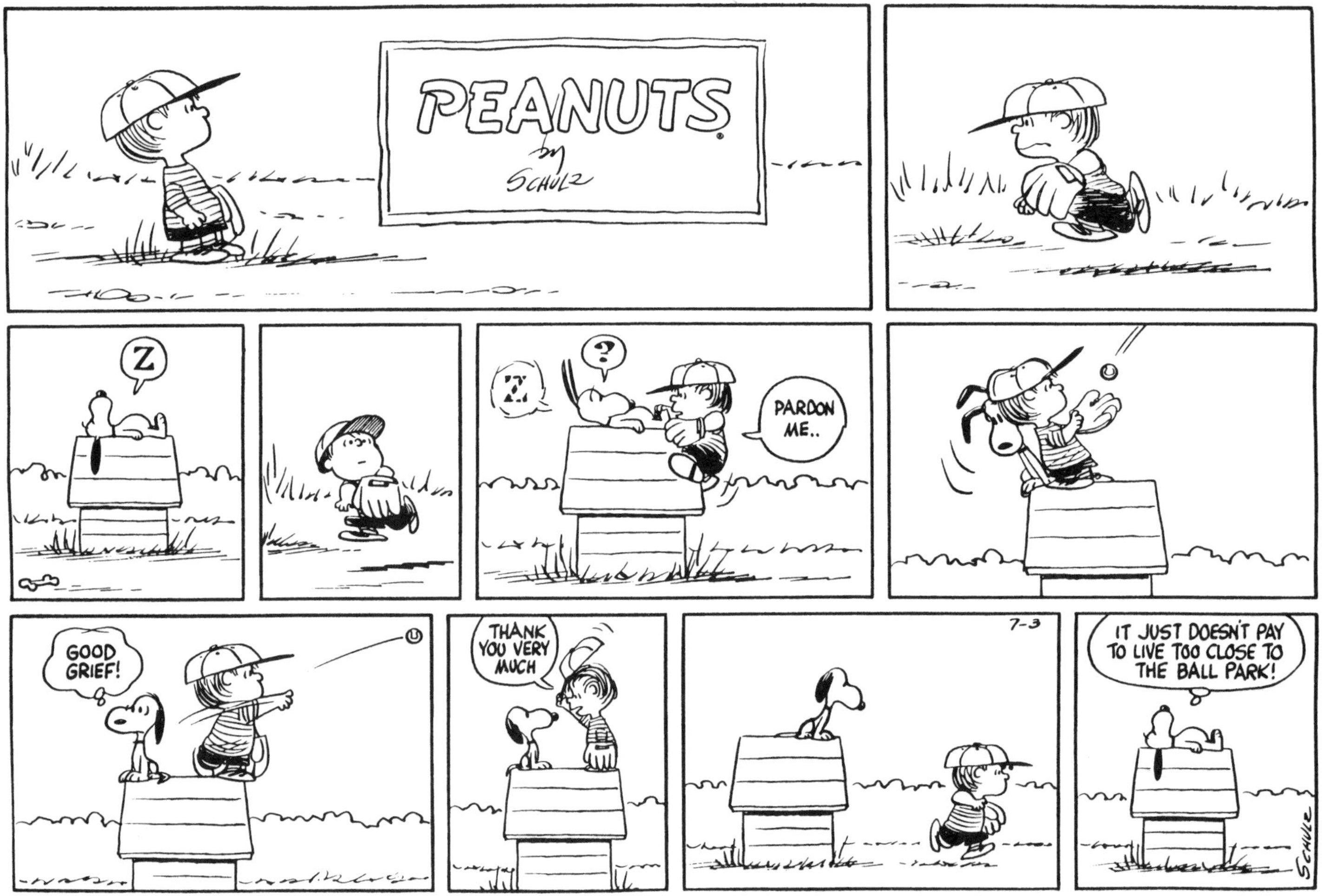
PEANUTS
by
SCHULZ
Z
Z
?
PARDON ME..
GOOD GRIEF!
THANK YOU VERY MUCH
7-3
IT JUST DOESN'T PAY TO LIVE TOO CLOSE TO THE BALL PARK!
SCHULZ

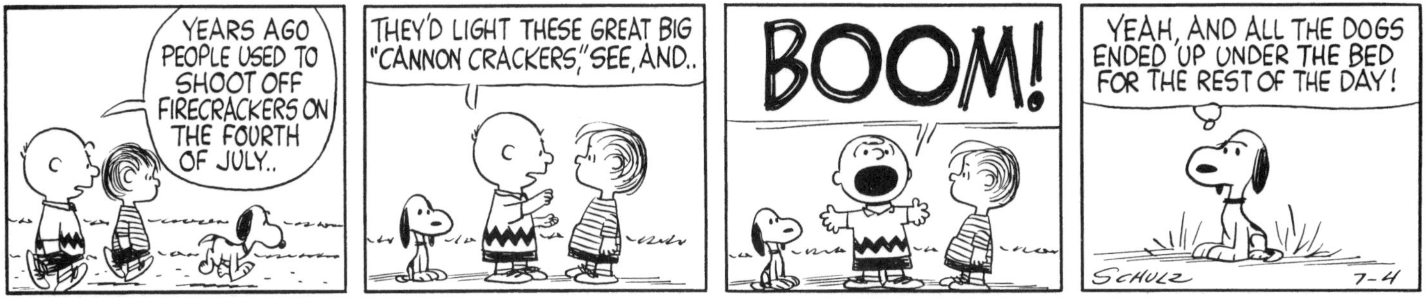
YEARS AGO PEOPLE USED TO SHOOT OFF FIRECRACKERS ON THE FOURTH OF JULY..
THEY'D LIGHT THESE GREAT BIG "CANNON CRACKERS," SEE, AND..
BOOM!
YEAH, AND ALL THE DOGS ENDED UP UNDER THE BED FOR THE REST OF THE DAY!
SCHULZ
7-4

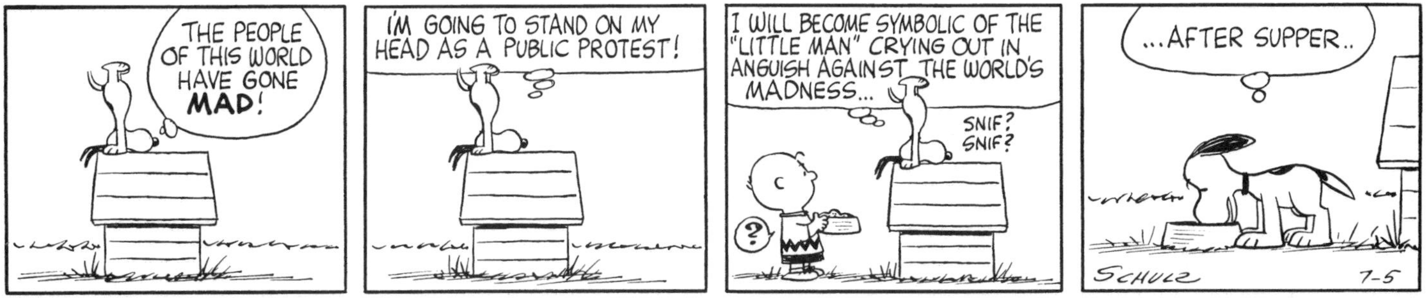
THE PEOPLE OF THIS WORLD HAVE GONE MAD!
I'M GOING TO STAND ON MY HEAD AS A PUBLIC PROTEST!
I WILL BECOME SYMBOLIC OF THE "LITTLE MAN" CRYING OUT IN ANGUISH AGAINST THE WORLD'S MADNESS...
SNIF? SNIF?
?
...AFTER SUPPER..
SCHULZ
7-5

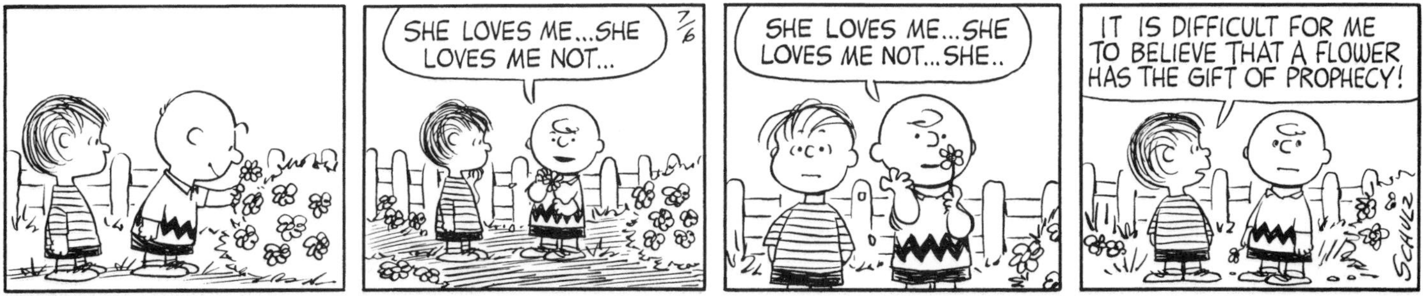
7/6
SHE LOVES ME...SHE LOVES ME NOT...
SHE LOVES ME...SHE LOVES ME NOT...SHE..
IT IS DIFFICULT FOR ME TO BELIEVE THAT A FLOWER HAS THE GIFT OF PROPHECY!
SCHULZ

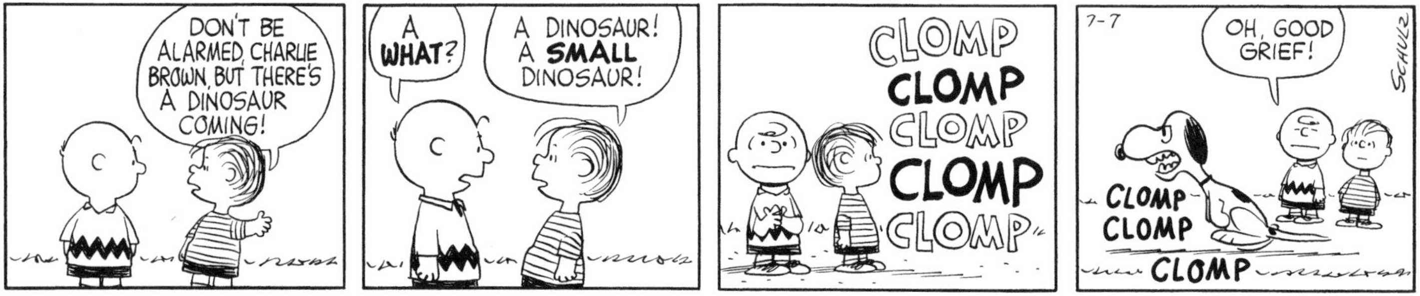
DON'T BE ALARMED, CHARLIE BROWN, BUT THERE'S A DINOSAUR COMING!
A WHAT?
A DINOSAUR! A SMALL DINOSAUR!
CLOMP CLOMP CLOMP CLOMP CLOMP
7-7
OH, GOOD GRIEF!
SCHULZ
CLOMP CLOMP CLOMP

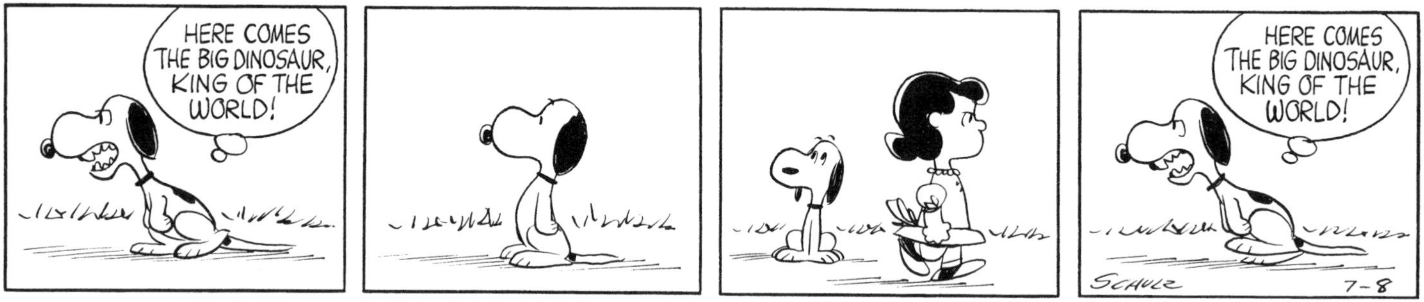
HERE COMES THE BIG DINOSAUR, KING OF THE WORLD!
HERE COMES THE BIG DINOSAUR, KING OF THE WORLD!
SCHULZ
7-8

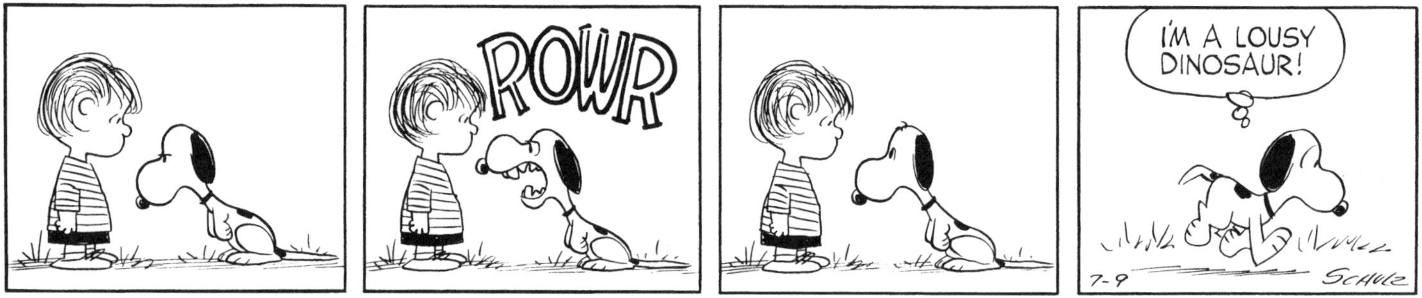
ROWR
I'M A LOUSY DINOSAUR!
7-9
SCHULZ

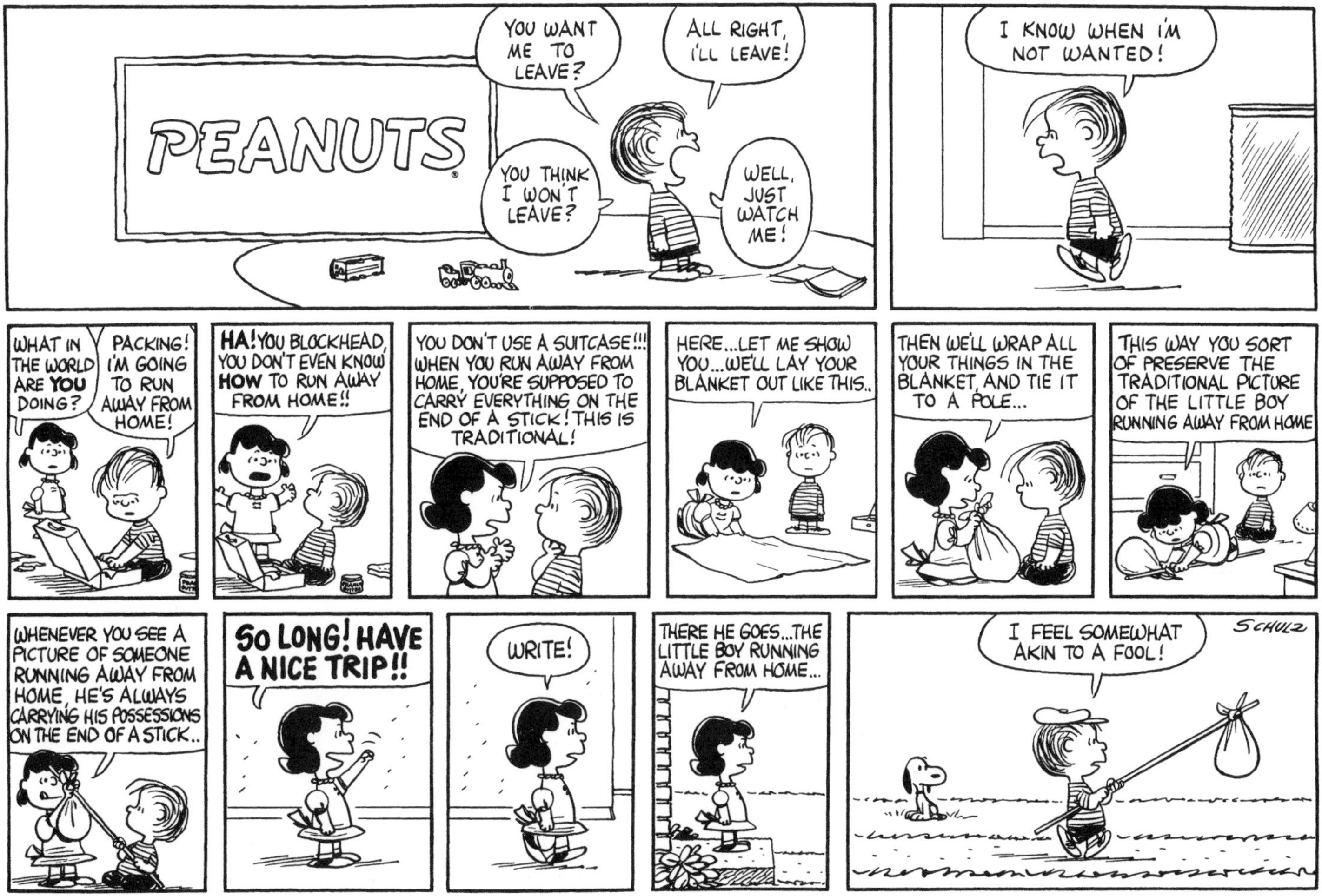
PEANUTS
YOU WANT ME TO LEAVE?
YOU THINK I WON'T LEAVE?
ALL RIGHT, I'LL LEAVE!
WELL, JUST WATCH ME!
I KNOW WHEN I'M NOT WANTED!
WHAT IN THE WORLD ARE YOU DOING?
PACKING! I'M GOING TO RUN AWAY FROM HOME!
HA! YOU BLOCKHEAD, YOU DON'T EVEN KNOW HOW TO RUN AWAY FROM HOME!!
YOU DON'T USE A SUITCASE!!! WHEN YOU RUN AWAY FROM HOME, YOU'RE SUPPOSED TO CARRY EVERYTHING ON THE END OF A STICK! THIS IS TRADITIONAL!
HERE...LET ME SHOW YOU...WE'LL LAY YOUR BLANKET OUT LIKE THIS..
THEN WE'LL WRAP ALL YOUR THINGS IN THE BLANKET, AND TIE IT TO A POLE...
THIS WAY YOU SORT OF PRESERVE THE TRADITIONAL PICTURE OF THE LITTLE BOY RUNNING AWAY FROM HOME
WHENEVER YOU SEE A PICTURE OF SOMEONE RUNNING AWAY FROM HOME, HE'S ALWAYS CARRYING HIS POSSESSIONS ON THE END OF A STICK..
SO LONG! HAVE A NICE TRIP!!
WRITE!
THERE HE GOES...THE LITTLE BOY RUNNING AWAY FROM HOME...
I FEEL SOMEWHAT AKIN TO A FOOL!
SCHULZ

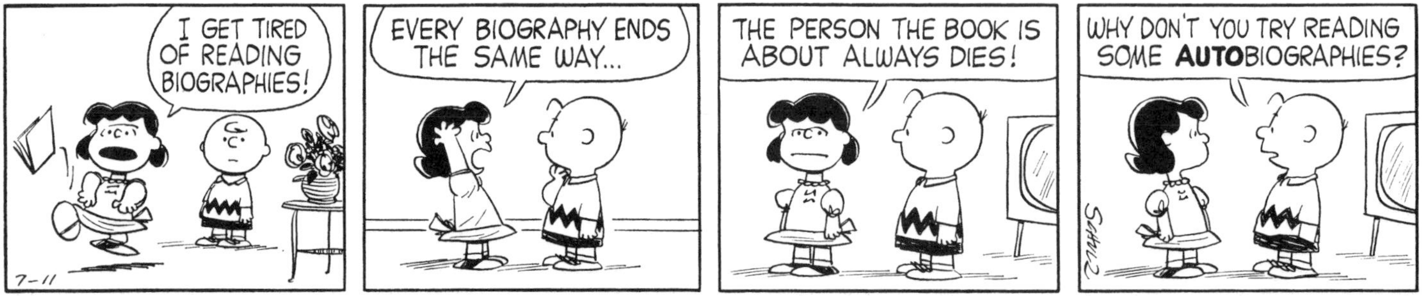
I GET TIRED OF READING BIOGRAPHIES!
EVERY BIOGRAPHY ENDS THE SAME WAY...
THE PERSON THE BOOK IS ABOUT ALWAYS DIES!
WHY DON'T YOU TRY READING SOME **AUTO**BIOGRAPHIES?

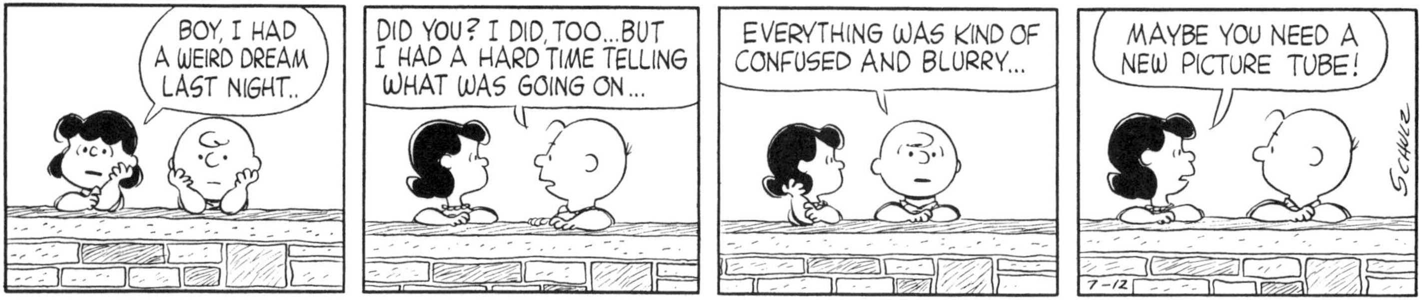
BOY, I HAD A WEIRD DREAM LAST NIGHT..
DID YOU? I DID, TOO...BUT I HAD A HARD TIME TELLING WHAT WAS GOING ON...
EVERYTHING WAS KIND OF CONFUSED AND BLURRY...
MAYBE YOU NEED A NEW PICTURE TUBE!

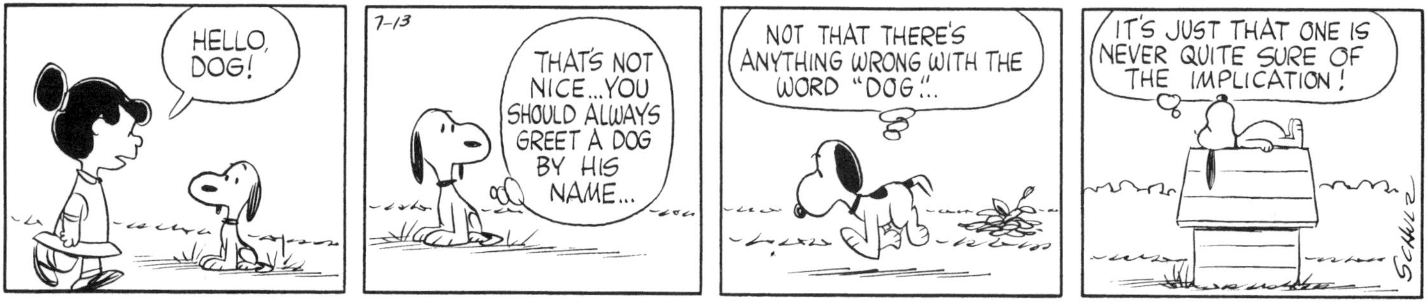
HELLO, DOG!
THAT'S NOT NICE...YOU SHOULD ALWAYS GREET A DOG BY HIS NAME...
NOT THAT THERE'S ANYTHING WRONG WITH THE WORD "DOG"!..
IT'S JUST THAT ONE IS NEVER QUITE SURE OF THE IMPLICATION!

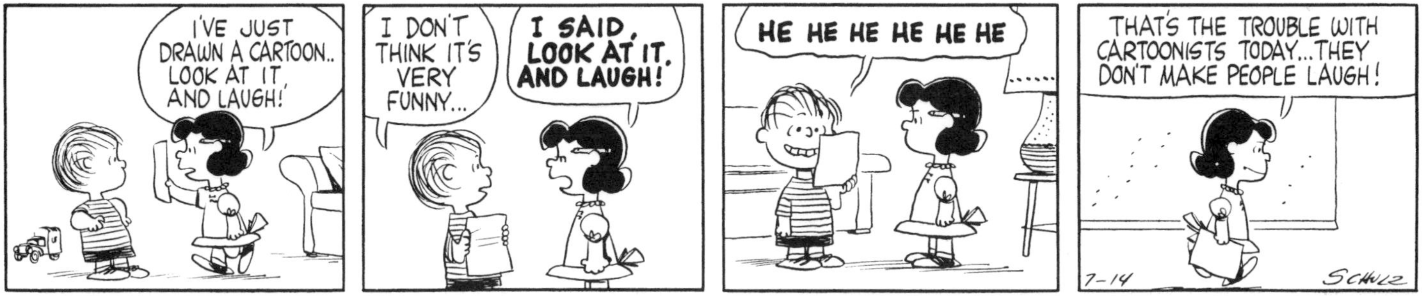
I'VE JUST DRAWN A CARTOON.. LOOK AT IT, AND LAUGH!
I DON'T THINK IT'S VERY FUNNY...
I SAID, LOOK AT IT, AND LAUGH!
HE HE HE HE HE HE
THAT'S THE TROUBLE WITH CARTOONISTS TODAY...THEY DON'T MAKE PEOPLE LAUGH!
7-14
SCHULZ

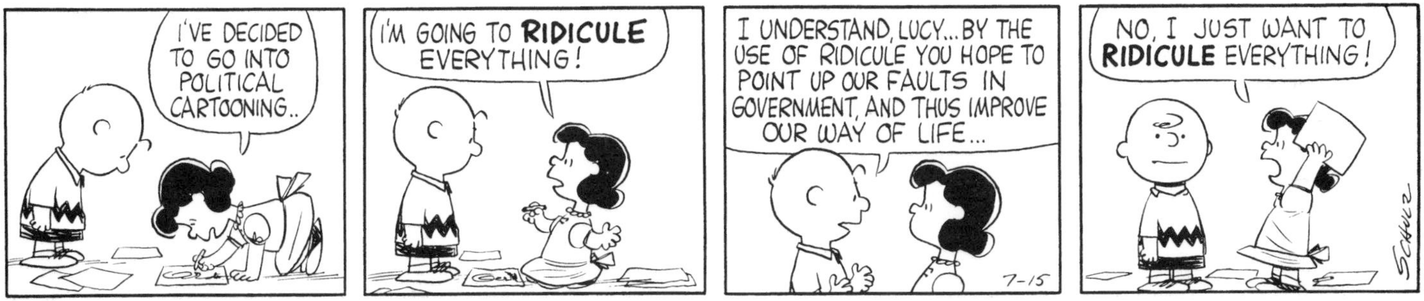
I'VE DECIDED TO GO INTO POLITICAL CARTOONING..
I'M GOING TO RIDICULE EVERYTHING!
I UNDERSTAND, LUCY...BY THE USE OF RIDICULE YOU HOPE TO POINT UP OUR FAULTS IN GOVERNMENT, AND THUS IMPROVE OUR WAY OF LIFE...
7-15
NO, I JUST WANT TO RIDICULE EVERYTHING!
SCHULZ

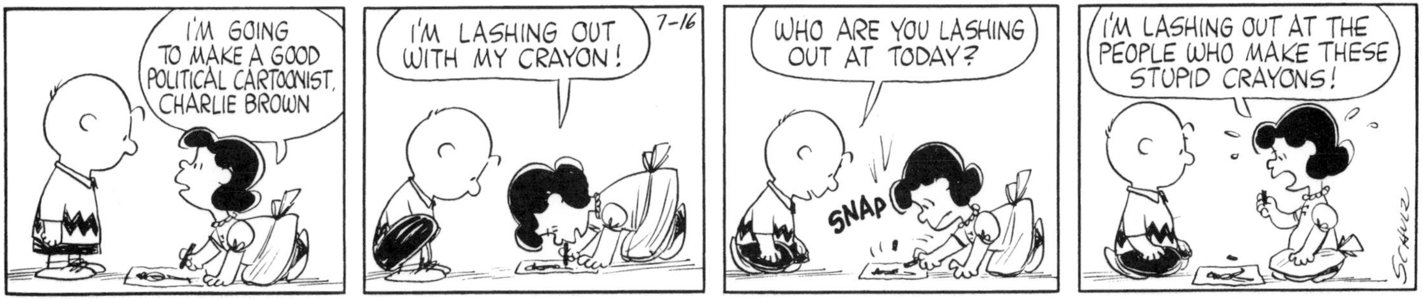
I'M GOING TO MAKE A GOOD POLITICAL CARTOONIST, CHARLIE BROWN
I'M LASHING OUT WITH MY CRAYON!
7-16
WHO ARE YOU LASHING OUT AT TODAY?
SNAP
I'M LASHING OUT AT THE PEOPLE WHO MAKE THESE STUPID CRAYONS!
SCHULZ

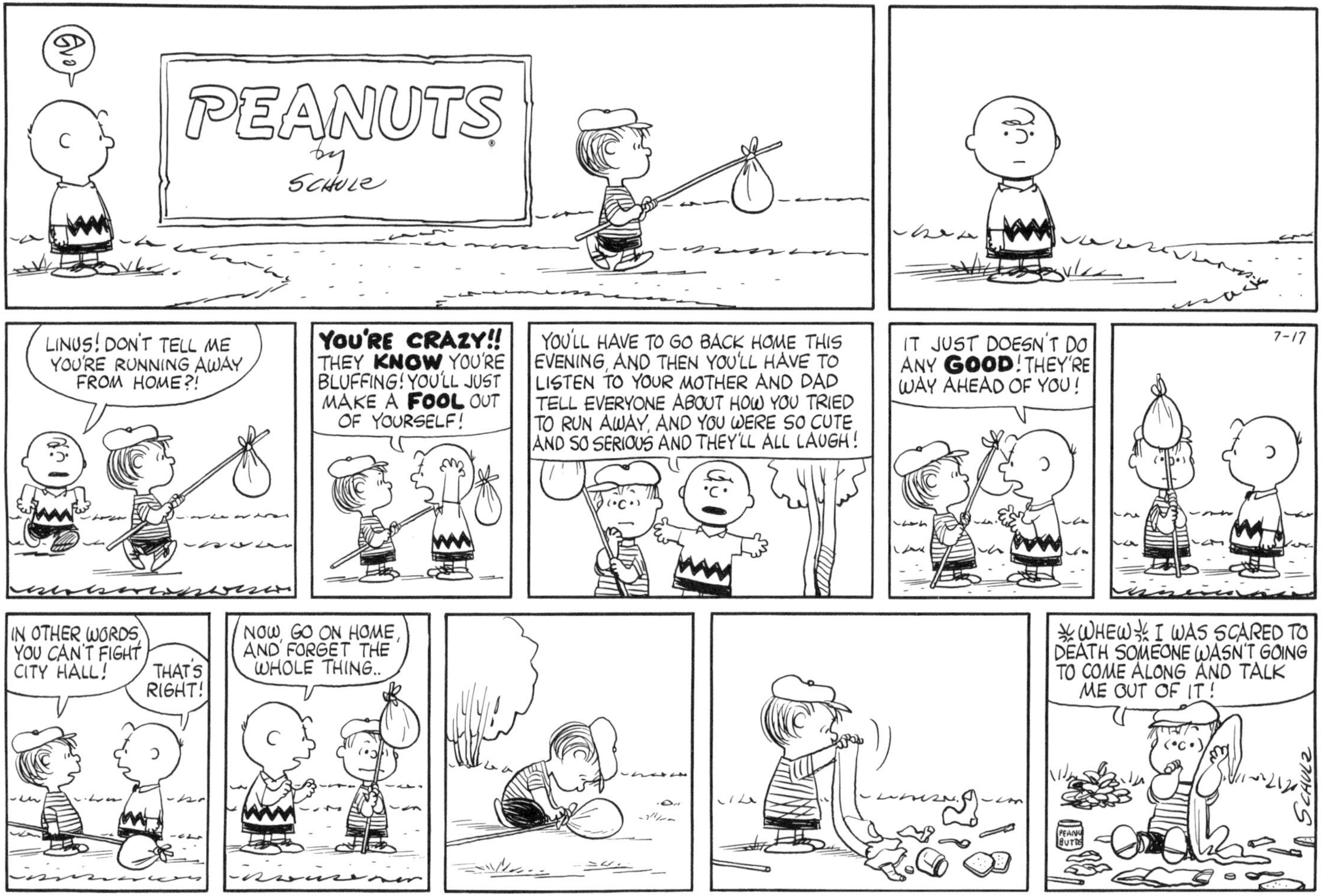
PEANUTS
by
SCHULZ
LINUS! DON'T TELL ME YOU'RE RUNNING AWAY FROM HOME?!
YOU'RE CRAZY!! THEY KNOW YOU'RE BLUFFING! YOU'LL JUST MAKE A FOOL OUT OF YOURSELF!
YOU'LL HAVE TO GO BACK HOME THIS EVENING, AND THEN YOU'LL HAVE TO LISTEN TO YOUR MOTHER AND DAD TELL EVERYONE ABOUT HOW YOU TRIED TO RUN AWAY, AND YOU WERE SO CUTE AND SO SERIOUS AND THEY'LL ALL LAUGH!
IT JUST DOESN'T DO ANY GOOD! THEY'RE WAY AHEAD OF YOU!
7-17
IN OTHER WORDS YOU CAN'T FIGHT CITY HALL!
THAT'S RIGHT!
NOW, GO ON HOME, AND FORGET THE WHOLE THING..
WHEW! I WAS SCARED TO DEATH SOMEONE WASN'T GOING TO COME ALONG AND TALK ME OUT OF IT!
PEANU BUTTE
SCHULZ

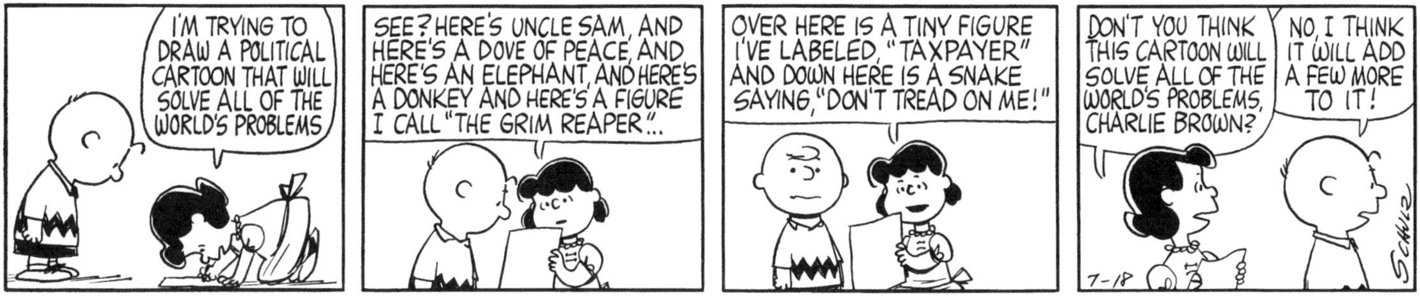
I'M TRYING TO DRAW A POLITICAL CARTOON THAT WILL SOLVE ALL OF THE WORLD'S PROBLEMS
SEE? HERE'S UNCLE SAM, AND HERE'S A DOVE OF PEACE, AND HERE'S AN ELEPHANT, AND HERE'S A DONKEY AND HERE'S A FIGURE I CALL "THE GRIM REAPER"...
OVER HERE IS A TINY FIGURE I'VE LABELED, "TAXPAYER" AND DOWN HERE IS A SNAKE SAYING, "DON'T TREAD ON ME!"
DON'T YOU THINK THIS CARTOON WILL SOLVE ALL OF THE WORLD'S PROBLEMS, CHARLIE BROWN?
NO, I THINK IT WILL ADD A FEW MORE TO IT!
7-18
SCHULZ

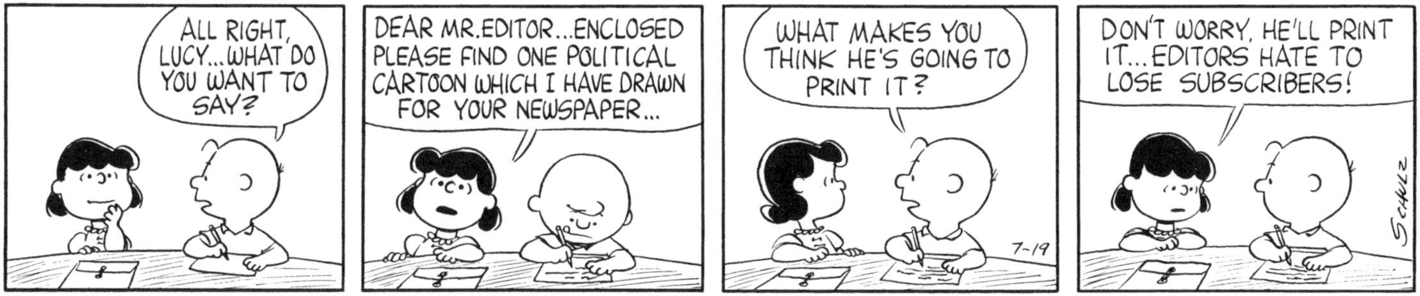
ALL RIGHT, LUCY...WHAT DO YOU WANT TO SAY?
DEAR MR. EDITOR...ENCLOSED PLEASE FIND ONE POLITICAL CARTOON WHICH I HAVE DRAWN FOR YOUR NEWSPAPER...
WHAT MAKES YOU THINK HE'S GOING TO PRINT IT?
7-19
DON'T WORRY, HE'LL PRINT IT... EDITORS HATE TO LOSE SUBSCRIBERS!
SCHULZ

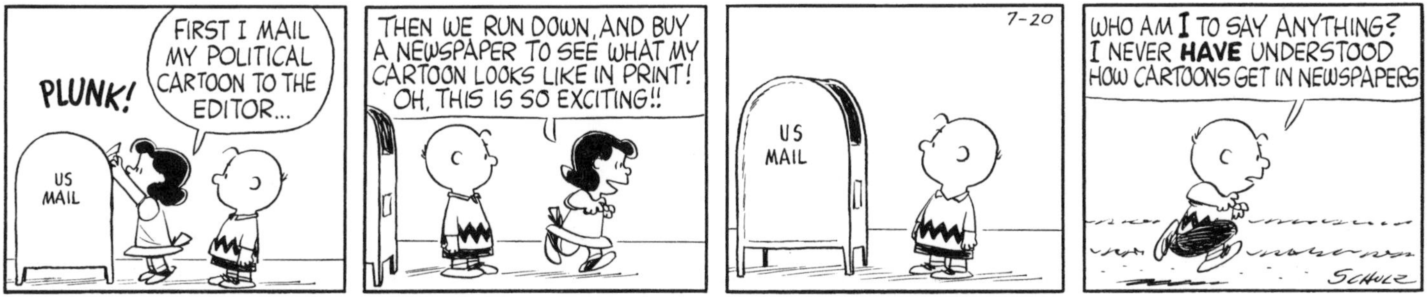
PLUNK!
FIRST I MAIL MY POLITICAL CARTOON TO THE EDITOR...
US MAIL
THEN WE RUN DOWN, AND BUY A NEWSPAPER TO SEE WHAT MY CARTOON LOOKS LIKE IN PRINT! OH, THIS IS SO EXCITING!!
7-20
US MAIL
WHO AM I TO SAY ANYTHING? I NEVER HAVE UNDERSTOOD HOW CARTOONS GET IN NEWSPAPERS
SCHULZ

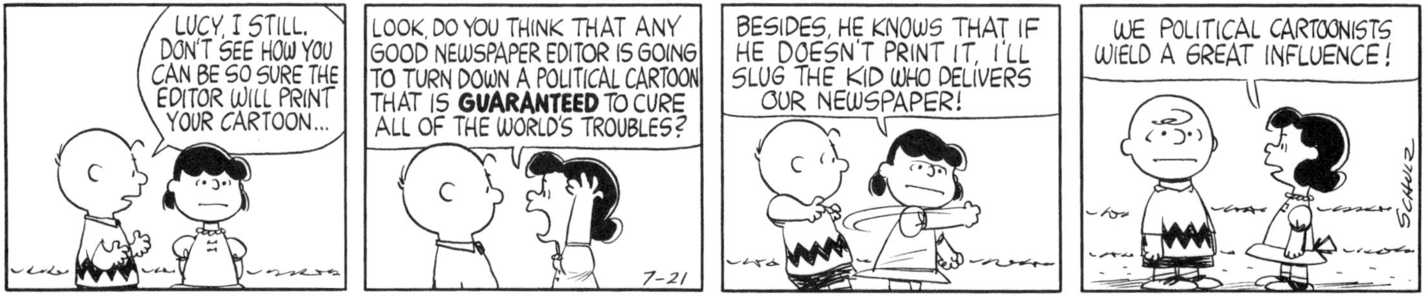
LUCY, I STILL DON'T SEE HOW YOU CAN BE SO SURE THE EDITOR WILL PRINT YOUR CARTOON...
LOOK, DO YOU THINK THAT ANY GOOD NEWSPAPER EDITOR IS GOING TO TURN DOWN A POLITICAL CARTOON THAT IS **GUARANTEED** TO CURE ALL OF THE WORLD'S TROUBLES?
7-21
BESIDES, HE KNOWS THAT IF HE DOESN'T PRINT IT, I'LL SLUG THE KID WHO DELIVERS OUR NEWSPAPER!
WE POLITICAL CARTOONISTS WIELD A GREAT INFLUENCE!
SCHULZ

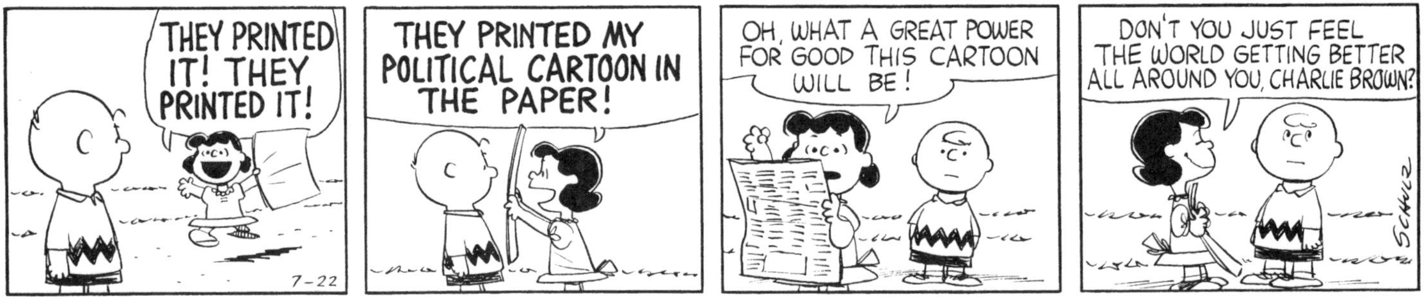
THEY PRINTED IT! THEY PRINTED IT!
7-22
THEY PRINTED MY POLITICAL CARTOON IN THE PAPER!
OH, WHAT A GREAT POWER FOR GOOD THIS CARTOON WILL BE!
DON'T YOU JUST FEEL THE WORLD GETTING BETTER ALL AROUND YOU, CHARLIE BROWN?
SCHULZ

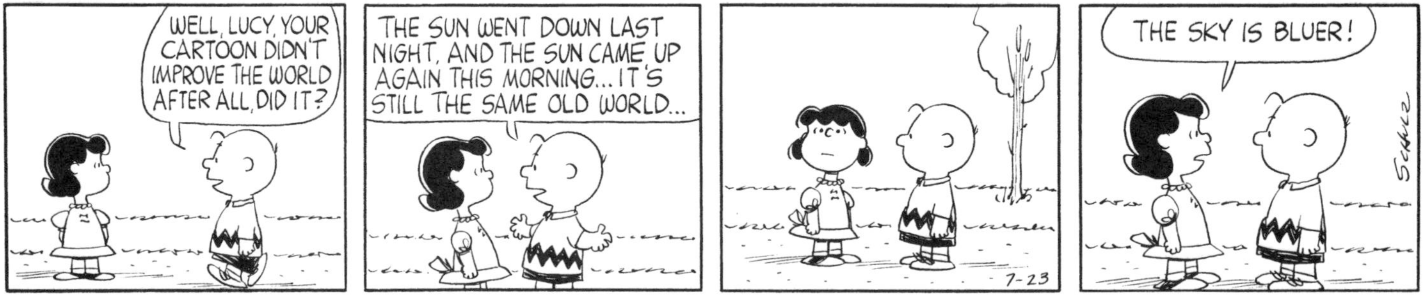
WELL, LUCY, YOUR CARTOON DIDN'T IMPROVE THE WORLD AFTER ALL, DID IT?
THE SUN WENT DOWN LAST NIGHT, AND THE SUN CAME UP AGAIN THIS MORNING... IT'S STILL THE SAME OLD WORLD...
7-23
THE SKY IS BLUER!
SCHULZ

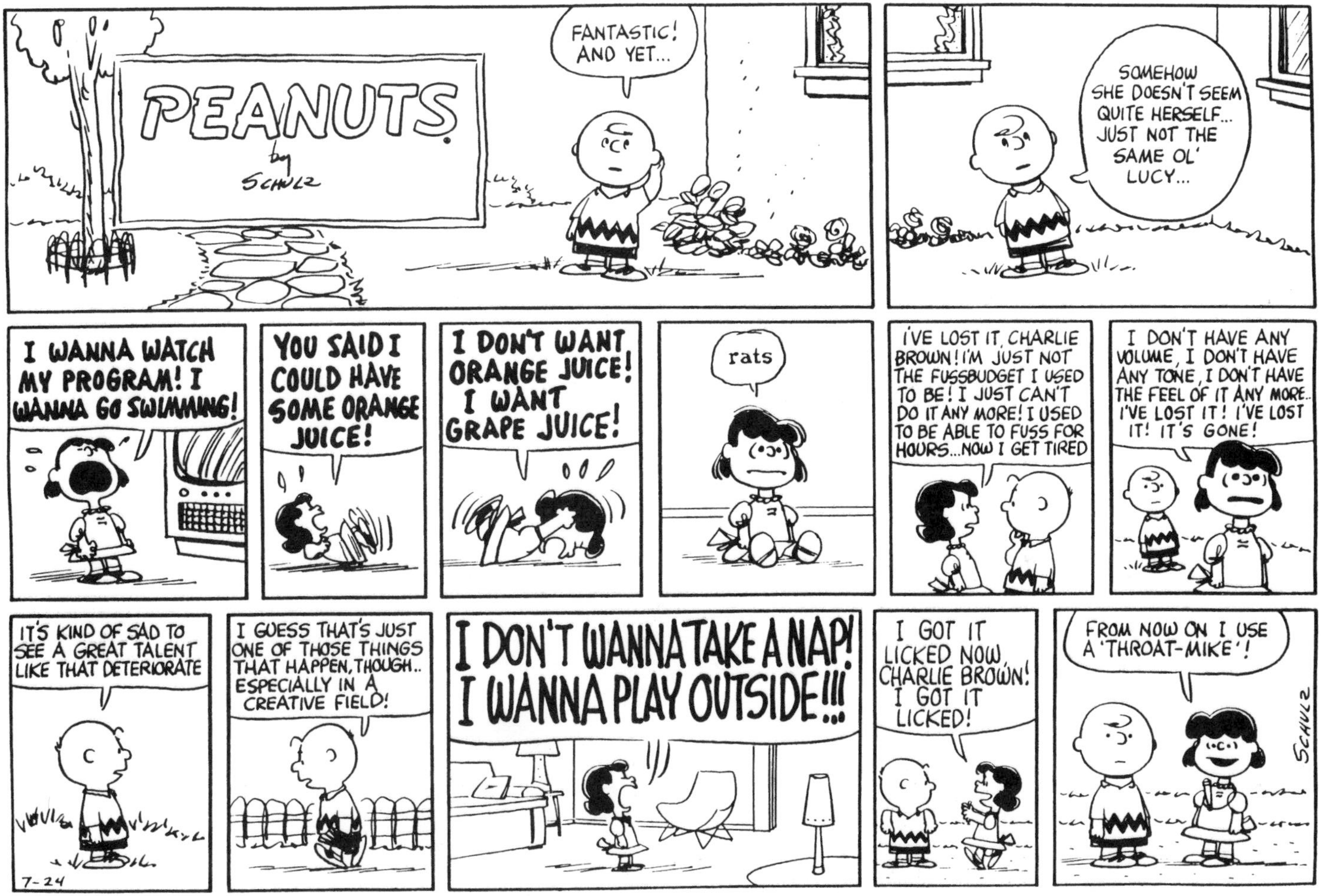
PEANUTS
by SCHULZ
FANTASTIC! AND YET...
SOMEHOW SHE DOESN'T SEEM QUITE HERSELF... JUST NOT THE SAME OL' LUCY...
I WANNA WATCH MY PROGRAM! I WANNA GO SWIMMING!
YOU SAID I COULD HAVE SOME ORANGE JUICE!
I DON'T WANT ORANGE JUICE! I WANT GRAPE JUICE!
rats
I'VE LOST IT, CHARLIE BROWN! I'M JUST NOT THE FUSSBUDGET I USED TO BE! I JUST CAN'T DO IT ANY MORE! I USED TO BE ABLE TO FUSS FOR HOURS...NOW I GET TIRED
I DON'T HAVE ANY VOLUME, I DON'T HAVE ANY TONE, I DON'T HAVE THE FEEL OF IT ANY MORE.. I'VE LOST IT! I'VE LOST IT! IT'S GONE!
IT'S KIND OF SAD TO SEE A GREAT TALENT LIKE THAT DETERIORATE
7-24
I GUESS THAT'S JUST ONE OF THOSE THINGS THAT HAPPEN, THOUGH.. ESPECIALLY IN A CREATIVE FIELD!
I DON'T WANNA TAKE A NAP! I WANNA PLAY OUTSIDE!!!
I GOT IT LICKED NOW, CHARLIE BROWN! I GOT IT LICKED!
FROM NOW ON I USE A 'THROAT-MIKE'!
SCHULZ

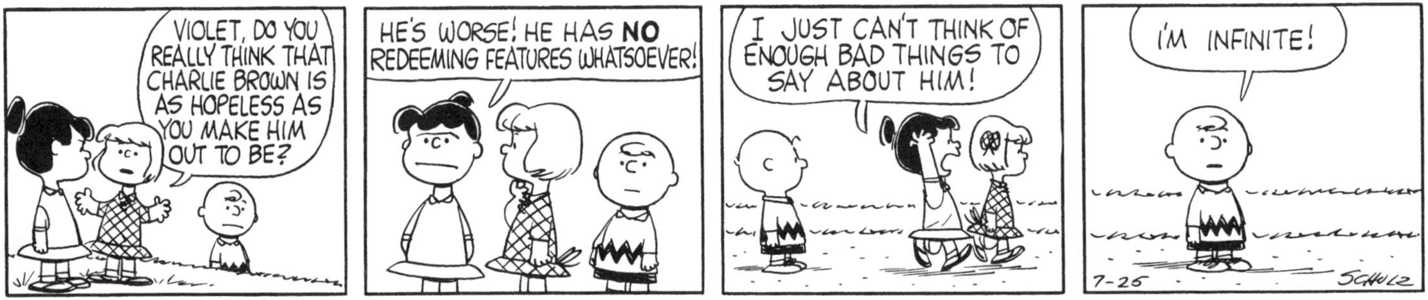
VIOLET, DO YOU REALLY THINK THAT CHARLIE BROWN IS AS HOPELESS AS YOU MAKE HIM OUT TO BE?
HE'S WORSE! HE HAS **NO** REDEEMING FEATURES WHATSOEVER!
I JUST CAN'T THINK OF ENOUGH BAD THINGS TO SAY ABOUT HIM!
I'M INFINITE!
7-25
SCHULZ

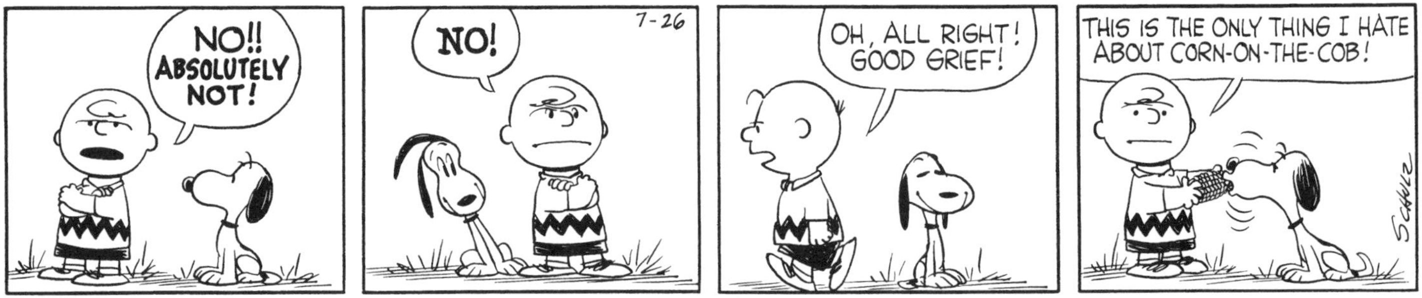
NO!! ABSOLUTELY NOT!
NO!
7-26
OH, ALL RIGHT! GOOD GRIEF!
THIS IS THE ONLY THING I HATE ABOUT CORN-ON-THE-COB!
SCHULZ

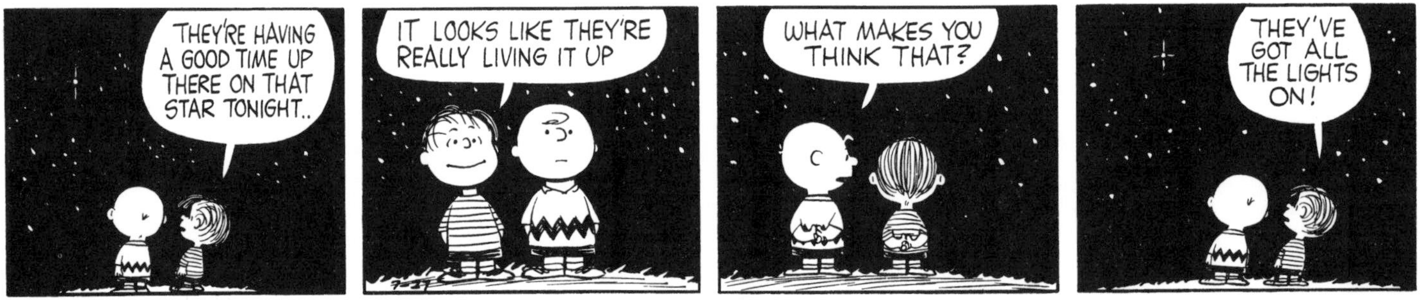
THEY'RE HAVING A GOOD TIME UP THERE ON THAT STAR TONIGHT..
IT LOOKS LIKE THEY'RE REALLY LIVING IT UP
WHAT MAKES YOU THINK THAT?
THEY'VE GOT ALL THE LIGHTS ON!

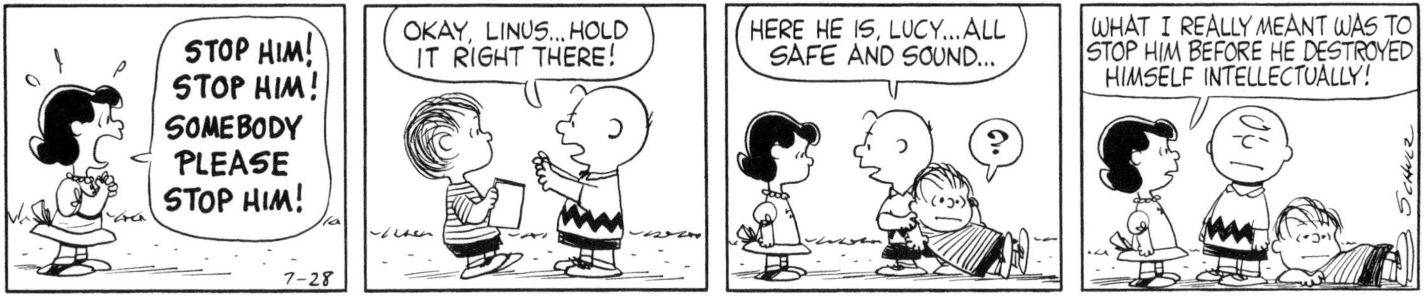
STOP HIM! STOP HIM! SOMEBODY PLEASE STOP HIM!
7-28
OKAY, LINUS...HOLD IT RIGHT THERE!
HERE HE IS, LUCY...ALL SAFE AND SOUND...
?
WHAT I REALLY MEANT WAS TO STOP HIM BEFORE HE DESTROYED HIMSELF INTELLECTUALLY!
SCHULZ

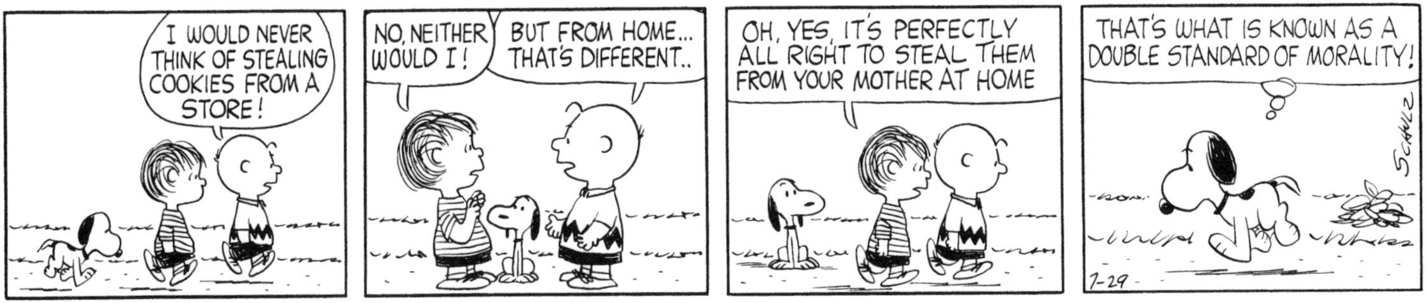
I WOULD NEVER THINK OF STEALING COOKIES FROM A STORE!
NO, NEITHER WOULD I!
BUT FROM HOME... THAT'S DIFFERENT..
OH, YES, IT'S PERFECTLY ALL RIGHT TO STEAL THEM FROM YOUR MOTHER AT HOME
THAT'S WHAT IS KNOWN AS A DOUBLE STANDARD OF MORALITY!
SCHULZ
7-29

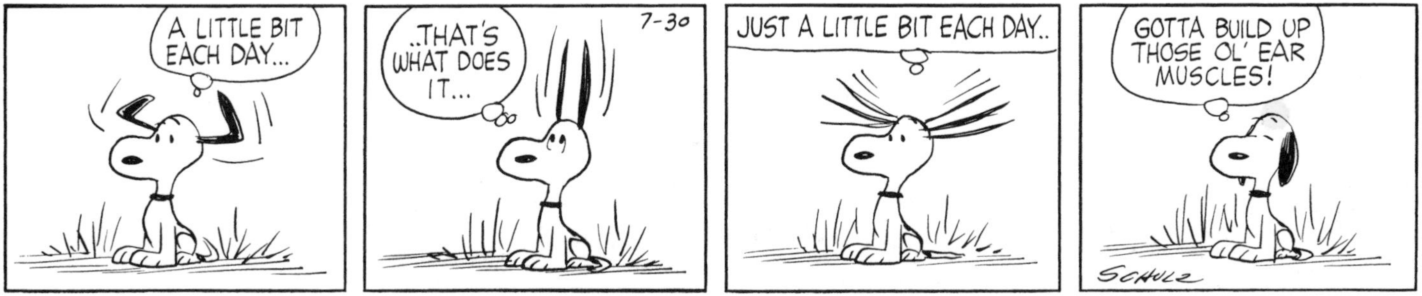
A LITTLE BIT EACH DAY...
..THAT'S WHAT DOES IT...
7-30
JUST A LITTLE BIT EACH DAY..
GOTTA BUILD UP THOSE OL' EAR MUSCLES!
SCHULZ

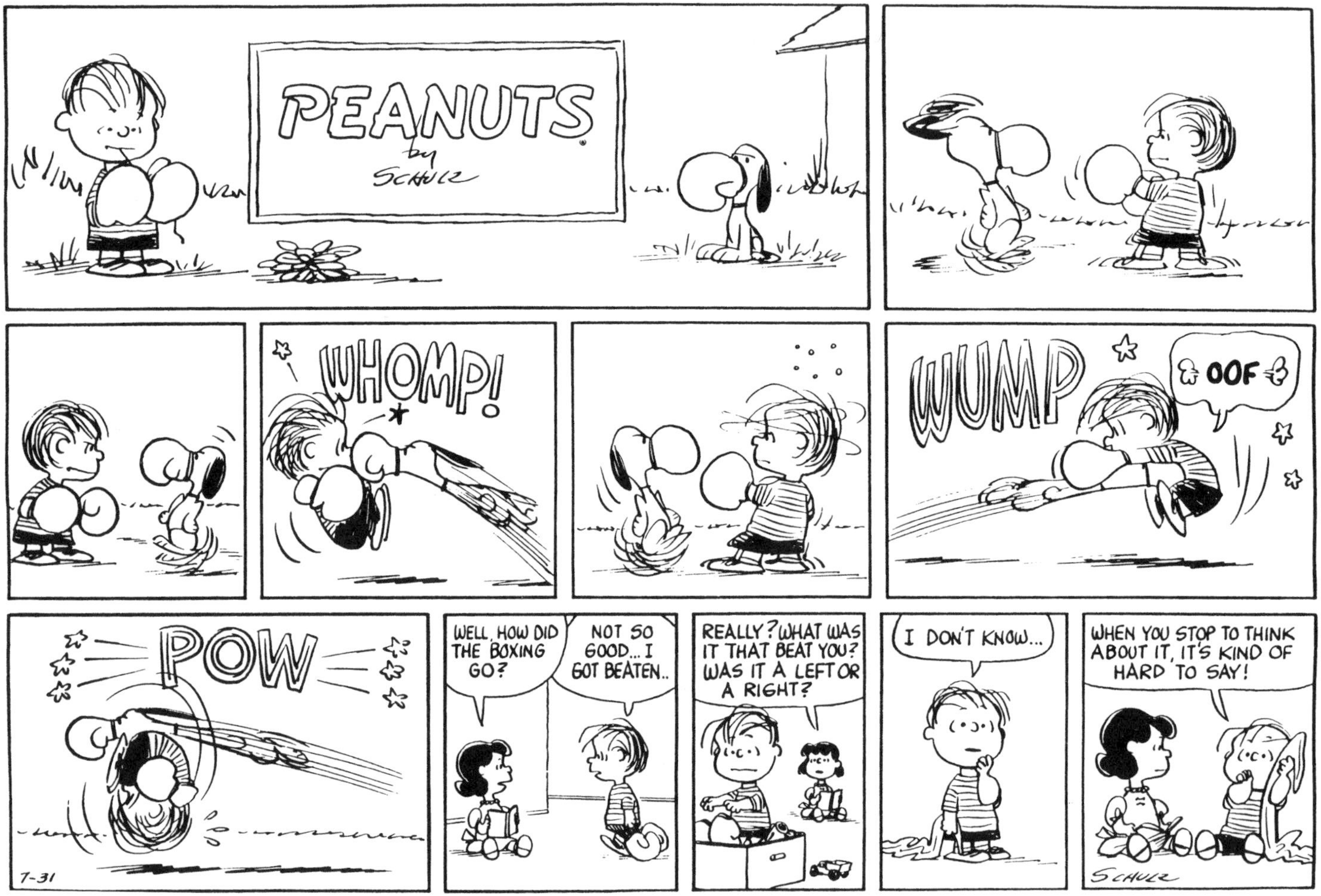
PEANUTS
by SCHULZ
WHOMP!
WUMP
OOF
POW
7-31
WELL, HOW DID THE BOXING GO?
NOT SO GOOD... I GOT BEATEN..
REALLY? WHAT WAS IT THAT BEAT YOU? WAS IT A LEFT OR A RIGHT?
I DON'T KNOW...
WHEN YOU STOP TO THINK ABOUT IT, IT'S KIND OF HARD TO SAY!
SCHULZ

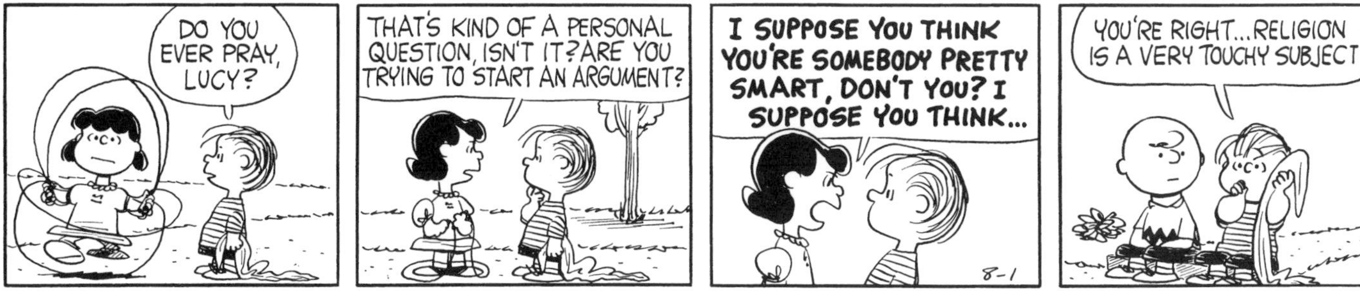
DO YOU EVER PRAY, LUCY?
THAT'S KIND OF A PERSONAL QUESTION, ISN'T IT? ARE YOU TRYING TO START AN ARGUMENT?
I SUPPOSE YOU THINK YOU'RE SOMEBODY PRETTY SMART, DON'T YOU? I SUPPOSE YOU THINK...
8-1
YOU'RE RIGHT...RELIGION IS A VERY TOUCHY SUBJECT!
SCHULZ

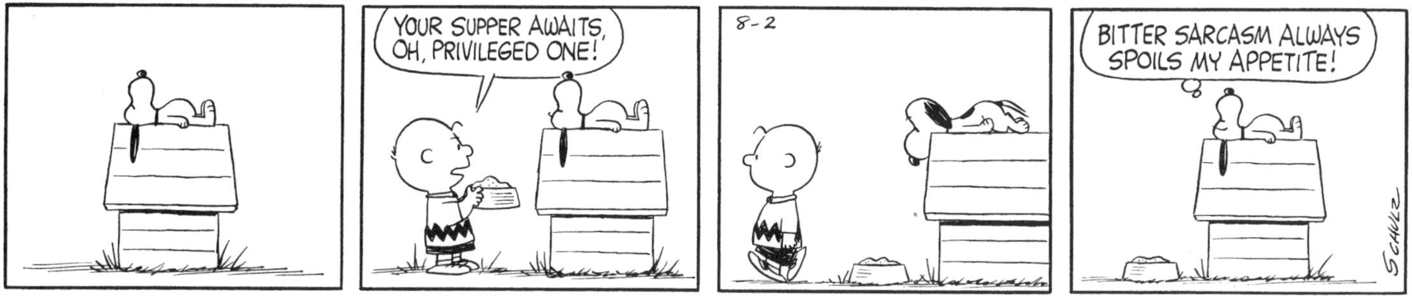
YOUR SUPPER AWAITS, OH, PRIVILEGED ONE!
8-2
BITTER SARCASM ALWAYS SPOILS MY APPETITE!
SCHULZ

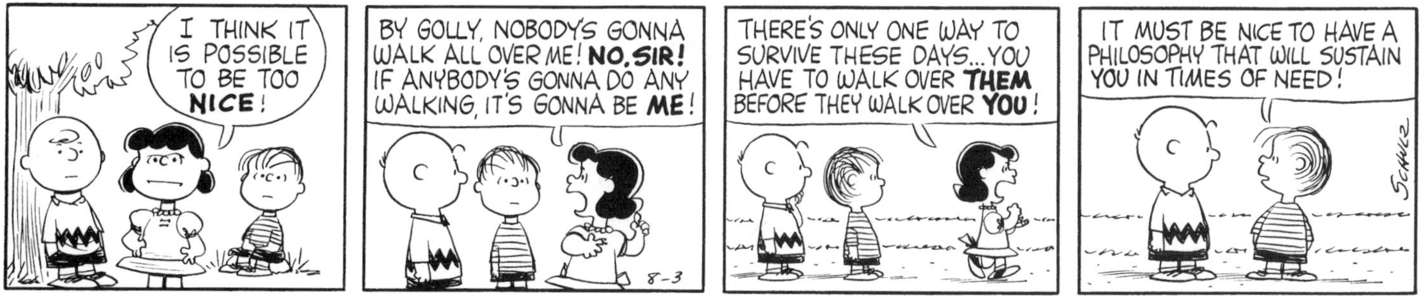
I THINK IT IS POSSIBLE TO BE TOO NICE!
BY GOLLY, NOBODY'S GONNA WALK ALL OVER ME! NO, SIR! IF ANYBODY'S GONNA DO ANY WALKING, IT'S GONNA BE ME!
8-3
THERE'S ONLY ONE WAY TO SURVIVE THESE DAYS...YOU HAVE TO WALK OVER THEM BEFORE THEY WALK OVER YOU!
IT MUST BE NICE TO HAVE A PHILOSOPHY THAT WILL SUSTAIN YOU IN TIMES OF NEED!
SCHULZ

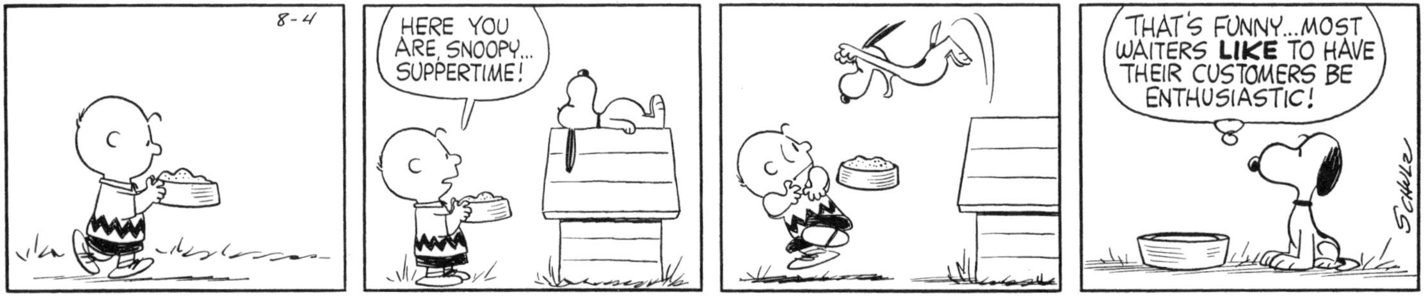
8-4
HERE YOU ARE, SNOOPY... SUPPERTIME!
THAT'S FUNNY...MOST WAITERS **LIKE** TO HAVE THEIR CUSTOMERS BE ENTHUSIASTIC!
SCHULZ

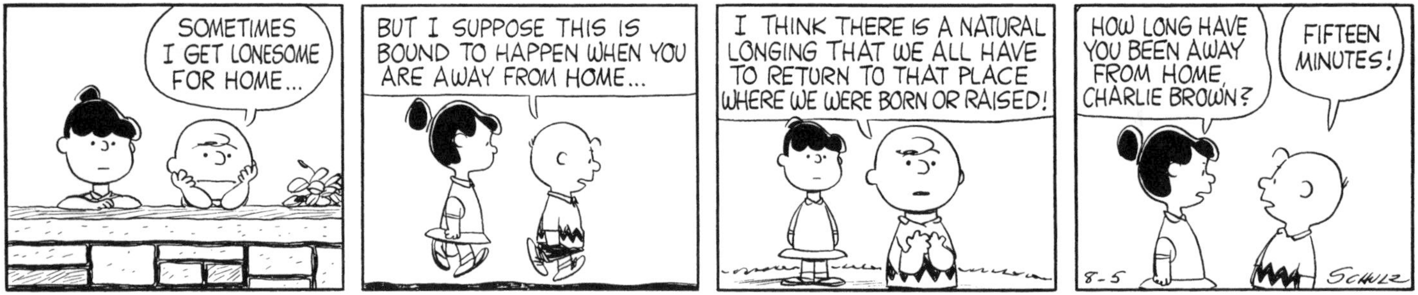
SOMETIMES I GET LONESOME FOR HOME...
BUT I SUPPOSE THIS IS BOUND TO HAPPEN WHEN YOU ARE AWAY FROM HOME...
I THINK THERE IS A NATURAL LONGING THAT WE ALL HAVE TO RETURN TO THAT PLACE WHERE WE WERE BORN OR RAISED!
HOW LONG HAVE YOU BEEN AWAY FROM HOME, CHARLIE BROWN?
FIFTEEN MINUTES!
8-5
SCHULZ

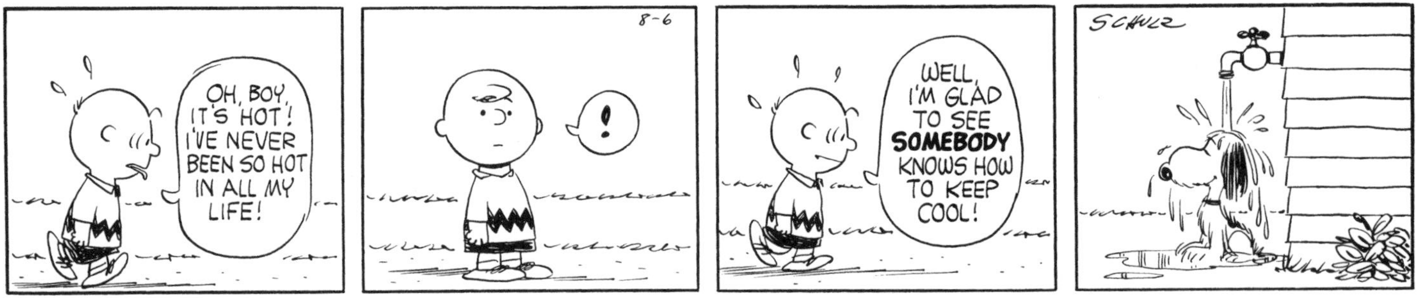
8-6
OH, BOY, IT'S HOT! I'VE NEVER BEEN SO HOT IN ALL MY LIFE!
!
WELL, I'M GLAD TO SEE **SOMEBODY** KNOWS HOW TO KEEP COOL!
SCHULZ

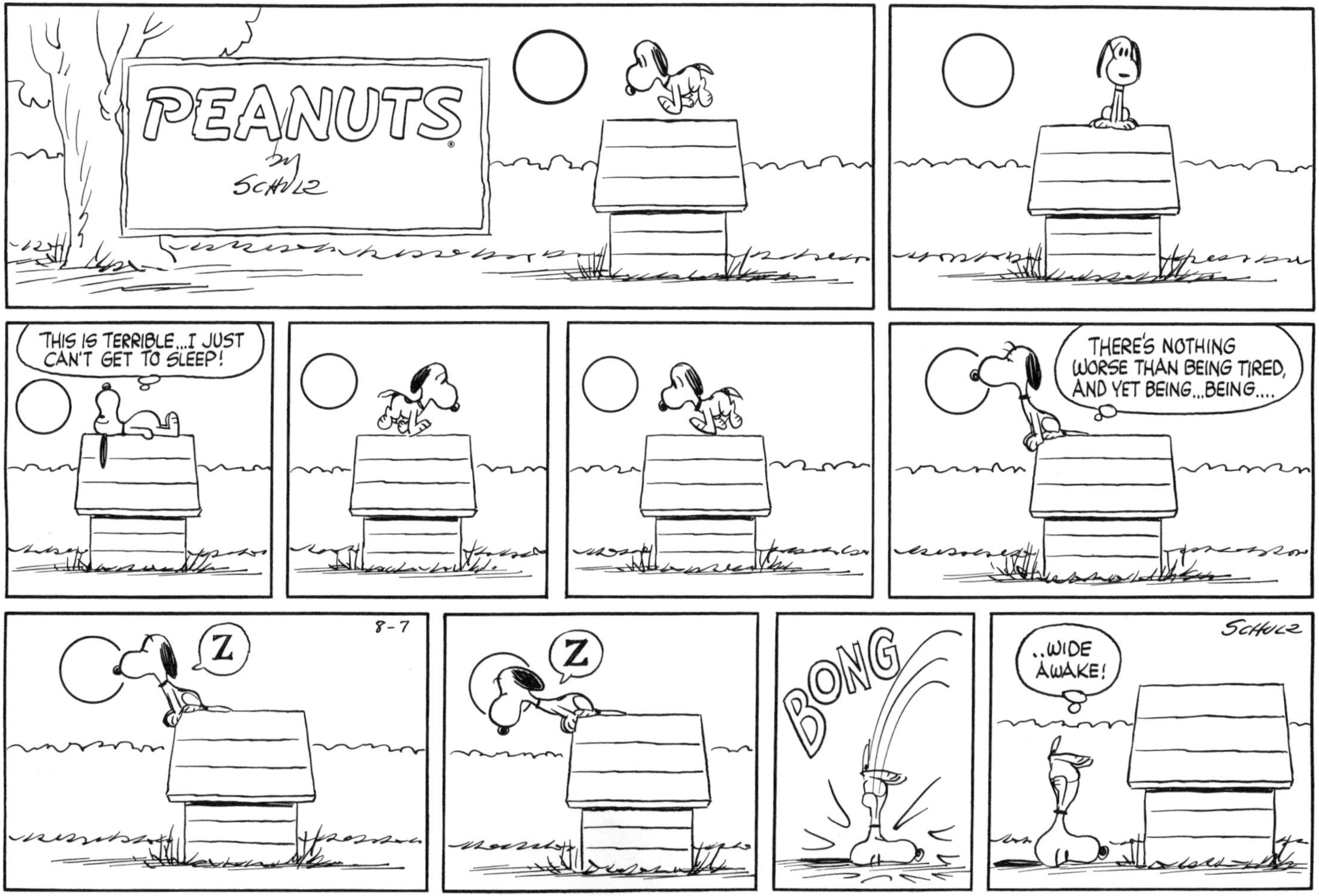
PEANUTS
by SCHULZ
THIS IS TERRIBLE...I JUST CAN'T GET TO SLEEP!
THERE'S NOTHING WORSE THAN BEING TIRED, AND YET BEING...BEING....
8-7
Z
Z
BONG
SCHULZ
..WIDE AWAKE!

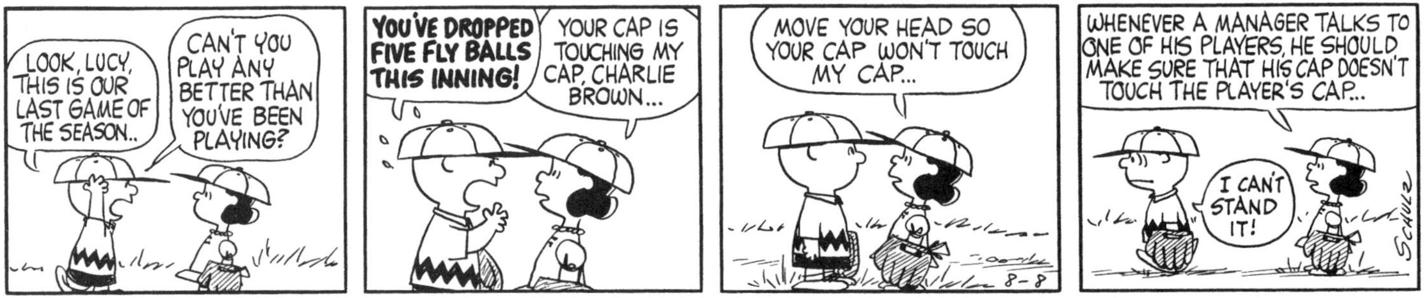
LOOK, LUCY, THIS IS OUR LAST GAME OF THE SEASON..
CAN'T YOU PLAY ANY BETTER THAN YOU'VE BEEN PLAYING?
YOU'VE DROPPED FIVE FLY BALLS THIS INNING!
YOUR CAP IS TOUCHING MY CAP, CHARLIE BROWN...
MOVE YOUR HEAD SO YOUR CAP WON'T TOUCH MY CAP...
8-8
WHENEVER A MANAGER TALKS TO ONE OF HIS PLAYERS, HE SHOULD MAKE SURE THAT HIS CAP DOESN'T TOUCH THE PLAYER'S CAP...
I CAN'T STAND IT!
SCHULZ

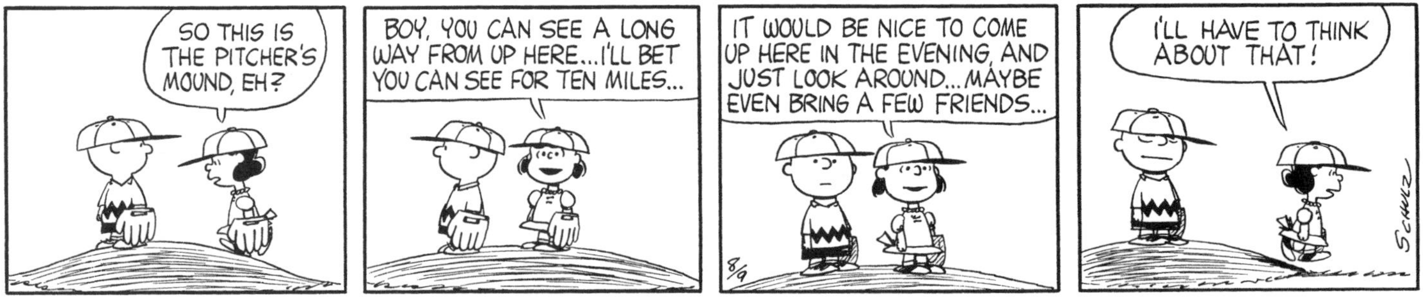
SO THIS IS THE PITCHER'S MOUND, EH?
BOY, YOU CAN SEE A LONG WAY FROM UP HERE...I'LL BET YOU CAN SEE FOR TEN MILES...
IT WOULD BE NICE TO COME UP HERE IN THE EVENING, AND JUST LOOK AROUND...MAYBE EVEN BRING A FEW FRIENDS...
8/9
I'LL HAVE TO THINK ABOUT THAT!
SCHULZ

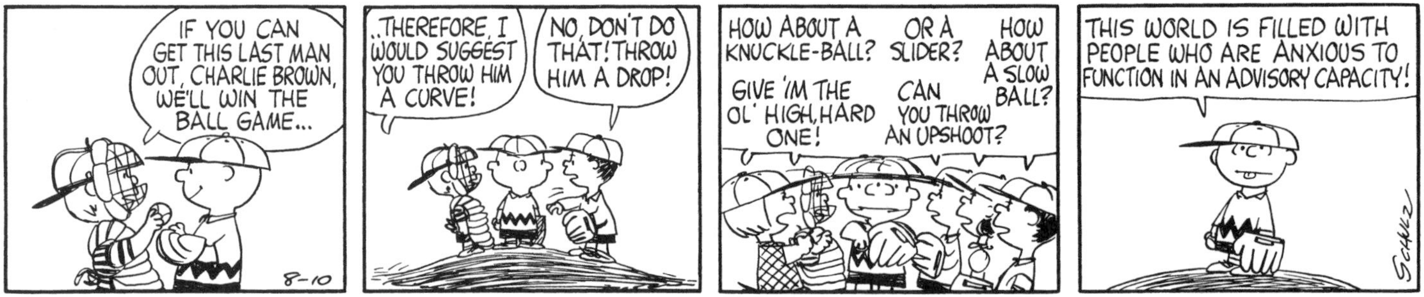
IF YOU CAN GET THIS LAST MAN OUT, CHARLIE BROWN, WE'LL WIN THE BALL GAME...
8-10
..THEREFORE, I WOULD SUGGEST YOU THROW HIM A CURVE!
NO, DON'T DO THAT! THROW HIM A DROP!
HOW ABOUT A KNUCKLE-BALL?
OR A SLIDER?
HOW ABOUT A SLOW BALL?
GIVE 'IM THE OL' HIGH, HARD ONE!
CAN YOU THROW AN UPSHOOT?
THIS WORLD IS FILLED WITH PEOPLE WHO ARE ANXIOUS TO FUNCTION IN AN ADVISORY CAPACITY!
SCHULZ

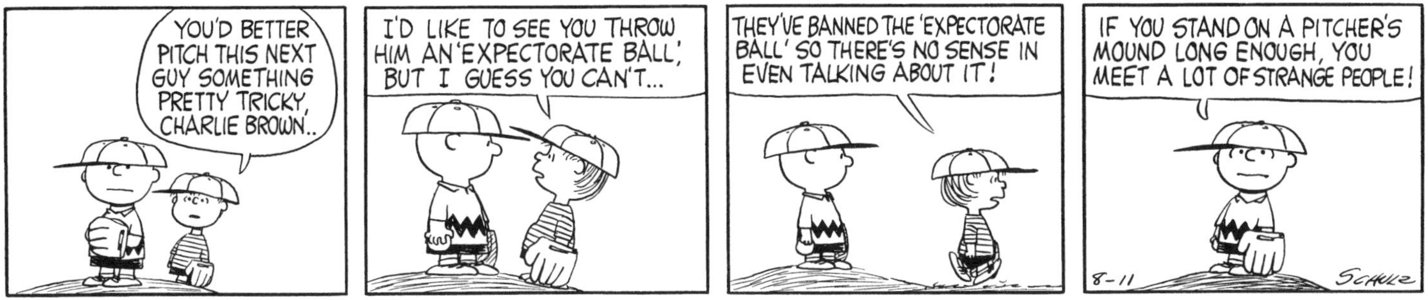
YOU'D BETTER PITCH THIS NEXT GUY SOMETHING PRETTY TRICKY, CHARLIE BROWN..
I'D LIKE TO SEE YOU THROW HIM AN 'EXPECTORATE BALL,' BUT I GUESS YOU CAN'T...
THEY'VE BANNED THE 'EXPECTORATE BALL' SO THERE'S NO SENSE IN EVEN TALKING ABOUT IT!
IF YOU STAND ON A PITCHER'S MOUND LONG ENOUGH, YOU MEET A LOT OF STRANGE PEOPLE!
8-11
SCHULZ

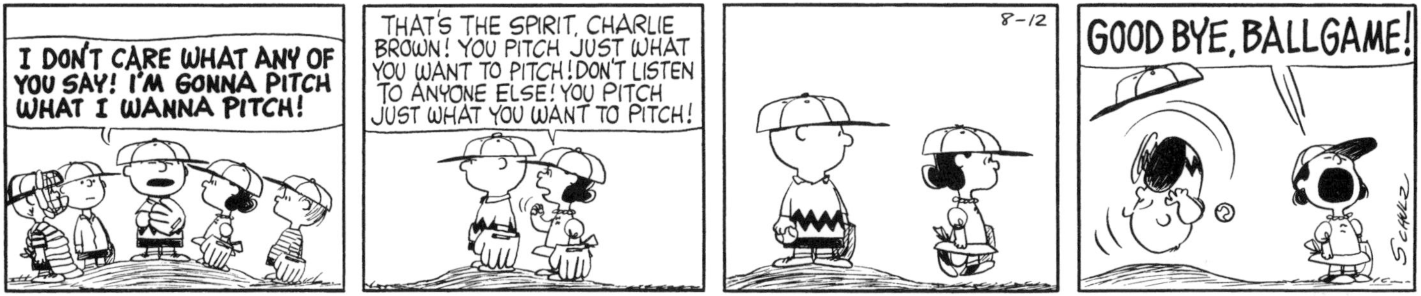
I DON'T CARE WHAT ANY OF YOU SAY! I'M GONNA PITCH WHAT I WANNA PITCH!
THAT'S THE SPIRIT, CHARLIE BROWN! YOU PITCH JUST WHAT YOU WANT TO PITCH! DON'T LISTEN TO ANYONE ELSE! YOU PITCH JUST WHAT YOU WANT TO PITCH!
8-12
GOOD BYE, BALLGAME!
SCHULZ

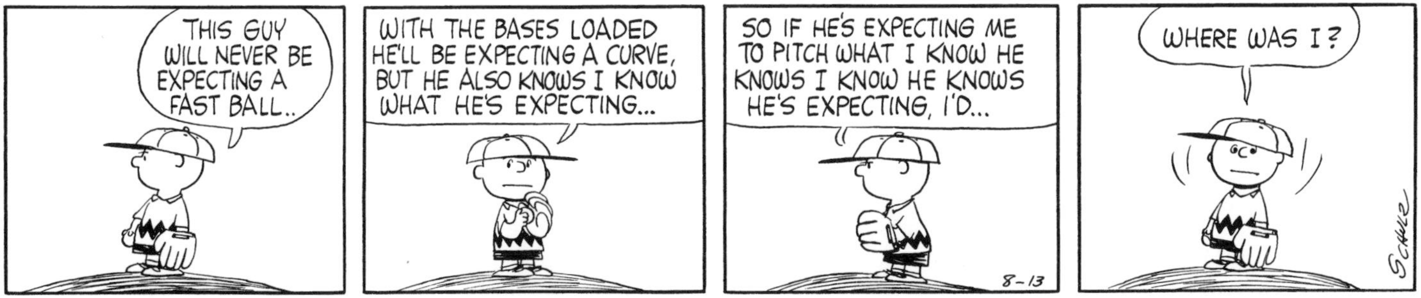
THIS GUY WILL NEVER BE EXPECTING A FAST BALL..
WITH THE BASES LOADED HE'LL BE EXPECTING A CURVE, BUT HE ALSO KNOWS I KNOW WHAT HE'S EXPECTING...
SO IF HE'S EXPECTING ME TO PITCH WHAT I KNOW HE KNOWS I KNOW HE KNOWS HE'S EXPECTING, I'D...
8-13
WHERE WAS I?
SCHULZ

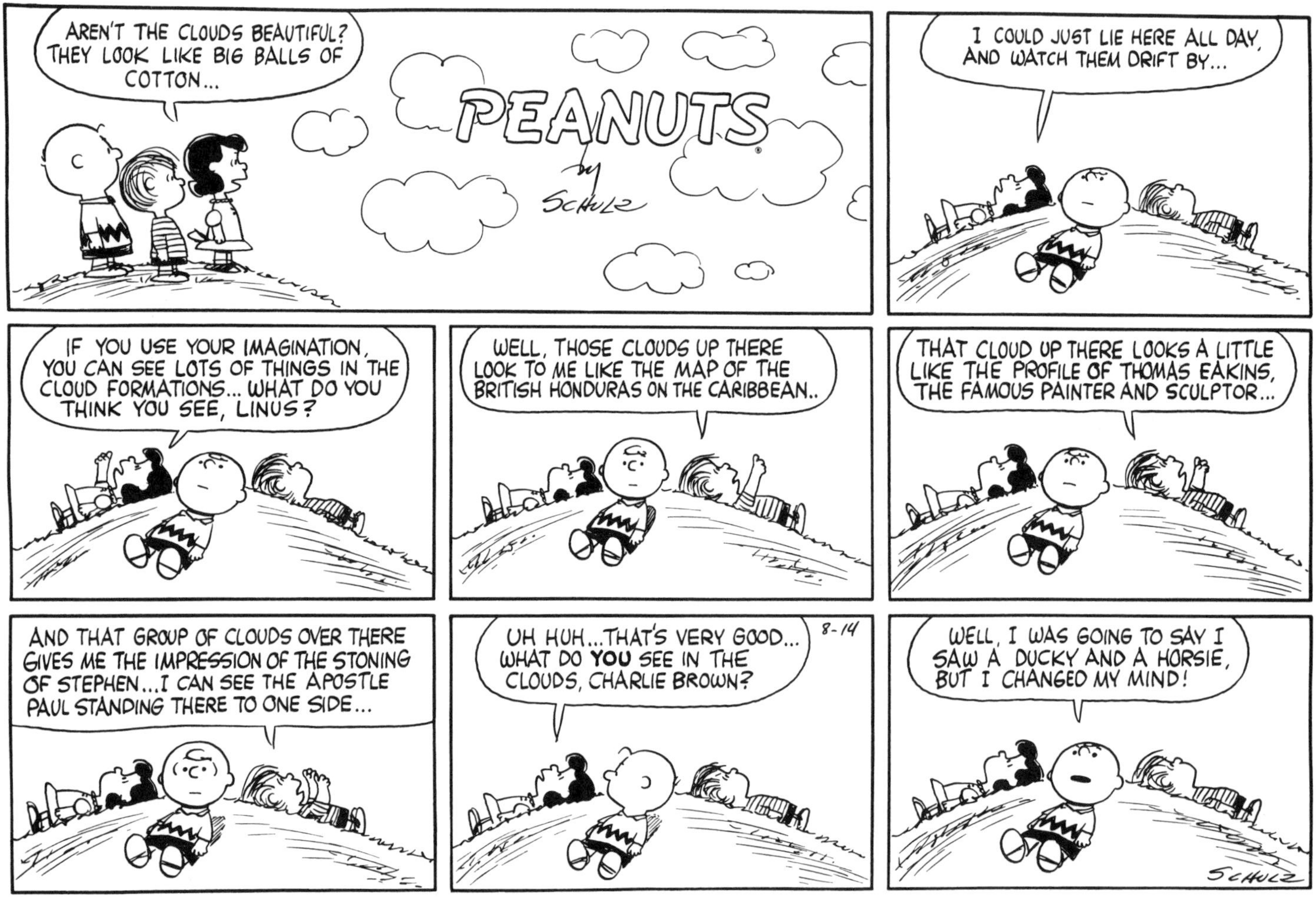
AREN'T THE CLOUDS BEAUTIFUL? THEY LOOK LIKE BIG BALLS OF COTTON...
PEANUTS
by SCHULZ
I COULD JUST LIE HERE ALL DAY, AND WATCH THEM DRIFT BY...
IF YOU USE YOUR IMAGINATION, YOU CAN SEE LOTS OF THINGS IN THE CLOUD FORMATIONS... WHAT DO YOU THINK YOU SEE, LINUS?
WELL, THOSE CLOUDS UP THERE LOOK TO ME LIKE THE MAP OF THE BRITISH HONDURAS ON THE CARIBBEAN..
THAT CLOUD UP THERE LOOKS A LITTLE LIKE THE PROFILE OF THOMAS EAKINS, THE FAMOUS PAINTER AND SCULPTOR...
AND THAT GROUP OF CLOUDS OVER THERE GIVES ME THE IMPRESSION OF THE STONING OF STEPHEN...I CAN SEE THE APOSTLE PAUL STANDING THERE TO ONE SIDE...
8-14
UH HUH...THAT'S VERY GOOD... WHAT DO **YOU** SEE IN THE CLOUDS, CHARLIE BROWN?
WELL, I WAS GOING TO SAY I SAW A DUCKY AND A HORSIE, BUT I CHANGED MY MIND!
SCHULZ

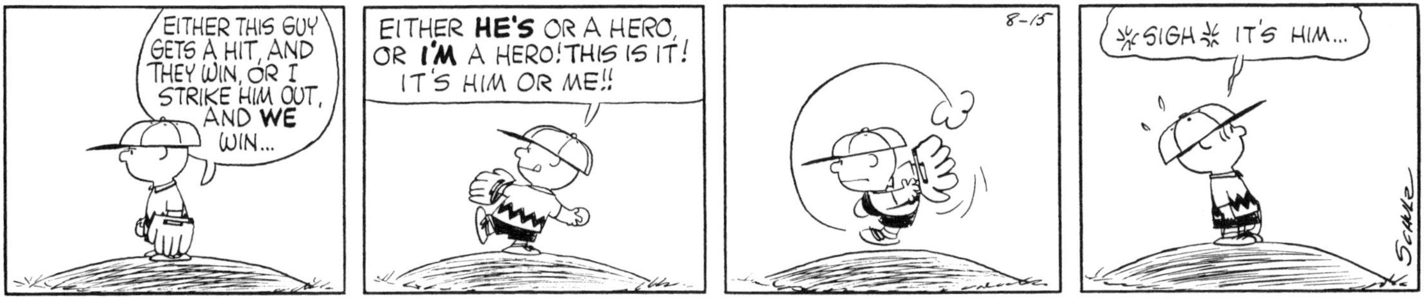
EITHER THIS GUY GETS A HIT, AND THEY WIN, OR I STRIKE HIM OUT, AND WE WIN...
EITHER HE'S OR A HERO, OR I'M A HERO! THIS IS IT! IT'S HIM OR ME!!
8-15
SIGH IT'S HIM...
SCHULZ

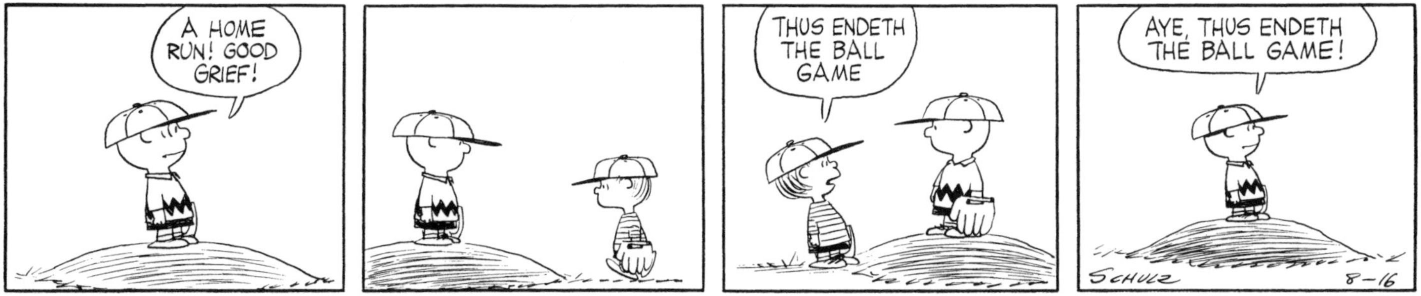
A HOME RUN! GOOD GRIEF!
THUS ENDETH THE BALL GAME
AYE, THUS ENDETH THE BALL GAME!
SCHULZ
8-16

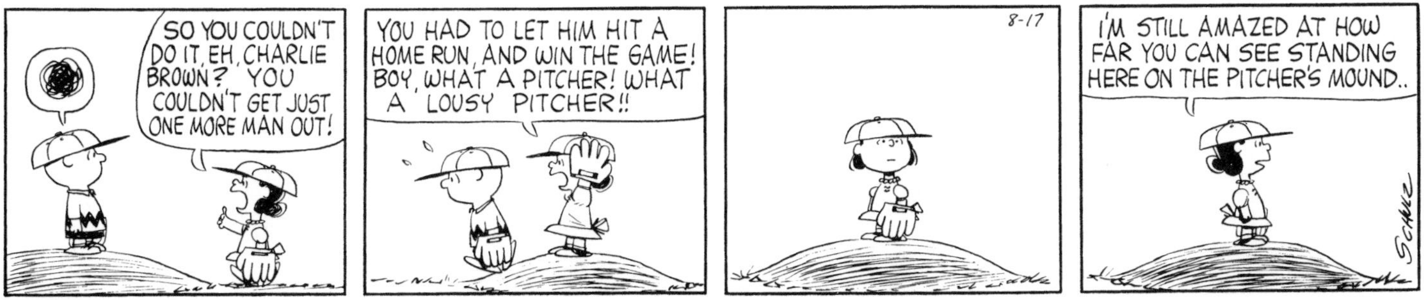
SO YOU COULDN'T DO IT, EH, CHARLIE BROWN? YOU COULDN'T GET JUST ONE MORE MAN OUT!
YOU HAD TO LET HIM HIT A HOME RUN, AND WIN THE GAME! BOY, WHAT A PITCHER! WHAT A LOUSY PITCHER!!
8-17
I'M STILL AMAZED AT HOW FAR YOU CAN SEE STANDING HERE ON THE PITCHER'S MOUND..
SCHULZ

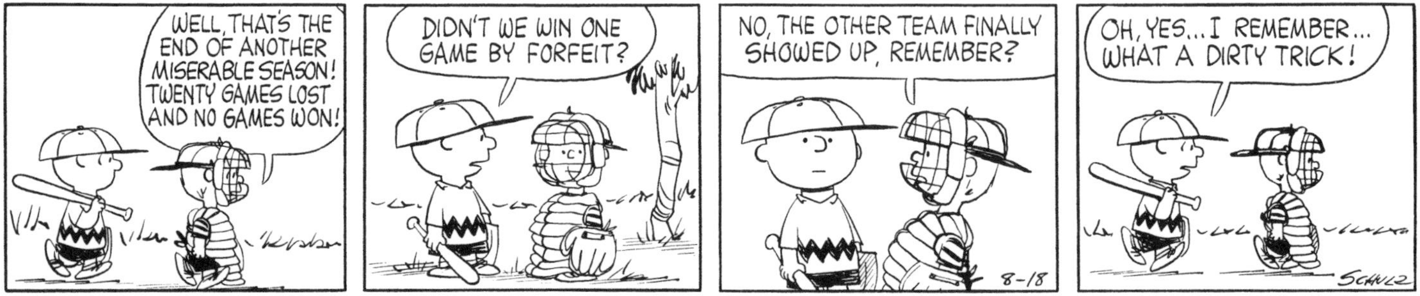
WELL, THAT'S THE END OF ANOTHER MISERABLE SEASON! TWENTY GAMES LOST AND NO GAMES WON!
DIDN'T WE WIN ONE GAME BY FORFEIT?
NO, THE OTHER TEAM FINALLY SHOWED UP, REMEMBER?
8-18
OH, YES... I REMEMBER... WHAT A DIRTY TRICK!
SCHULZ

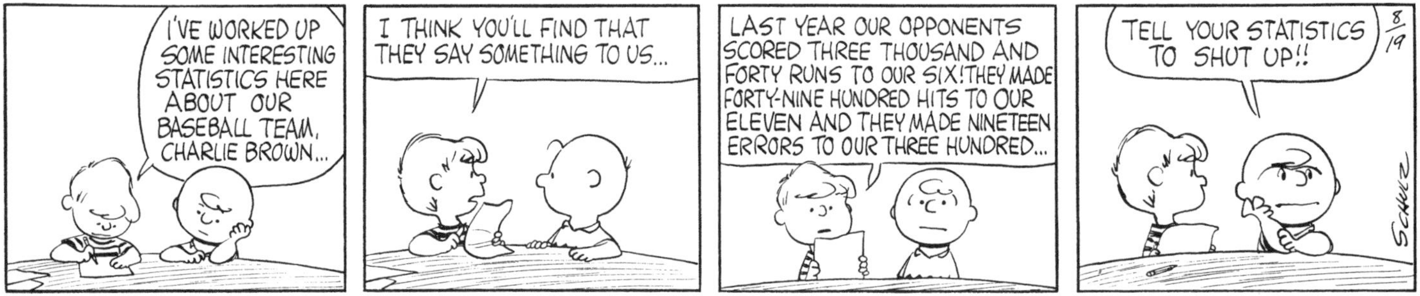
I'VE WORKED UP SOME INTERESTING STATISTICS HERE ABOUT OUR BASEBALL TEAM, CHARLIE BROWN...
I THINK YOU'LL FIND THAT THEY SAY SOMETHING TO US...
LAST YEAR OUR OPPONENTS SCORED THREE THOUSAND AND FORTY RUNS TO OUR SIX! THEY MADE FORTY-NINE HUNDRED HITS TO OUR ELEVEN AND THEY MADE NINETEEN ERRORS TO OUR THREE HUNDRED...
TELL YOUR STATISTICS TO SHUT UP!!
8/19
SCHULZ

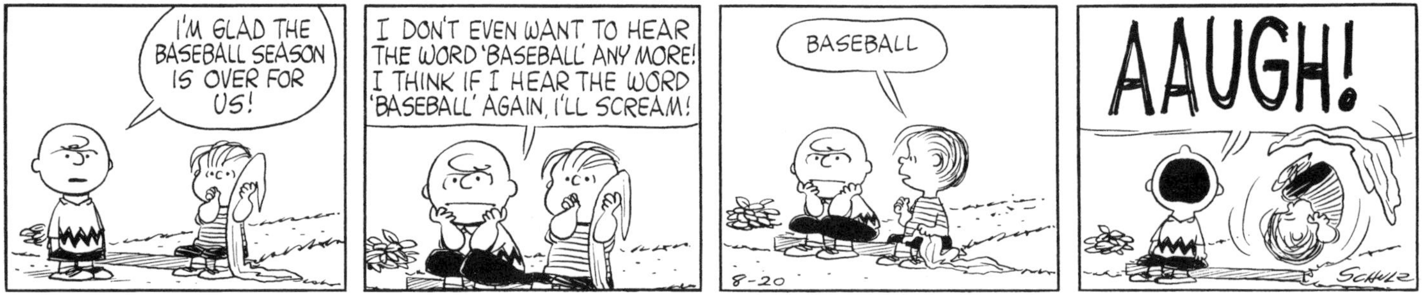
I'M GLAD THE BASEBALL SEASON IS OVER FOR US!
I DON'T EVEN WANT TO HEAR THE WORD 'BASEBALL' ANY MORE! I THINK IF I HEAR THE WORD 'BASEBALL' AGAIN, I'LL SCREAM!
BASEBALL
8-20
AAUGH!
SCHULZ

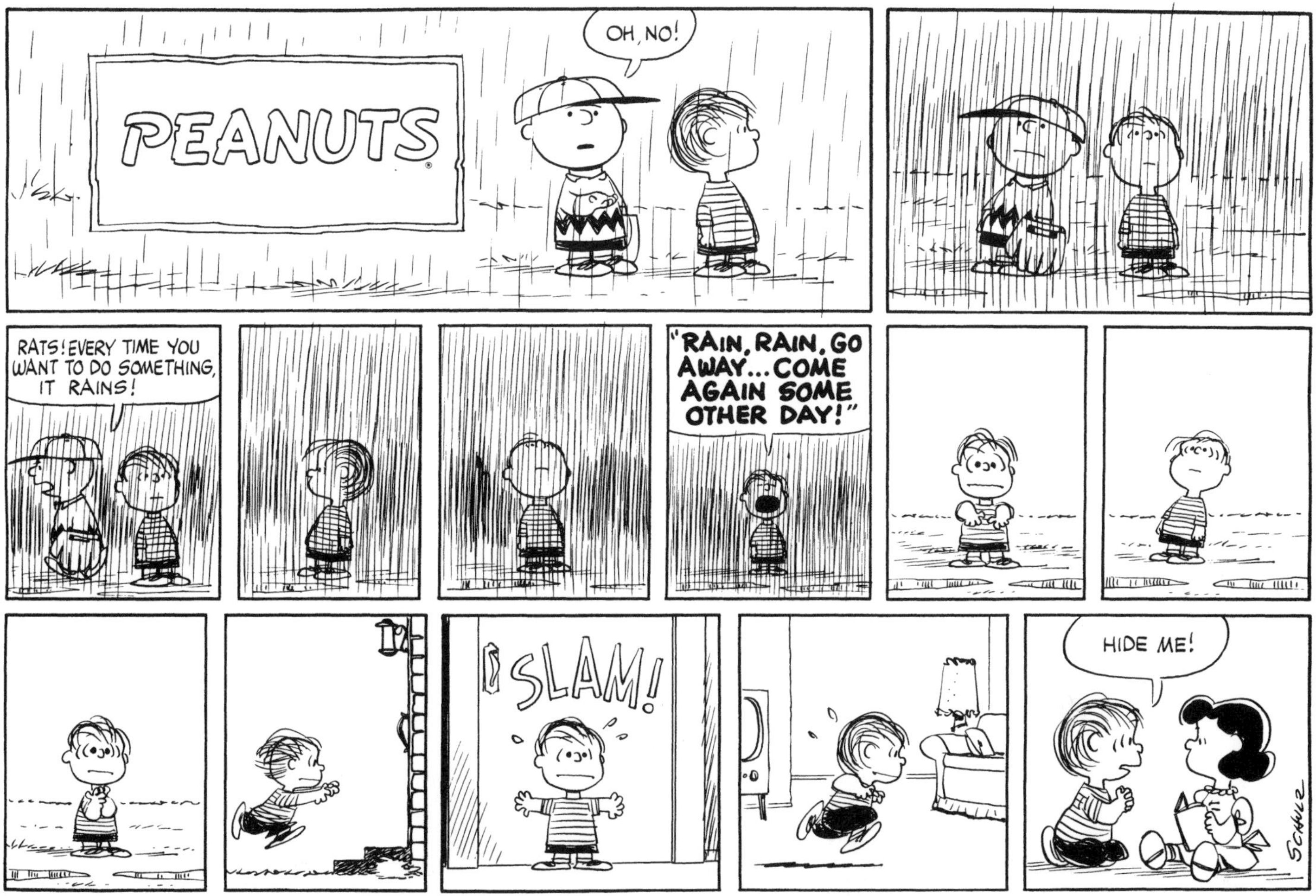
PEANUTS
OH, NO!
RATS! EVERY TIME YOU WANT TO DO SOMETHING, IT RAINS!
"RAIN, RAIN, GO AWAY... COME AGAIN SOME OTHER DAY!"
SLAM!
HIDE ME!
SCHULZ

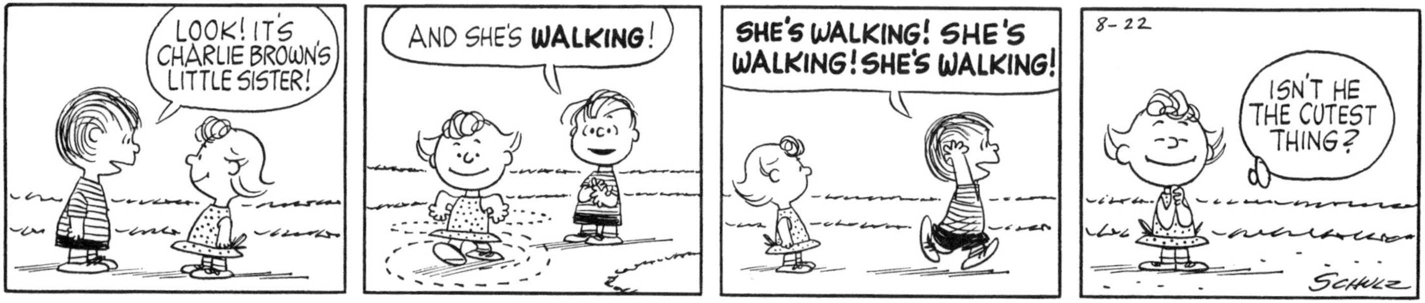
LOOK! IT'S CHARLIE BROWN'S LITTLE SISTER!
AND SHE'S **WALKING**!
SHE'S WALKING! SHE'S WALKING! SHE'S WALKING!
8-22
ISN'T HE THE CUTEST THING?
SCHULZ

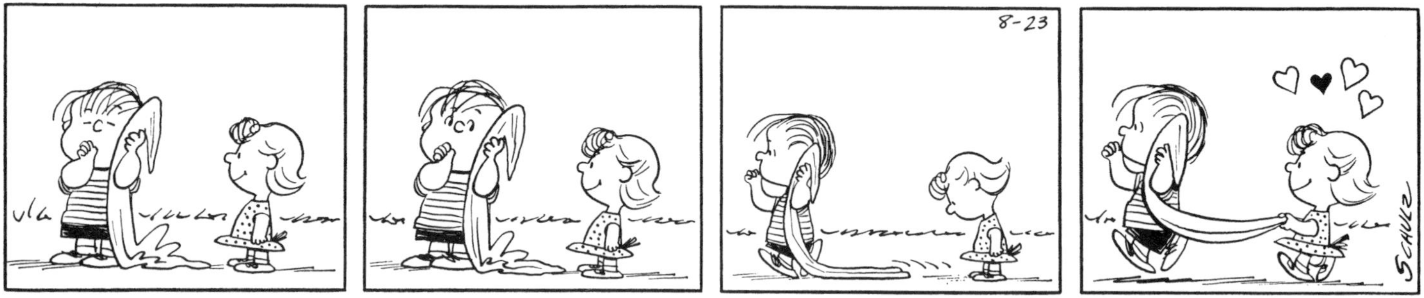
8-23
SCHULZ

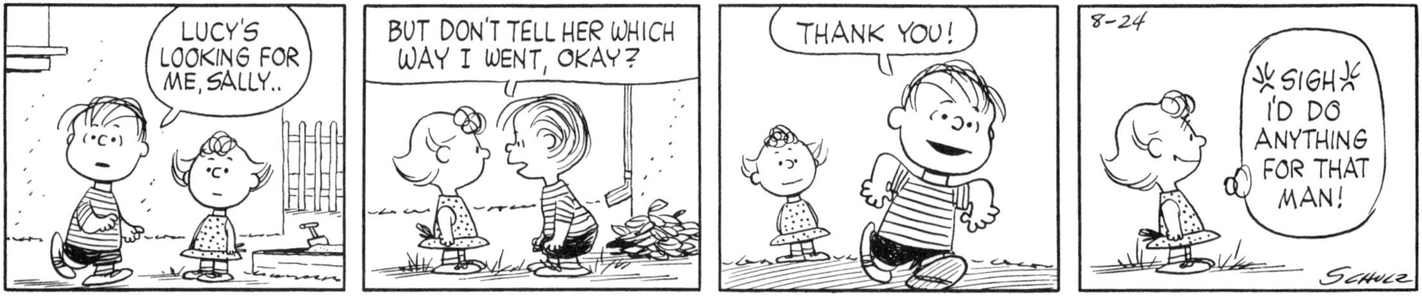
LUCY'S LOOKING FOR ME, SALLY..
BUT DON'T TELL HER WHICH WAY I WENT, OKAY?
THANK YOU!
8-24
SIGH
I'D DO ANYTHING FOR THAT MAN!
SCHULZ

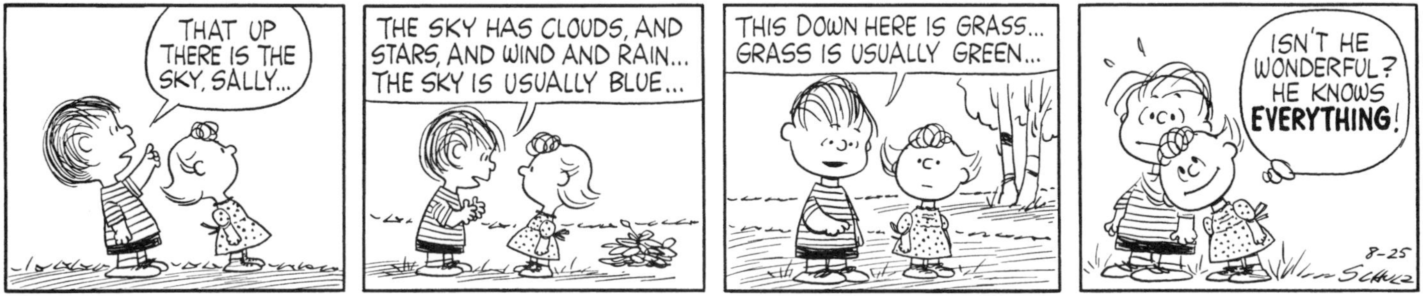
THAT UP THERE IS THE SKY, SALLY...
THE SKY HAS CLOUDS, AND STARS, AND WIND AND RAIN... THE SKY IS USUALLY BLUE...
THIS DOWN HERE IS GRASS... GRASS IS USUALLY GREEN...
ISN'T HE WONDERFUL? HE KNOWS **EVERYTHING**!
8-25
SCHULZ

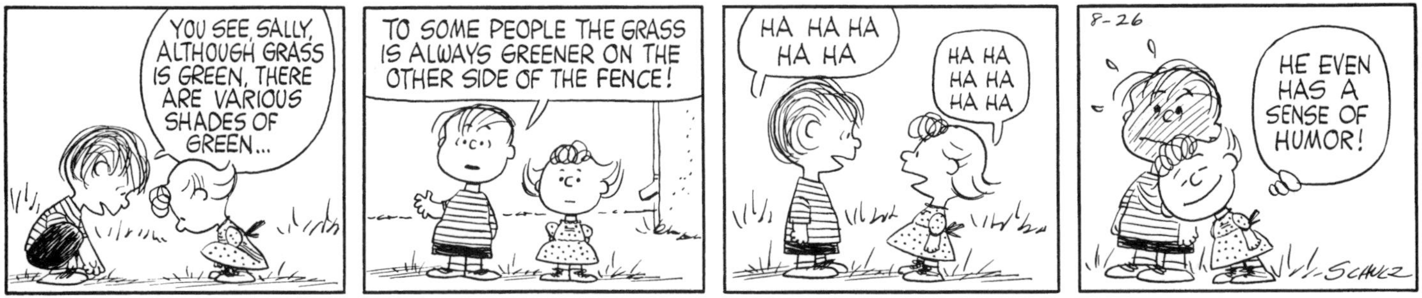
YOU SEE, SALLY, ALTHOUGH GRASS IS GREEN, THERE ARE VARIOUS SHADES OF GREEN...
TO SOME PEOPLE THE GRASS IS ALWAYS GREENER ON THE OTHER SIDE OF THE FENCE!
HA HA HA HA HA
HA HA HA HA HA HA
8-26
HE EVEN HAS A SENSE OF HUMOR!
SCHULZ

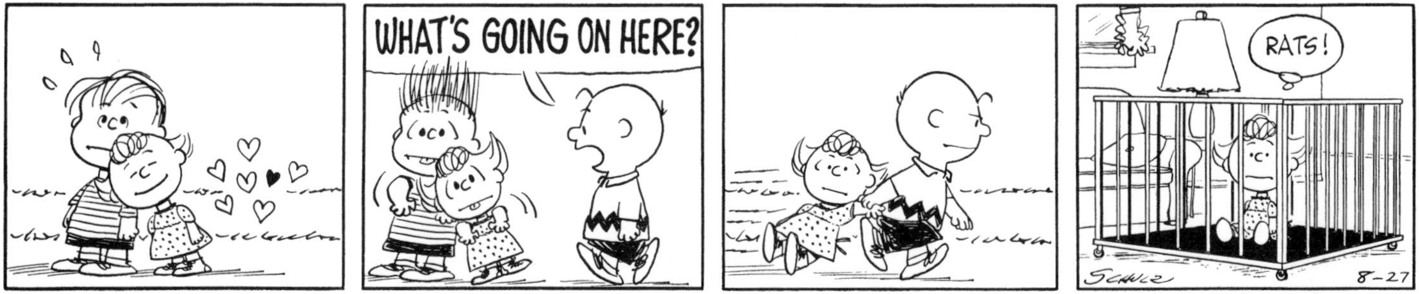
WHAT'S GOING ON HERE?
RATS!
SCHULZ
8-27

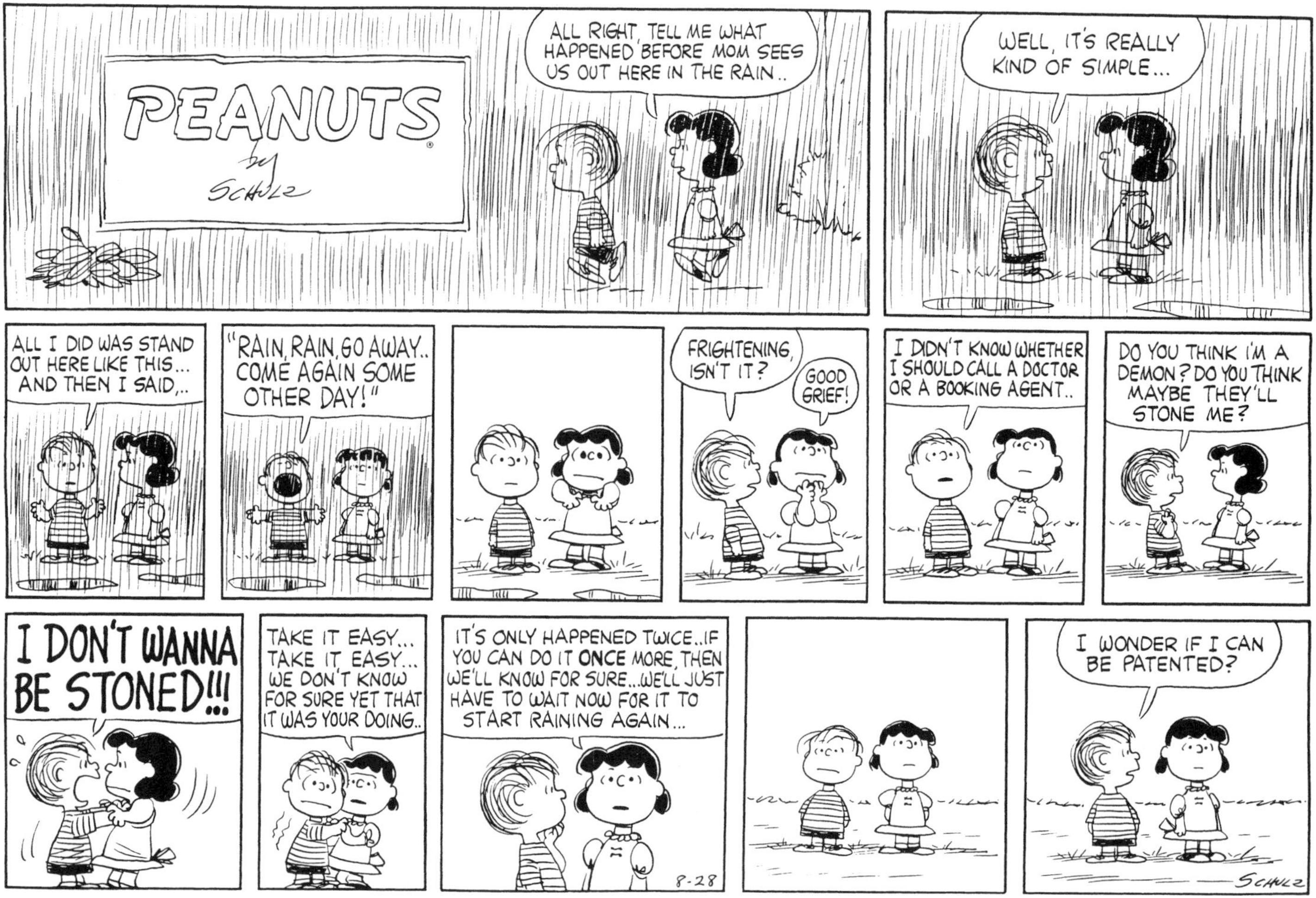
PEANUTS
by SCHULZ
ALL RIGHT, TELL ME WHAT HAPPENED BEFORE MOM SEES US OUT HERE IN THE RAIN..
WELL, IT'S REALLY KIND OF SIMPLE...
ALL I DID WAS STAND OUT HERE LIKE THIS... AND THEN I SAID,..
"RAIN, RAIN, GO AWAY.. COME AGAIN SOME OTHER DAY!"
FRIGHTENING, ISN'T IT?
GOOD GRIEF!
I DIDN'T KNOW WHETHER I SHOULD CALL A DOCTOR OR A BOOKING AGENT..
DO YOU THINK I'M A DEMON? DO YOU THINK MAYBE THEY'LL STONE ME?
I DON'T WANNA BE STONED!!!...
TAKE IT EASY... TAKE IT EASY... WE DON'T KNOW FOR SURE YET THAT IT WAS YOUR DOING..
IT'S ONLY HAPPENED TWICE..IF YOU CAN DO IT ONCE MORE, THEN WE'LL KNOW FOR SURE...WE'LL JUST HAVE TO WAIT NOW FOR IT TO START RAINING AGAIN...
8-28
I WONDER IF I CAN BE PATENTED?
SCHULZ

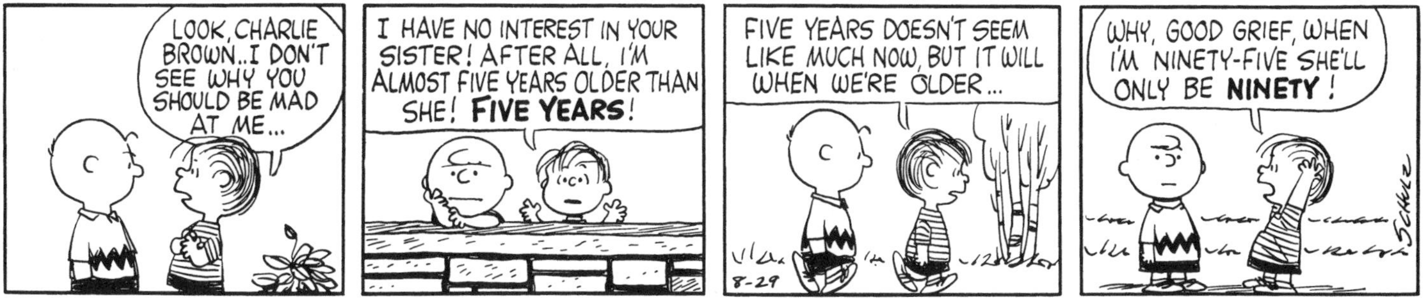
LOOK, CHARLIE BROWN..I DON'T SEE WHY YOU SHOULD BE MAD AT ME...
I HAVE NO INTEREST IN YOUR SISTER! AFTER ALL, I'M ALMOST FIVE YEARS OLDER THAN SHE! FIVE YEARS!
FIVE YEARS DOESN'T SEEM LIKE MUCH NOW, BUT IT WILL WHEN WE'RE OLDER...
8-29
WHY, GOOD GRIEF, WHEN I'M NINETY-FIVE SHE'LL ONLY BE NINETY!
SCHULZ

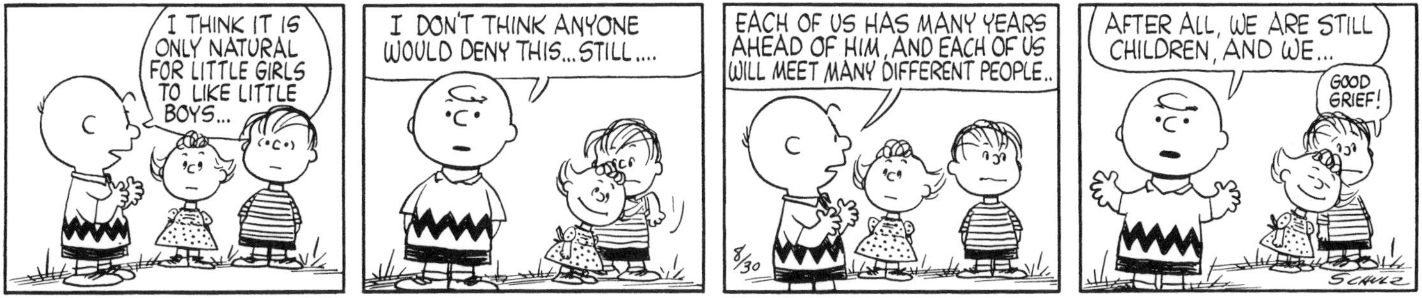
I THINK IT IS ONLY NATURAL FOR LITTLE GIRLS TO LIKE LITTLE BOYS...
I DON'T THINK ANYONE WOULD DENY THIS...STILL....
EACH OF US HAS MANY YEARS AHEAD OF HIM, AND EACH OF US WILL MEET MANY DIFFERENT PEOPLE..
8/30
AFTER ALL, WE ARE STILL CHILDREN, AND WE...
GOOD GRIEF!
SCHULZ

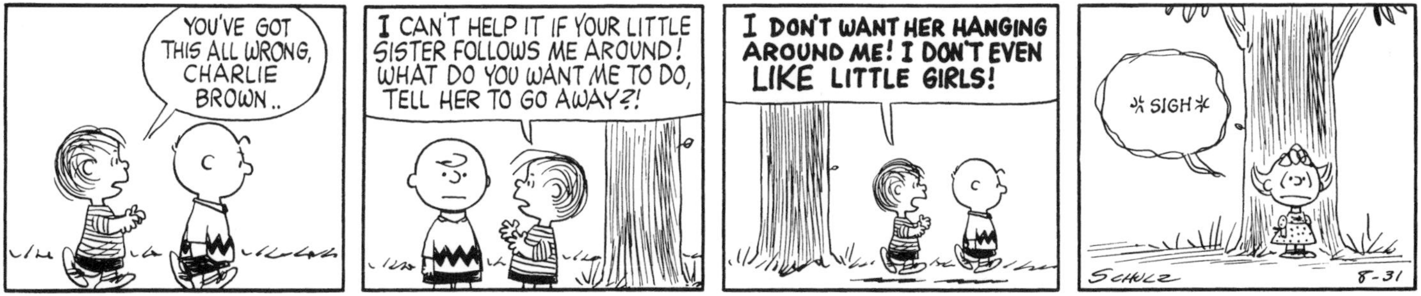
YOU'VE GOT THIS ALL WRONG, CHARLIE BROWN..
I CAN'T HELP IT IF YOUR LITTLE SISTER FOLLOWS ME AROUND! WHAT DO YOU WANT ME TO DO, TELL HER TO GO AWAY?!
I DON'T WANT HER HANGING AROUND ME! I DON'T EVEN LIKE LITTLE GIRLS!
SIGH
SCHULZ
8-31

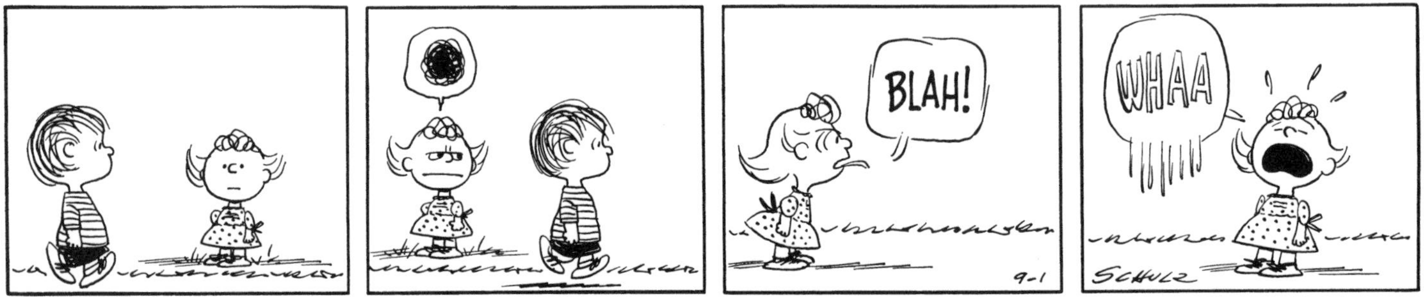
BLAH!
WHAA
9-1

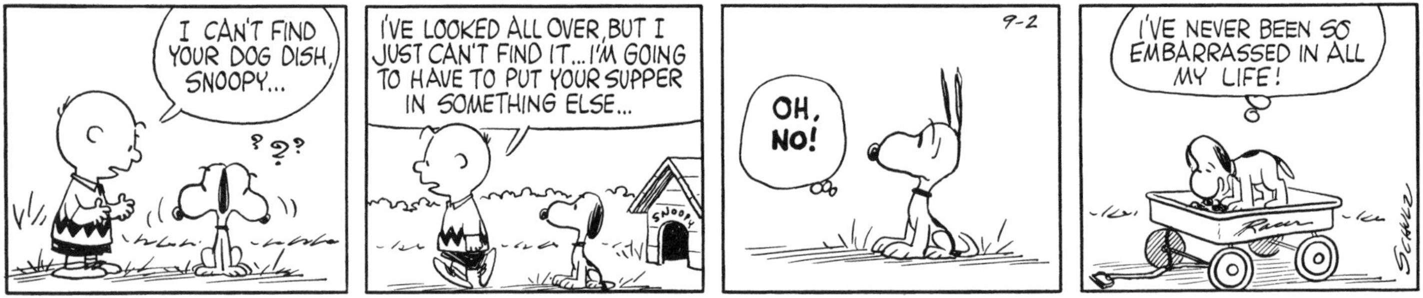
I CAN'T FIND YOUR DOG DISH, SNOOPY...
I'VE LOOKED ALL OVER, BUT I JUST CAN'T FIND IT... I'M GOING TO HAVE TO PUT YOUR SUPPER IN SOMETHING ELSE...
SNOOPY
9-2
OH, NO!
I'VE NEVER BEEN SO EMBARRASSED IN ALL MY LIFE!

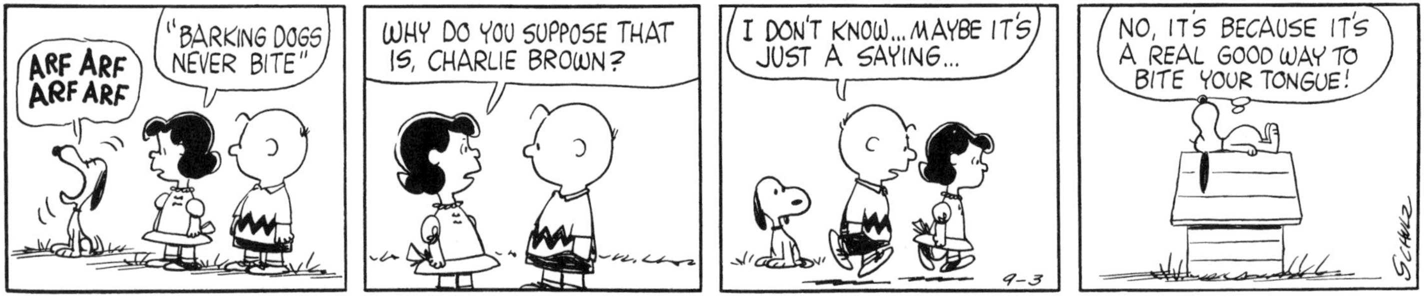
ARF ARF ARF ARF
"BARKING DOGS NEVER BITE"
WHY DO YOU SUPPOSE THAT IS, CHARLIE BROWN?
I DON'T KNOW... MAYBE IT'S JUST A SAYING...
9-3
NO, IT'S BECAUSE IT'S A REAL GOOD WAY TO BITE YOUR TONGUE!

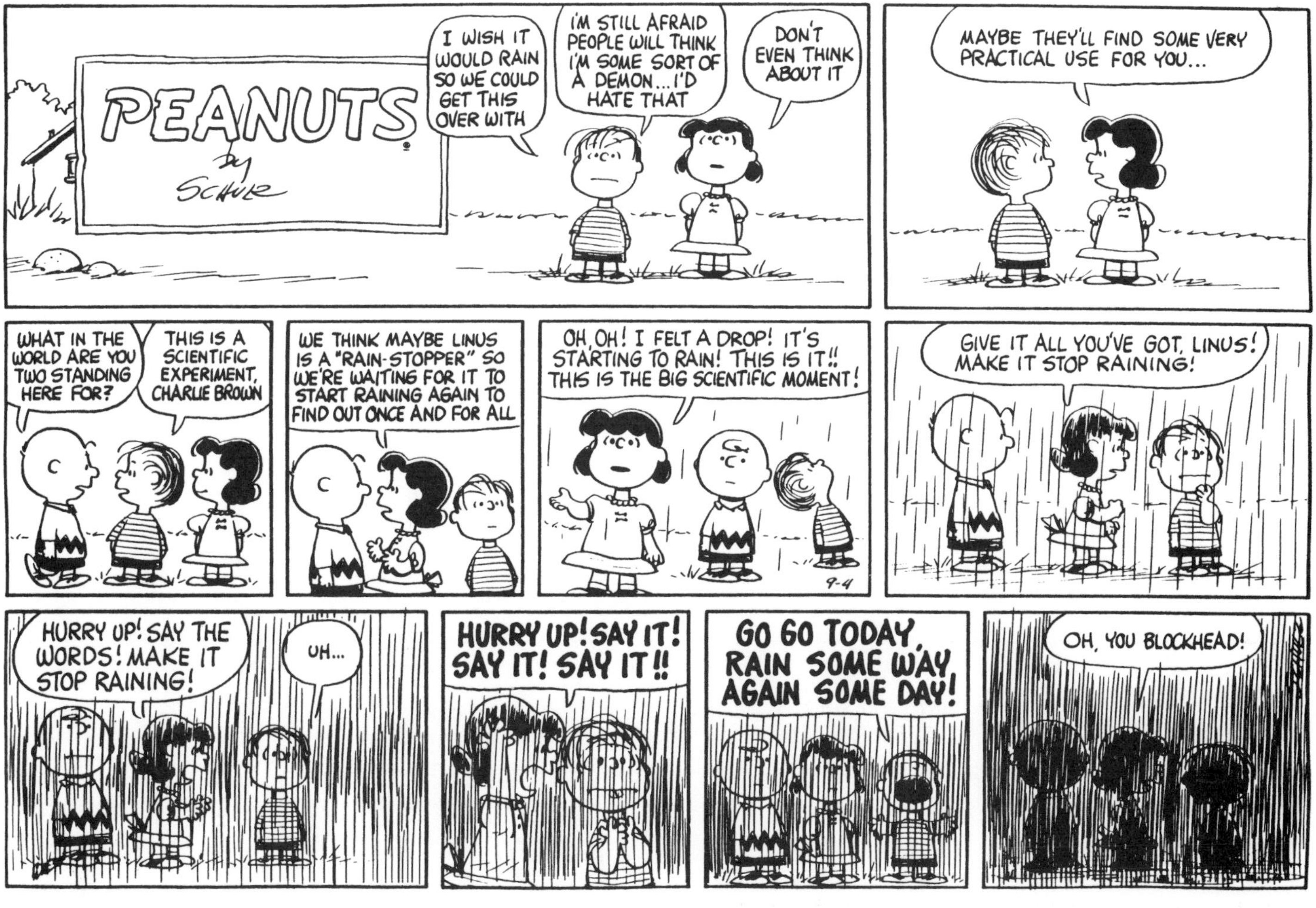
PEANUTS
by SCHULZ
I WISH IT WOULD RAIN SO WE COULD GET THIS OVER WITH
I'M STILL AFRAID PEOPLE WILL THINK I'M SOME SORT OF A DEMON... I'D HATE THAT
DON'T EVEN THINK ABOUT IT
MAYBE THEY'LL FIND SOME VERY PRACTICAL USE FOR YOU...
WHAT IN THE WORLD ARE YOU TWO STANDING HERE FOR?
THIS IS A SCIENTIFIC EXPERIMENT, CHARLIE BROWN
WE THINK MAYBE LINUS IS A "RAIN-STOPPER" SO WE'RE WAITING FOR IT TO START RAINING AGAIN TO FIND OUT ONCE AND FOR ALL
OH, OH! I FELT A DROP! IT'S STARTING TO RAIN! THIS IS IT!! THIS IS THE BIG SCIENTIFIC MOMENT!
9-4
GIVE IT ALL YOU'VE GOT, LINUS! MAKE IT STOP RAINING!
HURRY UP! SAY THE WORDS! MAKE IT STOP RAINING!
UH...
HURRY UP! SAY IT! SAY IT! SAY IT!!
GO GO TODAY, RAIN SOME WAY, AGAIN SOME DAY!
OH, YOU BLOCKHEAD!

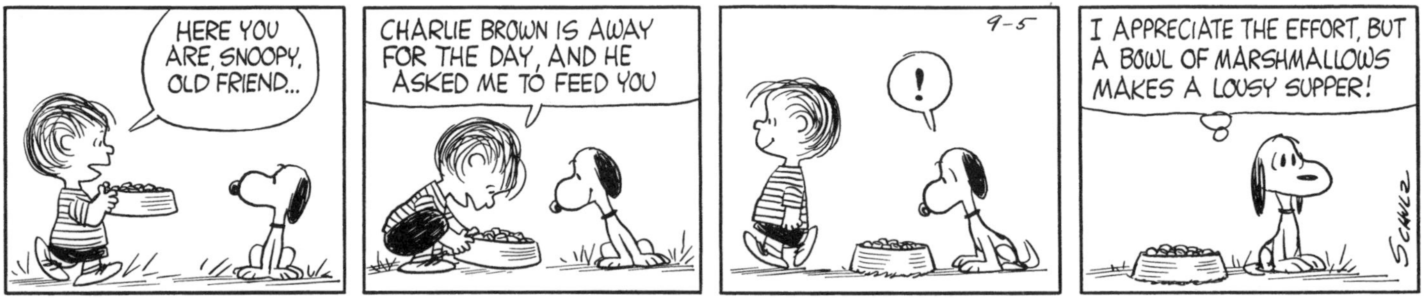
HERE YOU ARE, SNOOPY, OLD FRIEND...
CHARLIE BROWN IS AWAY FOR THE DAY, AND HE ASKED ME TO FEED YOU
9-5
!
I APPRECIATE THE EFFORT, BUT A BOWL OF MARSHMALLOWS MAKES A LOUSY SUPPER!
SCHULZ

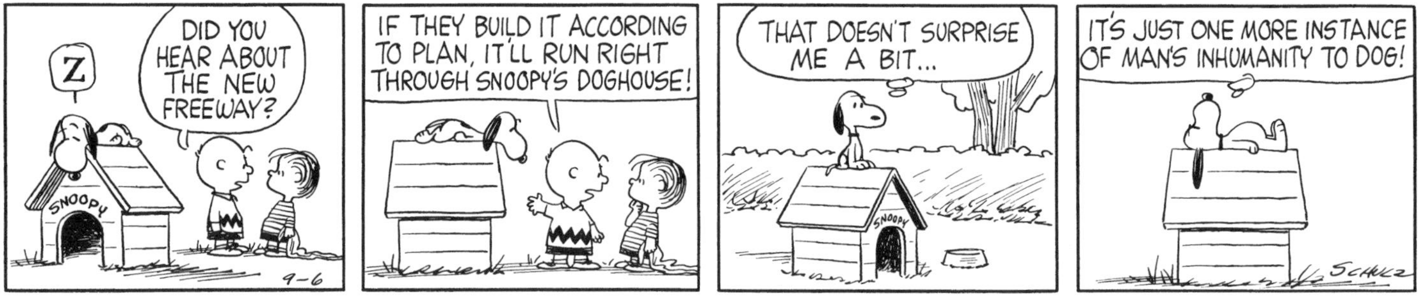
Z
DID YOU HEAR ABOUT THE NEW FREEWAY?
SNOOPY
9-6
IF THEY BUILD IT ACCORDING TO PLAN, IT'LL RUN RIGHT THROUGH SNOOPY'S DOGHOUSE!
THAT DOESN'T SURPRISE ME A BIT...
SNOOPY
IT'S JUST ONE MORE INSTANCE OF MAN'S INHUMANITY TO DOG!
SCHULZ

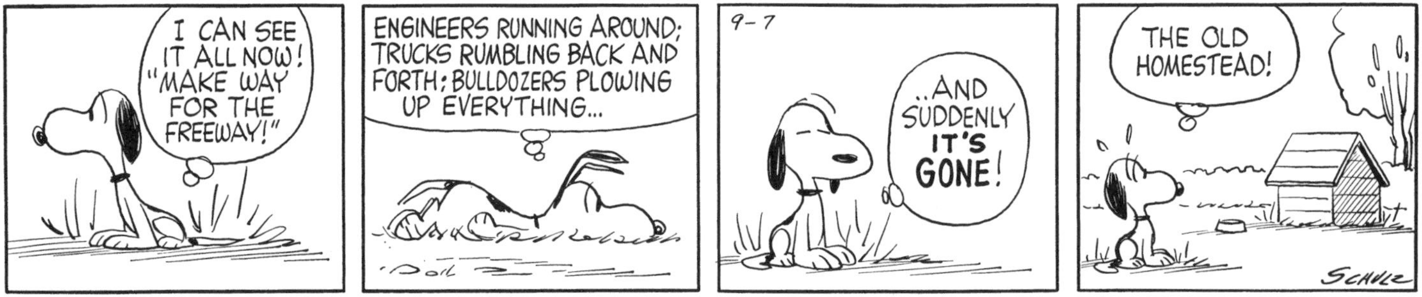
I CAN SEE IT ALL NOW! "MAKE WAY FOR THE FREEWAY!"
ENGINEERS RUNNING AROUND; TRUCKS RUMBLING BACK AND FORTH; BULLDOZERS PLOWING UP EVERYTHING...
9-7
..AND SUDDENLY IT'S GONE!
THE OLD HOMESTEAD!
SCHULZ

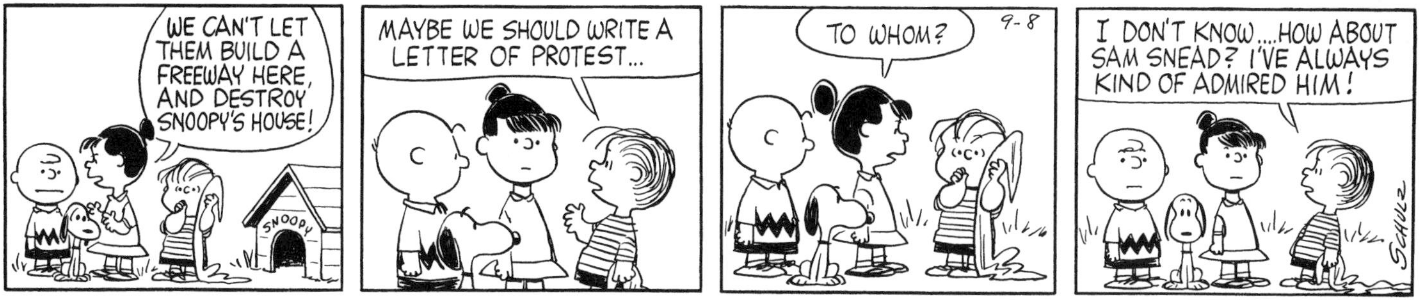
WE CAN'T LET THEM BUILD A FREEWAY HERE, AND DESTROY SNOOPY'S HOUSE!
SNOOPY
MAYBE WE SHOULD WRITE A LETTER OF PROTEST...
TO WHOM?
9-8
I DON'T KNOW....HOW ABOUT SAM SNEAD? I'VE ALWAYS KIND OF ADMIRED HIM!
SCHULZ

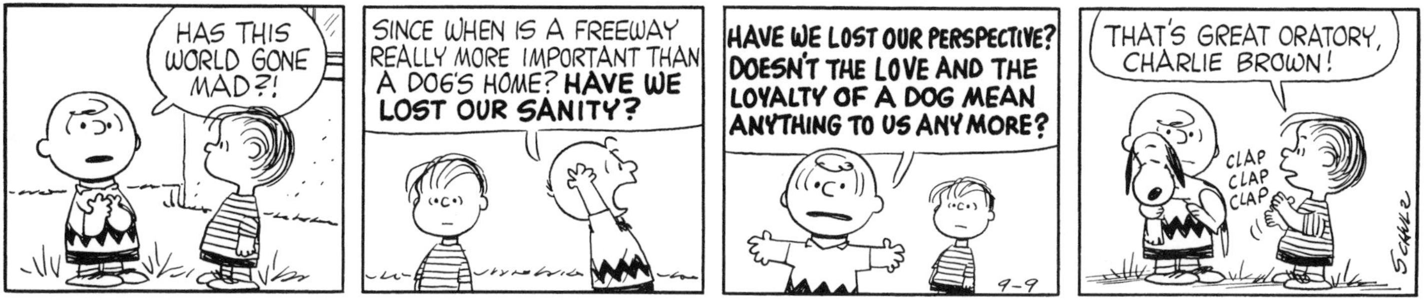
HAS THIS WORLD GONE MAD?!
SINCE WHEN IS A FREEWAY REALLY MORE IMPORTANT THAN A DOG'S HOME? HAVE WE LOST OUR SANITY?
HAVE WE LOST OUR PERSPECTIVE? DOESN'T THE LOVE AND THE LOYALTY OF A DOG MEAN ANYTHING TO US ANY MORE?
9-9
THAT'S GREAT ORATORY, CHARLIE BROWN!
CLAP CLAP CLAP
SCHULZ

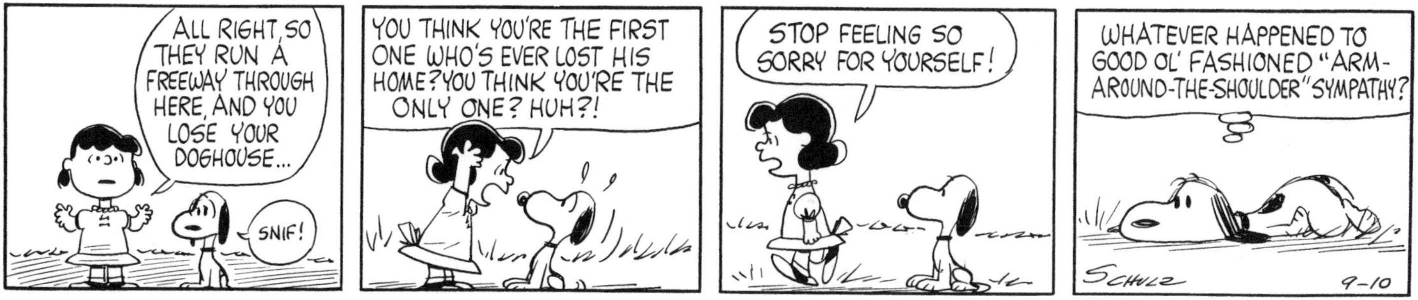
ALL RIGHT, SO THEY RUN A FREEWAY THROUGH HERE, AND YOU LOSE YOUR DOGHOUSE...
SNIF!
YOU THINK YOU'RE THE FIRST ONE WHO'S EVER LOST HIS HOME? YOU THINK YOU'RE THE ONLY ONE? HUH?!
STOP FEELING SO SORRY FOR YOURSELF!
WHATEVER HAPPENED TO GOOD OL' FASHIONED "ARM-AROUND-THE-SHOULDER" SYMPATHY?
SCHULZ
9-10

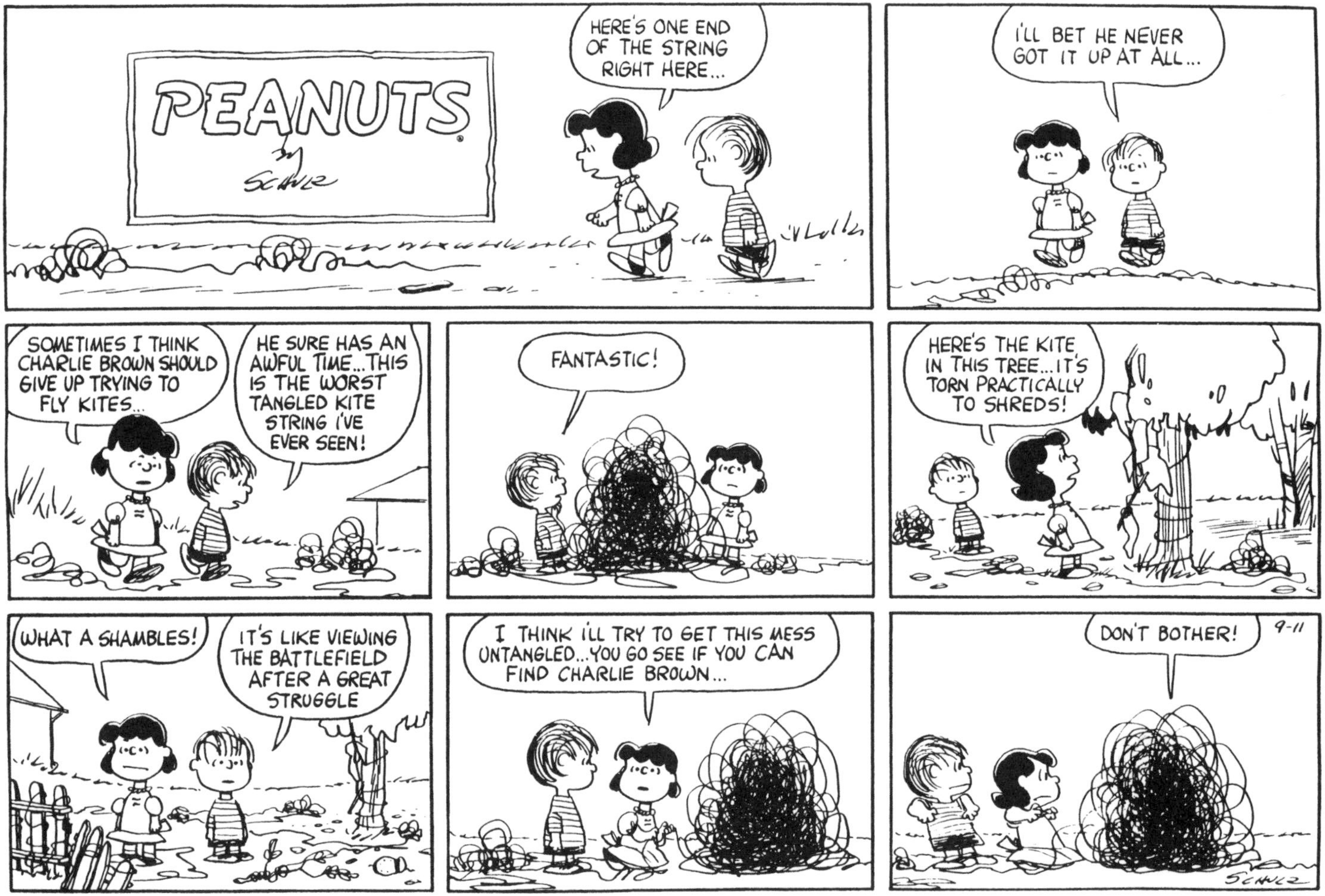
PEANUTS
by SCHULZ
HERE'S ONE END OF THE STRING RIGHT HERE...
I'LL BET HE NEVER GOT IT UP AT ALL...
SOMETIMES I THINK CHARLIE BROWN SHOULD GIVE UP TRYING TO FLY KITES...
HE SURE HAS AN AWFUL TIME...THIS IS THE WORST TANGLED KITE STRING I'VE EVER SEEN!
FANTASTIC!
HERE'S THE KITE IN THIS TREE...IT'S TORN PRACTICALLY TO SHREDS!
WHAT A SHAMBLES!
IT'S LIKE VIEWING THE BATTLEFIELD AFTER A GREAT STRUGGLE
I THINK I'LL TRY TO GET THIS MESS UNTANGLED...YOU GO SEE IF YOU CAN FIND CHARLIE BROWN...
DON'T BOTHER!
9-11
SCHULZ

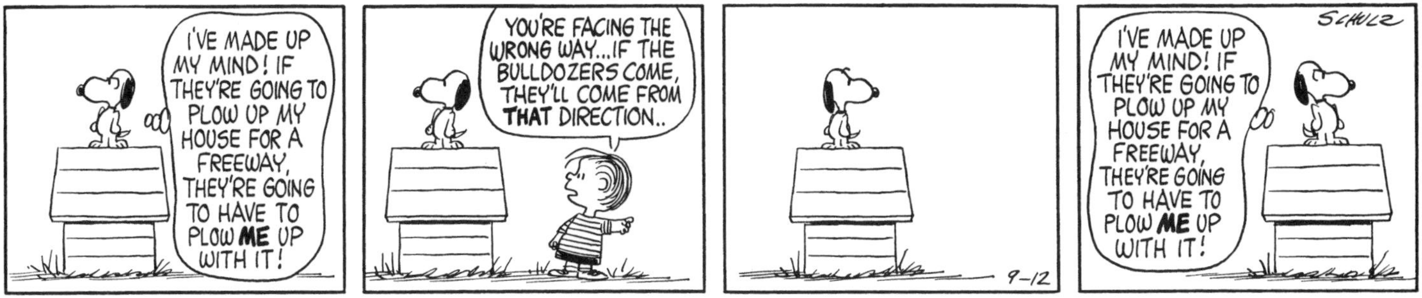
I'VE MADE UP MY MIND! IF THEY'RE GOING TO PLOW UP MY HOUSE FOR A FREEWAY, THEY'RE GOING TO HAVE TO PLOW **ME** UP WITH IT!
YOU'RE FACING THE WRONG WAY...IF THE BULLDOZERS COME, THEY'LL COME FROM **THAT** DIRECTION..
9-12
SCHULZ
I'VE MADE UP MY MIND! IF THEY'RE GOING TO PLOW UP MY HOUSE FOR A FREEWAY, THEY'RE GOING TO HAVE TO PLOW **ME** UP WITH IT!

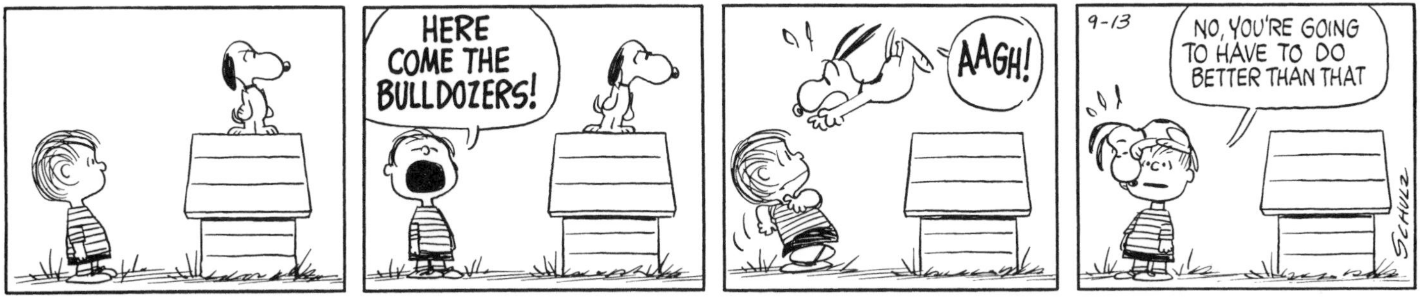
HERE COME THE BULLDOZERS!
AAGH!
9-13
NO, YOU'RE GOING TO HAVE TO DO BETTER THAN THAT
SCHULZ

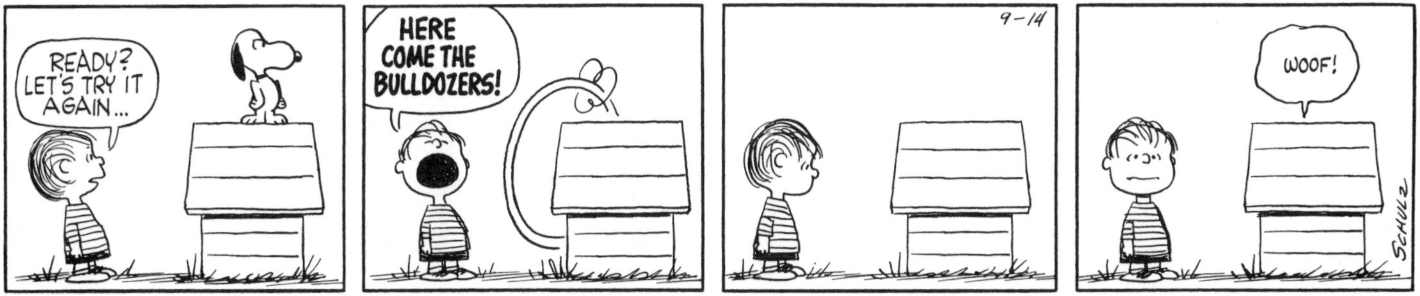
READY? LET'S TRY IT AGAIN...
HERE COME THE BULLDOZERS!
9-14
WOOF!
SCHULZ

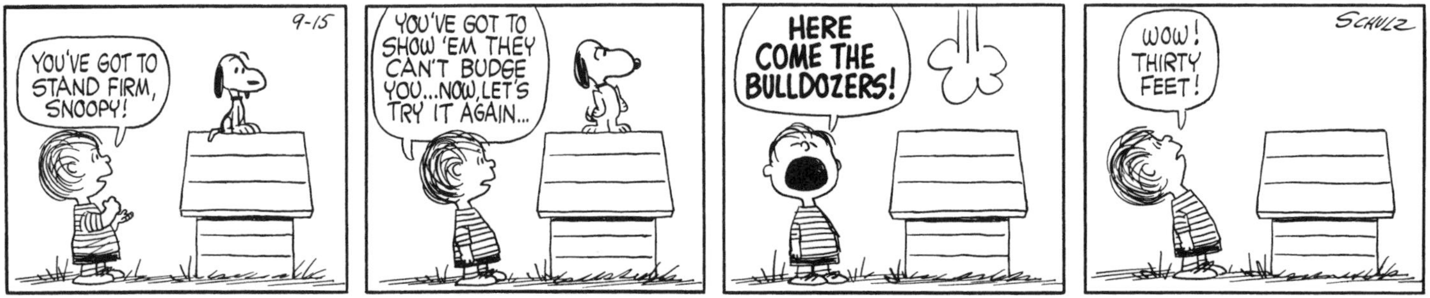
9-15
YOU'VE GOT TO STAND FIRM, SNOOPY!
YOU'VE GOT TO SHOW 'EM THEY CAN'T BUDGE YOU...NOW, LET'S TRY IT AGAIN...
HERE COME THE BULLDOZERS!
WOW! THIRTY FEET!
SCHULZ

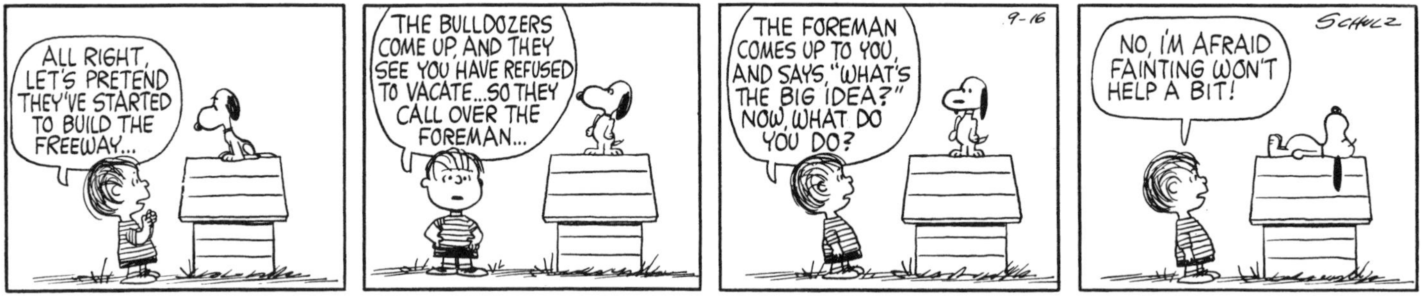
ALL RIGHT, LET'S PRETEND THEY'VE STARTED TO BUILD THE FREEWAY...
THE BULLDOZERS COME UP, AND THEY SEE YOU HAVE REFUSED TO VACATE...SO THEY CALL OVER THE FOREMAN...
9-16
THE FOREMAN COMES UP TO YOU, AND SAYS, "WHAT'S THE BIG IDEA?" NOW, WHAT DO YOU DO?
SCHULZ
NO, I'M AFRAID FAINTING WON'T HELP A BIT!

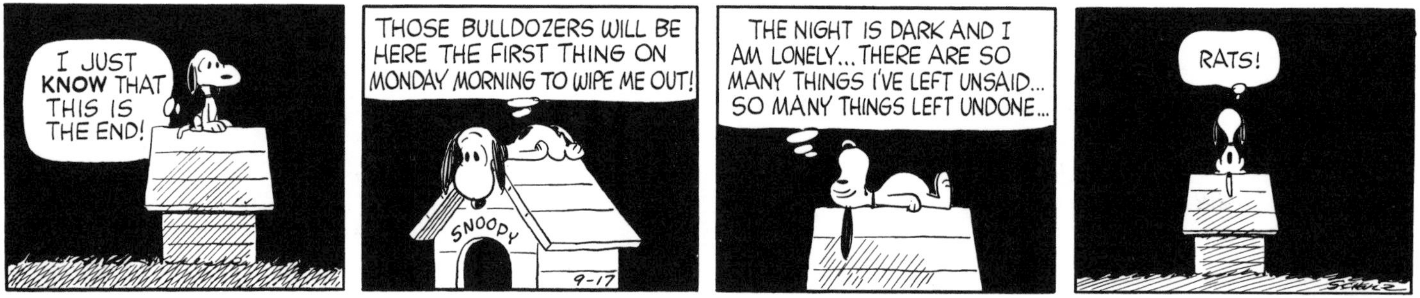
I JUST **KNOW** THAT THIS IS THE END!
THOSE BULLDOZERS WILL BE HERE THE FIRST THING ON MONDAY MORNING TO WIPE ME OUT!
SNOOPY
9-17
THE NIGHT IS DARK AND I AM LONELY... THERE ARE SO MANY THINGS I'VE LEFT UNSAID... SO MANY THINGS LEFT UNDONE...
RATS!
SCHULZ

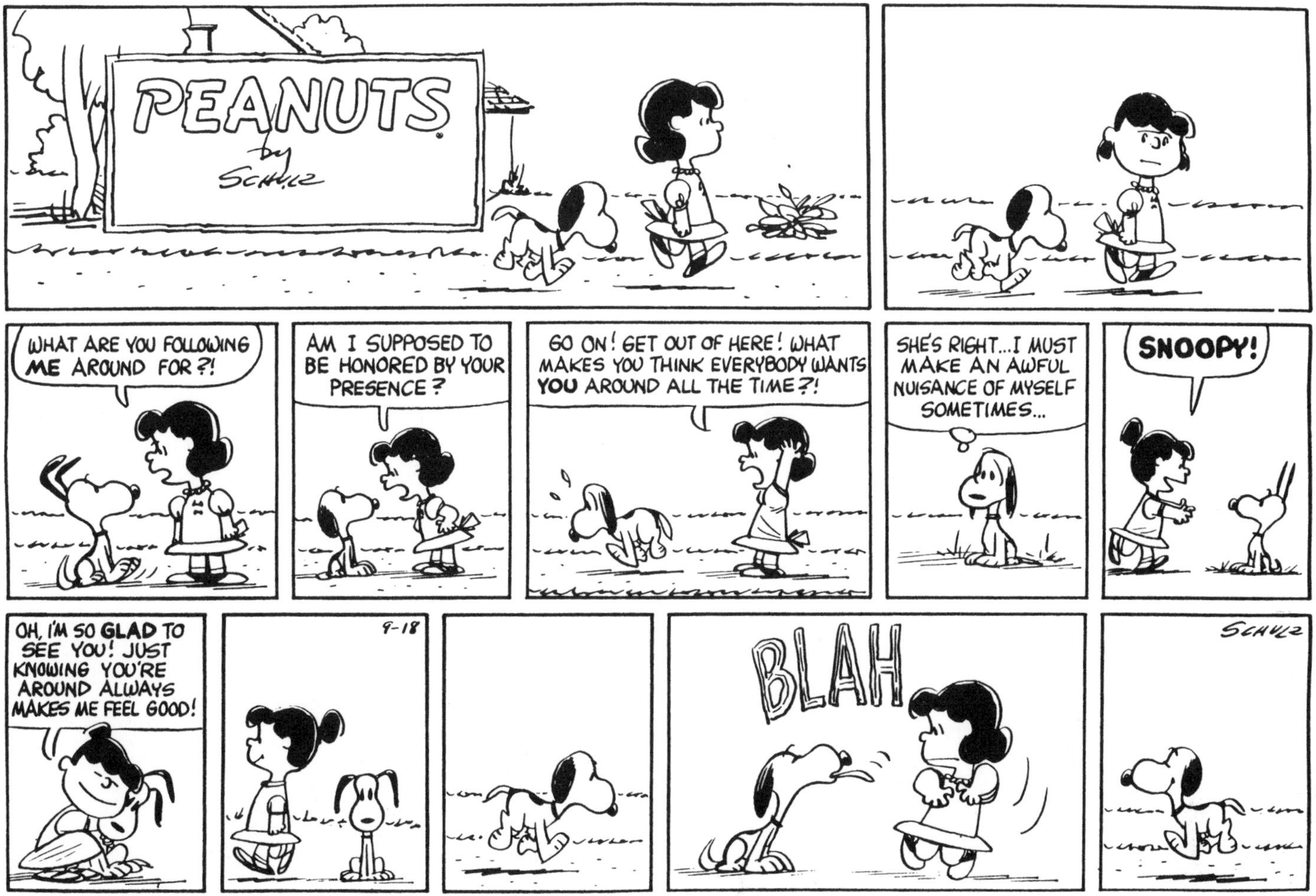
PEANUTS
by SCHULZ
WHAT ARE YOU FOLLOWING ME AROUND FOR?!
AM I SUPPOSED TO BE HONORED BY YOUR PRESENCE?
GO ON! GET OUT OF HERE! WHAT MAKES YOU THINK EVERYBODY WANTS YOU AROUND ALL THE TIME?!
SHE'S RIGHT...I MUST MAKE AN AWFUL NUISANCE OF MYSELF SOMETIMES...
SNOOPY!
OH, I'M SO GLAD TO SEE YOU! JUST KNOWING YOU'RE AROUND ALWAYS MAKES ME FEEL GOOD!
9-18
BLAH
SCHULZ

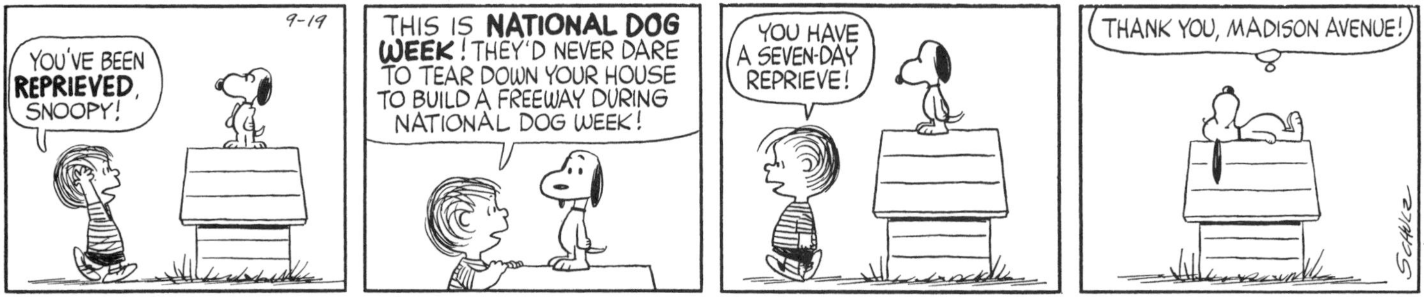
9-19
YOU'VE BEEN **REPRIEVED**, SNOOPY!
THIS IS **NATIONAL DOG WEEK**! THEY'D NEVER DARE TO TEAR DOWN YOUR HOUSE TO BUILD A FREEWAY DURING NATIONAL DOG WEEK!
YOU HAVE A SEVEN-DAY REPRIEVE!
THANK YOU, MADISON AVENUE!
SCHULZ

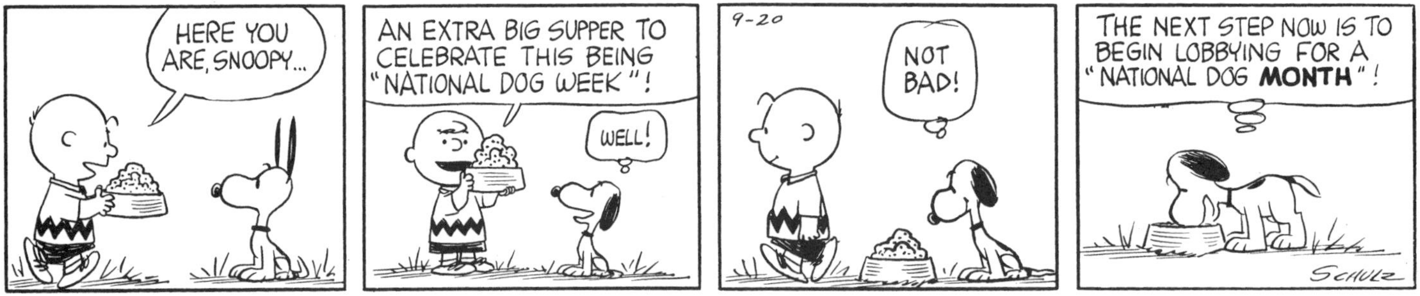
HERE YOU ARE, SNOOPY...
AN EXTRA BIG SUPPER TO CELEBRATE THIS BEING "NATIONAL DOG WEEK"!
WELL!
9-20
NOT BAD!
THE NEXT STEP NOW IS TO BEGIN LOBBYING FOR A "NATIONAL DOG **MONTH**"!
SCHULZ

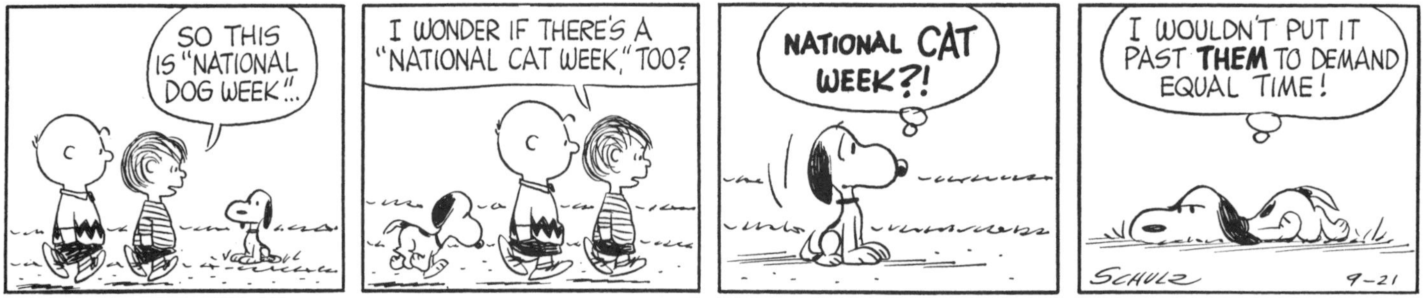
SO THIS IS "NATIONAL DOG WEEK"...
I WONDER IF THERE'S A "NATIONAL CAT WEEK," TOO?
NATIONAL CAT WEEK?!
I WOULDN'T PUT IT PAST **THEM** TO DEMAND EQUAL TIME!
SCHULZ
9-21

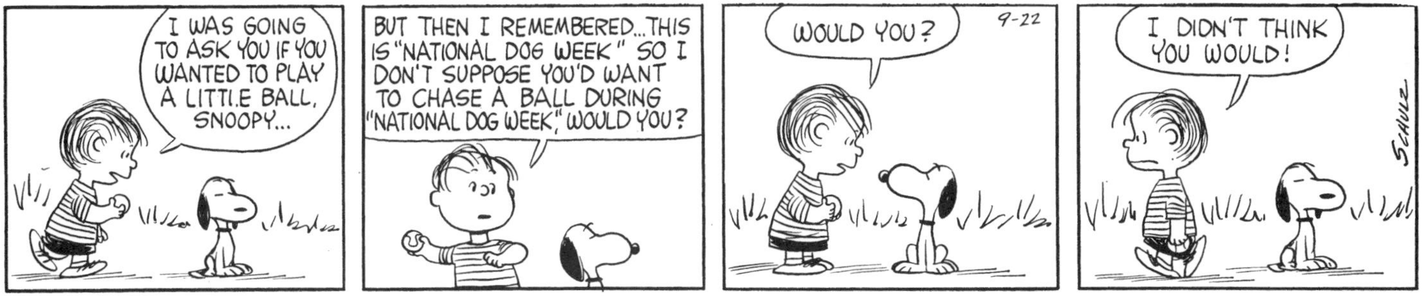
I WAS GOING TO ASK YOU IF YOU WANTED TO PLAY A LITTLE BALL, SNOOPY...
BUT THEN I REMEMBERED...THIS IS "NATIONAL DOG WEEK" SO I DON'T SUPPOSE YOU'D WANT TO CHASE A BALL DURING "NATIONAL DOG WEEK," WOULD YOU?
WOULD YOU?
9-22
I DIDN'T THINK YOU WOULD!
SCHULZ

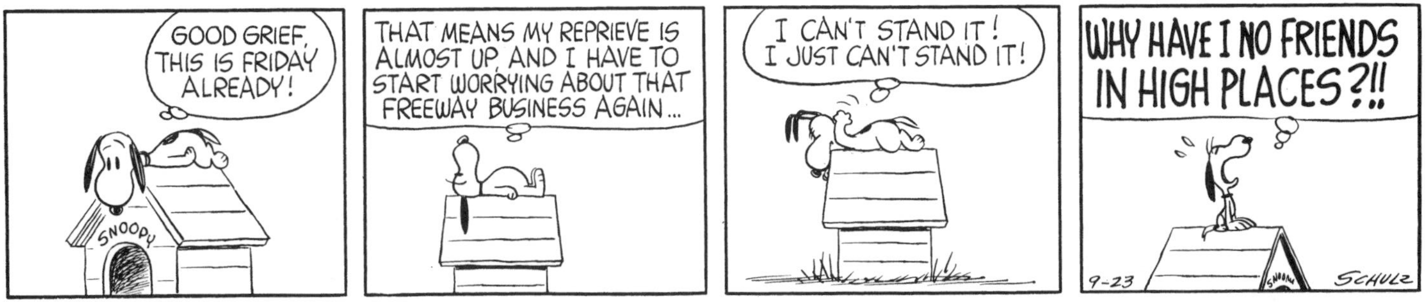
GOOD GRIEF, THIS IS FRIDAY ALREADY!
SNOOPY
THAT MEANS MY REPRIEVE IS ALMOST UP, AND I HAVE TO START WORRYING ABOUT THAT FREEWAY BUSINESS AGAIN...
I CAN'T STAND IT! I JUST CAN'T STAND IT!
WHY HAVE I NO FRIENDS IN HIGH PLACES?!!
9-23
SCHULZ

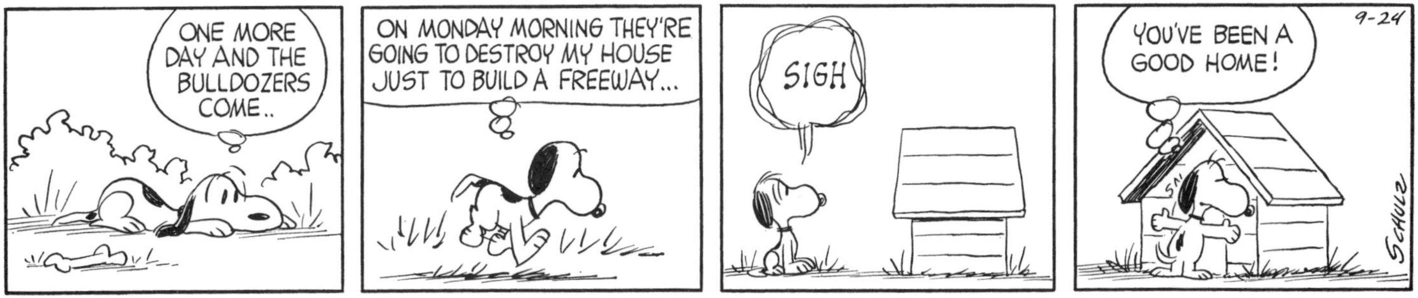
ONE MORE DAY AND THE BULLDOZERS COME..
ON MONDAY MORNING THEY'RE GOING TO DESTROY MY HOUSE JUST TO BUILD A FREEWAY...
SIGH
YOU'VE BEEN A GOOD HOME!
9-24
SCHULZ

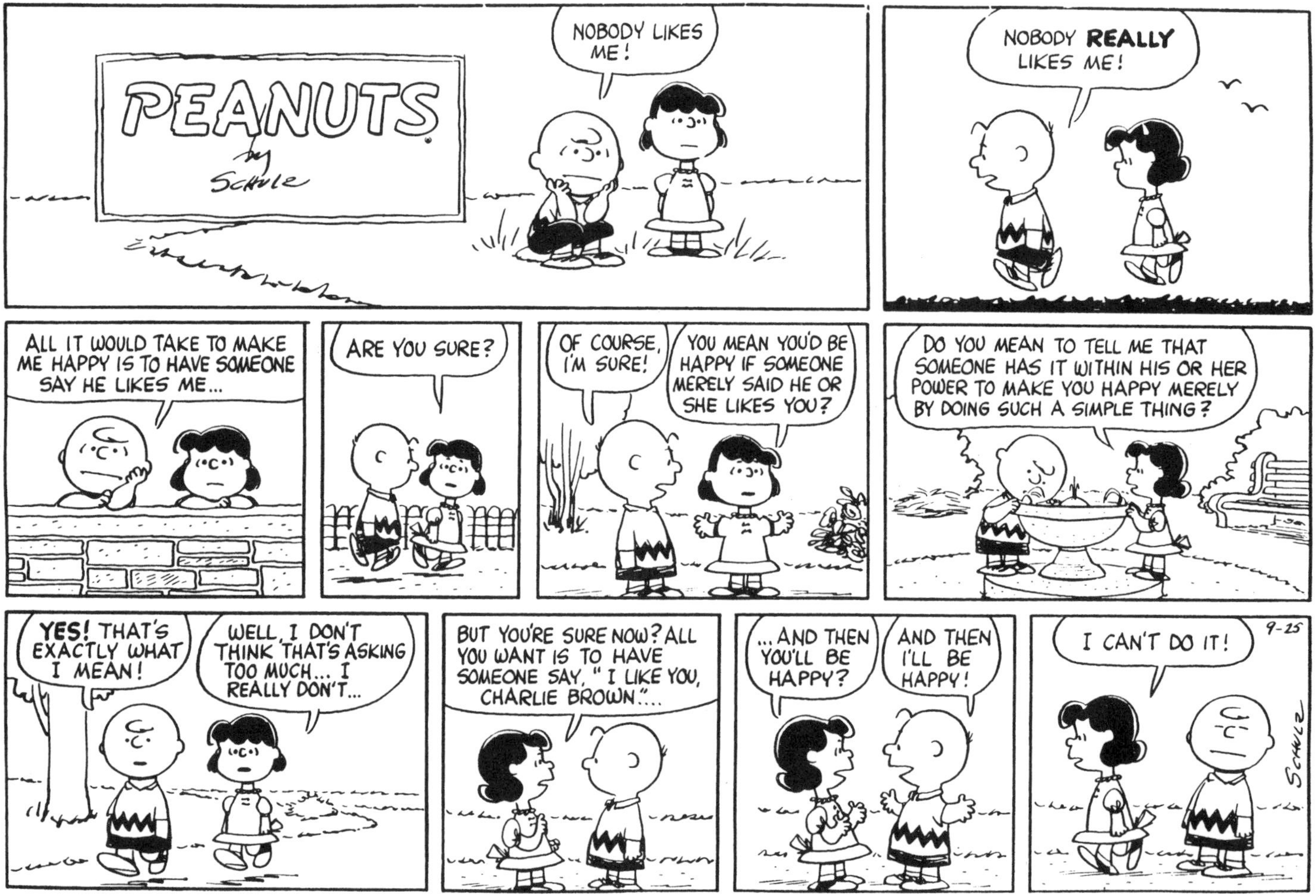
PEANUTS
by Schulz
NOBODY LIKES ME!
NOBODY REALLY LIKES ME!
ALL IT WOULD TAKE TO MAKE ME HAPPY IS TO HAVE SOMEONE SAY HE LIKES ME...
ARE YOU SURE?
OF COURSE, I'M SURE!
YOU MEAN YOU'D BE HAPPY IF SOMEONE MERELY SAID HE OR SHE LIKES YOU?
DO YOU MEAN TO TELL ME THAT SOMEONE HAS IT WITHIN HIS OR HER POWER TO MAKE YOU HAPPY MERELY BY DOING SUCH A SIMPLE THING?
YES! THAT'S EXACTLY WHAT I MEAN!
WELL, I DON'T THINK THAT'S ASKING TOO MUCH... I REALLY DON'T...
BUT YOU'RE SURE NOW? ALL YOU WANT IS TO HAVE SOMEONE SAY, "I LIKE YOU, CHARLIE BROWN."...
...AND THEN YOU'LL BE HAPPY?
AND THEN I'LL BE HAPPY!
9-25
I CAN'T DO IT!
SCHULZ

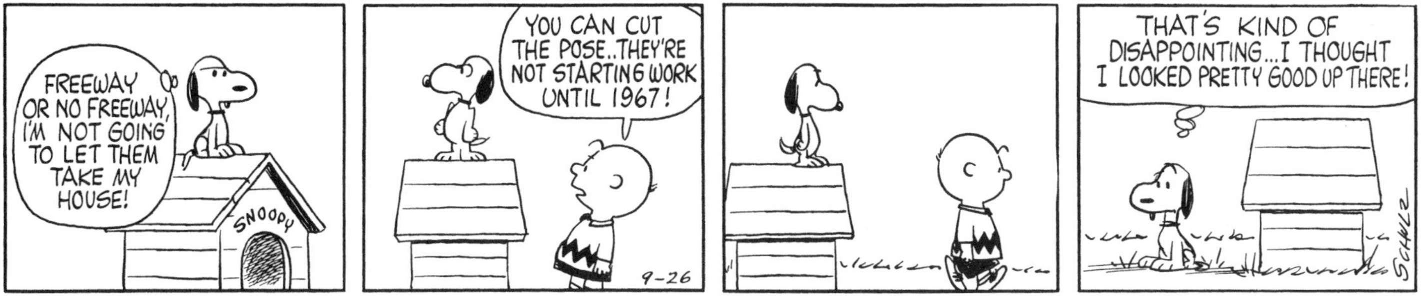
FREEWAY OR NO FREEWAY, I'M NOT GOING TO LET THEM TAKE MY HOUSE!
SNOOPY
YOU CAN CUT THE POSE..THEY'RE NOT STARTING WORK UNTIL 1967!
9-26
THAT'S KIND OF DISAPPOINTING...I THOUGHT I LOOKED PRETTY GOOD UP THERE!
SCHULZ

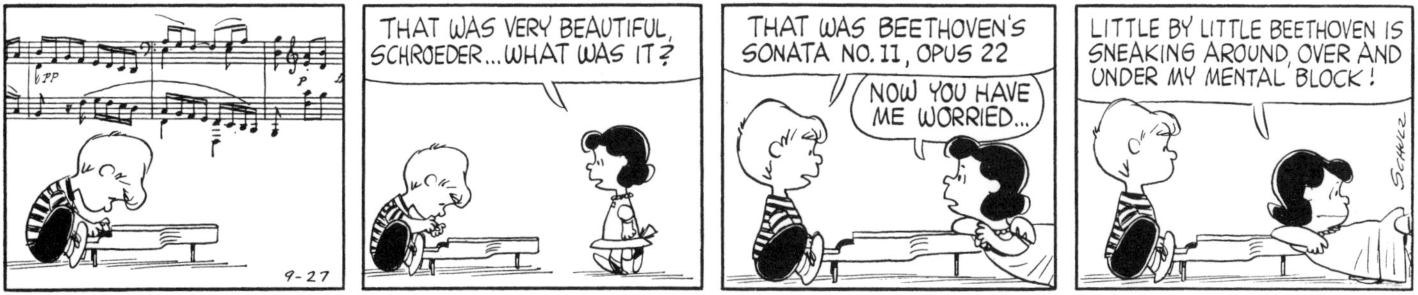
9-27
THAT WAS VERY BEAUTIFUL, SCHROEDER...WHAT WAS IT?
THAT WAS BEETHOVEN'S SONATA NO. 11, OPUS 22
NOW YOU HAVE ME WORRIED...
LITTLE BY LITTLE BEETHOVEN IS SNEAKING AROUND, OVER AND UNDER MY MENTAL BLOCK!
SCHULZ

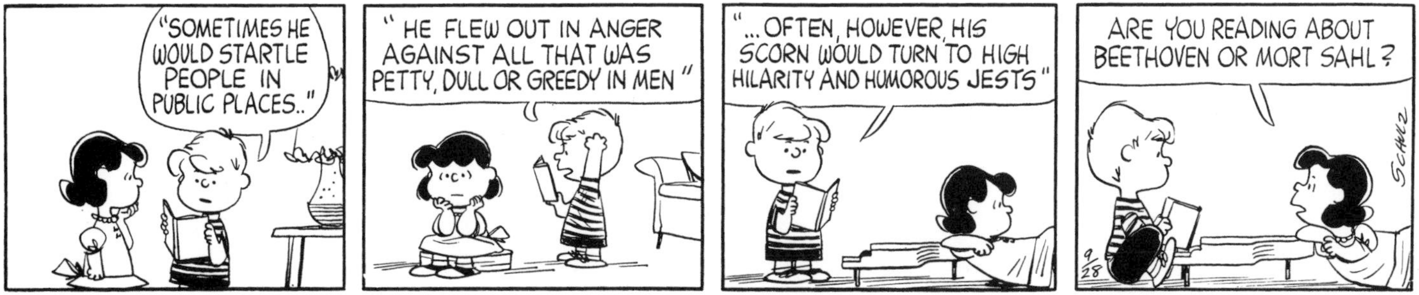
"SOMETIMES HE WOULD STARTLE PEOPLE IN PUBLIC PLACES.."
" HE FLEW OUT IN ANGER AGAINST ALL THAT WAS PETTY, DULL OR GREEDY IN MEN "
"...OFTEN, HOWEVER, HIS SCORN WOULD TURN TO HIGH HILARITY AND HUMOROUS JESTS"
ARE YOU READING ABOUT BEETHOVEN OR MORT SAHL?
SCHULZ
9/28

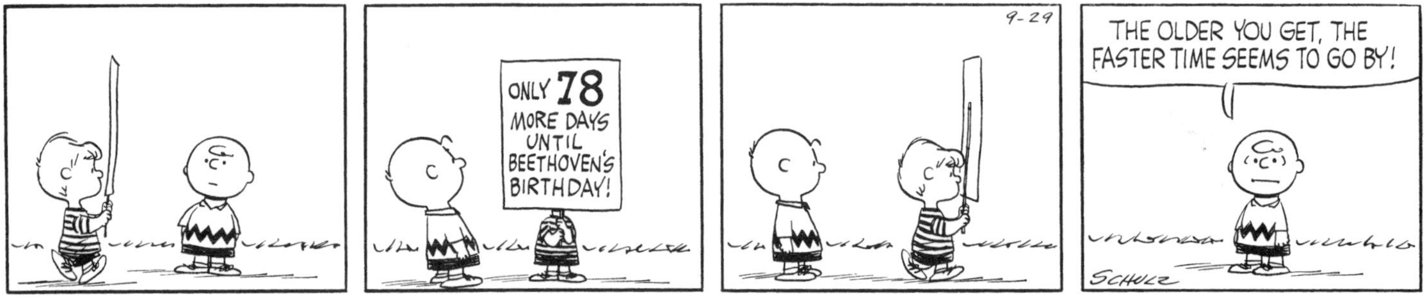
ONLY 78 MORE DAYS UNTIL BEETHOVEN'S BIRTHDAY!
9-29
THE OLDER YOU GET, THE FASTER TIME SEEMS TO GO BY!
SCHULZ

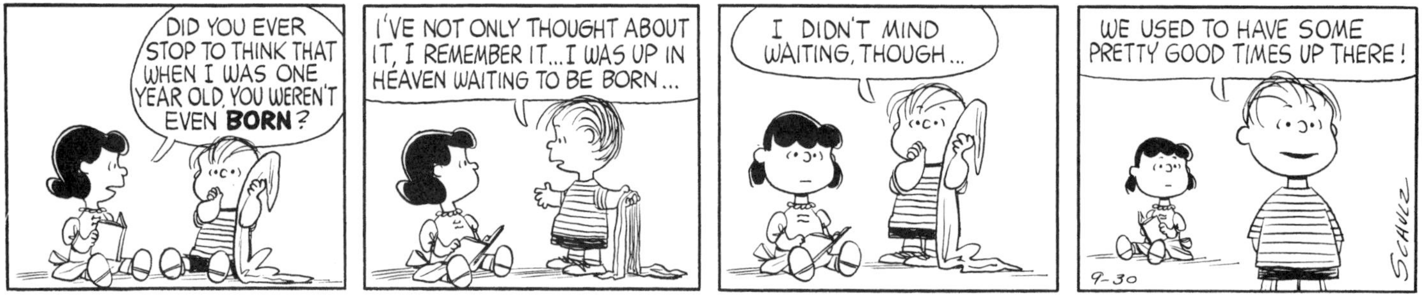
DID YOU EVER STOP TO THINK THAT WHEN I WAS ONE YEAR OLD, YOU WEREN'T EVEN **BORN**?
I'VE NOT ONLY THOUGHT ABOUT IT, I REMEMBER IT...I WAS UP IN HEAVEN WAITING TO BE BORN...
I DIDN'T MIND WAITING, THOUGH...
WE USED TO HAVE SOME PRETTY GOOD TIMES UP THERE!
9-30
SCHULZ

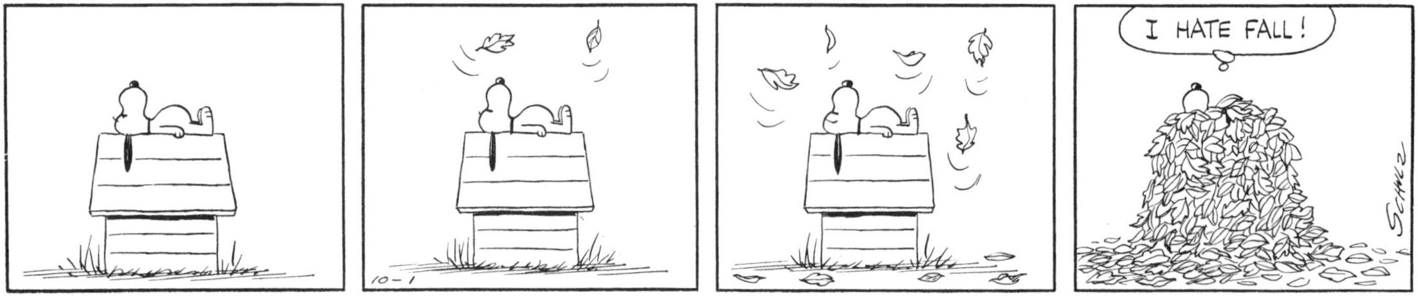
10-1
I HATE FALL!
SCHULZ

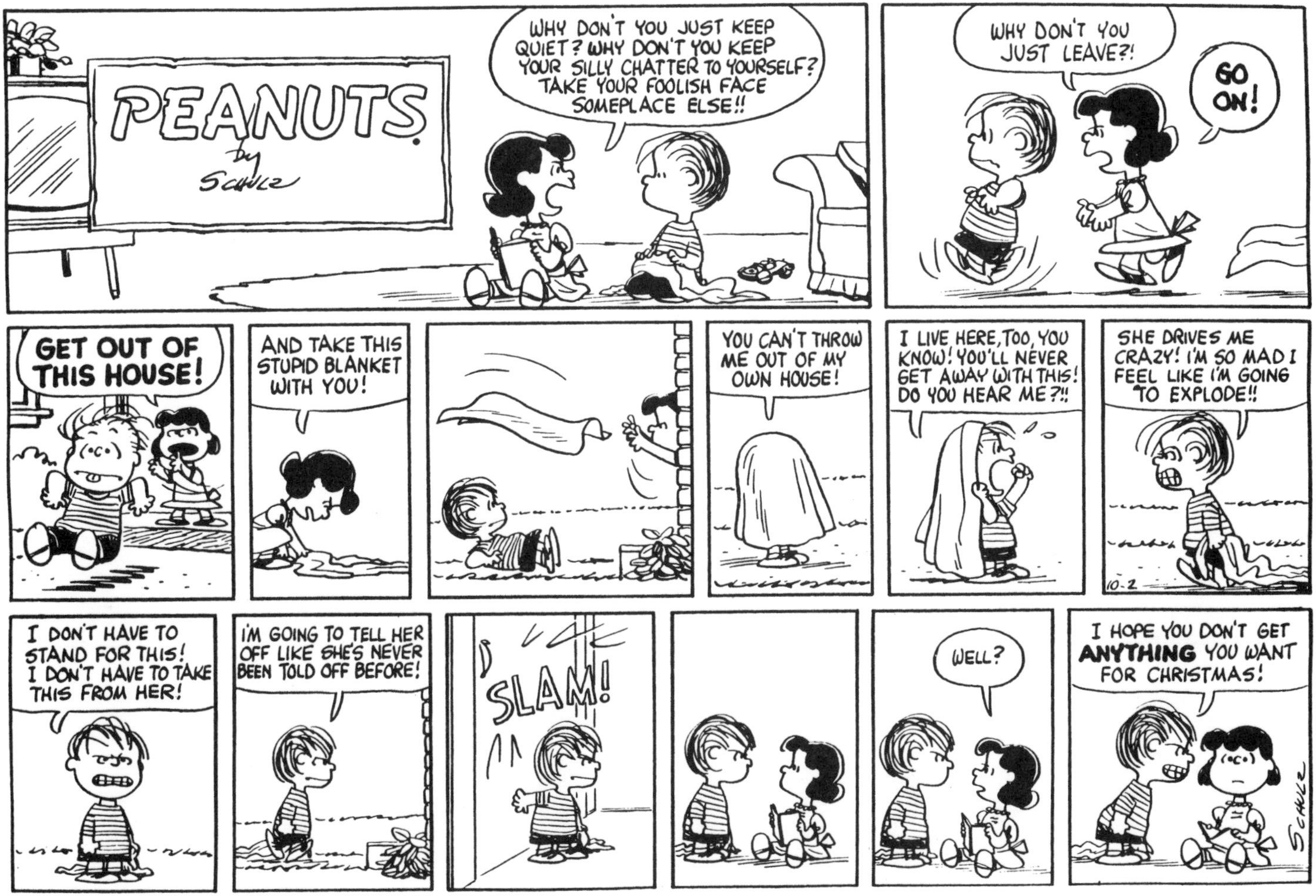
PEANUTS
by SCHULZ
WHY DON'T YOU JUST KEEP QUIET? WHY DON'T YOU KEEP YOUR SILLY CHATTER TO YOURSELF? TAKE YOUR FOOLISH FACE SOMEPLACE ELSE!!
WHY DON'T YOU JUST LEAVE?!
GO ON!
GET OUT OF THIS HOUSE!
AND TAKE THIS STUPID BLANKET WITH YOU!
YOU CAN'T THROW ME OUT OF MY OWN HOUSE!
I LIVE HERE, TOO, YOU KNOW! YOU'LL NEVER GET AWAY WITH THIS! DO YOU HEAR ME?!!
SHE DRIVES ME CRAZY! I'M SO MAD I FEEL LIKE I'M GOING TO EXPLODE!!
10-2
I DON'T HAVE TO STAND FOR THIS! I DON'T HAVE TO TAKE THIS FROM HER!
I'M GOING TO TELL HER OFF LIKE SHE'S NEVER BEEN TOLD OFF BEFORE!
SLAM!
WELL?
I HOPE YOU DON'T GET ANYTHING YOU WANT FOR CHRISTMAS!
SCHULZ

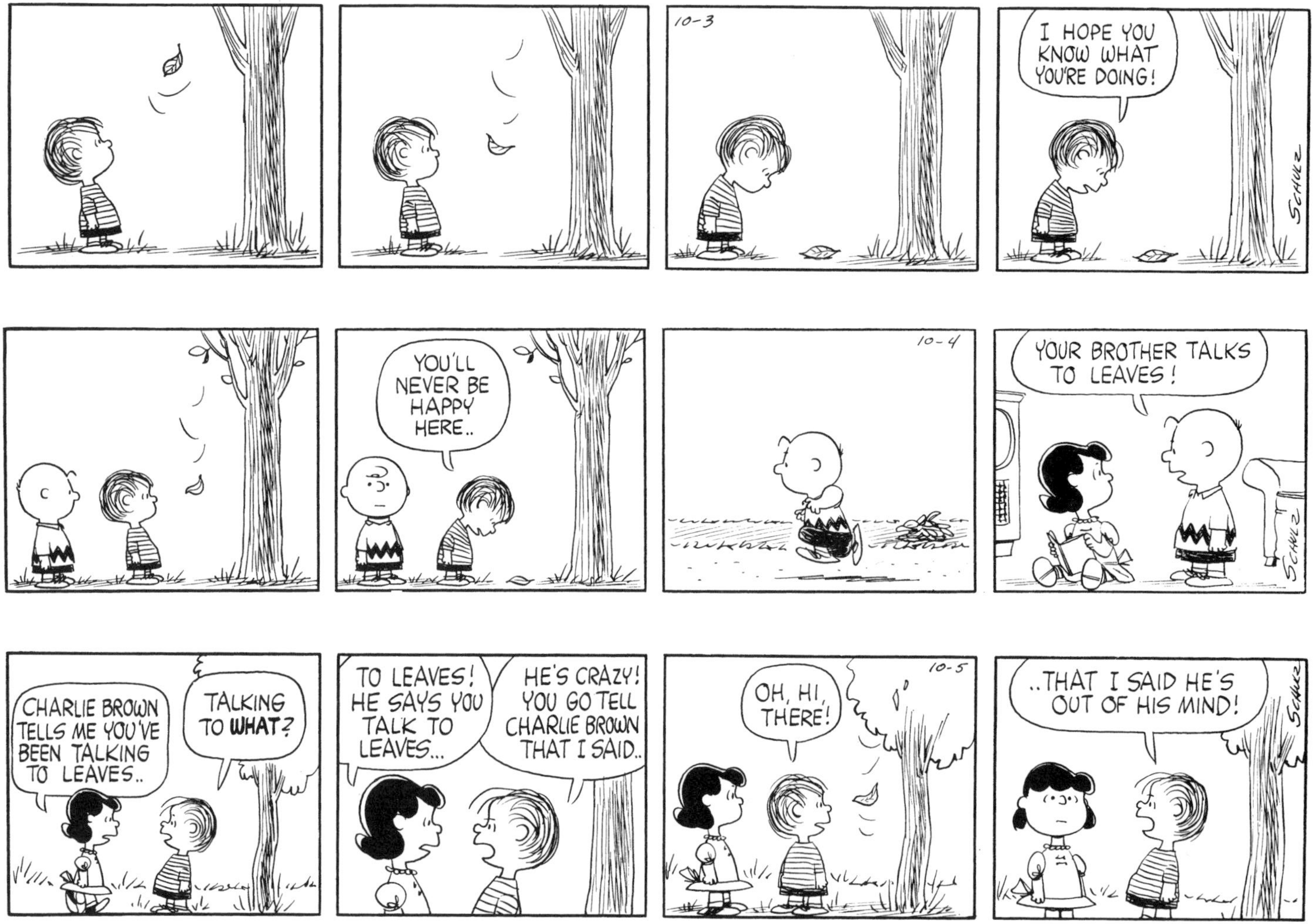
10-3
I HOPE YOU KNOW WHAT YOU'RE DOING!
SCHULZ
YOU'LL NEVER BE HAPPY HERE..
10-4
YOUR BROTHER TALKS TO LEAVES!
SCHULZ
CHARLIE BROWN TELLS ME YOU'VE BEEN TALKING TO LEAVES..
TALKING TO **WHAT**?
TO LEAVES! HE SAYS YOU TALK TO LEAVES...
HE'S CRAZY! YOU GO TELL CHARLIE BROWN THAT I SAID..
10-5
OH, HI, THERE!
..THAT I SAID HE'S OUT OF HIS MIND!
SCHULZ

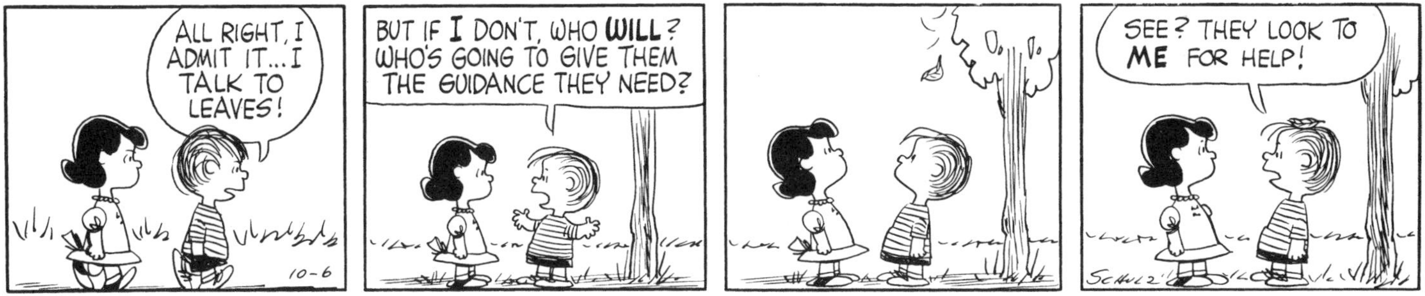
ALL RIGHT, I ADMIT IT... I TALK TO LEAVES!
10-6
BUT IF I DON'T, WHO WILL? WHO'S GOING TO GIVE THEM THE GUIDANCE THEY NEED?
SEE? THEY LOOK TO ME FOR HELP!
SCHULZ

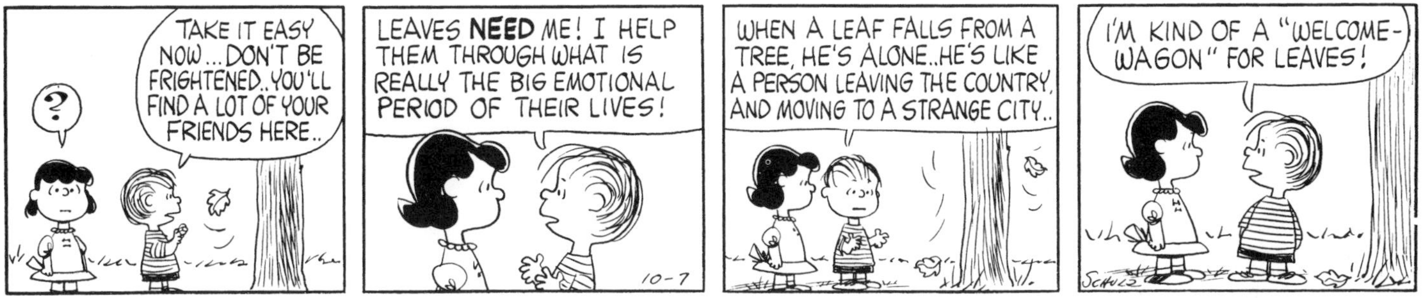
?
TAKE IT EASY NOW... DON'T BE FRIGHTENED.. YOU'LL FIND A LOT OF YOUR FRIENDS HERE..
LEAVES NEED ME! I HELP THEM THROUGH WHAT IS REALLY THE BIG EMOTIONAL PERIOD OF THEIR LIVES!
10-7
WHEN A LEAF FALLS FROM A TREE, HE'S ALONE..HE'S LIKE A PERSON LEAVING THE COUNTRY, AND MOVING TO A STRANGE CITY..
I'M KIND OF A "WELCOME-WAGON" FOR LEAVES!
SCHULZ

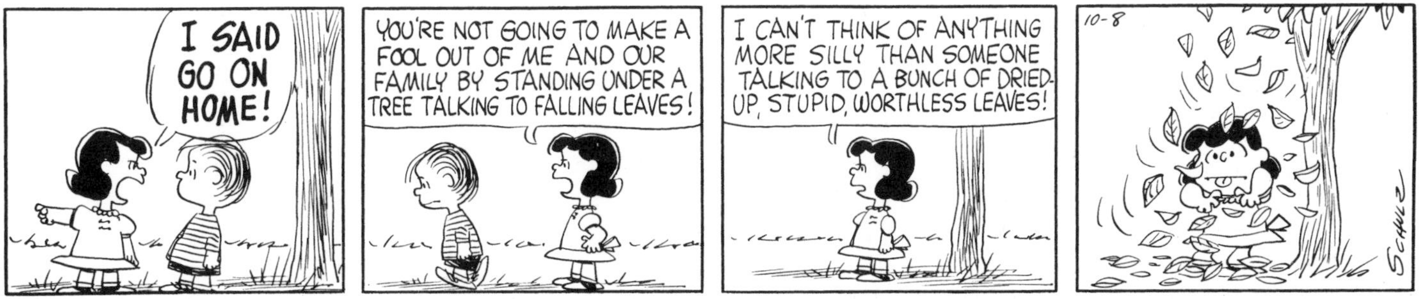
I SAID GO ON HOME!
YOU'RE NOT GOING TO MAKE A FOOL OUT OF ME AND OUR FAMILY BY STANDING UNDER A TREE TALKING TO FALLING LEAVES!
I CAN'T THINK OF ANYTHING MORE SILLY THAN SOMEONE TALKING TO A BUNCH OF DRIED-UP, STUPID, WORTHLESS LEAVES!
10-8
SCHULZ

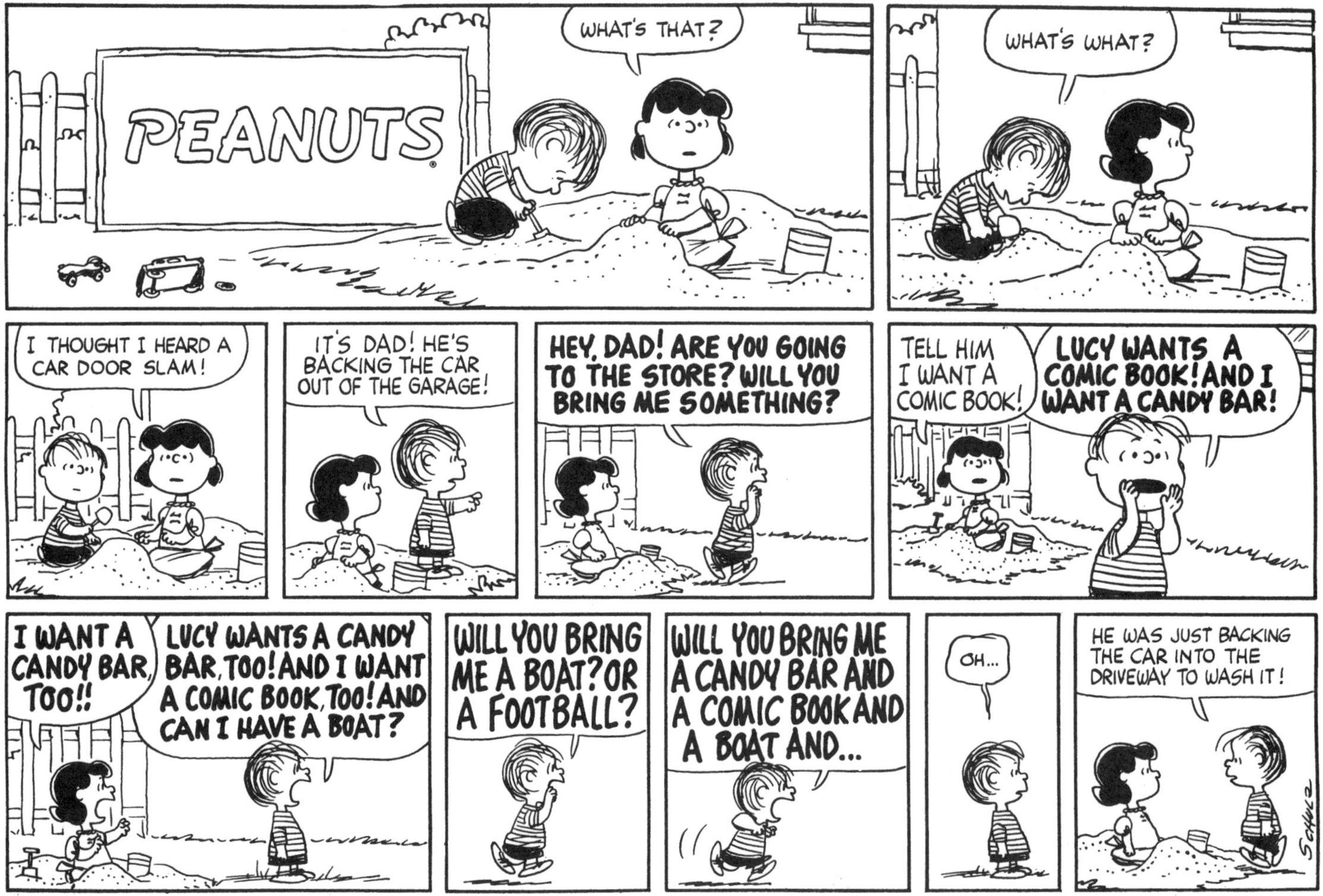
PEANUTS
WHAT'S THAT?
WHAT'S WHAT?
I THOUGHT I HEARD A CAR DOOR SLAM!
IT'S DAD! HE'S BACKING THE CAR OUT OF THE GARAGE!
HEY, DAD! ARE YOU GOING TO THE STORE? WILL YOU BRING ME SOMETHING?
TELL HIM I WANT A COMIC BOOK!
LUCY WANTS A COMIC BOOK! AND I WANT A CANDY BAR!
I WANT A CANDY BAR, TOO!!
LUCY WANTS A CANDY BAR, TOO! AND I WANT A COMIC BOOK, TOO! AND CAN I HAVE A BOAT?
WILL YOU BRING ME A BOAT? OR A FOOTBALL?
WILL YOU BRING ME A CANDY BAR AND A COMIC BOOK AND A BOAT AND...
OH...
HE WAS JUST BACKING THE CAR INTO THE DRIVEWAY TO WASH IT!
SCHULZ

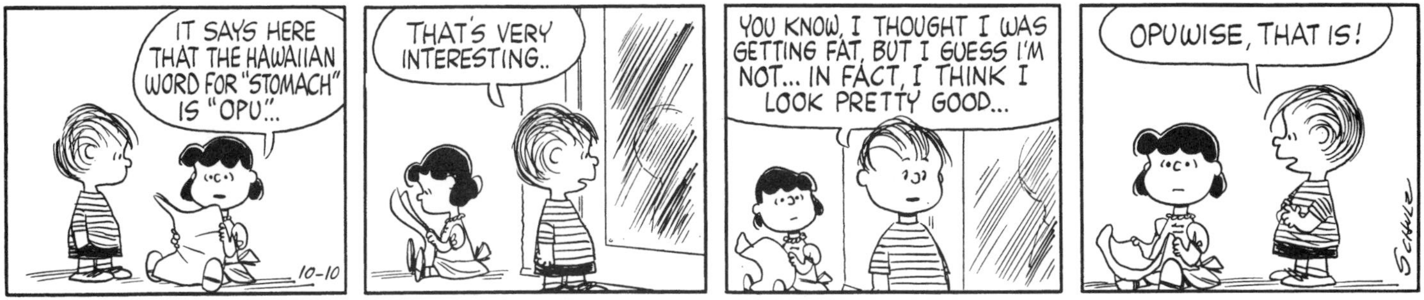
IT SAYS HERE THAT THE HAWAIIAN WORD FOR "STOMACH" IS "OPU"...
10-10
THAT'S VERY INTERESTING..
YOU KNOW, I THOUGHT I WAS GETTING FAT, BUT I GUESS I'M NOT... IN FACT, I THINK I LOOK PRETTY GOOD...
OPUWISE, THAT IS!
SCHULZ

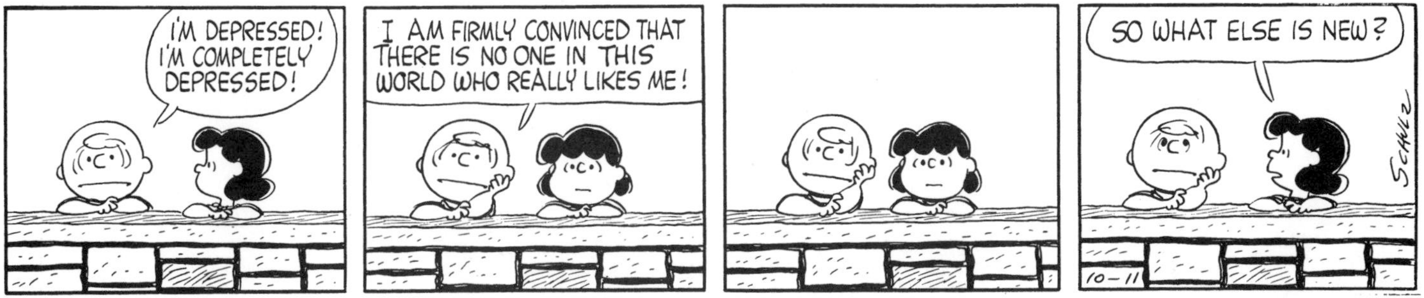
I'M DEPRESSED! I'M COMPLETELY DEPRESSED!
I AM FIRMLY CONVINCED THAT THERE IS NO ONE IN THIS WORLD WHO REALLY LIKES ME!
SO WHAT ELSE IS NEW?
SCHULZ
10-11

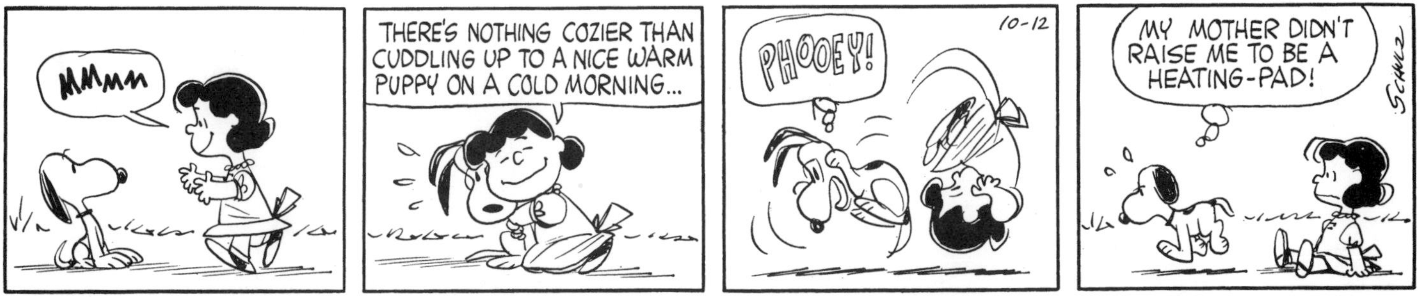
MMmn
THERE'S NOTHING COZIER THAN CUDDLING UP TO A NICE WARM PUPPY ON A COLD MORNING...
10-12
PHOOEY!
MY MOTHER DIDN'T RAISE ME TO BE A HEATING-PAD!
SCHULZ

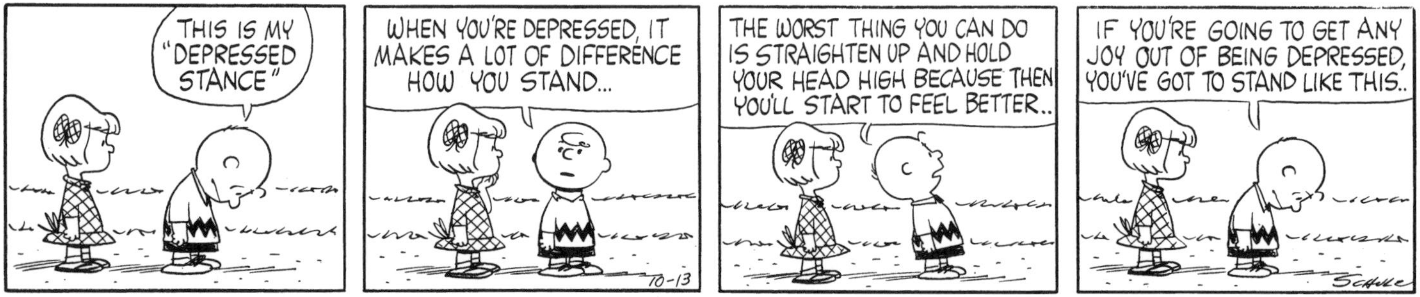
THIS IS MY "DEPRESSED STANCE"
WHEN YOU'RE DEPRESSED, IT MAKES A LOT OF DIFFERENCE HOW YOU STAND...
10-13
THE WORST THING YOU CAN DO IS STRAIGHTEN UP AND HOLD YOUR HEAD HIGH BECAUSE THEN YOU'LL START TO FEEL BETTER..
IF YOU'RE GOING TO GET ANY JOY OUT OF BEING DEPRESSED, YOU'VE GOT TO STAND LIKE THIS..
SCHULZ

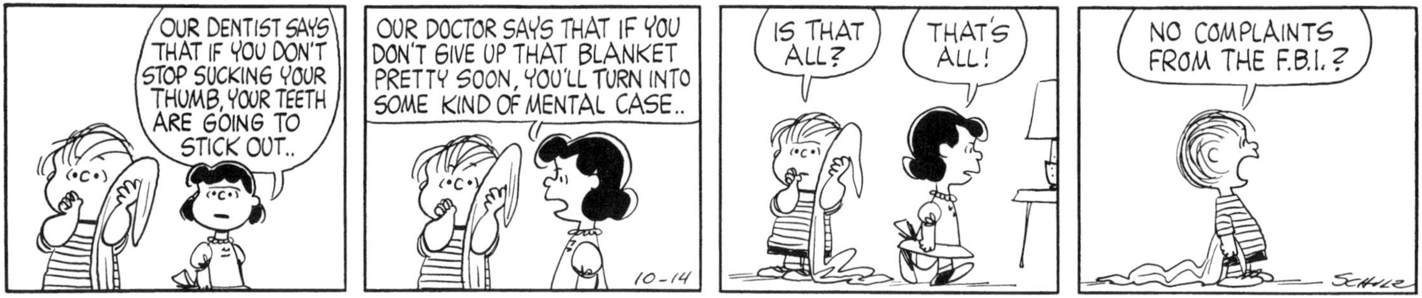
OUR DENTIST SAYS THAT IF YOU DON'T STOP SUCKING YOUR THUMB, YOUR TEETH ARE GOING TO STICK OUT..
OUR DOCTOR SAYS THAT IF YOU DON'T GIVE UP THAT BLANKET PRETTY SOON, YOU'LL TURN INTO SOME KIND OF MENTAL CASE..
10-14
IS THAT ALL?
THAT'S ALL!
NO COMPLAINTS FROM THE F.B.I.?
SCHULZ

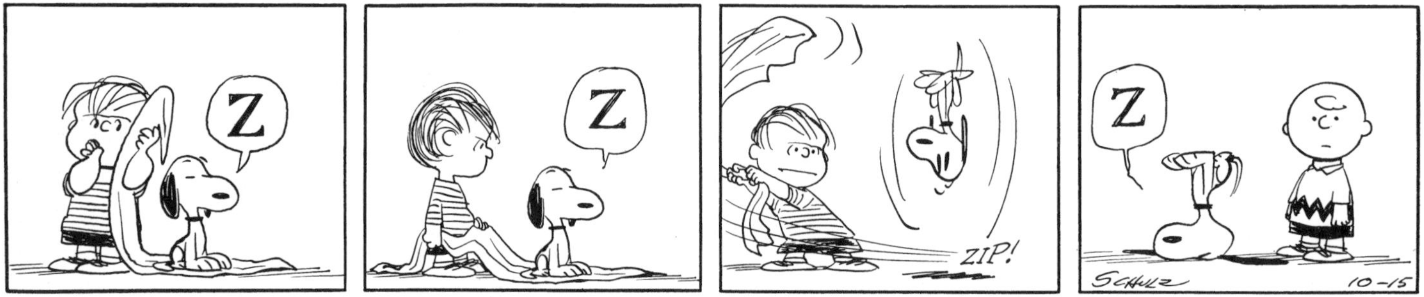
Z
Z
ZIP!
Z
SCHULZ
10-15

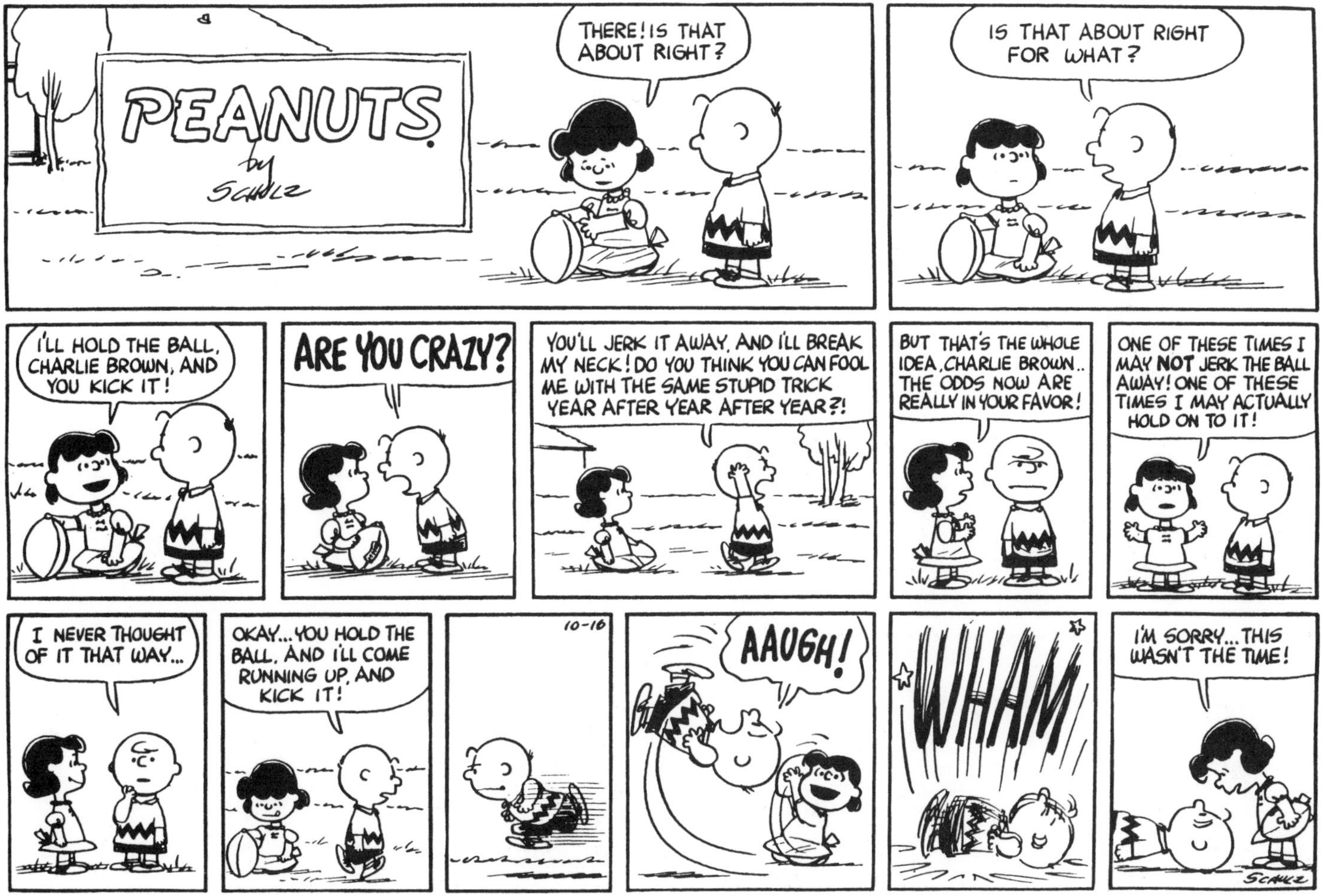
PEANUTS
by SCHULZ
THERE! IS THAT ABOUT RIGHT?
IS THAT ABOUT RIGHT FOR WHAT?
I'LL HOLD THE BALL, CHARLIE BROWN, AND YOU KICK IT!
ARE YOU CRAZY?
YOU'LL JERK IT AWAY, AND I'LL BREAK MY NECK! DO YOU THINK YOU CAN FOOL ME WITH THE SAME STUPID TRICK YEAR AFTER YEAR AFTER YEAR?!
BUT THAT'S THE WHOLE IDEA, CHARLIE BROWN.. THE ODDS NOW ARE REALLY IN YOUR FAVOR!
ONE OF THESE TIMES I MAY NOT JERK THE BALL AWAY! ONE OF THESE TIMES I MAY ACTUALLY HOLD ON TO IT!
I NEVER THOUGHT OF IT THAT WAY...
OKAY... YOU HOLD THE BALL, AND I'LL COME RUNNING UP, AND KICK IT!
10-16
AAUGH!
WHAM
I'M SORRY... THIS WASN'T THE TIME!
SCHULZ

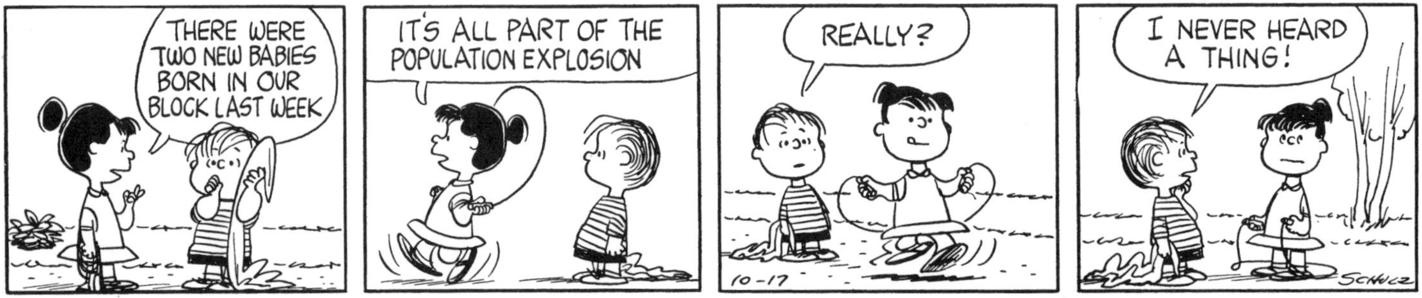
THERE WERE TWO NEW BABIES BORN IN OUR BLOCK LAST WEEK
IT'S ALL PART OF THE POPULATION EXPLOSION
REALLY?
10-17
I NEVER HEARD A THING!

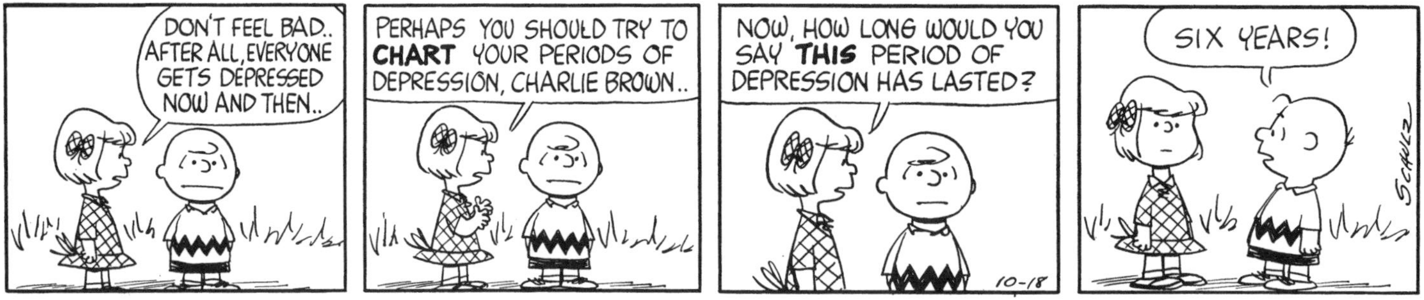
DON'T FEEL BAD.. AFTER ALL, EVERYONE GETS DEPRESSED NOW AND THEN..
PERHAPS YOU SHOULD TRY TO CHART YOUR PERIODS OF DEPRESSION, CHARLIE BROWN..
NOW, HOW LONG WOULD YOU SAY THIS PERIOD OF DEPRESSION HAS LASTED?
10-18
SIX YEARS!

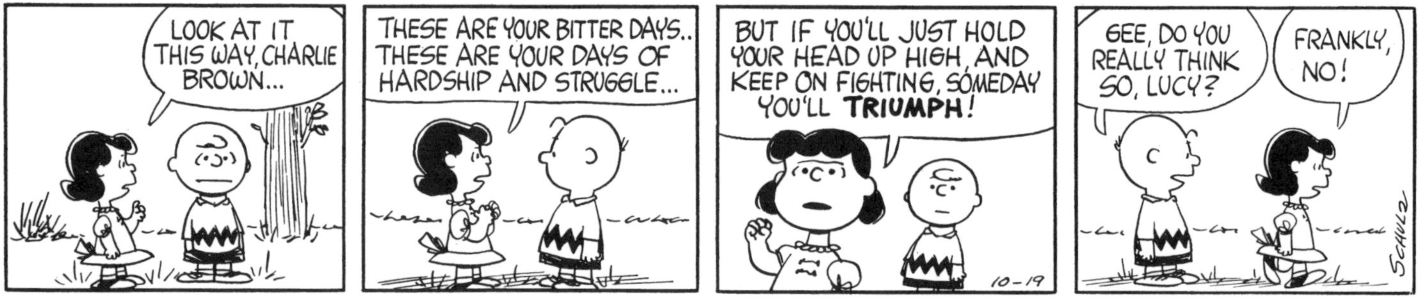
LOOK AT IT THIS WAY, CHARLIE BROWN...
THESE ARE YOUR BITTER DAYS.. THESE ARE YOUR DAYS OF HARDSHIP AND STRUGGLE...
BUT IF YOU'LL JUST HOLD YOUR HEAD UP HIGH, AND KEEP ON FIGHTING, SOMEDAY YOU'LL TRIUMPH!
10-19
GEE, DO YOU REALLY THINK SO, LUCY?
FRANKLY, NO!

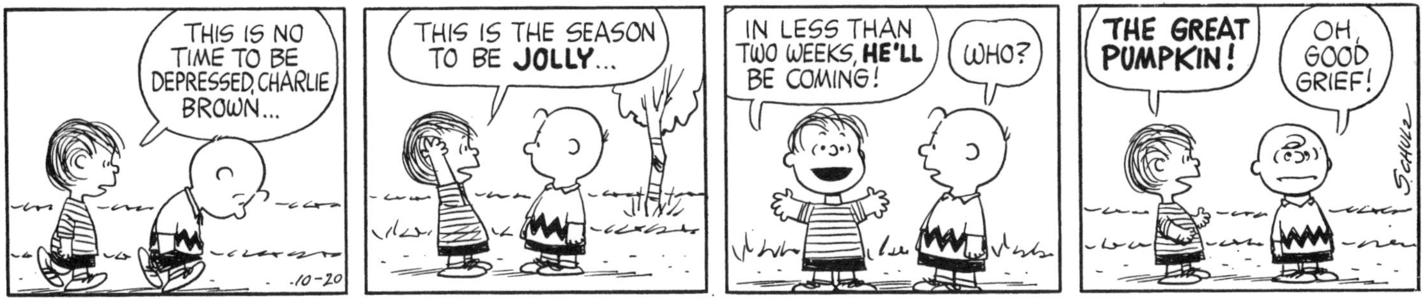
THIS IS NO TIME TO BE DEPRESSED, CHARLIE BROWN...
THIS IS THE SEASON TO BE JOLLY...
IN LESS THAN TWO WEEKS, HE'LL BE COMING!
WHO?
THE GREAT PUMPKIN!
OH, GOOD GRIEF!

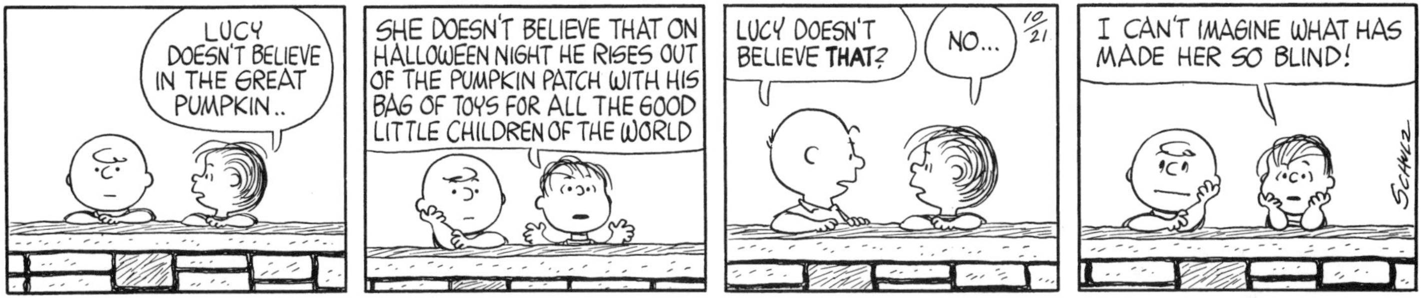
LUCY DOESN'T BELIEVE IN THE GREAT PUMPKIN..
SHE DOESN'T BELIEVE THAT ON HALLOWEEN NIGHT HE RISES OUT OF THE PUMPKIN PATCH WITH HIS BAG OF TOYS FOR ALL THE GOOD LITTLE CHILDREN OF THE WORLD
LUCY DOESN'T BELIEVE THAT?
NO...
I CAN'T IMAGINE WHAT HAS MADE HER SO BLIND!

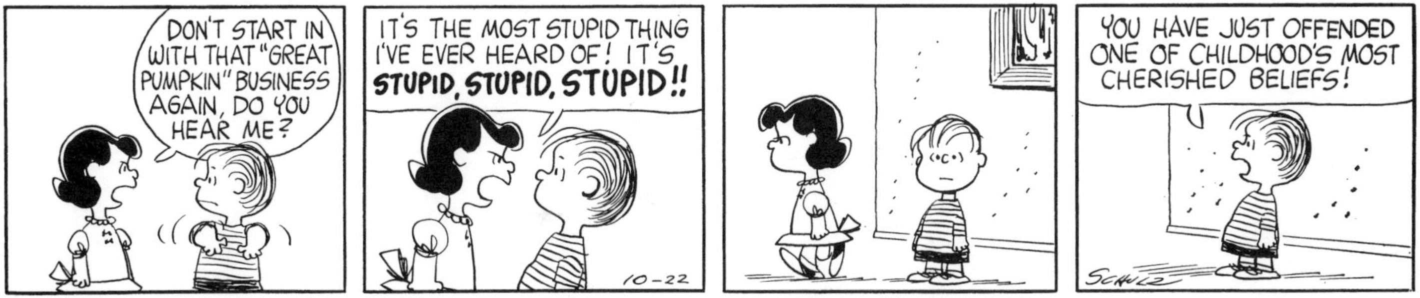
DON'T START IN WITH THAT "GREAT PUMPKIN" BUSINESS AGAIN, DO YOU HEAR ME?
IT'S THE MOST STUPID THING I'VE EVER HEARD OF! IT'S STUPID, STUPID, STUPID!!
YOU HAVE JUST OFFENDED ONE OF CHILDHOOD'S MOST CHERISHED BELIEFS!

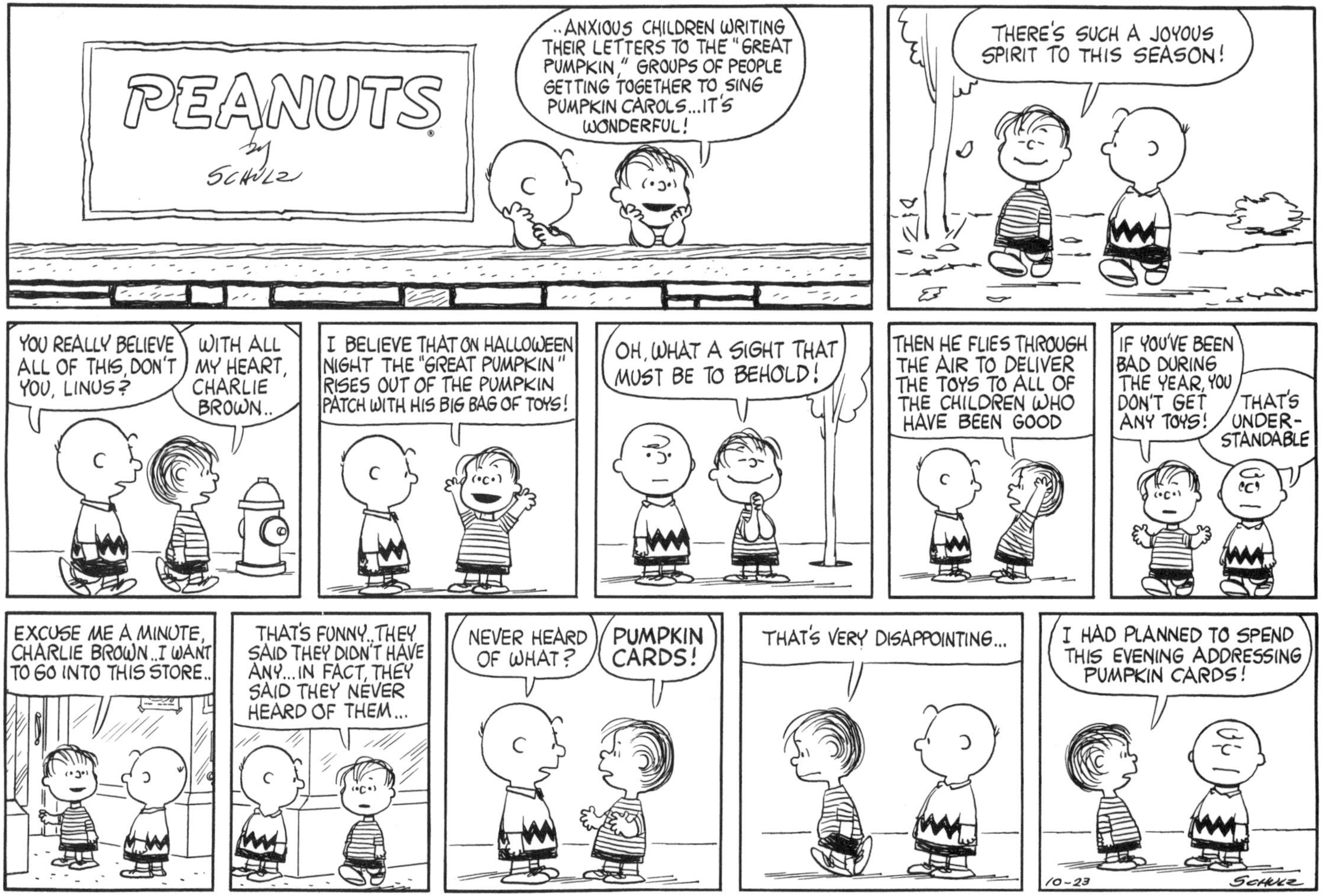
PEANUTS
by SCHULZ
..ANXIOUS CHILDREN WRITING THEIR LETTERS TO THE "GREAT PUMPKIN," GROUPS OF PEOPLE GETTING TOGETHER TO SING PUMPKIN CAROLS...IT'S WONDERFUL!
THERE'S SUCH A JOYOUS SPIRIT TO THIS SEASON!
YOU REALLY BELIEVE ALL OF THIS, DON'T YOU, LINUS?
WITH ALL MY HEART, CHARLIE BROWN..
I BELIEVE THAT ON HALLOWEEN NIGHT THE "GREAT PUMPKIN" RISES OUT OF THE PUMPKIN PATCH WITH HIS BIG BAG OF TOYS!
OH, WHAT A SIGHT THAT MUST BE TO BEHOLD!
THEN HE FLIES THROUGH THE AIR TO DELIVER THE TOYS TO ALL OF THE CHILDREN WHO HAVE BEEN GOOD
IF YOU'VE BEEN BAD DURING THE YEAR, YOU DON'T GET ANY TOYS!
THAT'S UNDER-STANDABLE
EXCUSE ME A MINUTE, CHARLIE BROWN..I WANT TO GO INTO THIS STORE..
THAT'S FUNNY..THEY SAID THEY DIDN'T HAVE ANY...IN FACT, THEY SAID THEY NEVER HEARD OF THEM...
NEVER HEARD OF WHAT?
PUMPKIN CARDS!
THAT'S VERY DISAPPOINTING...
I HAD PLANNED TO SPEND THIS EVENING ADDRESSING PUMPKIN CARDS!
10-23
SCHULZ

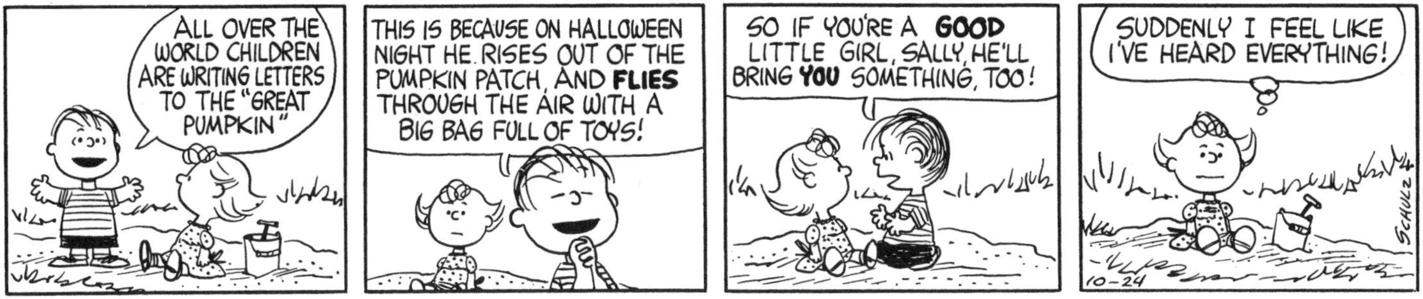
ALL OVER THE WORLD CHILDREN ARE WRITING LETTERS TO THE "GREAT PUMPKIN"
THIS IS BECAUSE ON HALLOWEEN NIGHT HE RISES OUT OF THE PUMPKIN PATCH, AND **FLIES** THROUGH THE AIR WITH A BIG BAG FULL OF TOYS!
SO IF YOU'RE A **GOOD** LITTLE GIRL, SALLY, HE'LL BRING **YOU** SOMETHING, TOO!
SUDDENLY I FEEL LIKE I'VE HEARD EVERYTHING!
SCHULZ
10-24

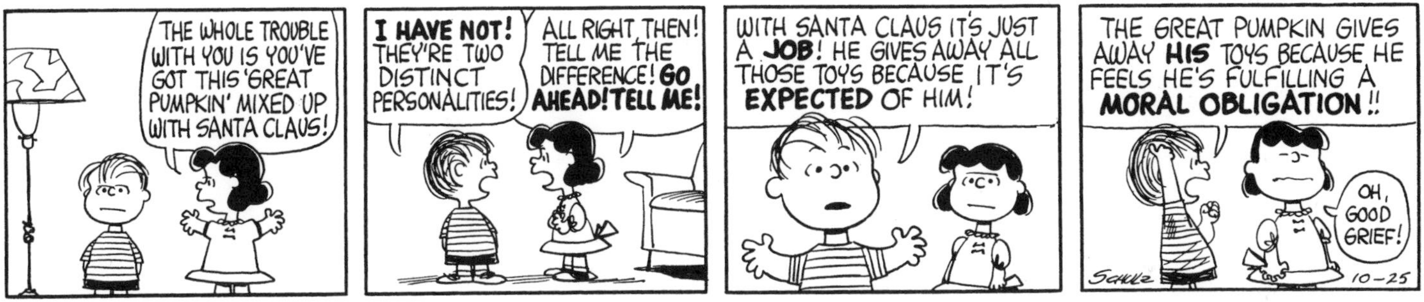
THE WHOLE TROUBLE WITH YOU IS YOU'VE GOT THIS 'GREAT PUMPKIN' MIXED UP WITH SANTA CLAUS!
I HAVE NOT! THEY'RE TWO DISTINCT PERSONALITIES!
ALL RIGHT, THEN! TELL ME THE DIFFERENCE! **GO AHEAD! TELL ME!**
WITH SANTA CLAUS IT'S JUST A **JOB**! HE GIVES AWAY ALL THOSE TOYS BECAUSE IT'S **EXPECTED** OF HIM!
THE GREAT PUMPKIN GIVES AWAY **HIS** TOYS BECAUSE HE FEELS HE'S FULFILLING A **MORAL OBLIGATION**!!
OH, GOOD GRIEF!
SCHULZ
10-25

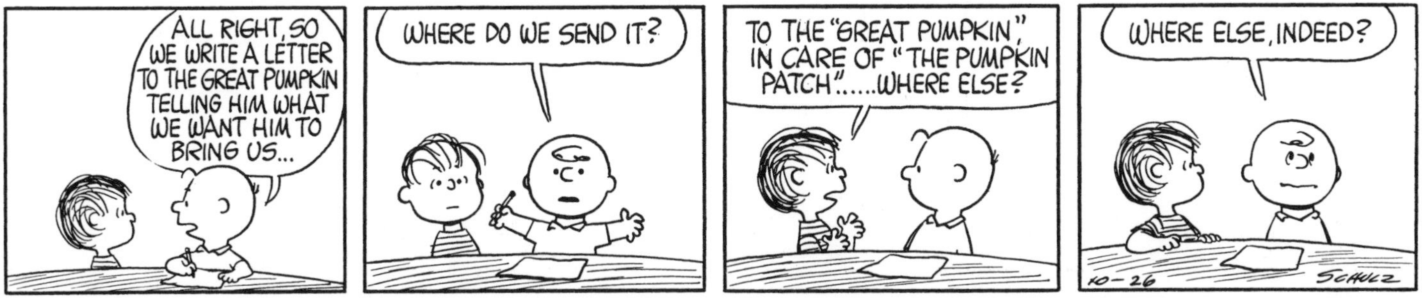
ALL RIGHT, SO WE WRITE A LETTER TO THE GREAT PUMPKIN TELLING HIM WHAT WE WANT HIM TO BRING US...
WHERE DO WE SEND IT?
TO THE "GREAT PUMPKIN," IN CARE OF "THE PUMPKIN PATCH"......WHERE ELSE?
WHERE ELSE, INDEED?
10-26
SCHULZ

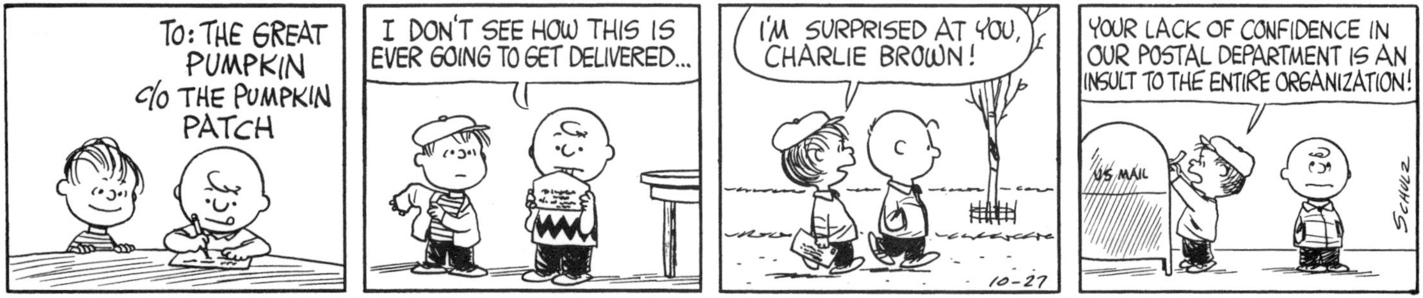
TO: THE GREAT PUMPKIN c/o THE PUMPKIN PATCH
I DON'T SEE HOW THIS IS EVER GOING TO GET DELIVERED...
I'M SURPRISED AT YOU, CHARLIE BROWN!
10-27
YOUR LACK OF CONFIDENCE IN OUR POSTAL DEPARTMENT IS AN INSULT TO THE ENTIRE ORGANIZATION!
US MAIL
SCHULZ

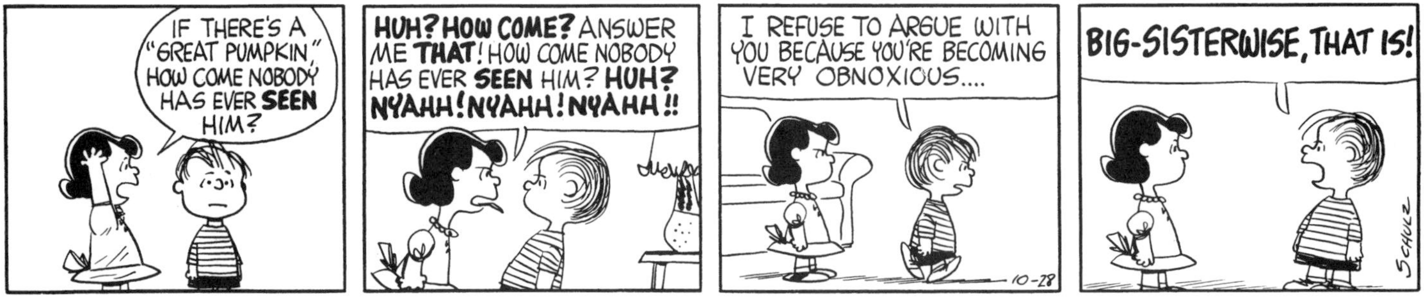
IF THERE'S A "GREAT PUMPKIN," HOW COME NOBODY HAS EVER **SEEN** HIM?
HUH? HOW COME? ANSWER ME **THAT**! HOW COME NOBODY HAS EVER **SEEN** HIM? **HUH? NYAHH! NYAHH! NYAHH!!**
I REFUSE TO ARGUE WITH YOU BECAUSE YOU'RE BECOMING VERY OBNOXIOUS....
10-28
BIG-SISTERWISE, THAT IS!
SCHULZ

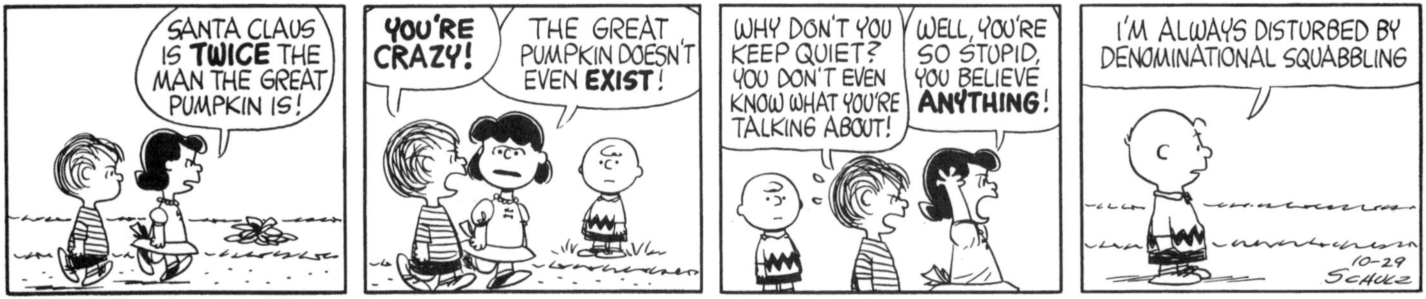
SANTA CLAUS IS **TWICE** THE MAN THE GREAT PUMPKIN IS!
YOU'RE CRAZY!
THE GREAT PUMPKIN DOESN'T EVEN **EXIST**!
WHY DON'T YOU KEEP QUIET? YOU DON'T EVEN KNOW WHAT YOU'RE TALKING ABOUT!
WELL, YOU'RE SO STUPID, YOU BELIEVE **ANYTHING**!
I'M ALWAYS DISTURBED BY DENOMINATIONAL SQUABBLING
10-29
SCHULZ

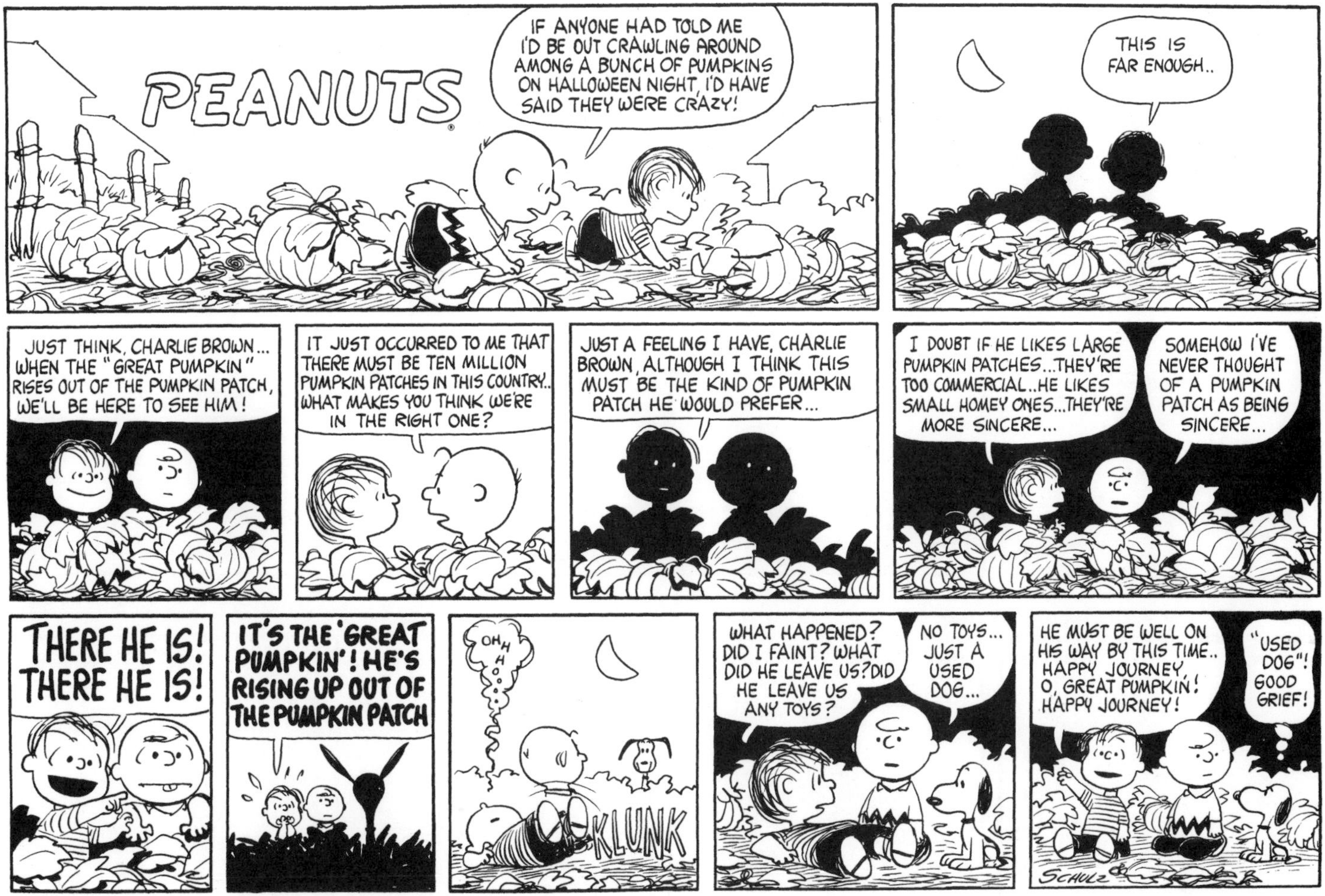
PEANUTS
IF ANYONE HAD TOLD ME I'D BE OUT CRAWLING AROUND AMONG A BUNCH OF PUMPKINS ON HALLOWEEN NIGHT, I'D HAVE SAID THEY WERE CRAZY!
THIS IS FAR ENOUGH..
JUST THINK, CHARLIE BROWN... WHEN THE "GREAT PUMPKIN" RISES OUT OF THE PUMPKIN PATCH, WE'LL BE HERE TO SEE HIM!
IT JUST OCCURRED TO ME THAT THERE MUST BE TEN MILLION PUMPKIN PATCHES IN THIS COUNTRY.. WHAT MAKES YOU THINK WE'RE IN THE RIGHT ONE?
JUST A FEELING I HAVE, CHARLIE BROWN, ALTHOUGH I THINK THIS MUST BE THE KIND OF PUMPKIN PATCH HE WOULD PREFER...
I DOUBT IF HE LIKES LARGE PUMPKIN PATCHES...THEY'RE TOO COMMERCIAL..HE LIKES SMALL HOMEY ONES...THEY'RE MORE SINCERE...
SOMEHOW I'VE NEVER THOUGHT OF A PUMPKIN PATCH AS BEING SINCERE...
THERE HE IS! THERE HE IS!
IT'S THE 'GREAT PUMPKIN'! HE'S RISING UP OUT OF THE PUMPKIN PATCH
OHHHOOOO
KLUNK
WHAT HAPPENED? DID I FAINT? WHAT DID HE LEAVE US? DID HE LEAVE US ANY TOYS?
NO TOYS... JUST A USED DOG...
HE MUST BE WELL ON HIS WAY BY THIS TIME.. HAPPY JOURNEY, O, GREAT PUMPKIN! HAPPY JOURNEY!
"USED DOG"! GOOD GRIEF!
SCHULZ

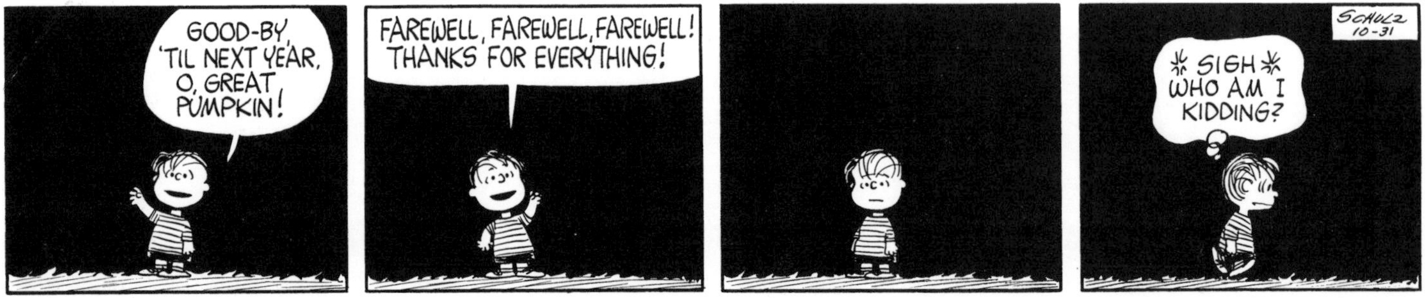
GOOD-BY, 'TIL NEXT YEAR, O, GREAT PUMPKIN!
FAREWELL, FAREWELL, FAREWELL! THANKS FOR EVERYTHING!
SCHULZ 10-31
* SIGH * WHO AM I KIDDING?

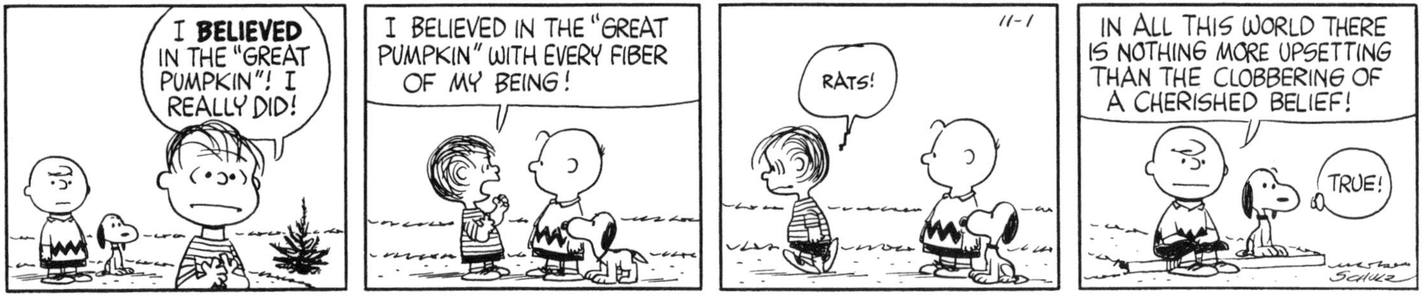
I **BELIEVED** IN THE "GREAT PUMPKIN"! I REALLY DID!
I BELIEVED IN THE "GREAT PUMPKIN" WITH EVERY FIBER OF MY BEING!
11-1
RATS!
IN ALL THIS WORLD THERE IS NOTHING MORE UPSETTING THAN THE CLOBBERING OF A CHERISHED BELIEF!
TRUE!
SCHULZ

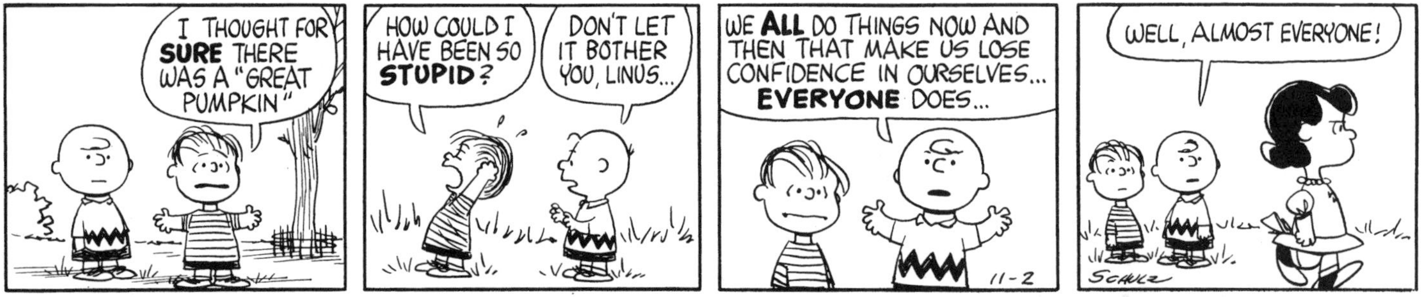
I THOUGHT FOR **SURE** THERE WAS A "GREAT PUMPKIN"
HOW COULD I HAVE BEEN SO **STUPID**?
DON'T LET IT BOTHER YOU, LINUS...
WE **ALL** DO THINGS NOW AND THEN THAT MAKE US LOSE CONFIDENCE IN OURSELVES... **EVERYONE** DOES...
11-2
WELL, ALMOST EVERYONE!
SCHULZ

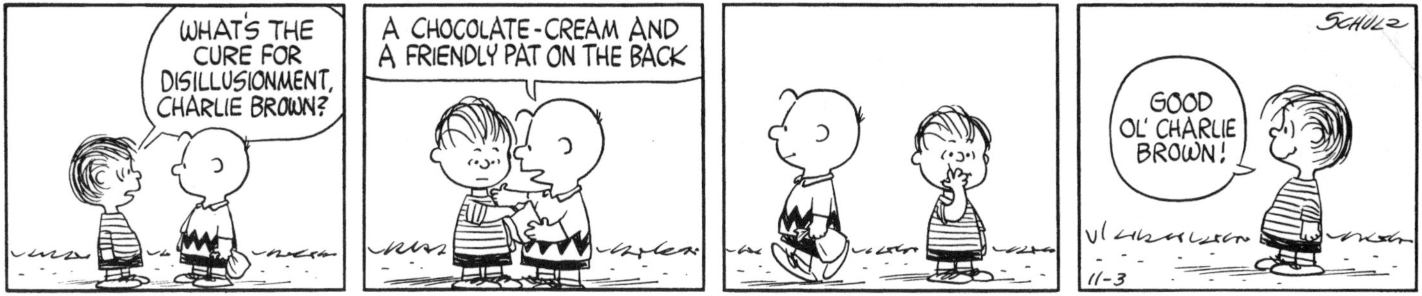
WHAT'S THE CURE FOR DISILLUSIONMENT, CHARLIE BROWN?
A CHOCOLATE-CREAM AND A FRIENDLY PAT ON THE BACK
GOOD OL' CHARLIE BROWN!
SCHULZ
11-3

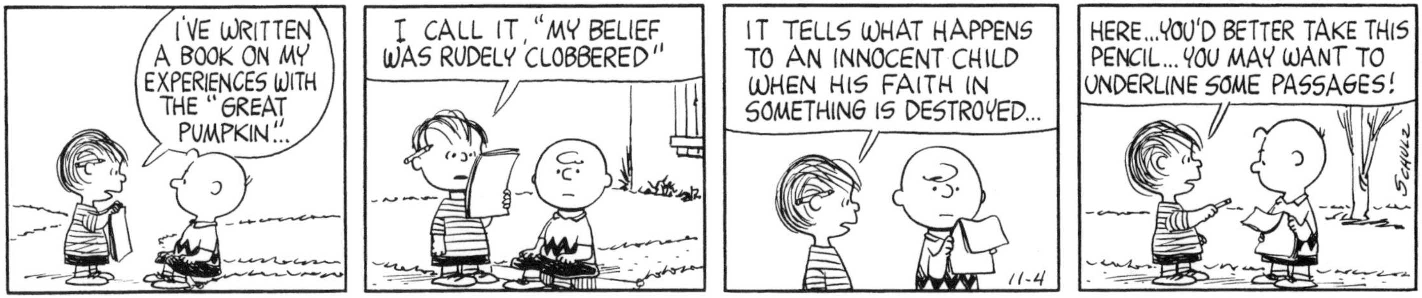
I'VE WRITTEN A BOOK ON MY EXPERIENCES WITH THE "GREAT PUMPKIN"..
I CALL IT, "MY BELIEF WAS RUDELY CLOBBERED"
IT TELLS WHAT HAPPENS TO AN INNOCENT CHILD WHEN HIS FAITH IN SOMETHING IS DESTROYED...
11-4
HERE...YOU'D BETTER TAKE THIS PENCIL...YOU MAY WANT TO UNDERLINE SOME PASSAGES!
SCHULZ

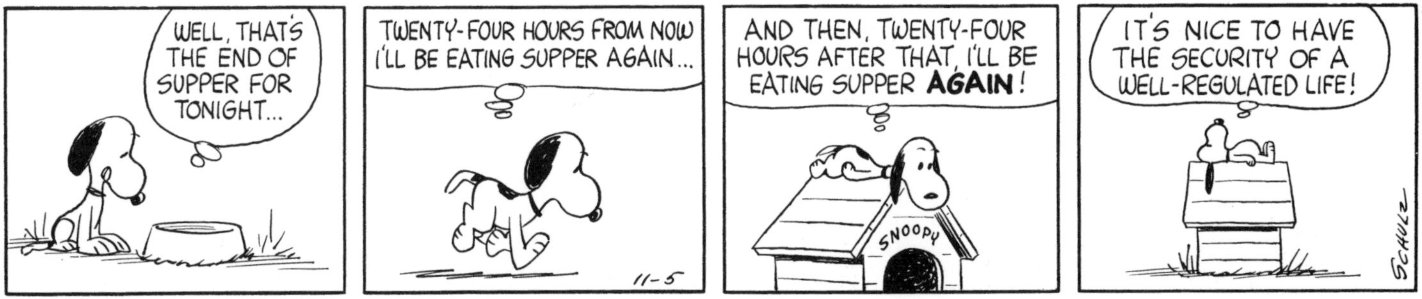
WELL, THAT'S THE END OF SUPPER FOR TONIGHT...
TWENTY-FOUR HOURS FROM NOW I'LL BE EATING SUPPER AGAIN...
11-5
AND THEN, TWENTY-FOUR HOURS AFTER THAT, I'LL BE EATING SUPPER **AGAIN**!
SNOOPY
IT'S NICE TO HAVE THE SECURITY OF A WELL-REGULATED LIFE!
SCHULZ

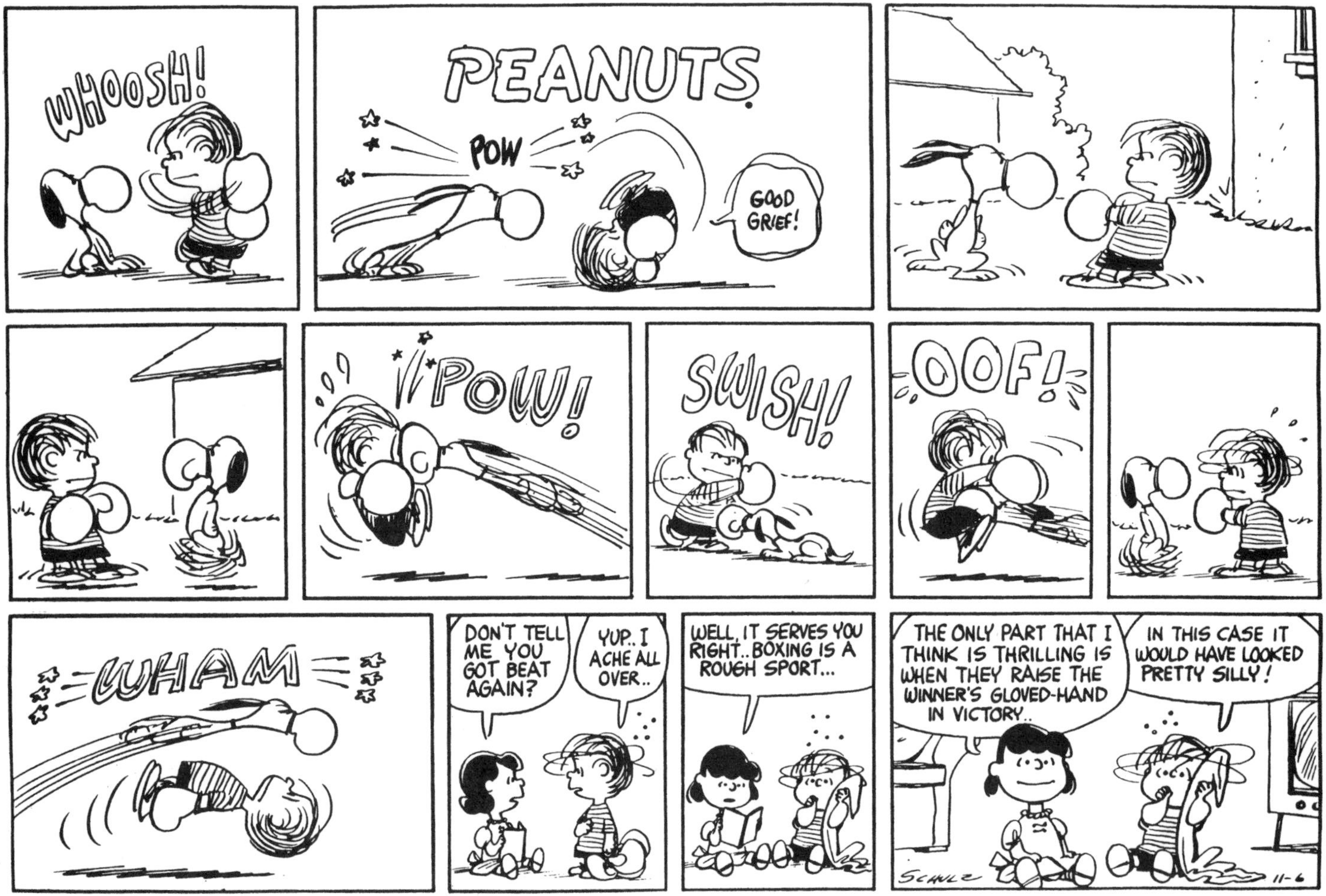
WHOOSH!
PEANUTS
POW
GOOD GRIEF!
POW!
SWISH!
OOF!
WHAM
DON'T TELL ME YOU GOT BEAT AGAIN?
YUP.. I ACHE ALL OVER..
WELL, IT SERVES YOU RIGHT.. BOXING IS A ROUGH SPORT...
THE ONLY PART THAT I THINK IS THRILLING IS WHEN THEY RAISE THE WINNER'S GLOVED-HAND IN VICTORY..
IN THIS CASE IT WOULD HAVE LOOKED PRETTY SILLY!
SCHULZ
11-6

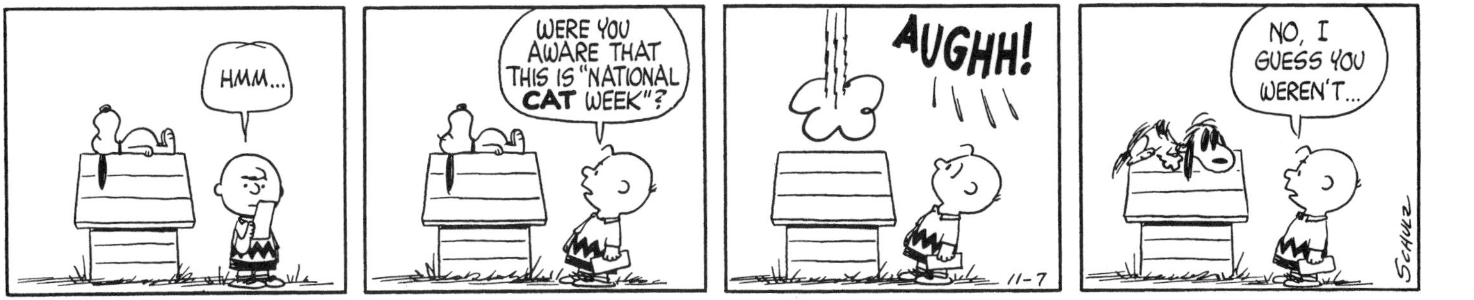
HMM...
WERE YOU AWARE THAT THIS IS "NATIONAL CAT WEEK"?
AUGHH!
NO, I GUESS YOU WEREN'T...
11-7
SCHULZ

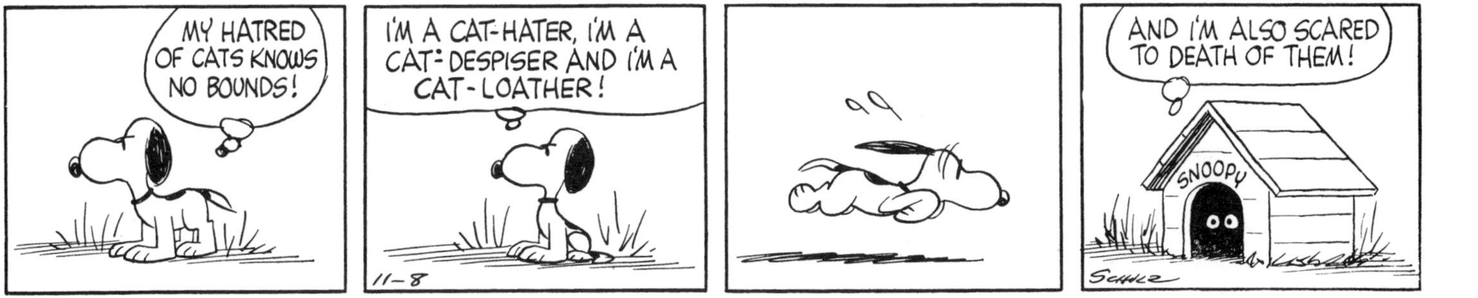
MY HATRED OF CATS KNOWS NO BOUNDS!
I'M A CAT-HATER, I'M A CAT-DESPISER AND I'M A CAT-LOATHER!
11-8
AND I'M ALSO SCARED TO DEATH OF THEM!
SNOOPY
SCHULZ

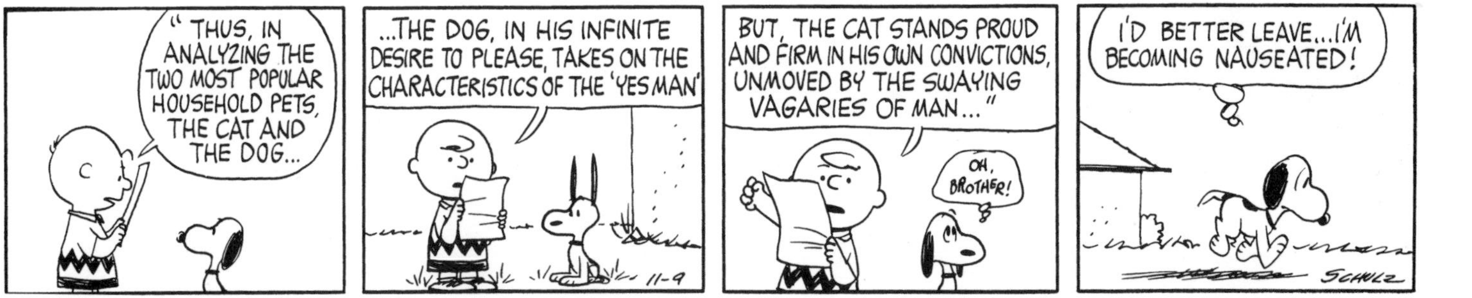
" THUS, IN ANALYZING THE TWO MOST POPULAR HOUSEHOLD PETS, THE CAT AND THE DOG...
...THE DOG, IN HIS INFINITE DESIRE TO PLEASE, TAKES ON THE CHARACTERISTICS OF THE 'YES MAN'
11-9
BUT, THE CAT STANDS PROUD AND FIRM IN HIS OWN CONVICTIONS, UNMOVED BY THE SWAYING VAGARIES OF MAN..."
OH, BROTHER!
I'D BETTER LEAVE...I'M BECOMING NAUSEATED!
SCHULZ

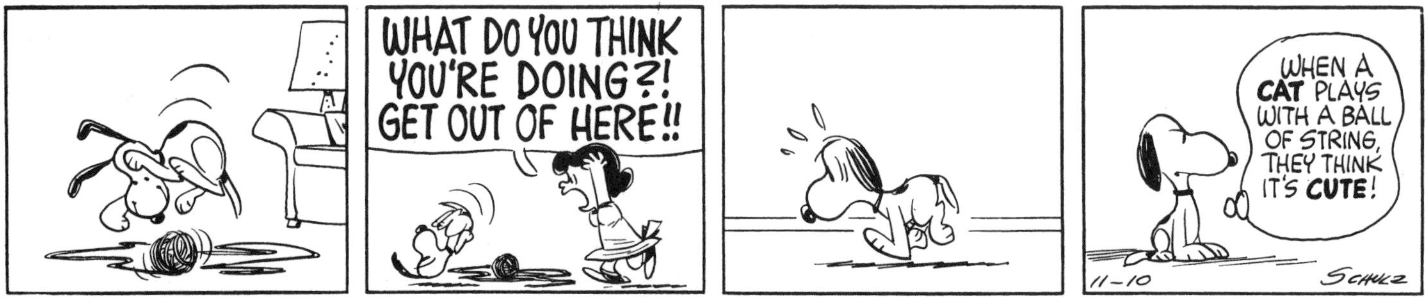
WHAT DO YOU THINK YOU'RE DOING?! GET OUT OF HERE!!
WHEN A **CAT** PLAYS WITH A BALL OF STRING, THEY THINK IT'S **CUTE**!
11-10
SCHULZ

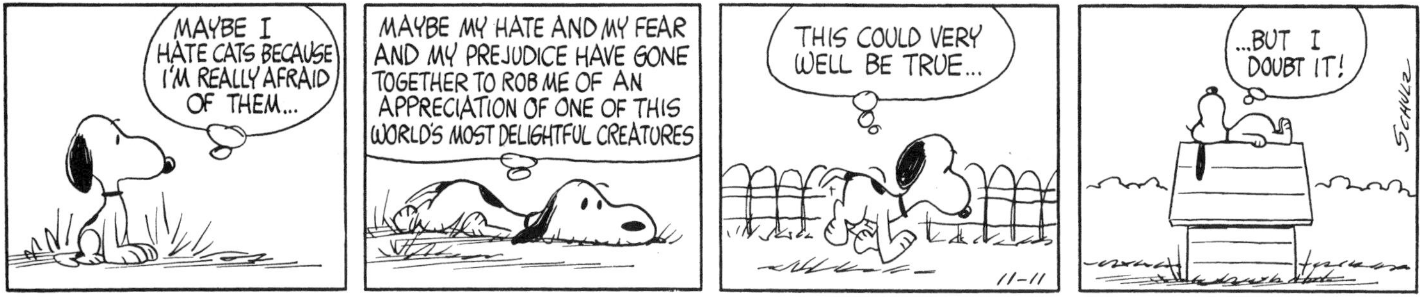
MAYBE I HATE CATS BECAUSE I'M REALLY AFRAID OF THEM...
MAYBE MY HATE AND MY FEAR AND MY PREJUDICE HAVE GONE TOGETHER TO ROB ME OF AN APPRECIATION OF ONE OF THIS WORLD'S MOST DELIGHTFUL CREATURES
THIS COULD VERY WELL BE TRUE...
11-11
...BUT I DOUBT IT!
SCHULZ

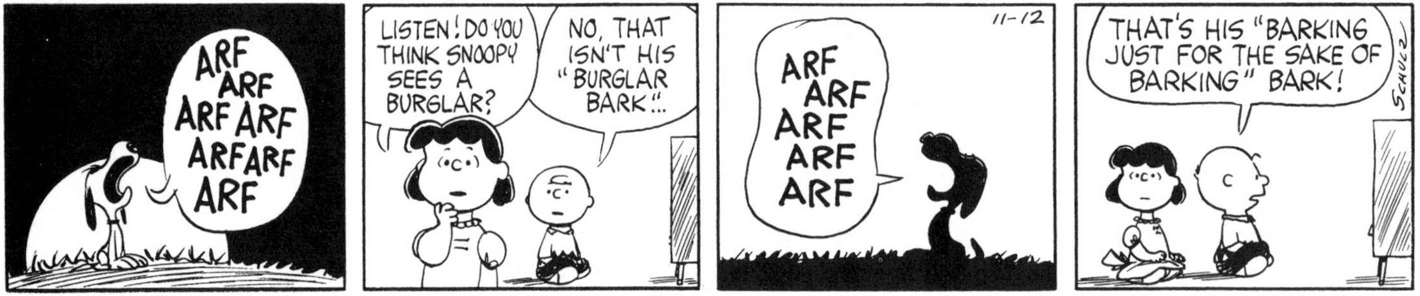
ARF ARF ARF ARF ARF ARF ARF
LISTEN! DO YOU THINK SNOOPY SEES A BURGLAR?
NO, THAT ISN'T HIS "BURGLAR BARK"!..
11-12
ARF ARF ARF ARF ARF
THAT'S HIS "BARKING JUST FOR THE SAKE OF BARKING" BARK!
SCHULZ

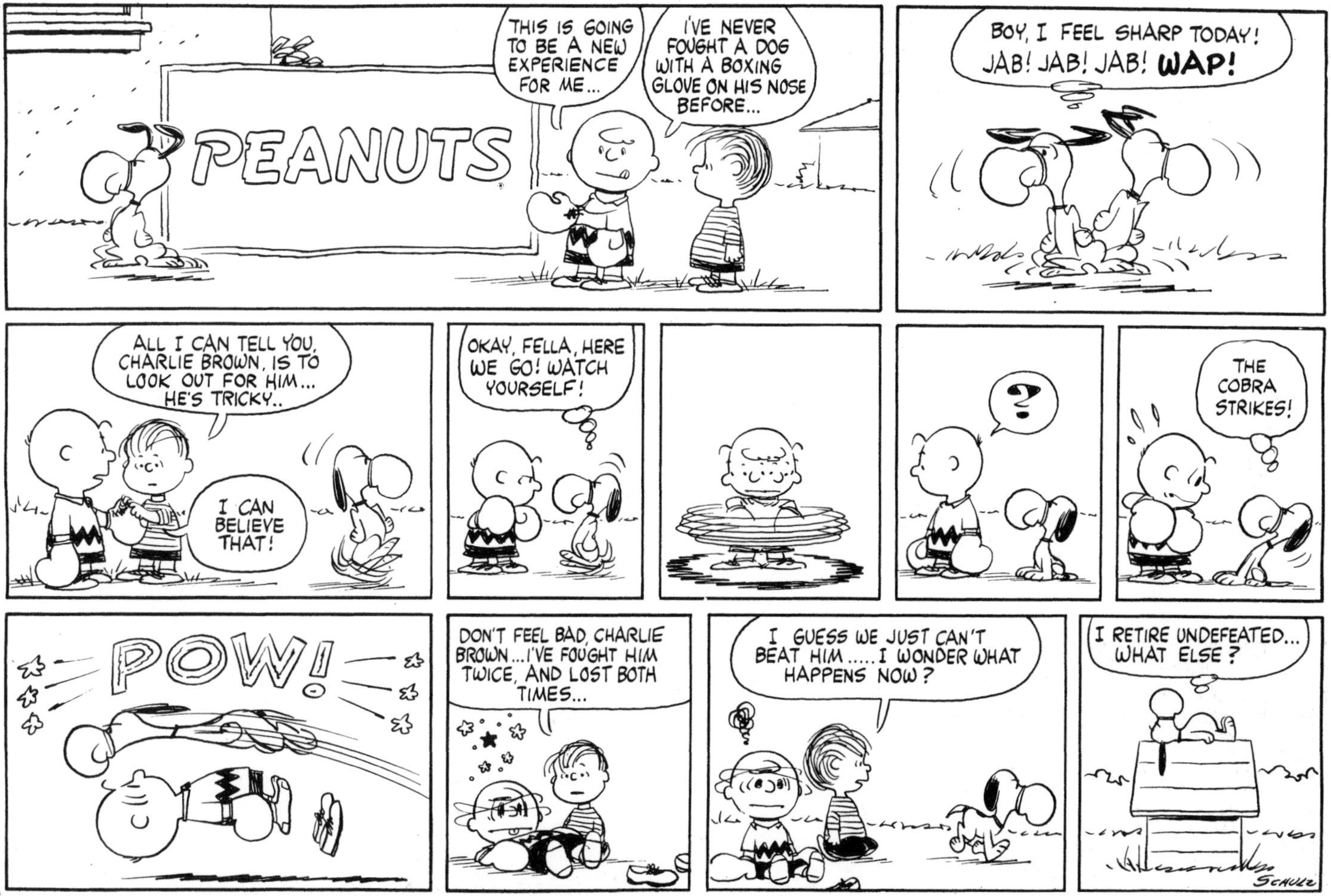
PEANUTS
THIS IS GOING TO BE A NEW EXPERIENCE FOR ME...
I'VE NEVER FOUGHT A DOG WITH A BOXING GLOVE ON HIS NOSE BEFORE...
BOY, I FEEL SHARP TODAY! JAB! JAB! JAB! WAP!
ALL I CAN TELL YOU, CHARLIE BROWN, IS TO LOOK OUT FOR HIM... HE'S TRICKY..
I CAN BELIEVE THAT!
OKAY, FELLA, HERE WE GO! WATCH YOURSELF!
?
THE COBRA STRIKES!
POW!
DON'T FEEL BAD, CHARLIE BROWN...I'VE FOUGHT HIM TWICE, AND LOST BOTH TIMES...
I GUESS WE JUST CAN'T BEAT HIM..... I WONDER WHAT HAPPENS NOW?
I RETIRE UNDEFEATED... WHAT ELSE?
SCHULZ

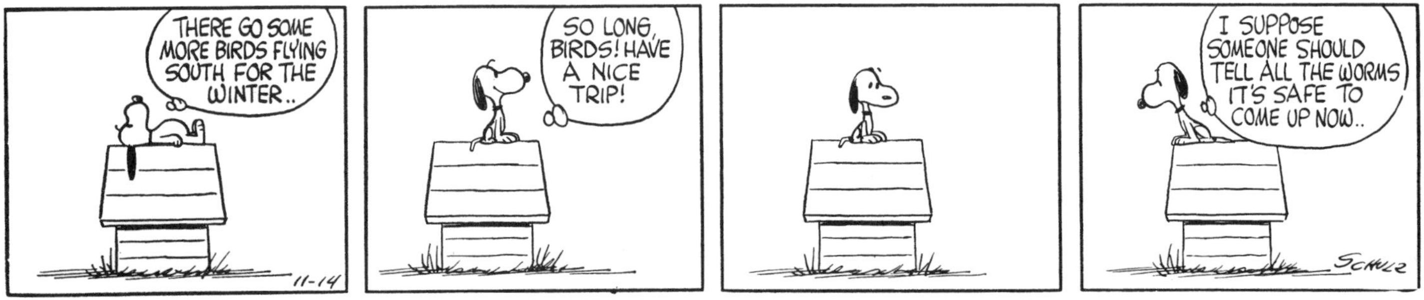
THERE GO SOME MORE BIRDS FLYING SOUTH FOR THE WINTER..
11-14
SO LONG, BIRDS! HAVE A NICE TRIP!
I SUPPOSE SOMEONE SHOULD TELL ALL THE WORMS IT'S SAFE TO COME UP NOW..
SCHULZ

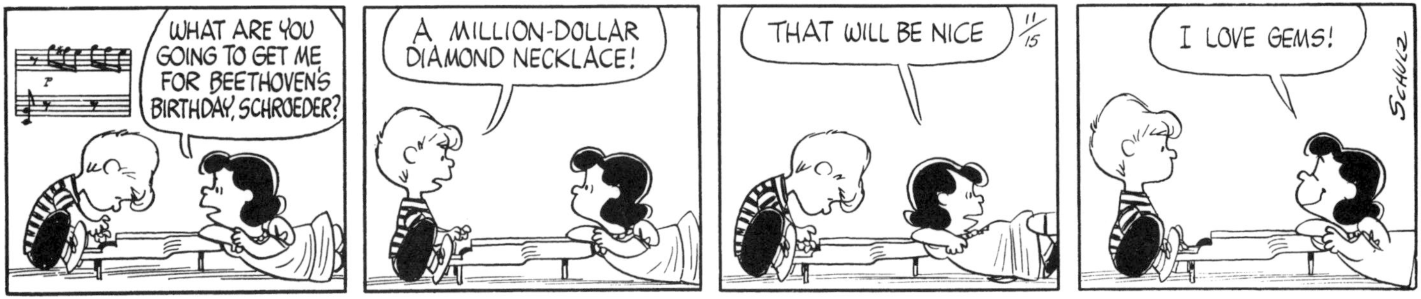
WHAT ARE YOU GOING TO GET ME FOR BEETHOVEN'S BIRTHDAY, SCHROEDER?
A MILLION-DOLLAR DIAMOND NECKLACE!
THAT WILL BE NICE
11/15
I LOVE GEMS!
SCHULZ

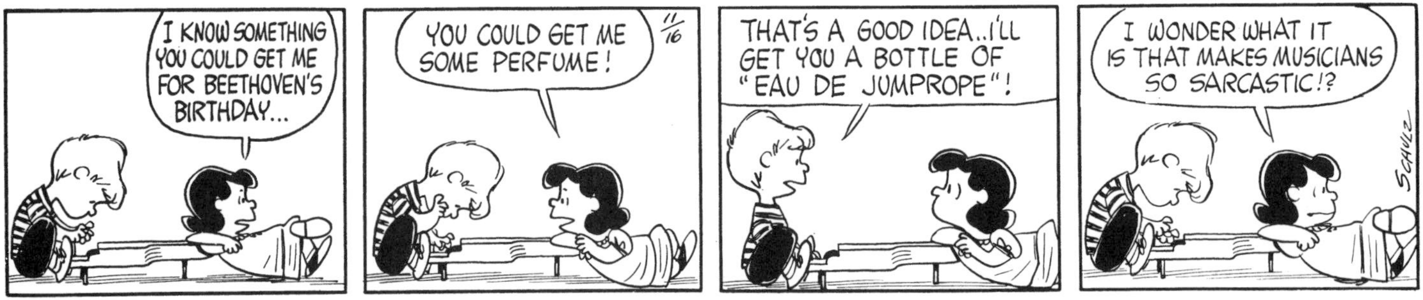
I KNOW SOMETHING YOU COULD GET ME FOR BEETHOVEN'S BIRTHDAY...
YOU COULD GET ME SOME PERFUME!
11/16
THAT'S A GOOD IDEA..I'LL GET YOU A BOTTLE OF "EAU DE JUMPROPE"!
I WONDER WHAT IT IS THAT MAKES MUSICIANS SO SARCASTIC!?
SCHULZ

WHY SHOULD I GIVE YOU SOMETHING FOR BEETHOVEN'S BIRTHDAY? I DON'T EVEN **LIKE** YOU!

WELL, I DON'T LIKE **YOU** EITHER!!

I DON'T EVEN KNOW WHAT'S GOING ON...

11/17

WELL, LOOK HERE! A BIG YELLOW BUTTERFLY!

IT'S UNUSUAL TO SEE ONE THIS TIME OF YEAR UNLESS, OF COURSE, HE FLEW UP FROM BRAZIL...I'LL BET THAT'S IT!

THEY DO THAT SOMETIMES, YOU KNOW...THEY FLY UP FROM BRAZIL, AND THEY...

THIS IS NO BUTTERFLY... THIS IS A POTATO CHIP!

WELL, I'LL BE! SO IT IS! I WONDER HOW A POTATO CHIP GOT ALL THE WAY UP HERE FROM BRAZIL?

11-18

THERE'S ONE THING I'VE ALWAYS BEEN PROUD OF, AND THATS THE FACT THAT I'M INDEPENDENT

WELL, MAYBE I'M SORT OF **SEMI**-INDEPENDENT!

11-19

1960

Page 295

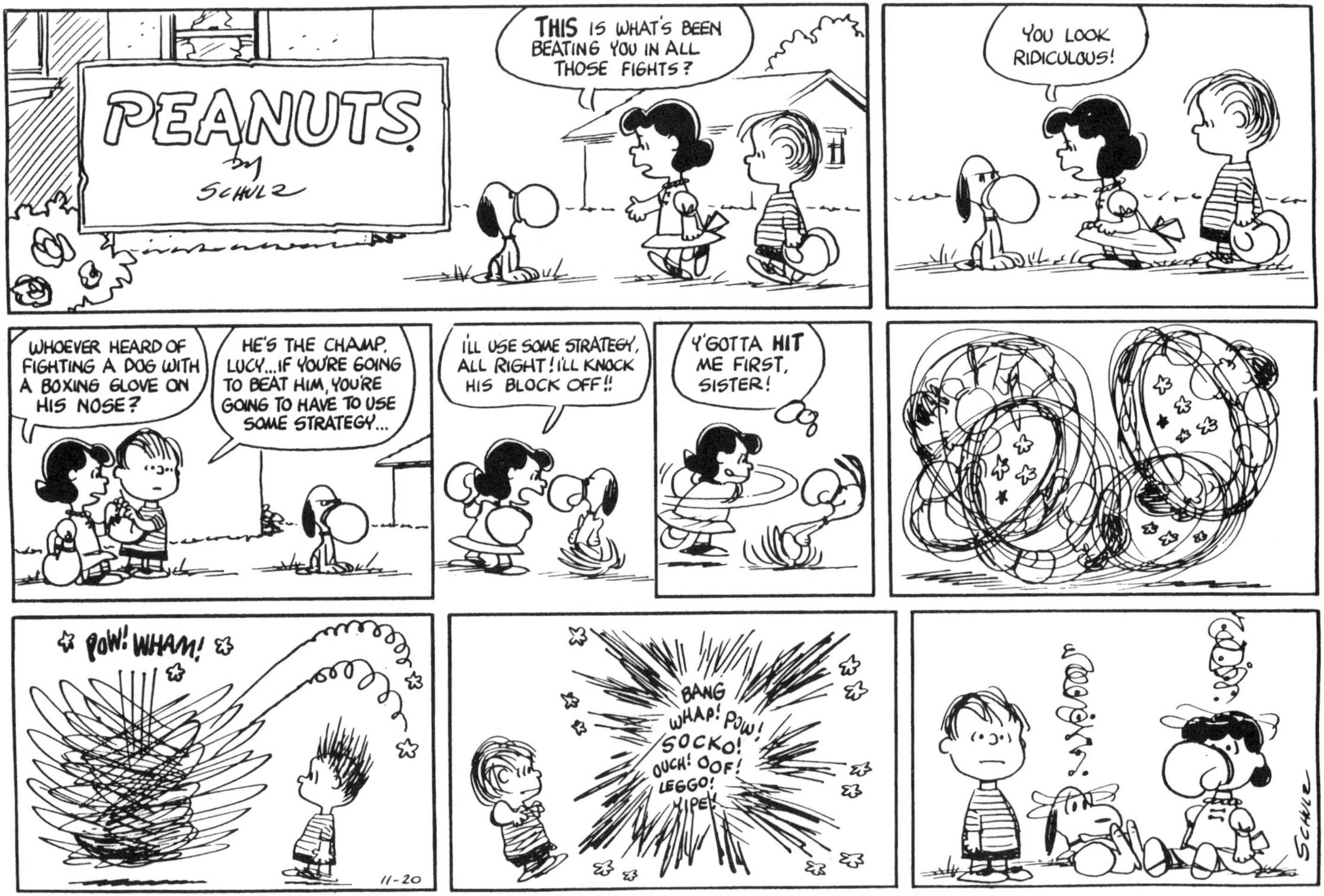
PEANUTS
by SCHULZ
THIS IS WHAT'S BEEN BEATING YOU IN ALL THOSE FIGHTS?
YOU LOOK RIDICULOUS!
WHOEVER HEARD OF FIGHTING A DOG WITH A BOXING GLOVE ON HIS NOSE?
HE'S THE CHAMP, LUCY...IF YOU'RE GOING TO BEAT HIM, YOU'RE GOING TO HAVE TO USE SOME STRATEGY...
I'LL USE SOME STRATEGY, ALL RIGHT! I'LL KNOCK HIS BLOCK OFF!!
Y'GOTTA HIT ME FIRST, SISTER!
POW! WHAM!
11-20
BANG
WHAP! POW!
SOCKO!
OUCH! OOF!
LEGGO!
YIPE!
SCHULZ

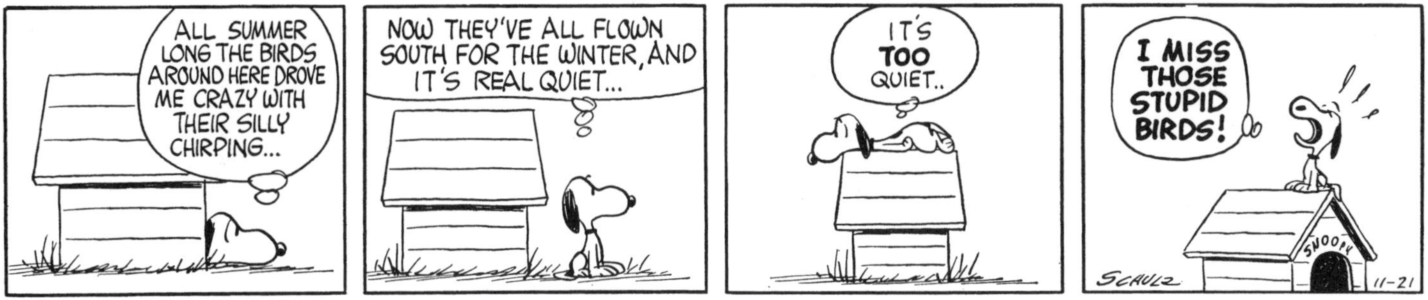
ALL SUMMER LONG THE BIRDS AROUND HERE DROVE ME CRAZY WITH THEIR SILLY CHIRPING...
NOW THEY'VE ALL FLOWN SOUTH FOR THE WINTER, AND IT'S REAL QUIET...
IT'S **TOO** QUIET..
I MISS THOSE STUPID BIRDS!
SNOOPY
SCHULZ
11-21

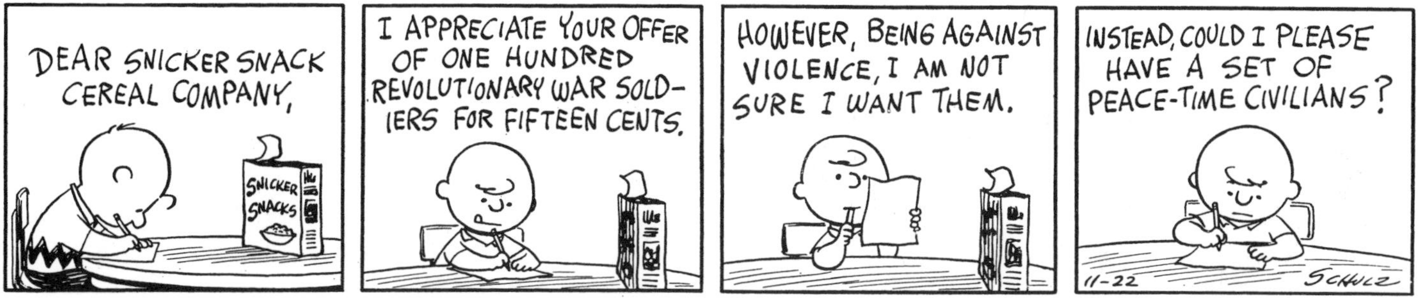
DEAR SNICKER SNACK CEREAL COMPANY,
SNICKER SNACKS
I APPRECIATE YOUR OFFER OF ONE HUNDRED REVOLUTIONARY WAR SOLDIERS FOR FIFTEEN CENTS.
HOWEVER, BEING AGAINST VIOLENCE, I AM NOT SURE I WANT THEM.
INSTEAD, COULD I PLEASE HAVE A SET OF PEACE-TIME CIVILIANS?
11-22
SCHULZ

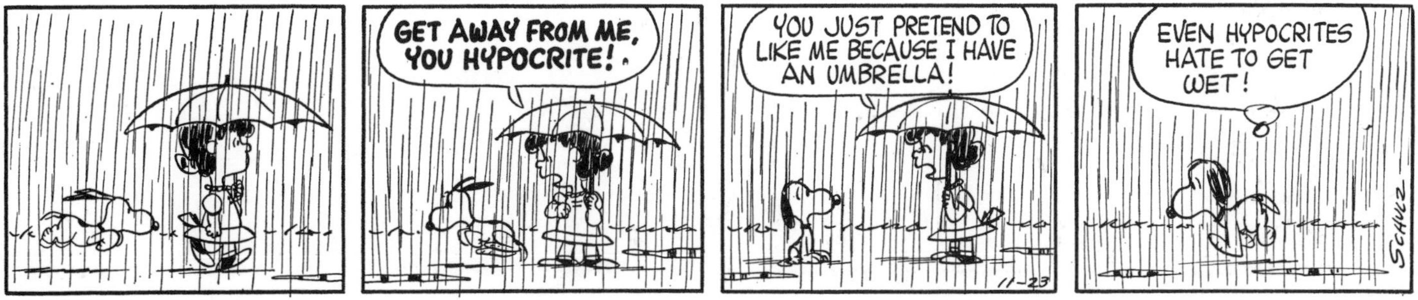
GET AWAY FROM ME, YOU HYPOCRITE!
YOU JUST PRETEND TO LIKE ME BECAUSE I HAVE AN UMBRELLA!
11-23
EVEN HYPOCRITES HATE TO GET WET!
SCHULZ

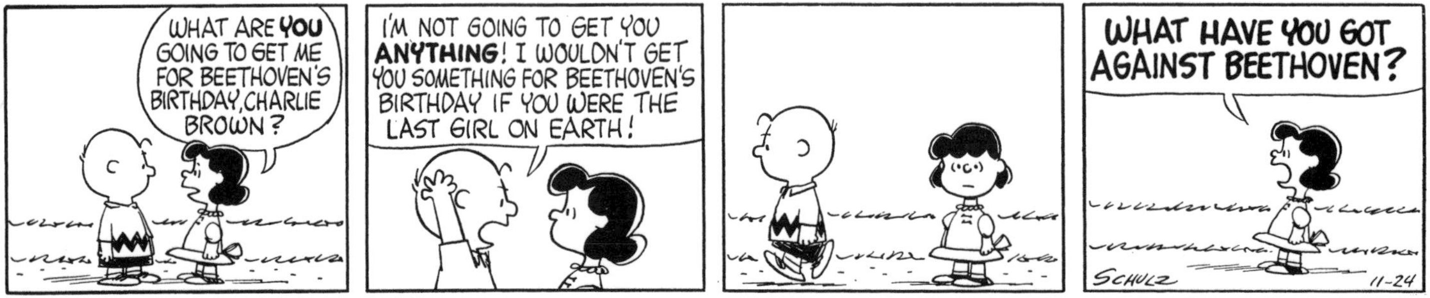
WHAT ARE **YOU** GOING TO GET ME FOR BEETHOVEN'S BIRTHDAY, CHARLIE BROWN?
I'M NOT GOING TO GET YOU **ANYTHING**! I WOULDN'T GET YOU SOMETHING FOR BEETHOVEN'S BIRTHDAY IF YOU WERE THE LAST GIRL ON EARTH!
WHAT HAVE YOU GOT AGAINST BEETHOVEN?
SCHULZ
11-24

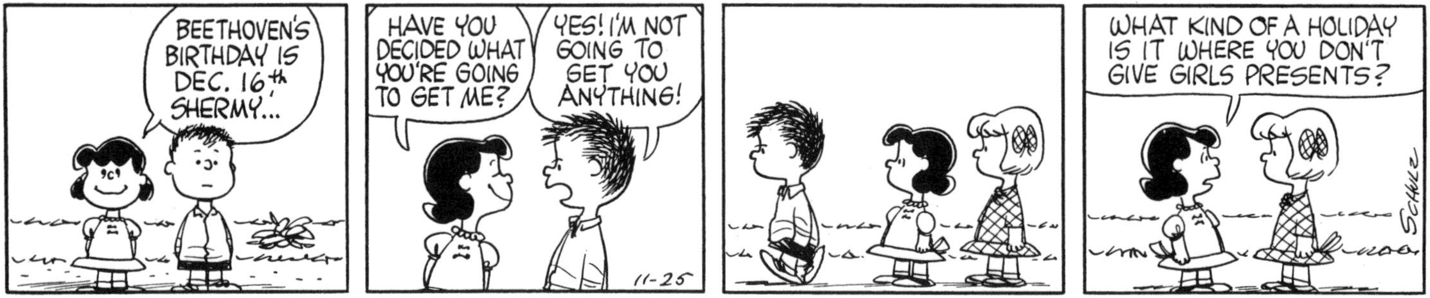
BEETHOVEN'S BIRTHDAY IS DEC. 16th, SHERMY...
HAVE YOU DECIDED WHAT YOU'RE GOING TO GET ME?
YES! I'M NOT GOING TO GET YOU ANYTHING!
11-25
WHAT KIND OF A HOLIDAY IS IT WHERE YOU DON'T GIVE GIRLS PRESENTS?
SCHULZ

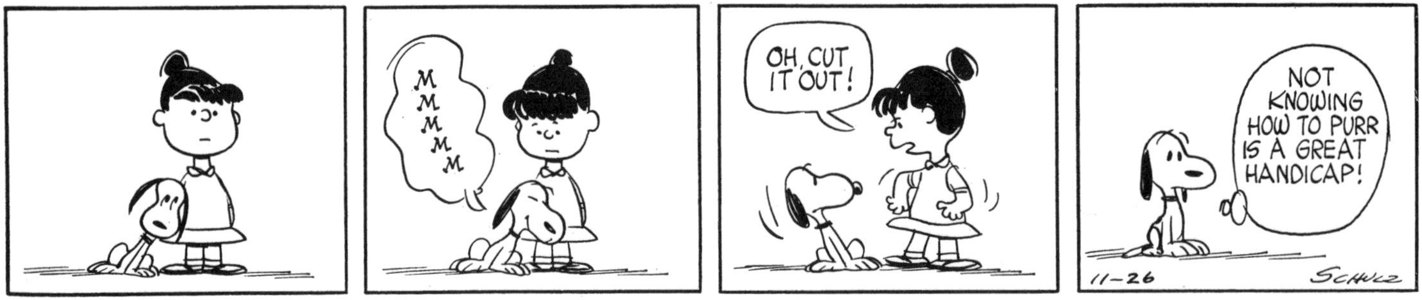
MMMMM
OH, CUT IT OUT!
NOT KNOWING HOW TO PURR IS A GREAT HANDICAP!
11-26
SCHULZ

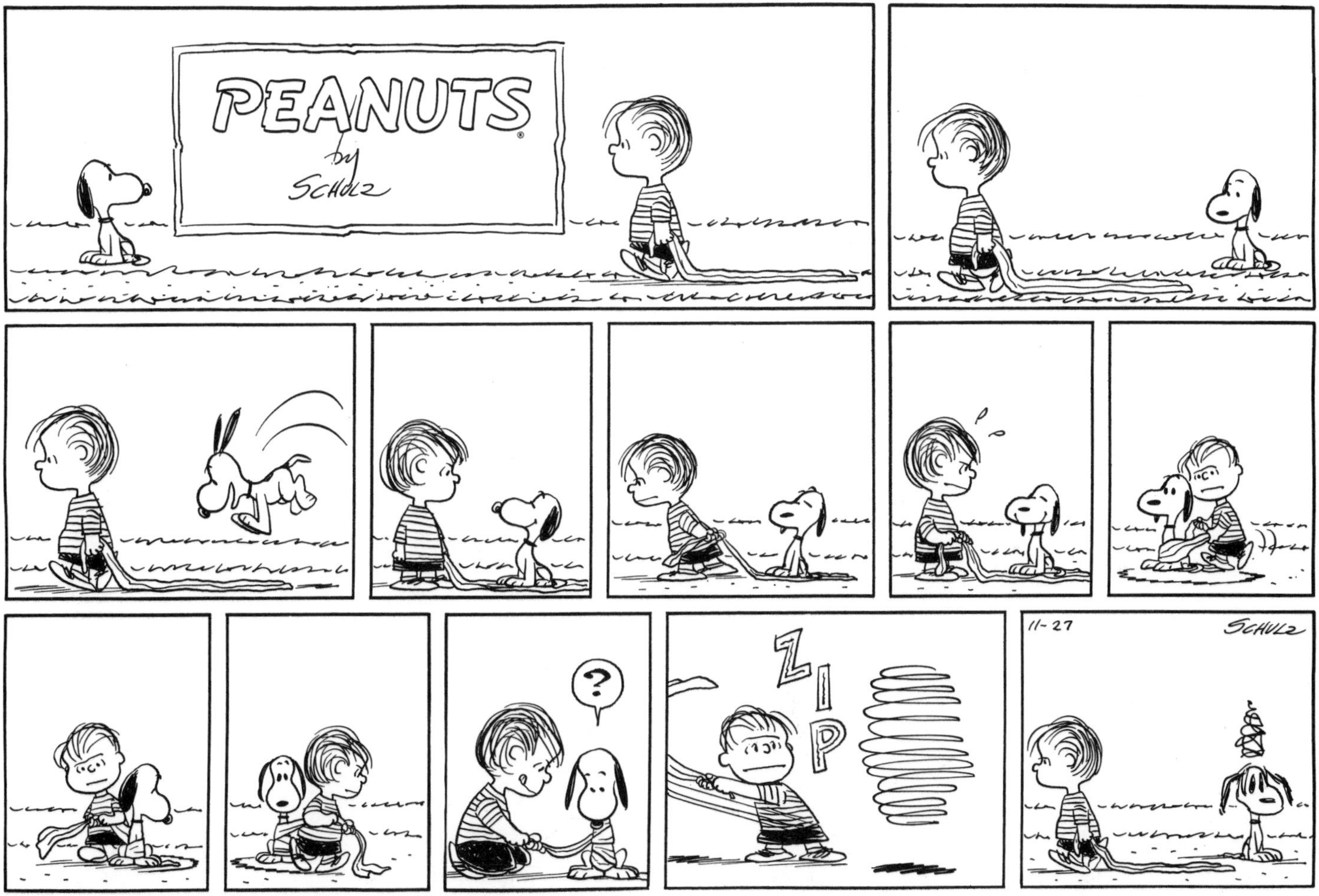
PEANUTS
by SCHULZ
?
ZIP
11-27
SCHULZ

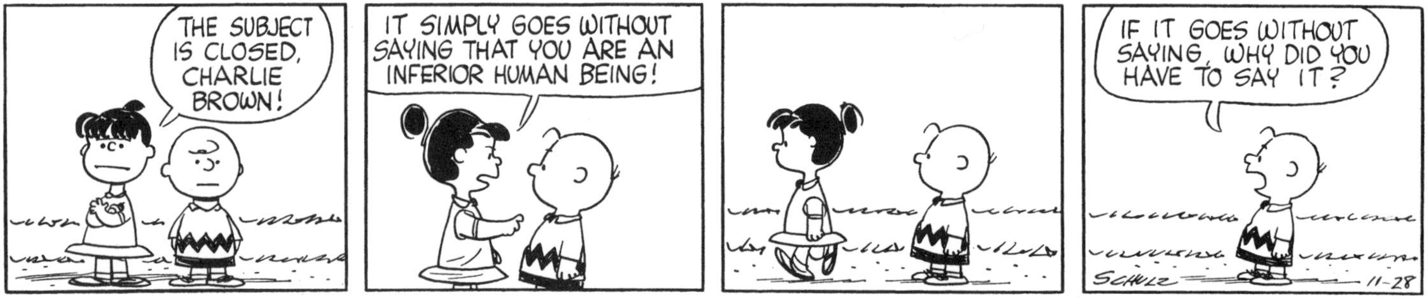
THE SUBJECT IS CLOSED, CHARLIE BROWN!
IT SIMPLY GOES WITHOUT SAYING THAT YOU ARE AN INFERIOR HUMAN BEING!
IF IT GOES WITHOUT SAYING, WHY DID YOU HAVE TO SAY IT?
SCHULZ
11-28

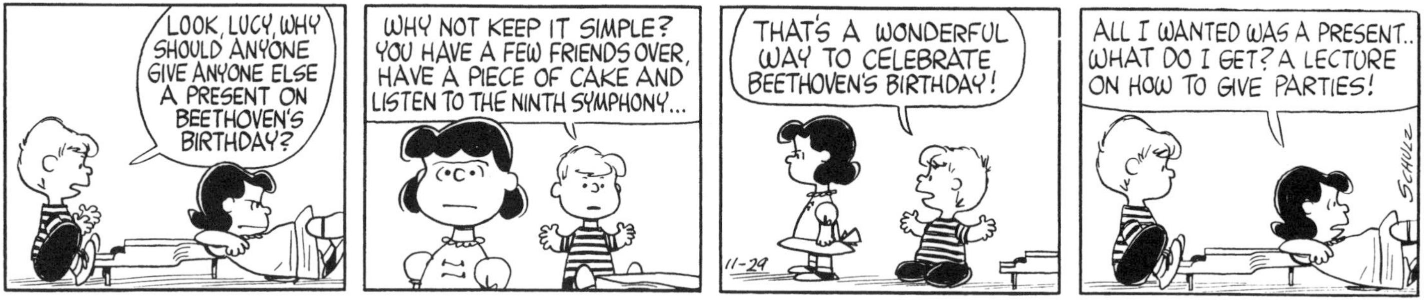
LOOK, LUCY, WHY SHOULD ANYONE GIVE ANYONE ELSE A PRESENT ON BEETHOVEN'S BIRTHDAY?
WHY NOT KEEP IT SIMPLE? YOU HAVE A FEW FRIENDS OVER, HAVE A PIECE OF CAKE AND LISTEN TO THE NINTH SYMPHONY...
THAT'S A WONDERFUL WAY TO CELEBRATE BEETHOVEN'S BIRTHDAY!
11-29
ALL I WANTED WAS A PRESENT.. WHAT DO I GET? A LECTURE ON HOW TO GIVE PARTIES!
SCHULZ

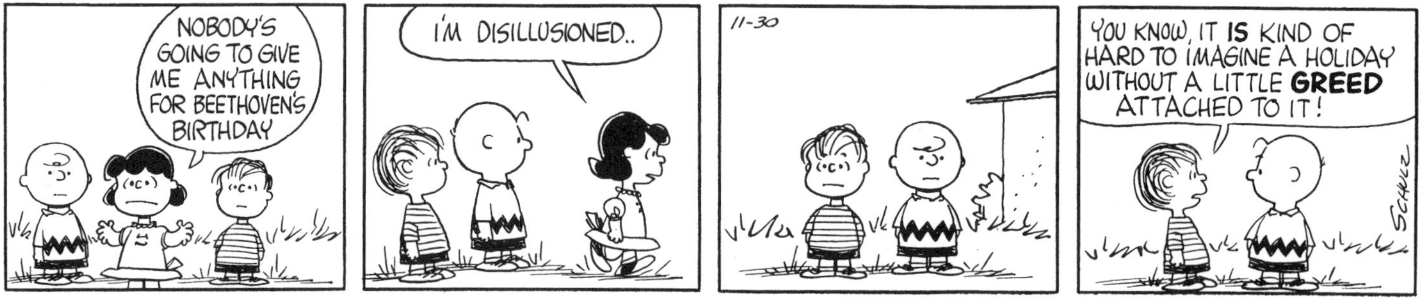
NOBODY'S GOING TO GIVE ME ANYTHING FOR BEETHOVEN'S BIRTHDAY
I'M DISILLUSIONED..
11-30
YOU KNOW, IT **IS** KIND OF HARD TO IMAGINE A HOLIDAY WITHOUT A LITTLE **GREED** ATTACHED TO IT!
SCHULZ

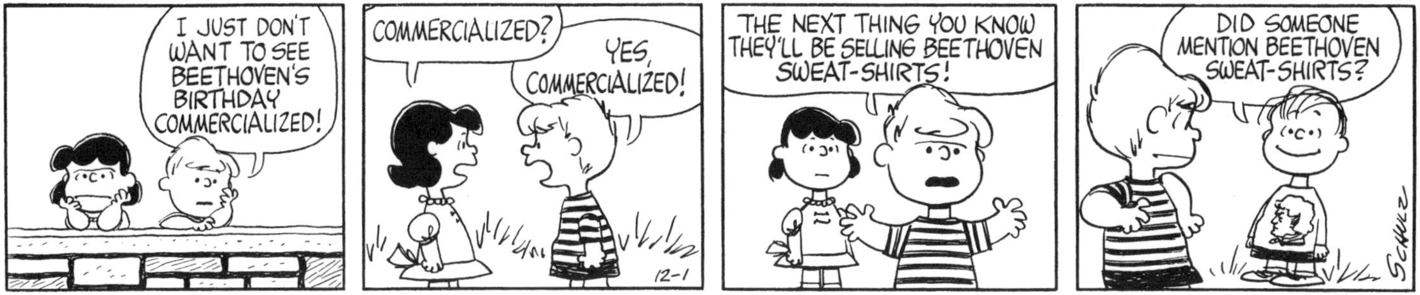
I JUST DON'T WANT TO SEE BEETHOVEN'S BIRTHDAY COMMERCIALIZED!
COMMERCIALIZED?
YES, COMMERCIALIZED!
12-1
THE NEXT THING YOU KNOW THEY'LL BE SELLING BEETHOVEN SWEAT-SHIRTS!
DID SOMEONE MENTION BEETHOVEN SWEAT-SHIRTS?
SCHULZ

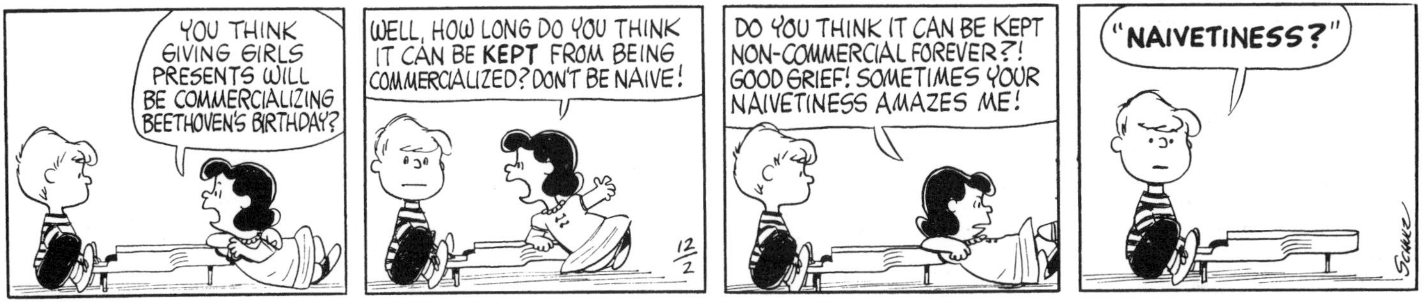
YOU THINK GIVING GIRLS PRESENTS WILL BE COMMERCIALIZING BEETHOVEN'S BIRTHDAY?
WELL, HOW LONG DO YOU THINK IT CAN BE **KEPT** FROM BEING COMMERCIALIZED? DON'T BE NAIVE!
12 2
DO YOU THINK IT CAN BE KEPT NON-COMMERCIAL FOREVER?! GOOD GRIEF! SOMETIMES YOUR NAIVETINESS AMAZES ME!
"**NAIVETINESS?**"
SCHULZ

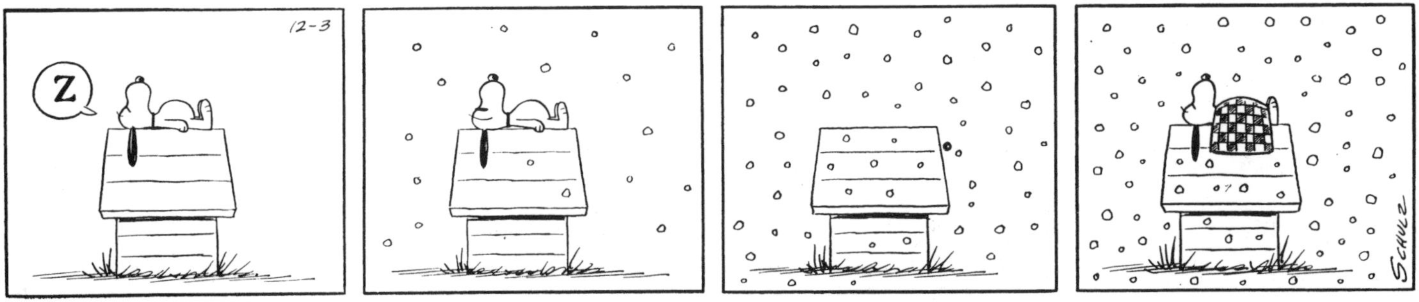
12-3
Z
SCHULZ

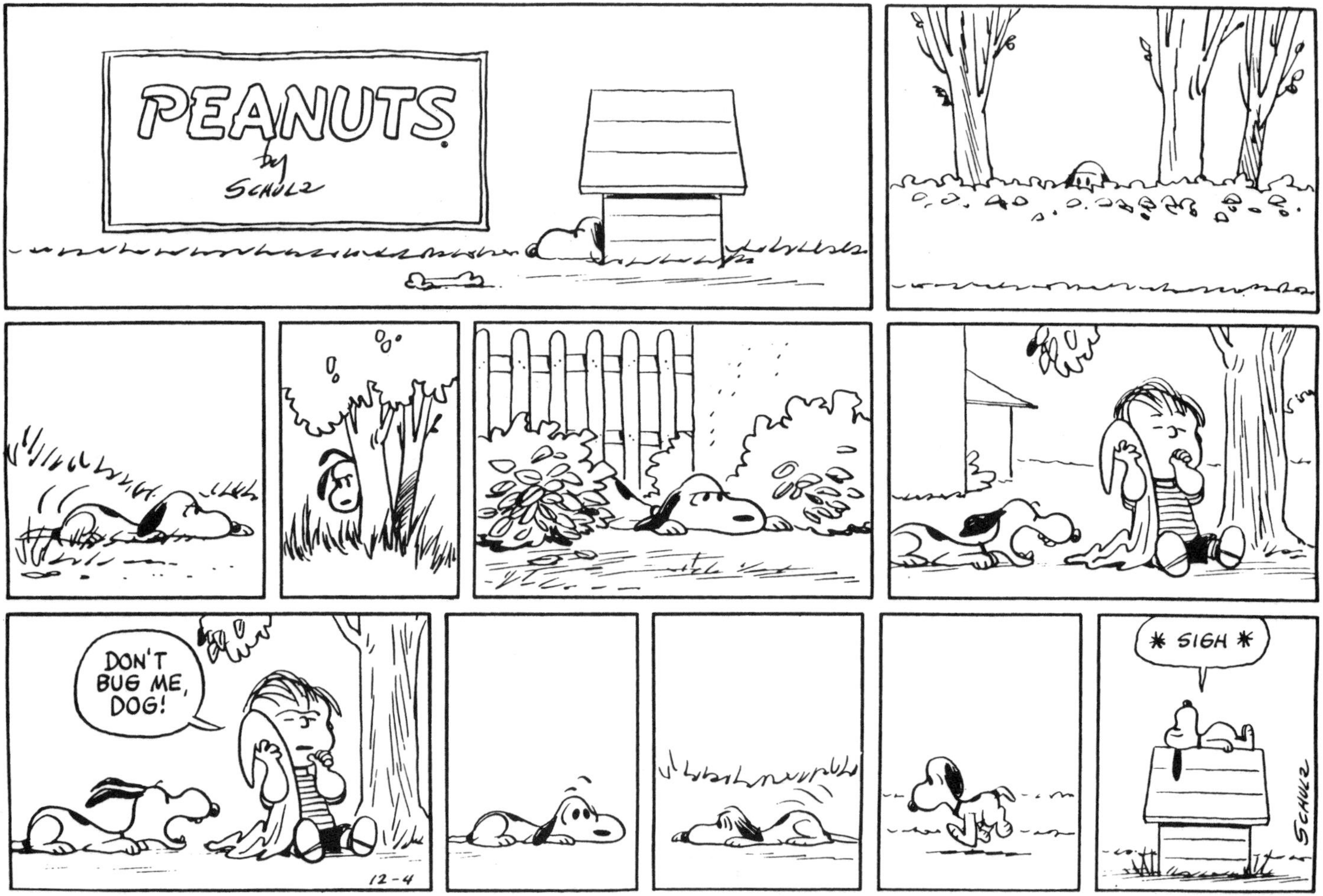
PEANUTS
by
SCHULZ
DON'T BUG ME, DOG!
12-4
* SIGH *
SCHULZ

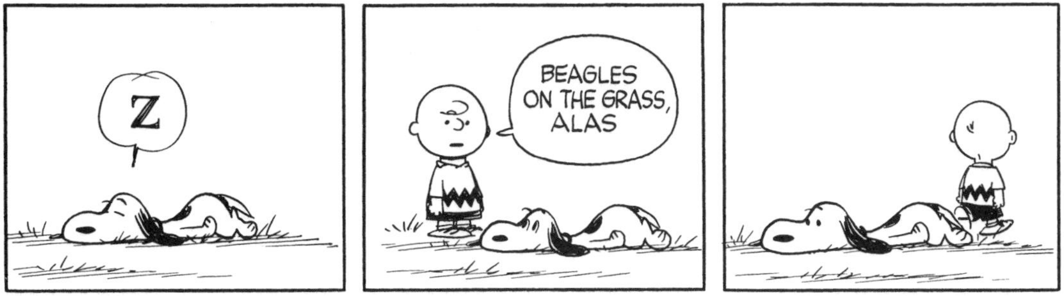
Z
BEAGLES ON THE GRASS, ALAS
SCHULZ 12-5
I AIN'T NO STUPID BEAGLE!

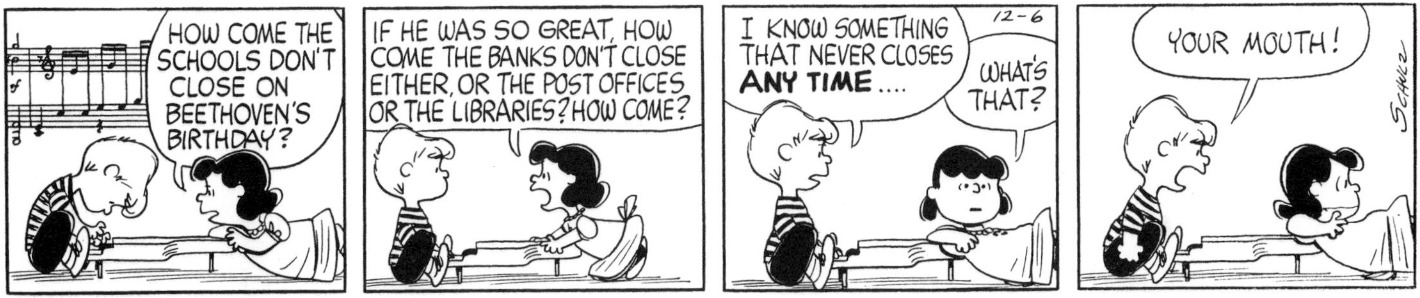
HOW COME THE SCHOOLS DON'T CLOSE ON BEETHOVEN'S BIRTHDAY?
IF HE WAS SO GREAT, HOW COME THE BANKS DON'T CLOSE EITHER, OR THE POST OFFICES OR THE LIBRARIES? HOW COME?
12-6
I KNOW SOMETHING THAT NEVER CLOSES **ANY TIME**....
WHAT'S THAT?
YOUR MOUTH!
SCHULZ

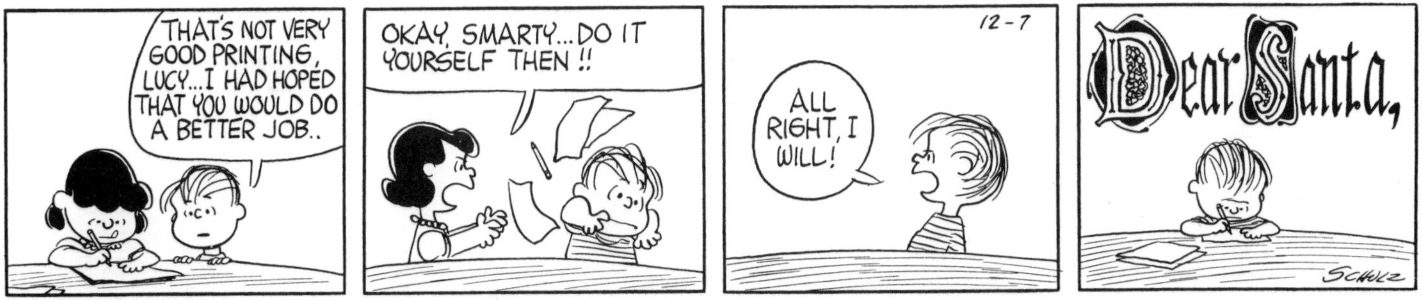
THAT'S NOT VERY GOOD PRINTING, LUCY...I HAD HOPED THAT YOU WOULD DO A BETTER JOB..
OKAY, SMARTY...DO IT YOURSELF THEN !!
12-7
ALL RIGHT, I WILL!
Dear Santa,
SCHULZ

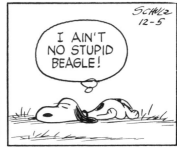

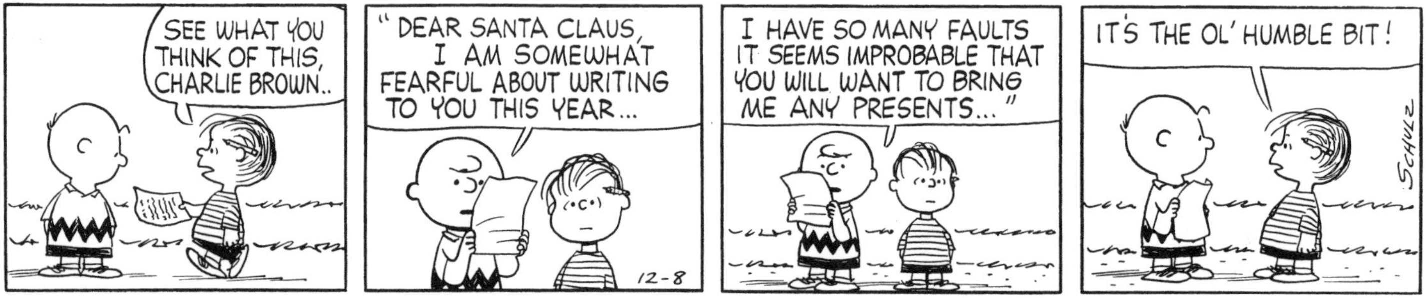
SEE WHAT YOU THINK OF THIS, CHARLIE BROWN..
" DEAR SANTA CLAUS, I AM SOMEWHAT FEARFUL ABOUT WRITING TO YOU THIS YEAR...
12-8
I HAVE SO MANY FAULTS IT SEEMS IMPROBABLE THAT YOU WILL WANT TO BRING ME ANY PRESENTS... "
IT'S THE OL' HUMBLE BIT!
SCHULZ

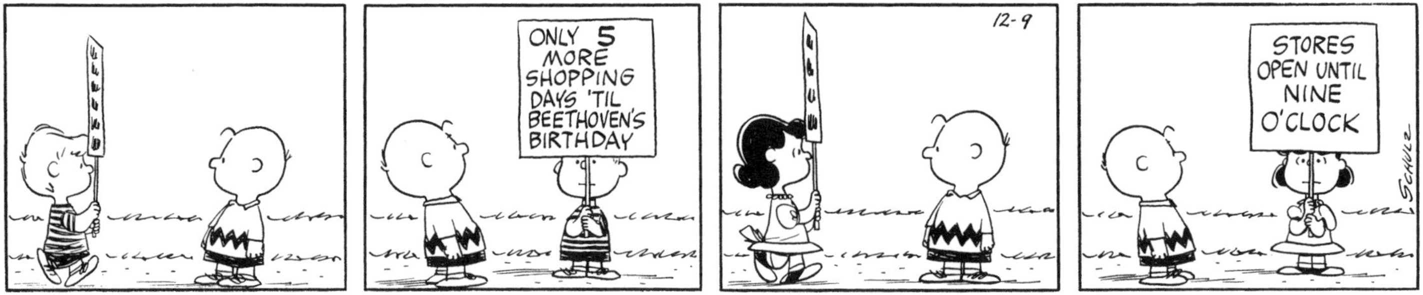
ONLY 5 MORE SHOPPING DAYS 'TIL BEETHOVEN'S BIRTHDAY
12-9
STORES OPEN UNTIL NINE O'CLOCK
SCHULZ

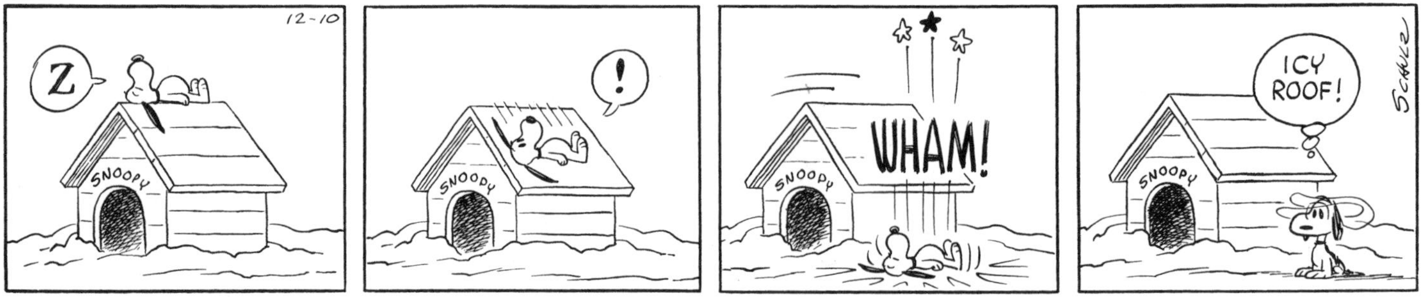
12-10
Z
SNOOPY
!
SNOOPY
WHAM!
SNOOPY
ICY ROOF!
SNOOPY
SCHULZ

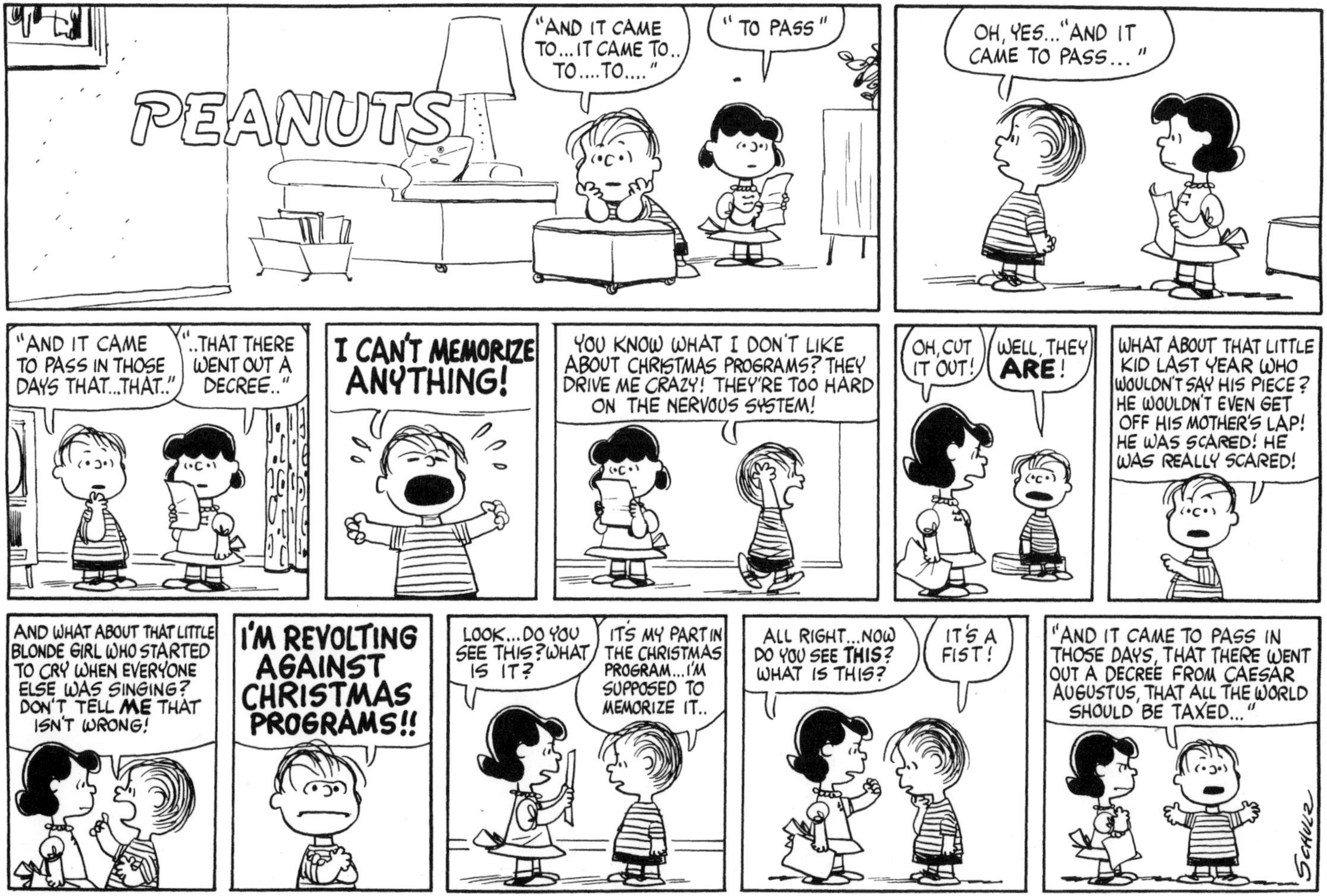
PEANUTS
"AND IT CAME TO... IT CAME TO.. TO....TO...."
" TO PASS "
OH, YES..."AND IT CAME TO PASS..."
"AND IT CAME TO PASS IN THOSE DAYS THAT...THAT.."
"..THAT THERE WENT OUT A DECREE.."
I CAN'T MEMORIZE ANYTHING!
YOU KNOW WHAT I DON'T LIKE ABOUT CHRISTMAS PROGRAMS? THEY DRIVE ME CRAZY! THEY'RE TOO HARD ON THE NERVOUS SYSTEM!
OH, CUT IT OUT!
WELL, THEY ARE!
WHAT ABOUT THAT LITTLE KID LAST YEAR WHO WOULDN'T SAY HIS PIECE? HE WOULDN'T EVEN GET OFF HIS MOTHER'S LAP! HE WAS SCARED! HE WAS REALLY SCARED!
AND WHAT ABOUT THAT LITTLE BLONDE GIRL WHO STARTED TO CRY WHEN EVERYONE ELSE WAS SINGING? DON'T TELL ME THAT ISN'T WRONG!
I'M REVOLTING AGAINST CHRISTMAS PROGRAMS!!
LOOK...DO YOU SEE THIS? WHAT IS IT?
IT'S MY PART IN THE CHRISTMAS PROGRAM...I'M SUPPOSED TO MEMORIZE IT..
ALL RIGHT...NOW DO YOU SEE THIS? WHAT IS THIS?
IT'S A FIST!
"AND IT CAME TO PASS IN THOSE DAYS, THAT THERE WENT OUT A DECREE FROM CAESAR AUGUSTUS, THAT ALL THE WORLD SHOULD BE TAXED..."
SCHULZ

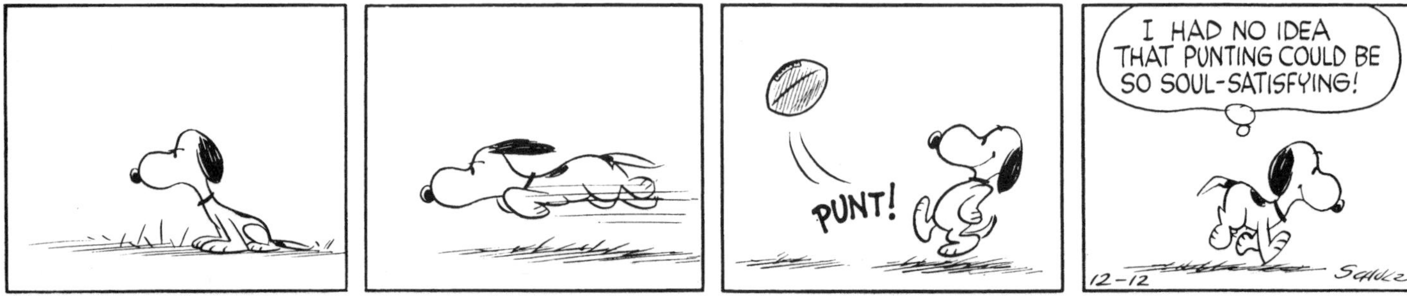
PUNT!
I HAD NO IDEA THAT PUNTING COULD BE SO SOUL-SATISFYING!
12-12
SCHULZ

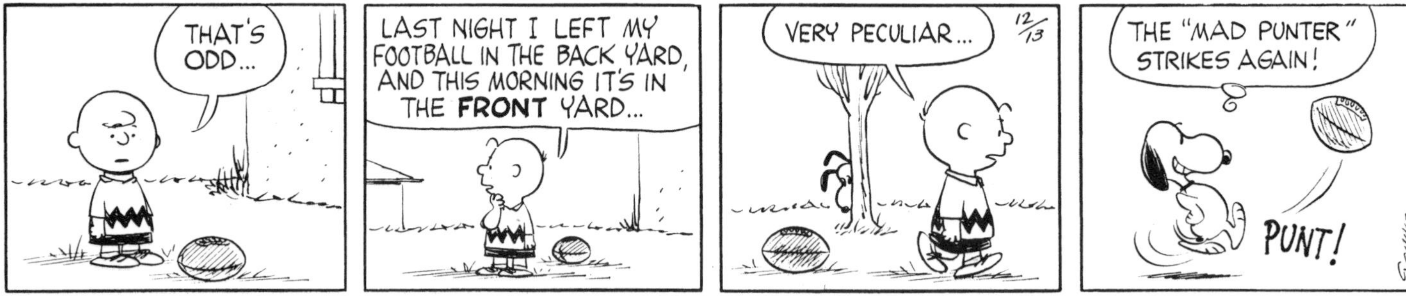
THAT'S ODD...
LAST NIGHT I LEFT MY FOOTBALL IN THE BACK YARD, AND THIS MORNING IT'S IN THE FRONT YARD...
VERY PECULIAR...
12/13
THE "MAD PUNTER" STRIKES AGAIN!
PUNT!
SCHULZ

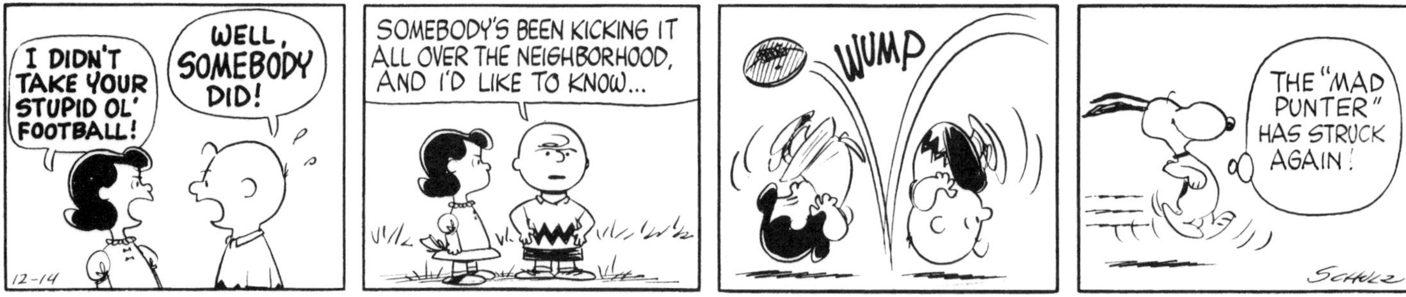
WELL, SOMEBODY DID!
I DIDN'T TAKE YOUR STUPID OL' FOOTBALL!
12-14
SOMEBODY'S BEEN KICKING IT ALL OVER THE NEIGHBORHOOD, AND I'D LIKE TO KNOW...
WUMP
THE "MAD PUNTER" HAS STRUCK AGAIN!
SCHULZ

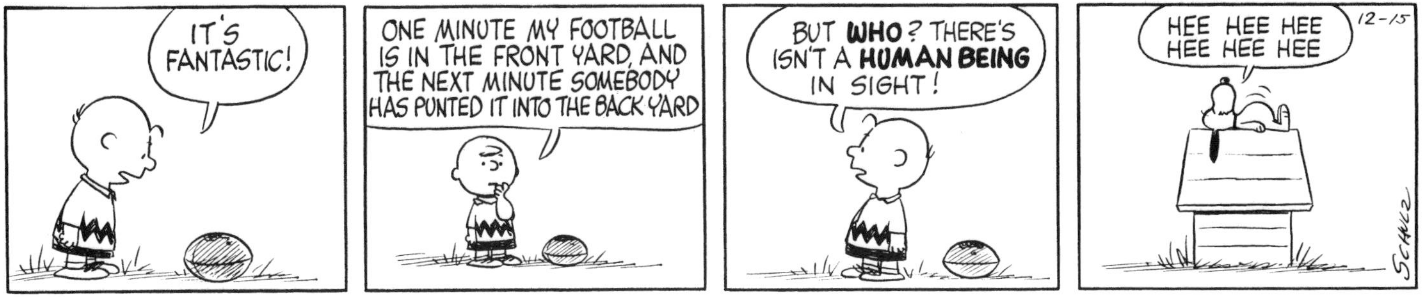
IT'S FANTASTIC!
ONE MINUTE MY FOOTBALL IS IN THE FRONT YARD, AND THE NEXT MINUTE SOMEBODY HAS PUNTED IT INTO THE BACK YARD
BUT **WHO**? THERE'S ISN'T A **HUMAN BEING** IN SIGHT!
HEE HEE HEE HEE HEE HEE
12-15
SCHULZ

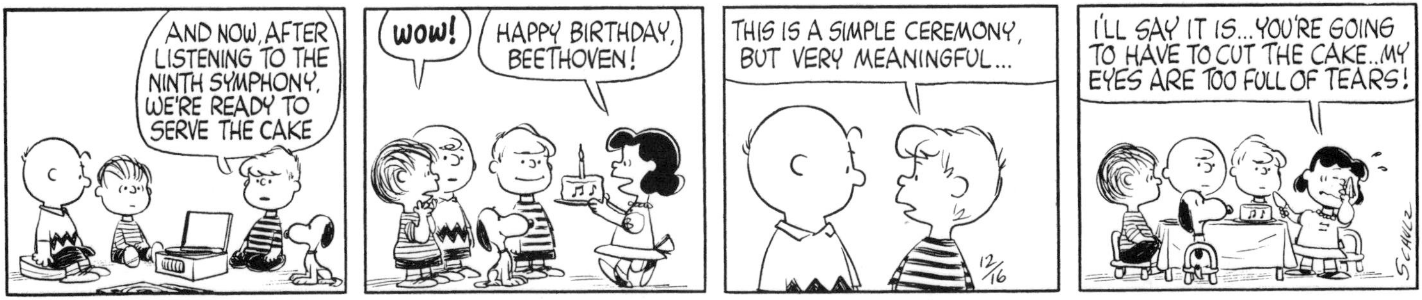
AND NOW, AFTER LISTENING TO THE NINTH SYMPHONY, WE'RE READY TO SERVE THE CAKE
WOW!
HAPPY BIRTHDAY, BEETHOVEN!
THIS IS A SIMPLE CEREMONY, BUT VERY MEANINGFUL...
12/16
I'LL SAY IT IS...YOU'RE GOING TO HAVE TO CUT THE CAKE..MY EYES ARE TOO FULL OF TEARS!
SCHULZ

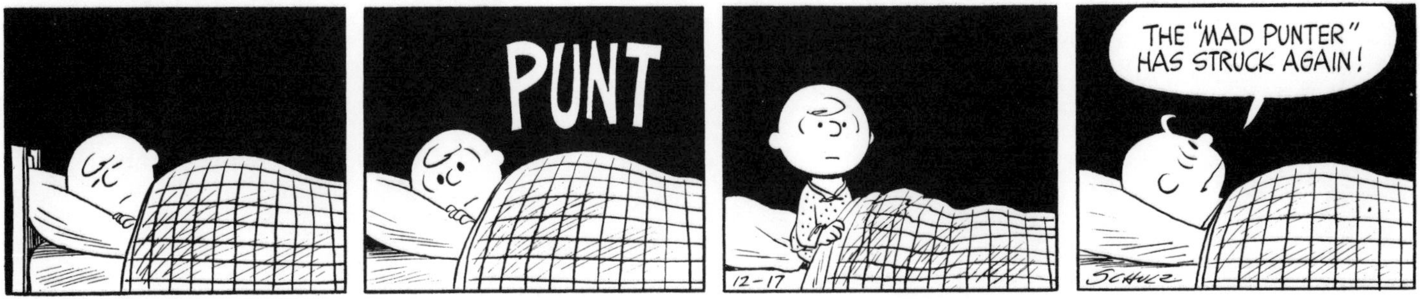
PUNT
12-17
THE "MAD PUNTER" HAS STRUCK AGAIN!
SCHULZ

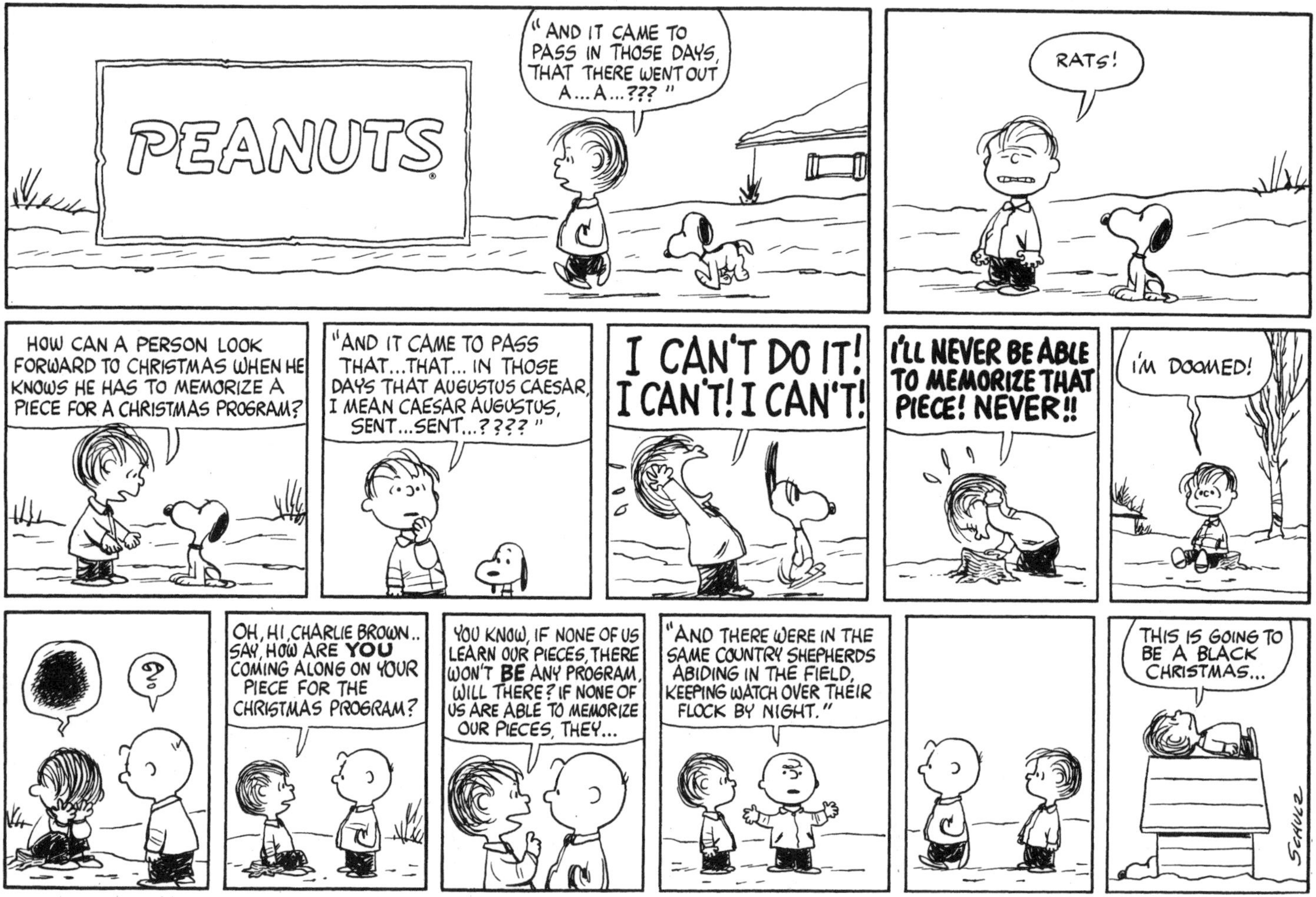
PEANUTS
"AND IT CAME TO PASS IN THOSE DAYS, THAT THERE WENT OUT A...A...???"
RATS!
HOW CAN A PERSON LOOK FORWARD TO CHRISTMAS WHEN HE KNOWS HE HAS TO MEMORIZE A PIECE FOR A CHRISTMAS PROGRAM?
"AND IT CAME TO PASS THAT...THAT... IN THOSE DAYS THAT AUGUSTUS CAESAR, I MEAN CAESAR AUGUSTUS, SENT...SENT...????"
I CAN'T DO IT! I CAN'T! I CAN'T!
I'LL NEVER BE ABLE TO MEMORIZE THAT PIECE! NEVER!!
I'M DOOMED!
?
OH, HI, CHARLIE BROWN.. SAY, HOW ARE **YOU** COMING ALONG ON YOUR PIECE FOR THE CHRISTMAS PROGRAM?
YOU KNOW, IF NONE OF US LEARN OUR PIECES, THERE WON'T **BE** ANY PROGRAM, WILL THERE? IF NONE OF US ARE ABLE TO MEMORIZE OUR PIECES, THEY...
"AND THERE WERE IN THE SAME COUNTRY SHEPHERDS ABIDING IN THE FIELD, KEEPING WATCH OVER THEIR FLOCK BY NIGHT."
THIS IS GOING TO BE A BLACK CHRISTMAS...
SCHULZ

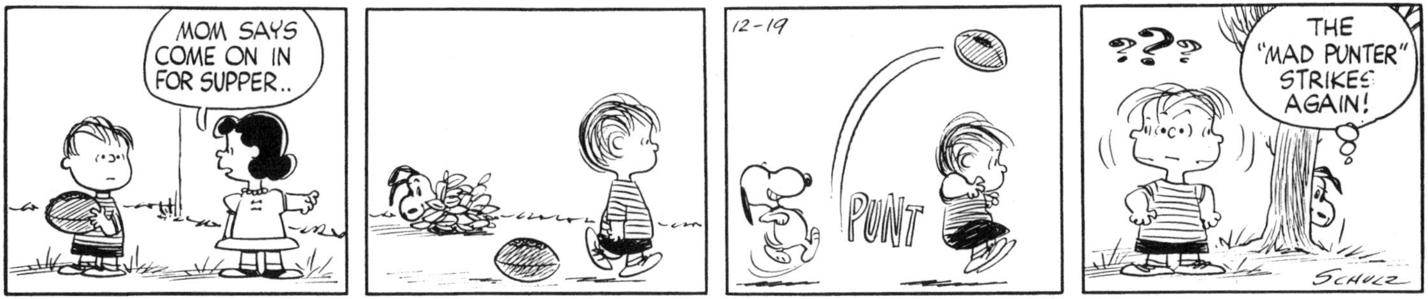
MOM SAYS COME ON IN FOR SUPPER..
12-19
PUNT
THE "MAD PUNTER" STRIKES AGAIN!
SCHULZ

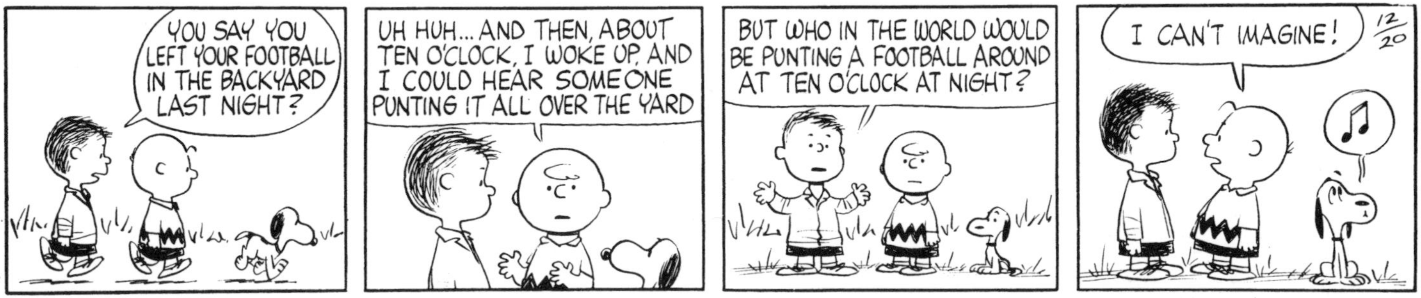
YOU SAY YOU LEFT YOUR FOOTBALL IN THE BACKYARD LAST NIGHT?
UH HUH... AND THEN, ABOUT TEN O'CLOCK, I WOKE UP, AND I COULD HEAR SOMEONE PUNTING IT ALL OVER THE YARD
BUT WHO IN THE WORLD WOULD BE PUNTING A FOOTBALL AROUND AT TEN O'CLOCK AT NIGHT?
I CAN'T IMAGINE!
12/20

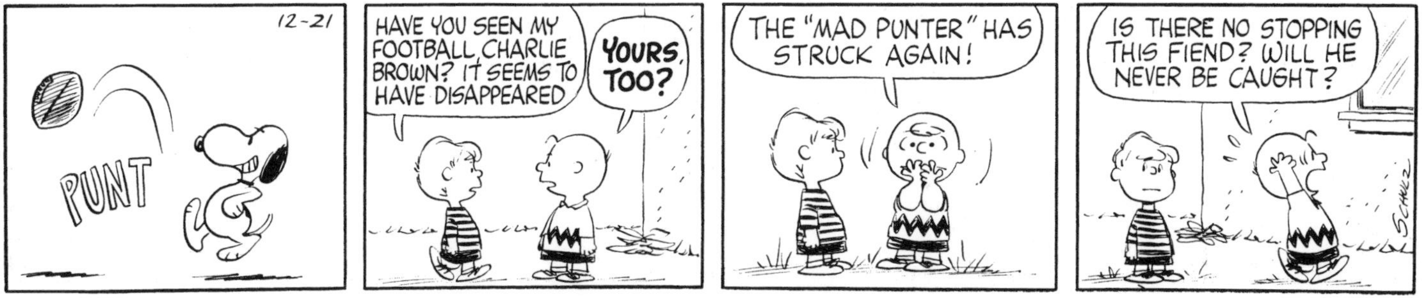
12-21
PUNT
HAVE YOU SEEN MY FOOTBALL, CHARLIE BROWN? IT SEEMS TO HAVE DISAPPEARED
YOURS, TOO?
THE "MAD PUNTER" HAS STRUCK AGAIN!
IS THERE NO STOPPING THIS FIEND? WILL HE NEVER BE CAUGHT?
SCHULZ

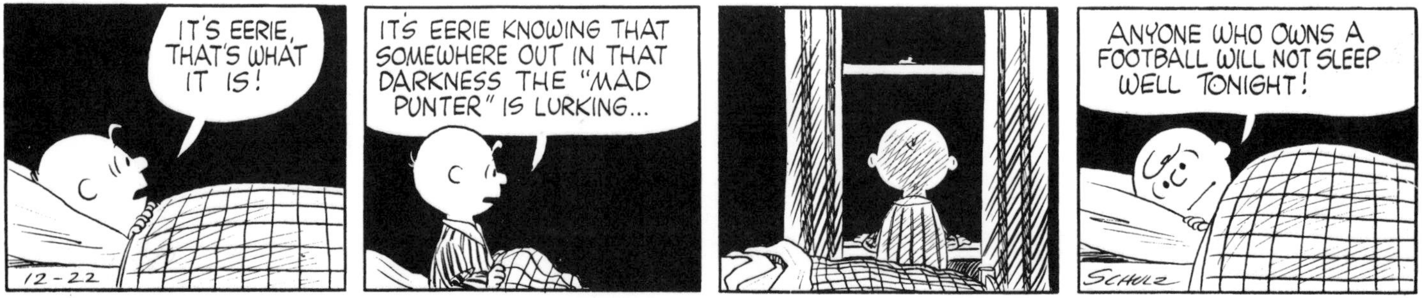
IT'S EERIE, THAT'S WHAT IT IS!
12-22
IT'S EERIE KNOWING THAT SOMEWHERE OUT IN THAT DARKNESS THE "MAD PUNTER" IS LURKING...
ANYONE WHO OWNS A FOOTBALL WILL NOT SLEEP WELL TONIGHT!
SCHULZ

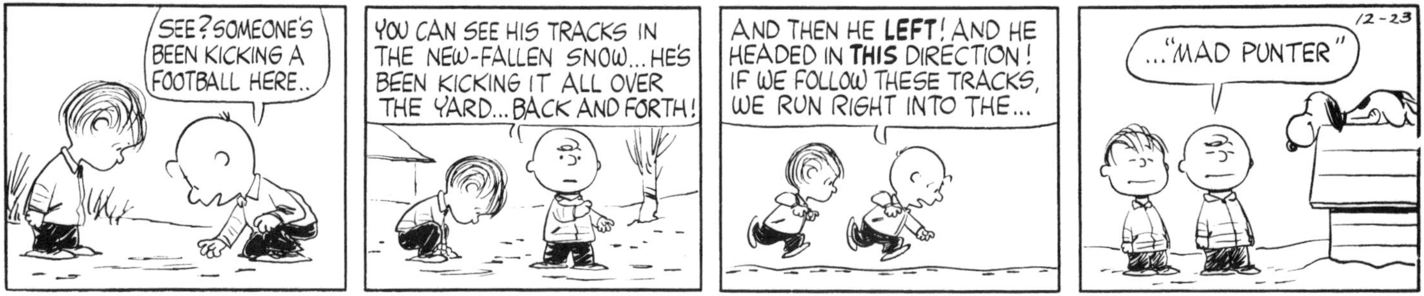
SEE? SOMEONE'S BEEN KICKING A FOOTBALL HERE..
YOU CAN SEE HIS TRACKS IN THE NEW-FALLEN SNOW... HE'S BEEN KICKING IT ALL OVER THE YARD... BACK AND FORTH!
AND THEN HE **LEFT**! AND HE HEADED IN **THIS** DIRECTION! IF WE FOLLOW THESE TRACKS, WE RUN RIGHT INTO THE...
12-23
..."MAD PUNTER"

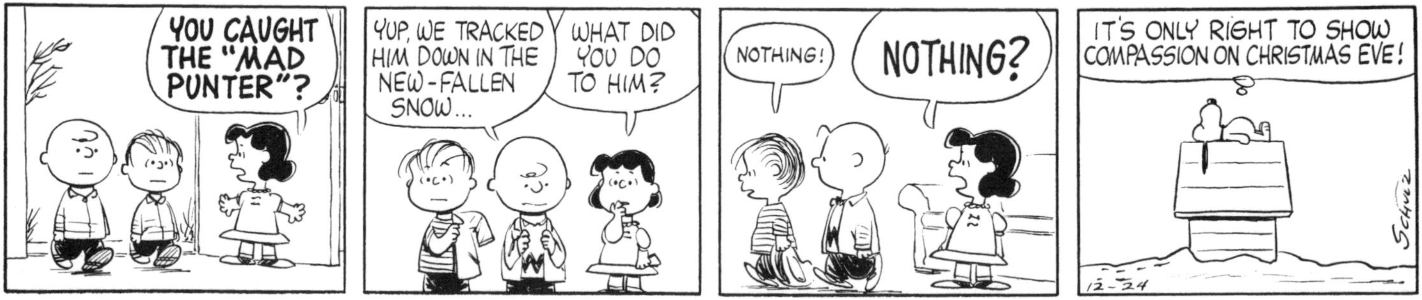
YOU CAUGHT THE "MAD PUNTER"?
YUP, WE TRACKED HIM DOWN IN THE NEW-FALLEN SNOW...
WHAT DID YOU DO TO HIM?
NOTHING!
NOTHING?
IT'S ONLY RIGHT TO SHOW COMPASSION ON CHRISTMAS EVE!
SCHULZ
12-24

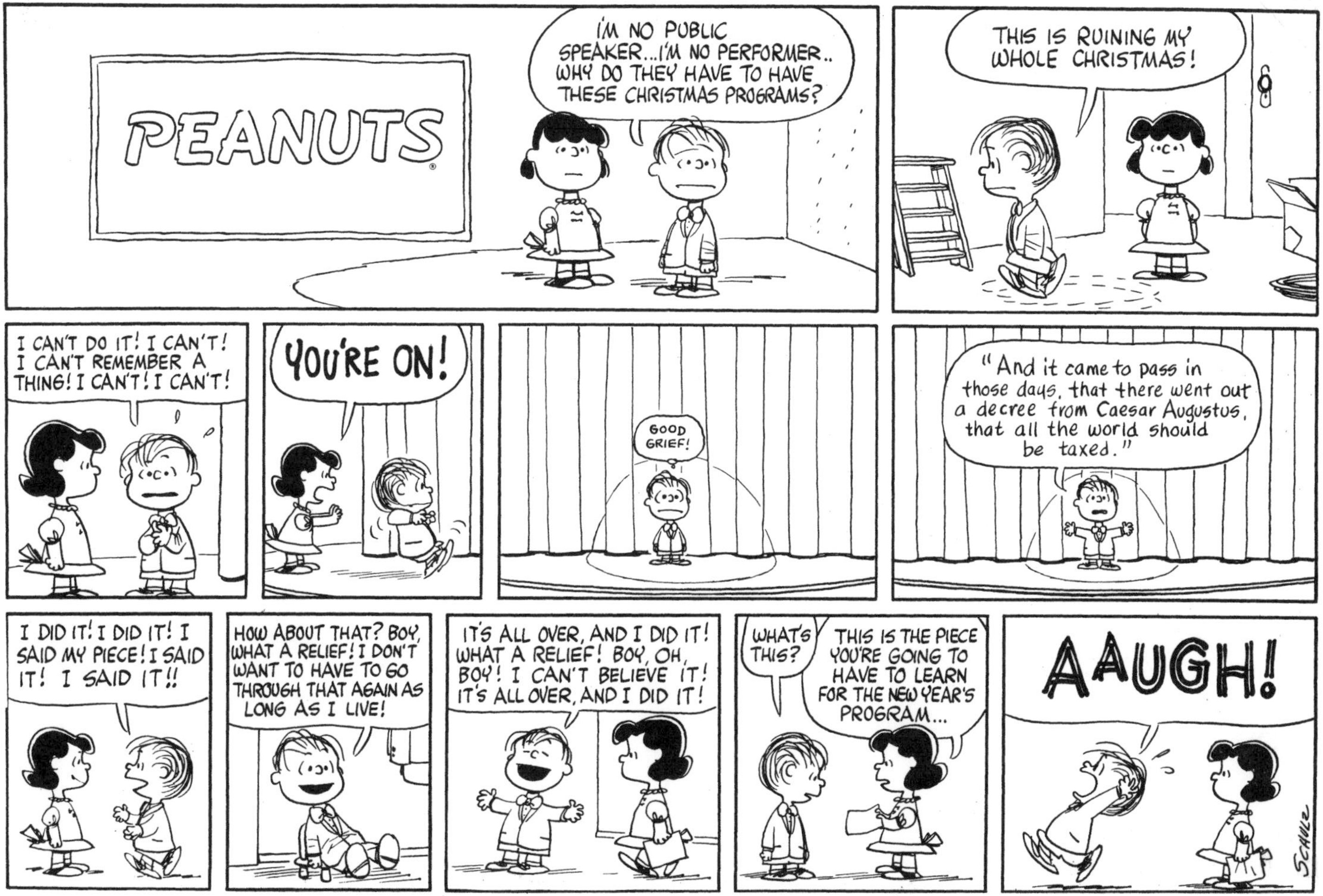
PEANUTS
I'M NO PUBLIC SPEAKER...I'M NO PERFORMER.. WHY DO THEY HAVE TO HAVE THESE CHRISTMAS PROGRAMS?
THIS IS RUINING MY WHOLE CHRISTMAS!
I CAN'T DO IT! I CAN'T! I CAN'T REMEMBER A THING! I CAN'T! I CAN'T!
YOU'RE ON!
GOOD GRIEF!
"And it came to pass in those days, that there went out a decree from Caesar Augustus, that all the world should be taxed."
I DID IT! I DID IT! I SAID MY PIECE! I SAID IT! I SAID IT!!
HOW ABOUT THAT? BOY, WHAT A RELIEF! I DON'T WANT TO HAVE TO GO THROUGH THAT AGAIN AS LONG AS I LIVE!
IT'S ALL OVER, AND I DID IT! WHAT A RELIEF! BOY, OH, BOY! I CAN'T BELIEVE IT! IT'S ALL OVER, AND I DID IT!
WHAT'S THIS?
THIS IS THE PIECE YOU'RE GOING TO HAVE TO LEARN FOR THE NEW YEAR'S PROGRAM...
AAUGH!
SCHULZ

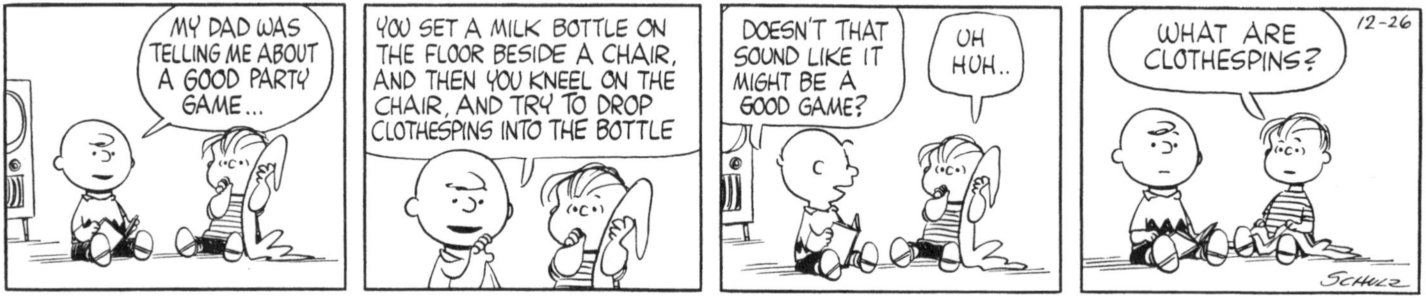
MY DAD WAS TELLING ME ABOUT A GOOD PARTY GAME...
YOU SET A MILK BOTTLE ON THE FLOOR BESIDE A CHAIR, AND THEN YOU KNEEL ON THE CHAIR, AND TRY TO DROP CLOTHESPINS INTO THE BOTTLE
DOESN'T THAT SOUND LIKE IT MIGHT BE A GOOD GAME?
UH HUH..
WHAT ARE CLOTHESPINS?
12-26
SCHULZ

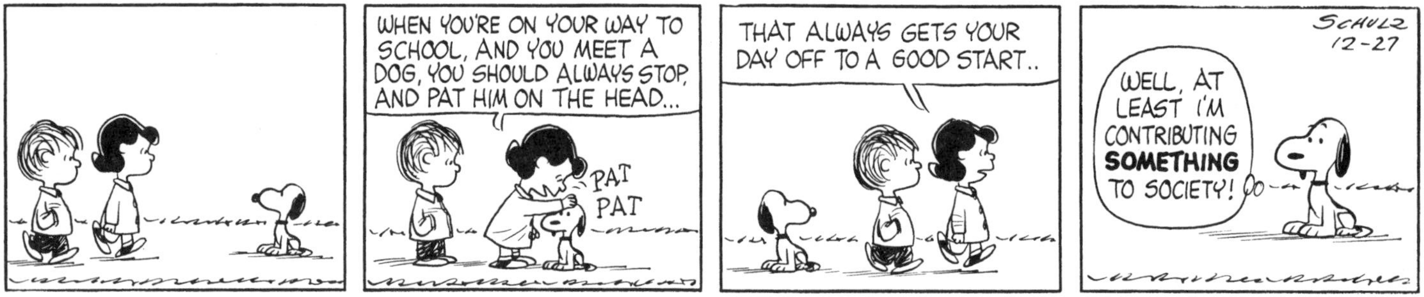
WHEN YOU'RE ON YOUR WAY TO SCHOOL, AND YOU MEET A DOG, YOU SHOULD ALWAYS STOP, AND PAT HIM ON THE HEAD...
PAT PAT
THAT ALWAYS GETS YOUR DAY OFF TO A GOOD START..
SCHULZ 12-27
WELL, AT LEAST I'M CONTRIBUTING **SOMETHING** TO SOCIETY!

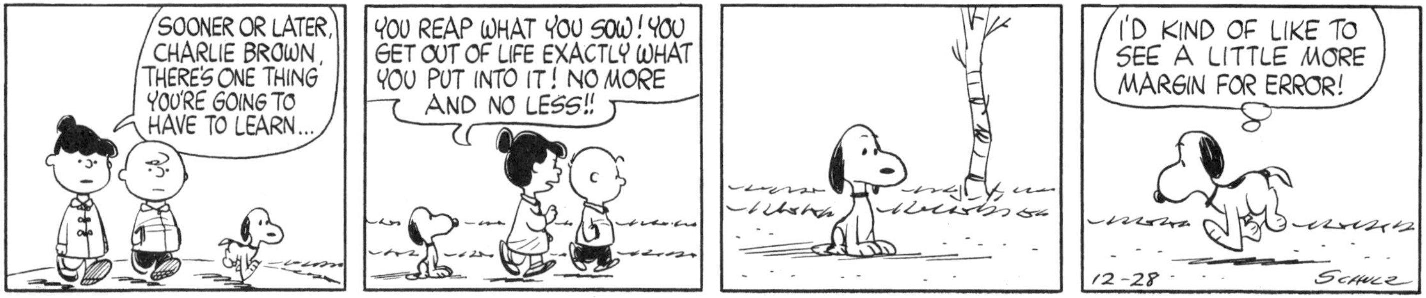
SOONER OR LATER, CHARLIE BROWN, THERE'S ONE THING YOU'RE GOING TO HAVE TO LEARN...
YOU REAP WHAT YOU SOW! YOU GET OUT OF LIFE EXACTLY WHAT YOU PUT INTO IT! NO MORE AND NO LESS!!
I'D KIND OF LIKE TO SEE A LITTLE MORE MARGIN FOR ERROR!
12-28
SCHULZ

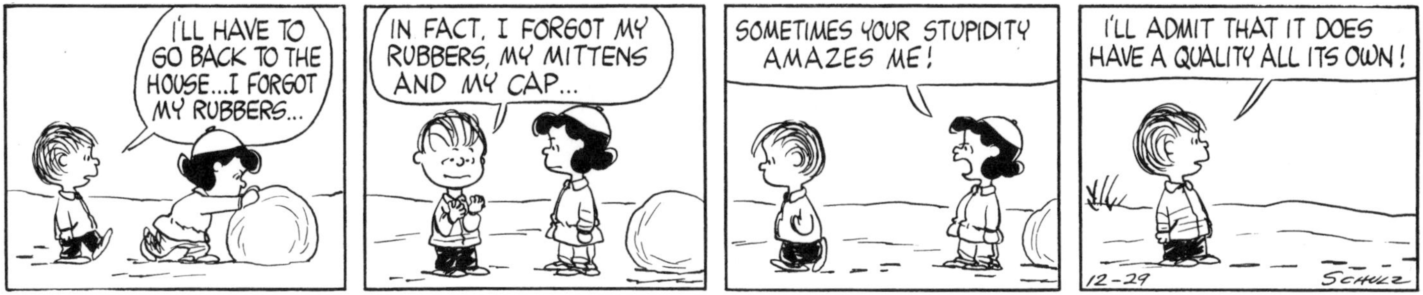
I'LL HAVE TO GO BACK TO THE HOUSE...I FORGOT MY RUBBERS...
IN FACT, I FORGOT MY RUBBERS, MY MITTENS AND MY CAP...
SOMETIMES YOUR STUPIDITY AMAZES ME!
I'LL ADMIT THAT IT DOES HAVE A QUALITY ALL ITS OWN!
12-29
SCHULZ

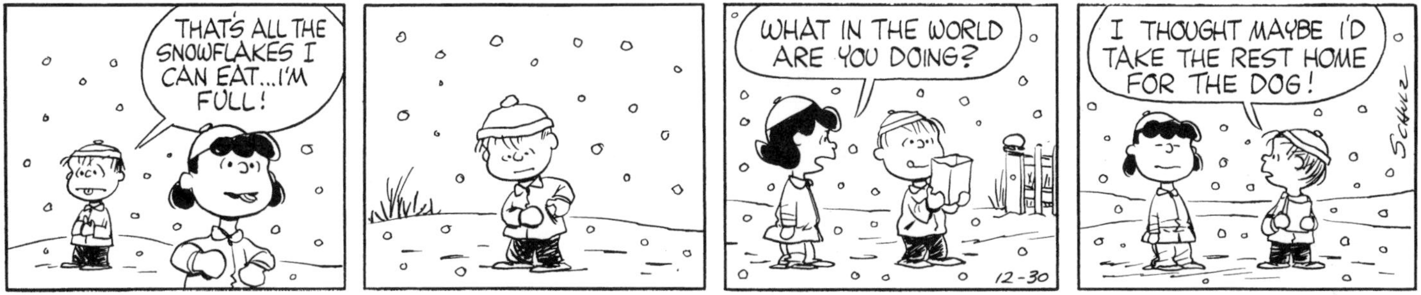
THAT'S ALL THE SNOWFLAKES I CAN EAT...I'M FULL!
WHAT IN THE WORLD ARE YOU DOING?
12-30
I THOUGHT MAYBE I'D TAKE THE REST HOME FOR THE DOG!
SCHULZ

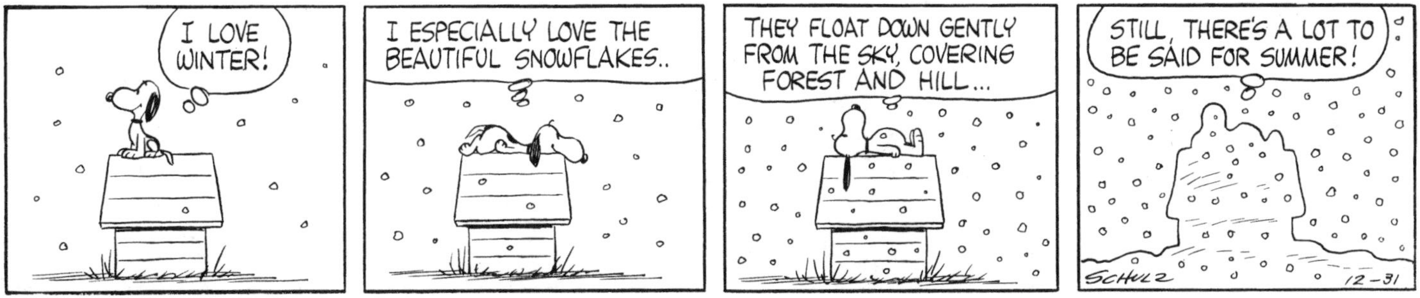
I LOVE WINTER!
I ESPECIALLY LOVE THE BEAUTIFUL SNOWFLAKES..
THEY FLOAT DOWN GENTLY FROM THE SKY, COVERING FOREST AND HILL...
STILL, THERE'S A LOT TO BE SAID FOR SUMMER!
SCHULZ
12-31

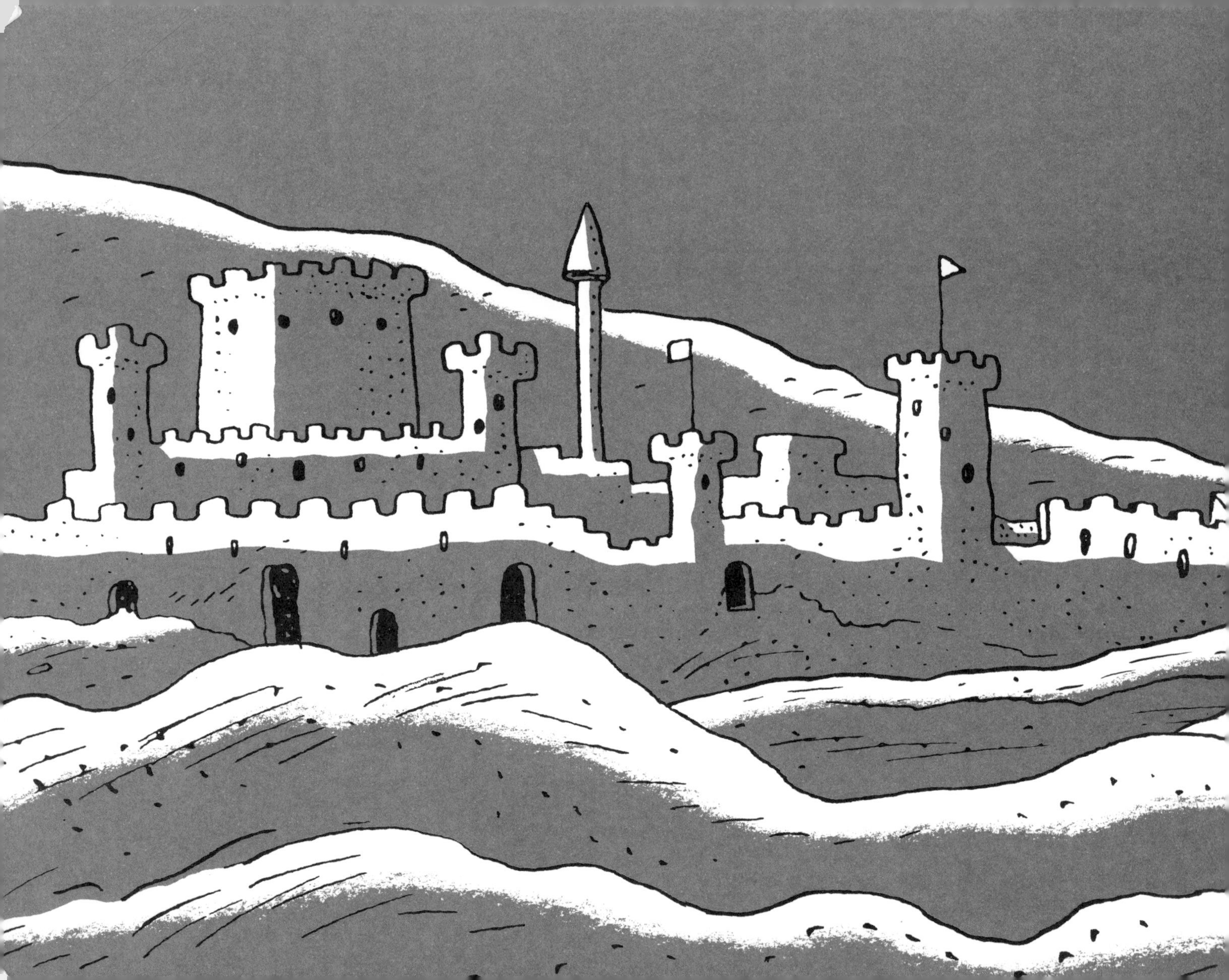

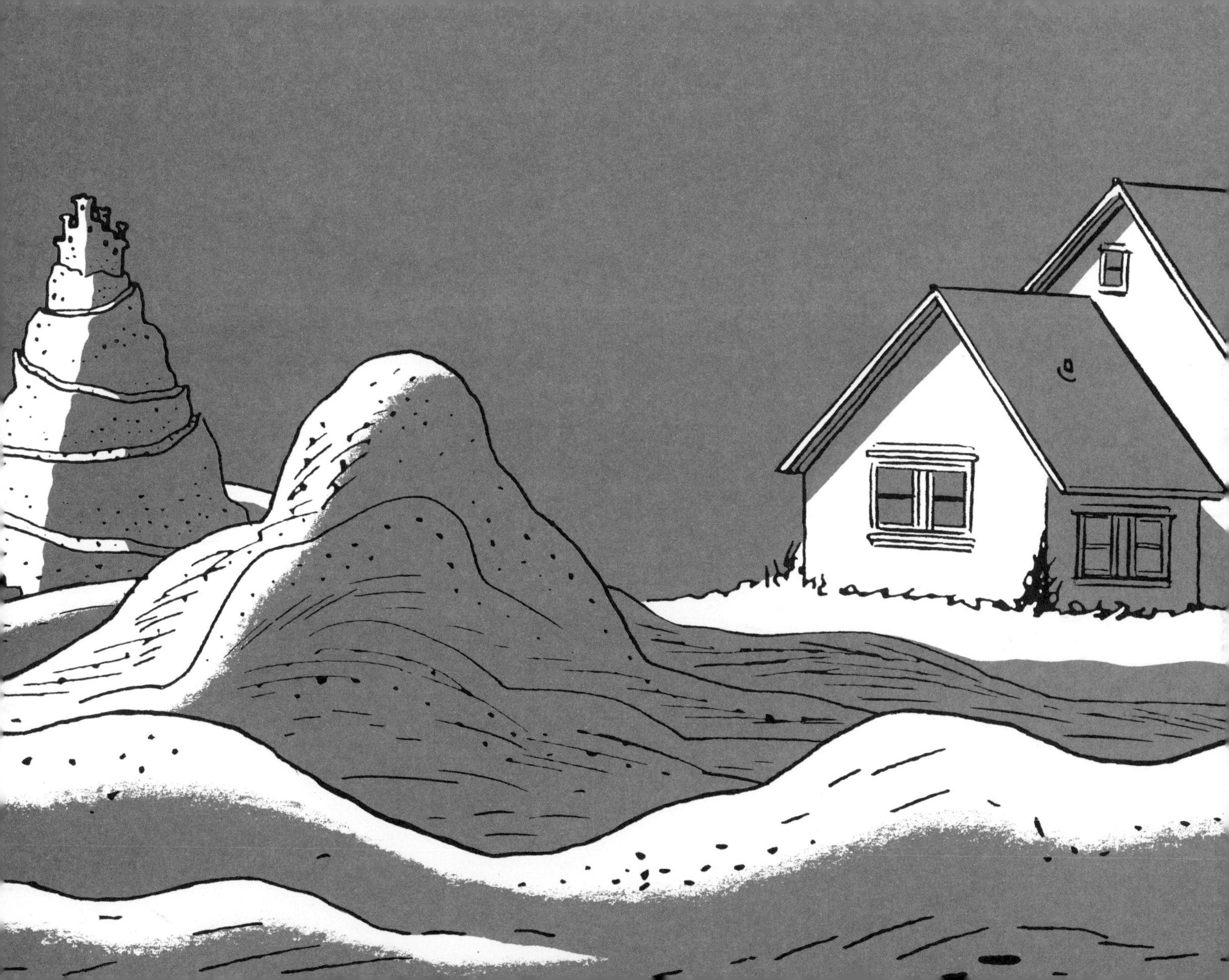

INDEX

HMMPF!

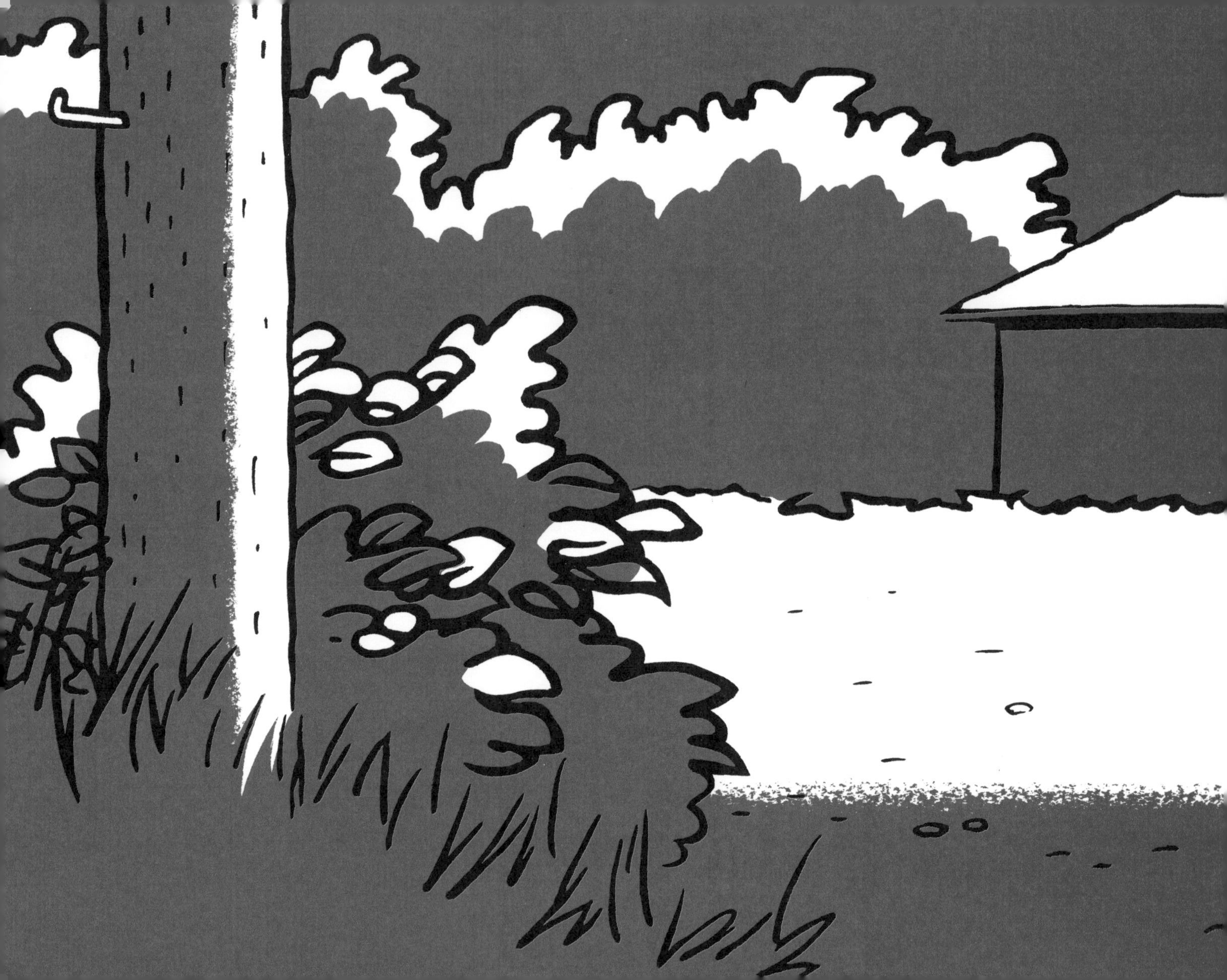

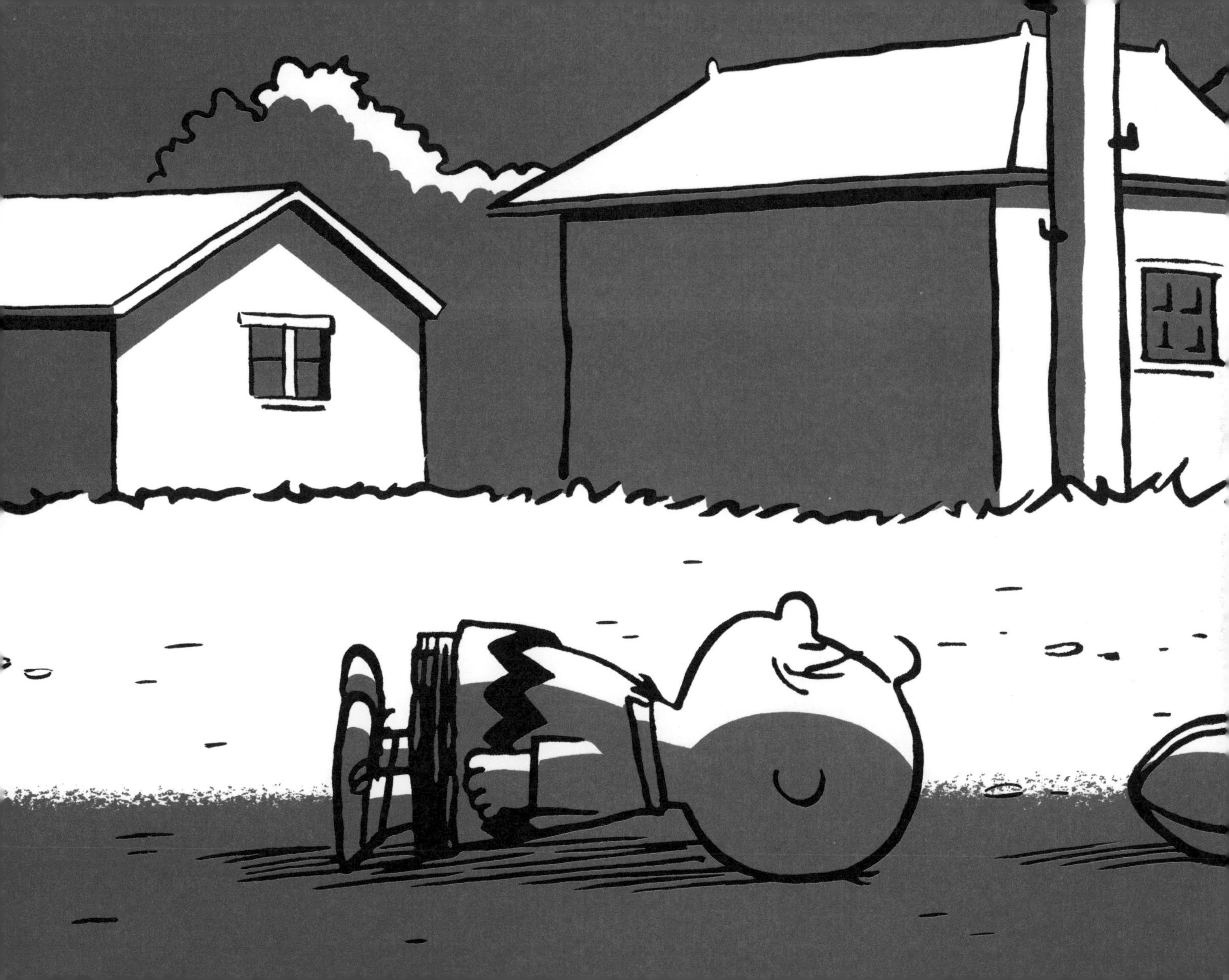

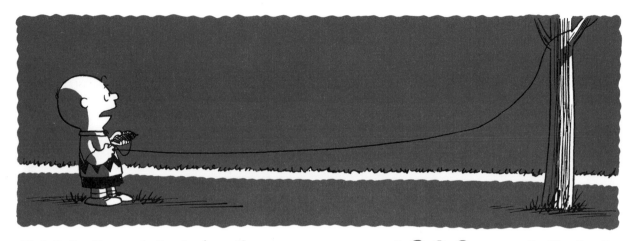

CHARLES M. SCHULZ · 1922 To 2000

Charles M. Schulz was born November 26, 1922 in Minneapolis. His destiny was foreshadowed when an uncle gave him, at the age of two days, the nickname Sparky (after the racehorse Spark Plug in the newspaper strip *Barney Google*).

Schulz grew up in St. Paul. By all accounts, he led an unremarkable, albeit sheltered, childhood. He was an only child, close to both parents, his eventual career path nurtured by his father, who bought four Sunday papers every week — just for the comics.

An outstanding student, he skipped two grades early on, but began to flounder in high school — perhaps not so coincidentally at the same time kids are going through their cruelest, most status-conscious period of socialization. The pain, bitterness, insecurity, and failures chronicled in *Peanuts* appear to have originated from this period of Schulz's life.

Although Schulz enjoyed sports, he also found refuge in solitary activities: reading, drawing, and watching movies. He bought comic books and Big Little Books, pored over the newspaper strips, and copied his favorites — *Buck Rogers*, the Walt Disney characters, *Popeye*, *Tim Tyler's Luck*. He quickly became a connoisseur; his heroes were Milton Caniff, Roy Crane, Hal Foster, and Alex Raymond.

In his senior year in high school, his mother noticed an ad in a local newspaper for a correspondence school, Federal Schools (later called Art

Instruction Schools). Schulz passed the talent test, completed the course and began trying, unsuccessfully, to sell gag cartoons to magazines. (His first published drawing was of his dog, Spike, and appeared in a 1937 Ripley's *Believe It Or Not!* installment.)

After World War II had ended and Schulz was discharged from the army, he started submitting gag cartoons to the various magazines of the time; his first breakthrough, however, came when an editor at Timeless Topix hired him to letter adventure comics. Soon after that, he was hired by his alma mater, Art Instruction, to correct student lessons returned by mail.

Between 1948 and 1950, he succeeded in selling 17 cartoons to the *Saturday Evening Post* — as well as, to the local *St. Paul Pioneer Press*, a weekly comic feature called *Li'l Folks*. It was run in the women's section and paid $10 a week. After writing and drawing the feature for two years, Schulz asked for a better location in the paper or for daily exposure, as well as a raise. When he was turned down on all three counts, he quit.

He started submitting strips to the newspaper syndicates. In the Spring of 1950, he received a letter from the United Feature Syndicate, announcing their interest in his submission, *Li'l Folks*. Schulz boarded a train in June for New York City; more interested in doing a strip than a panel, he also brought along the first installments of what would become *Peanuts* — and that was what sold. (The title, which Schulz loathed to his dying day, was imposed by the syndicate). The first *Peanuts* daily appeared October 2, 1950; the first Sunday, January 6, 1952.

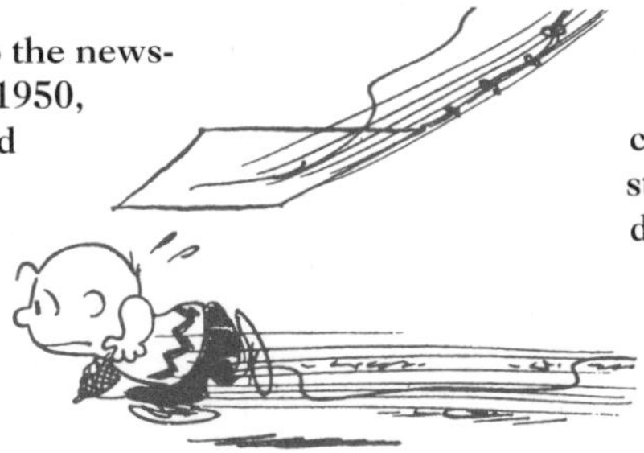

Prior to *Peanuts*, the province of the comics page had been that of gags, social and political observation, domestic comedy, soap opera, and various adventure genres. Although *Peanuts* changed, or evolved, during the 50 years Schulz wrote and drew it, it remained, as it began, an anomaly on the comics page — a comic strip about the interior crises of the cartoonist himself. After a painful divorce in 1973 from which he had not yet recovered, Schulz told a reporter, "Strangely, I've drawn better cartoons in the last six months — or as good as I've ever drawn. I don't know how the human mind works." Surely, it was this kind of humility in the face of profoundly irreducible human question that makes *Peanuts* as universally moving as it is.

Diagnosed with cancer, Schulz retired from *Peanuts* at the end of 1999. He died on February 12th 2000, the day before Valentine's day — two days before his last strip was published — having completed 17,897 daily and Sunday strips, each and every one fully written, drawn, and lettered entirely by his own hand — an unmatched achievement in comics. *—Gary Groth*

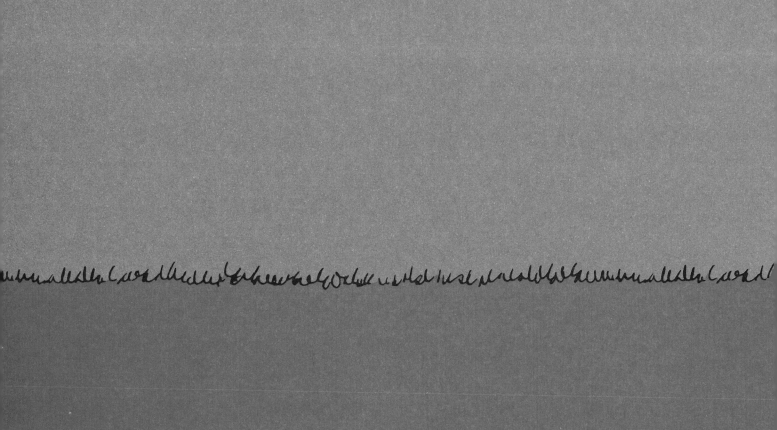

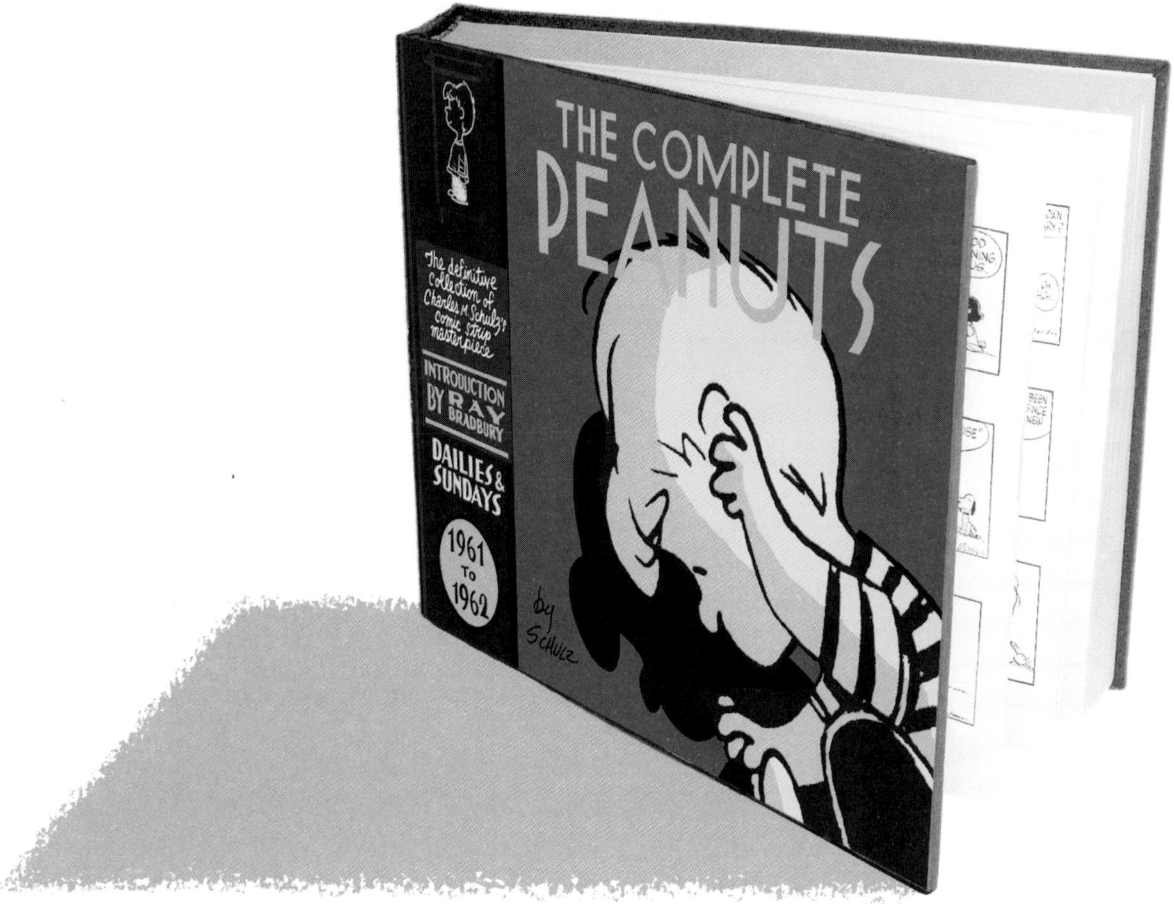
THE COMPLETE PEANUTS
The definitive collection of Charles M. Schulz's comic strip masterpiece
INTRODUCTION BY RAY BRADBURY
DAILIES & SUNDAYS
1961 To 1962
by Schulz

COMING IN *THE COMPLETE PEANUTS: 1961-1962*

Two new cast members: Frieda of the "naturally curly hair" and her cat Faron... Lucy buries Linus's blanket, turns it into a kite... The Van Pelt parents acquire a tangerine-colored pool table... Miss Othmar returns... Sally starts kindergarten... Linus gets glasses... Snoopy endures a doomed friendship with a snowman and a family crisis involving birds... plus baseball, Beethoven, and the Great Pumpkin!

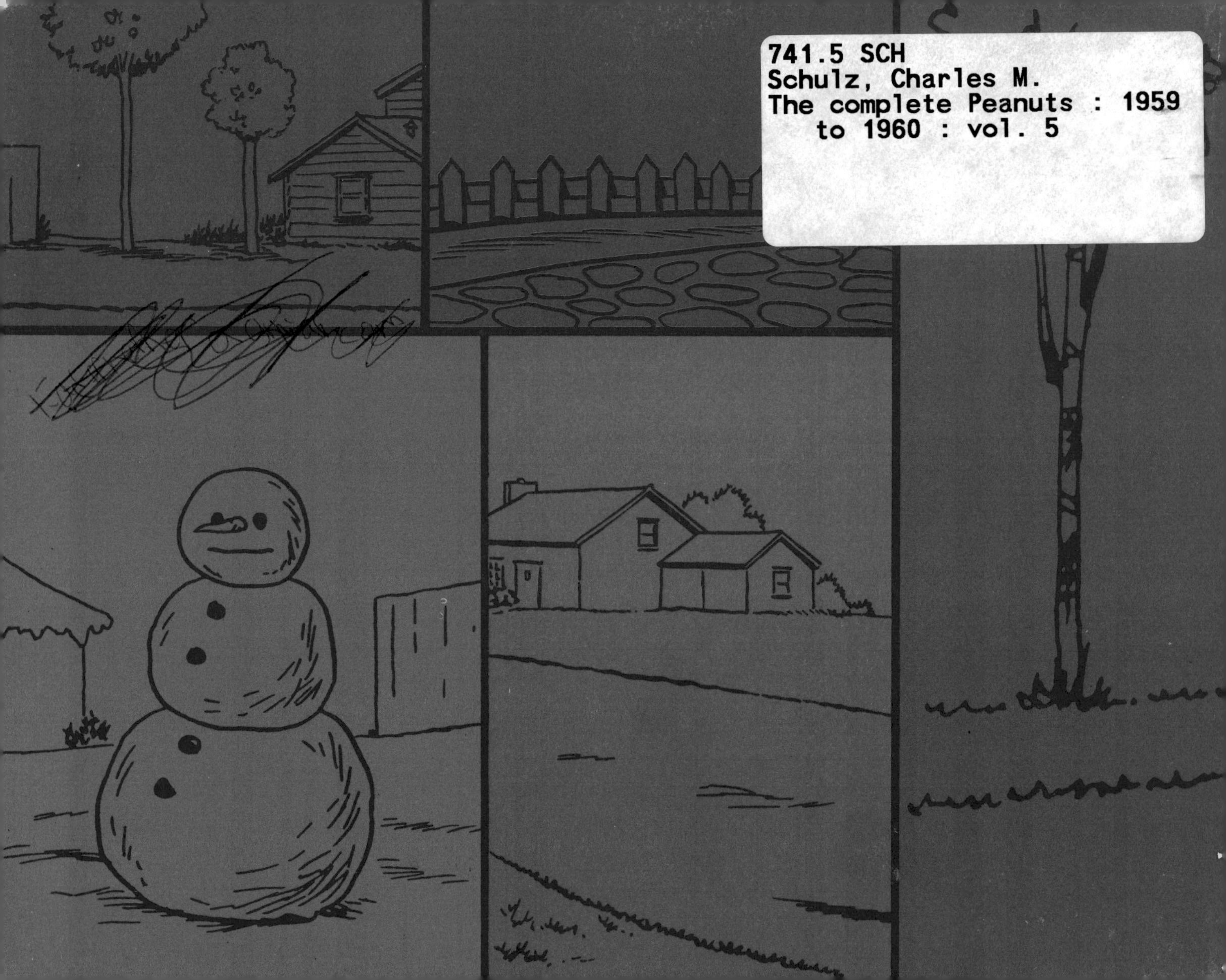